SELECTED LETTERS OF
MARY WOLLSTONECRAFT SHELLEY

SELECTED LETTERS

of

Mary Wollstonecraft Shelley

EDITED BY

BETTY T. BENNETT

THE JOHNS HOPKINS UNIVERSITY PRESS

BALTIMORE AND LONDON

© 1995 The Johns Hopkins University Press
All rights reserved. Published 1995
Printed in the United States of America on acid-free paper
03 02 01 00 99 98 97 96 95   5 4 3 2 1

The Johns Hopkins University Press
2715 North Charles Street
Baltimore, Maryland 21218-4319
The Johns Hopkins Press Ltd., London

Frontispiece: Mary Wollstonecraft Shelley, a miniature
by Reginald Easton, courtesy of the Bodleian Library

Design and composition: Wilsted & Taylor Publishing Services

Library of Congress Cataloging-in-Publication Data
will be found at the end of this book.
A catalog record for this book is available from the British Library.

CONTENTS

PREFACE

Mary Shelley was born in London on 30 August 1797. Her life was filled with adventure, from her early days as the child of two of the most prominent reformers in an era of political and social upheaval, to her elopement at age sixteen with the married poet-reformer Shelley and their unconventional existence in Britain and on the Continent, to a widowhood at twenty-five from which she shaped a life unlike that of other nineteenth-century women. For most people this would have been enough. But at the same time, Mary Shelley lived another adventure, equally important to her: that of the imagination, which brought forth the novel *Frankenstein* when she was eighteen years old and a series of other works, both before and after that first, monumental work.

In selecting these 231 letters from the 1,276 letters in the three-volume edition of *The Letters of Mary Wollstonecraft Shelley,* I have been guided by those central adventures of Mary Shelley's life—parents, husband, children; writing, editing, publishing; culture and politics—lived and translated through an extraordinary imagination and intellect.

The introduction, together with the biographical and historical notes, is designed to provide sufficient background to place the letters in the larger context of Mary Shelley's life and times. By seeing each letter in its entirety, readers may be able to better imagine for themselves the author's mind and spirit and perhaps the responses of those who received her letters. The chronological rather than topical organization of the volume makes it easier to see how sustained and intertwined her interests were and how they related to her professional writing. To those readers who become absorbed in Mary Shelley's story, I recommend turning to the full edition of the *Letters,* her *Journals,* and her novels and other professional writing—all of which reflect a very remarkable woman in a very remarkable era.

The three-volume edition, which contains some five hundred previously unpublished letters, was assembled from libraries and private collections in the United States, Britain, Europe, Australia, Africa, and New Zealand. While I had the opportunity to express my acknowledgment and gratitude earlier, I wish again to thank the Carl and Lily Pforzheimer Collection, Lord and Lady Abinger, and the Bodleian Library for their continued and special generosity.

In preparing this edition, I have taken the opportunity to correct errors that occurred in the three-volume edition. I have also reedited several letters for which the manuscripts have become available.

A brief description of editorial principles follows:

1. The name of the addressee is given at top left, and the place and date of writing at top right, regardless of where it appeared in the letter. The complimentary close is separated from the letter except when it is followed by additional text or when it is so informal as to be considered part of the text.

2. Postscripts, which appear on envelopes and address sheets, in margins, and cross-written, follow the signature.

3. Mary Shelley's irregularities in spelling, abbreviations, and punctuation have been retained. Where clarity requires, the correctly spelled word follows in brackets.

4. Obvious slips have been silently omitted. Deleted words that appear to have significance are enclosed in angled brackets.

5. Where possible, words missing due to holes or deterioration of the manuscript are supplied in square brackets. Wholly conjectural words appear in square brackets followed by a question mark. Empty square brackets indicate missing words for which there is no sound basis for conjecture.

6. Portions of letters that contain cross-writing—that is, horizontal writing crossed by vertical writing, giving a gridlike effect—are preceded by the indication [cross-written].

7. Letters in French and Italian are followed by translations.

8. Persons included in the section entitled "Biographical Names" in Webster's Seventh New Collegiate Dictionary are not identified unless the context requires additional information.

[?]	Unidentified addressee
{London}	Non-given but certain addressee, place, or date
{?London}	Editorial conjecture of addressee, place, or date
[ ]	Word torn from text or otherwise obliterated
mo[on}	Editorial conjecture of word torn from text or otherwise obliterated
{*moon?*}	Uncertain editorial conjecture of word torn from text or otherwise obliterated
[*?moon*]	Uncertain reading
[*P. 1, top*]	Editorial information
M^rs G [*Godwin*]	Abbreviated name supplied
and [*an*]	Clarification of word
{ }	Word or letter omitted
{moon}	Editorial conjecture of omitted word or letter
⟨ ⟩	Deletion restored

Finally, I wish to thank a number of people who have particularly assisted me in this selected edition of the letters. I am grateful to Edward Kessler, Kermit Moyer, and Kay Mussell, colleagues and friends at the American University, who commented on the introduction in various stages of development. Anne James, of the American University, patiently and kindly dealt with a variety of details, as did Elizabeth Storch and Eileen Pereira. And it is with pleasure that I acknowledge the overall continued support of my scholarship by the American University.

I wish to extend special thanks to Eric Halpern, of the Johns Hopkins University Press, who also oversaw the second and third volumes of the complete letters and has provided valuable suggestions throughout the process of editing this volume, and to copyeditor Joanne Allen.

For the pleasure and privilege of her company, I thank Mary Shelley. And for the pleasure and privilege of their company, and their love, I thank my parents, Jennie and Meyer Edelman, and my sons, Matthew and Peter Bennett.

INTRODUCTION

Mary Shelley's letters tell the story of an extraordinary nineteenth-century woman. Her singular intelligence and imagination shaped her first publication, when she was eleven, and her most famous work, *Frankenstein,* when she was eighteen. Philosophically convinced that love, not law, must determine marriage, she eloped with the married Shelley a month before her seventeenth birthday, sealing her lifelong commitment to art and to democratic social reform based on universal love. But these letters take us even beyond her celebrated family and immediate circle. A product and a creator of the revolutionary age in which she lived, she reflects in her letters the spirit of a society in flux: the stagecoach yields to the railroad; wealth shifts from landholding to centers of industry; the aristocracy surrenders an increasing share of its control to the rising middle class. Mary Shelley's letters express her perceptions of the complex issues of power and responsibility that developed in the wake of these social and economic upheavals, upheavals that precipitated our contemporary legacy.

Her accounts of so many aspects of the period, particularized in relation to her individual experiences and expectations, make nineteenth-century history direct and alive. Observations on living conditions, politics, royalty, manners, customs, housing, diet, dress, recreation, travel, schooling, finance, and transportation are often couched in comparative terms—past with present, one country played against another—adding historical and cultural perspective to her insights. Not surprisingly, many of the letters deal with her particular interests—literature foremost but also opera, theater, music, ballet, and art. The scope of the letters, which date from the Shelleys' return to London in September 1814 until a few months before Mary Shelley died, on 1 February 1851, and the variety of her correspondents reveal a remarkably cosmopolitan daughter of the era.

The letters begin with Mary Shelley as a young author who relied on

Shelley to negotiate publication of her works. After Shelley's death in July 1822, she relied for introductions and recommendations to publishers on the assistance of established writers in her circle, among them Charles Lamb, Horace Smith, and, of course, Godwin. But she quickly developed the self-reliance that allowed her to negotiate directly and persistently for her own and her friends' works with leading publishers and editors of the day, including Henry Colburn, John Murray, Alaric A. Watts, and John Bowring. Not incidentally, the letters often reveal the pressures on a woman who had to represent herself in a Victorian world that was intent on relegating women to the home.

She writes of projects finished and unfinished, aspirations, feelings of failure and satisfaction, efforts to publish, reactions to reviews and friends' opinions, exhaustion from overwork, deadlines, lost manuscripts, revisions, self-appraisal. After Shelley's death she expressed confidence in her ability to earn a living through her writing: "I think that I can maintain myself, and there is something inspiriting in the idea" (*7 March 1823).[1] She found solace in continuing her already established habits of writing and study: "I study—I write—I think even to madness & torture of the past—I look forward to the grave with hope—but in exerting my intellect—in forcing myself to real study—I find an opiate which at least adds nothing to the pain of regret that must necessarily be mine for ever" (*28 February 1823).

Protracted negotiations with Sir Timothy, Shelley's father, wrung from him towards the close of 1823 only a modest allowance for her son, Percy Florence, repayable to Sir Timothy's other heirs when she inherited Shelley's estate at Sir Timothy's death (9–11 September 1823, nn. 11 and 12). Needing additional income, Mary Shelley was aware that, as with many professional authors, some of her writing was motivated primarily by financial gain. Her letters show, however, that she was determined to develop and fulfill her aesthetic ideals. When she advised Leigh Hunt to write for magazines to earn the money he needed, she characterized her own situation: "I write bad articles which help to make me miserable— but I am going to plunge into a novel, and hope that its clear water will wash off the ⟨dirt⟩ mud of the magazines" (*9 February 1824).

In her preface to the 1831 edition of *Frankenstein* she speaks of writing as a young girl. Her first publication, *Monsieur Nongtongpaw*, a satirical parody, appeared in 1809, when she was eleven years old. In 1817, draw-

---

1. References to letters in the three-volume edition of *The Letters of Mary Wollstonecraft Shelley* cited but not included in the *Selected Letters* are preceded by an asterisk.

ing on the journal that she and Shelley began together when they eloped (which Mary Shelley soon took over), she wrote her first travel work, *A Six Weeks' Tour* (1817), the adventurous story of the Shelleys' unconventional tour through war-torn Europe. In 1818 *Frankenstein* was published. Her next work, *Mathilda,* was written in 1819 but not published until 1959. This novella explores the catastrophic results of a father's incestuous love for his daughter. *Valperga* (1823), a historical political novel, advocates democratic governance and individual courage, personified by a woman, in opposition to unlimited power.

After Shelley's death she wrote *The Last Man* (1826), an apocalyptic novel that interweaves personal and political struggle. *Perkin Warbeck* (1830), a second historical novel that opposes unlimited power, again emphasizes female heroism. Her final novels, *Lodore* (1835) and *Falkner* (1837), both consider the uses of power versus love within familial conflicts, with special focus on the values and actions of young women.

From 1835 to 1839 Mary Shelley wrote five volumes of essays about the lives of eminent Italian, Spanish, Portuguese, and French literary and scientific figures in the setting of their sociopolitical context for Lardner's *Cabinet Cyclopedia.* In 1844, seven years before her death, she ended her publishing career with the personal and political *Rambles in Germany and Italy,* drawn from her travels in 1840–43 with her son (20 July [1840]). In addition to the longer works, she published the mythological drama *Proserpine* and at least two dozen short stories, as well as essays, translations, reviews, and poems. As Shelley's editor, she brought out Shelley's *Posthumous Poems* (1824), *Poetical Works* (1839, two-volume edition, and revised, one-volume edition [see her letter of 14 July (1841)]), and *Essays, Letters* (1839, dated 1840). These volumes contain her biographical notes, which remain an invaluable resource for Shelley scholarship.

All of her works except *Monsieur Nongtongpaw* are chronicled in the letters. They indicate the names of her literary, political, and historical printed sources as well as the names of colleagues she drew on for information. They recount the often difficult contexts in which she wrote, political as well as personal. And, perhaps most fascinating, they relate the artistic and the pragmatic struggle of a nineteenth-century female author.

Mary Shelley came early to the world of literature and politics through the works of her parents, both leading radical writers of their day. William Godwin (1756–1836), her father, is best known for *An Enquiry into Political Justice* and *Caleb Williams,* the first detective novel in the English language. Her mother, Mary Wollstonecraft (1759–97), who died ten days after the birth of her namesake, achieved enduring fame with her *Vindication of the Rights of Woman* and *Letters from Sweden, Norway, and*

Denmark. In 1814 Mary Shelley added a third, equally important influence to her life. On 28 July she eloped to the Continent with the radical, already married poet-philosopher Percy Bysshe Shelley (1792–1822), a disciple of her parents' reformist concepts. Mary Shelley's legacy as a Romantic was determined at birth. It was through choice, however, that she accepted and fulfilled that legacy and developed a literary voice quite her own, which was nurtured rather than subsumed by the achievements of Godwin, Wollstonecraft, and Shelley.

Godwin's influence on Mary Shelley and her works can be traced throughout her letters. She often reread his political tracts and novels, deriving much of her vision of an egalitarian social order from his theories of political and social justice. Mary Shelley wrote that before her relationship with Shelley began, she had an "excessive & romantic attachment" to her father (*30 October 1834).

The letters underscore her almost unfaltering devotion to her father, her unhappiness when he refused to accept her elopement with Shelley, her reconciliation with her father, and her distress to the point of illness in 1820–22 because of his incessant demands on the Shelleys for money (*30 June 1820). As close as her relationship to her father was, however, her initial decision after Shelley's death was to remain in Italy, where as an expatriate she was free from the restraints of English society. Forced to live in England as a condition of her allowance from Sir Timothy Shelley (7 January 1823, n. 1; *c. 5 April 1823), she reentered Godwin's close circle. Through him she renewed the literary friendships of her youth, and she gladly accepted from these friends recommendations of her work to publishers and editors. But this closeness also led to Godwin's financial reliance on the young widow and his wish, reinforcing Sir Timothy Shelley's injunction, that she remain in England against her own ardent desire to return to Italy.

From Mary Shelley's earliest years, Godwin also exerted another influence on his daughter: he taught her to idolize her mother. Although many contemporaries deplored the unconventional life and radical ideas of Mary Wollstonecraft, Godwin and a number of his friends encouraged her daughter to worship this pioneer of equal rights for men and women and to measure herself and others against the heritage of her mother's ideals. On 3 November 1814 Mary Shelley praised her friend Isabella Booth by writing that "she adores the shade of my mother." On *18 August 1823 she wrote: "Mrs K [Kenney] says that I am grown very like my Mother, especially in Manners . . . the most flattering thing anyone c^d say to me." Her friendship with the abolitionist Frances Wright was based in part on praise of Wollstonecraft: "The memory of my Mother has been always been the pride & delight of my life; & the admiration of others for her, has been the cause of most of the happiness ⟨of my life⟩ I have enjoyed. Her greatness of soul & my father high talents have perpetually reminded me that I ought to degenerate as little as I could from those from whom I derived my being" (12 September 1827).

Mary Shelley's letters and her professional writings demonstrate her early and consistent concern with political events, articulating a vehement antimonarchism and an abiding commitment to the freedom of the individual. The many letters she wrote expressing enthusiastic support of uprisings against tyrannical acts of government in Spain, Italy, Greece, and England substantiate her *24 March 1820 self-depiction: "You see what a John or rather Joan Bull I am so full of politics—." She formed a close friendship with Prince Alexander Mavrocordato, a leader in the Greek war of independence against Turkey, and was his confidante before he left Italy for Greece in June 1821. Her political propensity did not end with Shelley's death, as some critics contend. She maintained her contact with Mavrocordato, and her letters to and about Trelawny testify to her continued attention to the Greek battle for freedom. And certainly, *The Last Man* and *Perkin Warbeck* are as explicitly political as the earlier *Valperga*.

Her letters preserve firsthand observations of the transitional years between the post-Napoleonic unrest and economic depression that followed the wars and the emergence of Victorian attitudes and standards. For example, in her 11 November 1830 letter to General Lafayette congratulating him and France on the successful July Revolution she commented: "May England imitate your France in its moderation and heroism." In her 27 December 1830 letter to Trelawny she referred to the burnings and alarms in England as well as to her belief that "the Autocrats would have the good sense to make the necessary sacrifices to a starving people." Her 30 December 1830 letter to Frances Wright celebrates the triumph of "the *Cause*" in Europe, which is expected to quell tyrants. Of England she said: "The people *will* be redressed—will the Aristocrats sacrifice enough to tranquillize them—if they will not—we must be revolutionized." Her letters of 1831 describe political unrest and her own excitement about, and support of, the impending Reform Bill. Of a threatened war in America in 1833 she wrote: "I am truly sorry—Brothers should not fight for the different & various portions of their inheritance. . . . War is the companion & friend of Monarchy—if it be the same of freedom—the gain is not much to Mankind between a Sovereign & a president" (*16 January 1833). In 1834 she attended Parliament to hear the debates on the Irish tithe issue and the revised poor laws, and she was

xv

angered at Lord Brougham for his support of these measures, which increased the plight of the poor (*19 August [1834]). Her letters throughout her life, including those to Alexander Berry in the 1840s, testify to how fully engaged and knowledgeable she was about the political issues of the day.

Not surprisingly, during the Shelleys' eight peripatetic years together they were strongly influenced by reformist politics. Their egalitarian ideals led them to support and encourage each other's writing within the shared intellectualism that was a major part of their daily life. In the conservative era following the Napoleonic Wars, their works also shared an advocacy of the reformist ideals prevalent among eighteenth-century Enlightenment philosophers.

Critics have seldom considered, however, the complexities of a relationship in which both parties are young and committed to literary careers. When they eloped, Mary Shelley had among her possessions some of her own writings, and on the tour she added a story called "Hate," as well as their travel journal. While *Six Weeks' Tour* was being printed, Shelley, in addition to attending to the publication of several of his own works, helped Mary Shelley see through the press the novel that is probably more familiar to people worldwide than any other Romantic work, *Frankenstein*. Some critics, beginning with Sir Walter Scott (14 June 1818) and continuing to the present, have believed that Shelley was entirely or largely the author of *Frankenstein*. Both Shelleys denied this attribution. Rather, Shelley contributed to *Frankenstein* the judgment and suggestions of an astute and committed editor, a favor Mary Shelley returned when she became his editor.

Critics have stressed that Mary Shelley's relationship with Shelley introduced into her life personal and Shelleyan philosophic love. They often ignore, however, other aspects of their relationship, often painful, that contributed significantly to the growth of a gifted and intelligent but dependent girl into an accomplished author and independent woman. Surely one of the central experiences in her life was motherhood. During the eight years the Shelleys lived together, Mary Shelley was pregnant five times, the last pregnancy ending in a nearly fatal miscarriage. Of the four children born, only Percy Florence, born 12 November 1819, survived both his parents.

Following the death of William, their second child, Mary Shelley, then childless, wrote: "I feel that I am no[t] fit for any thing & therefore not fit to live but how must that heart be moulded which would not be broken by what I have suffered—" (29 June 1819). At that time she seemed almost to wish she had forgone her union with Shelley rather than have endured the deaths of their children (MWS *Journal*, 4 August 1819).

Shelley drowned in the Bay of Spezia on 8 July 1822, a month before his thirtieth birthday. Devastated by his death, but with the energy of youth —she was not quite twenty-five—Mary Shelley proceeded to reshape her life, supporting herself and her small son while maintaining her commitment to her own writing and to achieving posthumous recognition for Shelley. Her 1822–23 letters express her half-wish, half-fear that she too would die young. These same letters also show how completely she erased all blemish from her memory of Shelley and began her devoted mission of gathering and publishing his writings, shortly after his death, and how she mobilized herself to gain the financial means to exist independently even as she suffered her great loss.

If the Shelleys' life together was marked by death, it was marked even more by love. Mary Shelley's letters are a primary source of information about her response to Shelley's philosophy of expansive rather than exclusive love, which became central to her own value system politically and personally. Her letters to Thomas Jefferson Hogg make clear that she participated in a three-sided love experiment with Shelley and Hogg in 1815. The degree of her involvement remains a matter of speculation, though these letters strongly suggest that the affair between Mary Shelley and Hogg was unconsummated (1 January 1815). Other letters refer to her awareness that throughout her union with Shelley other women, including her stepsister Claire Clairmont, Sophia Stacey, Teresa Emilia Viviani, and Jane Williams, became Shelley's temporary love objects and inspirations, although she remained his "best Mary." However, it is important to note that each of these women was, to a greater or lesser degree, a member of the Shelley circle with whom Mary Shelley had her own special friendship.

The woman against whom Mary Shelley reacted most strongly during Shelley's life and after was her stepsister. Aspects of Shelley's relationship with Claire Clairmont remain unresolved to this day. Many Shelley biographers have thought it quite possible that he and Claire Clairmont had a liaison in 1814–15, the period during which Mary Shelley was pregnant and Shelley encouraged her and Hogg in their relationship. Aside from the amount of time Shelley and Claire Clairmont spent together and Mary Shelley's open annoyance at the attention her stepsister demanded and received in their household, there is no clear evidence to document such a liaison (1 January 1815, n. 1). Nor is there any clear evidence that Shelley and Claire Clairmont were the parents of Shelley's "Neapolitan child" (*18 June 1820, n. 1).

In the years 1823–28 Mary Shelley's adult love was in great measure transferred to a number of women. Her strong feelings for female friends (a tendency of her mother's as well) began before she met Shelley, with her girlhood friendship with Isabella Baxter Booth, a friendship that endured throughout her life (26 May 1850; 15 November 1850). But her letters make clear that the primary object of Mary Shelley's adoration and confidence following Shelley's death was Jane Williams, who to Mary Shelley's great shock proved to be deeply disloyal. Mary Shelley's letters of July and August 1827 show how she tried to disguise her anguish at the insincerity of her friend, whom she loved for herself and as a living bond to their days in Italy with Shelley and Edward Williams (*18 October [1823]). Her feelings of loss were renewed and in a sense made more final as she was again deprived of a trusted companion and denied the solace of shared memories. It was at this point that Mary Shelley turned outward from reliance on the circle of "the Elect" (3 October 1824) to create an independent life on her own. Despite this, the somewhat shadowed friendship between the two women endured.

Mary Shelley also had to adjust to Jane Williams's union with Thomas Jefferson Hogg, with whom, after their initial intimacy of 1814–15, Mary Shelley did not get along with very well. The letters following this crisis, always to "dearest Jane," tell of friendship injured and reestablished, the Hoggs' relationship, their daughters, the growth to adulthood of Edward and Dina Williams, Mary Shelley's attempt to help Hogg publish a novel (*4 November 1830) or find a job (*[?18 January–2 April 1836]), Hogg's assistance to Mary Shelley in legal matters. Moreover, they show that the women continued to aid each other in times of distress. For example, Mary Shelley wrote of her severe illness in 1835: "I can never forget nor cease to be grateful to Jane, for her excessive kindness to me when I needed it most, confined as I was to my sopha, unable to move" (*13 October 1835). But that she never forgot Jane Williams Hogg's disloyalty is underscored by her ironic response of 11 February [1839] to Hogg's criticism of her omission of the dedication to *Queen Mab:* "I thank you for your kindly expressed insinuations. I began to be fed on poison at Kentish Town—it almost killed me at first—now I am used to it."

The lives of the two young widows provide interesting parallels and telling differences: both were left with almost no financial means; both tenaciously refused to give up the guardianship of their children to affluent relatives; both returned to England; both sought and gained financial assistance from the families of their spouses. But whereas Mary Shelley regarded herself as a writer capable of selling her work, Jane Williams had neither independence nor the expectation of a career. In keeping with the conventions of the day, she again took the role most readily available to women by living with Thomas Jefferson Hogg as his wife, though legally she was still married to her very much alive first husband.

After the poison at Kentish Town, Mary Shelley, however reluctantly, entered a social and literary world far different from the Pisan circle. During the dozen years after 1827 her closest friends were the young daughters of Joshua Robinson, first Isabella, then Julia and Rosa (*[19 February 1827]). The most startling aspect of these new friendships, revealed through the letters and supplemented by other evidence, was the role Mary Shelley played in assisting Isabella Robinson's charade as the "wife" of "Sholto Douglas." In the summer of 1827 Mary Shelley, Isabella Robinson Douglas, and their entourage were in the south of England awaiting Isabella Robinson Douglas's husband so that the couple could complete their plans to go abroad. The fact is that the "husband" they waited for was actually their friend Mary Diana Dods, or "Doddy," a woman who wrote under the pseudonym David Lyndsay (30 October [1826] to Alaric A. Watts, n. 2). The letters surreptitiously unfold the strange story of Mary Diana Dods's transition into the role and attire of a man called Sholto Douglas, who traveled with Isabella Robinson Douglas as her husband and as the father of her infant daughter and who was accepted in French society as a man (17 September [1827]).

Mary Shelley was a pivotal player in this hoax, which remained a secret until the publication of *The Letters of Mary Wollstonecraft Shelley,* vols. 1 and 2. She looked after Isabella Robinson Douglas, who was quite ill in the summer of 1827; she obtained false passports for the group through John Howard Payne; she secured letters of introduction for them to French society from an unaware Frances Wright; she visited them in Paris, where they all maintained their charade, in 1828. Here then is another example, perhaps the most extraordinary, that should dispel past assessments that after Shelley's death Mary Shelley led a conventional, conservative life.

Mary Shelley invested a great deal of her emotional life in her friendships with women. She valued them in themselves and because she was basically unwilling or unprepared for anyone to take Shelley's place in her life. This may be one of the reasons she was not interested in men who pursued her but rather seemed drawn to men who did not reciprocate her feelings. Thus, after her return to England she was courted by John Howard Payne, whose suit she rejected, but was attracted to Washington Irving, who lived mostly on the Continent and only occasionally visited England during these years. In the period 1827–40 other men appeared to fit into this pattern of ensured singleness, for a variety of reasons. She firmly rejected Trelawny, who romantically commented that his and Mary Shelley's fates might still be intertwined. His suggestion and her response became a topic of repartee in their letters (14 June 1831). In the summer of 1828 she met Prosper Mérimée, with whom she maintained a correspondence into 1829. Her one known letter to him appears to be a rejection of a marriage proposal, though in her letters to friends she seemed charmed by this talented author and his interest in her. Most of the information about their interaction is contained in Mérimée's letters to Mary Shelley, first published in 1977, which make clear that they shared confidences about their personal lives as well as their careers. It seemed that the more pressing Mérimée's letters, the more distant Mary Shelley's responses. He was gratified by her willingness to assist his career by reviewing his latest work in the *Westminster Review,* but he complained of her melancholy, of her failure to write often enough, of rumors that she had married Trelawny, of her insistence that they keep their correspondence secret. Mérimée, ever consolable, soon turned his attentions elsewhere, and there seems to be nothing in the letters or her journal to suggest a sense of loss on her part.

Far different, it has been suggested, were her feelings for Major Aubrey Beauclerk, brother of her beloved friend Georgiana Beauclerk Paul (*16 January 1833), whose circle she entered in the 1830s. On the basis of evidence in her *Journal* it has been argued that Mary Shelley was in love with him from the early 1830s until the early 1840s. The letters make no explicit reference to her feelings about Beauclerk, though it is possible to attribute some of the melancholy she experienced in the mid-1830s to her disappointment at Beauclerk's marriage in February 1834 to Ida Goring. After Beauclerk's wife died in 1838, he married, in 1841, Rosa Robinson, who was quite possibly introduced to the Beauclerks by Mary Shelley. Claire Clairmont described Rosa Robinson as having been selected by Beauclerk because he needed a wife young and energetic enough to care for the four young children born of his first marriage. The full story of Mary Shelley and Beauclerk is yet to be told.

Of all her friendships within the Shelley circle, the one that altered most dramatically during the 1830s was that with Trelawny. In 1828, elated over Trelawny's return to England from Greece, Mary Shelley referred to him as "Dear dear darling—once again to find the true and good one" ([5 June 1828]).

A number of events led to the breach in their friendship, apparently more the result of Trelawny's actions than of hers. Although he claimed that he disapproved of her because she had become conservative and wasted her time in the company of such friends as the Robinsons, the crux of his arguments with her seems to have been her refusal to assist him in writing a biography of Shelley (April 1[829]). From this point on his letters to her, as well as his letters to Claire Clairmont about her, take on a new tone of critical sharpness. This, however, did not prevent him from asking her to assume the responsibility of arranging for the publication of his *Adventures of a Younger Son,* negotiating the contract, and seeing it through the press while he remained in Italy. Both her letters to him and those on his behalf show that she expended a great deal of time and energy in attempting to fulfill this voluntary obligation to Trelawny's best advantage.

Trelawny, however, complained that she had not obtained enough money for him for the book, that she was overfastidious in her judgment that parts of the books would be unacceptable to publisher and public (though he acceded when Horace Smith gave the same opinion), that she did not title the book as he had wished. Finally, he responded to Mary Shelley's first-edition deletions in *Queen Mab* by returning his copy of the book to Moxon with a rude note (11 February [1839]). In his revised edition of *Records of Shelley, Byron, and the Author* (1878) he entirely forgot the "dear Mary" to whom he had so often pledged his love and friendship and instead vilified her.

The years 1827–40 were Mary Shelley's most prolific as an author and editor. She wrote three more full-length novels, bringing her total to six. *Perkin Warbeck,* the first of these, she based on wide reading and consultation. She wrote to Thomas Crofton Croker for Irish sources (30 October 1828), to Sir Walter Scott for references to Scottish source material (25 May 1829), and to Godwin and others for additional details that she could distill into her fiction. In her final two novels, *Lodore* and *Falkner,* she shifted her focus to domestic life, spelling out her prevalent themes of the importance of love and the necessity to set aside self-interest in favor of serving others. On 8 November 1835 she confided to Maria Gisborne that she looked on fidelity as the first of human virtues and would write a novel to voice that conviction. Although Mary Shelley said she could "see its defects" (*26 April [1837]), *Falkner,* the story of an unconventional woman's strength and loyalty, was one of her favorite works.

The titles of the two final novels notwithstanding, the heroic figure in each is female. Their feelings and actions, which bear at times more than a passing resemblance to Mary Shelley's, reflect the author's self-respect and her respect for other women. Beginning with her admiration for Mary Wollstonecraft, she early recognized the important contributions women could make to society, though she also recognized the many barriers to those contributions.

During these same years, Mary Shelley also wrote the five volumes of Lardner's *Lives*. These studies of significant French, Spanish, Portuguese, and Italian literary and scientific figures occasioned many letters from her to famous contemporaries, such as Sir John Bowring and Gabriele Rossetti, from whom she sought accurate and learned sources of biographical, historical, and critical material.

Other letters refer to Mary Shelley's many short stories, poems, reviews, and essays and suggest that more of her shorter works than as yet have been ascribed to her have been published. She deals with questions of length of story, deadlines, payments, competing journals, contents, and editors, affording considerable insight into contemporary publishing procedures. Her opinions of contemporary authors are derived from her book reviews and, far more extensively, from her letters, in which she mentions, among others, Jane Austen, Edward Bulwer, Thomas Campbell, Benjamin Disraeli, Catherine Gore, Keats, Leigh Hunt, Washington Irving, Letitia Elizabeth Landon (L. E. L.), Harriet Martineau, Thomas Moore, Caroline Norton, John Howard Payne, Edward John Trelawny, William Wordsworth, and, of course, Shelley, Godwin, and Byron.

Among projects left unfinished was her life of Godwin, who died on 7 April 1836. His will appointed Mary Shelley his literary executor and requested that she determine which of his papers and letters should be published after his death (20 April 1836). She accordingly signed an agreement with Colburn to publish Godwin's memoirs and correspondence for the benefit of his widow, who, despite their differences over the years, she greatly assisted after Godwin's death. Mary Shelley began to annotate Godwin's early memoirs and to solicit his letters from friends and acquaintances. But she intended to defer publication until after Percy Florence's matriculation at Trinity College, Cambridge, in spring 1837, to prevent injury to his career from "a cry . . . raised against his Mother" ([26 January 1837]) on religious grounds. Perhaps for this reason, the edition was never completed. Or perhaps it was set aside in favor of first completing the Shelley editions and then was not resumed because she was unwilling or unable to undergo again the physical and psychological stress that she endured in the preparation of her editions of Shelley's poetry and prose in 1838–40.

Her intention to gather, preserve, and publish Shelley's works is expressed repeatedly in her letters, beginning almost immediately after his death. The first phase of this project led to the 1824 *Posthumous Poems,* which were suppressed at Sir Timothy's insistence in exchange for continuation of Percy Florence's allowance. The 1827–40 letters detail the subsequent history of her plans, which culminated in the 1839–40 editions. After *Posthumous Poems,* Mary Shelley's next major involvement with publishing Shelley was in 1829, when she assisted Cyrus Redding in editing Galignani's pirated *Poetical Works of Coleridge, Shelley, and Keats.* Prohibited by agreement with Sir Timothy from bringing Shelley's name before the public, she obviously believed that she could aid this French publication with impunity and thereby keep both her commitments; *she* would not bring Shelley forward, yet his works would be kept in the public notice.

Ten years elapsed between the Galignani edition and Mary Shelley's 1839 editions, though negotiations for those editions began at least as early 22 January 1834, when she informed Edward Moxon of her willingness to publish with him once "family reasons" no longer prevented her. Mary Shelley's letters between 1834 and 1840 record the development of this project. They provide a wealth of information about the problems, constraints, editorial decisions, and exhaustive labor, as well as the ideals and objectives that shaped the volumes. These letters also provide a far more accurate depiction than heretofore available of Mary Shelley's motives and actions and of contemporary publishing processes. For instance, Mary Shelley has been attacked almost universally for her omissions of the atheistical passages in *Queen Mab* in the four-volume *Poetical Works* (11 December 1838). The letters disclose, however, that although she disagreed with atheism and believed that Shelley himself had changed his mind about this subject, she was persuaded by the publisher Edward Moxon to omit those passages to protect his copyright, which he could lose if he were found guilty of publishing a work containing blasphemy. Nor was her omission of the dedication to Harriet Shelley in *Queen Mab* the result, as critics have suggested, of her reluctance to display Shelley's feelings for his first wife. Rather, it was made on the reasonable editorial principle of authorial intent. Years before, she had decisive evidence that Shelley himself preferred the omission (11 February [1839]).

The letters reveal that Mary Shelley was a more than responsible editor. She searched for first editions from which to correct proofs; she inquired after additional manuscripts of Shelley's works and letters; she asked advice and guidance from friends, including Hunt and Hogg. Her letters tell of her efforts in "turning over Manuscript books—full of scraps of finished or unfinished poems—half illegible" (*11 November [1839]), the questions of her claim to copyright (12 January 1839); and the frustrations of the work.

Mary Shelley circumvented Sir Timothy's injunction that she not include a biography of Shelley by notes she appended to the poems that trace their origins and history. What she could not circumvent was the severe illness caused by the editorial and personal strains of preparing Shelley's manuscripts in context. The achievement of the four-volume *Poetical Works,* the *Essays, Letters from Abroad, Translations and Fragments,* and the one-volume *Poetical Works* testifies as much to her commitment to achieve posthumous fame for Shelley as to her commitment as a professional, deliberate editor.

Subsequent editors have acknowledged their indebtedness to Mary Shelley for her arduous labors in transcribing often illegible and seemingly undecipherable manuscripts. And Shelley scholars have looked to her notes and her introductions as an invaluable source of biographical and critical detail. As is true for all editors, some decisions she made are open to criticism. But the letters show that even her most serious error, the failure to use first editions consistently as copy-text when manuscripts were not available, was not the result of amateurishness or indifference. In fact, Mary Shelley's letters reveal that her editorial principles, stated or implied, stand up well even by modern standards.

As editor, Mary Shelley became Shelley's collaborator, returning to him the assistance he had given her when she wrote *Frankenstein* and other earlier works. She gathered and preserved his writings. She brought the experience of a professional author to the editing of his works. Finally, Mary Shelley's commitment to bring Shelley the notice she believed his works merited was, biographers and critics agree, the single major force that established Shelley's reputation as a poet during a period when he almost certainly would have faded from public view.

But however significant writing and editing were in her life, Mary Shelley's daily responsibilities centered on the welfare of the Shelleys' one surviving child, Percy Florence. Mary Shelley was resolved, in accordance with Shelley's wish (*17 November 1834), that their son attend a public school. Because her own means were extremely limited and were frequently strained to assist Godwin and others, she was placed in the position of constantly importuning an ever-reluctant Sir Timothy for increases in the allowance borrowed against the estate as Percy Florence's educational expenses mounted. Mary Shelley's letters record her continual negotiations with him, conducted on his behalf by his attorneys, William Whitton and then John Gregson, because their client was determined never to communicate directly with his daughter-in-law.

Family, literary life, friendships, politics, travel, art, nature, finances —all central to the younger Mary Shelley—continued as the major subjects in her last years. But circumstances changed, and these years were marked by four important turning points that reflect at once her past and present, her public and private self. To these is joined the issue of Mary Shelley's health, an increasingly present motif from 1839 until her death in 1851.

The first of these major changes was in her relationship with Percy Florence Shelley. In November 1840 Percy Florence celebrated his twenty-first birthday, acknowledged by his grandfather by an outright allowance of £400 a year. The following January, he graduated from Trinity College and returned home to live with his mother. The two, always devoted to each other as mother and son, now became companions as well.

In the summer preceding his twenty-first birthday, Mary Shelley and Percy Florence, accompanied by two of his friends, embarked on the first of their several tours of the Continent, which became the basis of her last full-length work, *Rambles in Germany and Italy* (*6 June [1840] to Marianne Hunt). For Mary Shelley, who all her life loved to travel, this meant both new exploration and especially a return to her beloved Italy. For Percy, who was amiable but reserved, it meant introductions to other people, other countries, and other ways of life, which he did not always welcome. Her letters trace her son's growth into manhood and his ability to choose and select for himself. At times these choices made his mother unhappy. His boating on Lake Como, for example, brought back old fears (20 July [1840]), but she adjusted to his "hereditary passion for the sea" (*17 August 1847), as she was to adjust to his choice to live in London in 1845 while he studied law for a short time and then briefly became involved in the political arena. Her letters indicate that she accepted the life her son shaped for himself, a life that would eventually center on family, boating, music, and the theater he built at Boscombe Manor, where he wrote and produced plays.

The second major change in Mary Shelley's later life was the death of Sir Timothy Shelley on 24 April 1844. Given her father-in-law's refusal to see her for nineteen years, it is no surprise that his death was greeted by her with some relief. She wrote to Claire Clairmont on 25 April: "Poor Sir Tim is gone at last—He died Yesterday Morning at 6 o'clock He went gradually out & died at last without a sigh. . . . worry enough will come—& money too I trust—seeing that we have none just now." Mary Shelley and her son were now financially independent for the first time. To their disappointment, however, they found the estate to be worth considerably less than they had anticipated. Sir Timothy Shelley had bequeathed everything he could to Lady Shelley, with her holdings to go to her son John Shelley on her death. In addition, Mary Shelley was required to pay back the allowance received for Percy Florence since 1823, as well as money she had borrowed to send her son to Cambridge.

The third major change in the decade of the 1840s occurred in 1848, when Percy Florence married Jane Gibson St. John, a marriage that proved to be as happy for the mother-in-law as for the bride and groom. The closeness of Mary Shelley and Jane Shelley was no doubt rooted in part in the story of Jane Shelley's life. Born Jane Gibson, Jane Shelley was one of nine illegitimate children of Thomas Gibson, a Newcastle-on-Tyne banker, and Ann Shevill. In 1841 Jane Gibson married Charles Robert St. John, son of George Richard St. John (third viscount Bolingbroke and fourth viscount St. John) and his second wife, Isabella Antoinette. Charles St. John's family background was even more extraordinary than his wife's. His father had at least fifteen children, only four of whom were legitimate (including Charles), by two marriages and an alliance with his half-sister. Charles, in turn, had fathered an illegitimate son, of whom Jane St. John became guardian on her husband's death in 1844 and to whom Mary Shelley referred as a young "relation" of Jane Shelley's first husband (*[5 February 1849]). Within these families no distinction appears to have been made on the basis of legitimacy. Rather, the unconventional relationships were probably one of the reasons why Mary Shelley was drawn to her daughter-in-law.

Here were echoes of the unconventional relationships in Mary Shelley's own life—her mother's liaison with Gilbert Imlay, resulting in the birth of the illegitimate Fanny, her parents' marriage just five months before she was born, followed by her mother's death ten days after giving birth to her, the unclear marital status of her stepmother and her two children, her elopement with the married Shelley, her own two illegitimate children, who died in early childhood, and her young widowhood. No doubt Jane Shelley was especially dear because she required the kind of social protection that Mary Shelley herself had so acutely felt the need of, "exiled from the good society of my own country on account of the outset of my life" (20 September [1843]).

Among the most dramatic events was the final and complete break in Mary Shelley's almost lifelong relationship with Claire Clairmont, Mary Shelley's stepsister/friend/nemesis, recorded in a correspondence that is almost coextensive with Mary Shelley's adult life. Impatience, mutual protection, care, anger, pain—all were woven into an association that was the result not of sympathy but of happenstance and was protracted out of mutual need and family and habit. Mary Jane Clairmont, Claire Clairmont's mother, the stepmother whom Mary Shelley disliked but to whom she gave attention and care, died in June 1841. Claire Clairmont, still struggling financially, took out an annuity against Sir Timothy Shelley's life and used the money to settle in Paris. Upon Sir Timothy Shelley's death, Claire Clairmont received Shelley's legacy of £12,000, and Mary Shelley offered assistance about investing the money. Claire Clairmont in turn aided and comforted Mary Shelley when the Italian expatriate Gatteschi tried to blackmail her. Their long connection ended, however, when Claire Clairmont's niece, while on a visit to the Shelleys in 1849, suddenly married Alexander Knox, Percy's school friend and a favorite of Mary Shelley's. Claire Clairmont blamed Mary Shelley, never forgiving either niece or stepsister. Perhaps she had forgotten her own and Mary Shelley's far more daring youthful adventures, or perhaps she remembered them only too well.

Unfortunately, the tranquility Mary Shelley found in the closeness to her children and the family's financial ease was disrupted by her illness that began in 1839, which was manifested by recurring and severe head pain and partial paralysis that varied in intensity and duration. For long periods she could neither read nor write, two activities that she considered essential to her existence. During the 1840s, however much she suffered, she optimistically expected to be "restored to my natural good health" (*12 November [1846]), but despite her courage, the battle was not to be won. In December 1850 intense head pain recurred, followed by paralysis and death on 1 February 1851. At the age of fifty-three Mary Shelley died of "Disease of the Brain Supposed Tumour in left hemisphere, of long standing, Certified."

Her lengthy struggle against ill health provides insight into Mary Shelley's literary activities from 1840 to 1850. It may well have been her physical suffering that prevented her from writing the biographies of Godwin (*[?22 October 1845]) and Shelley that she had so long intended to write. But there were other reasons as well. To write truthfully about Godwin required discussion of his constant impecunity. To write truthfully about Shelley required discussion of his unconventional ideas about free love and religion. In 1846 she told Medwin that she believed "the time has not yet come to recount the events of my husband's life" without doing great harm to the living ([?13–16 May 1846]).

Even without these biographies, Mary Shelley and her family remained the subject of public interest and curiosity. Still, she was determined to maintain as much privacy as possible about their personal lives, past and present. Preying on this commitment to privacy, in the mid-1840s two men threatened her with blackmail and extortion. The first carried with him the trappings of an Italian expatriate and a talented writer. Ferdinand Gatteschi, along with other expatriates, fled to Paris after the defeat of their cause of liberation from the Austrian empire. In 1843 Claire Clairmont introduced Mary Shelley to Gatteschi and his circle, now homeless and poor heroes. Gatteschi, defender of her beloved Italy, personified the earlier dreams of European freedom she and Shelley had shared. She responded to him with empathy, money, and assistance in finding employment. She encouraged him to write and called on him to write details of the fight for Italian freedom, which she incorporated into her *Rambles*. In the course of their friendship she corresponded with him openly and sufficiently for her letters to become the instruments of his blackmail. What the letters actually said we will never know. The Paris police raided Gatteschi's home and confiscated the letters (*[15–16 October 1845]); returned to Mary Shelley, they were burned.

Within two weeks, however, other letters and more consternation arose. One George "Byron," who claimed to be the illegitimate son of Lord Byron and proved to be a notorious forger, offered to return to Mary Shelley eleven letters (or copies of letters) by Shelley and Mary Shelley in exchange for "a loan" ([?3 November 1845], n. 1). Mary Shelley entered a period of protracted negotiations through Thomas Hookham, bookseller and a friend of Shelley's, who purchased a number of the letters on her behalf.

What Mary Shelley intended to be known about her family's personal life she would say herself. She had secretly assisted Cyrus Redding in his 1829 edition of Shelley's poems; she refused to aid Trelawny and George Henry Lewes in biographies; she included her biographical notes in the 1839 editions. The last time she willingly shared information with the public about her family was in her own *Rambles in Germany and Italy*. Her first published book, the *History of a Six Weeks' Tour,* recorded her elopement with Shelley. With *Rambles* she came full circle, back to the Continent, with another Shelley—Percy Florence. Although the travelers, the events, and the years are different, throughout the *Rambles* there is an overlay of memories of earlier days, and occasionally Mary Shelley explicitly refers to the time long gone.

Her letters written on her travels also reflect those memories: "There is something strange & dreamlike in returning to Italy after so many many years—the language the mode of life the people—the houses the vegetation are as familiar to me as if I had left them only yesterday—yet since I saw them Youth has fled—my baby boy become a man—& still I have struggled on poor & alone" (20 July [1840]). In October she told Abraham Hayward of her happiness at being again in Italy, with "its dear, courteous, lying, kind inhabitants," and of her unhappiness at the thought of returning to England, which she had ever found inhospitable (26 October [1840]). Those dreamlike memories also included the deepest grief. In Venice she is made melancholy remembering the death of her dear Clara (1–2 October [1842]); in Rome she reflects on William's death.

Just as her memoirs circle back, the *Rambles* reflect Mary Shelley's basic methodology of *History of a Six Weeks' Tour*. In the earlier work she drew on her journal and her letters. Now, again writing in the first person, she worked from observation, calling upon the letters she had written to supply her with specifics (*13–[16] October [1843]). *Rambles*, published less than seven years before her death, is Mary Shelley's last book. Although her motivation for writing the book was financial—to assist Gatteschi—she did not look upon the writing of it as perfunctory. In negotiating with Moxon, publisher of the book, she reminded him that her "6 weeks tour brought me many compliments & my present Twelvemonths tour will, I feel sure, procure me many more" (27 September [1843]). Her interests in writing and in assisting others were strong enough to induce her as late as 1846 and 1849 to offer to translate and edit the Italian works of Laura Galloni (*[?March 1846]; *[6 April 1849]). For Mary Shelley, writing was the language of imagination, and it was her imagination that sustained and nourished her through her life.

Only her letters preserve her imagination during the remaining six and a half years of her life. They are the single source we have to trace her life through to its relatively early end. All the more a loss are her letters that have not been found, to Godwin, Percy Florence, the Robinsons, Prosper Mérimée. Many letters were no doubt casually destroyed; others, like those to Gatteschi, were purposely destroyed by Mary Shelley herself. Letters continue to surface. And perhaps there are bundles of her letters tucked away in someone's attic, neatly ribboned and awaiting their time.

Mary Shelley wrote of herself: "A pen in hand my thoughts flow fast" (*6 January 1825), which partially explains the air of spontaneity as well as the many minor errors in her letters. But the haste was not motivated by indifference to letter writing. On the contrary, Mary Shelley frequently commented in her letters on the high value she placed on letters as literature, as literary and biographical source, and as personal communication. During Shelley's lifetime she asked Thomas Love Peacock to save Shelley's letters because she intended to copy them when the couple returned to England (*10 November 1818). After Shelley's death she gathered his letters, originals and copies, and published a selection of them in *Essays, Letters*. She and Shelley included two letters each in *Six Weeks' Tour*, and she revised passages from letters for her fiction and for *Rambles in Germany and Italy*.

Her letters, diverse in tone and topic, display a letter-writing style that is frank about her feelings to her closest friends but reserved and private with all others. The melancholia and depression of many of her letters have long been a subject for critics, who have cited them to argue that Mary Shelley had little or no sense of humor. A number of the letters, however, are marked by humor and playfulness (c. 13 November 1819; *11 June 1826). The letters also call into question another canard of Mary Shelley criticism: that as a person she was cold. These letters exhibit a wide range of engaged and enthusiastic impulses: joy of her love of Shelley and of their children; optimism about her writing; pride in Shelley's writing and her own; love of friends; amusement over human foibles; excitement over books, theater, opera, art; exhilaration in nature. These contrast and sometimes commingle with grief over the deaths of Shelley and their children, dismay and anger at accusations of incest against Shelley (10 August 1821 to Shelley; 10 August 1821 to Isabella Hoppner), wryness at the outcome of Shelley's friendship with Emilia Viviani (*7 March 1822), fatigue resulting from overwork, hostility towards Claire Clairmont, disappointment over lost friendships, frustration at financial pressures and her ostracism by Shelley's family until Sir Timothy's death in 1844. Her commentaries on these experiences may be faulted for their occasional repetitiveness, but not for their want of feeling.

Mary Shelley's explicit and implicit self-revelations in the letters reflect a woman of great strength and energy. This is nowhere more movingly demonstrated than in her 1822–23 mourning letters interfaced with her persistent request that Sir Timothy grant her an allowance for his grandson. Her career intentions, her demands on her father-in-law, and her dealings with publishers all mark Mary Shelley as a most unconventional woman in her day, and her letters bring to light many examples of her unconventional behavior, the most dramatic being her role in the lives of Mary Diana Dods and Isabella Robinson Douglas.

Her letters place Mary Shelley in the tradition of Romantic letter writing not because they are creative and reflective in the same way as Lamb's or Byron's, Shelley's or Keats's are but because their own creativity and reflectiveness add a different, equally important perspective to our understanding of the Romantic period. Her elopement and life with Shelley, her writing career, her self-dependence in widowhood, her ambivalence as she faced a world inhospitable to independent women, and her publications of Shelley's works and her own are rooted in a Romantic defiance of conventions and a belief in the ability of the individual to change those conventions.

Mary Shelley's Romantic voice was also expressed in her reverence for nature as regenerative as well as in her belief in the value of the individual. At times she used copies of these letters as sources for details for her fiction and travel books (see, for example, 17 May 1816 and 20 July [1840]), just as Wordsworth sometimes used his sister Dorothy Wordsworth's journal observations for his poetry. Some of the letters, particularly those written after Shelley's death, resemble the topographical-meditative poetry so popular in the period—characterized by a description of a specific place followed by associations and reflections that it inspired.

Her confessional tendency to a number of correspondents, including Jane Williams, Leigh Hunt, John Howard Payne, and Maria Gisborne, is another indication of the influence of an age that celebrated self-revelation as art, typified by Jean-Jacques Rousseau, Wordsworth, and Lord Byron. Her letters as well as her professional writing also place her in the Romantic tradition in their expression of an aesthetic dependent on the curative role of nature and the dignity of the individual; to this, both Shelleys added the concept that love, not force, was the only valid means of restructuring the life of the individual and society.

Following her breach with Jane Williams Hogg, Mary Shelley emerged, despite her self-doubts, as a woman of determination and accomplishment rather than the chronically mournful widow presented in many biographies. Her achievements are all the more notable in the context of a society far from hospitable to a female on her own who could write: "The best is that the very thing which occasions the difficulty makes it interesting—namely—the treading in unknown paths and dragging out unknown things" (3 October 1835). Although she was referring to literary research, her comment may serve equally well to characterize Mary Shelley's personal life and career.

Perhaps the most important Romantic characteristic of Mary Shelley, confirmed by her letters, was her enduring will not merely to survive but to create and help shape the world in which she lived. Readers interested exclusively in literary or historical detail or in the state of women will value parts of her letters more than others. But the diversity of her concerns develops a counterpoint, the minor themes giving depth and nuance to the major themes of her life and letters: the Godwin, Shelley, and Byron circles; her career; her responses to and reflections on nineteenth-century European society.

Although Mary Shelley was a highly regarded author in her own era, after her death the significance of her works was eclipsed, and she was written about mainly as Shelley's wife. In the last fifteen years, however, Mary Shelley's professional and personal writings, which so forcefully reflect the very sociopolitical debates we engage in today, have been accorded new, and enthusiastic, assessment. Through her own letters, we may better situate this complex figure within her own era and understand her role among the leading Romantic figures of the nineteenth century.

ABBREVIATIONS

Abinger MSS.

The manuscripts and letters of William Godwin, Mary Wollstonecraft Shelley, Percy Bysshe Shelley, and others in the possession of Lord Abinger (many of which are now on deposit at the Bodleian Library).

Altick, *The Cowden Clarkes*

Richard D. Altick. *The Cowden Clarkes*. London: Oxford University Press, 1948.

Alumni Cantabrigienses

Alumni Cantabrigienses. Edited by John Venn and J. A. Venn. 10 vols. Cambridge: At the University Press, 1922–47.

Annual Register

The Annual Register, or a View of the History, Politics, and Literature. London: Baldwin, Cradock, and Joy [various dates].

Bennett and Little, "Seven Letters from Mérimée to Mary Shelley"

Betty T. Bennett and William T. Little. "Seven Letters from Prosper Mérimée to Mary Shelley." *Comparative Literature* 31 (Spring 1979): 134–53.

Blunden, *"Examiner" Examined*

Edmund Blunden. *Leigh Hunt's "Examiner" Examined*. London: Cobden-Sanderson, 1928.

Blunden, *Leigh Hunt*

Edmund Blunden. *Leigh Hunt, A Biography*. London: Cobden-Sanderson, 1930.

Boyle's Court Guide

Boyle's Fashionable Court and Country Guide. London: Eliza Boyle & Son. Published under various titles throughout the nineteenth century and continued into the twentieth century.

Brewer, *The Holograph Letters* — *My Leigh Hunt Library, the Holograph Letters*. Edited by Luther A. Brewer. Iowa City: University of Iowa Press, 1938.

Brown, *Godwin* — Ford K. Brown. *The Life of William Godwin*. London: J. M. Dent & Sons, 1926.

Brown, *Letters* — *The Letters of Charles Armitage Brown*. Edited by Jack Stillinger. Cambridge, Mass.: Harvard University Press, 1966.

Burke's Peerage — John Burke *et al.*, eds. *Genealogical and Heraldic History of the Peerage, Baronetage and Knightage*. London [various dates].

Byron, *Letters and Journals* — *Byron's Letters and Journals*. Edited by Leslie A. Marchand. 12 vols. Cambridge, Mass.: The Belknap Press of Harvard University Press, 1973–82.

Byron, *Works* — *The Works of Lord Byron: Letters and Journals*. Edited by Rowland E. Prothero. 6 vols. London: John Murray, 1898–1901.

Cameron, *The Golden Years* — Kenneth Neill Cameron. *Shelley: The Golden Years*. Cambridge, Mass.: Harvard University Press, 1974.

CC Journals — *The Journals of Claire Clairmont, 1814–1827*. Edited by Marion Kingston Stocking with the assistance of David Mackenzie Stocking. Cambridge, Mass.: Harvard University Press, 1968.

Cline, *Pisan Circle* — C. L. Cline. *Byron, Shelley and their Pisan Circle*. London: John Murray, 1952.

Dean, "Mary Shelley and Gideon Mantell" — Dennis Dean. "Mary Shelley and Gideon Mantell." *Keats-Shelley Journal* 30 (1981): 21–29.

DNB — Edgar Williams and Helen M. Palmer, eds. *The Compact Edition of the Dictionary of National Biography*. 2 vols. Oxford: Oxford University Press, 1975.

Dowden, *Shelley* — Edward Dowden. *The Life of Percy Bysshe Shelley*. 2 vols. London: Kegan Paul, Trench & Co., 1886.

Dunbar, *PBS Bibliography*

Clement Dunbar. *A Bibliography of Shelley Studies: 1823–1950.* New York: Garland, 1976.

Fenner, *Leigh Hunt and Opera Criticism*

Theodore Fenner. *Leigh Hunt and Opera Criticism: The "Examiner" Years, 1808–1821.* Lawrence: University Press of Kansas, 1972.

Galignani, *Poetical Works of Coleridge, Shelley, and Keats*

The Poetical Works of Coleridge, Shelley, and Keats. Edited by Cyrus Redding. Paris: A. and W. Galignani, 1829.

Garnett Letters

Cecilia Payne-Gaposchkin, ed. *The Garnett Letters.* Privately printed, 1979.

Genest, *English Stage*

John Genest, ed. *Some Account of the English Stage from the Restoration in 1660 to 1830.* 10 vols. Bath, 1832.

Gisborne, *Journals and Letters*

Maria Gisborne & Edward E. Williams, Shelley's Friends, Their Journals and Letters. Edited by Frederick L. Jones. Norman: University of Oklahoma Press, 1951.

Godwin, Journal

Manuscript journal of William Godwin, 1788–1836 (Abinger MSS.).

Grylls, *Mary Shelley*

R. Glynn Grylls. *Mary Shelley: A Biography.* London: Oxford University Press, 1938.

Hayward, *Correspondence*

A Selection from the Correspondence of Abraham Hayward, Q.C. Edited by Henry E. Carlisle. 2 vols. New York: Scribner and Welford, 1887.

Hogg, *Shelley*

Thomas Jefferson Hogg. *The Life of Percy Bysshe Shelley.* In *The Life of Percy Bysshe Shelley . . .,* edited by Humbert Wolfe. 2 vols. London: J. M. Dent & Sons, 1933.

Hunt, *Autobiography*

The Autobiography of Leigh Hunt. Edited by Roger Ingpen. 2 vols. New York: E. P. Dutton & Co., 1903.

Hunt, *Correspondence*

The Correspondence of Leigh Hunt. Edited by Thornton Hunt. 2 vols. London: Smith, Elder and Co., 1862.

Hunt, *Lord Byron and Some of His Contemporaries*

Leigh Hunt. *Lord Byron and Some of His Contemporaries*. London: Henry Colburn, 1828.

Ingpen, *Shelley in England*

Roger Ingpen. *Shelley in England: New Facts and Letters from the Shelley-Whitton Papers*. 2 vols. London: Kegan Paul, Trench, Trubner & Co., 1917.

Irving, *Journals and Notebooks*

Washington Irving. *Journals and Notebooks*. Edited by Henry A. Pochmann. Vol. I, *1803–1806*, edited by Nathalia Wright (Madison: University of Wisconsin Press, 1969–70); vol. II, *1807–1822*, edited by Lillian Schlissel and Walter A. Reichart (Boston: Twayne Publishers, 1981); vol. III, *1819–1827*, edited by Walter A. Reichart (Madison: University of Wisconsin Press, 1969–70).

Lamb, *Letters*

The Letters of Charles Lamb to Which Are Added Those of His Sister Mary Lamb. Edited by E. V. Lucas. 3 vols. London: J. M. Dent & Sons, 1935.

Locke, *Godwin*

Don Locke. *A Fantasy of Reason: The Life and Thought of William Godwin*. London: Routledge & Kegan Paul, 1980.

Lovell, *Medwin*

Ernest J. Lovell, Jr. *Captain Medwin: Friend of Byron and Shelley*. Austin: University of Texas Press, 1962.

Lyles, *MWS Bibliography*

W. H. Lyles. *Mary Shelley: An Annotated Bibliography*. New York: Garland, 1975.

McAleer, *The Sensitive Plant*

Edward C. McAleer. *The Sensitive Plant: A Life of Lady Mount Cashell*. Chapel Hill: University of North Carolina Press, 1958.

Marchand, *Byron*

Leslie A. Marchand. *Byron: A Biography*. 3 vols. New York: Alfred A. Knopf, 1957.

Marshall, *Mary Shelley*

Mrs. Julian {Florence A.} Marshall. *The Life and Letters of Mary Wollstonecraft Shelley*. 2 vols. London: Richard Bentley & Son, 1889.

Marshall, *The Liberal*   William H. Marshall. *Byron, Shelley, Hunt and the Liberal*. Philadelphia: University of Pennsylvania Press, 1960.

Medwin, *Conversations*   *Medwin's Conversations of Lord Byron*. Edited by Ernest J. Lovell, Jr. Princeton: Princeton University Press, 1966.

Medwin, *Shelley*   Thomas Medwin. *The Life of Percy Bysshe Shelley*. Edited by H. Buxton Forman. London: Oxford University Press, 1913.

Merriam, *Moxon*   Harold G. Merriam. *Edward Moxon: Publisher of Poets*. New York: Columbia University Press, 1939.

Moore, *Accounts Rendered*   Doris Langley Moore. *Lord Byron: Accounts Rendered*. London: John Murray, 1974.

Moore, *Journal*   *The Journal of Thomas Moore*. Edited by Wilfred S. Dowden. 6 vols. Newark: University of Delaware Press, 1983–1991.

Moore, *The Late Lord Byron*   Doris Langley Moore. *The Late Lord Byron*. New York: Harper & Row, 1961.

Moore, *Letters*   *The Letters of Thomas Moore*. Edited by Wilfred S. Dowden. 2 vols. Oxford: Clarendon Press, 1964.

Moore, *Memoirs*   Thomas Moore. *Memoirs, Journal and Correspondence*. Edited by Lord John Russell. 8 vols. Boston: Little, Brown and Co., 1853.

MWS, *Falkner*   Mary Wollstonecraft Shelley. *Falkner: A Novel*. 3 vols. London: Saunders and Otley, 1837.

MWS, *Frankenstein*   Mary Wollstonecraft Shelley. *Frankenstein; or, The Modern Prometheus*. 3 vols. London: Lackington, Hughes, Harding, Mavor, & Jones, 1818.

MWS Journal   Manuscript journal of Mary Shelley (Abinger MSS.).

MWS *Journal*   *Mary Shelley's Journal*. Edited by Paula R. Feldman and Diana Scott-Kilvert. 2 vols. Oxford: Clarendon Press, 1987.

MWS, *The Last Man*	Mary Wollstonecraft Shelley. *The Last Man*. 3 vols. London: Henry Colburn, 1826.
MWS *Letters*	*The Letters of Mary Wollstonecraft Shelley*. Edited by Betty T. Bennett. 3 vols. Baltimore: Johns Hopkins University Press, 1980–88.
MWS, *Lives* (1835–37)	Mary Wollstonecraft Shelley (with others). *Lives of the most Eminent Literary and Scientific Men of Italy, Spain, and Portugal*. Vols. I–III. The Cabinet of Biography, edited by the Rev. Dionysius Lardner, vols. 86–88. London: Longman, Orme, Brown, Green, & Longman; and John Taylor, 1835–37.
MWS, *Lives* (1838–39)	Mary Wollstonecraft Shelley. *Lives of the most Eminent Literary and Scientific Men of France*. Vols. I and II. The Cabinet of Biography, edited by the Rev. Dionysius Lardner, vols. 102 and 103. London: Longman, Orme, Brown, Green & Longman; and John Taylor, 1838–39.
MWS, *Lodore*	Mary Wollstonecraft Shelley. *Lodore*. 3 vols. London: Richard Bentley, 1835.
MWS, *Matilda*	Mary Wollstonecraft Shelley. *Mathilda*. Edited by Elizabeth Nitchie. Chapel Hill: University of North Carolina Press, 1959.
MWS, *Midas*	Mary Wollstonecraft Shelley. *Midas*. In *Proserpine & Midas. Two Unpublished Mythological Dramas by Mary Shelley*, edited by A[ndré] [Henri] Koszul. London: Humphrey Milford, 1922.
MWS, *Perkin Warbeck*	Mary Wollstonecraft Shelley. *The Fortunes of Perkin Warbeck, A Romance*. 3 vols. London: Henry Colburn and Richard Bentley, 1830.
MWS, *Proserpine*	Mary Wollstonecraft Shelley. *Proserpine, a Mythological Drama in Two Acts*. In *The Winter's Wreath*. London: G. and W. B. Whittaker, 1832 [1831].
MWS, *Rambles in Germany and Italy*	Mary Wollstonecraft Shelley. *Rambles in Germany and Italy, in 1840, 1842, and 1843*. 2 vols. London: Edward Moxon, 1844.

MWS, *Six Weeks' Tour*   Mary Wollstonecraft Shelley with Percy Bysshe
                            Shelley. *History of a Six Weeks' Tour through a Part of
                            France, Switzerland, Germany, and Holland: with
                            Letters Descriptive of a Sail round the Lake of Geneva,
                            and of the Glaciers of Chamouni*. London: T.
                            Hookham, Jun. and C. and J. Ollier, 1817.

MWS, *Valperga*   Mary Wollstonecraft Shelley. *Valperga: or, the Life
                            and Adventures of Castruccio, Prince of Lucca*. 3 vols.
                            London: G. and W. B. Whittaker, 1823.

New Grove Dictionary of   Stanley Sadie, ed. *The New Grove Dictionary of
Music and Musicians   Music and Musicians*. 20 vols. London: Macmillan,
                            1980.

Nicoll, *English Drama*   Allardyce Nicoll. *A History of English Drama,
                            1660–1900*. Vol. IV, *Early Nineteenth Century
                            Drama, 1800–1850*. London: Cambridge
                            University Press, 1960.

Nitchie, *Mary Shelley*   Elizabeth Nitchie. *Mary Shelley: Author of
                            "Frankenstein."* New Brunswick: Rutgers
                            University Press, 1953.

Norman, *After Shelley*   *After Shelley: The Letters of Thomas Jefferson Hogg to
                            Jane Williams*. Edited by Sylva Norman. London:
                            Oxford University Press, 1934.

Norman, *Flight of the*   Sylva Norman. *Flight of the Skylark: The
Skylark*   Development of Shelley's Reputation*. London: Max
                            Reinhardt, 1954.

Origo, *The Last*   Iris Origo. *The Last Attachment*. London: Jonathan
Attachment*   Cape & John Murray, 1949.

Overmyer, *America's*   Grace Overmyer. *America's First Hamlet*.
First Hamlet*   New York: New York University Press, 1957.

Owen, *Threading My*   Robert Dale Owen. *Threading My Way: An
Way*   Autobiography*. 1874. Reprint. New York:
                            Augustus M. Kelley, 1967.

Paul, *Godwin*   C. Kegan Paul. *William Godwin: His Friends and
                            Contemporaries*. 2 vols. London: Henry S. King &
                            Co., 1876.

Payne, Letterbook

Manuscript letterbooks of John Howard Payne. Columbia University Library [various dates].

PBS Letters

The Letters of Percy Bysshe Shelley. Edited by Frederick L. Jones. 2 vols. Oxford: Oxford University Press, 1964.

Peacock, *Works*

The Works of Thomas Love Peacock. Edited by H. F. B. Brett-Smith and C. E. Jones. (Halliford Edition). 10 vols. London: Constable & Co., 1924–34.

Perkins, *Mrs. Norton*

Jane Gray Perkins. *The Life of the Honourable Mrs. Norton.* New York: Henry Holt & Co., 1909.

Perkins and Wolfson, *Frances Wright*

A. J.G. Perkins and Theresa Wolfson. *Frances Wright: Free Inquirer.* New York and London: Harper & Brothers, 1939.

Redding, *Fifty Years' Recollections*

Cyrus Redding. *Fifty Years' Recollections: Literary and Personal.* 3 vols. London: Charles J. Skeet, 1858.

Reiman, *The Romantics Reviewed*

Donald H. Reiman, ed. *The Romantics Reviewed: Contemporary Reviews of British Romantic Writers.* 9 vols. New York: Garland, 1972.

Rennie, *Traits of Character*

Eliza Rennie. *Traits of Character: Being Twenty-Five Years' Literary and Personal Recollections By A Contemporary.* 2 vols. London: Hurst and Blackett, 1860.

Robinson, *On Books*

Henry Crabb Robinson. *On Books and Their Writers.* Edited by Edith J. Morley. 3 vols. London: J. M. Dent & Sons, 1938.

The Romance

The Romance of Mary W. Shelley, John Howard Payne and Washington Irving. Edited by F. B. Sanborn. Boston: Boston Bibliophile Society, 1907.

St Clair, *Trelawny*

William St Clair. *Trelawny: The Incurable Romancer.* London: John Murray, 1977.

S&M

Shelley and Mary. 4 vols. London: privately printed, 1882.

SC   Kenneth Neill Cameron and Donald H. Reiman,
                                eds. *Shelley and his Circle, 1773–1822*. 8 vols.
                                Cambridge, Mass.: Harvard University Press,
                                1961–86.

Shelley, *Essays, Letters*   *Essays, Letters from Abroad, Translations and
                                Fragments, By Percy Bysshe Shelley*. Edited by Mrs.
                                Shelley. 2 vols. London: Edward Moxon, 1840
                                [1839].

Shelley, *Poetical Works*   *The Poetical Works of Percy Bysshe Shelley*. Edited by
(1839)   Mrs. Shelley. 4 vols. London: Edward Moxon,
                                1839.

Shelley, *Poetry and Prose*   *Shelley's Poetry and Prose*. Edited by Donald H.
                                Reiman and Sharon B. Powers. New York: Norton
                                & Co., 1977.

Shelley, *Posthumous Poems*   *Posthumous Poems of Percy Bysshe Shelley*. Edited by
                                Mary W. Shelley. London: John and Henry L.
                                Hunt, 1824.

Smith, *A Sentimental   Harry B. Smith. *A Sentimental Library*. Privately
Library*   printed, 1914.

Steffan, *Byron's Don Juan*   Truman Guy Steffan. *Byron's Don Juan*. 2d ed.
                                4 vols. Austin: University of Texas Press, 1971.

Taylor, *Early Collected   Charles H. Taylor, Jr. *The Early Collected Editions of
Editions*   Shelley's Poems*. New Haven: Yale University Press,
                                1958.

Trelawny, *Adventures*   Edward John Trelawny. *Adventures of a Younger Son*.
                                Edited by William St Clair. London: Oxford
                                University Press, 1974.

Trelawny, *Letters*   *Letters of Edward John Trelawny*. Edited by H.
                                Buxton Forman. London: Oxford University Press,
                                1910.

Trelawny, *Recollections*   *Trelawny's Recollections of the Last Days of Shelley and
                                Byron*. With an Introduction by Edward Dowden.
                                London: Humphrey Milford, 1931.

Trelawny, *Records*   Edward John Trelawny. *Records of Shelley, Byron,
                                and the Author*. 2 vols. London: Basil Montagu
                                Pickering, 1878.

Wardle, *Hazlitt*

Ralph M. Wardle. *Hazlitt*. Lincoln: University of Nebraska Press, 1971.

White, *Shelley*

Newman Ivey White. *Shelley.* 2 vols. London: Secker & Warburg, 1947.

Williams, *Journals and Letters*

Maria Gisborne & Edward E. Williams, Shelley's Friends, Their Journals and Letters. Edited by Frederick L. Jones. Norman: University of Oklahoma Press, 1951.

LIST OF LETTERS

xliii

xlv

xlvii

SELECTED LETTERS OF
MARY WOLLSTONECRAFT SHELLEY

To Shelley[1]

[5 Church Terrace, Pancras   25 October 1814][2]

For what a minute did I see you yesterday—is this the way my beloved that we are to live till the sixth[3] in the morning I look for you and when I awake I turn to look on you—dearest Shelley you are solitary and uncomfortable why cannot I be with you to cheer you and to press you to my heart oh my love you have no friends why then should you be torn from the only one who has affection for you—But I shall see you tonight and that is the hope that I shall live on through the day—be happy dear Shelley and think of me—why do I say this dearest & only one   I know how tenderly you love me and how you repine at this absence from me—when shall we be free from fear of treachery?—

I send you the letter I told you of from Harriet and a letter we received yesterday from fanny[4] the history of this interview I will tell you when I come—but perhaps as it is so rainy a day Fanny will not be allowed to come at all—

My love my own one be happy—

I was so dreadfully tired yesterday that I was obliged to take a coach home forgive this extravagance but I am so very weak at present[5] & I had been so agitated through the day that I was not able to stand a morning rest however will set me quite right again and I shall be quite well when I meet you this evening—will you be at the door of the coffee house at five oclock as it is disagreeable to go into those places and I shall be there exactly at that time & we will go into St. Pauls where we can sit down

I send you Diogenes as you have no books—Hookham[6] was so ill tempered as not to send the books I asked for

TEXT: MS., Bodleian Library.

1. On 28 July 1814 William Godwin wrote in his journal, "Five in the morning," thereby noting the elopement of his daughter Mary Wollstonecraft Godwin with Percy Bysshe Shelley. Accompanied by Jane (also called Mary Jane) Clairmont (1798–1879), Mary Godwin's stepsister, the couple toured Europe for six weeks and kept an account of their travels, published as *History of a Six Weeks' Tour through a*

Part of France, Switzerland, Germany, and Holland: with Letters Descriptive of a Sail round the Lake of Geneva, and of the Glaciers of Chamouni (London: T. Hookham, Jun.; and C. and J. Ollier, 1817), hereinafter cited as *Six Weeks' Tour*. On 13 September they returned to London without funds to find that almost all of their former friends disapproved of their elopement and of Shelley's treatment of his wife, Harriet Westbrook Shelley (1795–1816), and daughter, Ianthe (1813–76). Shelley and Mary Godwin's residence in London was marked by constant financial embarrassment until May 1815 (see 26 April 1815). Shelley had to pay past debts and immediate living expenses not only for his current household, which included Jane Clairmont, but also for his wife and daughter and for Godwin, who refused to see the elopers but used go-betweens to continue to draw on Shelley's resources. Shelley and Mary Godwin often changed their lodgings while Shelley tried to negotiate for funds. From the night of 23 October until 9 November 1814, aided by his friend Thomas Love Peacock, Shelley lived apart from Mary Godwin in order to avoid arrest for debt. To elude detection by bailiffs, Shelley and Mary Godwin met daily at different hours and locations, including St. Pancras, Holborn Street, Southampton Buildings, and a number of coffeehouses. The first four letters printed here were written during this period of forced separation. In *Lodore* (1835) Mary Shelley wrote a fictionalized account of the tribulations and restorative love of these days. (The dates and details of the events reflected in these letters are found in MWS *Journal*, *CC Journals*, and *PBS Letters*. For an account of the six-week tour, see *SC*, III, 342–75.)

2. Mary Godwin's letters were written from the lodgings she, Shelley, and Jane Clairmont had taken on 27 September.

3. Bailiffs were not permitted to make arrests from midnight Saturday until midnight Sunday, allowing debtors to come from hiding for a twenty-four-hour period each week. If Mary Godwin had been referring to their Sunday meeting, she would have named 30 October, the first Sunday after separation and the writing of this letter. The text suggests rather that Mary Godwin expected to be permanently reunited with Shelley on 6 November, an expectation he shared (see *PBS Letters*, #269, #270).

4. Fanny Imlay (1794–1816), Mary Godwin's half sister through Mary Wollstonecraft's liaison with Gilbert Imlay (1754–?1828). The letter was to Jane Clairmont asking her to meet Fanny the next day. Jane Clairmont complied and found that Fanny had been sent as an emissary bearing Godwin's proposal that she leave Mary Godwin and Shelley and "go into a family" (*CC Journals*, 24 October 1814; *MWS Journal*, 25 October 1814).

5. Mary Godwin was often indisposed during this period due to pregnancy.

6. Thomas Hookham, Jr. (1787–1867), publisher and friend of Shelley and Peacock. Hookham and his brother, Edward T. Hookham, were Peacock's publishers, and they introduced Shelley to Peacock (Carl Dawson, *His Fine Wit: A Study of Thomas Love Peacock* [Berkeley: University of California Press, 1970], pp. xiii, 37). Hookham and Shelley were briefly estranged because Hookham disapproved of the elopement.

To Shelley

[5 Church Terrace, Pancras   27 October 1814]

My own love

I do not know by what compulsion I am to answer you but your porter says I must so I do—

By a miracle I saved your £5[1] & I will bring it—I hope indeed; oh my loved Shelley we shall indeed be happy

I meet you at three and bring heaps of Skinner street news[2]—Heaven bless my love & take care of him

his own Mary

TEXT: MS., Lily Library, Indiana University.

1. Shelley had pawned his microscope at Davidson's for £5 on 24 October. Writing to his wife of his dire financial straits, Shelley alludes to this sale of their "last valuable" and implores her to "send quick supplies" (*PBS Letters*, #269). According to *MWS Journal*, *CC Journals*, and Mary Godwin's letter of [25 October 1814], Mary Godwin and Jane Clairmont had taken a coach on 24 October. Since prior to pawning the microscope they had no money, perhaps Peacock supplied them with their fare, or perhaps they spent some small part of the £5.

2. Early in the day, Fanny Imlay left a letter from herself and Charles Gaulis Clairmont (1795–1850), Jane Clairmont's brother and Mary Godwin's stepbrother, which Mary Godwin carried to Shelley that afternoon (*MWS Journal*; *CC Journals*).

To Shelley

[5 Church Terrace, Pancras   28 October 1814]

So this is the end of my letter—dearest love what do they mean—I detest M[rs] G. [*Godwin*][1] she plagues my father out of his life & then—well no matter—why will not Godwin follow the obvious bent of his affections & be reconciled to us—no his prejudices the world & she—do you not hate her my love—all these forbid it—what am I to do trust to time of course—for what else can I do

Goodnight my love—tomorrow I will seal this blessing on your lips dear good creature press me to you and hug your own Mary to your heart perhaps she will one day have a father till then be every thing to me love— & indeed I will be a good girl and never vex you any more   I will learn Greek[2] and—but when shall we meet when I may tell you all this & you will so sweetly reward me—oh we must meet soon for this is a dreary

3

life   I am weary of it—a poor widowed deserted thing no one cares for her—but—ah love is not that enough—indeed I have a very sincere affection for my own Shelley—

But Good night   I am woefully tired & so sleepy—I shall dream of you ten to one when naughty one—you have quite forgotten me—

Take me—one kiss—well that is enough—tomorrow

TEXT: MS., Bodleian Library.

  1. Very little is known about Mary Jane Vial (?Devereux) Clairmont Godwin (1768–1841) before her marriage to Godwin on 21 December 1801 in two separate ceremonies, first under the (probably assumed) name Clairmont and then under the name Vial. The paternity of her children, Charles Gaulis Clairmont and Jane Clairmont, remains obscure, although evidence suggests that both may have been illegitimate. Mrs. Godwin was credited with being an industrious woman who established and ran the M. J. Godwin Company, a publishing firm that specialized in children's books. Henry Crabb Robinson's description of her as a "meritorious wife" but of doubtful sincerity and integrity in her dealings with others seems generally accurate (Robinson, *On Books*, I, 235; *CC Journals*, pp. 13–16; White, *Shelley*, I, 667–68, 671, 673, 674, 683; Dowden, *Shelley*, II, 541–49). The relationship between Mary Godwin and her stepmother was never amicable. In this instance, Mary Godwin's ire concerned a letter she had received from Mrs. Godwin this same evening at six (*MWS Journal*).

  2. Mary Godwin was a most willing and apt student to Shelley, who in turn was a most committed mentor (see the lists in *MWS Journal* indicating their combined readings).

❖

To Shelley

[5 Church Terrace, Pancras   3 November 1814]

Dearest Love—I am so out of spirits   I feel so lonely but we shall meet tomorrow so I will try to be happy—Grays inn Gardens is I fear a dangerous place yet can you think of any other.

I received your letter tonight   I wanted one for I had {not} received one for almost two day but do not think I mean any thing by this my love—I know you took a long long walk yesterday so you could not write but I who am at home who do not walk out I could write to you all day love—

Another circumstance has made me feel more solitary that letter I received today¹—dear Shelley you will say I was deceived   I know I am not—I know her unexampled frankness and sweetness of character but what must that character be who resists opinions preach——

Oh dear what am I writing   I am indeed disappointed—I did think

4

Isabel perfectly unprejudiced—she adores the shade of my mother—but then a married man it is impossible to knock into some peoples heads that Harriet is selfish & unfeeling and that my father might be happy if he chose—by that cant concerning selling his daughter I should half suspect that there has been some communication between ⟨my⟩ the Skinner St. folks and them

Higho love such is the world

How you reason & philosophize about love—do you know if I had been asked I could not have given one reason in its favour—yet I have as great an opinion as you concerning its exaltedness and love very tenderly to prove my theory—adieu for the present it has struck eight & in an hour or two I will wish you goodnight.

Well so now I am to write a goodnight with the old story of I wish I could say it to you—yes my love it has indeed become an old story but I hope the last chapter is come—I shall meet you tomorrow love & if you do but get money love which indeed you must we will defy our enemies & our friends (for aught I see they are all as bad as one another) and we will not part again—Is not that a delightful word it shall cheer my dreams

No answer from Hooper[2]—I wish he would write oh how I long {to} be at our dear home where nothing can trouble us neither friends or enemies—dont be angry at this you know my love they are all a bad set—But Nantgwilt do you not wish to be settled there at a home you know love—with your own Mary nothing to disturb you studying walking & other such like amusements—oh its much better {I} believe not to be able to see the light of the sun for mountains than for houses

You dont say a word in your letter—you naughty love to ease one of my anxietie not a word of Lambert of Harriet of Mrs Stuart[3] of money or anythink [*anything*]—but all the reasonings you used to persuade Mr Peacock love was a good thing   Now you know I did not want converting—but my love do not be displeased at my chattering in this way for you know the expectation of a letter from you when absent always makes my heart jump so do you think it says nothing when one actually arrives.

Your own Mary who loves you so tenderly

TEXT: M.S., Bodleian Library.

1. From David Booth (1766–1846), lexicographer. In 1812 and 1813, for reasons of health, Mary Godwin had been sent by Godwin to live with the family of William Thomas Baxter, a manufacturer of canvas, in Dundee, Scotland. There she formed a deep friendship for Isabella Baxter, who in 1814 married Booth, widower of Isabella's sister Margaret and some twenty years her senior. According to contemporary law, it was illegal for Booth to marry his deceased wife's sister. On 4 and 23 October Mary Godwin had written to Isabella Booth (the letters are unlocated), but Booth, dis-

approving of the elopement and probably concerned about his own questionable matrimonial status, refused to allow the continuation of the friendship. In 1817 and 1818 attempts were made to change Booth's mind, but the friendship of Isabella Booth and Mary Shelley was not renewed until after Shelley's death (see *SC*, II, 558–59; 9–11 September [1823]; and 26 May 1850).

2. Shelley had lived in Mr. Hooper's House at Nantgwillt, Wales, in 1812. Before or on 28 October 1814 Shelley had written to Mr. Hooper to learn whether the house was available (*PBS Letters*, #274).

3. John Lambert, Godwin's creditor, was threatening Godwin with arrest (*PBS Letters*, #277). Mrs. Stewart was one of the most pressing of Shelley's creditors (*PBS Letters*, #278).

<hr>

To Thomas Jefferson Hogg[1]

[2 Nelson Square, Blackfriars Road]
January 1 1815[2]

Dearest Hogg

As they have ⟨all⟩ both[3] left me and I am here all alone I have nothing better to do than take up my pen and say a few words to you—as I do not expect you this morning.

You love me you say—I wish I could return it with the passion you deserve—but you are very good to me and tell me that you are quite happy with the affection which from the bottom of my heart I feel for you—you are so generous so disinterested that no one can help loving you   But you know Hogg that we have known each other for so short a time and I did not think about love—so that I think that that also will come in time & then we shall be happier I do think than the angels who sing for ever or even the lovers of Janes[4] world of perfection. There is a bright prospect before us my dear friend—lovely—and—which renders it certain—wholly dependant on our selves—for Shelley & myself I need promise nothing—nor to you either for I know that you are persuaded that I will use every effort to promote your happiness & such is my affection for you that it will be no hard task—

But this is prattle—I tell you what you know so well already—besides you will be here this evening—The sun shines it would be a fine day to visit the divine Theoclea[5] but I am not well enough—I was in great pain all night & this morning & am but just getting better

Affectionately yours
Mary

You need not answer this scrall

ADDRESS: Thomas Jefferson Hogg Esq. / Arundel Street / 34 Strand. POSTMARKS: (1) Two Py Post / Unpaid / West Lambth; (2) 7 o'clock / 1 Ja / 1815 NT. TEXT: MS., Pforzheimer Library.

1. Thomas Jefferson Hogg (1792–1862) and Shelley became close friends while at Oxford, from which both were expelled on 11 March 1811 for refusing to answer questions about Shelley's pamphlet *The Necessity of Atheism*. In October 1811 Hogg attempted to seduce Harriet Shelley, which caused a temporary rift in the friendship. Shelley's unconventional views of marriage, however, allowed him to forgive Hogg, whom Shelley held culpable mainly because he tried to force a relationship on an unwilling Harriet Shelley (White, *Shelley*, I, 170–74).

On 14 November 1814 Hogg paid his first call on the elopers. Uncertain about Hogg's ability to sympathize with his radical views, Shelley decided that a renewal of their friendship would depend on Hogg's response to Mary Godwin. Hogg, "pleased with Mary" (Shelley entry, *MWS Journal*), became a frequent caller. In the spirit of Shelley's philosophy of disinterested love and with Shelley's knowledge and encouragement, on 1 January 1815 Hogg sent Mary Godwin a gift accompanied by a declaration of love. Mary Godwin reciprocated, in this letter, indicating her willingness to "think about love" and the "bright prospect" before them. Evidently she came to enjoy Hogg's attentions. Her strongest motivation in this experimental relationship, however, seems to have been to please Shelley by embodying his doctrine of love unrestrained by social convention, and typically her expressions of affection for Hogg are overshadowed by her love for Shelley (see *SC*, III, 423–57, 461–73; and White, *Shelley*, I, 388–93, 400–402).

Some scholars have speculated that during this period Shelley and Claire Clairmont (see below, n. 4) had a love affair. Reviewing the various analyses of the Mary Godwin–Hogg and the Claire Clairmont–Shelley relationships, Kenneth N. Cameron argues that the journals and letters of 1815 offer evidence that "love affairs were planned" in accord with "Shelley's sex ethic . . . that although sensuality without love as a basis for sexual relations was abhorrent, people genuinely in love should have relations regardless of marriage ties; sexual relations must be viewed only as one segment of a complex emotional relationship." Cameron also suggests that if the affairs "materialized," they were of brief duration ("A New Shelley Legend," in *An Examination of the Shelley Legend*, ed. Newman I. White [Philadelphia: University of Pennsylvania Press, 1951], pp. 107–10). The question of a sexual relationship between Claire Clairmont and Shelley arose again in the scandal of the Neapolitan child (see 10 August 1821).

2. Mary Godwin, Shelley, and Claire Clairmont lived at 2 Nelson Square from 9 November 1814 to 10 January 1815.

3. Shelley had invited Hogg to call on Mary Godwin before evening, indicating that he and Claire Clairmont would be gone for the day, since Mary Godwin wished to speak with Hogg alone (*PBS Letters*, #283).

4. In November 1814 Jane Clairmont changed her name to Clara; she later changed it to Clary, then to Clare, and finally to Claire. The elder Godwins always referred to her as Jane, but Mary Godwin and Shelley complied with her wishes, although in the transitional period they sometimes reverted to Jane. From this point, I will refer to her as Claire Clairmont, the name by which she was generally known.

5. Apparently one of the statues John Bacon (1777–1859) exhibited at his studio/home at 17 Newman Street. Bacon, who exhibited at the Royal Academy from 1792 to 1824, was famous in his day primarily for sculpting monuments, which he produced in prolific numbers.

❧

To Thomas Jefferson Hogg

[13 Arabella Road, Pimlico   6 March 1815]

My dearest Hogg my baby is dead[1]—will you come to me as soon as you can—I wish to see you—It was perfectly well when I went to bed—I awoke in the night to give it suck it appeared to be <u>sleeping</u> so quietly that I would not awake it—it was dead then but we <u>did not find that</u> out till morning—from its appearance it evedently died of convulsions—

Will you come—you are so calm a creature[2] & Shelley is afraid of a fever from the milk—for I am no longer a mother now

Mary

ADDRESS: T. J. Hogg Esq. / Holroyd Esq. / Holborn Cou[r]t / 4 Grays Inn. TEXT: MS., Pforzheimer Library.

1. On 22 February 1815 Shelley recorded in the MWS Journal: "Maie perfectly well & at ease. The child is not quite 7 months. The child not expected to live." On 6 March Mary Godwin wrote in her Journal: "find my baby dead—Send for Hogg—talk—a miserable day—in the evening read fall of the Jesuits. H. sleeps here—" Hogg remained through the next day while Shelley and Claire Clairmont went into town, most likely to make burial arrangements. The infant's name, the cause of her death, and her burial place are unknown.

2. This quality of Hogg's made him especially welcome to the Shelley household, distressed not only by the death of the child but also by a recent medical opinion that Shelley was dying of consumption. Hogg spent his holidays, from 9 March until his return to courts on 17 April, with Mary Godwin and Shelley (White, *Shelley*, I, 393; *MWS Journal*).

❧

Thomas Jefferson Hogg

[Windmill Inn, Salt Hill   25 April 1815]

My dear Jefferson

I am no doubt a very naughty Dormouse ⌒ but indeed you must forgive me—Shelley is now returned—he went to Longdills[1]—did his busi-

8

ness & returned he heard from Harriets attorney that she meant (if he did not make a handsome settlement on her) to prosecute him for atheism.—

How are you amusing yourself with the Pecksie away very doleful no doubt but my poor Jefferson I shall soon be up again & you may remember that even if we had staid you would not have seen much of me as you must have been with me—

Do you mean to come down to us—I suppose not Prince Prudent well as you please but remember I should be very happy to see you. If you had not been a lawyer you might have come with us—

Rain has come after a mild beautiful day but Shelley & I are going to walk as it is only showery

How delightful it is to read Poetry among green shades   Tintern Abbey thrilled me with delight—

> But Shelley calls me to come for
> The sun it is set
> And Night is coming

I will write perhaps by a night coach or at least early tomorrow— I shall return soon & remain till then an affectionate but

Runaway Dormouse

ADDRESS: ⟨Mr⟩ Jefferson Hogg Esq / Arrundel Street / 34 / Strand. POSTMARKS: (1) COLNBROOK / Penn[y Post]; (2) B / 26 AP 26 / 1815. TEXT: MS., Pforzheimer Library.

1. Pynson Wilmont Longdill, Shelley's solicitor, was negotiating with William Whitton, Shelley's father's solicitor, for an agreement by which Shelley would sell to Sir Timothy Shelley his reversionary interest in part of his grandfather's estate valued at £18,000 in return for an annual income of £1,000 and a lump sum of £7,400. These negotiations resulted from the death of Shelley's grandfather, Sir Bysshe Shelley (b. 1752), on 6 January 1815. Sir Bysshe left an estate of £220,000 and a will that tried to force Sir Timothy Shelley, Shelley, and their heirs to keep the family fortune intact. Shelley, however, concerned with his present circumstances rather than with his future income, refused to comply with the terms of the will. In order to retain full control of an eventual inheritance valued at £80,000, he disclaimed his rights to that part of the estate valued at £140,000, believing, correctly, that his father, fearing that Shelley would deplete the estate through post-obit bonds, would negotiate a settlement with him (see Ingpen, *Shelley in England*, pp. 449–54, 644–45; and *SC*, IV, 605–7).

To Thomas Jefferson Hogg

Windmill Inn   Salt Hill
April 26th 1815

Dear Jefferson

You must not go to courts very early tomorrow as it is most likely we shall be with you about nine—We shall try to get a place in the mail which comes into London about seven so you must rise early to receive the Dormouse all fresh from grubbing under the oaks.

But you must know that I think it very dangerous for Shelley to remain in London—the Bailiffs know Longdill to be his attorney and of course will place spies there and indeed what part of London can he walk about free in—none I fear—Have you not thought of this & what do you think of it now—but more of this when we meet.

The Dormouse is going to take a long ramble to day among green fields & solitary lanes as happy as any little Animal could be in finding herself in her native nests again—I shudder to think of breathing the air of London again—Jefferson Jefferson it is your duty {to} not keep any creature away from its home so come—I shall expect you tonight and if you do not come I am off—not for London I promise you—

But dear Jefferson all things considered the danger of Shelley remaining in London and my hatred of it do you not think that you ought to come to Salt Hill incontinently—Remember I shall believe that your love is all a farce if you do not—so I expect you   Adieu—though he is but a bad sort of a personage yet he is good enough for you   A Dieu[1] therefore

Yours—as we shall see when we know how you behave

A Runaway Dormouse

you have not chosen to write to me very well I know by this what you are good for

I wish if there is time that you would send us some money as I do not think we shall have quite enough[2]

ADDRESS: Jefferson Hogg Esq. / Arrundel Street / 34 Strand. TEXT: MS., Pforzheimer Library.

1. An irreverent pun on *A Dieu* as "a God."

2. The frank manner of this request suggests that Hogg had been called on to provide assistance before. This period of financial distress ended on 13 May, when Shelley and Sir Timothy Shelley signed an agreement that brought Shelley £4,500.5.6 in cash, payment of Shelley's debts in the amount of £2,899.14.6, and

an annual income of £1,000, in quarterly payments. From his annuity, Shelley arranged for his estranged wife to receive an annual payment of £200. Shelley received his first quarter's payment on 24 June 1815 (White, *Shelley*, I, 397–98). A year later the Court of Chancery ruled that Sir Timothy could not purchase the reversion, whereupon Shelley and Sir Timothy came to a new agreement. Shelley's allowance was to continue and, on a post-obit bond, Shelley would receive funds sufficient to cover debts incurred during the year of negotiations (White, *Shelley*, I, 429–30).

<hr/>

To {?Fanny Imlay}[1]

Hôtel de Sécheron, Geneva.   17 May 1816[2]

We arrived at Paris on the 8th of this month, and were detained two days for the purpose of obtaining the various signatures necessary to our passports, the French government having become much more circumspect since the escape of Lavalette.[3] We had no letters of introduction, or any friend in that city, and were therefore confined to our hotel, where we were obliged to hire apartments for the week, although when we first arrived we expected to be detained one night only; for in Paris there are no houses where you can be accommodated with apartments by the day.

The manners of the French are interesting, although less attractive, at least to Englishmen, than before the last invasion of the Allies: the discontent and sullenness of their minds perpetually betrays itself. Nor is it wonderful that they should regard the subjects of a government which fills their country with hostile garrisons, and sustains a detested dynasty on the throne, with an acrimony and indignation of which that government alone is the proper object. This feeling is honourable to the French, and encouraging to all those of every nation in Europe who have a fellow feeling with the oppressed, and who cherish an unconquerable hope that the cause of liberty must at length prevail.

Our route after Paris, as far as Troyes, lay through the same uninteresting tract of country which we had traversed on foot nearly two years before, but on quitting Troyes we left the road leading to Neufchâtel, to follow that which was to conduct us to Geneva. We entered Dijon on the third evening after our departure from Paris, and passing through Dôle, arrived at Poligny. This town is built at the foot of Jura, which rises abruptly from a plain of vast extent. The rocks of the mountain overhang the houses. Some difficulty in procuring horses detained us here until the evening closed in, when we proceeded, by the light of a stormy moon, to Champagnolles, a little village situated in the depth of the mountains.

The road was serpentine and exceedingly steep, and was overhung on one side by half distinguished precipices, whilst the other was a gulph, filled by the darkness of the driving clouds. The dashing of the invisible mountain streams announced to us that we had quitted the plains of France, as we slowly ascended, amidst a violent storm of wind and rain, to Champagnolles, where we arrived at twelve o'clock, the fourth night after our departure from Paris.

The next morning we proceeded, still ascending among the ravines and vallies of the mountain. The scenery perpetually grows more wonderful and sublime: pine forests of impenetrable thickness, and untrodden, nay, inaccessible expanse spread on every side. Sometimes the dark woods descending, follow the route into the vallies, the distorted trees struggling with knotted roots between the most barren clefts; sometimes the road winds high into the regions of frost, and then the forests become scattered, and the branches of the trees are loaded with snow, and half of the enormous pines themselves buried in the wavy drifts. The spring, as the inhabitants informed us, was unusually late, and indeed the cold was excessive; as we ascended the mountains, the same clouds which rained on us in the vallies poured forth large flakes of snow thick and fast. The sun occasionally shone through these showers, and illuminated the magnificent ravines of the mountains, whose gigantic pines were some laden with snow, some wreathed round by the lines of scattered and lingering vapour; others darting their dark spires into the sunny sky, brilliantly clear and azure.

As the evening advanced, and we ascended higher, the snow, which we had beheld whitening the overhanging rocks, now encroached upon our road, and it snowed fast as we entered the village of Les Rousses, where we were threatened by the apparent necessity of passing the night in a bad inn and dirty beds. For from that place there are two roads to Geneva; one by Nion, in the Swiss territory, where the mountain route is shorter, and comparatively easy at that time of the year, when the road is for several leagues covered with snow of an enormous depth; the other road lay through Gex, and was too circuitous and dangerous to be attempted at so late an hour in the day. Our passport, however, was for Gex, and we were told that we could not change its destination; but all these police laws, so severe in themselves, are to be softened by bribery, and this difficulty was at length overcome. We hired four horses, and ten men to support the carriage, and departed from Les Rousses at six in the evening, when the sun had already far descended, and the snow pelting against the windows of our carriage, assisted the coming darkness to deprive us of the view of the lake of Geneva and the far-distant Alps.

The prospect around, however, was sufficiently sublime to command our attention—never was scene more awfully desolate. The trees in these regions are incredibly large, and stand in scattered clumps over the white wilderness; the vast expanse of snow was chequered only by these gigantic pines, and the poles that marked our road: no river or rock-encircled lawn relieved the eye, by adding the picturesque to the sublime. The natural silence of that uninhabited desert contrasted strangely with the voices of the men who conducted us, who, with animated tones and gestures, called to one another in a patois composed of French and Italian, creating disturbance where, but for them, there was none.

To what a different scene are we now arrived! To the warm sunshine and to the humming of sun-loving insects. From the windows of our hotel we see the lovely lake, blue as the heavens which it reflects, and sparkling with golden beams. The opposite shore is sloping and covered with vines, which however do not so early in the season add to the beauty of the prospect. Gentlemen's seats are scattered over these banks, behind which rise the various ridges of black mountains, and towering far above, in the midst of its snowy Alps, the majestic Mont Blanc, highest and queen of all. Such is the view reflected by the lake; it is a bright summer scene without any of that sacred solitude and deep seclusion that delighted us at Lucerne.

We have not yet found out any very agreeable walks, but you know our attachment to water excursions. We have hired a boat, and every evening at about six o'clock we sail on the lake, which is delightful, whether we glide over a glassy surface or are speeded along by a strong wind. The waves of this lake never afflict me with that sickness that deprives me of all enjoyment in a sea voyage; on the contrary, the tossing of our boat raises my spirits and inspires me with unusual hilarity. Twilight here is of short duration, but we at present enjoy the benefit of an increasing moon, and seldom return until ten o'clock, when, as we approach the shore, we are saluted by the delightful scent of flowers and new mown grass, and the chirp of the grasshoppers, and the song of the evening birds.

We do not enter into society here, yet our time passes swiftly and delightfully. We read Latin and Italian during the heats of noon, and when the sun declines we walk in the garden of the hotel, looking at the rabbits, relieving fallen cockchaffers, and watching the motions of a myriad of lizards, who inhabit a southern wall of the garden. You know that we have just escaped from the gloom of winter and of London; and coming to this delightful spot during this divine weather, I feel as happy as a new-fledged bird, and hardly care what twig I fly to, so that I may try my

13

new-found wings. A more experienced bird may be more difficult in its choice of a bower; but, in my present temper of mind, the budding flowers, the fresh grass of spring, and the happy creatures about me that live and enjoy these pleasures, are quite enough to afford me exquisite delight, even though clouds should shut out Mont Blanc from my sight. Adieu!

M.[4]

TEXT: *Six Weeks' Tour*, pp. 85–97.

1. This letter, as well as that of 1 June (following) and two letters by Shelley, was published in *Six Weeks' Tour*. Shelley's letters, dated 12 July and 22 July–2 August, identify the addressee as T. P., Thomas Love Peacock. Shelley's second letter (*S&M*, I, 104–13) and the first (*SC*, VII) both show that the contents as published in *Six Weeks' Tour* are largely those of the actual letters, but with considerable literary emendations and the omission of personal matters (finances, housing, and so on). Because Mary Godwin's letters contain no addressee, it has been assumed that hers were not actual letters but a travel narrative in the epistolary form then popular. Two letters written by Fanny Imlay to Mary Godwin strongly suggest that they are answers to Mary Godwin's letters in *Six Weeks' Tour*. On 29 May Fanny Imlay wrote: "Papa has given to me this space of paper to fill & seal. I received Mary's letter on Monday morning   I can assure you, it was very precious to me—France is in so strange a state that I could not feel easy for your safety till I heard that you had actually arrived—" Mary Godwin's 17 May letter begins by announcing their arrival and giving details of France that could well mesh with Fanny Imlay's remarks about the strange state of France at that time. In closing her letter of 29 May, Fanny Imlay expressed her hope that there was a letter already en route to her in response to one she had written about a fortnight earlier (Abinger MS.; *S&M*, I, 93–94). Fanny Imlay's letter of 29 July indicates that she had just received a letter from Mary Godwin describing the weather in Switzerland, a subject treated in Mary Godwin's letter of 1 June in *Six Weeks' Tour*. These letters clearly establish that a steady correspondence was carried on by the sisters, and it is quite likely that Mary Godwin's letters to Fanny Imlay formed the basis of her letters in *Six Weeks' Tour*, as Shelley's letters to Peacock were the basis of his. Mary Godwin may have omitted any identification of her correspondent because of the notoriety attached to Fanny Imlay's birth or in fear of stimulating fresh notoriety in connection with her suicide on 9 October 1816, an event Godwin wished to keep secret. In 1844 Mary Shelley again combined notes from her travels with lengthy passages from actual correspondence to publish them as *Rambles in Germany and Italy, in 1840, 1842, and 1843*, 2 vols. (London: Edward Moxon, 1844).

2. On 3 May, with their son William (born 24 January 1816) and again accompanied by Claire Clairmont, Shelley and Mary Godwin sailed from Dover en route to Geneva. In the spring of 1816 Claire Clairmont had formed a secret liaison with Byron. When Byron left England for Geneva on 25 April, Claire Clairmont determined to follow him. She revealed the affair to Shelley, who for her sake and because of his own interest in meeting Byron, agreed to go to Geneva instead of Italy (*SC*, IV, 677–79, 720–21).

3. Antoine-Marie Chamans, comte de La Valette (1769–1830), French politi-

cian, held political and military posts under Napoleon. When Louis XVIII came to power, La Valette was arrested and condemned to death, but with the aid of his wife and three Englishmen (Sir Robert Wilson; Michael Bruce; and Captain John Hely-Hutchinson, afterwards third earl of Donoughmore), he escaped from prison in December 1815 and was safely conveyed out of France.

4. In later editions of *Six Weeks' Tour* Mary Shelley altered this signature to "M.S."

❧

To {?Fanny Imlay}[1]

Campagne C[hapuis], near Coligny.
1 June 1816[2]

You will perceive from my date that we have changed our residence since my last letter. We now inhabit a little cottage on the opposite shore of the lake, and have exchanged the view of Mont Blanc and her snowy aiguilles for the dark frowning Jura, behind whose range we every evening see the sun sink, and darkness approaches our valley from behind the Alps, which are then tinged by that glowing rose-like hue which is observed in England to attend on the clouds of an autumnal sky when daylight is almost gone. The lake is at our feet, and a little harbour contains our boat, in which we still enjoy our evening excursions on the water. Unfortunately we do not now enjoy those brilliant skies that hailed us on our first arrival to this country. An almost perpetual rain confines us principally to the house; but when the sun bursts forth it is with a splendour and heat unknown in England. The thunder storms that visit us are grander and more terrific than I have ever seen before. We watch them as they approach from the opposite side of the lake, observing the lightning play among the clouds in various parts of the heavens, and dart in jagged figures upon the piny heights of Jura, dark with the shadow of the overhanging cloud, while perhaps the sun is shining cheerily upon us. One night we enjoyed a finer storm than I had ever before beheld. The lake was lit up—the pines on Jura made visible, and all the scene illuminated for an instant, when a pitchy blackness succeeded, and the thunder came in frightful bursts over our heads amid the darkness.[3]

But while I still dwell on the country around Geneva, you will expect me to say something of the town itself: there is nothing, however, in it that can repay you for the trouble of walking over its rough stones. The houses are high, the streets narrow, many of them on the ascent, and no public building of any beauty to attract your eye, or any architecture to gratify your taste. The town is surrounded by a wall, the three gates of which are shut exactly at ten o'clock, when no bribery (as in France) can open them. To the south of the town is the promenade of the Genevese, a grassy plain planted with a few trees, and called Plainpalais. Here a small obelisk is erected to the glory of Rousseau, and here (such is the mutability of human life) the magistrates, the successors of those who exiled him from his native country, were shot by the populace during that revolution, which his writings mainly contributed to mature, and which, notwithstanding the temporary bloodshed and injustice with which it was polluted, has produced enduring benefits to mankind, which all the chicanery of statesmen, nor even the great conspiracy of kings, can entirely render vain. From respect to the memory of their predecessors, none of the present magistrates ever walk in Plainpalais. Another Sunday recreation for the citizens is an excursion to the top of Mont Salêve. This hill is within a league of the town, and rises perpendicularly from the cultivated plain. It is ascended on the other side, and I should judge from its situation that your toil is rewarded by a delightful view of the course of the Rhone and Arve, and of the shores of the lake. We have not yet visited it.

There is more equality of classes here than in England. This occasions a greater freedom and refinement of manners among the lower orders than we meet with in our own country. I fancy the haughty English ladies are greatly disgusted with this consequence of republican institutions, for the Genevese servants complain very much of their scolding, an exercise of the tongue, I believe, perfectly unknown here. The peasants of Switzerland may not however emulate the vivacity and grace of the French. They are more cleanly, but they are slow and inapt. I know a girl of twenty, who although she had lived all her life among vineyards, could not inform me during what month the vintage took place, and I discovered she was utterly ignorant of the order in which the months succeed one another. She would not have been surprised if I had talked of the burning sun and delicious fruits of December, or of the frosts of July. Yet she is by no means deficient in understanding.[4]

The Genevese are also much inclined to puritanism. It is true that from habit they dance on a Sunday, but as soon as the French government was abolished in the town, the magistrates ordered the theatre to be closed, and measures were taken to pull down the building.

We have latterly enjoyed fine weather, and nothing is more pleasant than to listen to the evening song of the vine-dressers. They are all women, and most of them have harmonious although masculine voices.

The theme of their ballads consists of shepherds, love, flocks, and the sons of kings who fall in love with beautiful shepherdesses. Their tunes are monotonous, but it is sweet to hear them in the stillness of evening, while we are enjoying the sight of the setting sun, either from the hill behind our house or from the lake.

Such are our pleasures here, which would be greatly increased if the season had been more favourable, for they chiefly consist in such enjoyments as sunshine and gentle breezes bestow. We have not yet made any excursion in the environs of the town, but we have planned several, when you shall again hear of us; and we will endeavour, by the magic of words, to transport the ethereal part of you to the neighbourhood of the Alps, and mountain streams, and forests, which, while they clothe the former, darken the latter with their vast shadows.—Adieu!

M.

TEXT: *Six Weeks' Tour*, pp. 98–106.

1. See 17 May 1816.

2. By the end of May Shelley and his party had moved to a cottage variously called Montalègre, Maison Chapuis, Campagne Chapuis. On 10 June Byron rented the Villa Diodati, a short walk away. The two poets and their companions spent the summer in each other's company. The Shelley party remained at Lake Geneva until 29 August.

3. Byron described such a storm in *Childe Harold* 3. 92. Mary Godwin included her impressions of Alpine storms and scenery in *Frankenstein*, which she began that June in fulfillment of a pact made by herself, Claire Clairmont, Shelley, Byron, and Byron's physician, John William Polidori (1795–1821), to each write a ghost story. Only Mary Godwin and John Polidori (who incorporated Byron's idea for a ghost story into *The Vampyre: A Tale* [London, 1819]) completed the agreement. The fragment Byron wrote was published at the end of *Mazeppa, A Poem* (London: John Murray, 1819; see Marchand, *Byron*, II, 628–29, 787).

4. Perhaps Mary Godwin's first impressions of Elise (Louise) Duvillard, the Swiss servant who returned with them to England as William's nurse (see 29 May 1817, n. 9).

❖

To Shelley[1]

December 5th 1816   Bath   New Bond Street[2]

Sweet Elf

I got up very late this morning so that I could not attend M[r] West.[3] I dont know any more   Good night.

Sweet Elf

I was awakened this morning by my pretty babe and was dressed time enough to take my lesson from Mr West and (Thank God) finished that tedious ugly picture I have been so long about—I have also finished the 4 Chap. of Frankenstein which is a very long one & I think you would like it.

And where are you? and what are you doing my blessed love; I hope and trust that for my sake you did not go outside this wretched day, while the wind howls and the clouds seem to threaten rain. And what did my love think of as he rode along—Did he think about our home, our babe and his poor Pecksie? But I am sure you did and thought of them all with joy and hope.—But in the choice of residence—dear Shelley—pray be not too quick or a⟨t⟩tach yourself too much to one spot—Ah—were you indeed a winged Elf and could soar over mountains & seas and could pounce on the little spot—A house with a lawn a river or lake—noble trees & divine mountains that should be our little mousehole to retire to—But never mind this—give me a garden & absentia Clariæ and I will thank my love for many favours.

If you, my love, go to London you will perhaps try to procure a good Livy, for I wish very much to read it—I must be more industrious especially in learning latin which I neglected shamefully last summer at intervals, and those periods of not reading at all put me back very far.

The morning Chronicle as you will see does not make much of the riots which they say are entirely quieted and you would almost be enclined to say out of the mountain comes forth a mouse[4] although I dare say poor Mrs Platt[5] does not think so.

The blue eyes of your sweet boy are staring at me while I write this he is a dear child and you love him tenderly, although I fancy your affection will encrease when he has a nursery to himself and only comes to you just dressed and in good humour—Besides when that comes to pass he will be a wise little man for he improves in mind rapidly—Tell me shall you be happy to have another little squaller? You will look grave on this, but I do not mean anything.

Leigh Hunt[6] has not written;—I would advis[e   ] letter addressed to him at the Examiner offic[e   ] if there is no answer tomorrow—he may not be at the vale of Health for it is odd that he does not acknowledge the receipt of so large a sum. There have been no letters of any kind today.

Now, my dear, when shall I see you? Do not be very long away! take care of yourself; & take a house. I have a great fear that bad weather will set in. My airy Elf, how unlucky you are! I shall write to Mrs G. [*Godwin*] but let me know what you hear from Hayward and Papa as I am greatly interrested in those affairs.[7] Adieu, sweetest, Love me tenderly and think of me with affection whenever any thing pleases you greatly

Your affectionate girl
Mary W. G.

[*P. 4, sideways*]   I have not asked Clare but I dare say she would send her love although I dare say she would scold you well if you were here   My compts & remembrances to Dame Peacock & son[8]—but {do} not let them see this—sweet, adieu

ADDRESS: Percy B. Shelley Esq / Great Marlow / Bucks. POSTMARK: [B]ATH / [DEC.] 5 / [18]16. TEXT: MS., Bodleian Library.

1. On their return to England on 8 September, Shelley first went to London on business and then to Marlow to find a house; Mary Godwin and Claire Clairmont went to Bath. This plan was devised to keep from the Godwins the fact that Claire Clairmont was expecting Byron's child.

2. The date of this letter appears in the manuscript prior to the second greeting, which suggests that the brief opening note was written on 4 December. However, both the MWS Journal and *PBS Letters* (#372) attest that Shelley was still at Bath on 4 December. The postmark date of 5 December confirms Mary Godwin's assigned date (thereby precluding the possibility that the letter was written on 5 and 6 December). Having found no evidence in the manuscript of the letter, the Journal, or elsewhere to substantiate any of my own speculations about the opening of this letter, I assign the authorial date to the letter and acknowledge the mystery of the first brief note.

3. Possibly John West (1772–1836), miniature painter and drawing master, who lived in Bath from at least 1795 to 1833. John West was the father of Joseph West (b. 1797).

4. Horace *Epistles* 3. #139.

5. The *Morning Chronicle* of 4 December reported that it was the intention of rioters, on 2 December, to collect arms, return to their meeting in Spa-field, and then proceed to Carlton House, the residence of the Prince Regent. Mr. Platt, a neighbor of Godwin's on Skinner Street, was wounded by rioters demanding firearms.

6. James Henry Leigh Hunt (1784–1859), poet, essayist, editor, and co-owner of the *Examiner*, a weekly newspaper. Shelley admired Hunt for his liberal views and had written to him on a number of occasions, at one time offering him money (which Hunt declined) when he was jailed for libeling the Prince Regent. A deep friendship developed between the two men after Hunt's article "Young Poets" (on Keats, Shelley, and Reynolds) appeared in the *Examiner* on 1 December, the same day on which Shelley received a letter from Hunt. Mary Godwin's letter suggests that Shelley sent funds to Hunt at that time (see *PBS Letters*, #373; *SC*, V, 401–3). On 12 December Shelley visited the Hunts at their home in the Vale of Health, Hampstead.

7. Fanny Imlay, in her letter of 3 October, had reminded Mary Godwin that Shel-

ley had promised Godwin £300 (*S&M*, I, 143–46). On 6 December Mrs. Godwin sent Mary Godwin £100. Dowden infers that Godwin negotiated on Shelley's behalf with Richard William Hayward (Godwin's, and sometimes Shelley's, solicitor) and obtained £100 more than the sum promised him, which he sent to Shelley for his own use (Dowden, *Shelley*, II, 63).

8. At Marlow, Shelley stayed with Peacock and his mother.

To Shelley[1]

Bath   Dec. 17th 1816

My beloved friend

I waited with the greatest anxiety for your letter—You are well & that assurance has restored some peace to me.

How very happy shall I be to possess those darling treasures that are yours—I do not exactly understand what Chancery has to do in this and wait with impatience for tomorrow when I shall hear whether they are with you—and then what will you do with them? My heart says bring them instantly here—but I submit to your prudence

You do not mention Godwin—When I receive your letter tomorrow I shall write to Mrs G. [*Godwin*]   I hope yet I fear that he will show on this occasion some disinterrestedness—Poor dear Fanny if she had lived until this moment she would have been saved for my house would then have been a proper assylum for her[2]—Ah! my best love to you do I owe every joy every perfection that I may enjoy or boast of—Love me, sweet, for ever—But I {do} not mean————I hardly know what I I mean I am so much agitated

Clare has a very bad cough but I think she is better today   Mr Cam[3] talks of bleeding if she does not recover quickly—but {she} is positively resolved not to submit to that—She sends her love

My sweet love deliver some message from me to your kind friends at Hamstead—Tell Mrs Hunt that I am extremely obliged to her for the little profile she was so kind as to send me[4] and thank Mr H. [*Hunt*] for his friendly message which I did no{} hear

These Westbrooks—But they have nothing to do with your sweet babes they are yours and I do not see the pretence for a suit but tomorrow I shall know all

Your box arrived today   I shall send soon to the upolsterer—for now I long more than ever that our house should be quickly ready for the reception of those dear children whom I love so tenderly then there will be

20

a sweet brother and sister for my William who will lose his pre-eminence as eldest and be helped third at table—as his Aunt Clare is continually reminding him—

Come down to me sweetest as soon as you can for I long to see you and embrace—As to the event you allude {to} be governed by your friends & prudence as to when it ought to take place—but it must be in London[5]

Clare has just looked in—she begs you not to stay away long—to be more explicit in your letters and sends her love

You tell me to write a long letter and [I] would but that my ideas wander and my hand trembles come back to reassure me my Shelley & bring with you Your darling Ianthe & Charles—Thank your kind friends   I long to hear about Godwin

Your Affectionate Companion
Mary—W.G.—

Have you called on Hogg   I would hardly advise you—Remember me sweet in your sorrows as well as your pleasures they will I trust soften the one and heighten the other feeling   Adieu

Be resolute for Desse[6] plainly wishes to procrastinate and make out a bill for his worthy ⟨children⟩ patron—How it would please me if old Westbrook were to repent in his last moments and leave all his fortune away from that miserable and odious Eliza[7]

ADDRESS: Percy Bysshe Shelley Esq / Messrs Longdill & Butterfield / 5 Gray's Inn Square / London. POSTMARKS: (1) BATH / 17 DE 17 / [1816]; (2) E / 18 DE 18 / 1816. TEXT: MS., Bodleian Library.

1. On 10 December Harriet Westbrook Shelley's body had been found in the Serpentine, Hyde Park, an apparent suicide. On 15 December a letter from Thomas Hookham, Jr., informing Shelley of her death took Shelley to London to obtain custody of his two children from this marriage, Ianthe and Charles (b. 30 November 1814). The Westbrook family refused to give the children to Shelley and took the matter to the Court of Chancery to prevent Shelley from ever having custody of his children. This letter is in response to Shelley's letter of 16 December, which describes his anguish at these events (PBS Letters, #374).

2. Fanny Imlay had committed suicide on 9 October 1816 at the Mackworth Arms Inn, Swansea, Wales, by taking an overdose of laudanum.

3. A surgeon who resided at 7 Alfred Street, Bath.

4. Marianne Kent Hunt (1788–1857) had married Leigh Hunt in 1809. One of her artistic hobbies was cutting profile silhouettes out of paper (see [?14 October–November 1826]).

5. Shelley had written: "I have seen Longdill . . . I told him that I was under contract of marriage to you; & he said that in such an event all pretences to detain the children would cease" (PBS Letters, #374). On 30 December Mary Godwin and Shelley were married at St. Mildred's Church, London, with the Godwins as witnesses. Longdill's opinion about custody of the children, however, proved incorrect.

6. Attorney to John Westbrook, Harriet Shelley's father.

7. Shelley had grown to dislike Eliza Westbrook, Harriet Shelley's older sister, prior to the dissolution of his relationship with his first wife. Now he wrote to Mary Godwin that "the beastly viper her sister" drove Harriet Shelley to suicide in order to be their father's sole heir, an accusation he repeated to Byron (*PBS Letters*, #374, #381). That Harriet Shelley did not share Shelley's feelings towards her sister is demonstrated by her suicide letter to Eliza Westbrook, in which she requested that Ianthe remain permanently with her "dear sister" (*PBS Letters*, #374, n. 1).

To Lord Byron

Bath—Jan. 13th 1817[1]

Dear Lord Byron

Shelley being in London upon business I take upon myself the task & pleasure of informing you that Clare was safely delivered of a little girl yesterday morning (Sunday · January 12) at four.[2] She sends her affectionate love to you and begs me to say that she is in excellent spirits and as good health as can be expected. That is to say that she has had a very favourable time and has now no other illness than the weakness incidental to her case.

A letter ought not to be sent so far with out a little more news. The people at present are very quiet waiting anxiously for the meeting of parliament—when in the Month of March, as Cobbett boldly prophesies a reform will certainly take place.

For private news if you feel interest in it, Shelley has become intimate with Leigh Hunt and his family. I have seen them & like Hunt extremely. We have also taken a house in Marlow to which we intend to remove in about two months—And where we dare hope to have the pleasure of your society on your return to England. The town of Marlow is about thirty miles from London.

My little boy is very well and is a very lively child.

It is a long time since Shelley has heard from you and I am sure nothing would give him greater pleasure than to receive news of your motions & enjoyments.

Another incident has also occurred which will surprise you, perhaps; It is a little piece of egotism in me to mention it—but it allows me to sign myself—in assuring you of my esteem & sincere friendship

Mary W. Shelley[3]

ADDRESS: To the Right Honourable / Lord Byron / M. Hentsch-Banquier / Genève / Switzerland. POSTMARKS: (1) E / PAID / 18 JA 18 / 1817; (2) F17 / 191. TEXT: MS., John Murray.

22

1. Because the letter is postdated 18 January and its postmark is from London rather than from Bath, it has been conjectured that it may have been forwarded in Mary Shelley's letter of 17 January to Shelley, along with her letter of 13 January to Marianne Hunt, and that Shelley, on receipt of these letters, also wrote to Byron (*PBS Letters*, #381) and sent his letter under cover of Mary Shelley's letter to Byron (*SC*, V, 83–84). While the conjecture that Shelley mailed both letters may be valid, the postal fee on Mary Shelley's letter of 17 January (9 pence, the fee of a single-sheet letter between Bath and London) establishes that her two letters of 13 January were not enclosed in her 17 January letter but were perhaps sent under cover of another (unlocated) letter.

2. The baby was first called Alba, a name similar to Albè, Claire Clairmont and the Shelleys' nickname for Byron. At Marlow she was referred to as "Miss Auburn" (Dowden, *Shelley*, II, 124; *SC*, V, 391–92), perhaps an allusion to her hair (see *PBS Letters*, #401). Byron wanted the child to be christened Allegra, but on 9 March 1818 Claire Clairmont had her christened as Clara Allegra Byron. Donald H. Reiman suggests that this name was chosen because Allegra was not on the approved lists of saints' names with which Catholics and Anglicans of the period could be christened (*SC*, V, 365). Although this may have been the reason, it is obvious that the Christian name selected would be a reminder of the child's mother.

3. See 17 December 1816, n. 5.

❖

To Leigh Hunt

Marlow[1]—March 2—1817

Dear Hunt

Shelley & Peacock have started a question which I do not esteem myself wise enough to decide upon—and yet as they seem determined to act on it I wish them to have the best advise. As a prelude to this you must be reminded that Hamden[2] was of Bucks and our two worthies want to be his successors for which reason they intend to refuse to pay the taxes as illegally imposed—What effect will this have & ought they to do it is the question? Pray let me know your opinion.

Our house is very political as well as poetical and I hope you will acquire a fresh spirit for both when you come here[3]   You will have plenty of room to indulge your self in and a garden which will deserve your praise when you see it—flowers—trees & shady banks—ought we not to be happy and so indeed me [we] are in spite of the Lord Chancellor and the suspension act.[4] But I can assure you we hope for a great addition to it when you are so kind as to come to us. By the bye could you not come down with Shelley and stay only a day or two—just to view your future abode—It would give me great delight to see you—and I think the tout

23

ensemble would give you some pleasure   But for all this I know you will not come—but if one or two would—M[rs] Hunt for instance would lose her headach I am quite certain in three minutes—

I have not yet seen the Examiner but when I do I shall judge if you have been disturbed since we left you—The present state of affairs[5] is sufficient to rouse any one I should suppose except (as I wish to be contemptuous) a weekly politician—This however as I have not seen your paper is rather cat's play—if you have been good it will pass off very well but if you have not I shall be very sorry but I send it depending that you have pleased yourself this week.

We will hasten every thing to have you down and you shall be indulged in sopha's hair brushes & hair brushers to you hearts content but then in return you & M[rs] Hunt must leave off calling me M[rs] S. for I do not half like the name[6]

Remember us all with kindness & believe me your very sincere friend

Mary W. S.

Let me know if you have been at peace since our departure—And if you all have taken advantage of these fine days to improve your health & spirits by exercise. S. has been very well. In one of the parcels will you send down the hair[7] that you have got for me—

Do you know if you could get in town a small ivory casket in which I could put those memorials—

ADDRESS: Leigh Hunt Esq / Vale of Health / Hampstead. TEXT: M.S., Huntington Library.

1. From 2 to 18 March, while arranging their new house at Marlow, the Shelleys resided with Peacock and his mother.

2. John Hampden (1594–1643) was an English Parliamentary leader famous for his opposition to Charles I, particularly in matters of taxation. Marlow is in Buckinghamshire, the county where Hampden lived and that he represented in Parliament in the last years of his life.

3. As an economy measure, the Hunts gave up their Vale of Health home and accepted the Shelleys' invitation to stay with them at Marlow for an extended visit. They remained at Marlow from 6 April through 25 June (*MWS Journal*; *SC*, V. 227–28).

4. John Scott, Baron Eldon (1751–1838), as Lord Chancellor of England had heard the case between Shelley and the Westbrooks for the custody of Ianthe and Charles on 24 January. Eldon's decision, handed down on 27 March, deprived Shelley of the custody of his children (Dowden, *Shelley*, II, 76–95). Shelley wrote to Mary Shelley: "The only manner in which I could get at the children in the common course of law, is by Habeas Corpus, & that supposes a delay of some weeks" (*PBS Letters*, #380). On 24 February an act to suspend habeas corpus was presented to Parliament. On 25 March the act was passed, and it was in effect until 29 January 1818.

5. The great agitation for reform in 1817 was reflected in Hunt's weekly *Examiner* and in Shelley's pamphlet *A Proposal for Putting Reform to the Vote throughout the Kingdom* (London: C. and J. Ollier, 1817).

6. Mary Shelley preferred to have less formality between herself and the Hunts. Subsequently the Hunts addressed her as Mary or by the pet name Marina.

7. Perhaps locks of hair from Leigh and Marianne Hunt, for which Mary Shelley requests the "small ivory casket."

◆

To Shelley

Skinner St.[1]   May 29th 1817

My best Love

I have not heard from you today nor indeed since you left me—nor did I write last night for in some way I entirely forgot all about writing untill it was too late.

We have bad weather now but it was fine during your voyage with south east winds; you are now arrived & I hope safe under covert with your pretty Will man whom kiss a million of times for me   Saturday I shall kiss him myself.

Papa is not in very good spirits the money affairs are at a stand—I wish I could see him happy; he is full of care and I fear that there is no way to relieve this. I suppose you have nothing more of the proposal made to Longdill[2]

I have been once to the play to see Kean in Barbarossa[3] teusday night but otherwise I have been at home. Yesterday evening Papa supped with Hazlitt at Dr. Walcots[4] and I amused myself with reading the 3rd Canto of Childe Harold.[5] It made me dreadfully melancholy—The lake—the mountains and the faces associated with these scenes passed before me— Why is not life a continued moment where hours and days are not counted—but as it is a succession of events happen—the moment of enjoyment lives only in memory and when we die where are we?

Manfred[6] is advertized—I long to see it{.}   if the weather is tolerable I shall call in Albermarle St. before I return and if possible see Murray and ask a question or two about our faithless Albe but do not say a word of this as I may learn nothing or worse.[7]

Of course Gifford did not allow this courtly bookseller to purchase F.[8] I have no hope on that score but then I have nothing to fear.

I am very well here but so intolerably restless that it {is} painful to sit still for five minutes—

Pray write—I hear so little from Marlow [tha]t I can hardly believe that you and Will man live there

Give my love to such of my guests as care about it—to Clare and <u>Miss</u> <u>Alba</u> Tell Elise I shall buy clothes for Aimée[9] and that I hope she has been a good girl.

Adieu dearest—Welcome me with smiles and health

Your affectionate

Pecksie

Send Charles's[10] letter—I will not close this letter just yet that if I feel in better spirits after dinner I may say so.

Good bye pretty one—I smile now and shall again when I see you saturday

ADDRESS: Percy B Shelley Esq. / Grt Marlow / Bucks. POSTMARK: [   ] MY / 29 / 1817. TEXT: MS., Bodleian Library.

1. From 22 to 31 May, while trying to arrange for the publication of *Frankenstein*, Mary Shelley stayed with her father (Mrs. Godwin was in France at the time [see *SC*, V, 204]). Shelley, who had come to London with her, had returned to Marlow on 26 May (*MWS Journal*).

2. Shelley first introduced himself to Godwin, whose works he greatly admired, in a letter of 3 January 1812. In his second letter he informed Godwin that he was "heir by entail to an estate of 6000£ per an" (*PBS Letters*, #157, #159). Godwin, always in debt, readily accepted the young heir's financial assistance, calling on Shelley for money even when Shelley was himself hard-pressed. In March and April 1817 Godwin again tried to secure money from Shelley (Dowden, *Shelley*, I, 395; *SC*, I, 14, IV, 600–602, V, 203–5). The proposal to Pynson Wilmot Longdill, Shelley's lawyer, to which Mary Shelley refers is probably in connection with Godwin's latest plan for Shelley to raise money in order to aid him.

3. Mary Shelley had seen Edmund Kean (1787–1833) in *Barbarossa*, by John Brown (1715–66), at the Theatre Royal, Covent Garden, on 27 May (MWS Journal).

4. John Wolcott (1738–1819), physician and author, who since the 1780s had written poetry on the Whig side under the name Peter Pindar.

5. Shelley had brought the manuscript to John Murray, Byron's publisher, in September 1816 (*PBS Letters*, #361, #362). Byron's friend Scrope Davies was also entrusted to bring a copy to Murray (Byron, *Letters and Journals*, V, 113). The copy Davies carried was discovered in a trunk in the vaults of Barclays Bank Ltd. in December 1976 (Elma Dangerfield, "The Literary Find of the Century," *The Byron Journal*, 1977, pp. 5–9). It has been argued that Davies delivered his copy after Shelley delivered his and that John Murray returned it because Byron had given it to Davies as a gift (John Clubbe, "Scrope Davies Reconsidered," *The Byron Journal*, 1978, pp. 4–6).

6. Published by John Murray on 16 June 1817.

7. The Shelleys had had no response from Byron about the birth of Alba. Mary Shelley means that Shelley should not mention her intended inquiry about the "faithless Albe" to Claire Clairmont, who was with Shelley at Marlow.

8. William Gifford (1756–1826), author of *The Baviad* (1794) and *The Maeviad*

(1795) and editor of the *Quarterly Review*, was chief literary advisor to John Murray. Mary Shelley believed that Gifford would advise John Murray against publishing *Frankenstein*. John Murray rejected it on 18 June.

9. Emily W. Sunstein, in "Louise Duvillard of Geneva, the Shelleys' Nursemaid" (*Keats-Shelley Journal*, 1980), identifies the Shelleys' nursemaid Elise as Louise Duvillard, born 28 April 1795 at Geneva; Aimée Romieux as Elise Duvillard's half sister, born 20 January 1816; and other family members.

10. Charles Clairmont.

To Shelley

Marlow.   Sept. 26. 1817

You tell me to decide between Italy and the sea[1]—I think—dearest—if, what you do not seem to doubt but which I do a little, our finances are in sufficiently good a state to bear the expence of the journey—our inclination ought to decide—I feel some reluctance at quitting our present settled state but as we <u>must</u> leave Marlow I do not know that stopping short on this side {of} the channel would be pleasanter to me than crossing it. At any rate, my love, do not let us encumber ourselves with a lease again. However consult in your own mind and say frankly in your next, if your feelings are decided enough on the subject—if Italy would not give you far more pleasure than a settlement on the coast of Kent—If it would say so & so be it—Perhaps A. [*Alba*] renders the thought of expence pretty nearly equal whichever way you decide.[2] Do you glow with the thoughts of a clear sky—pure air & burning sun—You would then enjoy life. For my own part I shall have tolerable health anywhere and for pleasure Italy certainly holds forth a charming prospect—But we are rich enough to enjoy ourselves when there.

I do not get strength so quickly as I could wish. I have finished the bottle of aperient medecine[3] and as I cannot get on at all without it I wish you would write to Furnival for more—I have not been out yet this day was too windy & rainy and indeed the season advances very fast which renders A.'s affairs pressing we must decide to go ourselves or send her within a month.

It is well that your poem was finished before this edict was issued against the imagination but my pretty eclogue will suffer from it[4]—By the bye talking of authorship do get a sketch of Godwin's plan from him—I do not think that I ought to get out of the habit of writing and I think that the thing he talked of would just suit me. I am glad to hear that G. [*Godwin*] is well   I told you that after what had passed he would

27

be particularly gracious. As to Mrs G. [*Godwin*] something very analogous to disgust arises whenever I mention her that last accusation of Godwins adds bitterness to every feeling I ever felt against her.

Send William[5] a present of fruit and a little money.—Pray also dearest do get the state of you{r} accounts from your banker—and also (for I might as well pack all my commissions into one paragraph send my broach down as soon as you can and as your hair is to be in it have a lock ready cut when you go to the jewellers—Get your hair cut in London— For any other commission be sure to consult your tablets.

You{r} babes are quite well but I have had some pain in perceiving or imagining that Willy has almost forgotten me—and seems to like Elise better—but this may be fancy & will certainly disappear when I can get out and aboutt again—Clara is well and gets very pretty. How happy I shall be when my own dear love comes again to kiss me and my babes— As it seems that your health principally depends upon care pray dearest take every possible precaution—I have often observed that rain has a very bad effect upon {you}— if therefore you have rain in London do not go out in it.

Clare told me to send Harry[6] today to Maidenhead to wait for her which I did but she has not come but I suppose I shall receive an explanation by tomorrow's post

Adieu—dearest—Come back as soon as you may and in the mean time write me long long letters—

Your own Mary

Mr B. [*Baxter*] thinks that Mr Booth keeps Isabel from writing to me he has written to her today warmly in praise of us both and telling her by all means not to let the acquaintance cool & that in such a case her loss would be much greater than mine. He has taken a prodigious fancy to us and is continually talking of & praising Queen Mab which he vows is the best poem of modern days.[7]

ADDRESS: P. B. Shelley Esq. TEXT: MS., Bodleian Library.

1. Dr. Lawrence had told Shelley that his best hope for recovery from his pulmonary illness was to cease writing and remove to a warmer climate (White, *Shelley*, I, 538).

2. If they decided on Italy, the Shelleys could take Alba to Byron themselves (*PBS Letters*, #411).

3. A laxative, which she requests Shelley to get from Dr. Furnivall, a surgeon of Egham who attended her at the birth of Clara. (Dr. Furnivall was the father of Frederick J. Furnivall, the Victorian literary scholar who founded the first Shelley Society.)

4. *Laon and Cythna* was complete, but *Rosalind and Helen*, an eclogue suggested to Shelley by Mary Shelley's friendship with Isabella Booth, remained unfinished

when Dr. Lawrence ordered Shelley to discontinue writing. Shelley completed *Rosalind and Helen* at the Bagni di Lucca (Baths of Lucca) during August 1818 (*PBS Letters*, #475).

5. William Godwin, Jr. (1803–32), the son of William Godwin and Mary Jane Clairmont Godwin and half brother to Mary Shelley.

6. The Shelleys' manservant at Marlow. He had a variety of household duties, including the care of the garden (Dowden, *Shelley*, II, 111, 123).

7. Shelley's *Queen Mab; A Philosophical Poem: with Notes* (London, 1813).

❧

Mary Shelley and Shelley
to Leigh and Marianne Hunt

Lyons, March 22 1818[1]

[*Cross-written by Mary Shelley, pp. 1–3 of Shelley's letter*]   Now, my dear Hunt & my dear Marianne, we see Jura & Mont Blanc again from the windows of our hotel and the Rhone rushes by our window—The sun shines bright and it is a kind of Paradise which we have arrived at through the valley of the shadow of death—for certainly the greater part of our journey here was not the most pleasant thing in the world—I think if Peacock had been with us he would have taken fright and returned. The first night after quitting Calais we slept at St. Omers—we arrived after the shutting the gates—The postillions craked their whips to give signs of our approach and a female voice was heard from the battlements demanding the name and number of the invaders she was told that it was some English ladies with their children and she departed to carry the intelligence to the Governor who lived half a mile off—In about half an hour the gates were thrown open and about a dozen soldiers came out headed by this female who demanded our passport—she received it and began to read it when recollecting herself she said—Mais, Medames you will remember the guard. We told her that we certainly would   Ah then—said she—you may enter directly—So we passed through the various windings of the fortifications and through three immense gates which were successively closed after us with a clanking sound. But these are the frontier towns and when we came to the middle of France we found nothing of this. The largest towns here are not fortified—but these kind of things appear to spring up in the north of France—that is that part of it that borders Flanders like mushrooms or toadstools great large round things with a ditch & wall round them swarming with people— There is Douai—with I do not know many thousand inhabitants—who

29

ever heard of Douai?[2] Why to be born in such a town is like living out of the circle of human things—an ambitious individual of Douai would almost like Erostratus[3] wish to burn down a fine building or two to let his fellow men know that there was such a place in the world. Now Lyons is a pleasant city and very republican—The people have suffered dreadfully—you know the horrors they went th{r}ough in the revolution and about six months ago they were not much better off.[4] If it had not been for Napoleon said one man to us, my head would not have been where it is he brought peace to us—and I say nothing but there are people who wish him back—When the Angouleme party had the lead dreadful atrocities were committed here mais ce Monsieur q'on appelle Louis XVIII is a better man and restrained them.[5]

This same man told us some horrible facts which could never have been committed if there was liberty of the press and such things could have been published. I do not relate them for you do not like to hear of inhumanities.

Such is our little history at present—Is yours a pleasant one—You have promised to write often—and I am sure that here your kindness would stand instead of promise or any thing else—it would bind you to us exiles who love you very sincerely and wish to hear every good news concerning you. Shelley's health is infinitely improved and I hope the fine climate we now enjoy and are proceeding to will quite restore him—The children bear the journey exceedingly well and thus far we are fortunate and in good spirits. La prima donna[6] desires her love to you and Bessy

Adieu—We will write again soon and hope to find a letter waiting for us from you at Milan

Most affectionately yours, my dear friends—MWS

ADDRESS: Mr Leigh Hunt / 13 Lisson Grove North / Paddington / London / Angleterre. POSTMARKS: (1) P 58 P / LYON; (2) FPO / MR. 30 / 1818; (3) 12 o'Clock / MR. 30 / 1818 Nn; (4) 4 o'Clock / 30. MR / 1818 EV. TEXT: MS., Pforzheimer Library.

1. On 13 March the Shelley party left Calais. They traveled through Saint Omer, Douai, La Fère, Rheims, Saint Dizier, Langres, Dijon, and [?Thounu(s) or Thomirey] and arrived at Lyons on 21 March. They remained at Lyons for four days, staying at the Hôtel de l'Europe (MWS Journal).

2. Douai was well known as a center of English Catholic scholarship from 1562 through 1793.

3. Erostratus (or Herostratus) burned down the temple of Artemis at Ephesus in order to gain a place in history.

4. The "horrors" six months past may have resulted from the revelation in June 1817 of a seditious conspiracy in Lyons (SC, VI, 529).

5. In 1816 Louis XVIII had suppressed the Angoulême party, an ultraroyalist group (SC, VI, 529).

6. A playful allusion to Claire Clairmont's singing artistry.

To Leigh and Marianne Hunt

Milan—[6] April 1818[1]

My dear Friends

We have at length arrived in Italy. After winding for several days through vallies & crossing mountains and passing Cenis we have arrived in this land of blue skies & pleasant fields. The fruit trees all in blossom and the fields green with the growing corn—Hunt already says—I should like this. Indeed as we passed along the mountainous districts of Savoy we often said—Hunt would not like this—but the first evening that we arrived in Italy every thing appeared changed. We arrived at Susa the first Italian town at the foot of Cenis about six in the evening and Shelley and I went to look at a triumphal arch that had been erected to the honour of Augustus—It was nearly in perfect preservation and most beautifully situated surrounded by mountains—The path under it was preserved in beautiful order a green lane covered with flowers a pretty Italian woman went with us and plucked us a nosegay of violets.

Italy appears a far more civilized place than France—you see more signs of cultivation and work and you meet multitudes of peasants on the road—driving carts drawn by the most beautiful oxen I ever saw—They are of a delicate dove colour with eyes that remind you of, and justify the Homeric epithet ox-eyed Juno. In France you might travel many miles and not meet a single creature. The inns are infinitely better and the bread which is uneatable in France is here the finest and whitest in the world. There is a disconsolate air of discomfort in France that is quite wretched   In Italy we breathe a different air and every thing is pleasant around us.—At Turin we went to the opera—it was a little shabby one and except the lights on the stage the house was in perfect darkness—there were two good singers and these the people heard but during the rest of the time you were deafened by the perpetual talking of the audience.—We have been also at the opera of Milan.[2] The house is nearly as large as that of London and the boxes more elegantly fitted up. The scenery and decorations much more magnificent   Madame Camporesi[3] is the Prima Donna but she was ill and we did not hear her—indeed we heard nothing   For the people did not like the opera which had been repeated for every night for these three weeks so not one air was heard. But the ballet was infinitely magnificent—It was (strange to say) the story of Othello—but it was rather a tragic pantomime than a ballet—There was no dancer like Mam^{lle} Milanie[4] but the whole was in a finer stile—

The corps de ballet is excellent and they throw themselves into groups fit for a scluptor [*sculptor*] to contemplate. The music of the ballet was very fine and the gestures striking. The dances of many performers which are so ill executed with us are here graceful to the extreme. The theatre is not lighted and the ladies dress with bonnets and pelisses which I think a great pity—The boxes are dear—but the pit—in which none but respectable people are admitted is only eighteen pence so that our amusement is very cheap.

I like this town—The ladies dress very simply and the only fault of their costume is the length of their petticoats so that Marianne's pretty feet would be quite hid. We think however of spending the summer on the banks of the lake of Como which is only twenty miles from here. Shelley's health is infinitely improved and the rest of the chicks are quite well—How are you all—And how do you like Don Garcia and il barbiere di Seviglia.[5] We half expected a letter to have arrived before us—but the posts travel very slowly here. Let us have long letters.—Do you see Peacock and is he in despair[6] Remember me to all friends and kiss your babes for me.

I almost forgot to mention that we spent one day at 30 miles from Geneva Elise's Mother and father-in-law and little girl came to see her [ ][7] Aimee is very beautiful with eyes something lik[e] but sweeter than William's—a perfect shaped nose and a more beautiful mouth than her Mothers expressive of the greatest sensibility

Adieu—My dear Hunt & Marianne La Prima Donna sends her Affectionate remembrances and Shelley his love

Most affectionately yours
Mary W Shelley

Direct to us
  Mess. Marietti-Banquiers
    Milano
      Italie
Tell Ollier that S. has not received his parcel but that he can send the proofs[8] to Peacock for revision.

We left several things at our lodgings in Great Russel St. to be sent you—among the rest have you received William's service—if not have {the} kindness to enquire for it.   for I should be very sorry that it should be lost.

Shelley wishes you to call at the first jewellers on the left hand side of the way in New Bond St—as you enter it from Oxford St. where we bough[t] Marianne's broach—Shelley left a ring to be mended and forgot to call for it.

Tell Peacock to send Beppo[9] & some pins with the first parcel—& sealing wax these things are so bad here

ADDRESS: Mr Leigh Hunt / 13 Lisson Grove North / Paddington / London / Angleterre / Inghilterra. POSTMARKS: (1) FPO / AP. 23 / 1818; (2) 12 o'Clock / AP. 23 / 1818 Nn; (3) 4 o'Clock / 23. AP / 1818 EV. TEXT: MS., Huntington Library.

1. Shelley wrote to Peacock telling him about the opera and ballet that he, Mary Shelley, and Claire Clairmont had seen the previous night (*MWS Journal*), which dates Shelley's letter as 6 April. In the same letter, Shelley asked for news of Hunt, "to whom Mary is now writing" (*PBS Letters*, #460). Both Shelley's and Mary Shelley's letters were received in England on 23 April. On 25 March the Shelley party had left Lyons. Traveling through Tour-du-Pin, Chambery, Saint Jean-de-Maurienne, Mt. Cenis, Susa, and Turin, they had arrived at Milan on 4 April.

2. La Scala.

3. Violante Camporese (1785–1839), a soprano who excelled in works by Mozart.

4. The Shelleys had been greatly impressed by the dancing of Mlle Milanie, whom they had seen during their last month in England (*PBS Letters*, #460, #462).

5. Leigh Hunt wrote a review of Manuel Garcia's performance in *Il Barbiere de Siviglia* for the *Examiner* of 12 April 1818 (Fenner, *Leigh Hunt and Opera Criticism*, pp. 216, 260).

6. Possibly an allusion to Claire Clairmont's rejection of Peacock's proposal of marriage, made in 1818 (*CC Journals*, p. 143, n. 41).

7. On 27 March at Chambéry they visited with Jeanne Elizabeth Duvillard Romieux, Louis Romieux, and Aimée Romieux (see 29 May 1817, n. 9). In accordance with the common usage of the day, "father-in-law" could refer to either a stepfather, as in this case, or the parent of one's spouse (see 9–11 September [1823], n. 14).

8. Of the incomplete *Rosalind and Helen*.

9. Shelley had undertaken to bring Byron's poem *Beppo*, published by John Murray in February 1818, to Byron. Having left it behind, Shelley arranged for Peacock to send it on (*PBS Letters*, #464).

To Maria Gisborne

H. di Malta   1. June 1818

Dear Madam

May I take the liberty to ask you to lend me your Ariosto? We had only one Volume of our's, and I have finished it.

I hope you feel no ill effects from last night's walk. It is the first of June, and we are longing for a fire here in Italy!

Your's truly obliged.   MWS.

TEXT: John Gisborne Notebook No. 2, Abinger MSS., Bodleian Library.

To {Sir Walter Scott}[1]

Bagni di Lucca[2]   14 June—1818

Sir

Having received from the publisher of Frankenstein the notice taken of that work in Blackwood's magasine, and intelligence at the same time that it was to your kindness that I owed this favourable notice I hasten to return my acknowledgements and thanks, and at the same time to express the pleasure I receive from approbation of so high a value as yours.

M[r] Shelley soon after its publication took the liberty of sending you a copy[3] but as both he and I thought in a manner which would prevent you from supposing that he was the author we were surprised therefore to see him mentioned in the notice as the probable author,[4]—I am anxious to prevent your continuing in the mistake of supposing M[r] Shelley guilty of a juvenile attempt of mine; to which—from its being written at an early age, I abstained from putting my name—and from respect to those persons from whom I bear it. I have therefore kept it concealed except from a few friends.

I beg you will pardon the intrusion of this explanation—

Your obliged &c &c

Mary Wollst[ft] Shelley.

TEXT: MS., National Library of Scotland.

1. *Frankenstein* was very favorably reviewed by Sir Walter Scott in *Blackwood's Edinburgh Magazine* 2 (March 1818): 613–20. For a discussion of the contemporary reviews of *Frankenstein*, most of which were favorable, see Grylls, *Mary Shelley*, pp. 315–19. For a listing of contemporary reviews, see Lyles, *MWS Bibliography*.

2. On 11 June the Shelley party had removed to Casa Bertini at the Bagni di Lucca.

3. *PBS Letters*, #443.

4. See *SC*, V, 471–73.

To Maria Gisborne

Casa Bertini   Bagni di Lucca   June 15—1818

My dear Madam

It is strange after having been in the habit of visiting you daily, now for so many days to have no communication with you; and after having been accustomed for a month to the tumult of Via Grande to come to this quiet scene, where we hear no sound except the rushing of the river in the valley below—While at Livorno I hardly heard the noise, but when I came here I felt the silence as a return to something very delightful from which I had been long absent. We live here in the midst of a beautiful scene and I wish that I had the imagination and expressions of {a} poet to describe it as it deserves and to fill you all with an ardent desire to visit it—We are surrounded by mountains covered with thick chestnut woods —they are peaked and picturesque and sometimes you see peeping above them the bare summit of a distant Appenine{.} vines a{re} cultivated on the foot of the mountains—The walks in the woods are delightful; for I like nothing so much as to be surrounded by the foliage of trees only peeping now and then through the leafy screen on the scene about me— You can either walk by the side of the river on [or] on commodious paths cut in the mountains, & for ramblers the woods are intersected with narrow paths in every direction—our house is small but commodious and exceedingly clean for it has just been painted and the furniture is quite new—we have a small garden and at the end of it is an arbour of laurel trees so thick that the sun does not penetrate it—Nor has my prediction followed us that we should every where find it cold—although not hot the weather has been very pleasant—we see the fire flies in an evening— somewhat dimmed by the brightness of the moon—

And now I will say a few words of our domestic economy—albeit I am afraid the subject has tired you out of your wits more than once—Signor Chiappa[1] we found perfectly useless—he would talk of nothing but himself and recommended a person to cook our dinner for us at 3 pauls a day—So, as it is, Paolo[2] (whom we found exceedingly useful) cooks and manages for us, and a woman comes at 1 paul a day to do the dirty work— we live very comfortably and if Paolo did not cheat us he would be a servant worth a treasure for he does everything cleanlily & exactly without teizing us in any way—So we lead here a very quiet pleasant life—reading our Canto of Ariosto[3]—and walking in the evening am[ong] these delightful woods—we have but one wish—you know what that is but you take no pity on us, and exile us from your presence so long—that I quite long to see you again—Now we see no one—the Signor Chi{a}ppa is a stupid fellow and the Casino is not open that I know of—at least it is not at all frequented, when it is every kind of amusement goes on there particularly dancing which is divided into four parts—English & french country dances; quadrilles; walzes; & Italian dances, these take place twice a week on which evenings the ladies dress but on others they go merely in a walking dress.

We have found among our books a volume of poems of Lord Byrons which you have not seen—some of them I think you will like—but this will be a novelty to recommend us on our return—I begin to be very much delighted with ariosto the beginning of the nineteenth canto is particularly beautiful—It is the wounding [*p. 1, cross-written*] of Medoro and his being relieved by Angelica who for a wonder shews herself in the light of {a} sympathizing and amiable person

Mr Shelley is tolerably well he desires to be most kindly rememembered to you & Mr Gisborne not forgetting the Macchinista[4] who although he has seen very little of him is {a} favourite of his from certain phisiognomonical reasons—you will also have the kindness to present my best remembrances both to him and M^r G—[*Gisborne*]   Clare desires to be remembered—But we all of us repine that we must send such messages and that you are not all here when I could express to {you} by words how much I am

My dear Mrs Gisborne

Most obliged & Affectionately yours

Mary Wollstonecraft Shelley

Has Mr Reveley made a Calleidoscope? and do you find as much pleasure as the Londone{r}s in looking through it?[5]

ADDRESS: Alla Signora / Signora Gisborne / 1091 Via Genesi / Fuore della porta di Capucini / Livorno. POSTMARKS: (1) LUCCA; (2) 19 GIUGNO. ENDORSED: Baths of Lucca / 15 June / Recd 19 Do / Ans 21st Do. TEXT: MS., Bodleian Library.

1. G. B. del Chiappa, owner of Casa Bertini (Dowden, *Shelley*, II, 211).

2. Paolo Foggi, the Shelleys' Italian servant, who later formed an illicit relationship with Elise, the Swiss nursemaid. In Naples, towards the end of 1818, the Shelleys discovered that Elise was pregnant and arranged for the marriage of Foggi and Elise prior to dismissing them sometime between the end of December 1818 and 22 January 1819 (MWS *Letters*, vol. I, 22 January 1819; *PBS Letters*, #491; White, *Shelley*, II, 67). Foggi subsequently spread scandalous rumors concerning Shelley and Claire Clairmont and tried to blackmail Shelley (18 June 1820; [10 August 1821] to Shelley; 10 August 1821 to Isabella Hoppner).

3. Mary Shelley read *Orlando Furioso* from 30 May through 19 July. On 15 June she read Canto 19 (*MWS Journal*).

4. "Engineer," that is, Henry Reveley.

5. On 21 June Maria Gisborne responded: "Kaleidoscopism is at this moment with us in a most triumphant state . . . but as we are not eagle eyed our initiation into this delightful science has occasioned us many a headache" (Abinger MS.; *S&M*, I, 289). Henry Reveley had built a kaleidoscope from a description sent to the Shelleys by Hogg (*SC*, VI, 764, 766–67).

To Lord Byron

I take advantage of an opportunity of a person going to Venise to send you Mazeppa and your ode with I hope not many errors and those partly from my not being able to decypher your M.S.[1]

It will give me great pleasure (if the Fornaretta will permit)[2] if you will send me your Don Juan[3] by the bearer—you may trust him as we often employ him—At any rate write a line to say that you have received this safe as I do not like to send your M.S. untill I know that my copy is in your hands—You will see by my copying Mazeppa so quickly that there is more of pleasure than labour in my task. MWS   Allegra is perfectly well[4]

TEXT: MS., John Murray.

1. Mary Shelley transcribed Byron's *Mazeppa* and *Ode on Venice* from 1 through 4 October (*MWS Journal*; Marchand, *Byron*, II, 754).

2. Margarita Cogni, one of Byron's mistresses at Venice, called La Fornarina because she was a baker's wife. Mary Shelley may be alluding to the fact that La Fornarina read and sometimes kept letters to Byron from other women (Byron, *Letters and Journals*, VI, 195).

3. Mary Shelley is perhaps offering to transcribe the first canto of *Don Juan*, which Byron had recently completed. Byron may have expressed to her what he wrote on 19 September to Thomas Moore about transcribing the canto: "But the bore of copying it out is intolerable; and if I had an amanuensis he would be of no use, as my handwriting is so difficult to decipher" (Byron, *Letters and Journals*, VI, 68). After Shelley's death, Byron paid Mary Shelley to copy some of his new cantos (Marchand, *Byron*, III, 1042).

4. The Shelleys returned Allegra to Byron on 29 October.

To Maria Gisborne

My Dear Mrs Gisborne

I have not heard from you since we parted[1]—but I hope that nothing has occasioned this, except your dislike of letter writing—Several events have occurred to us since then, and the principal one, the death of my little Clara—I wrote to tell you of her illness, and the dreadful state of weakness that succeeded to it—In this state she began to cut all her teeth at once—pined a few weeks, and died—

Soon after this, William grew rather ill, and as we were now soon frightened, and there is no good doctor at Este, Shelley and I took him to Venice, where we staid about a fortnight.[2] It is a pleasant town to visit—it's appearance is so new and strange: but the want of walks and variety must render it disagreeable for a continuous residence—The Hoppners[3] find it so—they have lived between four and five years here, and are heartily sick of it. We liked almost every thing,—however I must here except three things, as the disagreements of the city—1st its inhabitants—2nd its streets to walk in—3rd its canals at low water. These are tolerable deductions, and yet there is enough to like without liking these. The inhabitants I dislike, because they are some of the worst specimens of Italians, and to you, who have lived so long in the country, and know their characteristics, this is saying every thing. The streets I dislike because they are narrow and dirty, and above all because they carry zucche[4] about to sell, the sight of which always makes me sick. and I dislike the canals at low water, because they are never cleaned, and the horrid smell makes my head ache, and so now, I daresay, you will think me reasonable enough in all my dislikes—

Well; tomorrow, god permitting, we set out for Naples[5]—but having been forced to delay our journey so long, we must give up the hope of seeing you until next June, when we think of coming north again. We go to Naples by Rimini and Ancona—Will you therefore be so kind as to direct our letters to (Ferma in Posta)[6] Napoli. Write to us also, and tell me if you have any further projects for returning to England. I have been speaking to Shelley, and he says that there is a very heavy tax upon books entering England—he thinks as much as 9^d per bk.

I will write to you again from Naples—I need not say, if you could send us any introductions for that place, you would infinitely oblige us. Shelley and Clare desire to be kindly remembered.

I hope Mr Reveley is entirely recovered, and that you and Mr G. [*Gisborne*] are in good health. What news of the Steam Engine? Mr Webb has received 200 Cr. on Shelley's account,[7] I enclose an order for you to receive it. You will be so kind as to pay yourselves and Mr Dunn, and to keep the rest for more letters and parcels. Have you received our's sent so long ago? The name of the ship it is sent by is—We have actually lost the letter in which it is mentioned. We think it was either the Sisters, or the Northumberland; and the Captain's name Nainor—Adieu—

> Your's affectionately and
> Sincerely
> M.W.S.

TEXT: John Gisborne Notebook No. 2, Abinger MSS., Bodleian Library.

1. When Mary Shelley went to join Shelley and Claire Clairmont at Este on 31 August, she was accompanied as far as Lucca by Maria Gisborne, who had been visiting her at the Bagni di Lucca (*MWS Journal*).

2. From 12 to 31 October. Shelley returned to Este from 24 to 29 October to take Allegra back to Venice (*MWS Journal*).

3. When Clara died, the Hoppners showed great kindness to the Shelleys (*PBS Letters*, #482). During the Shelleys' stay in Venice they were almost daily in the Hoppners' company (*MWS Journal*).

4. Gourds.

5. They left Este on 5 November, stopping at Bologna from 8 to 10 November and at Rome from 20 through 27 November. Shelley left Rome on 27 November; the others followed the next day. On 1 December Mary Shelley recorded: "A long and fatiguing journey. We arrived at Naples about 6 o'clock" (*MWS Journal*).

6. Meaning "Hold at Post Office."

7. Webb & Co. was a banking firm at Leghorn (*SC*, VI, 942–43).

To Maria Gisborne

Naples [c. 3] Dec. 1818[1]

My dear Mrs. Gisborne

I hasten to answer your kind letter as soon as we are a little recovered from the fatigue of our long journey although I still feel wearied and overcome by it—so you must expect a very stupid letter. We set out from Este the day after I wrote to you—we remained one day at Ferrara & two at Bologna looking at the memorials preserved of Tasso and Ariosto in the former town and at the most exquisite pictures in the latter—Afterwards we proceeded along the coast Road by Rimini Fano Fossombrone &c—We saw the divine ⟨acquaduct⟩ waterfall of Terni—And arrived safely at Rome. We performed this journey with our own horses with Paolo to drive us which we found a very œconomical & a very disagreable way so we shall not attempt it again—To you who have seen Rome I need not say how enchanted we were with the first view of Rome and its antiquities—one draw back they have at present which I hope will be fully compensated for in the future—The ruins are filled with galley slaves at work—They are propping the Coliseum & making very deep excavations in the forum. We remained a week at Rome and our fears for the journey to Naples were entirely removed they said there that there had not been a robbery on the road for 8 months—This we found afterwards to be an exageration but it tranquillized us so much that Shelley went on first to secure us lodgings and we followed a day or two after—We found the road guarded and the only part of the road where there was any talk of fear was between Terracina and Fondi where it was not thought advisable that we should set out from the former place before daylight—Shelley travelled with a Lombard merchant & a Neapolitan priest—he remained only two nights {on} the road—and he went veterino,[2] so you may guess he had to travel early & late—The priest—a great strong muscular fellow was almost in convulsions with fear—to travel before daylight along the Pomptine Marshes—There was talk of two bishops murdered & that touched him nearly—The Robbers spare foreigners but never Neapolitan men if they are young & strong so he was the worst off of the party—the Merchant did not feel very comfortable & they were both surprised at Shelley's quietness—That quiet was disturbed however between Capua & Naples by an assassination committed in broad daylight before their eyes—{a} young man ran out of a shop on the road followed by a woman armed with a great stick & a man with a great knife—the man overtook him & stabbed him in the nape of the neck so that he fell down instantly stone dead—The fearful priest laughed heartily at Shelley's horror on the occasion—

Well we are now settled in comfortable lodgings which S. took for 3 louis a week opposite the Royal gardens[3]—you no doubt remember the situation—we have a full view of the bay from our windows—so I think we are well off—As yet we have seen nothing but we shall soon make some excu{r}sions in the environs—

I will write soon again but the journey has quite knocked me up—Be so kind as to send our parcel as soon as you can directed to the care of M. Falconet Bankers—Naples

Use our little purse in paying for our letters & parcels—William is very well—S. & Clare send their kindest remembrances—Excuse this stupid scrawl

Ever yours affectionately
Mary W. Shelley

Shelley left his card at the door of Sig. Castellani but he has not returned his call.

ADDRESS: Alla Signora / La Signora Gisborne / Via Genesi / Fuore della Porta dei Capucini / Livorno. POSTMARKS: (1) NAP 1818 / [   ] DIC; (2) 18 DICEMBRE. ENDORSED: Naples Dec. 1818 / recd 26 Dec / Ans 15th Jany. TEXT: MS., Bodleian Library.

1. They arrived at Naples at about 6:00 P.M. on 1 December. Mary Shelley's statements in this letter that she writes as soon as they "are a little recovered" from travel fatigue but while they have yet "seen nothing" suggests that the letter was written

before 5 December, when they began their sightseeing excursions with a visit to a museum and the theater (MWS Journal).

2. A *vetturino* was the owner of a coach who contracted to take passengers a certain distance and provide them with food and shelter, all for a fixed price (see 23 July [1823]; and MWS *Letters*, vol. I, 26 [–27] July [1823] through 7 August [1823] for Mary Shelley's description of travel by *vetturino*).

3. Their lodgings were at 250 Riviera di Chiaia.

<hr/>

To Maria Gisborne

Naples.   22nd Jany 1819

My Dear Mrs Gisborne

We received your Bill of Lading last night, and we hope soon to have the box—It will be a great amusement to us, although I read almost all the books that it contains, at Venice. Another parcel is on its way, but we have not yet heard by what ship it sails.

Naples is, I can easily conceive, to most people, a delightful residence—We live on the Chiaiia, just opposite the royal gardens, so that we have a full view of the lovely bay, and can hear the dashing of the waves of the sea. We have been to Vesuvius, Herculaneum, Pompeii, the Studii,[1] so that you may guess, we have enjoyed ourselves somewhat here; especially since Shelley, partly through the prescriptions of our English surgeon,[2] and partly by riding on horseback, enjoys better health than he ever did before during the winter season; and has some hopes of an entire cure. Yet we have been dreadfully teized, and that has, in some degree, taken away from our gusto for this place, and besides, I long to return to Rome, which city I like better than any I was ever in.

We are very studious here, and we are all reading "Sismondi's Histoire des Republiques Italiennes du moyen âge,"[3] which since we have visited many of the towns, the history of which he treats of, is exceedingly interesting. I have been reading also Virgil's Georgics, which is, in many respects, the most beautiful poem I ever read—He wrote it at Baiæ; and sitting at the window, looking almost at the same scene that he did—reading about manners little changed since his days, has made me enjoy his poem, more, I think, than I ever did any other.

I should think that you must find Livorno very dull—I, although continually seeing novelties, begin to get home-sick. The Italians are so very disagreeable, and you live in the same kind of solitude that we do—There is no life here—They seem to act as if they had all died fifty years ago, and now went about their work like the ghostly sailors of Coleridge's enchanted ship[4]—except indeed when they cheat. Yet no doubt, there would be many things to teize one in England, and I remember when I set my foot on the shore at Calais, I seemed to break the thread of my annoyances. but I find care to be the thing that Horace describes it to be[5]—and yet mine came from outward circumstances in a great part, and not from my self. The reports, you mention, have nothing to do with these—I seldom suffer them to torment me.[6] When we see you again, we can talk them over, if you have any curiosity on the subject—but it was a kind of treat when we came to Italy to be acquainted with friends who knew nothing of us, as it were, in a public light—and that kept me silent.

You see I am not in very good spirits today—how can one be, when the scirocco blows, especially as I am made stiff by riding a very pretty, but very hard gallopping horse yesterday. We have got rid of our Italian Paolo,[7] after he has made, I fancy, £100—by us. lately he has cheated us through thick and thin.

You ask me news of my father. We have not had a letter from him for above a month. When he wrote last, he said, that he was over head and ears in his answer to Malthus. M[rs] G.—'s [*Godwin's*] health seems to be getting worse daily—

I have several anecdotes to tell you about Lord Byron's particular friend, who is no Colonel.[8] He must bore you dreadfully, I should think—

Have you heard the news from Spain?[9] A plot was discovered at Madrid by the Inquisition, and seven hundred people killed—but the insurgents, to the number of 18,000, have surrounded Madrid—The Queen, who was far advanced in pregnancy, died of fright. The King attempted to escape, and, it is universally believed here, is killed—besides the old King of Spain, who lived here, has died of the gout, and they are very busy in trying to find out how to bury him[10]—Some of their ceremonies are ghastly and laughable at the same time—On account of these misfortunes happening to their relations, the Royal Family have forbidden Carnival to be celebrated.

Shelley and Miss Clairmont desire their kindest remembrances—We shall see you, the good spirit willing, next June—but the devil is getting more and more power in the world every day—I hope however his antagonist will allow you to return to England when we do, so that we shall not lose the Fine Arts, and our friends at the same time—

Ever affectionately your's
M. WS

TEXT: John Gisborne Notebook No. 2, Abinger MSS., Bodleian Library.

1. These visits were made on 16, 5, 22, and 19 December, respectively (*MWS Journal*).

2. Almost certainly identified as Dr. Roskilly in *SC*, VI, 768.

3. Simonde de Sismondi, *Histoire des republiques italiennes du moyen âge* (Paris, 1808–18).

4. *The Rime of the Ancient Mariner* 5. 329–44.

5. *Odes* 3. 1. 40: "Post equitem sedent atra Cura" (Behind the horseman sits black Care), which means that no matter what the speed of distance, one cannot escape from care.

6. Perhaps rumors about the Shelleys' elopement.

7. Elise, recently married to Paolo Foggi and about to give birth, was also dismissed at Naples (see 15 June 1818, n. 2).

8. Robert Finch (1783–1830) was a self-conferred colonel. The Shelleys referred to him as Colonel Calicot, after a fraudulent character in Thomas Moore's *The Fudge Family in Paris, Edited by Thomas Brown, the Younger* (London: Longman, 1818). For an account of Finch as Colonel Calicot, see Elizabeth Nitchie, *The Reverend Colonel Finch* (New York: Columbia University Press, 1940).

9. A Carbonari conspiracy in Valencia, not Madrid, against the local authorities, headed by General Francisco Elío, at the beginning of January 1819. The conspiracy was discovered, and Elío ordered thirteen executed and some twenty-two imprisoned. The Inquisition aided in the prosecution and trials (Iris M. Zavala, *Masones, cumuneros y carbonarios* [Madrid: Siglo XXI Editores, 1971], p. 27). Queen Isabel of Portugal, second wife of Ferdinand VII of Spain, died at the end of December 1818 from a miscarriage or from illness resulting from a previous miscarriage. The miscarriage has been attributed to poor health rather than to political fears (Miguel Morayta, *Historia general de España*, 9 vols. [Madrid, 1896] VI, 490). Rumors of Ferdinand's death proved false.

10. Charles IV, king of Spain from 1788 to 1808, died on 19 January 1819, while visiting the court of his brother Ferdinand I, King of the Two Sicilies, at Naples.

To Maria Gisborne

Rome   April 9th 1819

My Dear Mrs Gisborne,

You will have received Shelley's letter inviting you to Naples[1]—but you will not come—I wish you would; but how many things do I wish as uselessly as I do this. We shall stay all the summer and perhaps the autumn somewhere on the shores of the Bay—I am with child—and an eminent English surgeon will be there[2]—that is one reason for going, for we have no faith in the Italians.

We are delighted with Rome, and nothing but the Malaria would drive us from it for many months—It is very busy now with the funzioni of the holy week, and the arrival of the Emperor of Austria,[3] who goes about to see these things preceded by an officer, who rudely pushes the people back with a drawn sword, a curious thing that a fellow, whose power only subsists through the supposed conveniences of the state of the complaisance of his subjects, should be thus insolent—Of course, we keep out of his track; for our English blood, would, I am afraid, boil over at such insolence.

The place is full of English, rich, noble—important and foolish. I am sick of it—I am sick of seeing the world in dumb show, and but that I am in Rome, in the city where stocks and stones defeat a million of times over my father's quoted maxim, "that a man is better than a stock or a stone,"[4] who could see the Apollo, and a Dandy spying at it, and not be of my opinion—Our little Will is delighted with the goats and the horses and the men rotti, and the ladie's white marbel feet.

We saw the illuminated cross in St Peter's last night, which is very beautiful; but how much more beautiful is the Pantheon by Moonlight![5] As superior, in my opinion, as is the ancient temple to the modern church! I don't think much of S. Peter's after all—I cannot—it is so cut up—it is large—and not simple.

I am very much grieved to hear that Mr Webb[6] is become your enemy! I am afraid he will check all your endeavours, and, be as steady as you will, the life of a contender with the wealthy must be, at least, an anxious one. I hate Livorno, and it always makes me melancholy to think that you are cooped up there, where you are confined from all that can interest you in life, or where there can be any field for Mr Reveley's industry, but I know you will not change it—perhaps you are right!

My father is now engaged in a lawsuit[7]—the event of which will be to him the loss or not of £1500—You may conceive how anxious I am, as well as he; for my part, I am so devoured by ill spirits, that I hardly know what or where I am.

Adieu my Dear Mrs Gisborne—Mr Shelley desires his kindest remembrances, and believe me,

Affectionately your's
MWS

TEXT: John Gisborne Notebook No. 2, Abinger MSS., Bodleian Library.
  1. *PBS Letters*, #497.
  2. John Bell.
  3. Francis II (1768–1835), Holy Roman Emperor from 1792 to 1806, as Francis I, emperor of Austria from 1804 to 1835 and former grand duke of Tuscany.
  4. Used here in the sense of graven images (see *Jeremiah* 2: 27).

5. The Shelleys had seen the Pantheon first in the daytime and then by moonlight on 9 March (*MWS Journal*).

6. A banker at Leghorn (see 2 November 1818).

7. Godwin had lived rent-free for many years in his Skinner Street house. The demand for the accumulated rent resulted in a lawsuit that Godwin finally lost on 1 May 1822 (Brown, *Godwin*, pp. 339–46, 349).

<hr />

To Marianne Hunt

Leghorn—June 29th 1819

My dear Marianne

Although we have not heard from you or of you for some time I hope you are going on well—that you enjoy our [*your*] health and see your children lively about you—

You see by our hap how blind we mortals are when we go seeking after what we think our good—We came to Italy thinking to do Shelley's health good—but the Climate is not any means warm enough to be of benefit to him & yet it is that that has destroyed my two children—We went from England comparatively prosperous & happy—I should return broken hearted & miserable—I never know one moments ease from the wretchedness & despair that possesses me—May you my dear Marianne never know what it is to loose two only & lovely children in one year— to watch their dying moments—& then at last to be left childless & for ever miserable.

It is useless complaining & I shall therefore only write a short letter for as all my thoughts are nothing but misery it is not kind to transmit them to you—Since Shelley wrote to Hunt we have taken a house in the neighbourhood of Leghorn be so kind as to inform Peacock of this—and that he must direct to us Ferma in Posta, Livorno & to let us know whether he has sent any letter to Florence—I am very anxious to know whether or not I am to receive the clothes I wrote to you about[1]—for if we do not I must provide others and although that will be a great expense & trouble yet it would be better for me to know as soon as possible if any one can or will send them—Peacock seems too much taken up in his new occupations[2] to think about us & he unfortunately is the only person whom I can have the slightest hope would do such a thing—If you would write to let me know whether you have them or indeed what you know about them it would exceedingly oblige me—but I know that your do-

45

mestic concerns leave you no time therefore I do not expect that you can do me this favour   I wish I had brought them with me—but one can only learn by experience how slowly & badly every thing is done for the absent—do not think that I reproach you by these words—I know that you can do nothing and who else is there that would care for my convenience or inconveniences

I am sorry to write to you all about thes[e] petty affairs [y] et if I would write any thi[ng] else about [my]self it would only be a list of hours spent [in] tears & grief—Hunt used to call me serious wh[a]t would he say to me now—I feel that I am no[t] fit for any thing & therefore not fit to live but how must that heart be moulded which would not be broken by what I have suffered—William was so good so beautiful so entirely attached to me—To the last moment almost he was in such abounding health & spirits—and his malady appeared of so slight a nature—and as arising simply from worms inspired no fear of danger that the blow was as sudden as it was terrible—Did you ever know a child with a fine colour—wonderful spirits—breedings worms (and those of the most innocent kind) that would kill him in a fortnight—we had a most excellent English surgeon to attend him and he allowed that these were the fruits of this hateful Italy—

But all this is all nothing to any one but myself & I wish that I were incapable of feeling that or any other sorrow—Give my love to Hunt keep yourselves well and happy

Yours—MWShelley

If the child's things are not sent at least as soon as this letter arrives they will come too late but if I had hopes that any one would take the trouble to send them at least—I would only make up the things perfectly necessary in expectation of the others

ADDRESS: Mrs. Hunt / 8 York Buildings / New Road / London / Angleterre. POSTMARKS: (1) LIVORNO; (2) FPO / JY. 17 / 1819; (3) 12 o'Clock / JY 17 / 1819 Nn. TEXT: MS., Huntington Library.

1. Clothes for the baby the Shelleys expected in November.

2. In May 1819, after a training period, Peacock was appointed Assistant to the Examiner in the East India Company. He remained with the company—as Senior Assistant to the Examiner from 1830 and Examiner from 1836—until his retirement in March 1856 (SC, VI, 710, 721).

To Amelia Curran

My dear Miss Curran

We certainly lost your first letter concerning the engraving of La Cenci so perhaps some good person is at work for us here as well as at Rome— I am sorry that you have had so much trouble especially, as it is in vain— of course if the two years were not inadmissible a 1,000 sequins[1] would be—What Shelley thought of was an engraving of a fit size to place as a frontispiece to his tragedy[2] but he has now given up the thought of its being done in Italy, as we trust to your copy—which you know you are to do very beautifully for us—it will be doing us both a very great favour—

We shall quit Leghorn in about a fortnight but as yet we do not know where we go—The autumn here is very delightful & not at all too hot— we are so much more north than you—I regret this for I regret Rome & God knows when we shall see it again—not this winter for we cannot stir before it will be too cold for travelling—not in the summer for then we shall not seek so hot a residence—the next winter is a possible thing— but then I fear you will be thinking of returning to England

Nothing more has been said about the tomb—we still encline to a pyramid as the most durable of simple monumental forms—when you return to Rome do not be angry with me for requesting you to inform yourself of the following particulars—What would be the size of a pyramid built of the most solid materials & covered with white marble at the price of £25 sterl—and also what would be the size of an obelisk built in the same manner & at the same price? When we know these things I think we can decide—You are so kind that you see I trouble you without ceremony & hope that you will accept our thanks & gratitude without being angry with us for the trouble we give you—I wish all the people that we depend upon were as good as you are—the most pressing entreaties on my part as well as Clares cannot draw a single line from Venise[3]—It is now 6 months since we have heard even in an indirect manner from there—God knows what has happened or what has not—I suppose S. must go to see what has become of the little thing—yet how or when I know not, for he has never recovered from his fatigue at Rome and continually frightens me by the approaches of a dysentery—besides we must remove—my lying in & winter are coming on so we are wound up in an inextricable dilemma—this is very hard upon us—& I have no consolation in any quarter for my misfortune has not altered the tone of my father's letters[4]—so I gain care every day & can you wonder that my spirits suffer terribly—that time is a weight to me—& I see no end to this—

Well to talk of something more interesting—Shelley has finished his tragedy & it is sent to London to be presented to the managers—it is still a deep secret & only one person, Peacock who presents it, knows anything about it in England—with S.'s public & private enemies it would certainly fall if known to be his—his sister in law[5] alone would hire enough people to damn it—It is written with great care & we have hopes that its story is sufficiently polished not to shock the audience—we shall see

Continue to direct to us at Leghorn for if we should be gone they will be faithfully forwarded to us—And when you return to Rome just have the kindness to enquire if there should be any stray letter for us at the post office

I hope the country air will do you real good—You must take care of yourself—remember that one day you will return to England & that you may be happier there—Affectionately Yours

MWS.

[*P. 1, top*]   Shelley desires his kindest remembrances & thanks—he will write soon—Clare &ce—Have you paid Bandeloni, her music master?— if not pray do—

ADDRESS: Miss Curran / Alla Casa della / Signora Rosalinda Rotonda / Roma / per Gensano. POSTMARKS: (1) LIVORNO; (2) 25 SETTEMBRE. TEXT: MS., Bodleian Library.

1. A sequin, the French form of the Italian *zecchino*, was worth at that time about nine shillings. The amount quoted, then, is approximately £450.

2. On 5 August Shelley had asked Amelia Curran to inquire about the cost of a good engraving of the portrait of Beatrice Cenci, then in the Colonna Palace in Rome (*PBS Letters*, #507). On 8 August Shelley finished *The Cenci* and arranged for 250 copies to be printed at Leghorn. On 9 September, having asked Peacock to offer it to Covent Garden for production with its authorship a secret, Shelley sent either a printed copy or proof sheets to Peacock (*SC*, VI, 895, 899). The play was rejected by Covent Garden. In March 1820 Charles Ollier published the printed copies that Shelley had sent to him (*PBS Letters*, #513; *SC*, VI, 926). Mary Shelley's "Note on *The Cenci*," in Shelley, *Poetical Works* (1839), II, 273–80, gives a detailed account of Shelley's intentions regarding the writing, proposed production, and printing of *The Cenci*.

3. From the Hoppners or Byron about Allegra. Shelley's letter of 18 October 1819 indicated that he had heard from Hoppner by that time (*PBS Letters*, #520).

4. Ever in debt and at this time particularly worried about the lawsuit for back rent, Godwin wrote pressing and unpleasant letters in his attempt to draw further upon Shelley's financial resources (*SC*, II, 852).

5. Eliza Westbrook.

To Maria Gisborne

[Florence   c. 13 November 1819][1]

The little boy takes after me, and has a nose that promises to be as large as his grandfather's—I have not yet seen his form, but I enput it to be the quintessence of beauty, entracted from all the Apollos, Bacchus's, Loves and dawns of the Study and the Vatican.

His health is good, and he is very lively, and even knowing for his age—although like a little dog I fancy his chief perfection lies in his nose, and that he smells me out, when he becomes quiet the moment I take him.

We have had for the last fifteen days a tempo patetico,[2] as Maria[3] calls it—true enough, it is always crying.   perhaps some little misfortune has happened la su, and that il figlio is infreddato,[4] or the padre got a stroke of the palsy, and all the pretty angels and cherubs are weeping.

Maria must depart—She does nothing, and is in every way disagreeable—Addio, Cara mia amica!

TEXT: John Gisborne Notebook No. 2, Abinger MSS., Bodleian Library.
  1. It is likely that these paragraphs (perhaps with a note by Shelley) announced the birth of Percy Florence on 12 November. In his letter to the Gisbornes of 16 November, Shelley comments, "Mary & the babe continue well" (*PBS Letters*, #532).
  2. "Melancholy weather."
  3. A servant.
  4. "The son is suffering from a cold."

To Marianne Hunt

Florence—Nov 24th (November 25th) 1819

My dear Marianne

At length I am afraid Hunt has got tired of his monday remembrances[1]—I cannot tell you how this vexes me; perhaps he thinks that my little Percy will serve instead—but why not have two pleasant things instead of one? Ask him to be very good, and to continue his practise, which was the pleasantest in the world—tell him we have few friends in any part of Italy—none in Florence—& none whom we we love as well as we love him: make him always consider it a black monday when he does not write a little to us.

49

A few days before we left Leghorn which is now 2 months ago Shelley sent ⟨an ode to Hunt⟩ a poem called the mask of anarchy² Hunt does not mention the reception of it—it was directed to York buildings—and he is anxious to know whether it has been received—you will have received several other large packets from him—you will ask Ollier for money to pay for these extra extraordinary letters—but just let us hear of their safe arrival—We have to thank Bessy for her kindness in transcribing Hunt's kindness³—but it so happened that the practical Peacock had thought it worth while to send those three Examiners themselves to us by post—pray how is the said gentleman going on—he is not yet married & says he does not think about it—I am afraid his Marianne⁴ does & somewhat bitterly—she had rather perhaps that he were still faithfully rusticating at Marlow; for this shepherd-King has I am afraid forgotten his crook & his mistress—do not shew him this gossip of mine concerning him on any account—

After writing this long page I need not tell you that I am very well— & the little boy also—he was born a small child but has grown so during this first fortnight that if his little face were not always the same one might almost think him a changed child he takes after me—You see I say more about him than Hunt did of his little Harry but he is my only one and although he is so healthy and promising that for the life of me I cannot fear yet it is a bitter thought that all should be risked on one yet how much sweeter than to be childless as I was for 5 hateful months—Do not lett us talk of those five months; when I look back on all I suffered at Leghorn I shudder with horror yet even now a sickening feeling steps in the way of every enjoyment when I think—of what I will not write about

I hope all your children are well—they must all be grown quite out of our knowledge—years can hardly give steadiness to Thornton—& Johnny & Mary are yet in the jumping age give them a kiss they & the three younger ones—including the little stranger—

You have no notion how many admirers Hunt has got here by means of his picture especially among our lady acquaintances (English) I had corked up in my memory a number of soft & tender exclamations concerning his eyes & his hair & his forehead &c—I have forgotten them unfortunately—but really from the effect his phisiognomy produces on all who see him & the warmth with which people defend him after seeing it who were cool before—and their vows that indeed he cannot be the Bristol Hunt⁵ I should think that his friends ought to club to have his picture painted by Owen or Lawrence⁶ & exhibited & then no one would think ill of him more—

Shelley in his last letter mentioned something about his return to

50

England[7]—but this is very vague—I hope—how ardently you may guess that it will not be—but in any case keep it quite a secret as if he came hardly a creature must know it.—We have been pursued by so much ill luck that I cannot hope & dare not that things will turn out well—but his return would be in so many ways so dreadful a thing that I can not dwell long enough upon the idea as to conceive it possible—We do not think of all returning—Since we have returned to Tuscany we have lived for the first time in an œconomical manner & it would be madness to break this up besides that arrests & a thousand other things render it impossible that we should be known to be in England—

(November 25th) Another post day & no letter from any of you who I must tell you are the only people from whom we receive any letters except concerning business—Peacock's corespondence having degenerated since the time he had nought to do but to tune his pipe in Bisham wood—I could ask a thousand questions about you & yours but I am afraid that they would not be answered & so instead I will talk to you of ourselves. You may judge by what Shelley has sent to England[8] that he has been very busily employed—and besides this he often spends many hours of the day at the gallery admiring & studying the statues & pictures—There are many divine ones—he says—for my part I have not seen any thing except one peep I took at the Venus di Medici which is not a striking statue— both from its size & the meaningless expression of the countenance the form requires study to understand its full merit.

Claire[9] has got now a very good singing master & is getting on exceedingly well—Tell Hunt that there is a beautiful song—Non temete, O Madre Amata—of Azziolis[10]—only a few copies of which were printed—I wish he could get it to sing to me when I return. When will that be? I must answer with the nursery rhyme—When I grow rich.

After having heard that the box you so kindly sent was shipped from Genoa we have heard no more of it—fortunately a box from Peacock contained the things I so indispensably needed—but I am now in great want of the flannel for the child—

I long to hear from you—I wish you could squeeze a hour for a letter— Love from all to all—Have you received Peter Bell 3[rd][11] &c—Yours affectionately & entirely

Mary WShelley.

ADDRESS: Mrs. Hunt / Examiner Office / 19. Catharine Street / Strand / London. POSTMARKS: (1) FIRENZE; (2) FPO / DE. 15 / 1819. TEXT: MS., Huntington Library.
1. Hunt had promised to write to the Shelleys every Monday.
2. The poem was sent on 23 September 1819 (MWS Journal).
3. The Examiners of 26 September, 3 October, and 10 October contained Hunt's

attack on the *Quarterly Review* for its vitriolic review of Shelley's *Laon and Cythna* in April 1819.

4. Marianne St. Croix. Whether Peacock ever proposed to Marianne St. Croix remains uncertain. However, on 20 November 1819 Peacock proposed marriage to Jane Gryffydh (Peacock, *Works*, VIII, 217–18); she accepted, and they were married in Wales in March 1820 (*SC*, I, 102).

5. Henry "Orator" Hunt (1773–1835), a leading radical spokesman imprisoned for two and a half years (1820–22) because of his participation in Manchester's "Peterloo" in August 1819.

6. William Owen (1769–1825) and Sir Thomas Lawrence (1769–1830).

7. Shelley had written to Hunt: "some circumstances have occurred, not necessary to explain by letter, which make my pecuniary condition a very difficult one . . . it is probable that I shall pay you a visit in the spring" (*PBS Letters*, #529). On 18 November Shelley had written Amelia Curran that he might have to return to England to arrange the large sum of money Godwin required because the lawsuit for back rent had been decided against him (*PBS Letters*, #534).

8. Between 14 August and 17 November 1819 Shelley had sent *Julian and Maddalo, The Cenci, The Mask of Anarchy*, "Letter to the Editor of the *Examiner*" (concerning Richard Carlile), *Prometheus Unbound, Peter Bell the Third*, and several shorter poems. Shelley had requested that the Gisbornes send *The Cenci* and *Prometheus Unbound* in mid-October, but they were not sent to Ollier until mid-December (*PBS Letters*, #551).

9. This marks the end of the evolution, begun in late 1814, of Mary Jane Clairmont's name to Claire Clairmont. (Marion Kingston Stocking points out that in old age she added the name Constantia in acknowledgment of Shelley's poem to her [*CC Journals*, p. 13].) Mary Shelley generally uses the spelling *Claire* from this time forward.

10. Possibly Bonifacio Asioli (1769–1832), the most famous of a family of composers and a prolific composer of songs, cantatas, operas, and duets.

11. Shelley had written the poem in Florence during the latter part of October and on 2 November had sent it to Hunt to give to Ollier for immediate publication (*PBS Letters*, #526). It was not published until 1840, when Mary Shelley included it in the second edition of Shelley, *Poetical Works* (1839).

To Maria Gisborne

Florence   Dec 28–1819

My dear Mrs Gisborne

I am glad that you are pleased with the Prometheus[1]—the last act though very beautiful is certainly the most mystic of the four—I am glad also that Spencer pleases you for he is a favourite author of mine—in his days I fancy translations & plagiarisms were not considered so disgraceful as they are now—You have not all of him & perhaps you have not read therefore the parts that I particularly admire—the snowy Florimel—Bel-phœbe and her squire lover who is half meant for Q. Elizabeth & Lord Essex—Britomart is only an imitation—she is cold & dull but these oth-ers & the lovely Una are his own creations & I own I like them better than Angelica although indeed the thought of her night scene with Medoro[2] came across me & made me pause as I wrote the opinion—but perhaps it is not in pathos but in the simple description of beauty that Spencer ex-cels—His description of the island of of bliss is an exact translation of Tasso's garden of Armida[3] yet how is it that I find a greater simplicity & spirit in the translation than in the original—yet so it is.

You cannot guess how busy & I may almost say now it is over uselessly busy I have been these last days—Milly has left us & for 3 days we were without a servant for the child (chi è bello e grasso) now we have a German-Swiss who speaks Italian perfectly who as much as I see of her I prefer to Milly[4] infinitely so we are fortunate so far & now I think of beginning to read again   Study I cannot for I have no books & I may not call simple reading study for Papa is continually saying & writing that to read one book without others beside you to which you may refer is mere childs work—but still I hope now to get on with latin & Spanish—Do you know that if you could borrow for us Rousseaus Emile & Voltaires essai sur l'eprit des nations[5] either or both you would oblige us very much & send them with the stripped cotons which I wish you to send if the duty is not intolerable but I dare say your <u>sage</u> (I mean Giuseppe)[6] can manage that.

Shelley has given up the idea of visiting Leghorn before the finishing of the steam boat—he is rather better these last 2 or 3 days but he has suffered dreadfully lately from his side—he seems a changed man his nu-merous weaknesses & ailments have left him & settled all in his side alone for he never any other winter suffered such constant pain there—It puts me in mind of the mountain of ills in the Spectator—where mankind exchange ills one with the other—there they all take up their old evils again as the most bearable[7]   I do not know whether this is Shelley's case.

Well—I hope the steam engine is getting on prosperously—give our best loves to it and our compts (as more respectful to the higher being) to its maker—I have a headach & will not scribble any more except to say that Papa's riddle[8] is not yet divined   Your way of cutting the knot we all think the best but it were easier to set Pelion upon Ossa than to make him think so

Adieu my dear <u>good</u> friend (& wise too & <u>upright</u>)   I cannot answer what you say about Zoide that must remain for gossip—Mad^me M. [*Mer-veilleux du Plantis*] might go on exceedingly well & gain if she had the brains of a goose but her head is a sive & her temper worse than wildfire it is gunpowder & blows up every thing—We see a great deal of Louise she is a good girl clever too but lazy—what say you to her jilting poor Charles[9] & marrying the steam boat (or its maker) tell it or him (if you are not afraid) that she has lovely hair pretty eyes—nice neck & shoulders for the rest non c'è male—

You see I chatter on & nonsense [to]o that is the worst of it—adieu

Affectionately yours

MWS.

Our best remembrances to Mr. G. [*Gisborne*] & Mr. R. [*Reveley*]   If by any chance you have not sent the Prometheus add the word bowers after from their obscurest[10] & in the other change it to it's mother fears awhile[11]

ADDRESS: A Madame / Madame Gisborne / Livorno. POSTMARKS: (1) FIRENZE; (2) 31 DECEMBRE. ENDORSED: Recd. 31st Dec., 1819. Ansd. TEXT: MS., Bodleian Library.

1. Shelley wrote the fourth act of *Prometheus Unbound* in the autumn of 1819 and sent it to the Gisbornes on 23 December to read and then mail to Charles Ollier (*PBS Letters*, #542).

2. Florimel, Belphoebe, Britomart, and Una are figures in Spenser's *The Faerie Queene* (1589–96); Angelica and Medoro are figures in Ariosto's *Orlando Furioso* (1532).

3. In *Gerusalemme liberata* (1575).

4. Amelia Shields, the Shelleys' servant from Marlow. Mrs. Mason helped them find their new servant, Carolina (McAleer, *The Sensitive Plant*, p. 132).

5. *Émile* (1762); *Essai sur les Mœurs et l'esprit des nations* (1753–56).

6. The Gisbornes' servant.

7. Joseph Addison, *The Spectator*, 23 and 25 June 1714.

8. Godwin's legal entanglement about his back rent.

9. Zoide and Louise, the daughters of Madame Merveilleux du Plantis. Charles Clairmont, who had visited the Shelleys until 10 November, had fallen in love with Louise, but she had rejected him (White, *Shelley*, II, 154).

10. *Prometheus Unbound* 4. 375.

11. *Prometheus Unbound* 4. 392.

To Maria Gisborne

Florence   Jany. 12th 1820

Here is a fine Tuscan winter! Are you not in a passion, my Dear M[rs] Gisborne? I am sure I am, and have every reason; for besides all pains in the side, of which Shelley has plenty, he had an attack last Friday of fever, just like, only more severe, the one he had on returning to Leghorn from Florence[1]—Wind! Frost! Snow! How can England be worse?

Are you yet reconciled to the idea that England is become a despotism? The freedom with which the newspapers talk of our most detestable governors is as mocking death on a death bed. The work of dissolution goes on, not a whit the slower—And cannot England be saved? I do hope it will—I enclose to you a letter we have received from a stock broker[2] on the subject—You see what he says, The rich alone support the government—The poor, and middling classes are, I believe, to a man, against them—But we have fallen, I fear, on evil days. There are great spirits in England. So there were in the time of Cesar and Rome. Athens flourished but just before the despotism of Alexander—Will not England fall? I am full of these thoughts;[3] but to talk of something else, what do you think of an idea that has crost our brains of taking a house, and settling, during our Exile, at Florence—We are tired of roving—We want our books— We dare not settle in a very warm climate on account of our child—It is true, it is cold at Florence, but seldom, they say, so cold as this. Do you think we could manage with two or three months in the summer at the baths of Lucca? We should then have some comforts about us, and when we felt ourselves en fonds, the steam boat would be our wings to carry us quickly there, and quickly back to see what curiosities we desired to visit.

I hope you have not been teazed any more by those rascally Italians— When you calculate a bargain with them, you ought always to put so much for law expences in your calculation—

I have not yet received the buff gown—you would much oblige me by letting me have it as soon as is convenient.

How does this cold weather agree with you, and your two Catastas[4] of wood? We are already in our fourth, but then we have two fires, and in our two first, to say nothing of the two last, were cheated above half by Maria, who sold it. She has left us long ago—She cheated us horribly— so does the one with us now—but she is a very good servant.

Adieu, dear M[rs] G—! The day will be benvenuto when I see you again, and this new year, if I see much of you within it. In any case may it be a fortunate one for you.—for us—I am tired of wishing or hoping. All goes on de pire en pire[5]—so let us shut our eyes—though the lightening of misfortune will pierce through our tight-closed lids.

So with this fine poetical image once more Adieu. I hope M[r] G— [*Gisborne*] does not suffer from the cold—Lord B— is at Ravenna—reforming—i.e. making love and becoming a methodist.—but tare! so again I recommend you to Jehovah. Your's affectionately.

M.WS.

Henry and his child[6] are not forgotten. A happy year to them both. May the boat have sailed 10,000 leagues, and he be married to an heiress of £10,000 within it. Return the letter that I send—By the bye, I send you none—for I have been looking it over and find it not worth sending. He is in a rage with Lord C—[7] and says that the finance must explode one day—Do sent the cotton for my gown—

TEXT: John Gisborne Notebook No. 2, Abinger MSS., Bodleian Library.

1. On 23 September 1819 Shelley had gone to Florence to find lodgings, and on 25 September he had returned to Leghorn "very unwell" (*MWS Journal*).

2. Horace Smith. (For a discussion of Smith's liberal politics expressed in his correspondence, see Stuart Curran, "The View from Versailles: Horace Smith on the Literary Scene of 1822," *Huntington Library Quarterly* 40 [1977]: 357–71.) Mary Shelley may have been reacting to news of the repressive "six acts" passed by Parliament in December 1819. Her letter of [24 March] 1820 to Marianne Hunt contains a lengthy satirical attack against the "enslaved state" of England.

3. That Mary Shelley expressed the same political concerns in an unlocated letter of 11 January 1820 to Mrs. Mason is evident from Mrs. Mason's response of 14 January (Abinger MS.).

4. "Piles."

5. "Worse and worse."

6. That is, his steam engine.

7. Robert Stewart (1769–1822), Viscount Castlereagh by courtesy—he succeeded his father as second marquess of Londonderry in 1821—was blamed by liberals for atrocities in Ireland following the rebellion of 1798 and, as Secretary of War (1805–9) and Foreign Secretary (1812–22), for the Tory government's generally reactionary policies at home and abroad, including the "six acts."

❧

To Marianne Hunt

Pisa.   Feb 24th [error for 24 March] 1820[1]

We have at last received Bessy's letter my dear Marianne, when the long protracted silence of our poor dear friend made us fear that he must be engaged in some plot or other with T—d[2] or others so to engross his time that for three months (& during cold weather too) he could not send one look to Italy. But it appears that he is only engaged in the same plot that exercises all the world—viz. care. & I would write a great deal to say how melancholy it makes me to see all my friends oppressed by the same load—but I wish letters from Italy to be a recreation & to draw you out of your cares as much as vain words, & kind remem{bran}ces can. Although before I leave the subject of your cares my dear, let me advert to your health—Bessy says in her letter that Percy from a sickly infant is grown a fine stout boy—he appears to have been in the same case as Swinburne & I am afraid from the same cause—I could say a great many things to prove to you that a woman is not a field to be continually employed either in bringing forth or enlarging grain—but I say only, take care of yourself. And so I pass on to something else.

We are now comfortably settled in Pisa for 3 months more than we have already staid & then we go again to the Baths of Lucca. Shelley's health is so very delicate that little as he can bear cold—heat is almost more injurious to him & he is ordered to seek the coolest climate Tuscany affords i.e. the Baths of Lucca: besides the Baths themselves are recommended for him   The most famous surgeon in all Italy lives at Pisa, Vaccà—he is a very pleasant man—a great republican & no Xtian—He tells Shelley to take care of himself & strengthen himself but to take no medecine. At Pisa we have an appartment on the Lung' Arno—a street that runs the length of the town on each side of the Arno, and the side which receives the southern sun is the warmest & freshest climate in the world—We have two bed rooms 2 sitting rooms kitchen servants rooms nicely furnished—& very clean & new (a great thing in this country for 4 guineas & a ½ a month—the rooms are light and airy—so you see we begin to profit by Italian prices—One learns this very slowly but I assure you a crown here goes as far in the conveniences & necessaries of life as £1 in England & if it were not for claims on us & expences that are as it were external or perhaps rather internal for they belong to ourselves & not to the Country we live in we sh^d be very rich indeed. As it is for the first time in our lives we get on easily—our minds undisturbed by weekly bills & daily expences & with a little care we expect to get the things into better order than they are.

Only one thing teazes us—Elise has married & Milly has quitted us & we have only Italian servants who teaze us out of our lives—I am trying to get a Swiss & hope that I shall succeed. We see no society it is true except one or two English who are friends & not acquaintances—we might if we pleased but it is so much trouble to begin & I am so much confined & my time is so much taken up with my child that I sh^d grudge the time—however in the summer or next winter we shall I think mix a little with the Italians   Pisa is a pretty town but its inhabitants w^d exercise all Hoggs vocabulary of scamps, raffs &c &c to fully describe their ragged-haired, shirtless condition. Many of them are students of the university & they are none of the genteelest of the crew. Then there are Bargees, beggars without number; galley slaves in their yellow & red dress with chains—the women in dirty cotton gowns trailing in the dirt—pink silk hats starting up in the air to run away from their ugly faces in this

manner 🐝 (for they always tie the bows at the points {of} their chins—
& white satiny shoes—& fellows with bushy hair—large whiskers, canes
in their hands, & a bit of dirty party coloured riband (a symbol of nobility) sticking in their button holes) that mean to look like the lords of
the rabble but who only look like their drivers—The Pisans I dislike more
than any of the Italians & none of them are as yet favourites with me.
Not that I much wish to be in England if I could but import a cargo of
friends & books from that island here. I am too much depressed by its
enslaved state, my inutility; the little chance there is for freedom; & the
great chance there is for tyranny to wish to be witness of its degradation
step by step, & to feel all the sensations of indignation & horror which I
know sh^d experience were I to hear daily the talk of the subjects or rather
the slaves of King Cant whose dominion I fear is of wider extent in England than any where else. At present I have it double distilled through
Galignani[3] & even thus frittered way it makes one almost sick. No—since
I have seen Rome, that City is my Country, & I do not wish to own any
other untill England is free & true that is untill the throne Cant the God
or if you will the abominable idol before whom at present the english are
offering up a sacrifize of blood & liberty, be over thrown. Cant has more
power in parliament, & over the Kingdom than fear or any other motive—a man now in England w^d as soon think of refusing a duel as of not
listening to & talking the language of Cant & from the same motive—
he w^d be afraid of being turned out of society.

Besides these reasons you know many others, my dear Marianne, of an
individual nature that keep us from returning. If we had no debts yet
they w^d instantly accumulate if we went back to England—& then Shelley's health—the more we see & hear the more we are convinced that this
climate is absolutely necessary to him. Not that this is a Paradise of
cloudless skies & windless air just now the libechio is blowing hurri-
canes—but they are equinoctial gales—but it {is} so much better than
your northern island. But do not think that I am unenglishifying myself—but that nook of ci devant free land, so sweetly surrounded by the
sea is no longer England but Castlereagh[4] land or New Land Castlereagh,—heaven defend me from being a Castlereaghish woman. What
say you to Hunt's gravely putting a letter in his Examiner as from a Cor-
respondant saying that on the approaching elections, & during the present state of the country it is dangerous to repeat the name of England
which has become the watchword of rebellion & irreligion—& that while
the land continues in its present demoralized & disturbed state that all
loyal persons should distinguish themselves by assuming for their country the demonination [*denomination*] I before mentioned   The more loyal

one, which w^d be Georgia is objectionable on account of the immorality of the women of the region that goes by that name,^{5} which by association might have a bad effect on the imaginations of our chaste country women of unblemished reputation!!!!!—Is not this the talk of God Cant? & of his prime council the Exxxxxh Parliament? & of his prime organ the Courier newspaper?—But I really think an excellent plan might be made of it—All those who wish to become subjects of the new kingdom ought to be obliged to take an oath of citizenship not as Irish English or Scotch but as Castlereaghish—all that refused sh^d be put on the alien list—besides the Government should have the right to refuse subjects—what a picnic kingdom it w^d become! One of the first things w^d be to import a cargo of subjects from all various oppressed countries on the earth—not to free them but as good examples for the rest—A man w^d only have to enter himself a slave—a fool—a bigot—& a tyrant where he can; to become a Castlereaghishman. The form of their oath sh^d be—The king shall have my wealth—Castlereagh my obedience—his parliament my love—the Courier my trust—the Quarter[l]y my belief—Murray my custom—down with the Whigs & Radicals—So God help me. Their belief may be asily [*easily*] exprest—I believe in Cant—the creator of ⟨God⟩ this kingdom the Supporter of Castlereagh & maker &c of all good fortunes; The sole rule of life & the life of all morality—created by fear, falsehood & hate; brought into fashion by Castlereagh, for the use of Castlereagishmen & women—detested by the Whigs yet used by them—detested by the Radicals whom it detests—[   ] born long ago, but grew much since the French Revolution, & more since the establishment of the most holy kingdom New Land Castlereagh—May it never die—As it has changed all truth to a lie, so does it live in & by lies & may its food never fail; nor can it while we exist. I believe in all that Cant teaches, as it is revealed to me by the Courier, & the Quarterly, & sold to me by Murray—whom Cant bless. I believe in all plots Cant feigns & creates & will use none but the language of Cant unto my last day—amen!"—I really think I will write to Castlereagh on the subject it w^d be a God send to him such a kingdom, & save him a world of trouble in grinding & pounding, & hanging & taxing, the English that remain into Castlereaghish for all that w^d not accede to the terms of his agreement w^d be aliens & so an end to them.—You see what a John or rather Joan Bull^6 I am so full of politics—But I entreat you to adopt my vocabulary & call all that can support so vile a wretch as that detested Irishman by their proper name—do not degrade—the name of British they are & ever must be Castlereaghish—which pronounced in a short way Castleraish wont be very uncouth & will be very apt.

I hope that we shall soon hear of your health & well-being, my dear Marianne. Little Percy has got the measles very lightly—it is a much milder malady in this climate than with you—& he has it mildly for this climate—Do pray you or Hunt write—Bessy's letter is dated the 6th Jan^ry so God knows what may have happened since then—nothing ill I trust— But we now begin to feel that we are not travellers but exiles—since our English friends neglect & forget us—What say you to this reproach? or will you consider it as one?

Adieu—dear Marianne

Pisa. (direct to us here.)   Affectionately y^s ever

Marina W.S.

We have just re^d Hunt's letter—it is dreadful to see how much he is teazed—I hope, how sincerely that you are now going on better. do you write—Does he think I c^d write for his Indicator & what kind of thing w^d he like. Shelley will answer his letter next week—adieu

ADDRESS: Mrs. Leigh Hunt / Examiner Office / 19 Catherine St. Strand / London / Inghilterra / Angleterre. POSTMARKS: (1) Pisa; (2) FPO / AP. 8 / 1820. TEXT: MS., Huntington Library.

1. Mary Shelley's date of 24 February 1820 is an error for 24 March 1820, for in this letter Mary Shelley refers to Percy's measles, which he contracted on 9 March, and to their comfortable apartments, to which they moved on 14 March (*MWS Journal*; *CC Journals*). Moreover, the letter from Bessy Kent to which this letter is a response was received on 19 March (*CC Journals*). Shelley answered Bessy Kent's and Hunt's letters mentioned in Mary Shelley's postscript on 5 April (*PBS Letters*, #557). These facts and the 8 April 1820 postmark all support 24 March as the probable date.

2. Arthur Thistlewood (1770–1820) was the leader of the Cato Street conspiracy, a radical plot to murder all the members of the British Cabinet on 23 February 1820. The conspirators were betrayed and arrested before they could execute their plan; Thistlewood and four others were condemned to death and were hanged on 1 May 1820. Shelley's letter to Ollier of 13 March 1820 also refers to the plot and Hunt's possible involvement in it (*PBS Letters*, #555).

3. *Galignani's Messenger*, a weekly Parisian English-language newspaper.

4. See 12 January 1820.

5. That is, the area of the Caucasus, now part of the former Soviet Union.

6. In Shelley's *Oedipus Tyrannus; or, Swellfoot the Tyrant*, written in August 1820, Queen Caroline is represented by Iona Taurina ("Joan Bull"), her enemy Castlereagh by Purganax (Greek transliteration for Castlereagh) (Carlos Baker, *Shelley's Major Poetry: The Fabric of a Vision* [Princeton: Princeton University Press, 1948], p. 179). Mary Shelley's attack in this letter and others and Shelley's *Oedipus Tyrannus* employ figures of speech, characters, and ideas common to a flood of satires, tracts, and cartoons of the period on the Queen Caroline controversy (see 19 July 1820).

To Maria Gisborne

Pisa.   Good Friday   [31 March] 1820

My dear Mrs Gisborne

I will send your box soon & perhaps a vol of Political Justice which I hear you have defended to the loss of ancient friendship. Shelley c^d not be persuaded to continue his subscription to Gaglignani untill he found the paper stopt so we shall not have it for some days—I suppose however that you have heard the news—that the Beloved Ferdinand has proclaimed the Constitution of 1812 & called the Cortes—The Inquisition is abolished—The dungeons opened & the Patriots pouring out—This is good. I sh^d like to be in Madrid now.[1]

Do you think that you c^d get me some little stockings or shoes that w^d wash for Percy—If not could not the Miss Riccis[2] manufacture some out of old ones—they new footed some very nicely for me so perhaps they could—his foot is the length of your middle finger—if it can be done w^d you set them to work—I want 4 p^{rs} Claires shoes I suppose are to cost 8 pauls—I sh^d not think he w^d not charge more.

You do not write but pray come   I think you c^d manage it in the way I mentioned—

How does Mr G. [*Gisborne*] get on with Homer has he nearly finished the Iliad? You ought to have read it with him.

Adieu dear Mrs G.   The sun shines & it is divine weather   Shelley is not very well if I c^d get a pretty boat & come down in 2 hours I w^d come but a carriage & a child are discords—But you will come surely.

Very since{re}ly & for ever yours
Mary WS.

After all, like a goose I closed my letter having forgot the most particular thing I had to say—A gentleman of our acquaintance is going to Casciano[3] in May he will want a sitting room a bed room for himself & another for his servant—a man of the name of Passetti has asked 15 seq. per month for these accommodations—w^d you have the kindness to tell me what he ought to pay and the names of some reasonable lodging people there to apply to—& another facility you can thing [*think*] of— & the nearest to the baths—in short if you w^d kindly send me the information you judge necessary on the subject.

Addio Cara Mia

ADDRESS: Alla Ornatissima Signora / La Signora Maria Gisborne / Livorno.
POSTMARKS: (1) Pisa; (2) 2 APRILE. ENDORSED: Pisa Good Friday / 1820 / Between
the 26th March and the 9th April. TEXT: MS., Bodleian Library.

1. In January 1820 a full-scale revolution against Ferdinand VII brought about
the reinstatement of the constitution.

2. Carlotta and Apollonia Ricci, daughters of the Gisbornes' landlord at Leghorn
(White, *Shelley*, II, 207).

3. Mrs. Mason had requested this information for Mr. Mason in her letter to Mary
Shelley of 14 January (Abinger MS.).

❖

To Amelia Curran

Leghorn   June 20th 1820

My dear Miss Curran

It is a very long time since I heard from you so that if I did not know
your dislike to writing I should be afraid that somthing had happened—
and that you were very ill—My heart—during all this time is at Rome—
But I cannot conjecture when I shall be really there—still a letter with
a Roman postmark would be a pleasant thing how much more welcome
if from you!

I am afraid that you find great difficulties in executing our unhappy
commission   Shelley & I are therefore induced to entreat you to have the
kindness to order a plain stone to be erected to mark the spot with merely
his name & dates—(William Shelley born January 24, 1816—June 7—
1819)—You would oblige us more than I can express if you w^d take care
that this should be done.

Our little Percy is a thriving forward child but after what has happened
I own it appears to me—a faded cloud—all these hopes that we so earnestly dwell upon.

How do you like the Cenci—It sells—you must know of which I am
verry glad—If I could hear of any one going to Rome I w^d send you some
other books to amuse you—for we had a parcel from England the other
day—but we are entirely out of the world—

It will give me great pleasure to hear from you—to know when you
leave Rome—and how your pictures encrease—Be sure I do not forget
your nice study & your kind hospitality   You{r} study how can I forget
when we have so valuable a specimen of it that is dearer to me than I can
well say[1]

Shelley desires his kindest remembrances what have become of our pictures—Claire is not yet reconciled to hers—How is St. George & all your

friends—I would give a very great deal to look upon the divine city from the Trinità dei Monti—Is not my heart there?—

From Papa I have not heard a very long time—affairs seem gowing [*going*] on there badly but slower than a tortoise   I hope not so surely towards their apparent end—

Farewell—I entreat you to write

Yours with affection
Mary WS.

I have heard your brothers life of your father much praised[2]—

ADDRESS: Miss Curran / 64 Via Sistina / Trinita de' Monti / Roma. POSTMARKS: (1) LIVORNO; (2) 26 GIUG[NO]. TEXT: MS., Bodleian Library.

1. The portrait of William. Mary Shelley then inquires about the portraits of Shelley, Claire Clairmont, and herself.

2. William Henry Curran, *The Life of the Right Honourable John Philpot Curran, Late Master of the Rolls in Ireland*, 2 vols. (London: Archibald Constable & Co., 1819).

❧

To Maria Gisborne

Leghorn   July 19th 1820

My Dear Friend!

Seeing what a large sheet of paper I have before me, I think I should do more than my duty if I were to fill it, which I do not promise—You have done so much less than your duty, and your promise, that I am seriously vexed—I could not have believed when we parted at Leghorn, that for three months nearly I should not have seen a single line indited by the fairest faithless Maria. Do you wish the word at the top of the letter to dwindle into a mere name? or do you think, as Hogg does, that there is an instinctive intercourse between congenial souls that needs not the slow and troublesome formality of letter-writing? I do not, for I am sure, if put to the rack, I could not have guessed at your employments and thoughts during this long interval—M[r] G—'s [*Gisborne's*] letter was very welcome, but it was not a journal[1]—I daresay you had the barbarity not to put down even any part of your talk with Papa—to leave it till your return is such a procrastination that you ought not even to have thought of, however, I expect a letter from you in a few days, and if one does not come, the fault will surely lie very heavy at your door—

I have now very seriously begun Greek—I pass five lines or more every day—reading them over again and again, so that now I may boast that I know perfectly sixty lines of Homer's Odyssey. I am much teazed from the want of a good grammar—S. wanted to persuade me to have Jones's sent out in sheets: but finding that a whole box would cost less than that, he has written to Peacock to beg him to send, without delay, a box.² If you have anything to send, pray consign it, as you will have several things to bring for us, perhaps you would like to send some of your books this way. But I should advise that nothing but books were sent. Pray do not forget to ask Mʳˢ Hunt for the remains of the flannel &c. that she bought for the last winter, but did not send. I wish you to bring that with you— as I shall want flannel next winter, and that will serve.

We are still at Casa Ricci, nor have we yet settled the date of our im-igration—Necessity brought us here—You know Leghorn is no favourite with me—The rascal, whom I mentioned in my first letter from here, came and laid an accusation, but, through the means of Del Rosso,³ he was ordered to quit Leghorn in four hours. The idea of going to Del Rosso was most fortunate, as otherwise we certainly should have been frightened again, if not excessively teazed. We now wait here until we receive our quarter, and afterwards perhaps for other arrangements; but we shall be guided by time. I wish very much to spend a month among mountains before the end of the summer—I think we shall go in a fortnight⁴—

I do not wonder you dislike the smoke and confinement of London. They say you are visited by some very hot weather. You can tell us how this weather is in comparison with Italy—

We have had some very hot hours, but the weather is so changeable that a very hot day we have not yet had—The country wants rain and the Cicalas sing in the trees, I suppose, entreating for dew, and telling the Gods that the dry leaves hurt the sweetness of their merry song. With this exception, the season is promising—the Vines are weighed down by their clusters, and the trees loaded with figs. Come and eat! Will you?

I am sorry to see an Advertisement in Galignani to say that on the first of the month a steam boat was to sail from Bourdeux to Leghorn and ply between here and Genoa—Will they have the start of us?

To ask something that has to do with business for us as you will guess—Will you tell me why the King of Naples set up a Confectioner's shop?⁵ That rascal Galignani gave you a pretty account of the sale of the Cenci⁶—We know that Copies were sent for, and he sent word that none were to be had—It was only advertised once, so the matter is clear. It has been suppressed, doubtless, through the representations of our moral Country-men, who, as we have reason to know, hate Shelley (I hope they will include me in the Compliment) with ardour, and this is why only four Copies were sold—

The Queen! The Queen! The Queen![7] Does it not rain Queens in England, or at least orations sent post from Heaven with pleadings in favour of our heroic—magnanimous—innocent—injured—virtuous—illustrious and lion-hearted British one—full of painful feelings, delicate subject (not any scandal of the V.M.[8] I hope). Tantini said he saw her at the Campo Santo—She had on a black pelisse, tucked up to her knees, and exhibiting a pair of men's boots. A fur tippet that seemed as if it would cover ten such—a white cap, and a man's hat set on sideways.—to be sure, she is injured, but it is too great a stretch of imagination to make a God of a Beef-eater, or a heroine of Queen Caroline.—but I wish with all my heart downfall to her enemies, and that is no great stretch of compassion. Besides her, you have the coronation to carry joy to the hearts of H.M.'s subjects. Oh! they are a pretty set! Castlereagh's impudence and Brougham[9] speechifying—I believe the latter to be a good man at bottom, but he is naturally cautious, canny, as they say in his Country.—Apropos of Scotland, Ask Papa if it were not well to introduce Henry to Mr Booth—and ask him also how those good folks are going on—If he sees Isabel &c—

Are you not, or will you not be delighted to hear of the Revolution at Naples.[10] The Duke of Campochiaro was at the head of it—They assembled before the gates of the palace, and the old pastry Cook ordered the Soldiers to fire on them—they refused, and he was obliged to compromise by turning out his old ministry and filling their places by popular nobles and entreating the people's patience until a constitution should be formed. Thirty years ago was the era for Republics, and they all fell—This is the era for constitutions, I only hope that these latter may in the end remove the [?mothes] of the former. What a glorious thing it will be if Lombardy regains its freedom—and Tuscany—all is so mild there that it will be the last, and yet in the end I hope the people here will raise their fallen souls and bodies, and become something better than they are.

The friend of Mrs Mason asking where she ought to apply to receive and pay for the Piano, I gave them the direction of Clementi's shop, 26 Cheapside.[11] You will therefore have the kindness to acquaint Clementi of this. She desires me to convey her thanks to you for your kindness—

Annunziata departed with her new-born last Monday, to take her to the mountains. While she was here, Fortunata screamed all day—Now, we do not know that the child is in the house. That woman is a real Devil—I could no more endure her than the perpetual sight of a dozen crawling toads. I will not conclude without mentioning Percy—he is well—lively, and thriving—Shelley gets on pretty well, he has just concluded the translation of Homer's Hymn to Mercury   I do not hear from you, and I am vexed—that is my last word, except indeed I add that I am ever your's

Mary WShelley

If your hearts did not very much encline you to Italy, I should say, accept C—'s offer.[12] Your instructions assuredly would be worth £100 p ann. and with the addition of one or two pupils, which you would easily get, you might be well and comfortably settled. But this is for your decision—I will just mention that our Parisian plan[13] has failed. It seems that the French are become surly having lost their politeness, and hating the English in an incredible manner—

TEXT: John Gisborne Notebook No. 2, Abinger MSS., Bodleian Library.

1. Mary Shelley evidently expected Maria Gisborne to send the *Journal* to her in installments.

2. See *PBS Letters*, #576. On 18 June Mary Shelley asked Maria Gisborne to have Peacock send a number of books, including Jones's Greek grammar.

3. A lawyer.

4. On 4 August the Shelleys and Claire Clairmont left Leghorn, spent the night of 4 August with the Masons, and then went to the Bagni di Pisa (also called Bagni di San Giuliano), which was a short distance from Pisa, Lucca, and Leghorn.

5. Ferdinand I (1751–1825). Maria Gisborne responded: "The old confectioner whom you inquire about had one principal and one secondary object in setting up business—gain and amusement" (Gisborne, *Journals and Letters*, p. 65).

6. Shelley believed (erroneously) that *The Cenci* had been piratically published by Galignani in Paris (*PBS Letters*, #561).

7. Caroline of Brunswick (1768–1821), separated from her husband the Prince of Wales (and from 1811 to 1820 Prince Regent) since 1796—they were married in 1795—returned to England in June 1820 to claim her rights as queen (George III had died on 29 January). The Prince Regent objected to her claims and instigated a bill in the House of Lords to dissolve the marriage on the basis of accusations of adultery; this resulted in a great public debate in which Caroline's partisans characterized the charges as victimization of Caroline by a debauched monarch. The bill of divorce was abandoned on 10 November 1820. The Shelleys regarded Caroline as a woman of poor character, but they were far more antipathetic towards George IV and his cabinet. The dispute came to an end with the death of Caroline on 7 August 1821, shortly after George IV's coronation on 19 July 1821. Shelley satirized the scandal in *Oedipus Tyrannus, or, Swellfoot the Tyrant*, written in August 1820 (see [24 March] 1820, n. 6).

8. For Virgin Mary, perhaps.

9. Henry Peter Brougham, Baron Brougham and Vaux (1778–1868), attorney, liberal politician, legal reformer, and one of the founders of the *Edinburgh Review* (to which he was a prolific contributor). He was Leigh and John Hunt's friend and defended them in their 1811 libel trials, but he was Byron's enemy (*SC*, III, 106–7, IV, 645–53; Marchand, *Byron*, II, 614).

10. Inspired by the success of the revolution in Spain in 1820, which forced Fer-

dinand VII to restore the constitution, a revolution began on 1 July in Naples under the leadership of General Guglielmo Pepe. The rebels demanded a democratic constitution, which Ferdinand I granted on 7 July and swore to on 13 July. On 23 March 1821, Austria, with the consent of Ferdinand I, crushed the revolution. The restoration of Ferdinand I as absolute monarch was followed by reprisals against the liberals under a police state.

11. Muzio Clementi (1752–1832), distinguished pianist, composer, and conductor. On 3 July 1811 he married Emma Gisborne, John Gisborne's sister. Clementi founded the firm of Clementi & Co., piano manufacturers and publishers of music.

12. In her *Journal* for 2 July, Maria Gisborne wrote: "Clementi has offered to instruct me, which would be an incalculable advantage to me should I determine to teach music."

13. A plan by which Claire Clairmont was to go to Paris. Following the text of Mary Shelley's letter is a cross-written addition by Shelley that refers to the poor relations between Mary Shelley and Claire Clairmont, the failure of the Paris plan, and the exertions of Mrs. Mason to find a substitute place for Claire Clairmont. (In her *Journal* for 4 July Claire Clairmont wrote: " 'Heigh-ho the Clare, & the Ma / Find something to fight about every day—' ".) In concluding, Shelley cautioned the Gisbornes: "Of course you will not suppose that Mary has seen the enclosed, or this transverse writing—so take no notice of it in any letter intended for her inspection." The enclosure is unidentified, but Jones speculates that it may have been one of the "sad" poems, "Time Long Past" (*PBS Letters*, #577).

❦

To Leigh Hunt

[Pisa]   December 29th—1820 (Jan. 1. 1821)

My dear Friend

We have been very anxious to hear from you since we saw that your paper had been honoured with the peculiar attention of the A.G.[1] Yet no letters comes. I am convinced that you will escape when it comes to trial—but an Acquittal must be bought not only with anxiety—fear & labour but also with the money you can so ill spare. Before this comes to hand you will of course have written—one of your letters which are as rare as Fountains in the Stony Arabia will have given us a brief pleasure —Why do you not writer oftener?—Ah! why are you not rich, peaceful and Enjoying? We have just been delighted with a parcel of your Indicators[2] but they also afford full proof that you are not as happy as you ought to be—Yet how beautiful they are. That one upon the deaths of young children was a piece of as fine writing & of as exquisite feeling as I ever read—To us you know it must have been particularly affecting— Yet there is one thing well apparent—You, my dear Hunt, never lost a child or the ideal immortality w^d not suffice to your immagination as it naturally does thinking only of those whom you loved more from the overflowing of affection, than from their being the hope, the rest, the purpose, the support, and the ⟨reward⟩ recompense of life.

I hardly know whether I do not teaze you with too many letters, yet you have made no complaint of that, and besides you always like to hear about Italy[3] and it is almost impossible not to write something pleasing to you from this divine country, if praises of its many beauties and its delights be interesting to you. I have now an account to give you of a wonderful and beautiful exhibition of talent which we have been witnesses of.[4]   An exhibition peculiar to the Italians and like their climate—their vegetation and their country fervent fertile and mixing in wondrous proportions the picturesque the cultivated & the wild until they become not as in other countries one the foil of the other but they mingle and form a spectacle new and beautiful   We were the other night at the theatre where the Improvisatore whom I mentioned in my last letter delivered an extempore tragedy. Conceive of a poem as long as a Greek Tragedy, interspersed with choruses, the whole plan conceived in an instant—The ideas and verses & scenes flowing in rich succession like the perpetual gush of a fast falling cataract. The ideas poetic and just; the words the most beautiful, scelte[5] and grand that his exquisite Italian afforded—He is handsome—his person small but elegant—and his motions graceful beyond description: his action was perfect; and the freedom of his motions outdo the constraint which is ever visible in an English actor—The changes of countenance were of course not so fine as those I have witnissed on the English stage, for he had not conned his part and set his features but it was one impulse that filled him; an unchanged deity who spoke within him, and his voice su{r}passed in its modulations the melody of music. The subject was Iphigenia in Tauris. It was composed on the Greek plan (indeed he followed Euripides in his arrangement and in many of his ideas)—without the devision of acts and with chorus's. Of course if we saw it written there would have been many slight defects of management, defects—amended when seen—but many of the scenes were perfect—and the recognition of Orestes and Iphigenia was worked up beautifully.

I do not know how this talent may be appreciated in the other cities of Italy, but the Pisans are noted for their want of love and of course entire ignorance of the fine arts—Their opera is miserable, their theatre the worst in Italy. The theatre was nearly empty on this occasion—The students of the University half filled the pit and the few people in the boxes were foreigners except two Pisan families who went away before it was half over. God knows what this man w[d] be if he laboured and become

68

a poet for posterity instead of an Improvisatore for the present—I am enclined to think that in the perfection in which he possesses this art it is by no means an inferior power to that of a printed poet—There have been few Improvisatores who have like him joined a cultivated education and acquirements in languages rare among foreigners—If however his auditors were refined—and as the oak or the rock to the lightning—feeling in their inmost souls the penetrative fire of his poetry—I sh^d not find fault with his making perfection in this art the aim of his exertions— But to Improvise to a Pisan audience is to scatter otto of roses among the overweighing stench of a charnel house:—pearls to swine were œconomy in comparison. As Shelley told him the other night He appeared in Pisa as Dante among the ghosts—Pisa is a city of the dead and they shrunk from his living presence. The name of this Improvisatore is Sgricci, and I see that his name is mentioned in your literary pocket book.[6] This has made me think that it were an interesting plan for this same pretty pocket book if you were to give some small interesting account—not exactly a biographical sketch, but anecdotical and somewhat critical of the various authors of the list. Sgricci has been accused of ca{r}bonarism whether truly or not I cannot judge—I should think not or he w^d be trying to harvest at Naples instead of extemporizing here. From what we have heard of him I believe him to be good and his manners are gentle and amiable—while the rich flow of his beautifully pronounced language is as pleasant to the ear as a sonata of Mozart. I must tell you that some wiseacre Professors of Pisa wanted to put Sgricci down at the theatre and their vile envy might have frightened the God from his temple if an Irishman who chanced to be in the same box with him had not compelled him to silence. The ringleader of this gang is called Rosini[7] a man, a speaker of folly in a city of fools—bad envious talkative presumptuous;—one— "chi mai parla bene di chichesisia—o di quei che vivono o dei morti."[8] He has written a long poem which no one has ever read and like the illustrious Sotherby[9] gives the law to a few distinguished Blues of Pisa Well good night; tomorrow I will finish my letter and talk to you about our unf[ortu]nate young friend, Emilia Viviani.

It is grievous to see this beautiful girl wearing out the best years of her life in a[n] odious convent where both mind and body are sick from want of the appropriate exercize for each—I think she has great talent if not genius—or if not an internal fountain how could she have acquired the mastery she has of her own language which she writes so beautifully, or those ideas which lift her so far above the rest of the Italians. She has not studied much and now hopeless from a five years confinement every thing disgusts her and she looks with hatred & distaste even on the alleviations of her situation. Her only hope is in a marriage which her parents tell her is concluded although she has never seen the person intended for her—Nor do I think the change of situation will be much for the better for he is a younger brother and will live in the house with his mother whom they say is molta secante[10]—Yet she may then have the free use of her limbs—she may then be able to walk out among the fields—vineyards & woods of her country and see the mountains and the sky and not be as now a dozen steps to the right and then back to the left another dozen which is the longest walk her convent garden affords—and that you may be sure she is very seldom tempted to take.

Winter began with us on Xmas day—not that we have yet had frost but a cold wind sweeps over us and the sky is covered with dark clouds and the cold sleet mizzles down—I understand that you have had as yet a mild winter—This and the plentiful harvest will keep the poor somewhat happier this year.—Yet I dare say you now see the white snow before your doors. Even warm as we are here Shelley suffers a great deal of pain in every way—perhaps more even than last winter.

(Jan 1. 1821)   Although I almost think it of bad augury to wish you a good new year yet as I finish my letter on this day I cannot help adding the Compliments of the Season and wishing all happiness peace & enjoyment for this comming year to you my dear dear Marianne and all who belong to you—I thank you for all the good wishes I know you have made for us—We are quiet now—last year there were many turbulencies—perhaps during this there will be fewer—

We have made acquaintance with a Greek, a Prince Mauro Codarti[11]—a very pleasant man profound in his own language and who although he has applied to English little more than a month begins to relish its beauties & to understand the genius of its expressions in a wonderful manner—He was done up [cross-written, p. 1] by some alliance I believe with Ali Pacha[12] and has taken refuge in Italy from the Constantinopolitan bowstring. He has related to us some very infamous conduct of the English powers in Greece of which I sh^d exceedingly like to get the documents & to place them in Grey Bennett's of [or] Sir F. B.'s [Francis Burdett][13] hands—they might serve to give another knock to this wretched system of things.

We are very anxious to hear the event of the meeting of parliament as I suppose you all are in England—but perhaps we exiles are ultrapolitical—but certainly I have some hopes that something fortunate will soon happen for the state of things in England.

And Italy! The King of Naples has gone to Trophau[14] with the consent of his parliament and that is the latest news—we begin, we hope to see

the ⟨golden⟩ crimson clouds of rising peace—And if all be quiet southward we have some thoughts of emigrating there next summer—

Adieu my dear Hunt

.   Most affectionately yours

Marina

[*Half-line deleted*] ⟨will⟩ be a better girl than last time—let her make
up a small parcel—a dozen papers of middle sized pins—an assortment
of good needles—a small pointed pair of Scissars—an excellent penknife
of several blades—a few sticks of sealing wax—let the needles be in a
very small morocco case such as they make on purpose for papers of
needles—a steel topped thimble and some ounces of stocking cotton—
[*half-line deleted*]—and send this to Horace Smith—asking him if he has
sent our parcel if he has let it be sent to Peacock written on the outside
to be sent to me by the next parcel—

Ollier will answer her demand for the amount of these things

Adieu

add also a few hundreds of Brama's pens.

ADDRESS: Leigh Hunt Esq. / Mess. Olliers. Booksellers / Vere St. Bond St. / London / Inghilterra / Angleterre. POSTMARKS: (1) PISA; (2) FPO / JA. 18 / 1821. TEXT:
MS., Huntington Library.

1. The Attorney General, who had prosecuted the *Examiner* for its comments concerning the trial of Caroline of Brunswick. On 25 February 1821 John Hunt (1775–
1848), Leigh Hunt's brother and proprietor of the *Examiner*, was sent to prison for
one year, and the sum of £1,000 was required as guarantee of proper future conduct
(Blunden, *"Examiner" Examined*, pp. 106–8).

2. The *Indicator* was a weekly literary periodical edited and published by Hunt
from 13 October 1819 to 21 March 1821 and continued by someone else under the
name Onewhyn from 28 March 1821 to 30 August 1821 (*SC*, VI, 912–13, 915–
16).

3. *Italy* is written over *Italians*.

4. On 21 December Mary Shelley, Shelley, and Claire Clairmont went to the theater to see Sgricci's improvisations of "a Canzone upon Pyramus & Thisbe" and a
tragedy, "Iphegenia in Tauris" (*CC Journals*).

5. "Select."

6. The *Literary Pocket-Book; or, Companion for the Lover of Nature and Art*, an annual
pocket calendar that contained a variety of useful data (currency rates; coach sched-
ules; shop addresses; lists of persons in the arts, science, and government), as well as
original prose and poetry. Begun by Leigh Hunt and printed for him by Charles and
James Ollier, it appeared for five years beginning in 1819.

7. A professor at the University of Pisa, Rossini was a man of wide learning and
a poet. He regarded Sgricci as mediocre and tried to stem his popularity (Dowden,
Shelley, II, 368–69).

8. "Who never speaks well of anybody whatsoever—living or dead."

9. William Sotheby (1757–1833), an author prominent in London literary society. Mary Shelley's allusion here is to Byron's satire of Sotheby as "Botherby" in *Beppo*, stanzas 72–76. For Byron's reason for satirizing Sotheby, who was once his friend, see Byron, *Letters and Journals*, VI, 34–36.

10. "Very tiresome."

11. Prince Alexander Mavrocordato (1791–1865), Greek patriot and statesman and a major figure in the cause of Greek liberty. Introduced to the Shelleys by Pacchiani on 2 December 1820, Mavrocordato became a friend and frequent visitor. Although Shelley admired him as a political hero and dedicated *Hellas* to him, he did not develop any true rapport with Mavrocordato (*PBS Letters*, #626). Mary Shelley, however, became his close friend. He aided her in her studies of Greek, and she gave him English lessons. Mary Shelley's letters to Mavrocordato remain unlocated, but seventeen of his letters to her are extant (Abinger MSS.) and reveal the deep and active interest she had in political events in Greece, as well as her role as confidante to Mavrocordato until his departure for Greece on 26 June 1821 (Herbert Huscher, "Alexander Mavrocordato: Friend of the Shelleys," *Keats-Shelley Memorial Bulletin* 16 [1965]: 29–38).

12. Ali Pasha (1741–1822), "The Lion of Janina," was a Turkish brigand who became pasha of Janina in 1788 and through ruthless, capricious rule eventually established independent authority over Albania, Macedonia, Epirus, Thessaly, and the Morea, all technically answerable to the sultan. In 1820 Ali Pasha, in an attempt to gain further power, openly revolted against Sultan Mahmud II, which preoccupied the Turks and gave the Greeks the opportunity to rebel against Turkish rule.

13. Henry Grey Bennet (1777–1836) and Sir Francis Burdett (1770–1844), radical political leader and advocate for reform whose strong criticism of the actions of the authorities at "Peterloo" brought him a fine of £2,000 and three months in prison.

14. The Congress of Troppau (in Silesia) of the Holy Alliance, attended by the emperors Alexander I of Russia and Francis I of Austria and representatives of Prussia and Great Britain, began on 20 October 1820. On 19 November Austria, Russia, and Prussia agreed to crush any changes of government due to revolution. At the subsequent Congress of Laibach (in Slovenia), from 26 January to 12 May 1821, the Holy Alliance authorized Austria to suppress the Neapolitan revolution, which it did by 7 March 1821.

❧

To Claire Clairmont

Ὑψιλάντι

†Ὑψιλάντι[1]

[Pisa]   April 2—1821

My dear Claire,

Greece has declared its freedom![2] Prince Mavrocordato had made us expect this event for some weeks pas{t}. Yesterday he came *rayonnant de joie*—he had been ill for some days but he forgot all his pains—Ipselanti,

72

a greek General in the service of Russia, has collected together 10,000 Greeks & entered Wallachia declaring the liberty of his country—The Morea—Epirus—Servia are in revolt. Greece will most certainly be free. The worst part of this news for us is that our amiable prince will leave us—he will of course join his countrymen as soon as possible—never did Man appear so happy—yet he sacrifices family—fortune every thing to the hope of freeing his country—Such men are repaid—such succeed. You may conceive the deep sympathy that we feel in his joy on this occasion: tinged as it must be with anxiety for success—made serious by the knowledge of the blood that must be shed on this occasion. What a delight it will be to visit Greece free.

April has opened with a weather truly heavenly after a whole week of libeccio—rain & wind it is delightful to enjoy one of those days peculiar to Italy in this early season—the clear sky animating sun & fresh yet not cold breeze—Just that delicious season when pleasant thoughts bring sad ones to the mind—when every sensation seems to make a double effect—and every moment of the day is divided, felt, and counted. One is not gay—at least I am not—but peaceful & at peace with all the world—

I write you a short letter today but I could not resist the temptation of acquainting you with the changes in Greece the Moment P^ce Mavrocordato gave us leave to mention it.

I hope that your spirits will get better with this favourable change of weather—Florence must be perfectly delightful send the white paint as soon as you can & two strisce's[3] for me—

Shelley says that he will finish this letter[4]—We hear from no one in England

Ever yours
MWS

ADDRESS: Miss Clairmont / presso al Profe Bojti / dirimpetto Palazzo Pitti / Firenze. TEXT: MS., Pforzheimer Library.

1. "Ipselanti, Ipselanti." Note the cross here and over *Ipselanti* in line four in the text of the letter.

2. On 6 March 1821 Greek rebels led by Prince Alexandros Ypsilanti rose against the Turks in Wallachia (now Rumania) but were defeated. On or about 25 March new uprisings broke out in the Morea, in Roumeli, and on several islands, beginning a period of war between Greek and Turkish forces (with England, France, and Russia aiding Greece at various times) that culminated in Greek independence in 1832. On 3 April Mavrocordato wrote to Mary Shelley telling her that he was writing a small article supporting Greek liberty, which Shelley had promised to have inserted in an English newspaper (Abinger MS.).

3. "Strips."

4. See *PBS Letters*, #617.

To Shelley[1]

My dear Shelley

Shocked beyond all measure as I was I instantly wrote the enclosed—
if the task be not too dreadful pray copy it for me I cannot—

send that part of you letter—which contains the accusation—I tried
but I could not write it—I think I could as soon have died—I send also
Elise's last letter[2]—enclose it or not as you think best.

I wrote to you with far different feelings last night—beloved friend—
our bark is indeed tempest tost but love me as you have ever done & God
preserve my child to me and our enemies shall not be too much for us.

Consider well if Florence be a fit residence for us[3]—I love I own to face
danger—but I would not be imprudent—

Pray get my letter to M[rs] H [*Hoppner*] copied for a thousand reasons

Adieu dearest take care of yourself all yet is well—the shock for me is
over and I now despise the slander—but it must not pass uncon-
tra{di}cted—I sincerely thank Lord Byron for his kind unbelief[4]

affectionately yours

Mary WS.

Do not think me imprudent in mentioning Clares illness at Naples[5]—It
is well to meet facts—they are as cunning as wicked—I have read over
my letter it is written in haste—but it were as well that the first burst
of feeling sh[d] be expressed—No letters—

TEXT: MS., Bodleian Library.

   1. When Shelley returned from Florence on 2 August, he found waiting for him
a letter from Byron asking that he come at once to Ravenna, since Byron intended
to leave there shortly. Concerned about Byron's plans for Allegra, Shelley departed
from the Baths of Pisa on 3 August, spent 4 August at Leghorn with Claire Clairmont (who on 19 June had gone "to bathe at Livorno for an Aneurism of the heart"
[*CC Journals*]), and arrived at Ravenna on 6 August. Shelley's letter to Mary Shelley
of 7 August informed her that Elise Foggi had told the Hoppners that Claire Clairmont had given birth to Shelley's child at Naples. The accusation was repeated by
Hoppner in his letter of 16 September to Byron: "You must know then that at the
time the Shelleys were here Clare was with child by Shelley: you may remember to
have heard that she was constantly unwell, and under the care of a Physician, and I
am uncharitable enough to believe that the quantity of medicine she then took was
not for the mere purpose of restoring her health. I perceive too why she preferred
remaining alone at Este, notwithstanding her fear of ghosts and robbers, to being
here with the Shelleys. Be this as it may, they proceeded from here to Naples, where
one night Shelley was called up to see Clara who was very ill. His wife, naturally,

thought it very strange that he should be sent for; but although she was not aware of the nature of the connexion between them, she had had sufficient proof of Shelley's indifference, and of Clara's hatred for her: besides as Shelly desired her to remain quiet she did not dare to interfere. A Mid-wife was sent for, and the worthy pair, who had made no preparation for the reception of the unfortunate being she was bringing into the world, bribed the woman to carry it to the Pietà, where the child was taken half an hour after its birth, being obliged likewise to purchase the physician's silence with a considerable sum. During all the time of her confinement Mrs. Shelley, who expressed great anxiety on her account, was not allowed to approach her, and these beasts, instead of requiting her uneasiness on Clara's account by at least a few expressions of kindness, have since increased in their hatred to her, behaving to her in the most brutal manner, and Clara doing everything she can to engage her husband to abandon her. Poor Mrs. Shelley, whatever suspicions she may entertain of the nature of their connexion, knows nothing of their adventure at Naples, and as the knowledge of it could only add to her misery, 'tis as well that she should not. This account we had from Elise, who passed here this summer with an English lady who spoke very highly of her. She likewise told us that Clara does not scruple to tell Mrs. Shelley she wishes her dead, and to say to Shelley in her presence that she wonders how he can live with such a creature" (*PBS Letters*, #650, n. 5).

2. See 10 August 1821 to Isabella Hoppner, n. 2.

3. Claire Clairmont made her home at Florence.

4. Byron believed the Hoppners' report at least through March 1821 (Byron, *Works*, V, 500–501). On 8 October 1820 he has written to Hoppner: "The Shiloh story is true no doubt, though Elise is but a sort of Queen's evidence. You remember how eager she was to return to them, and then she goes away and abuses them. Of the facts, however, there can be little doubt; it is just like them. You may be sure that I keep your counsel" (Byron, *Works*, V, 86).

5. *MWS Journal*, 27 December 1818, records: "Claire is not well."

To Isabella Hoppner

Pisa. August 10th 1821

My dear Mrs Hoppner—

After a silence of nearly two years I address you again, and most bitterly do I regret the occasion on which I now write. Pardon me that I do not write in french; you understand English well, and I am too much impressed to shackle myself in a foreign language; even in my own, my thoughts far outrun my pen, so that I can hardly form the letters. I write ⟨in⟩ to defend ⟨of⟩ him to whom I have the happiness to be united, whom I love and esteem beyond all creatures, from the foulest calumnies; and to you I write this, who were so kind, to Mr Hoppner; to both of whom I indulged the pleasing ⟨hope⟩ idea that I have every reason to feel gratitude. This is indeed a painful task.

⟨M^r⟩ Shelley is at present on a visit to Lord Byron at Ravenna and I received a letter[1] from him today containing accounts that make⟨s⟩ my hand tremble so much that I can hardly hold the pen. It tells me that Elise wrote to you relating the most hideous stories against him, and that you have believed them. Before I speak of these falsehoods permit {me} to say a few words concerning this miserable girl. You well know that she formed an attachment with Paolo when we proceeded to Rome, & at Naples their marriage was talked of—We all tried to dissuade her; we knew Paolo to be a rascal and we thought so well of her that we believed him to be unworthy of her. An accident led me to the knowledge that without marrying they had formed a connexion; she was ill we sent for a docter who said there was danger of a miscarriage—I w^d not turn the girl on the world without in some degree binding her to this man—we had them married at Sir W. A'Courts—she left us; turned catholic at Rome, married him & then went to Florence. After the disastrous death of my child we came to Tuscany—we have seen little of them; but we have had knowledge that Paolo has formed a scheme of extorting money from Shelley by false accusations—he has written him threatning letters saying that he w^d be the ruin of him &c—we placed these in the hands of a celebrated lawyer here who has done what he can to silence him. Elise has never interfered in this and indeed the other day I received a letter[2] from her entreating with great professions of love that I w^d send her money—I took no notice of this; but although I knew her to be in Evil hands I w^d not believe that she was wicked enough to join in his plans without proof.

And now I come to her accusations—and I must indeed summon all my courage while I transcribe them; for tears will force their way, and how can it be otherwise? You knew Shelley, you saw his face, & could you believe them? Believe them only on the testimony of a girl whom you despised? I had hopes that such a thing was impossible, and that although ⟨stange⟩ strangers might believe the calumnies that this man propogated, that none who had ever seen my husband could for a moment credit them.

She says Claire was Shelley's ⟨miss⟩ mistress, that—Upon my word, ⟨I vow by all that I hold⟩ I solemnly assure you that I cannot write the words, I send you a part of Shelleys letter that you may see what I am now about to refute—but I had rather die that [than] copy any thing so vilely so wickedly false, so beyond all imagination fiendish.

I am perfectly convinced, in my own mind that Shelley never had an improper connexion with Claire—At the time specified in ⟨Claires⟩ Elise's letter, the winter after we quited ⟨Nap⟩ Este, I suppose while she was was with us, and that was at Naples, we lived in lodgings where I had momentary entrance into every room and such a thing could not have passed unknown to me. The malice of the girl is beyond all thought—I now do remember that Claire did keep her bed there for two days—but I attended on her—I saw the physician—her illness was one that she had been accustomed to for years—and the same remedies were employed as I had before ministered to her in England.

Claire had no child—the rest must be false—but that you should believe it—⟨I th⟩ That my beloved Shelley should stand thus slandered in your minds—⟨He⟩ He, the gentlest & most humane of creatures, is more painful to me, oh far more painful than any words can express.

It is all a lie—Claire ⟨if anything⟩ is timid; she always shewed respect even for me—poor dear girl! she has ⟨many⟩ some faults—you know them as well as I—but her heart is good—and if ever we quarelled, which was seldom, it was I, and not she, that was harsh, and our instantaneous reconciliations were sincere & affectionate.

Need I say that the union between my husband and ⟨hims⟩ myself has ever been undisturbed—Love caused our first imprudences, love which improved by esteem, a perfect trust one in the other, a confidence and affection, which visited as we have been by severe calamities (have we not lossed two children?) has encreased daily and knows no bounds.

I will add that Claire has been seperated from us for about a year[3]—She lives with a respectable German family at Florence—The reasons of this were obvious—her connexion with us made her manifest as the Miss Clairmont, the Mother of Allegra—besides we live much alone—she enters much into society there—and solely occupied with the idea of the welfare of her child, she wished to ⟨be⟩ appear such that she may not be thought in aftertimes to be unworthy of fulfilling the maternal duties—you ought to have paused before you tried to convince the father of her child of such unheard of atrocities on her part—If his generosity & knowledge of the world had not made him reject the slander with the ridicule it deserved ⟨of⟩ what irretrievable mischief you would have occasioned her.

Those who know me ⟨we⟩ well believe my simple word—it is not long ago that my father said in a letter to me, that he had never known me utter a falsehood—but you, easy as you have been to credit evil, who may be more deaf to truth—to you I swear—by all that I hold sacred upon heaven & earth by a vow which I should die to write if I affirmed a falsehood—I swear by the life of my child, by my blessed & beloved child, that I know these accusations to be false—

Shelley is as incapable of cruelty as the softest woman—To those who know him his humanity is almost as a proverb.—He has been unfortunate as a father. the laws of his country & death has cut him off from his dearest hopes—⟨But⟩ His enemies have done him incredible mischief—but that you should believe such a tale coming from such a hand, is beyond all belief, a blow quite unexpected, and the very idea of it beyond words shockings—

But I have said enough to convince you   And are you not convinced? Are not my words the words of truth? Repair—I conjure you the evil you have done by retracting you confidence in one so vile as Elise, and by writing to me that you now reject as false every circumstance of her infamous tale.[4]

You were kind to us, and I shall never forget it; now I require justice; You must believe me, and do me, I solemnly entreat you, the justice to confess that you do so.

Mary W. Shelley

I send this letter to Shelley at Ravenna, that he may see it. For although I ought, the subject is too odious to me to copy it. I wish also that Lord Byron should see it—He gave no credit to the tale, but it is as well that he should see how entirely fabulous it is.   ⟨,and I⟩

ADDRESS: A Madame / Madme Hoppner. TEXT: MS., John Murray.
    1. *PBS Letters*, #650.
    2. Elise Foggi's letter is written in highly imperfect French. In an attempt to keep the character of the original, I give here an idiomatic translation based on a transcription and literal translation by Linette F. Brugmans (MS. of Elise Foggi letter, John Murray):
Dear and kind madam
    I have not had the pleasure of getting dear news from you in more than 20 months: I wrote you at livorno and pisa without ever having received an answer and I cannot understand what has prevented me from getting a dear letter from you and to know how your dear little passett is as well as the rest of your kind family. I heard from my doctor that monsieur was still in very poor health which pains me very much to know that he has remained ill for such a long time, but I think he will get better and that you, madam are always in good health as well as your little one.
    I must tell you that I have given birth to a pretty little girl who is very fat and very cheerful she will be 6 months old on the 3rd of the coming month   I am still nursing her and as I said she is coming along very well but I will soon have to wean her since for the past 10 months I have earned nothing and especially for almost the last 3 months I find myself in critical circumstances and if it were only possible for me to find a position as wet-nurse, as I have a lot of milk, or as a chamber maid to support my dear little girl for without the help of one or the other it is impossible to live.
my dear madam as I know your kind heart and your affection for me in view of the confidence my dear mistress always had in me I believe that you will be willing to have the kindness to protect me always and if you need anyone you will give me preference   if it is not imposing too much on your kindness to ask you if it is pos-

sible to lend me some money for which I will give you a note and when I have a position I will pay you back: I know my dear kind madam that your heart is always open to the voice of nature and always so charitable that you will not refuse to help a mother who beseeches you and will always be grateful to you and will repay you as soon as she has a position believe me my dear lady it is only great need that makes me beg this favor of you since my little one is teething and it will take me another 3 months to wean her because she suffers so much   I beg you to excuse my boldness but so kind a soul as you will pardon me   please do me the favor of an answer as soon as possible   you will oblige your devoted servant and I am for life your Elise Foggi

florence 26 July 1821

via maggio 1927

3. Claire Clairmont had gone to live with the Bojti family on 20 October 1820: (*CC Journals*).

4. Shelley wrote to Mary Shelley on 16 August that he had given her letter to Mrs. Hoppner, that is, "to Lord Byron, who has engaged to send it with his own comments to the Hoppners" (*PBS Letters*, #656). After Byron's death, Mary Shelley's letter to Mrs. Hoppner was found among his papers, and to date there is no clear evidence to settle the question of whether Byron forwarded it to the Hoppners, as requested (and had it returned), or never sent it. Nor is there any evidence that Mary Shelley ever received a response from Mrs. Hoppner. In 1843 Mary Shelley met Mrs. Hoppner in Florence and deliberately snubbed her (*Mary Shelley to Claire Clairmont, 20 February 1843).

To Maria Gisborne

Pisa   Nov. 30th 1821[1]

My Dear M[rs] Gisborne—

Although having much to do be a bad excuse for not writing to you, yet you must in some sort admit this plea on my part—Here we are in Pisa, having furnished very nice apartments for ourselves, and what is more paid for the furniture out of the fruits of two year's economy. We are at the top of the Tre Palazzi di Chiesa—I daresay you know the house, next door to la Scoto's house on the North side of Lung' Arno: but the rooms we inhabit are South, and look over the whole country towards the Sea, so that we are entirely out of the bustle and disagreeable puzzi &c— of the town, and hardly know that we are so envelopped until we descend into the street. The Williams's have been less lucky, though they have followed our example in furnishing their own house, but renting it of M[r] Webb, they have ben treated scurvily.—So here we live, Lord B just opposite to us in Casa Lafranchi[2] (the late Sig[ra] Filicchi's house)—So Pisa you see has become a little nest of singing birds—You will be both surprised and delighted at the work just about to be published by him.—his Cain[3]—which is in the highest style of imaginative Poetry. It made a great impression upon me, and appears almost a revelation from its power and beauty—Shelley rides with him—I, of course, see little of him. The lady, whom he serves, is a nice pretty girl, without pretensions, good-hearted and amiable[4]—her relations were banished {from} Romagna for Carbonarism.

Do you hear any thing of Shelley's Hellas?[5] Ollier treats us abominably—I should much like to know when he intends to answer S—'s last letter concerning my affair.[6] I had wished it to come out by Christmas—now there is no hope—We are warned on all hands not to trust him, and more to secure his attention and care than for any other reason, I wish to be sure of the money before he gets the book. I should not be sorry that we broke with him, although it would be difficult to bargain with another bookseller, at the distance we are. What do you know of Hunt? About two months ago he wrote to say that on the 21st October he should quit England,[7] and we have heard nothing more of him in any way. I expect that some day he and six children[8] will drop in from the clouds—trusting that God will temper the wind to the shorn lamb. Pray when you write tell us every thing you know concerning him. Do you get any intelligence of the Greeks—Our worthy Countrymen take part against them in every possible way, yet such is the spirit of freedom, and such the hatred of these poor people for their oppressors, that I have the warmest hopes—μάντις εἴμ' ἐσθλῶν ἀγώνων.[9]—Mavro cordato is there justly revered for the sacrifice he has made of his whole fortune to the cause, and besides for his firmness and talents. If Greece be free, Shelley and I have vowed to go, perhaps to settle there, in one of those beautiful islands where earth, ocean, and sky form the Paradise—

You will, I hope, tell us all the news of old friends when you write—I see no one that you knew. We live in our usual retired way, with few friends, and no acquaintances—Claire is returned to her usual residence, and our tranquillity is unbroken in upon, except by those winds, scirocco or tramontana, which now and then will sweep over the ocean of one's mind, and disturb or cloud its surface.

Since this must be a double letter, I save my self the trouble of copying the enclosed, which was a part of a letter written to you a month ago, but which I did not send—Will you attend to my requests—Every day increases my anxiety concerning the desk—Do have the goodness to pack it off as soon as you can.

How do you all get on? Have you yet embarked, and what is Henry about? I need not tell you how anxious we are to have these questions answered. I hope that you do not regret your journey to England, and that neither the climate, nor its more freezing accompaniments make you regret dear Italy. For this last month we have been enjoying a warm scirocco, which has rendered fires unnecessary—sometimes the days are surpassingly fine, and the burning sun of winter drives us to seek the shade.

Shelley was at your hive yesterday[10]—it is as dirty and busy as ever, so people live in the same narrow circle of space and thought, while time goes on, not as a race-horse, but "a six-inside dilly,"[11] and puts them down softly at their journey's end; while they have slept and ate, and "ecco tutto"—with this piece of morality, Dear M^{rs} G—, I end. Shelley begs every remembrance of his to be joined with mine to M^r G— [*Gisborne*] and Henry. Ever your's. Mary WS.

And now, my Dear Mrs Gisborne, I have a great favour to ask of you— Ollier writes to say that he has placed our two desks in the hands of a merchant of the City, and that they are to come—God knows when! Now as we sent for them two years ago, and are tired of waiting, will you do us the favour to get them out of his hands, and to send them without delay—If they can be sent without being opened, send them in statu quo; if they must be opened, do not send the smallest, but get a key (being a patent lock, the key will cost half a guinea) made for the largest and send it, and return the other to Peacock—If you send the desk, will you send with it, the following things—a few Copies of all Shelley's works, par- ticularly of the 2nd edition of the Cenci—my mother's posthumous works, and letters from Norway[12]—from Peacock, if you can, but do not delay the box for them—then get money from Ollier to buy a good pen- knife with several blades—needles in a case, pins, minnikin pins, sealing wax, scissors, a dozen skeins of white netting silk, not too fine for purses, a tortoise shell comb for combing out the hair—half a dozen ditto such as you gave me—a good spy-glass set in a gold rim for short sight, one to suit Papa, or any person of your acquaintance of the like sight—N° 10 I think they call it. Ask Peacock if he have any thing to send us— new books we hardly want, since we get them from L^d B Doing this, particularly in sending us the desk, you would do us a real service, for I have long waited in vain for it—You might also send me a doz. pair of stockings for a child of 3 years old—some of the best vellum drawing paper for miniatures—½ doz. Brookman and Langdon's pencils, marked H.B. and a cake of carmine from Smith's and Warner's. If you could get the money from Ollier, I should like very much a cornelian seal with S—'s coat of arms—

TEXT: John Gisborne Notebook No. 2, Abinger MSS., Bodleian Library.

1. The Shelleys had moved to the Tre Palazzi di Chiesa in Pisa on 25 October (*CC Journals*; Williams, *Journals and Letters*). Although in this letter Mary Shelley states that their new home was on the north side of the Arno, it was actually on the south side.

2. Byron had arrived in Pisa on 1 November.

3. Published by John Murray on 19 December 1821.

4. Countess Teresa Guiccioli, née Gamba (c. 1800–1873), was married to Count Alessandro Guiccioli, forty years her senior. She and Byron became lovers in 1819 and continued their relationship until Byron's death (see Origo, *The Last Attachment*, for a study of the Byron-Guiccioli relationship. See also Countess Teresa Guiccioli, *My Recollections of Lord Byron*, trans. Hubert E. H. Jerningham, 2 vols. [London: Richard Bentley, 1869]; and Marchand, *Byron*).

5. Shelley had completed *Hellas* in late October. From 6 to 10 November Edward Williams made a fair copy of it (Williams, *Journals and Letters*, pp. 106, 110–11). On 11 November Shelley sent it to Ollier, who published it in February 1822.

6. The publication of *Valperga*.

7. While Shelley was at Ravenna, he and Byron agreed to establish a liberal periodical. It was to be owned by Byron and Hunt; and Byron, Hunt, and Shelley would contribute (*PBS Letters*, #660). Hunt accepted the proposal, which included the plan for the Hunts to go to Italy. Inclement weather and illness delayed their arrival until 15 June 1822 at Genoa and 1 July 1822 at Leghorn. Four issues of *The Liberal, Verse and Prose from the South* were published, between October 1822 and July 1823 (Marshall, *The Liberal*, pp. 21–28, 50, 81, 196).

8. Thornton, John, Mary, Swinburne, Percy, and Henry.

9. "Prophet I am of noble combats" (Sophocles *Oedipus Coloneus*, line 1080).

10. Shelley and Williams were at Leghorn on 29 November (*MWS Journal*).

11. A quotation from Thomas Moore's *Fudge Family in Paris*: "Beginning gay, desperate, dashing down-hilly; / And ending as dull as a six-inside Dilly" (letter 10, line 35). "Dilly" was the familiar name for a diligence, or public stagecoach.

12. *Posthumous Works* and *A Short Residence*.

To Maria Gisborne

Pisa   Jan\[y\] [?-] 18 1822

My Dear M\[rs\] Gisborne:

Many thanks for your long letter, and so you see I am going to follow your example, and begin in a small hand at the very top of my paper. First, let me tell you that the Hunts are not come.   We wait anxiously for them, still more anxiously after having heard the wind whistle, and the distant sea roar; but I am sure they are safe—it is but hope delayed— Pisa today ha cambiato viso;[1] all was allegrezza,[2] the Court here, balls

&c—when a brother of the Dutchess, a promising young man, has suddenly died of a mal maligno, so the Court has left us. The ladies look in despair at their new gowns, the gentlemen, among them Medwin,[3] sigh to think of the wal{t}zing they might have had—Oh plaisirs! un long adieu!—You know us too well not to know that we have not lost any thing by this change—I had thought of being presented, mais J'ai beau faire—Shelley would not take the necessary steps, and so we go on in our obscure way—the Williams's lead the same life as us, and without a sigh, we see Medwin depart for his evening assemblies—Yet though I go not to the house of feasting, I have gone to the house of prayer—In the piano sotto di nos there is a Reverend Divine who preaches and prays, and sent me so many messages that I now make one of his congregation, and that from a truly Christian motive—Vaccà reported that this Doct.r Nott[4] said in Society that Shelley was a scelerato[5]—We told Taaffe and the little gossip reported it to all the world. Doct.r Nott heard of it, and sent a message by Medwin to deny it, and put our absence from Church on the score of this report, so to prove that I forgave or disbelieved, I went once, and then that I might not appear to despise his preaching, I went again and again—

What think you of Cain?[6] Is it not a wonderful work? It appears to me to be his finest, and that which he has written since, though beautiful, has not the sublimity of Cain. He is, at present employed in writing another Tragedy[7]—Do you remember some newspaper verses of Lord Carlisle, addressed to Lady Holland, begging her not to accept Napoleon's Snuff-box? Lord Byron began a parody on it, of which this is the first verse,

> Lady! accept the Box the Hero wore,
> In spite of all this elegiac stuff;
> Nor let seven Verses written by a Bore,
> Prevent your Ladyship from taking snuff.[8]

By the bye—Has Hogg yet got over his dislike of Lord B—I do not see much of him; but he is very amiable when we do meet—he knows that I am a great admirer of his poetry—We see a good {   } of La Guiccioli—She is a good amiable girl, and her brother Pierino[9] is one of the most gentlemanly Italians I have met with. You know the Italian manieres de compagnie—when Williams first saw this lady, they made him almost mad, and in vain do I try to drub into him a few of the expressions which fill up an Italian visit. I wrote them down, but he would not learn them; "ora la levo l'incomodo." "Incomodo! no, anzi è un piacare."[10]— the answer alone makes him mad; but reply follows reply "Il piacere è tutto mio" "bontà sua," and some dozen more.[11]

83

I am vexed to hear that you do not get on as you hoped; but I have better hopes than you—such undertakings always look desparingly at the beginning; but lay ever so small a foundation, and you will see the edifice rise of itself—You do not mention Henry's employments—however, since Mr Gisborne has regained his health, I look upon your removal to England as a great advantage to you. You talk of a sea-coal fire—We dined today in a room without a fire, with all the windows open—To be sure, that will not do for any time—and besides these are the first sunny days after a series of rain, which so caused the Arno to rise that the upper bridge was nearly choked up.

Jan. 18. So far we are advanced in 1822—yet the Hunts are not arrived—The Storms have been horrible and universal. At Genoa, forty ships were cast away, and 125 Souls lost; but I will not augur ill. And in a very few days I hope the memory will be all that will remain to them of their tedious and stormy sea-voyage—

Shelley is better this winter than he has been a long, long time—I have suffered from rheumatism in the head, very much indeed. It has been a sort of epidemic in Pisa. Percy is quite well. "Galliardo e sano, se Dio vuole"[12]—I hope, by this time, my desk[13] is en route—I own I am anxious to hear that it is safe out of Ollier's hands, who treats us infamously in every way. Now you are in England, we have some hope of hearing really something about his literary affairs—I hear that he is talked of. The Cenci most—I hope Charles the I^st[14] which is now on the anvil, will raise his reputation—I long to see Sardanapalus,[15] which I hear praised. You may soon expect other deeds from the same pen—His poetry is an overflowing river, without argini,[16] which makes a continual piena.[17] Sometimes it only floods a field—sometimes it is as a Cataract—Do you know, as a last Commission, if my desk be not sent, and you could get the money from Ollier, I should like a few large damask table-clothes, and napkins—The table Cloths 3 ½ braccia wide and long as the last, last Codicil, send a few quires of gilt-edged note-paper; it will be very useful to me—Be sure to ask Peacock if he has anything to send. Do you remember what I wrote about Matilda[18]—

Pray write often and fully—My Compliments to Emma Clementi. All the time I write, a duo of Rossini's is running in my head, now singing at the Opera—Sinclair[19] sings one part, and cuts an amazingly fine figure among them. It is hummed about as much as merivedone was, Do you know it? "Nati in ver noi siamo"—Adieu. Success attend you. Ever your's, MWS. Send an address for your letters. I do not wish to send any more through Ollier—

TEXT: John Gisborne Notebook No. 2, Abinger MSS., Bodleian Library.

1. "Changed its expression."
2. "Cheerfulness."
3. Medwin had returned to Pisa on 14 November 1821 (*MWS Journal*).
4. George Frederick Nott (1767–1841), cleric and author. Dr. Nott lived on a lower floor of the Tre Palazzi and conducted chapel services on Sundays for a small English congregation (Cline, *Pisan Circle*, p. 70). Mary Shelley attended on 9 and 16 December 1821; 24 February and 3 March 1822. On 30 December 1821 Dr. Nott had christened Rosalind Williams, the Williamses' second child (born on 16 March), to whom Mary Shelley was godmother (Williams, *Journals and Letters*, pp. 103, 121; *MWS Journal*, 16 March 1821).
5. "Scoundrel."
6. See 30 November 1821.
7. *Werner, A Tragedy* (London: John Murray, 1823), which Mary Shelley was copying for the printer (Marchand, *Byron*, III, 965).
8. Thomas Medwin wrote the following account of Byron's verse to Lady Holland: " 'I [Lord Byron] observe, in the newspapers of the day, some lines of his Lordship's, advising Lady Holland not to have any thing to do with the snuff-box left her by Napoleon, for fear that horror and murder should jump out of the lid every time it is opened! It is a most ingenious idea—I give him great credit for it.' He then read me the first stanza, laughing in his usual suppressed way,—'Lady, reject the gift,' &c. and produced in a few minutes the following parody on it:

> Lady, accept the box a hero wore,
>   In spite of all this elegiac stuff:
> Let not seven stanzas, written by a bore,
>   Prevent your Ladyship from taking snuff!"

(Medwin, *Conversations*, pp. 234–35). Ernest J. Lovell, Jr., points out that these lines are a parody of Carlisle's first stanza:

> Lady, reject the gift! 'tis tinged with gore!
>   Those crimson spots a dreadful tale relate;
> It has been grasp'd by an infernal Power;
>   And by that hand which seal'd young Enghein's fate.

9. Count Pietro Gamba (?1801–27) was an activist in the cause of Italian liberty in Ravenna and a leader of the revolutionary society of the Carbonari (Marchand, *Byron*, II, 780). He accompanied Byron to Greece in 1823, and in 1825 he expressed his friendship and admiration for Byron in his book, *A Narrative of Lord Byron's Last Journey to Greece* (London: John Murray, 1825). In 1825 he returned to Greece, where he died in 1827.
10. "Now I'll annoy her no longer." "Annoy! no, rather it's a pleasure."
11. "The pleasure is all mine"; "your goodness."
12. "Strong and healthy, if God wills."
13. Mary Shelley's lap desk had been left behind at Marlow in 1818, and for two years she had been trying to recover it. It finally arrived at Albaro on 7 October 1822 (*MWS Journal*).
14. *Charles the First*, a drama Shelley did not complete.

15. Byron's *Sardanapalus* was published with *Cain* and *The Two Foscari* by John Murray on 19 December 1821.

16. "Riverbanks."

17. "Fullness."

18. The Gisbornes had taken Mary Shelley's novella to England in May 1820 and left it with Godwin. In her letter of 9 February 1822, which answers many points of this letter by Mary Shelley, Maria Gisborne wrote: "With regard to Mathilda (another impediment), as your father has put a stop to all intercourse between us, I am at a loss what step to take" (Gisborne, *Journals and Letters*, p. 76).

19. John Sinclair (1791–1857), English tenor.

❧

To Maria Gisborne

Pisa   Feb 9. 1822

My dear Mrs Gisborne

Not having heard from you I am anxious about my desk[1]—It would have been a great convenience to me if I could have received it at the beginning of the winter   But now I should like it as soon as possible— I hope that it is out of Ollier's hands—I have before said what I would have done with it—if both desks can be sent without being opened let them be sent—if not give the small one back to Peacock—get a key made for the larger & send it I entreat you by the very next vessel. This key will cost half a guinea & Ollier will not give you the money—but give me credit for it I entreat you—& pray let me have the desk as soon as possible.

Shelley is now gone to la Spezia to get houses for our Colony for the summer[2]—It will be a large one—too large I am afraid for unity—yet I hope not—there will be Lord Byron who will have a large & beautiful boat built on purpose by some English navy officers at Genoa[3]—There will be the Countess Guiccioli and her brother—The Williams', whom you know—Trelawny[4]—a kind of half Arab Englishman—whose life has been as changeful as that of Anastatius[5] & who recounts the adventures of his youth as eloquently and well as the imagined Greek—he is clever— for his moral qualities I am yet in the dark he is a strange web which I am endeavouring to unravel—I would fain learn if generosity is united to impetuousness—Nobility of spirit to his assumption of singularity & independence—he is six feet high—raven black hair which curls thickly & shortly like a Moors dark, grey—expressive eyes—overhanging brows upturned lips & a smile which expresses good nature & kindheartedness—his shoulders are high like an Orientalist—his voice is monotonous yet emphatic & his language as he relates the events of his life en-

86

ergetic & simple—whether the tale be one of blood & horror or of irrisistable comedy   His company is delightful for he excites me to think and if any evil shade the intercourse that time will unveil—the sun will rise or night darken all.—There will be besides a Captain Roberts[6] whom I do not know—a very rough subject I fancy—a famous angler—&c— We are to have a smaller boat[7] and now that these first divine spring days are come (you know them well) the sky clear—the sun hot—the hedges budding—we sitting without a fire & the window open—I begin to long for the sparkling waves the olive covered hills & vine shaded pergolas of Spezia—however it would be madness to go yet—yet as ceppo[8] was bad we hope for a good Pascua[9] and if April prove fine we shall fly with the swallows

The Opera here has been detestable—The English Sinclair is the primo tenore & acquits himself excellently—but the Italians after the first have enviously selected such operas as give him little or nothing to do— We have English here & some English balls & parties to which I (mirabile dictú!) go sometimes. [We][10] have Taaffe who bores us out of our [senses][11] when he comes & writes complimentary verses telling a young lady that her eyes shed flowe{r}s why therefore should he send any

Lovely flowers from heavenly bowes
Love & friendship are what are due.

I have sent my novel[12] to Papa—I long to hear some news of it—as with an authors vanity I want to see it in print & hear the praises of my friends—I should like as I said when you went away—a Copy of Matilda—it might come out with the desk.

I hope as the town fills to hear better news of your plans—We long to hear from you—What does Henry do—how many times has he been in love—

Ever Yours Mary WS.
Shelley w[d] like to see the review of the Prometheus in the Quarterly[13]

ADDRESS: Mrs. Gisborne / 33 King Street West / Bryanstone Square / Inghilterra London / Londres. POSTMARKS: (1) PISA; (2) FPO / FE. 23 / 1822; (3) 12 o'Clock / FE. 23 / 1822 Nn. ENDORSED: Recd. 23rd Feb. 1822. TEXT: MS., Bodleian Library.

1. On 9 February Maria Gisborne wrote: "We applied too late to get your desk out of this man's rapacious clutches; he assured us that he had sent it off" (Gisborne, *Journals and Letters*, p. 75).

2. Shelley and Williams were house-hunting from 7 to 11 February but found only one suitable house. On 17 April Shelley and Williams again looked; and from 23 to 25 April Williams, Jane Williams, and Claire Clairmont looked for summer residences for the colony. The unavailability of appropriate housing caused them to

give up their plan, and the Shelleys and Williamses ended up sharing the same house, Casa Magni, at San Terenzo, near Lerici (see 2 June 1822, n. 5).

3. The *Bolivar*, completed in June and delivered to Byron shortly after 18 June (Williams, *Journals and Letters*, pp. 154–55).

4. Edward John Trelawny (1792–1881), the younger son of a retired lieutenant colonel, was enrolled by his family as a volunteer first class in the Royal Navy. He served from 1805 to 1812 but left without achieving a commission. Unhappy at home, at school (he was expelled at the age of ten), in the navy, and in marriage, he found refuge in an expansive fantasy life, in which he amplified his experiences as a midshipman into the imaginary adventures of a corsair. After his divorce in 1819, Trelawny went to live in Paris and then Switzerland, supported by an annual allowance of £300 provided by his father. At Geneva in 1820 he became friends with the Williamses and Medwin, and at their invitation he went to Pisa on 14 January 1822 to join them and to meet Byron and Shelley, whose works he greatly admired. Trelawny was welcomed into the Pisan circle and became the particular friend of the Shelleys, who were taken with his unconventional character and tales of adventure. After the deaths of the poets, Trelawny's written and spoken accounts of Byron and Shelley brought him attention throughout his long life as their special friend. Trelawny's accounts of himself and others present a decided problem, for they entangle truth and fiction to an almost indistinguishable degree (see Trelawny, *Recollections*, revised and reissued as *Records of Shelley, Byron, and the Author* [Trelawny, *Records*]; St Clair, *Trelawny*; *SC*, V, 37–81).

5. *Anastasius* (1819), a picaresque novel in autobiographical form by Thomas Hope (?1770–1831). The central figure is a courageous but unscrupulous Greek who has numerous extraordinary adventures in Greece, Constantinople, Egypt, Smyrna, and Arabia.

6. Captain Daniel Roberts, Trelawny's friend, built both the *Bolivar* and Shelley's boat, the *Don Juan*.

7. The *Don Juan* was delivered to Shelley on 12 May (Williams, *Journals and Letters*).

8. "Christmas."

9. "Easter."

10. Word taken from John Gisborne Notebook No. 4, Abinger MS., Bodleian Library.

11. Word taken from John Gisborne Notebook No. 4, Abinger MS., Bodleian Library.

12. *Valperga*.

13. A foolish review by William Sidney Walker (1795–1846) in the *Quarterly Review* 26 (October 1821): 168–80, which appeared in December 1821 (Reiman, *The Romantics Reviewed*, II, 780–86).

Mary Shelley and Shelley
To Claire Clairmont[1]

My dear Claire

Shelley and I have been consulting seriously about your letter received this morning, and I wish in as orderly a manner as possible to give you the result of our reflections. First as to my coming to Florence; I mentioned it to you first, it is true, but we have so little money, and our calls this quarter for removing &c will be so great that we had entirely given up the idea. If it would be of great utility to you, as a single expence we might do it—but if it be necessary that others sh^d follow, the crowns w^d be minus. But before I proceed further on this part of the subject let me examine what your plans appear to be. You anxiety for A's [*Allegra's*] health is to a great degree unfounded; Venice, its stinking canals & dirty streets, is enough to kill any child; but you ought to know, & any one will tell you so, that the towns of Romagna situated where Bagnacavallo[2] is, enjoy the best air in Italy—Imola & the neighbouring paese are famous. Bagnaca{va}llo especially, being 15 miles from the sea & situated on an eminence is peculiarly salutary. Considering the affair reasonably A. is well taken care of there, she is in good health, & in all probability will continue so.

No one can more entirely agree with you than I in thinking that as soon as possible A. ought to be taken out of the hands of one as remorseless as he is unprincipled. But at the same time it appears to me that the present moment is exactly the one in which this is the most difficult— time cannot add to these difficulties for they can never be greater. Allow me to enumerate some of those which are peculiar to the present instant. A. is in a convent, where it is next to impossible to get her out, high walls & bolted doors enclose her—& more than all the regular habits of a convent, which never permits her to get outside its gates & would cause her to be missed directly. But you may have a plan for this and I pass to other objections. At your desire Shelley urged her removal to LB. and this appears in the highest degree to have exasperated him—he vowed that if you annoyed him he would place A. in some secret convent, he declared that you sh^d have nothing to do with her & that he w^d move heaven & earth to prevent your interference. LB is at present a man of 12 or 15 thousand a year, he is on the spot, a man reckless of the ill he does others, obstinate to desperation in the pursuance of his plans or his revenge. What then would you do—having A. on the outside of the convent walls? w^d you go to America? the money we have not, nor does this seem to be your idea. You probably wish to secret yourself. But LB would use any means to find you out—& the story he might make up—a man stared at by the Grand Duke[3]—with money at command—above all on the spot to put energy into every pursuit, w^d he not find you? If he did not he comes upon Shelley—He taxes him; Shelley must either own it or tell a lie{.} in either case he is open to be called upon by LB to answer for his conduct—and a duel—I need not enter upon that topic, your own imagination may fill up the picture.

On the contrary a little time, a very little time, may alter much of this. It is more than probable that he will be obliged to go to England within a year—then at a distance he is no longer so formitable—What is certain is that we shall not be so near him another year—He may be reconciled with his wife, & though he may bluster he may not be sorry to get A. off his hands; at any rate if we leave him perfectly quiet he will not be so exasperated, so much on the qui vive as he is at present—Nothing remains constant, something may happen—things cannot be worse. Another thing I mention which though sufficiently ridiculous may have some weight with you. Spring is our unlucky season. No spring has passed for us without some piece of ill luck. Remember the first Spring at Mrs Harbottles.[4] The second when you became acquainted with LB. the Third We went to Marlow—no wise thing at least—The fourth our uncomfortable residence in London—The fifth our Roman misery—The sixth Paolo at Pisa—the seventh a mixture of Emilia & a Chancery suit[5]— Now the aspect of the Autumnal Heavens has on the contrary been with few exceptions, favourable to us—What think you of this? It is in your own style, but it has often struck me. W^d it not be better therefore to wait, & to undertake no plan until circumstance bend a little more to us.

Then we are drearily behind hand with money at present Hunt[6] & our furniture has swallowed up more than our savings. You say great sacrifices will be required of us. I would make many to extricate all belonging to me from the hands of LB, whose hypocrisy & cruelty rouse one's soul from its depths. We are of course still in great uncertainty as to our summer residence—we have calculated the great expence of removing our furniture for a few months as far as Spezia, & it appears to us a bad plan— to get a furnished house we must go nearer Genoa, probably nearer LB. which is contrary to our most earnest wishes. We have thought of Naples.[7]

ADDRESS: A Mademoiselle / Madlle de Clairmont / Chez M. le Professeur Bojti / Florence. POSTMARK: PISA. TEXT: MS., Humanities Research Center, University of Texas at Austin.

1. See *PBS Letters*, #691. Jones corrected his dating and all previous datings of this letter in "A Shelley and Mary Letter to Claire," *Modern Language Notes* 65 (1950): 121–23.

2. On 15 March Claire Clairmont was greatly agitated by information from Shelley and Mary Shelley that Byron, who had placed the four-year-old Allegra in the Convent of St. Anna at Bagnacavallo in 1821, had not brought Allegra with him when he moved to Pisa. (For Byron's justification for placing Allegra in the convent, see Byron, *Works*, V, 262–64; for Shelley's response to Byron on hearing that Allegra was in the convent, see *PBS Letters*, #621.)

3. On 8 July 1827 Mary Shelley told Thomas Moore about "the Grand Duke of Tuscany and his family walking past Byron's house at Pisa to get a glimpse of him" (Moore, *Memoirs*, V, 189–90).

4. A reference to the death of the Shelleys' first baby on 6 March 1815.

5. Chancery proceedings were brought against Shelley—and Shelley was given no notice—by Dr. Thomas Hume, guardian of Ianthe and Charles Shelley, when he did not receive the quarterly allowance for the children's keep. Because of this, Shelley's allowance was stopped (*MWS Journal*, 11 April 1821). Horace Smith, acting on Shelley's behalf, quickly clarified the matter, and Shelley's allowance was reinstated. The suit was unnecessary, for the money was available all the while, and a direct inquiry to Shelley would have resolved the problem (White, *Shelley*, II, 284–85, 610 n. 57).

6. Leigh Hunt, ill for months, had given up the *Indicator* and contributed almost nothing to the *Examiner*. On 24 January 1821 Marianne Hunt had written of their plight to the Shelleys, asking them to bring the Hunts to Italy (*S&M*, III, 578–79). Shelley responded by sending the Hunts whatever money he could manage (White, *Shelley*, II, 284).

7. Letter completed by Shelley (see above, n. 1).

To Maria Gisborne

Casa Magni, presso a Lerici   June 2nd 1822[1]

My Dear Mrs Gisborne

We received a letter from Mr G— [*Gisborne*] the other day, which promised one from you—It is not yet come, and although I think that you are two or three in my debt, yet I am good enough to write to you again, and thus to increase your debit—nor will I allow you, with one letter, to take advantage of the Insolvent act, and thus to free yourself from all claims at once. When I last wrote, I said, that I hoped our spring visitation had come and was gone—but this year we were not quit so

91

easily—however, before I mention anything else, I will finish the story of the Zuffa,[2] as far as it is yet gone. I think that in my last I left the Serjeant recovering; one of Lord B—'s and one of the Guiccioli's servants in prison, on suspicion, though both were innocent. The Judge or Advocate, called a Cancelliere, sent from Florence to determine the affair, disliked the Pisans, and having poca paga, expected a present from Milordo, and so favoured our part of the affair, was very civil, and came to our houses to take depositions, against the law.[3] For the sake of the Lesson, Hogg should have been there, to learn to cross question   The Cancelliere, a talkative buffoon of a Florentine, with "mille scuse per l'incomodo," asked, "Dove fu lei la sera del 24 Marzo"? "Andai a spasso in carozza, fuori della Porta della Piaggia—"[4]   A little clerk, seated beside him, with a great pile of papers before him, now dipt his pen in his Inkhorn—and looked expectant, while the Cancelliere, turning his eyes up to the ceiling repeated, "Io fui a spasso &c"   This scene lasted two, four, six hours, as it happened—In the span of two months, the depositions of fifteen people were taken—and finding Tita (Lord B—'s servant) perfectly innocent, the Cancelliere ordered him to be liberated, but the Pisan Police took fright at his beard—they called him "il barbone," and although it was declared that on his exit from prison he should be shaved, they could not tranquillize their mighty minds, but banished him—We, in the meantime were come to this place, so he has taken refuge with us. He is an excellent fellow, faithful, courageous and daring—How could it happen that the Pisans should not be frightened at such a mirabile mostro of an Italian, especially as the day he was let out of secreto, and was a larga in prison, he gave a feast to all his fellow prisoners, hiring chandeliers and plate—But poor Antonio, the Guiccioli's servant, the meekest hearted fellow in the world is kept in secret, not found guilty, but punished as such—e chi sa when he will be let out—so rests the affair—

About a month ago Claire came to visit us at Pisa, and went, with the Williams's to find a house in the Gulph of Spezia; when, during her absence, the disastrous news came of the death of Allegra[5]—She died of a typhus fever, which had been raging in the Romagna; but no one wrote to say it was there—she had no friends, except the nuns of the Convent, who were kind to her, I believe, but you know Italians—If half of the Convent had died of the plague, they would never have written to have had her removed, and so the poor child fell a sacrifice. Lord B— felt the loss, at first, bitterly—he also felt remorse, for he felt that he had acted against every body's councils and wishes, and death had stamped with truth the many and often urged prophecies of Claire, that the air of the Romagna, joined to the ignorance of the Italians, would prove fatal to

92

her. Shelley wished to conceal the fatal news from her, as long as possible, so when she returned from Spezia, he resolved to remove thither without delay—with so little delay, that he packed me off with Claire and Percy the very next day. She wished to return to Florence, but he persuaded her to accompany me—The next day, he packed up all our goods and chattels, (for a furnished house was not to be found in this part of the world) and like a torrent, hurrying every thing in it's course, he persuaded the W's [*Williamses*] to do the same.—They came here—but one house was to be found for us all—It is beautifully situated on the sea shore, under a woody hill.—But such a place as this is! The poverty of the people is beyond anything—Yet, they do not appear unhappy, but go on in dirty content, or contented dirt, while we find it hard work to purvey, miles around for a few eatables—We were in wretched discomfort at first, but now we are in a kind of disorderly order, living from day to day as we can—After the first day or two, Claire insisted on returning to Florence—so S— was obliged to disclose the truth—You may judge of what was her first burst of grief, and despair—however she reconciled herself to her fate, sooner than we expected; and although of course, until she form new ties, she will always grieve, yet she is now tranquil—more tranquil than, when prophesying her disaster, she was forever forming plans for getting her child from a place she judged, but too truly, would be fatal to her. She has now returned to Florence, and I do not know whether she will join us again. Our colony is much smaller than we expected, which we consider a benefit—Lord B— remains with his train at Monte Nero—Trelawny is to be the commander of his vessel, and, of course, will be at Leghorn—He is, at present at Genoa, awaiting the finishing of this boat—Shelley's boat is a beautiful creature. Henry would admire her greatly—though only 24 feet by 8, she is a perfect little ship, and looks twice her size—She had one fault—she was to have been built in partnership with Williams and Trelawny—T—y chose the name of the Don Juan, and we acceded; but when Shelley took her entirely on himself, we changed the name to the Ariel—Lord B— chose to take fire at this, and determined she should be called after the poem—wrote to Roberts to have the name painted on the mainsail, and she arrived thus disfigured—for days and nights full twenty one did Shelley and Edward ponder on her anabaptism, and the washing out the primeval stain.   turpentine, spirits of wine, buccata, all were tried, and it became dappled and no more— at length the piece has been taken out, and reefs put, so the sail does not look worse. I do not know what L^d B— will say, but Lord and poet as he is, he could not be allowed to make a coal-barge of our boat.[6] As only one house was to be found habitable in this gulph, the W's's have taken up their abode with us, and their servants and mine quarrel like cats and dogs; and besides you may imagine how ill a large family agrees with my laziness, when accounts and domestic concerns come to be talked of.— "Ma pazienza"—after all, the place does not please me—the people are rozzi,[7] and speak a detestable dialect.—and yet it is better than any other Italian sea-shore north of Naples—the air is excellent, and you may guess how much better we like it than Leghorn, where besides we should have been involved in English Society, a thing we longed to get rid of at Pisa. Mʳ G— talks of your going to a distant country. Pray write to me in time before this takes place, as I want a box from England first, but cannot now exactly name its contents. I am sorry to hear you do not get on; but perhaps Henry will, and make up for all. Percy is well and S— singularly so, his incessant boating does him a great deal of good. I had been very unwell for some time past, but am better now.

I have not even heard of the arrival of my novel; but I suppose, for his own sake, Papa will dispose of it to the best advantage[8]—If you see it advertized, pray tell me—also its publisher &c &c. We have heard from Hunt the day he was to sail, and anxiously and daily now await his arrival—S— will go over to Leghorn to him, and I also, if I can so manage it—We shall be at Pisa next winter, I believe—fate so decrees—Of course you have heard that the lawsuit went against my father.—this was the summit and crown of our spring misfortunes—but he writes in so few words, and in such a manner, that any information that I could get, through anyone, would be a great benefit to me.[9]

Adieu—Pray write now, and at length—remember both S— and I to Hogg—Did you get Matilda from Papa?

Your's ever,
Mary W. Shelley.

Continue to direct to Pisa

TEXT: John Gisborne Notebook No. 4, Abinger MSS., Bodleian Library.

1. The Shelleys had moved to Casa Magni at San Terenzo, near Lerici, on the Gulf of Spezia on 30 April (*MWS Journal*).

2. For details, see MWS *Letters*, I, 6–10 April 1822.

3. Byron's courier was questioned on 18 April; Mary Shelley and Teresa Guiccioli were questioned on 19 April; on 20 April further depositions were taken at Byron's house, and Williams wrote: "It is singular enough that suspicion should fall on me as the murderer" (Williams was not present at the affray); on 22 April Trelawny was questioned; and on 26 April Williams was questioned (Williams, *Journals and Letters*, pp. 144–45).

4. "A thousand apologies for the inconvenience . . . Where were you on the night of the 24th of March?" "I went for a diversion in a carriage, outside the Porta della Piaggia."

5. Claire Clairmont arrived at Pisa on 15 April. On 23 April she and the Williamses went to Spezia to seek summer quarters. On the same day, news came of Allegra's death at Bagnacavallo on 19 April. Anxious that Claire Clairmont not learn of the death while in the vicinity of Byron, Shelley rushed Claire Clairmont, Mary Shelley, and Percy to Spezia on 26 April, and he and the Williamses followed the next day. On 1 May the Williamses, unable to find other accommodations, moved in with the Shelleys at Casa Magni. On 2 May Claire Clairmont was told of Allegra's death. She returned to Florence on 21 May, but on 7 June she rejoined the Shelleys and the Williamses (Williams, *Journals and Letters*; Marchand, *Byron*, III, 991–96; *PBS Letters*, #702, #703).

6. Although Shelley had wanted to change the name of his boat to the *Ariel*, he accepted the name *Don Juan*; however, he objected to its name being painted in large letters across the mainsail (White, *Shelley*, II, 366).

7. "Coarse."

8. Shelley's letter of 29 May to Mrs. Godwin indicates that Godwin had written to Mary Shelley about *Valperga*. The information about the novel, however, was in one of many letters from Godwin outlining his dire financial situation as a result of the Skinner Street–rent lawsuit decision given against him. By the end of May Mary Shelley was approximately three months pregnant. Because Godwin's letters seriously upset her already poor health, it was agreed by the Shelleys' that Godwin's letters to Mary Shelley would be received and read by Mrs. Mason, who would then send all or parts of the letters to Shelley, who would then relate to Mary Shelley whatever information he thought appropriate. From Shelley's letter of 29 May we learn that that Godwin intended to withhold *Valperga* from publication for fear that booksellers might give him less than its worth because of his publicized financial distress. Shelley must have suppressed this information, knowing Mary Shelley's interest in having her novel published and perhaps concerned that *Valperga*, like *Matilda*, might come to nought in Godwin's hands (*PBS Letters*, #709, #710, #711; Mrs. Mason to Shelley, *S&M*, III, 800–802).

9. Godwin's letters of 19 April and 3 May and William Godwin, Jr.'s letter of 24 June, published together with Shelley's 29 April letter to Mrs. Godwin, his c. 21 May letter to Horace Smith, and Smith's 5 June response to Shelley, offer many details of the pressure exerted on the Shelleys by Godwin, as well as details of the Shelleys' efforts on Godwin's behalf (*PBS Letters*, #708, #710).

To Maria Gisborne

Pisa   August 15th 1822

I said in a letter to Peacock, my dear Mrs Gisborne, that I would send you some account of the last miserable months of my disastrous life. From day to day I have put this off, but I will now endeavour to fulfill my design. The scene of my existence is closed & though there be no pleasure in retracing the scenes that have preceded the event which has crushed my hopes yet there seems to be a necessity in doing so, and I obey the impulse that urges me. I wrote to you either at the end of May or the beginning of June. I described to you the place we were living in:—Our desolate house, the beauty yet strangeness of the scenery and the delight Shelley took in all this—he never was in better health or spirits than during this time. I was not well in body or mind. My nerves were wound up to the utmost irritation, and the sense of misfortune hung over my spirits. No words can tell you how I hated our house & the country about it. Shelley reproached me for this—his health was good & the place was quite after his own heart—What could I answer—that the people were wild & hateful, that though the country was beautiful yet I liked a more countryfied place, that there was great difficulty in living—that all our Tuscans would leave us, & that the very jargon of these Genovese was disgusting—This was all I had to say but no words could describe my feelings—the beauty of the woods made me weep & shudder—so vehement was my feeling of dislike that I used to rejoice when the winds & waves permitted me to go out in the boat so that I was not obliged to take my usual walk among tree shaded paths, allies of vine festooned trees—all that before I doated on—& that now weighed on me. My only moments of peace were on board that unhappy boat, when lying down with my head on his knee I shut my eyes & felt the wind & our swift motion alone. My ill health might account for much of this—bathing in the sea somewhat relieved me—but on the 8th of June (I think it was) I was threatened with a miscarriage, & after a week of great ill health on sunday the 16th this took place at eight in the morning. I was so ill that for seven hours I lay nearly lifeless—kept from fainting by brandy, vinegar eau de Cologne &c—at length ice was brought to our solitude—it came before the doctor so Claire & Jane were afraid of using it but Shelley overuled them & by an unsparing application of it I was restored. They all thought & so did I at one time that I was about to die—I hardly wish that I had, my own Shelley could never have lived without me, the sense of eternal misfortune would have pressed to heavily upon him, & what would have become of my poor babe? My convalescence was slow and during it a strange occurence happened to retard it. But first I must describe our house to you. The floor on which we lived was thus

1 is a terrace that went the whole length of our house & was precipitous to the sea. 2 the large dining hall—3, a private staircase. 4 my bedroom 5 Mrs [*Williams's*] bedroom, 6 Shelleys & 7 the entrance from the great staircase. Now to return. As I said Shelley was at first in perfect health but having over fatigued himself one day, & then the fright my illness gave him caused a return of nervous sensations & visions as bad as in his

worst times. I think it was the saturday after my illness while yet unable to walk I was confined to my bed—in the middle of the night I was awoke by hearing him scream & come rushing into my room; I was sure that he was asleep & tried to waken him by calling on him, but he continued to scream which inspired me with such a panic that I jumped out of bed & ran across the hall to M^{rs} W's room where I fell through weakness, though I was so frightened that I got up again immediately—she let me in & Williams went to S. who had been wakened by my getting out of bed'— he said that he had not been asleep & that it was a vision that he saw that had frightened him—But as he declared that he had not screamed it was certainly a dream & no waking vision—What had frightened him was this—He dreamt that lying as he did in bed Edward & Jane came into him, they were in the most horrible condition, their bodies lacerated— their bones starting through their skin, the faces pale yet stained with blood, they could hardly walk, but Edward was the weakest & Jane was supporting him—Edward said—["]Get up, Shelley, the sea is flooding the house & it is all coming down." S. got up, he thought, & went to the his window that looked on the terrace & the sea & thought he saw the sea rushing in. Suddenly his vision changed & he saw the figure of himself strangling me, that had made him rush into my room, yet fearful of frightening me he dared not approch the bed, when my jumping out awoke him, or as he phrased it caused his vision to vanish. All this was frightful enough, & talking it over the next morning he told me that he had had many visions lately—he had seen the figure of himself which met him as he walked on the terrace & said to him—"How long do you mean to be content"—No very terrific words & certainly not prophetic of what has occurred. But Shelley had often seen these figures when ill; but the strangest thing is that Mrs W. saw him. Now Jane though a woman of sensibility, has not much imagination & is not in the slightest degree nervous—neither in dreams or otherwise. She was standing one day, the day before I was taken ill, at a window that looked on the Terrace with Trelawny—it was day—she saw as she thought Shelley pass by the window, as he often was then, without a coat or jacket—he passed again—now as he passed both times the same way—and as from the side towards which he went each time there was no way to get back except past the window again (except over a wall twenty feet from the ground) she was struck at seeing him pass twice thus & looked out & seeing him no more she cried—"Good God can Shelley have leapt from the wall? Where can he be gone?" Shelley, said Trelawny—"No Shelley has past— What do you mean?" Trelawny says that she trembled exceedingly when she heard this & it proved indeed that Shelley had never been on the terrace & was far off at the time she saw him. Well we thought {no} more of these things & I slowly got better. Having heard from Hunt that he had sailed from Genoa, on Monday July 1ˢᵗ S., Edward & Captain Roberts (the Gent. who built our boat) departed in our boat for Leghorn to receive him—I was then just better, had begun to crawl from my bedroom to the terrace; but bad spirits succeded to ill health, and this departure of Shelley's seemed to add insuferably to my misery. I could not endure that he should go—I called him back two or three times, & told him that if I did not see him soon I would go to Pisa with the child—I cried bitterly when he went away. They went & Jane, Claire & I remained alone with the children—I could not walk out, & though I gradually gathered strength it was slowly & my ill spirits encreased; in my letters to him I entreated him to return—"the feeling that some misfortune would happen," I said, "haunted me": I feared for the child, for the idea of danger connected with him never struck me—When Jane & Claire took their evening walk I used to patrole the terrace, oppressed with wretchedness, yet gazing on the most beautiful scene in the world. This Gulph of Spezia is subdivided into many small bays of which ours was far the most beautiful—the two horns of the bay (so to express myself) were wood covered promontories crowned with castles—at the foot of these on the furthest was Lerici on the nearest Sanᶜ Arenzo—Lerici being above a mile by land from us & San Arenzo about a hundred or two yards—trees covered the hills that enclosed this bay & then beautiful groups were picturesquely contrasted with the rocks the castle on [*and*] the town—the sea lay far extended in front while to the west we saw the promontory & islands which formed one of the extreme boundarys of the Gulph—to see the sun set upon this scene, the stars shine & the moon rise was a sight of wondrous beauty, but to me it added only to my wretchedness—I repeated to myself all that another would have said to console me, & told myself the tale of love peace & competence which I enjoyed—but I answered myself by tears—did not my William die? & did I hold my Percy by a firmer tenure?—Yet I thought when he, when my Shelley returns I shall be happy—he will comfort me, if my boy be ill he will restore him & encourage me. I had a letter or two from Shelley mentioning the difficulties he had in establishing the Hunts,[2] & that he was unable to fix the time of his return. Thus a week past. On Monday 8ᵗʰ Jane had a letter from Edward, dated saturday, he said that he waited at Leghorn for S. who was at Pisa   That S's return was certain, "but" he continued, "if he should not come by monday I will come in a felucca, & you may expect me teusday evening at furthest."[3] This was monday, the fatal monday, but with us it was stormy all day & we did not at all suppose that they could put to sea. At twelve at night we had a thunderstorm; Teusday it rained all day & was calm—the sky wept on their graves—on Wednesday—the wind was fair from Leghorn & in the evening several felucca's arrived thence—one brought word that they had sailed monday, but we did not believe them—thursday was another day of fair wind & when twelve at night came & we did not see the tall sails of the little boat double the promontory before us we began to fear not the truth, but some illness—some disagreeable news for their detention. Jane got so uneasy that she determined to proceed the next day to Leghorn in a boat to see what was the matter—friday came & with it a heavy sea & bad wind— Jane however resolved to be rowed to Leghorn (since no boat could sail) and busied herself in preparations—I wished her to wait for letters, since friday was letter day—she would not—but the sea detained her, the swell rose so that no boat would venture out—At 12 at noon our letters came— there was one from Hunt to Shelley, it said—"pray write to tell us how you got home, for they say that you had bad weather after you sailed monday & we are anxious"—the paper fell from me—I trembled all over— Jane read it—"Then it is all over!" she said. "No, my dear Jane," I cried, "it is not all over, but this suspense is dreadful—come with me, we will go to Leghorn, we will post to be swift & learn our fate." We crossed to Lerici, despair in our hearts; they raised our spirits there by telling us that no accident had been heard of & that it must have been known &c— but still our fear was great—& without resting we posted to Pisa   It must have been fearful to see us—two poor, wild, aghast creatures—driving (like Matilda)[4] towards the sea to learn if we were to be for ever doomed to misery. I knew that Hunt was at Pisa at Lord Byrons' house but I thought that L. B. was at Leghorn. I settled that we should drive to Casa Lanfranchi that I should get out & ask the fearful question of Hunt, "do you know any thing of Shelley?" On entering Pisa the idea of seeing Hunt for the first time for four years under such circumstances, & asking him such a question was so terrific to me that it was with difficulty that I prevented myself from going into convulsions—my struggles were dreadful—they knocked at the door & some one called out "Chi è?" it was the Guiccioli's maid   L.B. was in Pisa—Hunt was in bed, so I was to see L.B. instead of him—This was a great relief to me; I staggered up stairs—the Guiccioli came to meet me smiling while I could hardly say— "Where is he—Sapete alcuna cosa di Shelley"—They knew nothing—he had left Pisa on sunday—on Monday he had sailed—there had been bad weather monday afternoon—more they knew not. Both LB & the lady have told me since—that on that terrific evening I looked more like a ghost than a woman—light seemed to emanate from my features, my face was very white   I looked like marble—Alas. I had risen almost from a bed of sickness for this journey—I had travelled all day—it was now 12 at night—& we, refusing to rest, proceeded to Leghorn—not in despair—no, for then we must have died; but with sufficient hope to keep up the agitation of the spirits which was all my life. It was past two in the morning when we arrived—They took us to the wrong inn—neither Trelawny or Cap^n Roberts were there nor did we exactly know where they were so we were obliged to wait until daylight. We threw ourselves drest on our beds & slept a little but at 6 o'clock we went to one or two inns to ask for one or the other of these gentlemen. We found Roberts at the Globe. He came down to us with a face which seemed to tell us that the worst was true, and here we learned all that had occurred during the week they had been absent from us, & under what circumstances they had departed on their return.——— Shelley had past most of the time a[t] Pisa—arranging the affairs of the Hunts—& skrewing LB's mind to the sticking place[5] about the journal. He had found this a difficult task at first but at length he had succeeded to his heart's content with both points. Mrs Mason said that she saw him in better health and spirits than she had ever known him, when he took leave of her sunday July 7th His face burnt by the sun, & his heart light that he had succeeded in rendering the Hunts' tolerably comfortable. Edward had remained at Leghorn. On Monday July 8th during the morning they were employed in buying many things—eatables &c for our solitude. There had been a thunderstorm early but about noon the weather was fine & the wind right fair for Lerici—They were impatient to be gone. Roberts said, "Stay until tomorrow to see if the weather is settled; & S. might have staid but Edward was in so great an anxiety to reach home—saying they would get there in seven hours with that wind—that they sailed! S. being in one of those extravagant fits of good spirits in which you have sometimes seen him. Roberts went out to the end of the mole & watched them out of sight—they sailed at one & went off at the rate of about 7 knots—About three—Roberts, who was still on the mole—saw wind coming from the Gulph—or rather what the Italians call a temporale anxious to know how the boat w^d weather the storm, he got leave to go up the tower & with the glass discovered them about ten miles out at sea, off Via Reggio, they were taking in their topsails—"The haze of the storm," he said, "hid them from me & I saw them no more—when the storm cleared I looked again fancying that I should see them on their return to us—but there was no boat on the sea."—This then was all we knew, yet we did not despair—they might have been driven over to Corsica & not knowing the coast & Gone god knows where. Reports favoured this belief.—it was even said that they had been seen in the Gulph—We resolved to return with all possible speed—We sent a courier to go from tower to tower along the coast to know if any thing had been seen or found, & at 9 AM. we quitted Leghorn—stopped but one moment at Pisa & proceeded towards Lerici. When at 2 miles from Via Reggio we rode down to that town to know if they knew any thing—here our calamity first began to break on us— a little boat & a water cask had been found five miles off—they had manufactured a piccolissima lancia of thin planks stitched by a shoemaker just to let them run on shore without wetting themselves as our boat drew 4 feet water.—the description of that found tallied with this—but then this boat was very cumbersome & in bad weather they might have been easily led to throw it overboard—the cask frightened me most—but the same reason might in some sort be given for that. I must tell you that Jane & I were not now alone—Trelawny accompanied us back to our home. We journied on & reached the Magra about ½ past ten P.M. I cannot describe to you what I felt in the first moment when, fording this river, I felt the water splash about our wheels—I was suffocated—I gasped for breath—I thought I should have gone into convulsions, & I struggled violently that Jane might not perceive it—looking down the river I saw the two great lights burning at the foce—A voice from within me seemed to cry aloud that is his grave. After passing the river I gradually recovered. Arriving at Lerici we {were} obliged to cross our little bay in a boat—San Arenzo was illuminated for a festa—what a scene—the roaring sea—the scirocco wind—the lights of the town towards which we rowed— & our own desolate hearts—that coloured all with a shroud—we landed; nothing had been heard of them. This was saturday July 13. & thus we waited until Thursday July 25^{th6} thrown about by hope & fear. We sent messengers along the coast towards Genoa & to Via Reggio—nothing had been found more than the lancetta; reports were brought us—we hoped— & yet to tell you all the agony we endured during those 12 days would be to make you conceive a universe of pain— each moment intolerable & giving place to one still worse. The people of the country too added to one's discomfort—they are like wild savages— on festa's the men & women & children in different bands—the sexes always separate—pass the whole night in dancing on the sands close to our door running into the sea then back again & screaming all the time one perpetuel air—the most detestable in the world—then the scirocco perpetually blew & the sea for ever moaned their dirge. On thursday 25^{th7} Trelawny left us to go to Leghorn to see what was doing or what could be done. On friday I was very ill but as evening came on I said to Jane— "If any thing had been found on the coast Trelawny would have returned to let us know. He has not returned so I hope." About 7 o'clock P.M. he did return—all was over—all was quiet now, they had been found washed on shore—Well all this was to be endured.

Well what more have I to say? The next day we returned to Pisa[8] And here we are still—days pass away—one after another—& we live thus. We are all together—we shall quit Italy together. Jane must proceed to London—if letters do not alter my views I shall remain in Paris.—Thus we live—Seeing the Hunts now & then. Poor Hunt has suffered terribly as you may guess. Lord Byron is very kind to me & comes with the Guiccioli to see me often.

Today—this day—the sun shining in the sky—they are gone to the desolate sea coast to perform the last offices to their earthly remains.[9] Hunt LB. & Trelawny. The quarantine laws would not permit us to remove them sooner—& now only on condition that we burn them to ashes. That I do not dislike—His rest shall be at Rome beside my child[10]— where one day I also shall join them—Adonais is not Keats's it is his own elegy—he bids you there go to Rome.—I have seen the spot where he now lies—the sticks that mark the spot where the sands cover him—he shall not be there it is too nea[r] Via Reggio—They are now about this fearful office—& I live!

One more circumstance I will mention. As I said he took leave of M[rs] Mason in high spirits on sunday—"Never," said she, "did I see him look happier than the last glance I had of his countenance." On Monday he was lost—on monday night she dreamt—that she was somewhere—she knew not where & he came looking very pale & fearfully melancholy— she said to him—"You look ill, you are tired, sit down & eat." "No," he replied, "I shall never eat more; I have not a soldo left in the world."— "Nonsense," said she, "this is no inn—you need not pay—"—"Perhaps,["] he answered, "it is the worse for that." Then she awoke & going to sleep again she dreamt that my Percy was dead & she awoke crying bitterly ⟨—so bitterly th⟩ & felt so miserable—that she said to herself— "why if the little boy should die I should not feel it in this manner." She [was] so struck with these dreams that she mentioned them to her servant the next day—saying she hoped all was well with us.

Well here is my story—the last story I shall have to tell—all that might have been bright in my life is now despoiled—I shall live to improve myself, to take care of my child, & render myself worthy to join him. soon my weary pilgrimage will begin—I rest now—but soon I must leave Italy—& then—there is an end of all despair. Adieu   I hope you are well & happy. I have an idea that while he was at Pisa that he received a letter from you that I have never seen—so not knowing where to direct

I shall send this letter to Peacock—I shall send it open—he may be glad to read it—

Your's ever truly Mary WS.—Pisa

I shall probably write to you soon again.

I have left out a material circumstance—A Fishing boat saw them go down—It was about 4 in the afternoon—they saw the boy at mast head, when baffling winds struck the sails, they had looked away a moment & looking again the boat was gone—This is their story but there is little down [*doubt*] that these men might have saved them, at least Edward who could swim. They c^d not they said get near her—but 3 quarters of an hour after passed over the spot where they had seen her—they protested no wreck of her was visible, but Roberts going on board their boat found several spars belonging to her.—perhaps they let them perish to obtain these. Trelawny thinks he can get her up, since another fisherman things [*thinks*] that he has found the spot where she lies, having drifted near shore. T. does this to know perhaps the cause of her wreck—but I care little about it

ADDRESS: [*by Mary Shelley*] Mrs. Gisborne / [*by Peacock*] 33 King Street West / Bryanstone Square / London. ENDORSED: [*by Peacock*] Combe near Wendover, Bucks; Septr. 2. 1822. / T.L.P.; [*by Mrs. Gisborne*] rec. 3rd Sept. / 1822 / Ans. POSTMARKS: (1) WENDOVER; (2) [   ] / 3 SE 3 / 1822. TEXT: MS., British Library.

1. Williams's *Journal* for 23 June records: "During the night Shelley sees *spirits* and alarms the whole house" (*Journals and Letters*, p. 155).

2. *PBS Letters*, #720.

3. Williams, *Journals and Letters*, p. 163.

4. The heroine of Mary Shelley's novella, Mathilda, in an unsuccessful effort to prevent her father's suicide, desperately follows his rush "towards the sea" (MWS *Mathilda*).

5. *Macbeth* 1. 60.

6. An error for Thursday, 18 July.

7. See n. 6.

8. On 20 July.

9. On 15 August Trelawny, Hunt, and Byron gathered at the beach a distance from Viareggio, where the bodies of Shelley and Williams had been temporarily interred in quick lime. They disinterred and cremated Williams's remains on 15 August. The next day they disinterred and cremated Shelley's remains. Trelawny left more than ten detailed accounts of the cremations (Trelawny, *Letters*, pp. 2–14; for a discussion of Trelawny's many accounts, see Leslie A. Marchand, "Trelawny on the Death of Shelley," *Keats-Shelley Memorial Bulletin* 4 [1952]: 9–34).

10. Shelley was not buried beside William, for the child's remains could not be found.

To Edward Dawkins

Pisa   21 Aug. 1822

Sir

Permit me on the present occasion to return you my most grateful thanks for the kindness with which you have attended to the many applications of Mʳ Trelawny on my account,[1] and to express my sorrow that we were obliged thus to annoy you. Mine indeed is a fate which may awaken the sympathy of a stranger; but the very affliction that causes that sympathy, renders me more sensible of the obliging attentions of others.

May I trouble you once more? I am ashamed to do so, but you will I trust forgive my importunity from its cause. It is my intention to forward the remains of him I have lost to Rome, to be buried there beside a darling boy whom we lost three years ago, near whom he always desired to be placed. Having no friend in that city, you would perhaps have the kindness to send me a letter for the consul there,[2] who thus called upon would be induced to see that my intentions are fulfilled, that the last honours are paid to him, and above all that he should really be placed close to our child; a tomb over him marks the spot.

Again, I must apologize for my new intrusion, and thank you for your attention to my past. I have the honour to be,

Sir,
Your obliged humble servant
Mary Shelley

ADDRESS: To His Excellency / Edward Dawkins Eq / Envoy Extraordinary of H.R.M. to the court of Tuscany / Florence. POSTMARKS: (1) PISA; (2) 22 / AGOSTO. TEXT: MS., Pforzheimer Library.

1. Edward Dawkins, Secretary to the Legation in Tuscany, who had assisted Byron in his exertions to free his servant Tita, made the arrangements with the Lucchese and Tuscan governments to permit the disinterment and cremation of Shelley and Williams (Trelawny, *Letters*, pp. 2–3; Cline, *Pisan Circle*, pp. 181–87.

2. The English Consul at Rome was John Parke. On 22 August Dawkins replied to Mary Shelley:

> According to your wishes I have written a letter to our Consul at Rome which will, I hope, remove every difficulty in the performance of your most melancholy duty.
>
> Should it be the intention of those who advise you on this occasion to carry this letter by land, I will request Mr Parke to send a Lascia passare to the frontier of the Roman States, which will prevent all enquiries at the Custom House—

I am much flattered, Madam, by the expression of your thanks; but I am not conscious of having deserved them—I have simply done my Duty; which, owing to the Laws of this Country, has not been so effective as I could have wished. (Abinger MS.)

After the cremation Shelley's ashes were put in an oak coffer and conveyed on the *Bolivar* to Leghorn, where they were consigned to an English merchant named Grant, who then consigned them to his correspondent at Rome, John Freeborn (H. Nelson Gay, "The Protestant Burial-Ground in Rome," *Keats-Shelley Memorial Bulletin* 2 [1913] 52–54). Although John Parke was British Consul, he did not live in Rome, and John Freeborn served as his consular agent there.

❖

To Maria Gisborne

[Pisa   c. 27 August 1822]

And so here I am! I continue to exist—to see one day succeed the other; to dread night; but more to dread morning & hail another cheerless day. My boy too is alas! no consolation; when I think how He loved him, the plans we had for his education, his sweet & childish voice strikes me to the heart. Why should he live in this world of pain and anguish? And if he went I should go too & we should all sleep in peace. At times I feel an energy within me to combat with my destiny—but again I sink—I have but one hope for which I live—to render myself worthy to join him—such a feeling sustains one during moments of enthusiasm, but darkness & misery soon overwhelms the mind when all near objects bring agony alone with them. People used to call me lucky in my star   You see now how true such a prophecy is—I was fortunate in having fearlessly placed by destiny in the hands of one, who a superior being among men, a bright planetary spirit enshrined in an earthly temple, raised me to the height of happiness—so far am I now happy that I would not change my situation as His widow with that of the most prosperous woman in the world—and surely the time will at length come when I shall be at peace & my brain & heart be no longer alive with unutterable anguish. I can conceive but of one circumstance that could afford me the semblance of content—that is the being permitted to live where I am now in the same house, in the same state, occupied alone with my child, in collecting His manuscripts—writing his life, and thus to go easily to my grave. But this must not be. Even if my circumstances did not compel me to return to England, I would not stay another summer in Italy with my child.—I will at least do my best to render him well & happy—& the idea that my circumstances may at all injure him is {the} fiercest pang my mind endures.

I wrote you a long letter containing a slight sketch of my sufferings I sent it directed to Peacock at the India House, because an accident led me to fancy that you were no longer in London. I said in that, that on that day (August 15) they had gone to perform the last offices for him—however I erred in this, for on that day those of Edward were alone fulfilled & they returned on the 16th to celebrate Shelley's. I will say nothing of the ceremony since Trelawny has written an account of it to be printed in the forthcoming journal[1]—I will only say that all except his heart (which was unconsumable)[2] was burnt, and that two days ago I went to Leghorn and beheld the small box that contained his earthly dress—that form, those smiles—Great God! No he is not there—he is with me, about me—life of my life & soul of my soul—if his divine spirit did not penetrate mine I could not survive to weep thus.

I will mention the friends I have here that you may form an idea of our situation. Mrs Williams Claire & I live all together, we have one purse, & joined in misery we are for the present joined in life. She poor girl, withers like a lily—she lives for her children, but it is a living death. Lord Byron has been [*several words canceled*] very kind—[*half-line canceled*] but the Guiccioli restrains him perhaps—she being an Italian is capable of being jealous of a living corpse such as I. Of Hunt I will speak when I see you. But the friend to whom we are eternally indebted is Trelawny. I have of course mentioned him in my letters to you—as one who wishes to be considered eccentric but who was noble & generous at bottom. I always thought so even when no fact proved it, & Shelley agreed with me, as he always did, or rather I with him. We heard people speak against him on account of his vagaries, we said to one another—"Still we like him—we believe him to be good." Once even when a whim of his led him to treat me with something like impertinence I forgave him, & have now been well rewarded. In my outline of events, you will see how unasked he returned with Jane & I from Leghorn to Lerici, how he staid with us miserable creatures twelve days there endeavouring to keep up our spirits—how he left us, on thursday, & finding our misfortune confirmed then without rest returned on friday to us, & again without rest returned with us to Pisa on saturday. These were no common services—Since that he has gone through by himself all the annoyances of dancing attendance on consuls & governors for permissions to fulfil the last duties to those gone, & attending the ceremony himself, all the disagreable part & all the fatigue fell on him—as Hunt said—"He worked with the meanest and felt with the best." He is generous to a distressing degree. But after all these benefits towards us what I most thank him for is this. When on that night of agony, that friday night he returned to announce that hope was dead for us—when he had told me that his earthly frame being found, his spirit was no longer to be my guide, protector & companion in this dark world—he did not attempt to console me, that would have been to{o} cruelly useless; but he launched forth into as it were an over-flowing & eloquent praise of my divine Shelley—until I almost was happy that I was thus unhappy to be fed by the praise of him, and to dwell on the eulogy that his loss thus drew from his friend.

Of my friends I have only Mrs Mason to mention. Her coldness has stung me—yet she felt his loss keenly, & would be very glad to serve me—but it is not cold offers of service that one wants—one's wounded spirit demands a number of nameless & slight but dear attentions that are a balm & wanting them one feels a bitterness which is a painful addition to one's other sufferings.

God knows what will become of me! My life is now very monotonous as to outward events—yet how diversified by internal feeling—How often in the intensity of grief does one instant seem to fill & embrace the universe. As to the rest, the mechanical spending of my time; of course I have a great deal to do preparing for my journey—I make no visits except one once in about ten days to Mrs Mason—I have not seen Hunt this nine days. Trelawny resides chiefly at Leghorn since he is captain of LordB.'s vessel, the Bolivar, he comes to see us about once a week; & LordB. visits me about twice a week, accompanied by the Guiccioli. But seeing people is an annoyance which I am happy to be spared. Solitude is my only help & resource; accustomed even when he was with me to spend much of my time alone, I can at those moments forget myself—until some idea, which I think I would communicate to him, occurs & then the yawning & dark gulph again displays itself unshaded by the rainbows which the imagination had formed. Despair, energy, love, despondency & excessive affliction are like clouds, driven across my mind, one by one, until tears blot the scene, & weariness of spirit consigns me to temporary repose.

I shudder with horror when I look on what I have suffered; & when I think of the wild and miserable thoughts that have possessed me, I say to myself "Is it true that I ever felt thus?"—And then I weep in pity of myself. Yet each day adds to the stock of sorrow & death is the only end. I would study, & I hope I shall—I would write—& when I am settled I may—But were it not for the steady hope I entertain of joining him what a mockery all this would be. Without that hope I could not study or write, for fame & usefulness (except as far as regards my child) are nullities to me—Yet I shall be happy if any thing I ever produce may exalt & soften sorrow, as the writings of the divinities of our race have mine. But how can I aspire to that?

The world will surely one day feel what it has lost when this bright child of song deserted her—Is not Adonais his own Elegy—& there does he truly depict the universal woe wh[ich] should overspread all good minds since he has ceased to be [their] fellow labourer in this worldly scene. How lovely does he [   ] paint death to be and with what heartfelt sorrow does one repeat that line—"But I am chained to time & cannot thence depart."[3] How long do you think I shall live? as long as my mother? then eleven long years must intervene—I am now on the eve of completing my five & twentieth year—how drearily young for one so lost as I! How young in years for one who lives ages each day in sorrow—think you that those moments are counted in my life as in other people's?—oh no! The day before the sea closed over mine own Shelley he said to Marianne—"If I die tomorrow I have lived to be older than my father, I am ninety years of age." Thus also may I say—The eight years I passed with him was spun out beyond the usual length of a man's life—And what I have suffered since will write years on my brow & intrench them in my heart—surely I am not long for this world—most sure should I be were it not for my boy—but God grant that I may live to make his early years happy.

Well adieu—I have no events to write about & can therefore can only scrawl about my feelings—this letter indeed is only the sequel of my last—In that I closed the history of all of event that can interest me. That letter I wish you to send my father[4]—the present one it is best not.

I suppose I shall see you in England some of these days—but I shall write to you again before I quit this place—Be as happy as you can, & hope for better things in the next world—by firm hope you may attain your wishes—again adieu

Affectionately yours
MWS

Do not write me again here. or at all until I write again

ADDRESS: Mrs. Gisborne / 33 King's Street West / Bryanstone Square / Inghilterra London / Londres. POSTMARKS: (1) PISA; (2) FPO / SE. 10 / 1822; (3) SE. 10 / 1822 Nn; (4) [   ] Clock / SP. 10 / 1822 Nn. ENDORSED: Recd. 10th Sept. 1822. TEXT: MS., Bodleian Library.

1. Trelawny's account was not published in the *Liberal*, but it was incorporated, in an altered form, into Hunt's *Lord Byron and Some of His Contemporaries* (Marshall, *The Liberal*, p. 75).

2. Shelley's heart, taken from the flames by Trelawny, was first given to Hunt, who intended to keep it. Mary Shelley's wish to have the heart precipitated a quarrel with Hunt. On 17 August he wrote: "I am sorry after what I said to you last night,

that you should have applied to Lord B. on this subject & in this manner. It is not that my self-love is hurt, for that I could have given up, as I have long [?learnt] to do; but it is my love,—my love for my friend; and for this to make way for the claims of any other love, man's or woman's, I must have great reasons indeed brought me— I do not say it is impossible for such reasons to be brought; but I say that they must be great, unequivocal, & undeniable. In his case above all other human beings, no ordinary appearance of rights, even yours, can affect me. . . . I begged it at the funeral pile; I had it; & his Lordship who happened to be at a distance at the moment, knew nothing of the matter till it was in my possession" (MS., British Library).

According to John Gisborne, Jane Williams's intercession, which stressed the bitterness between Mary Shelley and Hunt that resulted from his unwillingness to give Mary Shelley the heart, finally persuaded Hunt to relent (Gisborne, *Journals and Letters*, pp. 88–89). When Mary Shelley died, the heart, dried to dust, was discovered in a copy of *Adonais*. In 1889 Sir Percy Florence died, and the relic of the heart was buried with him in the vault that also contained the remains of Mary Shelley, William Godwin, and Mary Wollstonecraft, in St. Peter's Churchyard, Bournemouth (White, *Shelley*, II, 635).

In "Shelley's Heart," *Journal of the History of Medicine* 10 (January 1955): 114, Arthur M. Z. Norman offers the following reason for the heart's impregnability to fire, as well as reasons for other physical discomforts Shelley suffered during his life: "It seems very probable that Shelley suffered from a progressively calcifying heart, which might well have caused diffuse symptoms with its increasing weight of calcium and which indeed would have resisted cremation as readily as a skull, a jaw, or fragments of bone. Shelley's heart, epitome of Romanticism, may well have been a heart of stone."

3. *Adonais* 26.9.

4. On 6 August Godwin had written Mary Shelley that he had heard "the most afflicting intelligence to you, & in some measure to all of us, that can be imagined, the death of Shelley on the 8th ult" through Hunt's letter of 20 July to Bessy Kent (Hunt, *Correspondence*, I, 189–91). Godwin offered his condolences and his assistance and requested direct word from her. Before sending his letter, he received an undated letter from Mary Shelley, and he added a postscript to note its receipt, delayed "some hours by being directed to the care of Monro, for which I cannot account. William wrote to you on the 14th of June & I on the 23rd of July. I will call on Peacock & Hogg, as you desire. Perhaps Williams letter, & perhaps others, have been kept from you. Let us now be open & unreserved in all things" (Abinger MS.). Godwin had obviously forgotten his instructions to Mary Shelley of 3 May 1822, the day the Godwins were "compelled by summary process, to leave the house we live in," to direct her letters, until further word, "to the care of Mr. Monro" (Abinger MS.). For Godwin's remarks about letters kept from Mary Shelley, see 2 June 1822. Since Mary Shelley was already in direct touch with Godwin, her request to show the 15 August letter to him was no doubt an expedient way of giving him a detailed account of events before and after Shelley's death, just as she had left the 15 August letter open for Peacock to read before he sent it on to Maria Gisborne.

To Thomas Jefferson Hogg

Pisa. Septr 9th 1822

My dear Hogg

This letter will be delivered to you by Mrs Williams,[1] the widow of the dear friend who was lost with mine own Shelley. You will find in her the friend whom he saw daily for nearly two years, to whom he was affectionately attached, & who more than any person can describe to you the last actions & thoughts of your incomparable friend. If you still retain the affection you once had for him, and think of him with that kindness which he always felt for you, her company will be invaluable to you— although you can in part repay her by talking of the former years of the life of one whom she loved, esteemed & admired beyond all her other friends.

You did not know Edward, & cannot tell what she has lost in losing him. They were enthusiastically attached to each other, and he by his talents, angelic disposition, his gentle, brave & generous nature fully merited all the tenderness which she, the model of all gentleness, (& elegance) and grace, bore him. If my own unhappiness had not penetrated my heart so entirely I could never have endured to see her divided from one she loved so well; and you who used to be a fervent admirer of that devotion which distinguishes the sentiment of love in a woman, will appreciate her virtues, although they are repaid, as all earthly virtue is, by desolation & misery.

I would say do all in your power to be of use to her, but to know her is sufficient to make the desire of serving her arise in an unselfish mind. Do what little you can to amuse her.

By the time you receive this you will probably have heard from me by the post, so I say nothing of such a nullity as I now am—Adieu

Truly yours
MaryW. Shelley.

ADDRESS: Jefferson Hogg Esq / 1 Garden Court & Temple. TEXT: MS., Abinger MSS., Bodleian Library.

   1. Jane Williams left Italy for England on 17 September.

To Thomas Love Peacock

Casa Negroto, Crosa di San Nazaro,
Albaro,—fuore delle[1] Porte all'Arco.
Genova   September 29th 1822

My dear Friend

Before you receive this letter you will have seen my father, who will have acquainted you with the change in my plans. I do not return to England. I thought this journey perfectly necessary at first but Lord Byron, & afterwards all my friends, combined to shew me the inexpediency of such a step. What have I to do there? If Sir Timothy allows me nothing,[2] I should be a burthen to my father, and have expended on a fruitless journey that money which will maintain me & my child a long time here. If he allows me any thing it will be so small a sum that I should live miserably in your dear country; while however small, I am sure it would maintain me comfortably here. As to the will, I am convinced that nothing can be done with it until after Sir Timothys death. How can I give it up?—if it is not valid I can only give it up to the heir at law, who is Charles Bysshe, & he is under the Chancellor's & the Westbrooks protection, & has no interests in common with his paternal grandfather. All that can be done now is, to be silent concerning the will, & that you (in your own & Lord Byron's name) should apply to Sir Timothy through Whitton, for a maintenance for me & my child. Lord Byron is very kind to me, promises to Do his duty as executor, & really appears interested in my fate. If it be judged expedient he will write to Whitton himself—or take any other step to secure me a fitting allowance, which you should point out as proper to be taken.

In the mean time {I} remain here with the Hunts, spending little & passing the miserable hours as I can: better here than in England: I shall spend little, occupy myself in literature, take care of my child and even be useful to the Hunts. I have taken with them an unfurnished house in the outskirts of this town, it is large, pleasantly situated, neat & very cheap—my share in the rent is about 30 crowns a year. Can I do better in the present moment than make the resources I have in hand last as long as possible? I hope Sir Timothy will allow me something or at the end of some months my situation will become very disagreable, but I trust that he will; I am sure, my dear Peacock, that you will exert your utmost to induce him;—a maintenance, An Italian Maintenance is all that I require.

111

I must explain to you more fully about this bill. It is for the June & not for the September quarter.[3] In the middle of June I saw a letter of Shelley's to B. & D. [*Brooks & Dixon*] ordering to pay the June quarter into the hands of Guebhard. B. & D. wrote to Guebhard in reply, that they were ready to honour a bill for the amount. Guebhard's answer to this was this very bill drawn July 8th. I believe therefore that this bill is already honoured, since B. & D. say that they have paid the June quarter; but if ⟨it is nece⟩ on the contrary they dishonour it you must learn particularly from them in what form they remitted the June quarter to Shelley. I am convinc[d] from having read his letters, that he never received it, except as this bill of July 8th is paid. His letter to B. & D. asking them to advance his next quarter's annuity had nothing in common with this bill. This request was made only in consequence of our having taken up our abode at Lerici, where it was difficult to get bills remitted to us, and he wished to have ready money in his hands. As I have said, this bill of July 8th, is I doubt not honoured with the funds accrueing from the June quarter; if not, pray let me know very particularly in what form the June quarter was remitted to Shelley, that I may endeavour to fathom this mystery. If all this goes well, as I trust it will, and B. & D. receive in addition the September quarter, I shall get on very well for the present; if it be so, let the money be remitted to me instantly here

You would oblige me by communicating this letter to my father; if your time should be so much taken up that you cannot give sufficient attention to what is indeed life & death to me, I am sure that he will exert himself to be become master of the true state of the affair. Tell him I will write to him very soon, very soon indeed.

I am impatient for the papers I mentioned.[4] If you get all our Mss. from Maddocks let them all be sent to me. I wish particularly also for my two journal books—(one a green covered book & the other a little one bound with red leather). I shall not be easy until I get all the books from Maddocks' hands—& the moment my affairs are at all arranged I shall endeavour to obtain them. M[rs] Williams, the widow of dear, lost Edward, is on her way to England. I have asked her to [*cross-written*] procure several things for me which she will give to the Gisbornes'; add to these the Mss. you have—& some others that I shall ask my father to send you, & making a case for all, send them to me here, forwarding me the bill of lading.

I have written you a letter entirely about business, when I hold a pen in my hand my natural impulse is to express the feelings that overwhelm me; but resisting that impulse I dare not for a moment stray from my subject or I should never find it again. I have written to the Gisbornes twice since that letter which I enclosed to you, they can tell you what the

real current of my mind is.—Alas! find in the whole world so transcen-
dant a being as mine own Shelley—& then tell me to be consoled & it is
not he alone I have lost, though that misery, swallowing up every other,
has hitherto made me forgetful of all others—my best friend, my dear
Edward, whom next to S. I loved—& whose virtues were worthy of the
warmest affection he also is gone—Jane (i.e. Mrs Williams) driven by her
cruel fate to England, has also deserted me,   What have I left? Not one
that can console me—not one that does not shew by comparison how deep
& irremediable my losses are. Trelawny is the only quite disinterested
friend I have here, the only one who clings to the memory of my loved
ones, as I do myself—but he alas! is not as one of them, though he is
really good & kind. Adieu my dear Peacock, be happy with your wife &
child—I hear that the first is deserving of every happiness & the second
a most interesting little creature   I am glad to hear this, desolate as I am
I cling to the idea that some of my friends at least are not like me. Again
adieu

Your attached friend
Mary W. Shelley

ADDRESS: Thomas L. Peacock Esq / India House / London / Inghilterra / Londres.
POSTMARKS: (1) GENOVA; (2) FPO / OC. 12 / 1822. TEXT: MS., Pforzheimer Library.
    1. "Outside the."
    2. Shelley's allowance ceased with his death. Through the intercession of Peacock
and Byron, Mary Shelley was attempting to receive a maintenance from Sir Timothy
Shelley for herself and Percy. On 6 August, in a letter informing Timothy Shelley
of his son's death, Peacock wrote: "He had not insured his life, and his widow and
her infant son are left without any provision" (Peacock, Works, VIII, 229). On 18
October Peacock wrote to Mary Shelley: "Your Father has communicated to you his
opinion that a personal application from Lord Byron's solicitor to Whitton on the
subject of a permanent provision for you and your child will be the most advisable
course" (Peacock, Works, VIII, 232). Shelley had appointed Byron and Peacock as
joint executors of his will.
    3. Peacock's response to Mary Shelley's inquiries about the June quarter are of
particular interest, since he refers to three letters from Mary Shelley two of which
have not been located; the third is Mary Shelley's letter of 15 August to Maria Gisborne. On 2 September Peacock had written: "I write from a cottage in the Chiltern
Hills, in which I am lodging with my wife and child. I shall return to London on
the 16th. Before I left town I received your letter, with the certificate of your little
boy's baptism, with which I did as you requested. I have now received two more
letters from you, the first relating to Guebhard's bill of 220l., the second enclosing
one for Mrs. Gisborne. . . . Brooks and Dixon have already fully explained to me
the state of affairs between them and Shelley. They have paid the whole of his June
quarter, with the exception of 8l., which they have still in hand. The bill of 220l.,
which was drawn on the 8th of July, must be for the September quarter, which he
had requested them, and which they had refused, to advance. I understand it is cus-

113

tomary, in cases of life annuity, to pay the full amount of the quarter in which an annuitant dies; therefore, I presume the quarter's annuity will be paid at Michaelmas; but Brooks and Dixon will not honour the bill unless, or until, they receive the money; and whether they will receive it or not cannot be known till the time arrives. I will do all that I can do in the matter when I return to town. I have been to Marlow, and have seen Maddocks. I am not yet in possession of the papers, but have no doubt that I shall be in about three weeks. I will procure the manuscripts from Ollier. I have the *Defence of Poetry*. Ollier lent it to me, and was to send for it when he wanted it for publication. He did not continue the *Miscellany*, and never applied for the manuscript. I have read your letter to Mrs. Gisborne with deep and painful interest. I forward it by this post. Her address is 33, King Street West, Bryanstone Square" (Peacock, *Works*, VIII, 230–31). In response to Mary Shelley's letter of 29 September, Peacock again saw Brooks and Dixon and found that Guebhard's bill was for the June quarter, that it had been accepted and would be paid by them. For the September quarter, however, it was necessary that application be made to Whitton, and Peacock suggested that Byron's solicitor should intercede (Peacock, *Works*, VIII, 231–32).

4. On 15 April 1823 Peacock sent Mary Shelley all the items she had requested, with the exception of the papers at Marlow (Peacock, *Works*, VIII, 232–34).

❖

To Jane Williams

Genoa   Oct 15th 1822

This letter will find you, dearest Jane, not only arrived in England, but I hope, somewhat reposed from your fatigue and from the agitation of your first arrival. It will find you in the midst of those friends, with whom your & dear Edward's lively descriptions have made me well acquainted. I anxiously wait to hear from you, my best girl, to sympathize in your sorrows, and yet in the mean time to hope the best for you. I know that you are so beloved by all that know you that I trust you find some consolation in your present society. As for me, dreadful as the idea of going to England was to me, I sometimes now think that I should be less miserable there than here; & yet I should not.—I wrote to you, my dear girl, from the Croce di Malta where I remained a week longer & then I removed (that change at least was for the better) to this house; where for another week I enjoyed tranquillity & perfect solitude. Enjoyed, I say; that is, each night was marked by tears & each day by a miserable & intolerable impatience which goaded me almost to madness. At the end of this week Pietro[1] & I began both of us to be somewhat uneasy at the non arrival of any of our friends whom we knew had left Pisa 8 days ⟨ago⟩ before.— Nor was the cause of this delay an agreable one, since Lord Byron had been confined to his bed at Lerici for four days by a rhumatic fever which made him suffer very much. Imagine He & train & the Hunts all at that most horrible place.—Since their arrival my mode of life has changed very litle. The Hunts live in the same house with me & I generally spend the evening with them, & often walk to Genoa with him. I have no cause to complain of either of them—Marianne is sick & goodtempered Motherly & industrious. Hunt taken up chiefly with his own thoughts, yet he has not annoyed me in any way. I hope I have not them; I know that neither of them would be indulgent to me if I did—I think of the life I lead with them and I weep to remember Pugnano. Do you remember him, my best girl, as he scrambled up the hills or listened to your music, do you remember your own Edward, how we used, like children, to play in the great hall or your garden & then sit under the cypresses & hear him read his play?—do you remember your own sweet self—breathing love & shedding happiness around you—nay you weep now—& so do I.— Three dear, beloved beings!—I am deserted by you all—but I must live—dearest, we may not rest.

—Well to the other personages of my uninteresting drama. I see nobody at all—Not even Trelawny—I wished to warn him away from Genoa, but I have only seen him 3 times since his return here. Once for half an hour the day after—once at his lodgings with Hunt—& once he came in the evening here with Gabrielle. I do not lament his absence for myself alone—perhaps not at all on that account; I know indeed that he is the only one in Italy who has a sincere affection for me, perhaps his society might amuse me; but I cannot take the trouble of wishing for any thing, life must run on in its course, I will not as formerly be at the pains of decorating its banks—it runs to its sea of repose—Eternity or the real sea—it is the same thing, & may be as dark & sullen as it will. But I cannot help lamenting the life he leads. He is at the Croce di Malta; Gabrielle sees him every day—generally dines with him there, & what will become of him when W. [*Wright*] comes home?—I have only seen LB. once & that by accident—his rhumatism has left him but has left him as the G— [*Guiccioli*] told me, very bilious, cross & sleepy. He was very complaisant to me however, after having teazed me about my having taken back one or two articles of the furniture I sold him.[2] I have copied for him the 10th Canto of Don Juan[3] It is not in his fine style, but there are some beautiful & many witty things in it—He calls Sir W. Curtis— "The witless Fallstaff of a hoary Hal"—the most severe satire I ever read—what is Fallstaff without his wit but a thing an old play must give a name to—and Hal without his youth but an unpardonable rake.—I have seen the G—i twice. This then is the whole history of my acquain-

tance & my life consequently would be sufficiently monotonous were it
not for the endless change of thought & feeling which varies every hour
of the day. I have chosen this as one of my best days to write to you: for
being yesterday night teazed with the toothach I took a little laudanum
which has quieted also a nervousness which preyed on me for a week,
rendering every action of my life an act of pain. I rise about eight—copy
S's Mss. work or read until 2. Dine and if I do not walk spend the afternoon as I spent the morning—and I pass the evening with the Hunts—
Thus the sun rises & sets, but my days are no longer Italian days, cloudless
& the same—look at your succession of fogs—rain—winds clouds—&
now & then a ray, the memory of better times, to paint a rainbow—and
this is my life.—

The Don Juan was sold—The Captain of the Palute at Via Reggio
made the bargain that her finders shd have a third—the men came to
Roberts to say that they had heard that half had been promised—R. [Rob-
erts] sent them to LB. & LB said they sh^d have half. As Trelawny had given
out at Leghorn that whoever found her sh^d have half I sh^d not have repined
at this; but the men finding so ready an acquiescence to their demand,
made a further one for their expences, which LB. also granted—so they
got more than two thirds & from more than 400 cr. I only got 97.^{4} the
greater part of this (since Trelawny refuses every payment) belongs to you,
dear Jane, & when I hear from you concerning Medwin I will see about
the best way of letting you have it. Trelawny found the whole affair disposed of & finished when he arrived—most of the things were sold—
some however were preserved though I have not yet received them & do
not exactly know what. I have only the Mss. among them Ned's journal
book. Trelawny made no enquiry about your things at Leghorn but as the
journal book is with me I do not know how to send it to you: it is in
excellent preservation nothing but the covers being destroyed. I copy for
you all that he wrote after his departure from Lerici—it is short but as I
cannot tell how to send the whole I am sure you wd like to see it. What,
my dear Jane am I to do about it?—You may be sure that I will seize the
first very safe opportunity of sending it to you—& I will let no one have
it, not even Medwin if he comes.—"Monday July 1st calm & clear; Rose
at four to get the topsails altered. At 12 a fine breeze from the westward
tempted us to weigh for Leghorn; at 2 stretched across to Lerici to pick
up Roberts, & ½ past found ourselves in the offing with a side wind. At
½ 9 arrived at Leghorn. A run of 45 to 50 miles in 7 hours & ½. An-
chored astern of the Bolivar, from whom we procured cushions & made
for ourselves a bed on board, not being able to get ashore after sunset; on
account of health office shutting up at that hour. Teusday, July 2nd Fine

weather. We heard this mg. [*morning*] that the Bolivar was about to sail for Genoa, & that Lord B was quitting Tuscany on account of Count G's [*Gamba's*] family having again been exiled thence. This on reaching the shore, I fo[und] really to be the case for they had just left the Police office, having there received their sentence. Met Lord B. a[t Dunns]⁵ & took leave of him. Was introduced to Mʳ Leigh Hunt & called on Mʳˢ H. shopped & strolled about all day. Met L[t.] Marsham of the Rochfort, an old school fellow & shipmate.—Wednesday. July 3ʳᵈ Fine. Strong sea breeze. called on Degough & reᵈ from him 220 crowns 3 p. 5 for a bill on Harvey for £50. drew on H for £25 more—on Paxtons for £50 and on Allat for £35. Wrote to each this day. Thursday—July 4ᵗʰ Fine. Processions of priests & religisi have for several days past been active in their prayers for rain—but the Gods are either angry or nature is too powerful."—And this, dear Jane, is all.

The Don Juan was found her topsails down and her other sails fast. Trelawny tells me that in his, Roberts & every other sailor's opinion that she was <u>run down</u>; of course by that Fishing boat—which confessed to have seen them. When I see Roberts I shall talk to him on this subject & tell you all he says—for I know that however painful you will wish to hear all. It may add a most bitter pang to know that they might have been saved—but so many circumstances have concurred to rob us of all we loved, that we can hardly put our finger on one solitary one & say that was it—a feather might have checked the progress of the chain—formed, no giant could break it.

As probably sometime will elapse before you can send me the things I asked for, will you in your next letter send me a drawing or description of Shelley's crest—a drawing it must be as I want to get it cut here on a stone I have: but it must be done by one who understands heraldy—it may be as small as possible, but pray send it in your next letter.

My little Percy is quite well and good—How are your children—how are you write often my dear Jane. I would not that the chain that binds us shᵈ be snapped We may draw closer one day—soon perhaps—may we not?—Claire left Pisa on the monday she mentioned—T. [*Trelawny*] consequently did not see her. I have had a letter from her brother. Madᵐᵉ Hennikstein⁶ is to receive her at her home. Gabrielle says that both Madᵐᵉ H & Madᵐᵉ Schwalb (the lady who wᵈ have received her if Madᵐᵉ H. had not) are friends of hers, highly respectable people.—Good night—God bless my sorrowing Jane—I will add another word before I close my letter. Do you sleep now? it is 11 o'clock.

I have received my desk⁷—with several letters in it from me to mine own S. when he left me at Marlow to go to London for a few days—they are full of William—Clara & Allegra—I was in another world while I read them—when I had done even my Percy seemed a dream—for they were here—warm & living as he—& I am still here but they are not—My diamond cross was there too—the pledge of his safety who is no longer safe. The desk had been sent to LB. He read the letters—Ma che vuole che la dico?[8] There were some things a <u>little</u> against him—& others in praise of his writings—there was a lock of my S's hair & one of my Clara's—There is a fearful agony in that name for me—she was like him—But long, long ago I was destined to be the most miserable of living beings   Percy w^d go too, only then I sh^d no longer be chained to time but sh^d depart[9]—without self violence (which I wd never use)   I know that I sh^d then die. I have assurance of that and it renders me very tranquil sometimes in the midst of despair.—I have written to Miss Curran & I hope you will hear from her—Adieu, dear Jane—Affectionately Y^s Mary W. Shelley

ADDRESS: Mrs. Williams / Mrs. Cleveland / 24 Alsop's Buildings / New Road—Marybone / Inghilterra—London. POSTMARKS: (1) GENOVA; (2) FPO / OC. 29 / 1822; (3) 12 o'Clock / OC. 29 / 1822 Nn. TEXT: MS., Pforzheimer Library.

1. Pietro Gamba awaited the Byron party at the Casa Saluzzo.
2. For discussion of items Byron bought from Mary Shelley and Jane Williams, see Moore, *Accounts Rendered*, pp. 350–51, 495–97; Byron, *Works*, VI, 119–20.
3. On 9 October Byron wrote to Murray that Canto 10 was finished but not yet transcribed and Canto 11 was begun. By 24 October both cantos had been transcribed. Byron paid Mary Shelley to make copies of his work (Byron, *Works*, VI, 121, 130; Marchand, *Byron*, III, 1042).
4. Also retrieved from the *Don Juan* were "ninety and odd crowns" that Shelley was taking to Casa Magni. This sum also was turned over to Mary Shelley (Byron, *Works*, VI, 119).
5. From printed text of Williams, *Journals and Letters*.
6. Jeannette de Henickstein, whom Claire Clairmont had known in Pisa, became her good friend in Vienna (*CC Journals*, pp. 293, 359).
7. On 7 October (*MWS Journal*).
8. "But what can I say?"
9. Variant of *Adonais* 26. 9.

To Lord Byron

[Genoa]   Monday   [21 October 1822]

My dear Lord Byron

The letters that I received today were from Jane, Claire, & Mrs Gisborne,[1] nothing about <u>business</u> in any of them; indeed I do not expect to hear from my father before the expiration of a week. Mrs Gisborne saw him; she says—"I saw him alone, we spoke of you & of the ever to be lamented catastrophe without any expression or outward sign of sorrow. I thought that he had erred in his memorable assertion & that we human beings really were 'stocks & stones.' When Peacock called upon me, a tear did force itself into my eye in spite of all my struggles."

—But I do not write to your Lordship to tell you this, but to mention another subject in her letter. She says—"When Mr Gisborne went to Harrow, to accompany a son of Mr Clementi's who is placed in the Harrow school, he saw the grave of poor Allegra. This was precisely the day your father called on me, the funeral had taken place the day preceding. There was a great outcry among the Ultra priests on the occasion, and at the time they seemed resolved that the inscription intended by her father, should not be placed in the church. These Gentlemen would willingly cast an eternal veil over King David's infirmities & their own, but the world will peep through, even though poor Allegra should be without the honours of her inscription."[2]

Would you tell me the Book, Chapter & verse of this ⟨inscription⟩ quotation for the Epitaph.

I send you Lordship two letters from Hunt—he says that—"there appears some mistake about the Preface to the "Vision," but he hopes the realizations on the 7,000 will compensate for all defects."[3]

Jane writes from Paris—She has been very ill, but intends proceeding to England without delay. She desires to be remembered to you & begs me to remind you of your promise of bidding Murray send her your works.

This then is all my news.—Teresa's visit caused me to be out yesterday when you called, otherwise I am always at home at that hour & when you feel inclined to prolong your ride to this house you will be sure to find me.

I have nearly finished copying your savage Canto[4]—You will cause Milman to hang himself—"non c'è altro rimedio"—I was much pleased with your notice of Keats—your fashionable World is delightful—& your dove—you mention eight years—exactly the eight years that comprizes all my years of happiness—Where also is he, who gone has made this quite, quite another earth from that which it was?—There might be something sunny about me ⟨now⟩ then, now I am truly *cold moonshine*.[5]

Adieu, Truly yours
Mary Shelley

Text: MS., John Murray.
    1. Maria Gisborne's letter of 8 October is Italian-postmarked 21 October (Abinger MS.; Gisborne, *Journals and Letters*, pp. 89–93).

2. The result of the objection by the churchwarden and some parishioners was that no tablet or monument was erected in memory of Allegra, who was buried just inside the church door on 10 September 1822 (Marchand, *Byron*, III, 1001). Byron had asked John Murray to have inscribed on a marble tablet: "In memory of / Allegra, / daughter of G. C. Lord Byron, who died at Bagnacavallo, in Italy, April 20th, 1822, / aged five years and three months. / 'I shall go to her, but she shall not return to me.' 2d Samuel, xii. 23" (Byron, *Works*, VI, 70–72).

3. Seven thousand copies of the first issue of the *Liberal* (dated 15 October 1822) were printed. Byron's preface, explaining that *The Vision of Judgment* was aimed at Robert Southey and not at George III, was not published with the poem, because John Murray failed to give it to John Hunt. The preface was printed in the second issue of the *Liberal*, 1 January 1823 (Marshall, *The Liberal*, pp. 53–54, 72–73, 78, 238). On 22 October Byron wrote John Murray an angry letter remonstrating with him for this omission (Byron, *Works*, VI, 126–27).

4. Canto 11 of *Don Juan*.

5. An identification of herself and the "cold chaste moon" of Shelley's poem *Epipsychidion* (line 281). In Mary Shelley's Journal entries of 5 and 10 October 1822 she refers to herself as "moonshine," not in a self-deprecating way but rather as a metaphor for her reflection of Shelley's sunshine and her commitment to "endeavour to consider my self a faint continuation of his being." A pertinent reference to Mary Shelley's seeming coldness appears in Emilia Viviani's letter to her of 24 December 1820: "Tu mi sembri un poco fredda, talvolta, e mi dai qualchè soggezione; ma conosco che tuo Marito disse bene, allorchè disse: che la tua apparente freddezza non è che la cenere che ricuopre un cuore affettuoso" (*S&M*, III, 559) ("You seem to me a little cold sometimes, and that causes me an uncomfortable feeling; but I know that your husband said well when he said that your apparent coldness is only *the ash which covers an affectionate heart*" [White, *Shelley*, II, 476]). The accusation of coldness troubled Mary Shelley throughout her life (see, for example, *MWS Journal*, 11 November 1822).

To Maria Gisborne

Albaro.   Nov. 6th 1822

This, my dear Friend, will I believe only be an excuse for a letter; I have determined to write every day since I received yours, but yet I have never been able to prevail on myself so to do—First I have been occupied by writing an article for the Liberal[1]—& then I have been out of spirits—out of all desire to exert myself—I write now more for business than aught else—

I have not heard of Jane's arrival in England & am very anxious—I fear she is ill—for she wrote from Paris as if she were ill—I have heard from Miss Curran who is at Paris—My own Shelley's picture is at Rome, so nothing can be done about that. As soon as Jane writes to me—I shall see about her getting the money for my other commissions—and then pray send the things I asked for as quickly as possible.

Peacock says that he has got Shelleys—"Defence of Poetry." I wish him to send it to Mr John Hunt at the Examiner office[2]—Will you let him know that.

I am well—but very nervous—My poor child is quite well—My excessive nervousness (how new a disorder for me—my illness in the summer is the foundation of it) is the cause I do not write—& even now that I do I am in a state of excessive irritation. Well forgive me—I will seize my first best moment to scribble to better purpose than this scrawl—let me have long & frequent letters from you I pray.

I asked Jane to get for me, but if she be not arrived pray do you get & send in your next letter, a drawing of Shelley's crest that I may get it engraved on a seal—do not confound the two baronatages Sir John & Sir Timothy—pray do this as it will be very easy to get a book with the Baronatage—the crest is all I want—but let it be well drawn that the people here may understand it—

I live as comfortably as I can—I do not wish for any change—except that I do not like Genoa ma pocca mi cale[3]—I am so thankful to Lord B. that he prevented my journey to England   how miserable I should have been there—We have here the most divine Italian skies—having first had a meteora cioè a rovina d'Acqua[4]—that forced all the torrents from their beds & did infinite guasto near us—but we are at the top of the {h}ill & so did not suffer. Houses were thrown down & many walls—which is good—for the type of Genoa is a lane 10 feet wide between 2 stone walls each 20 feet hig[h][5] There is one pretty walk—Mrs Hunt is not I h[ope][6] worse than the season renders reasonable that she should be[7]—

This as I said is only an excuse for a letter—I write principally that Mr John Hunt may get the defence of poetry & that you may hear that I am well—so adieu—If I could get over the intense hatred I feel to every thing I think, do, or see I might get on—but day after day I long only more & more to go where all I love are save my poor boy who chains me here—

Adieu

Affectionately yours,
Mary W. Shelley

Will you add to the things sent out to me a bottle of lavender water?

ADDRESS: Mrs. Gisborne / 33 Kings Street West / Bryanstone Square / Inghilterra, London. POSTMARKS: (1) GENOVA; (2) FPO / NO. 23 / 1822; (3) 12 o'Clock / No.

121

23 / 1822 Nn. ENDORSED: Recd. 23rd Nov. 1822 Ans. TEXT: MS., Bodleian Library.

1. On 10 November Mary Shelley recorded in her Journal: "I have made my first probation in writing & it has done me great good, & I get more calm." Mary Shelley's contribution to the second number of the *Liberal* was "A Tale of the Passions," a short story that, according to Elizabeth Nitchie, bears an endorsement of Shelley's and thus must have been written prior to Shelley's death (Nitchie, *Mary Shelley*, p. 156). On 5 December Mary Shelley informed Jane Williams that she had written "an Article (a Tale)" for the next *Liberal*. The location of the manuscript of "A Tale of the Passions" is presently unknown.

2: By 22 November Mary Shelley had received word that Peacock had given John Hunt the manuscript of *A Defence of Poetry* for inclusion in the second issue of the *Liberal*. It remains unclear why it was not included in that issue or in either of the final two issues (Marshall, *The Liberal*, pp. 141–42).

3. "But it doesn't matter much to me."

4. "Meteor, that is, a heavy downpour."

5. Taken from John Gisborne Notebook No. 4, Abinger MSS., Bodleian Library.

6. See n. 5.

7. Marianne Hunt was severely ill when she arrived in Italy. Vaccà, who was consulted immediately after the Hunts arrived at Pisa, misjudged her condition as hopeless (*PBS Letters*, #720).

To Lord Byron

[Albaro]   Saturday.   [?14 December 1822][1]

Your Lordships MS. was very difficult to decypher, so pardon blunders & omissions

I like your Canto extremely; it has only touches of your highest style of poetry, but it is very amusing & delightful. It is a comfort to get anything to gild the dark clouds now my sun is set.—Sometimes when very melancholy I repeat your lyric in "The Deformed", & that for a while enlivens me:—But—

But I will not scrawl nonsense to you

Adieu   Yours   MaryS.

ADDRESS: To the Rt Honble / Lord Byron. TEXT: MS., John Murray.

1. By 24 October Mary Shelley had copied Canto 11. She copied Canto 12 between 7 and 14 December, and Cantos 13 through 16, as well as further scenes from *The Deformed Transformed*, before 21 May 1823 (Steffan, *Byron's Don Juan*, I, 307–9). This letter is placed at its earliest possible date.

To Edward John Trelawny

Albaro.   Jan. 7ᵗʰ [1823]

A letter, my dear Trelawny, from this solitary & wind striken hill of Albaro—may well appear to you a letter from the dead to the living. And shut out as I am from all communication with life I feel as if a letter from you would be to me a token sent from a world of flesh & blood to one of shadow. Here I am just as you left me—the wind whistling, & myself as comfortless as then. Forgotten by every body I cannot forget them & much less you—since the scenes that are ever present to my memory are those in which you bore a principal part, & cold as my heart is it warms then with gratitude—What should we, poor Jane & I, wild & desolate as we were, have done without you. We saw sorrow in other faces but we found help only from you.

I would not make you sorrowful by recalling those heavy hours but I have nothing so near my heart—and when I write that subject seems by right to tyrannize over my pen & to force me to write concerning it. I will conclude all allusion to it however by mentioning that soon after your departure Hunt had a letter from Mᵣ Brown[1] at Pisa telling him that he had received a letter from Mᵣ Severn (Keats' friend) at Rome who said that he was about to fulfill the last scene of misery for me by—by doing that which was to be done for me in that city—You understand me—so all the difficulties seem to be surmounted though I anxiously wait for the letter which will say that all is done.

What are you doing? And does the wind blow as bleakly & is the weather as cruelly sharp with you as with us? I can go no where & have not been to Genoa once since you left us. The only thing that could take me there, would be my desire to call on Mᵣˢ Thomas[2] to learn news of you (if she is more lucky than I in having heard from you) & of G.W. [*Gabrielle Wright*] & the first day that the sun shines I shall certainly go. I hate this place more than ever and shall be delighted to get away—for indeed I shall be wretched until then but I must stay with Marianne for some months,[3] & besides Sir T. Shelley has declined giving any answer to the application made to him for an allowance for me. LB. is now writing to him directly for a decisive answer—until that is decided I must be very economical, although as yet my money is far from being expended, & I expect to receive some also from the Liberal

I do not mention any thing of Claire's affairs since she says in a letter

123

I received from her yesterday that she has written to you directed to the Post office of Leghorn. I have not heard from Jane. And the only news I have is that the 2ⁿᵈ number of the Liberal was published the 1ˢᵗ of this month & promises to be a good number. There is in it the "Heaven & Earth" of LB. Shelley's Defence of Poetry—2 articles by Hazlitt 1 by Hogg—1 of mine &c⁴—Will you have the kindness to lend your copy of the 1ˢᵗ number to Mʳˢ Mason⁵—if you direct it to her Casa Silva, Pisa, Dunn can send it—& I promise you that it will be speedily & safely returned.

Just this time last year, my dear Friend, you left Genoa to find us happy & enjoying all the goods of life at Pisa. You found two who have now deserted us—You found me, so full of spirits & life that methinks when you first saw me you must have thought me even a little wild—now all is changed & surely he who is now beside my beloved boy at Rome is n[ot] more altered than I. I desire only solitude—I live only [   ] sorrow & my imagination then so fond of sharring with [   ] the shores of the sweet waters of life now only dwells under funereal shades— unless it peep beyond them to something that will be when I am not here. But may you long enjoy that delight which the stirring of one's warm blood—& the sense of life & the emotions of love may & do bestow— You deserve every happiness & I trust that {   } do enjoy a part at least

Adieu—trust to the feelings of gratitude & affection with which I am yours & when you are too melancholy to do any thing else write to

Mary Shelley

I have received a letter from Jane—she is well & enquires kindly after you—She is in low spirits & longs for Italy.

ADDRESS: Edward Trelawny Esq. / Presso al Signor Dunn / Via Grande / Livorno. POSTMARKS: (1) GENOVA; (2) 10 GENNAIO. TEXT: MS., Bodleian Library.

1. Charles Armitage Brown (1787–1842) was a friend of Hunt, Joseph Severn, and Keats. He arrived in Pisa at the end of August 1822, and he met Byron through Hunt. His correspondence with Severn indicates that he played an intermediary role between Mary Shelley and Severn in the arrangement of Shelley's funeral. In Brown's letter of 23 September 1822 to Severn he wrote: "I will also mention your offer concerning Shelley's grave" (Brown, Letters, pp. 102–6, 111, 119–20).

2. It is quite likely that Mary Shelley met Mrs. Thomas through John Taaffe, who had asked Shelley to read Mrs. Thomas's verses in 1821—Shelley called them "insufferable trash" (PBS Letters, #600). Mrs. Thomas tended to several commissions on Mary Shelley's behalf, and Mary Shelley gave her copies of the Liberal and an autographed copy of Frankenstein that contains corrections and additions for a second edition (Cline, Pisan Circle, pp. 22, 226). On the title page of her copy of Frankenstein Mrs. Thomas wrote: "My Acquaintance with this very interesting Person—arose from her being introduced to Me under Circumstances of so Melancholy a Nature

(which attended her Widowhood)—that it was impossible to refuse the Aid Asked of me—I gave her All I could and Passed Many delightful hours with her at Albaro—She left Genoa in a few Months for England   I called on her in London in 1824—but as My friends disliked her Circle of Friends—and Mrs Shelley was then No longer in a Foreign Country helpless, Pennyless, and broken hearted—I Never Returned Again to her but I preserve this Booke and her Autograph Notes to me—as at some future day they will be literary Curiosities—" (Pierpont Morgan Library).

On 4 October 1823 Marianne Hunt wrote a letter to Mary Shelley complaining about Mrs. Thomas: "Mrs Thomas has sent for your direction   I paid her as you desired or at least she paid herself for she stopt 6 or 7 crowns for freight of boxes &c out of what Mr Saunders was to send us I mention it that you may know how to deal with such a lady and if it may please you to unite voices—She has done for herself in Mr Hunt's good graces I dont know if that was the cause or no" (MS., Bodleian Library).

3. Mary Shelley had promised to stay with Marianne Hunt through her confinement with her seventh child, expected in June.

4. The second issue of the *Liberal*, published on 1 January 1823, included Byron's "Heaven and Earth"; Hazlitt's "On the Spirit of Monarchy" and "On the Scotch Character"; Hogg's "Longus"; and Mary Shelley's "A Tale of the Passions." For *A Defence of Poetry*, see 6 November 1822; and Marshall, *The Liberal*, pp. 135–63.

5. On 14 January Mrs. Mason wrote to Mary Shelley: "No letter from Mrs G [*Godwin*]—I suppose she waits to tell me that the Novel [*Valperga*] is out—I shall be very anxious to hear of its success—Have you begun another? Or does the Liberal prevent you from thinking of any other occupation? Mr. T— does not obey your orders about the first number—pray remind him of it—I will return it safe & speedily you may be sure" (Abinger MS.).

❧

To Lord Byron

Albaro   Teusday— [25 February 1823]¹

My dear Lord Byron

I am indeed at a loss to conceive of what is at present to be done; there is no law to help me, & certainly no feeling that can be of service to me with a man who could make that insolent & hardhearted proposition about my poor boy.—That did a little overcome my philosophy. If the persecuted Liberal² still continues that may in some degree prevent my burthening any one in my present evil fortune—if not some other means may be thought of. Perhaps if I were in England he might be shamed into doing something, but the difficulty of getting there, & the dearness of living when arrived, would I think destroy all good that could accrue from such a journey; though doubtless my being in Italy does my cause no good.

125

I sent a copy of the letter last night to my father that I might as soon as possible have his opinion & advice upon it. Your Lordship's also would of course be gratifying to me—but I fancy that you feel as I do, that the affair is hopeless.

I have been expecting Don Juan but I fear your Lordship's illness has been the cause of its delay[3]—perhaps this fine weather will cure you—

Very truly Yours

Mary Shelley

ADDRESS: To the Rt Honble / Lord Byron. TEXT: MS., John Murray.

1. On 24 February Byron sent Mary Shelley Sir Timothy Shelley's letter stating his refusal to aid her and his willingness to maintain Percy only if she gave up custody of him (Byron MS., Pierpont Morgan Library). That day she wrote in her Journal: "But today melancholy would invade me—& I thought the peace I enjoyed (such a word indeed does not befit) me) was transient—and that fate which has so re-lent[l]essly brought me to this lowest pitch of fortune, would not permit me to es-tablish myself in my airy height, but make me feel my mortality in every trembling nerve. Then that letter came to place its seal on on my prognostications—Yet it was not the refusal or the insult heaped on me that stung me to tears—it was their bitter words about our boy—Why I live only to keep him from their hands—How dared they dream that I held him not—far more precious than all save the hope of again seeing you—my lost one—but for his smiles—where should I now be?—"

On 14–18 February Godwin wrote Mary Shelley that he had received a copy of Sir Timothy Shelley's response to Byron (Abinger MS.). Godwin's letter is Italian-postmarked "3 Marzo." Mary Shelley's mention in this letter of sending her father "a copy of the letter last night" is in reference to a letter that would have been written on the Tuesday before she received Godwin's letter.

2. John Hunt, as publisher of the *Liberal*, had been indicted in December 1822 for printing Byron's *The Vision of Judgment*, which the Constitutional Association claimed to be a vilification of the memory of George III. News of the indictment reached Genoa on 23 December, and Byron arranged for legal counsel to defend Hunt and also offered to return to England himself if that would help. John Hunt was brought to trial and found guilty on 15 January. On 19 June 1824 he was sentenced to pay a fine of £100, considered by the *Examiner* as a kind of victory in that it did "not bear any proportion to the pretended flagrancy of the offence" (Marshall, *The Liberal*, pp. 126–31, 205–9).

3. Byron's letter of 24 February refers to his being ill for three days. Truman Guy Steffan infers that Mary Shelley had by this time copied Canto 13, written by Byron between 12 and 19 February (*Byron's Don Juan*, I, 308).

To Lord Byron

Albaro   Sunday   [30 March 1823][1]

My dear Lord Byron

The 15th Canto was so long coming even after I had heard that it was finished, that I began to suspect that you thought that you were annoying me by sending me employment. Be assured however on the contrary, that besides the pleasure it gives me to be in the slightest manner useful to your Lordship, the task itself is a delightful one to me.

Is Aurora a portrait?[2] ⟨She is⟩ Poor Juan I long to know how he gets out or rather into the net. Are the other Cantos to be published soon?

I have had no letters. I wait with no pleasant expectation for the result of my father's deliberations—it little matters which way he decides for either to go or stay are equally disagreable to me in the situation I now am. But the present state of things cannot & shall not last, though I see but dimly what is to come in lieu of it. I think it will be England after all—that will be best for my boys health & perhaps the least unexceptionable part for me to take.

I hope this fine weather has cured all your incommodi

Truly Yours obliged
Mary Shelley

Will you lend me those verses on Lady B. that Hunt had a few weeks ago[3]

ADDRESS: To the Right Honble / Lord Byron. TEXT: MS., John Murray.
   1. Mary Shelley's references to Canto 15 suggest that this letter was written on 30 March. Byron completed Canto 15 on 25 March (Steffan, *Byron's Don Juan*, I, 319).
   2. Aurora Raby, *Don Juan* 15. 43.
   3. Possibly "The Charity Ball."

To Maria Gisborne

May 3rd (May 6th)   Albaro   [1823]

My dear M[rs] Gisborne

Your letter[1] was very pleasing to me since it shewed me, that it was not want of affection that caused your silence: Utter solitude is delightful to me, but in the midst of the waste, I am much comforted when I hear the quiet voice of friendship telling me that I am still loved by some one,

& especially by those who knew my Shelley and have been his companions. You do well to say that it is an <u>almost</u> insurmountable difficulty in expressing your thoughts that causes you to be silent. For though occupation or indolence may often prevent your exerting yourself, yet when you do write, yours are the best letters I receive, especially as far as clearness & information goes.

I had a letter today from Trelawny at Rome concerning the disposition of the earthly dress of my lost one. He is in the Protestant burying ground at that place, which is beside, & not before, the tomb of Cestius. The old wall with an Ancient tower bounds it on one side & beneath this tower, a weed grown & picturesque ruin, the excavation has been made. T—y has sent me a drawing of it—& he thus writes,—"is placed apart, yet in the centre, & the most conspicuous spot in the burying Ground. I have just planted six young cypresses & 4 laurels, in the front of the recess, which you see in the drawing, which is caused by the projecting part of the old ruin. My own stone"—(T—y you know, one of the best & most generous of creatures, is eccentric in his way) "a plain slab, till I can decide upon some fitting inscription, is placed on the left hand—I have likewise dug my grave—so that when I die, there is only to lift up the coverlet, & roll me into it—You may lay on the other side, or I will share my narrow bed with you, if you like. It is a lovely spot. The only inscription on S. stone, besides the cor cordium of Hunt, are three lines I have added, from Shakespeare

> —"Nothing of him that doth <u>fade</u>,
> But doth suffer a sea-change
> Into something <u>rich</u> & <u>strange</u>

"This quotation by its double meaning alludes both to the manner of his d—h & his genius. And I think the element on which his soul took wing, & the subtle essence of his being mingled, may still retain him in some other shape. The water may keep the dead, as the earth may, & fire, & air. His passionate fondness might have arisen from some sweet sympathy in his nature; thence the fascination which so forcibly attracted him, without fear or caution to trust an element, which almost all others hold in superstitious dread, & venture as cautiously on as they would in a lair of Lions"—

This quotation is pleasing to me also, because a year ago, T—y came one afternoon in high spirits with news concerning the building of the boat—saying—oh—we must all embark—all live aboard—"We will all suffer a sea-change," and dearest Shelley was delighted with the quotation—saying that he w^d have it for the motto of his boat—Try—says in another part of his letter, "I have been digging & planting myself—there are 7 or 8 cypresses & as many laurels, about the tomb or rather I should say tombs, for I have completed one for myself & yesterday laid it down on the left of S. as they both stand on a very steep bank, I thought it necessary to put additional security to prevent their being moved, either by rain or otherwise—every thing is now most satisfactorily arranged."

Captain Roberts (Jane will tell you who he is) is just come from Rome. He confirms all that is said in this letter. Tell Jane I passed yesterday evening with him & talked a great deal of her & dearest Edward. I was pleased by the enthusiasm with which he spoke—He declared that he had never met a man to be compared him—in Nobleness & amiability of Nature—together with a nameless charm that pervaded all his converse. Roberts had bought the hulk of that miserable boat—new rigged her—even with higher Masts than before—he has sailed with her at the rate of 8 knots an hour—& on such occasions tried various experiments, hazardous ones, to discover how the catastrophe that closed the scene for us two poor creatures happened. It is plain to every eye. She was run down from behind. On bringing her up from 15 fathom all was in her—books, telescope ballast, lying on each side of the boat without any appearance of shifting or confusion—the topsails furled—topmasts lowered—the false stern (Jane can explain) broken to pieces & a great hole knocked in the stern timbers. When she was brought to Leghorn every one went to see her—& the same exclamation was uttered by all—She was run down. by that wretched fishing boat which owned that it had seen them.[2]

I have written myself into a state of agitation—if I continued my letter it would only be to pour out the bitterness of my heart. Oh this spring is so beautiful the clear sky shines above the calm murderer—the trees are all in leaf & a soft air is among them—The stars tell of other spheres where I pray to be—for all this beauty while at times it elevates me—yet in stronger words tells me—that he, the best & most beautiful is gone

> Oh follow! follow!—
> And on each herb, from which heavens dew had fallen
> The like was stamped, as with a with a withering fire,
> —And then
> Low, sweet, faint sounds, like the farewel of ghosts
> Were heard: oh, follow, follow, follow me.[3]

I will finish my letter Monday—God bless you: good night. I often see him—both he & dear Edward in dreams—perhaps I shall tonight—at least I shall not be in sleep as I am now—the clinging present is so odious—

(May 6th) I finish my letter. You will soon see me in England. It is not my own desire, or for my own advantage that I go—but for my boy's—So I am fixed—and enjoy these blue skies & the sight of vines & olive groves for the last time. I hope indeed to return—all my hopes are set upon that but that is in case I get richer one day—if not I trust I return for my repose. I am sorry to hear the melancholy account you give of your situation & am truly sorry that Henry does {not} gain the success that his talents deserve. I wait here to see Mrs Hunt safe through her confinement—In her critical situation among strangers & not speaking a word of Italian—without an English servant (the one she brought over has made a scapatura)   Hunt speaking badly—& this vile Genoese destroying that little, my presence is necessary at least to keep up her spirits. That passed, the fear of the advancing season will make me begin my journey as quickly as possible. I should in any case have feared an Italian summer for my delicate child—the climate of England will agree with him. LB. is very kind to me, & promises that I shall make my journey at my ease, which on Percy's account, I am glad of. He is much improved poor boy—& cannot speak a word of English—Remember me to Mr G [Gisborne] & Henry

Did the End of Beatrice[4] surprise you. I am surprised that none of these Literary Gazettes are shocked—I feared that they would stumble over a part of what I read to you & still more over my Anathema.[5] I wish much to see it—as my father has made some curtailments—but the vessel has not yet arrived. Is not the catastrophe strangely prophetic[6]   But it seems to me that in what I have hitherto written I have done nothing but prophecy what has arrived to. Matilda[7] fortells even many small circumstances most truly—& the whole of it is a monument of what now is—

Adieu, My dear Friend—Give my very tenderest love to Jane when you see her

Affectionately Yours,
Mary W. Shelley

ADDRESS: Mrs. Gisborne / 33 Kings St. West, / Bryanstone Square / London / Inghilterra / Londres. POSTMARKS: (1) GENOVA; (2) FPO / MY. 20 / 1823; (3) 12 NOON 12 / MY. 20 / 1823. TEXT: MS., Bodleian Library.

1. Dated 17 March 1823 (Gisborne, *Journals and Letters*, pp. 93–98).
2. See 15 August 1822.
3. *Prometheus Unbound* 2. 1. 153–55, 157–59.
4. *Valperga*, vol. 3, chap. 7.
5. *Valperga*, vol. 3, chap. 3, in which Beatrice curses the "author of her being."
6. Euthanasia, the heroine of Mary Shelley's *Valperga*, drowns at sea.
7. See 15 August 1822.

To Jane Williams

My very dear Jane

   I have delayed writing both to you and my father a long time, hoping
that I might mention the date of my departure in my letters. But I wait
in vain, and things have taken so strange a turn, and the delay is so much
greater than I expected that I find at last I must write while still in a state
of uncertainty. I write to you in preference to my father, because you to
a great degree understand the person I have to deal with, & in communicating what I say concerning him, you can viva voce add such comments, as will render my relation more intelligible

   The day after Mariannes confinement, (the 9th of June)[1] seeing all went
so prosperously, I told LB. that I was ready to go, & he promised to provide means. When I talked of going post, it was because he said that I
should go so, at the same declaring that he would regulate all himself. I
waited in vain for these arrangements—But not to make a long story,
since I hope soon to be able to relate the details, he chose to transact our
negotiation through Hunt; and gave such an air of unwillingness & sense
of the obligation he conferred, as at last provoked H. to say that there
was no obligation, since he owed me a £1000[2]—"Glad of a quarrel
straight I clap the door!—"[3] still keeping up an appearance of amity with
H. he has written notes & letters—so full of contempt against me & my
lost Shelley that I could stand it no longer, and have refused to receive
his still proffered aid for my journey[4]—This of course delays me I can
muster about £30[5] of my own; I do not know whether this is barely sufficient, but as the delicate constitution of my child may oblige me to rest
several times on the journey, I cannot persuade myself to commence my
journey with what is barely necessary, I have written therefore to Trelawny
for the sum requisite, and must wait till I hear from him.

   I see you, my poor girl, sigh over these my mischances—but never
mind; I do not feel them. My life is a shifting scene, & my business is to
play the part alotted for each day well—& not liking to think of tomorrow, I never think of it at all—except in an intellectual way—and as to
money difficulties—why having nothing, I can lose nothing. Thus as far
as regards what are commonly called worldly concerns, I am perfectly
tranquil, & as free or freer from care as if my signature should be able to
draw £1,000 from some banker;—⟨I want for⟩ The Extravagance & anger

of LB's letters also relieves me from all pain that his deriliction might occasion me. And that his conscience twinges him is too visible from his impatient kicks & unmannerly curvets—You w^d laugh at his last letter to H— where he says concerning his connection with Shelley that "he let himself down to the level of the democrats."

In the mean time Hunt is all kindness, consideration and friendship— all feeling of alienation towards me has disappeared even to its last dreg— He perfectly approves of what I have done. So I am still in Italy—And I doubt not that it is its sun, & vivifying geniality that relieves me from those biting cares which would be mine in England, I fear, if I were destitute there. But I feel above the mark of fortune and my heart, too much wounded to feel these pricks, on all occasions that does not regard its affections "s'arma di se, e d'intero diamante"[6]—thus am I changed—too late alas! for what ought to have been, but not too late, I trust, to enable me, more than before, to be some stay & consolation {to} you, my own dear Jane.

I very much wished not {to} have been in a crow[d   ] these melancholy days—now that the year is fulfill[ed] every hour & feeling reminds me of what is ever & for ever before me. How quickly this year has past—methinks it was but yesterday we parted—but why should I renew in you thoughts that must eat into your soul, & haunt you through every recess of your mind. I live in that world & in those scenes, & thus the present & its capricious changes appear dreams not worthy my attention.—One only thing afflicts me—to leave Italy—& if I could in any way dispose of my writings without being in England, I w^d remain here, but that cannot be.

I have not heard from Claire a long time—& have not written to her from the same causes that has prevented my writing to you. Will you let my father know what I have said of my affairs, & explain to him at the same time the primum mobile of LB actions—Meaness—the Greek Expedition will not blind you—thus he walks off triumphantly from these shores with his untouched thousands, and he has already p{r}e-pared many designs for their safe anabasis from their Greek journey— the Reatreat of his 9,000 will be worthy of the pen of another Zeno-phon.[7] I have already sent packages by sea.—2 cases with books & one box of clothes—they go by the Jane—Captain Whitney, & are directed to my father's house.

God bless you, my best girl. I shall set out the moment I hear from Trelawny, so somewhat poorer in cash—but rich to overflow in all the many feelings—sorrow—love & futurity that make my world, I shall embrace you & give you all the comfort [*p. 1, top*] that you can receive from

Your affectionate friend
Mary Shelley

I should come by sea if Hunt w^d let me

ADDRESS: Mrs Williams / Mrs Cleveland / 24 Alsop's Buildings / New Road / London / Londres / Inghilterra. POSTMARKS: (1) GENOVA; (2) FPO / JY. 15 / 1823; (3) 12 NOON 12 / JY. 15 / 1823. TEXT: MS., Abinger MSS., Bodleian Library.

1. With the Hunts' seventh child, Vincent Leigh Hunt.

2. Edward Williams recorded in his *Journals* for 25 December 1821: "It was on this day that Lord B. and S. proposed to give a thousand pounds to the other who first came to their estate" (p. 119). Hunt's claim of the debt owing was the result of the death of Lady Noel on 22 January 1822.

3. Pope, *Epistle to Dr. Arbuthnot*, line 67.

4. Marchand (*Byron*, III, 1085–86) and Moore (*The Late Lord Byron*, pp. 404–22) recount details of the quarrel. Moore places the responsibility for the quarrel with Hunt and contends that Hunt secretly appropriated for his own use a provision of £30 made by Byron for Mary Shelley.

5. Trelawny and Mrs. Mason gave Mary Shelley funds (Trelawny, *Letters*, pp. 67–68; McAleer, *The Sensitive Plant*, p. 182). On 1 July Hunt informed Byron that "under certain circumstances" Mary Shelley would ask Trelawny for the money and that she "is not aware of my saying a word to you on this point" (Moore, *The Late Lord Byron*, p. 441).

6. Unidentified.

7. Xenophon (c. 430–after 355 B.C.), Greek historian, whose *Anabasis* records the story of the ten thousand Greek troops who, deserted by their commanders in Persia, made their way safely back to Greece after a five-month march.

To Jane Williams

Albaro   July 23rd [1823]

Dearest Jane

I have at length fixed with the Vetturino;[1] I depart on the 25th My best girl, I leave Italy—I return to the dreariest reality after having dreamt away a year in this blessed and beloved country.

Lord Byron, Trelawny Pierino Gamba &c sailed for Greece on the 17th Ult. I did not see the former. His unconquerable avarice prevented his supplying me with money, & a remnant of shame caused him to avoid me. But I have a world of things to tell you on that score when I see you. If he were mean T—y [*Trelawny*] more than balanced the moral account.

His whole conduct during his last short stay here has impressed us all with an affectionate regard and a perfect faith in the unalterable goodness of his heart. They sailed together: LB with £10,000 Ty with £50—and LB cowering before his eye for reasons you shall hear soon. The Guiccioli is gone to Bologna—e poi cosa fara? Chi lo sa? Cosa vuol che la dico?[2] He talks seriously of returning to her, and may if he finds none of equal rank to be got as cheaply—She cost him nothing & was thus invaluable.

I travel without a servant. I rest first at Lyons. But do you write to me at Paris. Hotel Nelson—it will be a friend to await me—Alas! I have need of consolation—Hunt's kindness is now as active & warm as it was dormant before; but just as I find a companion in him I leave him. I lea[ve] him in all his difficulties, with his head throbbing with over-wrought thought, & his frame sometimes sinking under his anxieties. Poor Marianne has found good medecine, facendo un bimbo,[3] & then nursing it, but she with her female providence is more beset by care than Hunt. How much I wished & wish to settle near them at Florence—but I must submit with courage and patience may at last come and give opiate to my irritable feelings.

Both Hunt and Trelawny say that Percy is much improved since Maria[4] left me. He is affectionately attached to Silvan[5] & very fond of il Bimbo nuovo, kisses him by the hour & tells me come il Signor Enrico ha com-prato un Baby nuovo a Genova forse ti dara il Baby Vecchio,[6] as he gives away an old toy on the appearance of a new one.

I will not write longer. In conversation, nay almost in thought, I can at this most painful moment, force my excited feelings to laugh at them-selve and my spirits raised by emotion to seem as if they were light; but the natural current and real hue overflows me & penetrates me when I write—and it w^d be painful to you & overthrow all my hopes of retaining my fortitude if I were to write one word that truly translated the agitation I suffer into language.

I will write again from Lyons where I suppose that I shall be on the 3rd of August—Dear Jane—can I render you happier than you are? The idea of that might console me. At least you will see one who truly loves you & who is for ever Your affectionately attached

MaryShelley

If there is any talk of my accommodations, pray let M^rs G [*Godwin*] un-derstand that I cannot sleep on any but a <u>hard</u> bed—I care not how hard so that it be matresses

ADDRESS: Mrs Williams / Mrs Cleveland / 24 Alsop's Buildings / New Road / Inghil-terra London / Londres. POSTMARKS: (1) GENOVA; (2) FPO / AU. 7 / 1823; (3) 12 NOON 12 / AU. 7 / 1823. TEXT: MS., Pforzheimer Library.

1. See [c. 3] December 1818, n. 2.
2. "And then what will she do? Who knows? What can I say?"
3. "Having a baby."
4. A servant. Mrs. Mason wrote on 24 June of Maria's arrival at Pisa (Abinger MS.).
5. The Hunts' sixth child, [James] Henry Sylvan, was the same age as Percy Florence.
6. "Since Mr. Henry has bought a new Baby at Genoa, maybe he will give you the Old Baby."

To Leigh Hunt

[14 Speldhurst Street   Brunswick Square]
September 9th (Sep. 11th) [1823]

My dear Hunt

Bessy promised me to relieve you from any inquietude you might suffer from not hearing from me, so I indulged myself with not writing to you until I was quietly settled in lodgings of my own. Want of time is not my excuse, I had plenty—but until I saw all quiet around me I had not the spirit to write a line—I thought of you all—how much! and often longed to write, yet would not till I called myself free. To turn Southward; to imagine you all, to put myself in the midst of you would have destroyed all my philosophy. But now I do so. I am in little neat lodge-ings—my boy in bed, I quiet—and I will now talk to you; tell you what I have seen and heard, and with as little repining as I can try, by making the best of what I have, the certainty of your friendship & kindness, to rest half content tho' I am not in the "Paradise of Exiles."[1]—Well—first I will tell you journal wise the history of my 16 days in London. I arrived monday the 25th of August—My father & William came for me to the Wharf. I had an excellent passage of 11½ hours—a glassy sea & a con-trary wind—the smoke of our fire was wafted right aft & streamed out behind us—but wind was of little consequence—the tide was with us—& though the Engine gave a "short uneasy motion"[2] to the vessel, the water was so smooth that no one on board was sick & Persino played about the deck in high glee. I had a very kind reception in the Strand[3] and all was done that could be done to make me comfortable—I exerted myself to keep up my spirits—the house though rather dismal, is infinitely bet-ter than the Skinner St. one—I resolved not to think of certain things, to take all as a matter of course and thus contrived to keep myself out of the gulph of melancholy, on the edge of which I was & am continually peeping.——

But lo & behold! I found myself famous!—Frankenstein had prodigious success as a drama & was about to be repeated for the 23ʳᵈ night at the English opera house.[4] The play bill amused me extremely, for in the list of dramatis personæ came,————by Mʳ T. Cooke:[5] this nameless mode of naming the un{n}ameable is rather good. On Friday Aug. 29ᵗʰ Jane My father William & I went to the theatre to see it. Wallack[6] looked very well as F [*Frankenstein*]—he is at the beginning full of hope & expectation—at the end of the 1ˢᵗ Act. the stage represents a room with a staircase leading to F workshop—he goes to it and you see his light at a small window, through which a frightened servant peeps, who runs off in terror when F. exclaims "It lives!"—Presently F himself rushes in horror & trepidation from the room and while still expressing his agony & terror ———— throws down the door of the laboratory, leaps the staircase & presents his unearthly & monstrous person on the stage. The story is not well managed—but Cooke played ————'s part extremely well— his seeking as it were for support—his trying to grasp at the sounds he heard—all indeed he does was well imagined & executed. I was much amused, & it appeared to excite a breathless eagerness in the audience— it was a third piece   a scanty pit filled at half price—& all stayed till it was over. They continue to play it even now.

On Saturday Aug. 30ᵗʰ I went with Jane to the Gisbornes. I know not why, but seeing them seemed more than anything else to remind me of Italy. Evening came on drearily, the rain splashed on the pavement, nor star, nor moon deigned to appear—I looked upward to seek an image of Italy but the blotted sky told me only of my change. I tried to collect my thoughts, and then again dared not think—for I am a ruin where owls & bats live only and I lost my last singing bird when I left Albaro. It was my birthday and it pleased me to tell the people so—to recollect & feel that time flies & what is to arrive is nearer, & my home not so far off as it was a year ago. This same evening on my return to the Strand I saw Lamb who was very entertaining & amiable though a little deaf. One of the first questions he asked me was whether they made puns in Italy—I said—{"}Yes, now Hunt is there"—He said that Burney made a pun in Otaheite,[7] the first that was ever made in that country: At first the natives could not make out what he meant, but all at once they discovered the pun & danced round him in transports of joy. L. [*Lamb*] said one thing which I am sure will give you pleasure. He corrected for Hazlitt a new collection of Elegant Extracts, in which the Living Poets are included.[8] He said he was much pleased with many of your things, with a little of

Montgomery[9] & a little of Crabbe—Scott he found tiresome—Byron had many fine things but was tiresome but yours appeared to him the freshest & best of all. These Extracts have never been published—they have been offered to Mr Hunter & seeing the book at his house I had the curiosity to look at what the extracts were that pleased L. There was the Canto of the Fatal Passion from Rimini several things from Foliage & from the Amyntas. L. mentioned also your conversation with Coleridge & was much pleased with it. He was very gracious to me, and invited me to see him when Miss L. should be well.

On the strength of the drama my father had published for my benefit a new edition of F.[10] & this seemed all I had to look to, for he despaired utterly of my doing anything with S.T.S. [*Sir Timothy Shelley*]—I wrote to him however to tell him I had arrived & on the following Wednesday had a note from Whitton where he invited me, if I wished for an explanation of S.T.S.'s intentions concerning my boy to call on him.[11] I went with my father. W. [*Whitton*] was very polite though long winded—his great wish seemed to be to prevent my applying again to STS, whom he represented as old, infirm & irritable—however he advanced me £100 for my immediate expences, told me that he c^d not speak positively until he had seen STS. but that he doubted not but that I should receive the same annually for my child, & with a little time & patience, I should get an allowance for myself.[12] This, you see relieved me from a load of anxieties—I hesitated no longer to quit the Strand and having secured neat cheap lodgings—removed hither last night. Such, dear Hunt is the outline of your poor Exile's history. After two days of rain the weather has been uncommonly fine cioè without rain, & cloudless I believe, though I trust to other eyes for that fact, since the whitewashed sky is any thing but blue to any but the perceptions of the Natives themselves. It is so cold however that the fire I am now sitting by is not the first that has been lighted, for my father had one two days ago. The wind is East and piercing—but I comfort myself with the hope that softer gales are now fanning your not throbbing temples, that the climate of Florence will prove kindly to you, & that your health & spirits will return to you.—Why am I not there? This is quite a foreign country to me; the names of the places sound strangely—the voices of the people are new & grating—the Vulgar English they speak particularly displeasing—but for my father, I should be with you next spring—but his heart & soul are set on my stay, and in this world it always seems one's duty to sacrifice one's own desires, & that claim ever appears the strongest which claims such a sacrifice.

On Tuesday (Sep. 2nd) I dined with Mr Hunter and Bessy & she afterwards drank tea with me at the Strand—She is certainly much improved in countenance. Her mouth which used always to express violence & anger now seems habitually to wear a good tempered smile—Mrs Godwin herself observed the change—this is certainly to Bessy's credit since she is far from happy as you may guess. It would be useless for me to repeat Bessy's news since doubtless she has told you all herself & you already know that the Novello's have from motives of economy, retired to the country.[13]—One thing at Mr Hunter's amused me very much—Your piping Fau[n] & kneeling Venus are on the piano, but, from a feeling {of} delicacy, they are turned with their backs [   ] company. I think of going down to Richmond on Friday & take a last peep at green fields & [   ] leaves before I return to my winter cage. You must know that Jane is a great favourite w[ith] Mrs H. [*Hunter*]—Poor thing she is much persecuted by Edward's Mother in Law[14] Who to save her own credit spreads false reports about her as much as she can. She even called on Mrs Godwin to warn her that I ought not to know her—at the same time that she tells other people that she can never forgive her, for knowing me. England is no place for Jane—how I wish we could leave it together next spring. Hogg & Peacock are both out of town.

I have now renewed my acquaintance with the friend of my girlish days[15]—she has been ill a long time, even disturbed in her reason, and the remains of this still hang over her. She is delighted to see me, although she is just now on the point of going to Scotland for a few weeks. The great affection she displays for me endears her to me & the memory of early days—Else all is so changed for me that I should hardly feel pleasure in cultivating her society. We never do what we wish when we wish it, and when we desire a thing earnestly, & it does arrive, that or we are changed so that we slide from the summit of our wishes & find ourselves where we were. Two years ago I looked forward with eagerness to your arrival, & pictured to myself all that I should enjoy with you & dear Marianne to make a part of our pleasures—You came, 12 dreary months past, I just began to regain your affection & to delight in your society & I am here, to pine for it again. This is life!—And what more have I {   } to you with its painful bitterness—sour sweets & sweet sours?—What will happen when I see you again?

Your brother has been out of town all this time. I heard that he was to return yesterday & expect him to call on me today. Of course I did not talk to Henry of all that I have to say to his father. Henry is not handsome. He is stiff in his manners though polite to me. They seem to be going on well and he says that the literary Examiner is succeeding. The truth however is, dear Hunt, that there is nothing in it Except the Indicator which is worth reading—but you will see them and judge. They have offered that I should contribute to fill up the few pages that follow the Criticism on books (which is written by a Mr Gordon, I think is his name) & when I can I will—but I have not that talent which enlivens a half page.—Do you know that your friend R^d Mr Collyer (who so shamefully attacked dearest S.) has been accused of the Bishop's crime[16] & has absconded.—This will become quite a clerical amusement, it unnaturalness befits their habitual hypocrisy & cant—When a man belies his conscience to the world—he will soon bely it to himself and what comes next, may easily be as bad as poor Joslin. Adieu dear friend I will finish the rest when I have seen your brother.

(Sep. 11th) I saw your brother yesterday. Being the first time that I saw him you may guess that I looked curiously at him. In features he is very like Henry, but softened from his immoveability of feature by time and suffering. He does not look so old as he is, & LB. w^d envy his unchanged looks, but I do not think him at all like your picture. He was all politeness & even kindness to me—I soon found that I had two feelings to remove in his mind[17]—one your not having managed well with the D in M Stores—the other poor dear M⟨a⟩r.'s [*Marianne's*] extravagance—I believe that I succeeded in both these points at least he said that I did. He spoke with great affection of you & when he went away said, that he was reserved & had the character perhaps of being more so than he was but that he did not wish to be so with you or with me—In fact though obstinacy is written on his brow, & reserve in all his solemn address yet he encouraged me so far that I look forward with less apprehension to the final result of my next conversation with him. I feel that I must not be reserved, nor shall I be so—I told him as it was that he ought to write oftenor, spoke of regular remittances—& urged him to send an immediate one; he said that he would write by the same post as that by which this letter will go, and that I trust will contain a permission for you to draw. I expect to see him soon again. Direct to me 14 Speldhurst St.— Brunswick Square. I will write again speedily—& wait anxiously to hear from you—Keep well—be all well, dear, dearest friends, be as happy as you can, &, while it be of value to you, & even after, depend upon the unremitting affection of your Exiled

Mary WS.

ADDRESS: Leigh Hunt Esq / Ferma in Posta / Firenze / Florence—Italy. POSTMARKS: (1) F23 / 113; (2) ANGLE[TERRE]; (3) CHAMBERY; (4) 27 / SETTEMBRE. TEXT: MS., Bodleian Library.
  1. Shelley, *Julian and Maddalo*, line 57.
  2. Coleridge, *The Ancient Mariner* 5. 386.
  3. At the Godwins'.

139

4. *Presumption, or the Fate of Frankenstein*, by Richard Brinsley Peake (1792–1847).

5. Thomas Potter Cooke (1786–1864). In 1825 Cooke presented *Le Monstre* (i.e., *Frankenstein*) in Paris on eighty successive nights (see MWS *Letters*, vol. I, 11 June 1826, n. 14).

6. James William Wallack (?1791–1864), actor and stage manager.

7. Tahiti. Lamb was referring to his friend Captain James Burney (1750–1821), rear admiral and man of letters, the son of Charles Burney.

8. *Select British Poets, or New Elegant Extracts from Chaucer to the Present Time, with Critical Remarks, by Wm. Hazlitt* (London: William C. Hall, 1824). Hazlitt stated in his preface that the anthology was meant to be an improvement on the Reverend Vicesimus Knox's *Elegant Extracts in Verse*, "at least a third" of which "was devoted to articles either entirely worthless, or recommended only by considerations foreign to the reader of poetry" (Wardle, *Hazlitt*, p. 387). Included in the collection were poems by Lamb, Keats, Shelley, and Hunt. The volume was withdrawn from circulation almost immediately after publication because the selections from contemporary poets had been reprinted without permissions. The volume was republished the following year, but the contemporary poets were omitted (Wardle, *Hazlitt*, p. 388).

9. James Montgomery (1771–1854), poet and newspaper editor.

10. MWS, *Frankenstein*.

11. In response to Mary Shelley's letters to Sir Timothy Shelley and Lady Shelley, Whitton wrote on 3 September inviting her to call on him that day or the next but making clear that Shelley's parents refused to see her (*S&M*, IV, 973–74).

12. Mary Shelley misunderstood Whitton, who recommended to Sir Timothy Shelley that he make an allowance of £100 per annum for Percy Florence but made no recommendation on Mary Shelley's behalf. By the end of November, however, Sir Timothy Shelley agreed to make an annual allowance of £100 for Mary Shelley as well. All funds provided by Sir Timothy Shelley were to be deducted from the estate Mary Shelley would inherit upon Sir Timothy Shelley's death (Ingpen, *Shelley in England*, pp. 574–75).

13. The Novellos had moved to Shacklewell Green. Vincent Novello (1781–1861) was a famous composer and performer of music. With his son Joseph Alfred he founded, in December 1828, the publishing firm of Novello & Co., which is still in existence today. In 1808 Novello married Mary Sabilla Hehl (?1787–1854), who wrote a number of stories and novels and was respected as a woman who possessed both intellect and charm. The Novellos had eleven children, four of whom died in infancy or childhood. The Novellos held frequent musical evenings in their home and were the friends of many noted figures in the world of literature and music, among them Hunt and Lamb. The Shelleys first met the Novellos on 8 March 1818 (*MWS Journal*). Upon her return to England, Mary Shelley was reintroduced into the Novello circle by a letter from Hunt, and she (along with Jane Williams, who had been introduced upon her return by a letter from Hunt) quickly became an intimate friend of the Novellos and members of their circle. The Novellos' eldest daughter was Mary Victoria (1809–98), who married Charles Cowden Clarke (1787–1877) on 5 July 1825. Clarke, an author and publisher, had numerous literary associations. He was a friend of the Lambs, the Hunts, and the Novellos and is credited with introducing the young Keats to poetry at his (Clarke's) father's school at Enfield.

Individually and jointly, the Clarkes wrote many stories, essays, and books, several of which give details of the lives of the Novellos and their circle, including Mary Cowden Clarke and Charles Cowden Clarke, *Recollections of Writers* (London, 1878); and Mary Cowden Clarke, *My Long Life: An Autobiographic Sketch* (London, 1896) (see Altick, *The Cowden Clarkes*, pp. 1–8, 42–47, 68).

14. *Mother-in-law* then referred to the mother of one's spouse or a stepmother. Since Jane Williams refers to Edward Williams's mother-in-law as "Mrs. Williams" (see, e.g., Jane Williams's letter to Mary Shelley, 27 March 1823, Abinger MS.), we may conclude that Mary Shelley was writing about Williams's stepmother, Mary Ann Williams.

15. Isabella Baxter Booth. Godwin recorded in his Journal that "Mrs. Booth & fille" dined with him and Mary Shelley on 3 September (Abinger MS.).

16. Reverend William Bengo Collyer (1782–1854), "Licentious Productions in High Life," *The Investigator, or Quarterly Magazine* 5 (October 1822): 315–73. Hunt denounced Collyer's vicious personal attack on Shelley in "Canting Slander, to the Reverend William Bengo Collyer," *Examiner*, 22 September 1822 (Reiman, *The Romantics Reviewed*, Part B, III, 1170–99). In the *Morning Chronicle* of 25 August 1823 Reverend Collyer publicly refuted accusations of homosexual activity, stating that the two instances cited were of a medical nature.

17. John and Leigh Hunt were divided over Leigh Hunt's claims to proprietary rights in the *Examiner*. On 3 October 1823 Leigh Hunt wrote to John Hunt: "I have so little time to write, and so great a desire to render the footing on which I am to stand in future, plain and simple, that I will say at once, that I will resume my station in *The Examiner*, to write for it all that I can write both political and literary; in return for which, all matters considered, I will also continue my old share of the profits. You will observe, that whatever I have written, in *The Examiner* or out of it, I have always considered it as my duty to you to take care that you should be the better for it, as far as lay in my power. When you set up the *Literary Examiner*, my notion was, that it was only a part of *The Examiner* in another shape, and that not being able to do more for us both with the *Liberal*, I returned to my *Examiner* tasks. I never dreamed of its being a "secession" from *The Examiner*, or most assuredly I should have paused before I struggled to get up a new paper in conjunction with new hands" (Brewer, *The Holograph Letters*, p. 158). On 14 October Leigh Hunt wrote to John Hunt: "I have received a letter from Mrs. Shelley, in which she exhorts me to draw upon you, being certain, she says, that you expect me to do so, and have been surprised at my not doing it. Not hearing from you on this point, and having had no friends near me to endorse a bill, if I had drawn it, I confess I never thought of such a thing: But I now do it, having no other alternative" (Brewer, *The Holograph Letters*, p. 158). The dispute resulted, however—despite the intervention over a number of years of Mary Shelley, Vincent Novello, William Hazlitt, Charles Armitage Brown, and others—in an estrangement of the brothers that was not resolved until 1837 (see Brown, *Letters*, for extensive details of the controversy).

To Charles Ollier

Speldhurst St.   Oct—28th [1823]

My dear Sir

Will you have the kindness to deliver into Mr John Hunt's hands such copies of Mr Shelley's works as you still retain.[1]—I should be very glad of a single copy of the Alastor if by any chance there should be one remaining.

I hope that Mrs Ollier[2] and yourself are in good health

Your obedient servant
Mary W. Shelley

ADDRESS: Mr Chas Ollier / &c &c &c. TEXT: MS., Pforzheimer Library.

1. Charles Ollier, Shelley's publisher, went out of business in the summer of 1823. On 17 November he responded. Noting that "the sale, in every instance, of Mr Shelley's works has been very confined," he indicated that he had forwarded the following list of works to John Hunt:

160	Epipsychidion	(stitched)	4	Hellas	(sewed)
12	Hellas	(quires)	15	Revolt of Islam	(Bds)
12	Rosalind	D°	41	Adonais	(quires)
12	Prometheus	D°	92	Six Weeks' Tour	D°
12	Cenci	D°	18	Proposal for Reform	(stitched)
3	D°	Bds 1st Edit.			

Ollier, seeking a copy of *Alastor* to complete his own collection of Shelley, had recently been offered the purchase of one, which he was willing to allow Mary Shelley to purchase instead (Abinger MS.; printed in *S&M*, IV, 990–91).

2. Maria Gattie Ollier, whose brothers were friends of Leigh Hunt and Charles Cowden Clarke (*SC*, V, 125).

To Charles Ollier

14 Speldhurst St—   Saturday.
Nov. 15th [1823]

Dear Sir

In the Literary Pocket Book for 1821 there appeared two extracts, entitled "Sun set" and "Grief"[1]—taken from a longer poem of Mr Shelley's. You would extremely oblige me if you could inform me where it is probable that I should obtain a copy of this poem.

Excuse this trouble. I hope Mrs Ollier & your family are well—

Your obedient Servant
MaryShelley

ADDRESS: Mr Chas Ollier / &c &c &c. TEXT: MS., Pforzheimer Library.

1. "Sun set" and "Grief" were excerpts from Shelley's "The Sunset"—lines 9–20 and 27–42, respectively—signed Δ in the *Literary Pocket-Book* (see 29 December 1820–1 January 1821, n. 6) for 1821 (pp. 120–21). Mary Shelley published "The Sunset" in *Posthumous Poems*, pp. 183–84.

❖

To Edward John Trelawny[1]

London—(March [?–] 22nd) [1824]

My dear Trelawny

I wish I could see you in your Ulyssean dress—your red and gold vest and sheep-skin capote—To you who are in Greece and see her foul as well as her fair side, she may appear barbarous & perhaps odious—but here, where all the every day annoyances of civilization press on one who has passed her best years out of its pale—that sunlit country and its energetic inhabitants seem so much more capable of bestowing pleasure on me that [*than*] the crowded houses of London; and minus the shooting Turks and Woodcocks[2] I do most deeply envy your situation; the opportunities of seeing human Nature, and the interest you must feel in the strange aspect of humanity among these Greeks and Trojans—One is always ready to throw the blame on the mere accidents of life—I might perhaps be as unhappy any where as here; and the delights of Italy might {be} torture to me—I cannot tell; I only know that as I am, I am miserable. The eight years that I passed with our lost Shelley does not appear a dream, for my present existence is more like that—surely his state is not more changed than mine. When I first came to England, change of scene, the seeing old friends and the excitement with which the uncertainty of my situation inspired me, made me, though not happy, yet pass the day unrepining. But now each hour seems to add a load of intolerable melancholy. While alone I can hardly support the weight—when with others, it is almost worse. I think of my converse with Shelley, his incomparable superiority, and besides that he was mine and loved me; I think of Edward; of his virtues and pure friendship, till my heart sinks—The greatest pleasure I have is in company with Jane—When we talk over old times for hours— My other friends are good and kind, but they are so perfectly unlike all that I have been accustomed to, that I enter into a new world when I see them—It is to Jane only that I ever mention Shelley—Do you remember, dear friend, our talks over the fire-side at Genoa?—God knows how wretched I was there; and yet it seems a happy time in comparison to the present—Am I indeed Mary Shelley? the Mary Shelley who gave you almond billêt doux during our Pisan regales? and who ⟨almost forgot⟩ erred into wildness, untamed as she was by any sorrow?—Mary Shelley now is but a ghost of that—but I will not vex you with my repinings—It is a pleasure to me at least to write to you—to recall images of the past, which you also will remember with pleasure—to think that I shall see you once more, & to know that in the mean time your kind, generous heart feels compassion & affection for me

But instead of these useless repinings I had better fill my paper with what news may interest you—and though that is not much, yet it is always agreable to learn something from the land of the living while in exile (though in pleasant exile) from it. First Jane has settled her affairs in India—she will have no great things—not sufficient to live upon in this country—but she has something secure. Her guardian is dead, & her guardian's heir is very kind to her; he is rich and generous, & although of course she would not avail herself of the qualities—yet it is pleasant to know that there is a post to lean on during the accidents of life.—No one has heard from Claire since last July—this is very cruel of her, since she must be aware that we must all be very anxious about her. I strive to think that her silence is occasioned only by her love of mystery or some other caprice—but I am made very uncomfortable about it. There has been no change in my situation,—except that some circumstances induce me to believe that my father-in-law intends to be more generous towards me than he professed—but I cannot tell until next June, when my quarter is due. As it is—living with the greatest economy, I do not want for money—I lead the same life writing & reading & seeing a few people— dull and monotonous enough, since very hour I detest London and its— infernal (one must use expressive words on some occasions) climate more & more. I saw Miss Whitehead[3] the other day. She is at Islington, but talks of going into the country soon—She said that your Cousin was well.—By the bye I wrote to Mrs Mason[4] about the remainder of the will which you say Mr H. Browne had from the people from whom we rented a house at the Baths of Pisa[5]—in her reply she says: "The result of my inquiries is that no papers whatever were found after your departure, consequently no person can be in possession of the Document you mention by that means: Mrs Turbati (the woman of the house) added that had there been any papers, she must have found them, as she always examines every part of her house herself, the moment strangers leave it."—There is probably some mistake in the place—you described the papers so accurately that I cannot doubt of their being those I sought—I wish I could have them as soon as possible & know exactly the place where M^r H Browne got them.

(March 22nd) Mr Hamilton Browne called on me today which was a great pleasure to me, since he is the only person I have seen who has been in your company since we parted on the hill of Albaro. He tells me that a vessel sails for Greece next thursday, so I finish this letter & will send it by this opportunity with a few books—I enquired for works upon Greece but could hear of none. Opinions vary very much with regard to these last Cantos of Don Juan;[6] they are usually considered as a falling off—& so they are in many respects, they want the deep & passionate feeling of the first—but they are unequalled in their strictures upon life & flashes of wit.—These are almost our only novelties; Lady Morgan's life of Salvator Rosa[7] is pronounced dull—St. Ronan's well[8]—one of the worst of the Great Unknown—The reviews I never read;—What more? I have been to the theatre several times to see Kean. I never was more powerfully affected by any representation than by his Sir Giles Overreach[9]—The best scene is worked up to a pitch of passion that I could not have imagined—His tones & looks often remind me of you—& [   ][10] but that is not your stage—You Greek dress—pistols—Suliotes & Woodcock shooting are more in your way. Covent Garden was nearly deserted till they brought out a comedy by that ranter Croly[11]— by which it would seem that the proverb is a true one, that says, that extremes meet—for this comedy is, they say, as broad, vulgar & farcical, as his tragic vein is high flown & bombastic—it succeeds prodigiously.— Parliament is met here and Canning[12] is making a figure—he does not seem at all to like the part he was forced to play with regard to Spain, & said in the House that he would not tacitly acquiesce in such another invasion as that of the French at the risk of any war. They are introducing some ammelioration in the state of the slaves in some parts of the West Indies—during the debate on that subject Canning paid a compliment to Frankenstein in a manner sufficiently pleasing to me. The town how- ever is not full as yet, & the Winter is not begun—And although the Opera House is crowded I have not seen there any of the first Grandees. Medwin is still in Paris—nor have either Jane or I heard from him since Christmas—a pretty fellow! Roberts is shooting in the Maremma with Cap^n Hay—The Hunts are still at Florence—longing for England.— How I wish I could change places with them! They would get on well if Hunt would write—but he does not—John Hunt has acted very well to- wards his brother in the main & I think him perfectly honourable though rough in manner. My volume of our Shelley's Poems is printing—it will be a good sized one.

After all this odious place agrees with me & I am very well. Indeed we have had a mild though rainy winter—& last week we had two really fine days—Percy is grown quite out of your knowledge—Poor Jane is by no means well just now & has during this winter grown fearfully thin—We shall go somewhere into the country in the summer, when I hope she will regain her health.—She has been a great deal annoyed by her sister Mrs Baird,—and I think that her illness has been to a great degree occasioned by this.

I heard the other day from the Guiccioli—She says LB's behaviour to the Greeks has been generous in the extreme! H.B. [*Hamilton Browne*] says that his £4000 has already been repaid to him he is lucky in this— but how will he bear the news that Lord Blessington's bills in payment for the yacht[13] have been protested—I hope you are somewhat richer than you were last autumn but you will never be rich—have as much money as you will—Tell me—by the bye if a Miss Anne Matthews ever resided with you & Mrs T. [*Trelawny*] in Wales—Is there any idea that Captain Shenley will join { } in Greece—or the slightest hope that I shall see you soon again—Could you [*p. 1, top*] Direct to me at the Examiner Office—38 Tavistock St. Covent Garden Or: through Hunt in Italy.—

TEXT: MS., Bodleian Library.

1. This letter was written in response to Trelawny's 24 October 1823 letter from the Isle of Hydra, Greece (*S&M*, IV, 981–89).

2. Trelawny had written of "excellent sport between Turk and woodcock shooting."

3. Ellen Whitehead. Trelawny had written in a postscript: "If Miss Whitehead calls on you let her read this letter."

4. Margaret King Moore, Lady Mount Cashell (1773–1835), separated from her husband in 1805 and then lived in Italy with George William Tighe as Mr. and Mrs. Mason. The Shelleys became close friends with the Masons and their daughters Laura and Nerina in 1819 (see MWS *Letters*, I, 110, n.5; McAleer, *The Sensitive Plant*).

5. On 6 September 1823 Trelawny wrote Mary Shelley that James Hamilton Browne, who was en route to Greece with him (see Marchand, *Byron*, III, 1093), had lived in lodgings that the Shelleys had occupied at the Baths of Pisa and had discovered "some loose sheets of paper"—a will or deed of Shelley's, each page signed and witnessed. Margaret Mason's response was written on 31 January 1824 and arrived in England on 19 February (Abinger MS.).

6. Cantos 12, 13, and 14 were published by John Hunt on 17 December 1823; Cantos 15 and 16 were published on 26 March 1824.

7. Lady Morgan (née Sydney Owenson), *The Life and Times of Salvator Rosa* (Paris, 1824). Lady Morgan (1776–1859) wrote a number of romances and travel books. Her travel books about France and Italy caused some controversy because of her liberal views. Mary Shelley and Lady Morgan became friends in the 1830s.

8. Sir Walter Scott, *St. Ronan's Well* (Edinburgh, 1824 [for 1823]).

9. A character in *A New Way to Pay Old Debts* (1633), by Philip Massinger.

10. A line and a quarter deleted by Mary Shelley.

11. George Croly (1780–1860). His comedy with songs, *Pride Shall Have a Fall*, opened at Covent Garden on 11 March (Nicoll, *English Drama*, IV, 285). A rector, Croly wrote romances, plays, books reviews (some containing attacks on Byron and Shelley), and poems (two of the latter imitations of Byron). Byron satirized Croly as the "Revd. Rowley Powley" in *Don Juan* 11. 57.

12. George Canning (1770–1827), a British statesman who was credited for his liberal policies while he served as Foreign Secretary, from 1822 to 1827. The Congress of Verona (October 1822) of the Quadruple Alliance gave France a mandate to suppress the Spanish Revolution begun in 1820. On 31 August 1823 the revolutionaries were defeated, and Ferdinand VII was restored to the Spanish throne. Canning, however, had refused to cooperate with the other members of the Alliance in this action, and this led to the dissolution of the Alliance. Canning alluded to *Frankenstein* on 16 March 1824 (Great Britain, *Hansard's Parliamentary Debates*, 2d ser., 10 [1824], col. 1103).

13. Byron wrote to his banker, Charles Barry: "I regret Ld Blessington's behaviour about the bill: you know that he insisted on buying the Schooner, and had the bargain at his own price. If his bill is not paid, I must make it public, and bring the business, moreover, to a personal discussion; he shan't treat me like a tradesman—that I promise him" (Byron, *Works*, VI, 290).

◈

To Teresa Guiccioli

16mo—Maggio [May 1824][1]—Londra

Carissima Amica

Come scrivervi? Come esprimere l'alto dolore che mi punge il core? Povera Teresa! siamo ormai sorelle nella infelicità! Temo che una mia lettera sara un raddoppiamento della vostra tristezza, e pur troppo sento che non vi rechera alcuna consolazione. Non posso addoperare i luoghi communi della consolazione, giacche so io che sono falsi. Come dirvi che la pace vi attendera quando il tempo abbia guarito le piaghe del dolore, e provo che queste piaghe sono immediabile dal tempo? Ogni giorno si sente più al di dentro quanto poco vale il mondo quando l'oggetto amato ci manca. Non ha detto il caro Byron se stesso (egli che conobbe al fondo il cor femenile) che tutta l'esistenza d'una donna dipende dall'amore, ed allorchè perdiamo un amante non ci sia altro rifugio che

To love again and be again undone[2]

Ma noi, cara Guiccioli, siamo private di questo rufugio. Il destino diede ad ambedue i primi spiriti del secolo, perduti loro, non v'è un secondo

147

amare; ed i cori nostri sempremai vedovati, non sono altri che monumenti per dimostrare la felicità ivi sepolta.

E l'ho veduto per l'ultima volta! Non vedro mai più il più bello di tutti gli uomini, quella gloriosa creatura che fu il vanto del mondo; mai piu sentiro la sua voce o leggero la nuova poesia figlia del suo imparagibile genio. Non devo forse sfogarmi in questo modo, e destare le vostre lagrimi ora che i miei occhi sono offuscati della dolorose acque. Ma quando persi la cara metà di me stessa niente mi recò tanta consolazione quanto i di lui lodi—mi pasceva di quei, e mi figuro che voi anche amarete sentire nell'espressione dell'afflizione d'una amica di Byron, l'eco dei tuoi pianti. Vorrei che fossi presso a te, cara Contessina; parleremmo insieme del diletto Byron, ci rementeremmo del tempo che abbiamo passato insieme— dei nostri passeggi, quando egli veniva devante di noi in tutta la gloria della sua beltà: sarebbero le nostre converzazioni interminabili. Ma non vi manca sicuramente la simpatia degli amici; mi è grata l'idea che siete fra dei cari, e godiate tutto il conforto che la tenera amicizia può dare.

Quanta paura aveste di questo viaggio! ogni giorno sono più sicura che Dio ci ha dottato col potere di prevedere i nostri mali. Ma siamo tutte quante delle Cassandre; e cosi cieche siamo che non diamo orreccho alla voce silenziale che si fa sentire nell'anima. Si conosce poi la verità allorchè sono le profezie addempite. Quante e quante cose dessero sicura notizia alla Williams ed a me della nostra disgrazia, e voi mille volte poi mi avete detto—Quanto temo questa spedizione.—Temo di annoiarvi ma vorrei sapere tutte le circonstanze di questo disgraziatissimo avvenimento. È la medesima malatia che ebbe a Lerici, non è vero? Esso seppe il suo pericolo? Mi figuro che Pierino vi abbia spedita la narrazione di tutto, e spero di non mostrarmi importuna pregandovi di mandarmi una copia di ciò. Quando vi ha scritto il caro Byron ultimamente? era ammalato allora. State sicura che ogni cosa che mi mandate, ogni copia delle sue lettere, sara sacra per me; nel chiedere questi monumenti dei suoi ultimi momenti sono mossa della vere affezione che sento per lui

La Williams vi prega di gradire l'espressione della sua simpatia. Poverina! Sta assai male lei: è dimagrita al punto di far orrore, e la salute pare affatto rovinato. Per noi altri settentrionalioti non v'è primavera per far risalire i corpi soffranti; il freddo, la pioggia e gli spessi cambiamenti dell'atmosfera indeboliscono e guastono le costituzioni i più robusti; il s[ole] è sempre oscur[ato]. Ma perche parlare di sifatte bagatelle. Questa disgrazia fare[bbe o]scurare il bel cielo d'Italia ed i di lei fiori saranno [per] voi solamente tanti ornamenti per il sepolcro di votro amore. Coraggio intanto, che pare che ci sia nuova legge della natura, e moriremo tutti giovani—Coraggio! sicchè per noi l'ignota via della morta è calcata dai

nostri più cari; se quando facciamo questo medesimo viaggio, giunge-
remo ad un paese sconosciuto, quei che amiamo sono già costà e si af-
frettarono di farci le benvenute. Morire per noi non sara una seperazione
dai bene della vità, ma un raggiungnimento ai tesori nostri rapiti ora dalla
Morte.

Beh! Carissima mia, scivetemi col prossimo Corriere. Aspettero con
somma impazienza la vostra lettera.—Se vi sia alcuna cosa che volete che
faccio—alcuna ambasciata alle genti qui, commandatemi schiettamente,
che mi ripeto pur sempe, Cara Guiccioli

Vostra Aff^{ma} Amica—Mary Shelley.

[*Translation*]
Dearest Friend
How shall I write to you. How can I express the deep pain that pierces
my heart? Poor Teresa! we are now sisters in misfortune! I fear that my
letter will make your sorrow more intense, and unfortunately I feel that
it will not bring you any comfort. I cannot use the commonplaces of consolation, since I know that they are false. How can I tell you that peace
awaits you when time has healed the wounds of pain, when I know that
these wounds are incurable by time? Every day one feels more within how
little the world is worth when the beloved object is gone. Didn't dear
Byron himself say (he who knew so thoroughly the female heart) that the
whole of a woman's existence depends on love, and therefore losing a love
there is no other refuge than

To love again and be again undone[2]

But we, dear Guiccioli, are deprived of this refuge. Destiny gave to both
of us the first spirits of the age, losing them, there is no second love; and
our hearts forever widowed, can only be monuments to demonstrate the
happiness buried there.

And I saw him for the last time! I will never again see the most beautiful of all men, that glorious creature who was the pride of all the world;
never again will I hear his voice or read his new poetry, the daughter of
his incomparable genius. Maybe I should not give vent to my feelings in
this way, and arouse your weeping now that my eyes are blurred by these
sorrowful tears. But when I lost the dear half of myself, nothing brought
me as much consolation as hearing his praises—I fed on those, and I suppose that you also will want to hear the echo of your own lamentations
in the expression of the suffering of a friend of Byron. I wish that I were
close to you, dear Contessina; we would talk together of beloved Byron,
we would recall the time that we have passed together—of our walks,

when he would come before us in all the glory of his beauty: these would be our interminable conversations. But surely you do not lack the sympathy of your friends; I am pleased by the idea that you are surrounded by those who are dear to you, and you will enjoy all the comfort that affectionate friendship can give you.

How much you feared this voyage! every day I am more certain that God has endowed us with the power to foresee our misfortunes. But we are all Cassandras; and we are so blind that we do not give heed to the silent voice that makes itself heard within our soul. We then know the truth when the prophecies are fulfilled. How many things gave certain notice to Signora Williams and myself of our misfortune, and you also told me a thousand times—How much I fear this expedition.—I am afraid of annoying you but I would like to know all the circumstances of this most unfortunate happening. It was the same malady that he suffered from at Lerici, isn't that right? Did he know of his danger? I imagine that Pierino has sent you an account of all, and I hope not to appear importunate asking you to send me a copy of it. When was the last time that dear Byron wrote to you? Was he ill at that time? Be assured that anything that you send me, any copy of his letters, will be sacred to me; in asking for these monuments of his final moments I am moved by the true affection that I feel for him.

Signora Williams asks you to accept the expression of her sympathy. Poor thing! She is very ill: she has grown so thin as to cause horror, and her health seems to be truly ruined. For we northerners there is no spring to restore our suffering bodies; the cold, the rain and the frequent changes in the atmosphere weaken and ruin the constitutions of the most robust; the sun is always clouded. But why talk of such trifles. Your misfortune would becloud the beautiful Italian sky and for you her flowers will be only so many ornaments for the sepulchre of your love. Courage meanwhile, for there seems to be a new law of nature, and we all will die young—Courage! since for us the unknown path of death has been tread by those dearest to us; if when we make this same journey, we arrive at an unknown country, those whom we love are already there and will hurry to make us welcome. For us death will not be a separation from the blessings of life, but a reunion with our dear ones carried off by Death.

Well! My dearest, write to me by the next Courier. I will be awaiting your letter with the utmost impatience.—If there is anything that you might want me to do—any message to people here, ask me frankly, as I again declare myself always, Dear Guiccioli

Your most affectionate friend   Mary Shelley.

150

ADDRESS: Alla Sua Eccellenza / La Signora Contessa Teresa Guiccioli / A Bologna / nei Stati Pontefici / Bologna—Italy. POSTMARKS: (1) F24 / 30; (2) ANGLETERRE; (3) CORRISPZA EST[ERA DA GENOVA]; (4) [   ]INSTR GENER[   ]LE POST PONT / S.E.O.F. / BOLOGNA; (5) BOLOGNA / 6. GIU. TEXT: MS., Pforzheimer Library. TRANSLATION: Ricki B. Herzfeld.

  1. The news of Byron's death at Missolonghi on 19 April 1824 reached Byron's closest friends on 14 May and the public on 15 May. Byron's body was shipped to England on the *Florida*, arriving there on 29 June. Pietro Gamba, Byron's companion in Greece, traveled to England at the same time, but on a different vessel so as to avoid attention being called to his sister's relationship with Byron. On 12 Byron's funeral procession went from London toward Nottingham (passing Mary Shelley's residence as it climbed up Highgate Hill), and on 16 July Byron was interred in the Byron family vault at Hucknall Torkard (Marchand, *Byron*, III, 1229, 1242–43, 1260–63).

  2. *Don Juan* I. 194.

To John Howard Payne[1]

14 Speldhurst Street   June 1st [1824]

My dear Sir

  I was unable to avail myself of the Tickets that you kindly sent last Thursday,—I do not know what day next week Charles II[2] will be performed—but as soon as I possibly can I shall with great pleasure pass an evening I am sure of infinite amusement at C.G [*Covent Garden*]—& shall apply to you for admissions   In the mean time, if you can spare 4 Orders for this evening, for any part of the house (I should prefer the boxes) you will very much oblige me

I am, dear Sir
Your obedient Servant
MaryShelley

[*Added by William Godwin, Jr.*]   Turn over
Dear H—

  This note was ready written when I arrived—but Mrs Shelley has just discovered that she wants a double order for the boxes for Friday

Ever yours
W.G. Junior

ADDRESS: J. Howard Payne Esq. TEXT: MS., Pforzheimer Library.

  1. John Howard Payne (1791–1852) was an American actor and playwright who

collaborated with his friend Washington Irving in writing several plays; from 1842 to 1845 and again in 1851 and 1852 he was American Consul at Tunis. Payne fell in love with Mary Shelley in 1825 (see [28 June 1825], n. 2), but finding that she did not reciprocate his feelings but expressed some interest in Washington Irving, Payne tried to encourage Irving's attentions by giving him Mary Shelley's letters to read. Irving, however, was impervious to his friend's matchmaking efforts. Payne continued to be Mary Shelley's friend until his return to America in 1832. His association with the theater gave him access to free admissions, which he generously provided for Mary Shelley throughout their friendship. *The Romance*, which first brought the relationship of the three to light, prints part of Mary Shelley and Payne's correspondence. Sylva Norman suggests that Mary Shelley and Payne met in Paris in 1823 through the Kenneys [*Flight of the Skylark*, p. 64]. For a full-length study of Payne, see Overmyer, *America's First Hamlet*. Overmyer gives a more objective account of the relationship of Mary Shelley and Payne than Sanborn, who characterizes Mary Shelley as rather opportunistic in her treatment of Payne. Payne had known Godwin since 1817 and was a friend of William Godwin, Jr., as well.)

2. Payne's comedy *Charles the Second; or, The Merry Monarch* opened at Covent Garden on Thursday, 27 May 1824 (Nicoll, *English Drama*, IV, 369). *Charles the Second*; *Cozening*; and *Clari* were advertised to be performed on 1 June. *Clari; or, The Maid of Milan*, by Payne, opened at Covent Garden on 8 May 1823 and contained Payne's famous song "Home, Sweet Home."

To {Bryan Waller Procter}[1]

[14 Speldhurst Street
Brunswick Square]   Saturday
[? 12 June 1824]

My dear Sir

You will I hope have received copies of the Poems by this time.—As I do not know the address of Mʳ Kelsall & Mʳ Beddoes, will you have the goodness to forward copies to them. I have made out the en{c}losed list of errata[2] which ought to be printed immediately—but I wished to ask you first, if in looking over the volume you found any additional errors

I am, dear Sir
Yours sincerly & obliged
Mary W Shelley

Errata

P. 77   1.5—for
The shapes which drew in thick lightnings
read
The shapes which drew it, in thick lightenings.

P. 139—15 for seem, read, seems.

16—for shrine read shine

P. 164—Insert a comma at the end of line 4

and then insert this line

The breath of the moist earth is light

---

p. 186   last line—for 1817—read 1819.

P. 221—1 11—for wait, read wail.

TEXT: MS., Pforzheimer Library.

1. *Posthumous Poems of Percy Bysshe Shelley* was published during the second week of June (Taylor, *Early Collected Editions*, p. 7). The evidence that this letter was addressed to Procter is found in his letter to Mary Shelley dated "Tuesday Morning," in which he writes: "I have sent to Kelsall about the errata—which he will attend to—I have been in a state of such nervousness as not to be able to read enough for the purpose." He also says, "I desired Kelsall to thank you for the beautiful volume of Poems—I hope he did so" (Abinger MS.).

2. The errata leaf, which was tipped into some copies of the *Posthumous Poems*, contained twenty-four corrections (Taylor, *Early Collected Editions*, p. 17).

To { ?Charles Ollier}[1]

Kentish Town—Friday
[?June 1824–August 1825][2]

Dear Sir

I am in great want of a book which describes minutely the Environs of Constantinople—Whether it be in French or English is no consequence; I do not know any such book—but if you cast your eye over Colburns Catalogue you will perhaps meet with one—& you would oblige me if you would send it without delay.—On second thoughts, as I am quite at a stand, I send a special Messenger   Can you give him the Volumes

I am extremely obliged to you for your polite offer of services & as you see take the liberty of availing myself of them—

I am your Ob' Ser'
MaryShelley

153

TEXT: MS., Pforzheimer Library.

1. After the publishing firm of Charles and James Ollier foundered in 1823, Charles Ollier became a literary adviser for Henry Colburn (*SC*, V, 127). Charles Ollier served as intermediary between Mary Shelley and Henry Colburn, and in many instances she called on Ollier to aid her in obtaining books for research.

2. Mary Shelley moved to Kentish Town on 21 June 1824. Constantinople is the setting of the opening of the second volume of *The Last Man*. Since Mary Shelley began *The Last Man* in February 1824 and completed it by November 1825, this letter may have been written as late as summer 1825.

To Leigh Hunt

Kentish Town—August 22nd [1824]

My dear Hunt

Although I know that you wish yourself in England, yet it seems to me as if I wrote to Paradise from Purgatory—Our summer is over and rain and perpetual cloud veil this dreary land. I wish you were here since you wish it, yet from all I hear the period does not seem near. Poor dear Marianne! She goes on suffering, and God knows what would become of her in this ungenial climate. Jane and I dream and talk only of our return, and I begin to think that next Autumn this may be possible. A Negociation is begun between Sir T. S. [*Timothy Shelley*] & myself by which, on sacrificing a small part of my future expectations on the will, I shall ensure myself a sufficiency, for the present, & not only that, but be able, I hope, to releive Claire from her disagreable situation at Moscow. I have been obliged however as an indispensable preliminary, to suppress the Post. Poems—More than 300 copies had been sold so this is the less provoking, and I have been obliged to promise not to bring dear S's name before the public again during Sir. T—'s life. There is no great harm in this, since he is above 70, & from choice I should not think of writing memoirs now and the materials for a volume of more works are so scant that I doubted before whether I could publish it.—Such is the folly of the world—& so do things seem different from what they are, since from Whitton's account Sir T. writhes under the fame of his incomparable son as if it were a most grievous injury done to him.—& so perhaps after all it will prove.—All this was pending when I wrote last, but until I was certain I did not think it worth while to mention it. The affair is arranged by Peacock, who though I seldom see him, seems anxious to do me all these kind of services, in the best manner that he can.

It is long since I saw your brother nor had he then any news for me—

I lead a most quiet life & see hardly any one. Mrs Novello, Vincent C.C.C. [*Charles Cowden Clarke*] & Werter went to Boulogne the other day, whence V. escaped & returned to England, & the other three posted on to Paris, earning pleasure hardly I should think, especially as Mrs N. [*Novello*] appears in a continual fever—The Gliddons are gone to Hastings for a few weeks.—Hogg is on the circuit—now that he is rich he is so very poor—so unamiable & so strange that I look forward to his return without any desire of shortening the term of absence.—Poor Pierino is now in London—Non fosse male questo paese, he says, se vedesse mai il Sole[1]—He is full of Greece to which he is going to return, and gave us an account of our good friend T— [*Trelawny*] which shew [th]at he is not at all changed. T.— had made a hero of the Greek Chief Ulysses—& declares that there is a great cavern in Attica which he & Ulysses have provisioned for 7 years & to which if the Cause fails he & this Chieftain are to retire[2]—but if the Cause is triumphant he is to build a city in the Negropont, colonize it & Jane & I are to go out to be Queens & Chieftanesses of the Island. When T.— first came to Athens—he took to a Turkish life bought 12 or 15 women—brutte mostre—Pierino says—one a Moor, of all things—& there he lay on his sopha, smoking, these gentle creatures about him—till he got heartily sick of idleness shut them up in his haram & joined & combated with Ulysses. He has quarrelled very violently with Mavrocordato, but I easily divine how all this is—poor Mavrocordato, beset by covetous Suliotes, disliked by the chieftains of the Morea—caballed against by the strangers—poor, while every other chief is getting rich, is drinking deep of the bitter cup of calumny & disappointment.

But to quit Greece & return to England. The Opera House is closed—before it shut I heard Pasta[3] & never was more affected by any scenic representation than by her acting of Romeo—She joins intellectual beauty, grace, perfect tragic action to a fine voice & a sentiment in singing I never saw equalled. When she sees Giulletta in the tomb—when she takes poison, when Giulletta awakes & her joy at meeting is changed to the throes of death, the whole theatre was in one transport of emotion.—The novelty now is the Der Freishutz of Weiber—performing at the Lyceum & the music is wild but often beautiful—when the magic bullets are cast they fill the stage with all sorts of horrors—owls flapping the[ir] wings—toads [hopp]ing about—fierly[4] serpents darting & the [   ] ghostly hunters in the clouds, while every now & then in the [   ] of a stream of wild harmony comes a crashing discord—all forms I assure you a very fine scene, while every part of the house except the stage is invelloped in darkness.

One of my principal reasons for writing just now is that I have just

155

heard Miss Curran's address (64, Via Sistina, Roma) & I am anxious that Marianne should (if she will be so very good) send one of the profiles already cut, to her, of Shelley, since I think that by the help of that Miss C— will be able to correct her portrait of S— and make for us, what we so much desire, a good likeness—I am convinced that Miss C— will return the profile immediately that she has done with it—so that you will not sacrifice it, though you may be the means of our obtaining a good likeness.

I will write soon to Marianne—in the mean time I wish she would write to me since I long to hear from her, & should be very glad whenever you will be kind enough to assure me of the continuance of your friendship although I fear it is gone to the tomb of the Capulets—but I do not deserve this catastrophe—Give my love to your children—Occhi Turchini among the rest—& believe me ever, my dear Hunt

Your faithful friend Mary W. Shelley

[*P. 1, top*]   Direct to me thro' y^r brother

ADDRESS: Leigh Hunt Esq / Ferma in Posta / Firenze / Italie / Florence—Italy. POSTMARKS: (1) F24 / 103; (2) ANGLET[ERR]E; (3) CHA[MBE]RY; (4) CORRISPZA ESTERA [DA GENOVA]. TEXT: MS., Bodleian Library.

1. "This country might not be bad . . . if one could see the sun sometime."

2. Odysseus Androutsos (d. 17 June 1825), a Greek chieftain who controlled most of eastern Greece from Parnassus to Athens. Odysseus betrayed the Greek cause by making a truce with the Turks but was captured and killed by Mavrocordato (St Clair, *Trelawny*, 102, 115–16; *SC*, V, 54–56). Trelawny married Odysseus's sister. In September 1824 Trelawny sent Mary Shelley "a Description of the Cavern Fortress of Mt Parnassus belonging to General Ulysses commanded by Cap^n E. Trelawny," with the request that she "make an article" of it and have John Hunt publish it in the *Examiner* (Abinger MS.; *S&M*, IV, 1027–31).

3. Giuditta Pasta (c. 1798–1865).

4. A miswriting of *fiery*.

❖

To {John Cam Hobhouse}

Kentish Town.   Feb. 19 [1825]

My dear Sir

I am going I am afraid to tresspass most unwarrantably on your politeness—I can only say in excuse—that the object to me is important, & since my difficulty arises from restrictions placed by you the virtual majority upon us the weaker portion, I feel as if I had some (the shadow of a shade)[1] claim upon your gallantry.

I have often wished to be present at a debate in the House of Commons—Two circumstances spur this wish at the present time. First I am engaged in a tale[2] which will certainly be more defective than it would otherwise be, if I am not permitted to be present at a debate—And besides the animated discussions now going on, the splendid eloquence displayed, are beyond words objects of attraction to me. I consider it a great misfortune not {to} have heard the debate of last tuesday.[3]

I hear that there is a place, over the roof of St. Stephens[4] where you senators permit us to hear, not seen. Could you introduce me to this enviable post?—would you?—I make the request frankly—deny me in the same manner if I be too intrusive.

Your's was a most powerful article in the W.R.[5]—Dallas[6] must feel rather uncomfortable & I know that Medwin does.—I think Gamba's book decidedly one of the most interesting upon LordByron[7]—it is simple, affecting & praises without praising—

I am, dear Sir

Yr. Obedient Servant
MaryShelley

TEXT: MS., John Murray.

   1. Aeschylus *Agamemnon* 1. 839.

   2. Mary Shelley's request to Hobhouse, a member of Parliament, that he arrange her admission was in order to gather details for the political debates in her novel *The Last Man*, published by Henry Colburn in February 1826.

   3. On 15 February Canning and Brougham had debated on a petition granting Catholic rights.

   4. The meeting hall of the House of Commons.

   5. The *Westminster Review*.

   6. Robert Charles Dallas (1754–1824), a distant relation to Byron by marriage, had aided Byron's early career. In gratitude, Byron had given Dallas the copyright of *Childe Harold* and *The Corsair*, as well as letters Byron had written to his mother from abroad. In June 1824 Dallas proposed to publish the latter in *Private Correspondence of Lord Byron including his letters to his Mother . . . connected by Memorandums and Observations, forming a Memoir of his Life, from the year 1808 to 1814.* Hobhouse's efforts to suppress this book failed, and it was published, first in French, then in English, by Galignani in Paris. Byron's one highly critical remark about Hobhouse, cited by Dallas, was used by Hobhouse's enemies to his mortification. One of the objects of Hobhouse's review article in the *Westminster Review* was to prove the deep friendship that actually existed between himself and Byron (Moore, *The Late Lord Byron*, pp. 68–73, 85–91).

   7. Pietro Gamba, *A Narrative of Lord Byron's Last Journey to Greece* (London: John Murray, 1825). Hobhouse arranged for the translation of Gamba's book into English, overseeing and doing some of the translating himself (Moore, *The Late Lord Byron*, p. 115).

To John Howard Payne

Kentish Town   Saturday Morning
[?30 April 1825]

My dear Sir

Thank you for your kind attention in sending me the books—though as far as I have yet gone they grievously disappoint me. It is a melancholy consideration that the Creator of Lawton, Leather-Stockings & my beloved Long Tom should consent to put Lionel Lincoln[1] forth to the world—

You are very good to say all that you do in your letter; you put too high a price upon what was the result of the instinct as it were of self-preservation which led me to cultivate the only society which could alleviate almost unendurable sorrow[2]—But while you disclaim vanity, you must not make me vain—or perhaps worse egoistical—That is the worst part of a peculiar situation, which by making you the subject of over attention to others creates an undue estimation of self in one's own mind—But I am resolved not to allow myself to be in my own way—but to talk and think of something less near at hand—Will you not allow me to preserve this laudable determination?

I was unable to go to the theatre Yesterday evening—But if Virginius[3] should be acted & the thing practicable I should like to see it—If I do not see you before I will write concerning the arrangements for the opera—By the bye—a box would be preferable wherever it might be, if it can be obtained.—

Do not talk of frowns—You are good & kind—& deserve therefore nothing but kindness—But we must step lightly on the mosaic of circumstance for if we press too hard the beauty & charm is defaced—The world is a hard taskmaster & talk as we will of independance we are slaves
Adieu

I am truly Yours
MaryShelley

TEXT: MS., Huntington Library.

1. James Fenimore Cooper's *Lionel Lincoln; or, the Leaguer of Boston* (New York, 1825). On [24 April] Payne had sent Mary Shelley the "remaining volumes of Cooper's last novel," indicating that the early part pleased him because it reminded him of boyhood memories: "You can scarcely share my interest even in that part, and the rest may strike you as rather common place" (*The Romance*, p. 29). Godwin's Journal

indicates that he read *Lionel Lincoln* from 5 May through 14 May, which suggests that Mary Shelley lent Godwin these volumes.

2. Payne, alluding to their conversation of the day before, called Mary Shelley "a heroine in love & friendship & duty to a parent." He referred to a conversation in which Mary Shelley said "she found herself excluded from the world by her devotedness to Mrs. Williams, whose history she explained," and "she also explained herself about her father" (*The Romance*, pp. 28, 30).

3. *Virginius*, by James Sheridan Knowles, was first produced in 1820, in Glasgow and then at Covent Garden on 17 May 1820 (Nicoll, *English Drama*, IV, 339).

To John Howard Payne

Tuesday   November 25th
[humorously for 28 June 1825]
Kentish Town

My dear Payne

M[rs] Williams begs me to thank you for her for the attention you have paid to The Drama—She has no idea of making the <u>radical</u> alterations that you suggest[1]—

I am very sorry to have seen you in such ill spirits lately. Methinks I could give you a world of good advice—but I am so little didactic that I do not know how to set about it—And then I hope that it would no{t} come too late—& that by this time you are gay & hopeful—I trust that you will see me before you leave town—if you do leave it, which I hope you will not though this hope is I fear purely selfish on my part—You are good & kind to all except yourself—If you took to being bounteously, as is you wont, courteous towards yourself I think you would arrive at being, as all other objects of your kindness are, quite in good humour, with & grateful for, your own society.—

You made me expect that <u>another letter</u>[2] would have accompanied the book on Sunday—is it indelicate in me to ask for this?—I should not of course unless you had first said that you would be good enough to shew it me—I hope to see you soon & am always your sincere friend

MaryShelley

With regard to Kean; the weather has been so bad that I have not been able to go to town to see the bills—but as I suppose he will play twice this week & no more—I should like to go both times provided it be to Sir Giles Brutus[3]—Hamlet—or in fact to any thing except Richard III— Shylock & Othello—I shall be at My fathers tomorrow evening, perhaps

159

you can call there, or if not, you will I dare say be good enough to write to tell me by the earliest post—What he acts on Thursday & whether you can obtain places & orders for me for that night. If it be inconvenient to you to get 4; 2 will suffice

TEXT: MS., Huntington Library.

1. Payne had suggested extensive revisions for Edward Williams's play and offered to help revise it.

2. Payne had sent Mary Shelley one of Irving's letters and had promised more. To this inquiry Payne responded: "I did not send the letter, because I thought I might find others which would answer your wishes quite as well, and which contained less about my petty affairs, with which you have, in one or two instances, been somewhat disgusted, though you have never said so, and never will. The simple truth is, you have generally seen me under the influence of feelings too deeply possessed to allow me to talk about anything which would give me the trouble of thinking, and I remember all the trash to which I have made you listen with a sort of remorse at having, as it were, thus dragged down a fine mind to the worst of commonplace. But, no doubt, it would happen again, so let it rest. I did not think of these things when I mentioned the letter, which cannot strike you as it does me. I will find others for you, but I send this, lest circumstances should give a false colouring to its being withheld. To understand it, it is necessary you should know that Irving's advice has been of great service to me in all literary points upon which I have had opportunities of consulting him. Since chance threw me among pens, ink and paper, he and his elder brother are the only persons who have ever boldly and unhesitatingly encouraged me with the hopes of ultimate success and prosperity" (The Romance, pp. 69–70).

On Saturday, 25 June 1825, Mary Shelley had gone to the Godwins' for tea and had afterwards met Payne (Godwin's Journal makes no mention of Payne on that day), who walked home with her. On this walk Payne declared his love, to which Mary Shelley responded that her feelings for him were not romantic in nature. In the course of their conversation, she told Payne that she was interested in a "friendship" with Irving, whose gentleness and cordiality had impressed her. As a result, Payne decided to try to effect a match between the two. On 16 August he gave Mary Shelley's letters to Irving to read, with a covering letter that read in part: "I do not ask you to fall in love—but I should even feel a little proud of myself if you thought the lady worthy of that distinction, and very possibly you would have fallen in love with her, had you met her casually—but she is too much out of society to enable you to do so—and sentiments stronger than friendship seldom result from this sort of previous earnestness for intimacy when it comes from the wrong side" (The Romance, pp. 18–19).

Irving entered in his Journal for 16 August 1825: "Read Mrs Shelleys correspondence before going to bed" (Irving, Journals and Notebooks, III, 510). There is no evidence to suggest that Mary Shelley was aware that Payne gave her letters to Irving to read. In fact, she asked Payne not to make her "appear ridiculous" by "repeating tales out of school" to Irving, and she might well have considered Payne's actions a betrayal of her trust.

3. Payne's play Brutus; or, The Fall of Tarquin was first produced at Drury Lane on 3 December 1818 (Nicoll, English Drama, IV, 368). On 7 July 1825 Kean selected Brutus for his benefit night at Drury Lane (Genest, English Stage, IX, 297).

To {John Bowring}[1]

Kentish Town.   October 31. [1825]

A thousand thanks, my dear Sir, for your intelligence concerning my friend—News more interesting has appeared in the Chronicle today[2]—stating his arrival at Zante—apparently if not in a dangerous at least in a very suffering state—May I ask you what you know of this—and whether there is a probability of his coming to England—Rochefoucault's now trite Maxim[3] will occur to you when I own that my sorrow for his pain will be much diminished if I have a hope that it will be instrumental to the bringing him back to his English friends—I am anxious to know as soon as possible all that is known concerning him—as I wish to write to him without delay. I trust to your usual kindness to excuse my unceremonious call on your very valuable time—

I trust that you & your family are well—This divine summer has had a most beneficial effect on my spirits   After an interval of two years I live again. God help me—I hope I shall never get back again to {   } chaos of melancholy in which I lived so long—

I am, my dear Sir
Yours faithfully & obliged
MaryShelley

ENDORSED: Kentish Town Oct / 31st / Mary Shelley / Recd [   ]. TEXT: MS., Pforzheimer Library.

   1. This letter was quite likely written to John Bowring, who as Honorary Secretary to the Greek Committee would have had early news of Trelawny's expected return and would have communicated the news to her.

   2. The *Morning Chronicle* of 31 October 1825 reported under the heading "Portsmouth, Oct. 29" the near-fatal attempt on Trelawny's life: "The Sparrowhawk conveyed to Zante the English Captain Trelawney, who took refuge with his brother-in-law Odysseus, from the revenge of the Greeks, in the fortified cave on the summit of Mount Parnassus. A treacherous attempt had been made by two fellows, employed by the Greeks, to assassinate him, for having betrayed their cause. He was shot in the back; one ball passed out in the front of his shoulder, by which he lost the use of his arm, and another passed through his neck and came out at his mouth." Trelawny had not become a traitor to the Greek cause, but Odysseus, whom he followed, had, and newspapers in Austria, France, and England linked the two together (see St Clair, *Trelawny*, pp. 120–25).

   3. "Nous avons tous assez de force pour supporter les maux d'autrui" (We all have strength enough to bear the sufferings of others), from *Réflexions ou sentences et maximes morales* (1665), by François, Duc de La Rochefoucauld (1613–80).

161

To {?Charles Ollier}

Kentish Town   15 Nov. [1825]

My dear Sir

The title of my book is to be simply "The Last Man, a Romance, by the Author of Frankenstein."[1]—As soon as Mr Colburn has made the communication of which he speaks it will be ready—that is two volumes are quite ready the third will be prepared long before those are printed—Mr Colburn can therefore send it to the press immediately—

My little Percy is convalescent but not quite well

I am, dear Sir, Y^s truly

MaryShelley

TEXT: MS., Fales Library, New York University.

1. *The Last Man* was published by Henry Colburn in January 1826.

To William Godwin, Jr.

Kentish Town   Saturday
[?14 October–November 1826][1]

My dear William—I send you the print of LB—the likeness grows on one—I fancy the very tones he used to utter when he wore that fastidious upturned expression of countenance[2]—If you can get a notice of it in other papers thro' your interest in Thwaites Mudford[3] &c—I should consider it a particular favour done to myself & feel truly obliged. Can you not?—pray try—

I wish you w^d always with an enitial mark in my copy of the O.G. your articles—Which were Payne's last week?

Yours Ever
MaryShelley

This likeness striking at [as] it is was cut from memory—merely with scissars—without any drawing at all.

ADDRESS: W. Godwin Esq Jun / &c &c &c. TEXT: MS., Pforzheimer Library.

1. The date of this letter is based on Mary Shelley's reference to "the O.G.," which was *The Opera Glass for Peeping into the Microcosm of the Fine Arts, and more especially the Drama*, a weekly publication under the editorship of John Howard Payne; it first appeared on 2 October 1826 and ceased publication after twenty-four issues, in March 1827 (Overmyer, *America's First Hamlet*, pp. 267–68).

2. On 5 November 1826 a silhouette of Byron by Marianne Hunt was published in the *Examiner* with a description of the silhouette by Robert Hunt and a description of Byron by Leigh Hunt. Hunt's description mentions Byron's "face turned gently upwards" (Blunden, *"Examiner" Examined*, pp. 242–43).

3. William Mudford (1782–1848), author, journalist, and editor of the evening *Courier*.

<hr>

To Alaric A. Watts[1]

Kentish Town—30 Oct. [1826]

Sir

The absence of Mr Lyndsay[2] from this country has occasioned considerable delay in his & my answer to your obliging letter. I now enclose you the packet, he has consigned to my care for you.

I have no small pieces either of my own or of Mr Shelley's which I can offer you—and I am too much occupied at this moment to attempt the composition of any. The only MS.S. I could offer you—are a prose tale which would about fill 9 pages, I should guess of your work—and 2 short mythological dramas—on the subject of Proserpina & Midas—I would send these now, but I am convinced that your work must be too far advanced to allow the admission of pieces of their length. If you please you can have them that you may judge how far they will be admissible in your next years publication.

I beg to return my thanks for the elegant little volume you have had the politeness to send me. I had of course seen it before—the plates are extremely beautiful, and superior to anything of the kind that I have seen.

I am, Sir,

Your Obedient Servant
MaryShelley

Will you excuse me if I say that in consequence {of} my habit of withdrawing my name from public notice, I should be glad that my signature were not added to your interesting autographs.[3]

ADDRESS: Alaric Watts Esq / &c &c &c. TEXT: MS., Pforzheimer Library.

1. Alaric A. Watts (1797–1864) was editor and proprietor of *The Literary Souvenir*, an annual.

2. Until *MWS Letters*, David Lyndsay has been accepted as the actual name of the author of *Dramas of the Ancient World*, which in 1822 was read and admired by many, including the Shelleys. Thirty-two letters, dated 1821 through 1829, to William Blackwood, publisher of Lyndsay's *Dramas* and a number of Lyndsay's short stories, reveal that David Lyndsay was a pseudonym and that the author was bound

by a promise not to acknowledge his authorship but that sometime in the future his true identity would be made known to Blackwood (Lyndsay's letters to Blackwood are at the National Library of Scotland). The letters also reveal that Lyndsay had the best Scottish blood in his veins; he was several years younger than Byron (whose fame he aspired to equal); he was fluent in many languages; and he was well acquainted with Charles Lamb, "though as Lyndsay he does not know me." In his 16 January 1825 letter Lyndsay informed Blackwood that he was "well-acquainted with Mrs. Shelley." In another letter, c. November–December 1825, he wrote: "with Mrs. Shelley, who is indeed a fine Creature and a million times too good for the party to which she is so unlucky as to belong—I am intimate she is publishing now with Colburn, and from the infinite care with which she has written, I imagine she is anxious to controvert some opinions that have gone abroad as to her cherishing those adopted by her Husband—she had incurr'd an idea that you had been severe in your strictures upon Shelley's writings and character, and I was well pleas'd to be able to prove the contrary, by whole pages of Maga [*Blackwood's Edinburgh Magazine*], in which Shelley is declar'd to be, and treated like, a Scholar and a Gentleman—she was much gratified by your review of Valperga, but declar'd that in her delineation of Castruccio Bonaparte (whom she hates) never enter'd her mind—she has a very powerful mind, and with the most gentle feminine manner and appearance that you can possibly imagine."

These letters, which deal largely with placing his works in *Blackwood's Magazine* or with other publishers, mention the titles of many of his short stories, including his collection *Tales of the Wild and Wonderful* (London: Hurst and Robinson, 1825).

In January 1822 Blackwood wrote Charles Ollier to learn of the reception of *Dramas* in London and to find out whether Ollier knew the identity of the author. He did not. Eliza Rennie, however, in *Traits of Character*, tells of meeting the author of the *Tales of the Wild and Wonderful*: "certainly Nature, in any of its wildest vagaries, never fashioned anything more grotesque-looking than was this Miss Dods. She was a woman apparently between thirty and forty years of age; with a cropped curly head of short, thick hair, more resembling that of a man than of a woman. She wore no cap, and you almost fancied, on first looking at her, that some one of the masculine gender had indulged in the masquerade freak of feminine habiliments and that 'Miss Dods' was an alias for Mr.—. . . . My astonishment at her appearance was unbounded, and I had some difficulty to keep myself from betraying this, and to conceal the laughter I longed to indulge in; but the charm and fascination of her manner, the extraordinary talent which her conversation, without pedantry or pretence, displayed, soon reconciled me to all the singularities of her appearance, and checked all inclination to mirth; and I quickly ceased to wonder at 'Doddy,' as she was familiarly termed by Mrs. Shelley and her intimate friends, being so especial a favourite. She was a great linguist, being thoroughly versed in almost every European language, and, taken altogether, a person of very remarkable mental endowments. She was a contributor, she said, to 'Blackwood's Magazine,' and announced herself as the author of a book called 'Tales of the Wild and Wonderful.'

The events of her own 'wild and wonderful' subsequent career I will not enter upon or touch. She resided many years at Paris where 'she died and was buried' " (I, 207–9).

I have examined the handwriting of the letters signed "David Lyndsay" and two Abinger Manuscript letters to Mary Shelley signed "D" and "MD Dods." The identity of the handwriting confirms that "David Lyndsay" was the pseudonym of Mary Shelley's friend M. D. Dods, or "Doddy." From the will of the fifteenth earl of Morton I have further learned that the author's full name was Mary Diana Dods and that she and her sister Georgiana Dods Carter were the "reputed" daughters of the fifteenth earl (Scottish Record Office, RD5 / 345, p. 416; for references to the will in these letters, see 28 July 1827, n. 6; 15 August 1827).

Mary Diana Dods was a writer and translator of stories, and at one point she tried her hand at a tragedy, which she expected to be presented by Charles Kemble (Lyndsay to Blackwood, 23 March 1823). Although the stories Mary Shelley forwarded to Alaric A. Watts on behalf of her friend were too late for inclusion in the *Literary Souvenir* (the preface of the 1827 edition notes Watts's regret that the articles received from "Mr. David Lindsay" and the author of Frankenstein were too late for inclusion), perhaps it was Mary Shelley who placed "Lyndsay's" "The Three Damsels: A Tale of Halloween" and "The Bridal Ornaments: A Legend of Thuringia" in Ackermann's *Forget-Me-Not* for 1827 (pp. 79–86, 393–416).

By the summer of 1827 Mary Diana Dods and Mary Shelley were assisting Isabel Robinson Douglas to leave England. Additional research gives evidence that Mary Diana Dods now took on a male guise, changed her name to Walter Sholto Douglas (the name Sholto Douglas is found in a number of Scottish families, including that of Dods's father), and proceeded to live in Europe as the purported husband of Isabel Robinson. A 13 November 1827 description of Mr. Douglas as "a little deformed but clever" (MS., Harriet Garnett to Julia Pertz, Garnett Letters, Houghton Library) may be compared with Rennie's description of Mary Diana Dods as someone who was extremely intelligent and whose "figure was short and, instead of being in proportion, was entirely out of all proportion" (*Traits of Character*, I, 207).

The decision to play this role may well have been reflected in Mary Shelley's comment to Jane Hogg: "I am glad for pretty Isabel's sake that D. [*Doddy*] now seriously thinks of les culottes." While the motivations for this charade are not fully known, one reason may have been to give legitimacy to Isabel Robinson Douglas's apparently illegitimate infant daughter. There is only an oblique mention of this child in Mary Shelley's letters. On 26 August 1827, in writing of her own and Isabel Douglas's distress at their sudden eviction from their Sompting lodgings, she complains: "In consequence we must go tomorrow to look for lodgings, & remove without milk— can any thing be so orribile, scelerato [*horrible, villainous*] & all that?" Confirmation of the existence of an infant who would have needed milk is provided by an entry in the *DNB* and the General Register's Office. The former indicates that Henry Drummond Wolff (1830–1908) married Adeline Douglas, the daughter of Walter Sholto Douglas. In 1909 she was awarded a civil list pension of £100. The latter records that Adeline Drummond Wolff died in the second quarter of 1916, at the age of 89. This would place her birth sometime between July 1826 and June 1827. (I am indebted to Emily W. Sunstein for the General Register information.)

The legitimacy given to the daughter was shared by the mother as well: she and her "husband" were accepted in a number of social circles in France. And the *DNB* reports that in 1840 the Rev. William Falconer (1801–85) married Isabella, widow of W. S. Douglas, and that she died at St. Alessi, Italy, in 1869. When Mary Diana Dods, alias Walter Sholto Douglas, died is still unknown. Her sister, Georgiana Dods Carter, who accompanied the Douglases to Paris, remained there and died in August 1842 (Préfecture du Département de la Seine, Acte de Décès, Paris). Whether Dods also remained and died in Paris is difficult to ascertain because many French records were destroyed in World War II. The only person in the extant records who might be Dods is listed as a male with the family name Douglas, born in Scotland, unmarried, who died on 13 August 1845 and who had lived in the same arrondissement as Georgiana Dods Carter.

On 26 September 1827 Mary Shelley wrote in her Journal: "how utterly have I shaken off the dead calm of my life—interesting myself deeply for one whose destiny is so strange." Mary Shelley's letters make it quite clear that she was an active participant in her friends' complex scheme and served to chart partially the course of their lives. (For further details on the story of Dods, Robinson, and Mary Shelley, see Betty T. Bennett, *Mary Diana Dods: A Gentleman and a Scholar* [New York: William Morrow, 1991].)

Little is known about the family of Joshua Robinson (d. 1842). Mary Shelley was particularly the friend of Isabella ("Mrs. Douglas"), Julia, and Rosa (who became the wife of Aubrey William Beauclerk in 1841). Others identified as family members are Louisa (who married Major Lockhard Maclean in 1834), Alfred (1804–58, a solicitor), George, Julian, and Eliza Agnes (who married Henry James Perry in 1844). Mary Shelley made frequent and lengthy visits to their home, Park Cottage, Paddington, and often used the Robinsons' address for mail when she was not permanently domiciled.

3. Watts included in his Annual facsimiles of autographs of living authors.

❧

To Henry Colburn

Kentish Town   Monday   [?30 October 1826]

Dear Sir

A friend of mine, Mr David Lyndsay,[1] who is now abroad, has written to me, requesting me to propose a work of his to you. You have of course heard of Mr Lyndsay as the Author of "Dramas of the Ancient World"— and latterly of "Tales of the Wild and Wond{er}ful{"}   The former work in particular met with considerable success & was highly spoken of in all literary circles—It is indeed a production of genius. His present work is of the same cast—though on even a more poetical plan. The title of some of the Dramas will convey some idea of it "The Revolt of the Wilderness"—"The Festival of the Earth"—"The Wedding of Undine" &c &c The work is not yet complete, but Mr Lyndsay informs me that it will be ready to send by the time he hears from me. If you should feel disposed to purchase this work he would be most happy to treat with you.

He begs me to add that he is already far advanced in a poetical translation of a German drama held in high estimation in Germany called Der Zauber Liebe—Magic Love.   the name of the Author (I think but he has forgotten to mention it) is Alarn. It is of the length of Faust, but M^r

Lynds{ay} intends somewhat to abridge it. He describes it as a poem of the highest imaginative order.

I shall be very glad if you should deem ⟨it⟩ fitting to enter into a negotiation with my friend—

I am, Dear Sir,
Your Ob' Servant
Mary   Shelley

ADDRESS: Henry Colburn Esq / New Burlington St. TEXT: MS., Huntington Library.

  1. See 30 October [1826] to Alaric A. Watts, n. 2.

❖

To Leigh Hunt

5 Bartholomew Place—Kentish Town
30th October 1826

My dear Hunt

Is it—or is it not right that these few lines should be addressed to you now? Yet if the subject be one, that you may judge better to have been deferred—set my undelay down to the account of overzeal in wishing to relieve you from a part of the care, which I know is just now oppressing you:—too happy I shall be if you permit any act of mine to have that effect.

I told you long ago that our dear Shelley intended on rewriting his will to have left you a legacy; I think the sum mentioned was £2,000. I trust that hereafter you will not refuse to ⟨receive this⟩ consider me your debtor for this sum, merely because I shall be bound to pay it {to} you by the laws of honour, instead of a legal obligation. You would of course been better pleased to have received it immediately from dear Shelley's bequest—but as it is well known that he intended to make such an one it is in fact the same thing, and so I hope by you to be considered.   besides your kind heart will receive pleasure from the knowledge that you are bestowing on me the greatest pleasure I am capable of receiving.

This is no resolution of today; but formed from the moment I knew my situation to be such as it is. I did not mention it, because it seemed almost like an empty vaunt, to talk and resolve on things so far off. But futurity approaches[1]—and a feeling haunts me as if this futurity were not far distant. I have spoken vaguely to you on this subject before—but now, you having had a recent disappointment, I have thought it as well to in-

167

form you in express terms of the meaning I attached to my expressions. I have as yet made no will; but in the mean time, if I should chance to die, this present writing may serve as a legal document to prove that I give and bequeath to you the sum of two thousand pounds sterling. But I hope we shall both live—I to accomplish Dear Shelley's intentions; you, to honour me so far as to permit me to be their executor.

I have mentioned this subject to no one; and do not intend; an act is not aided by words—especially an act unfulfilled. Nor does this letter, methinks, require any answer—at least not till after the death of Sir Timothy Shelley[2]—when perhaps this explanation would have come with better grace—but I trust to your kindness to put my writing now to a good motive

I am, My dear Hunt
Yours affectionately & obliged
Mary Wollstonecraft Shelley

To Leigh Hunt Esq.

Text: MS., Bodleian Library.
   1. Charles Bysshe Shelley had died of tuberculosis at Field Place and was buried on 16 September, leaving Percy Florence Shelley as his father's heir.
   2. See 20 April 1844.

To Sir Timothy Shelley

Kentish Town—29. May. 1827

Sir

It is the subject of great anxiety to me that the period of my signing the deed drawn by M'r Whitton is again delayed,—and I am the more mortified since it appears that this delay is occasioned by a communication of mine. When M'r Whitton proposed to me that on the contingency of my inheriting on Bysshe's will, I should repay the sums advanced and to be advanced by you to me and my child, I immediately acceded to this arrangement as being just and proper. M'r Whitton wished that the deed he should draw, should be seen and approved by a Solicitor on my part. M'r Peacock named M'r Amory, and M'r Whitton was satisfied with this nomination. As soon as the affair was put into the hands of a Solicitor, I of course considered myself obliged to act under his directions, and in consequence of M'r Amory's objections all this delay has occurred.

For myself I do not hesitate to say that I put every confidence in you,

Sir Timothy, and that I feel perfectly secure that my interests are safe in your hands, and I am ready to confide them to your direction. It is hard therefore that while I am satisfied with the arrangements you make, that the objections of my advisers should subject me to the dreadful embarassments with which I am now struggling. It was in February last that Mr Whitton announced to me your intention of allowing me £250 per ann. since then I have received no supply—I have lived on credit—the bills incurred are now presented for payment, and neither have I funds to defray them, nor any by which I can continue to exist.

I do not understand business; and I do not mean to bring this subject before you as a question of business. The interest you shewed for my son encouraged me in the hope that you also will be desirous of facilitating my earnest wish of bringing him up properly. As by Bysshe's confidence in me I inherit a considerable property I consider it perfectly right that I should repay the sums you advance to me for his support—but the means for his support I can only obtain through you. I am sure that you will not permit a question of forms merely to interfere with the welfare of your Grandson and the respectability of his Mother. It is a great misfortune to me that I am not permitted to see you.[1] It would have been a great happiness to me if, left a widow, I could have been under the protection of Bysshe's father. This good is denied to me; but let me entreat you to enter into my situation, and not to delay in relieving me from the humiliations & distresses to which I am subjected. I believe that Mr Whitton feels assured that confidence may be safely placed in me and will not advise any further postponement in the desired settlement.

Let me entreat you therefore, Sir Timothy, to direct that the deed in question may be immediately prepared for my signature. Every day is of consequence to me; your kind feelings will I do not doubt, cause as few to intervene as possible before I am relieved from my embarassments.

Percy is quite well, and often speaks of you; I hope it will not be long before he has the honour of seeing you again

I am your obliged & ob^t Servant
MaryShelley

ADDRESS: Sir Tim. Shelley Bart. ENDORSED: 29th May 1827. TEXT: MS., Bodleian Library.

1. Although Sir Timothy Shelley saw Percy Florence from time to time, he adamantly refused to meet Mary Shelley.

To Teresa Guiccioli

3ᶻᵒ Luglio [July]—1827—Kentish Town

Cara Mia Contessina

Quanto tempo c'è che non siamo scritte! Quasi due anni! Ma non mi
sono scordata di voi—parlo continuamente di voi colla Williams—e pen-
siamo sempre al felice tempo quando fummo tutte vicine l'una a l'altra.
Voleva scrivervi quando sentii da Medwin che foste partita da Roma—ed
ora mi dice il medesimo che vi siete di ritorno. Mi spiccio a ricomminciare
la corispondenza interrotta. Ahime—Amica cara—non siamo scordate
dalle disgrazie—il Vostro amato fratello![1] l'abbiamo perduto—che colpo
per voi ed il povero Pappa—Questa vita si chiama bene un passo doloroso,
quanto abbiamo noi penate—giovane ancora.

Comminciava una lunga lettera per voi—raccontando gli avvenimenti
di questi lunghi mesi di silenzio—ma se non siate a Roma—se non vi
giunga questo foglio, non vorrei dare tal detaglio a chi che sia che forse
leggera questo vergare mio. Vi diro adunque solamente che sto bene,
io ed il mio figlio—e subito che tengo la vostra risposta a questa vi
riscrivero.

V'è una cosa pero che bisogna aggiungere a queste poche linèe—per
che preme il tempo. E vi prego mia cara, di rispondere senza indugio.
L'Amico intrinseco di Bÿron—Moore,—scrive ora la vita del vostro
Amante.[2] Mi è venuto vedere—Mi parlava di voi—diceva che dopo il libro di Medwin era inutile che voi cercaste l'oscurità, ma che in parlando
di voi—voleva sentire primamente da voi il vostro sentimento e se vi fosse
cosa alcuna che vorreste dire. Tengo dal Caro Pietro il fagotto delle tue
lettere a Bÿron—se mi permetterle potrei da queli far un ebauche della
vostra storia per Moore—Ma non vorrei far nulla senza il vostro
consentimento   Moore e gran'amico del Caro Bÿron—Vi stima—e gli
fara caso parlare di voi in un modo degno—E poi mi promette che io legga
quel che scrivera di voi—e che non stampera cosa che io non approva—
Potete fidarvi adunque, Cara Guiccioli, alla mia amicizia—ed alla sua
delicatezza—all'onore suo. Che dite. Forse avete lettere di Byron che vorreste contribuire—Rispondete subito e state sicurra che io staro vigi-
lantissima—e se mi mandate la vostra volonta—quella sara legge per
me.   Hobhouse dà ogni facilita a Moore—Cosi questo suo libro avra un
carattere autentico—Moore vi saluta rispettosamente e vi prega di accon-
sentire a questo proponimento.

Non potrei dirvi—Mia Cara Amica—quanto piacere reco dalla società di Moore—Non parliamo di altro quasi che di Bÿron—e non ci ne stanchiamo mai—Ma più di questo—no—fin' che sapro se voi riceverete sicuramente questa lettera.

Addio Mia Cara Contessa—Mi par mill'anni che non vi vedo—che non rivedo la mia Italia   Amate me sempre—che mi ripeto sempre

V^{ra} Aff^{ma} A^{ca}   Mary Shelley

Vi rammentate di quella letterina Inglese che Egli scrisse al fine della Vostra Corinna?³ Vi dispiacerebbe di darmi una copia—Indrizzate la Vostra lettera

Mrs Shelley
W. Godwin Esq.
44 Gower Place.—Bedford Sq.
London

[*Translation*]

My Dear Contessina

How long it's been since we have written to each other! Almost two years! But I have not forgotten you—I continually speak about you with Signora Williams—and we always think of the happy time when we were all near to one and other. I wanted to write you when I heard from Medwin that you might have left Rome—and now he tells me that you have returned. I hasten to begin again our interrupted correspondence. Alas—dear Friend—we have not been forgotten by misfortune—Your beloved brother!¹ we have lost him—what a blow for you and your poor Father—This life is justly called a sorrowful passage, how much we have suffered—young still.

I started a long letter for you—recounting the events of these long months of silence—but if you are not at Rome—if this letter does not reach you, I do not want to give such detail to whomever might read this letter of mine. I will tell you therefore only that I am well, I and my son—and as soon as I have your reply to this I will write again.

There is one thing however that it is necessary for me to add to these few lines—because time is important. And I beg you my dear, to reply without delay. The intimate friend of Byron—Moore—is now writing the life of your Lover.² He came to see me—He spoke to me of you—he said that after Medwin's book it was useless for you to seek obscurity, but that in speaking about you—he wanted to hear chiefly from you your feeling and if there might be anything that you would want to say. I have from Dear Pietro the bundle of your letters to Byron—if you allow me I could make from these a rough outline of your story for Moore—But I do not want to do anything without your consent. Moore is a great friend of Dear Byron—He respects you—and it will please him to speak of you in a deserving way—And then he promises me that I can read that which he will write about you—and that he will not print anything that I do not approve—You may have confidence then, Dear Guiccioli, in my friendship—and in his tact—in his honor. What do you say. Perhaps you have some letters of Byron's that you might want to contribute—Reply immediately and be assured that I will be extremely vigilant—and if you send me your wish—this will be the law for me. Hobhouse gives every accommodation to Moore—Therefore this book will have an authentic character—Moore respectfully sends you his regards and begs you to consent to this purpose.

I cannot tell you—My Dear Friend—how much pleasure I receive from Moore's company—We speak of almost nothing besides Byron—and we never tire of it—But more than this—no—until I know that you will receive this letter for certain.

Farewell My Dear Countess—It seems a thousand years to me since I have seen you—since I have seen my Italy—Love me always—as I again declare myself always

        Your most affectionate friend   Mary Shelley

Do you recall that little English letter that he wrote at the end of your Corinne?[3] Would you mind giving me a copy—Address your letter

M[rs] Shelley

W. Godwin Esq.

44 Gower Place.—Bedford Sq.

    London

ADDRESS: Alla Sua Eccellenza / La Contessa Teresa Guiccioli / a Roma / Rome. Italy. POSTMARKS: (1) PAID / 5 JY / 182[7]; (2) F27 / 229; (3) ANGLETERRE; (4) PONT / BEAUVOISIN; (5) 19 LUGLIO. TEXT: MS., Pforzheimer Library. TRANSLATION: Ricki B. Herzfeld.

    1. Upon his return to Greece, Pietro Gamba became a colonel in the Greek Army. He died of typhoid in 1827 (Origo, *The Last Attachment*, p. 387).

    2. Mary Shelley wrote in her Journal on 26 June: "I have just made acquaintance with Tom Moore—He reminds me delightfully of the past and I like him much— There is something warm & genuine in his feelings & manner which is very attractive—and redeems him from the sin of worldliness with which he has been charged." On 2 July she wrote in her Journal that she had breakfasted with Moore the day before and they had spoken about Shelley and Byron; she also wrote that she felt perfectly at ease with Moore and welcomed his company because "I have been so long exiled from the style of society in which I spent the better part of my life." On 11 July her Journal entry notes that Moore had left town; that his singing "is something new & strange & beautiful!"; and, again, that his visits gave her much pleasure. Moore's purpose in calling on Mary Shelley was to secure her aid in acquiring material for his biography of Byron, a favor she willingly provided. Only two fragments of Mary

Shelley's letters to Moore have been located, but his many letters to her, spanning the years 1827 through 1841, are evidence of the long friendship that developed between the two writers (see Moore, *Letters*, II; and Betty T. Bennett, "An Unpublished Letter from Thomas Moore to Mary Shelley," *Notes and Queries* 23, no. 3 [March 1976]: 114).

3. (1807), by Madame de Staël.

※

To Jane Williams Hogg[1]

Mrs. Burry—Sompting near Shoreham—
Sussex.   28 July 1827

Loveliest Janey—to thee tranquillity and health! How are you? You were far from well[2]—I do not fear any new disease, but how is the old one—does the bright lily raise its head lightly & cheerfully?—God send it may never in the slightest degree droop! it is—ma pero I am not sure that male eyes will not trace these lines, so I will endeavour to be as demure as an old maid—I wonder if you will understand the fitting supplement to that unfinished sentence. It is a pleasant thing to turn in one's mind's eye to a friend's sweet home & know that there is tranquillity there—I have now your drawing-room before me, with all its adornments—the kind & happy Giver of Good & the Fairy girl who has created the kindness—the happiness, the gift—the Good—the all. Is my pretty Filleule[3] with you & brave Med?—kiss both the dear children for me.

We are here calm & I trust contented—at least every outward & visible sign betokens peace. I did not tell you that Mary Hunt was to go with us—indeed it was only arranged the day before I saw you for the last time & then my head was full of—Sono veramente grato per questo piacere—incuramente mio procurero questo bene—The cosa fir questa[4]—I was in the Kentish Town Stage with M^arianne & she gave me so dreadful an account of Mary in so careless a tone, that I felt impelled to put in my feeble aid to endeavour to save a child of whose dispositions I have a favourable opinion—Doddy & Isabel[5] did not object—& she is in fact a great resource to us here being old enough to be the gouvernante to Percy & young enough to amuse herself in his game[   ] Monday we begin schooling—Heaven send that indeed we do—we intend it—& hope not to add another stone to the pavement of l'Inferno.

I am happy to find sweet Isabel well—she is anxious about D—[*Doddy*] from whom we had a most melancholy letter this morning—poor pet—she is very dreary & alone—She cannot visit you till she has quatrini

173

& they arrive far slower than the snail of the story—still though circumstances must make her* [*p. 3, upside-down*] *(I am stupid to have left these blanks to be so awkwardly fill up—it was thro' inadvertance) gloomy—good will come soon—Lord M. [*Morton*] is to be buried on Monday—the will will be read—& certainty will come.[6]

I must tell you all our plans hazard à merveille[7]—We arrived tired to death at Worthing at 4 on Tuesday—had tea—& slept—Worthing by the bye is a horror—the best dressed young ladies go about in scanty nankeen pelisses—straw pokes with pea green ribbons—& green crape veils made blue here & there as the sea [*p. 4, upside-down*] spray—on Wednesday morning we Fly it to Sompting with our traps—the lodgings were empty—we took them & established ourselves directly the people are civil & apparently honest—indeed all the villagers & country people are courteous à l'Italienne—we have beautiful walks—& shady embowered places where {we} sit & work & read. In truth so much am I delighted with my life here that I dwell more & more on a plan which I have long cherished—of living wholey in the country about 15 miles from town—Whitton certainly made out that Sir Tim would like this—I should see my family seldomer perhaps but far more comfortably—& even you—bright friend—but this is all en l'air as yet—I fear the future far—far too much to like to dwell on it.

Adieu then—take care of the prettiest, most graceful—blue-eyed Bride this world ever saw—For every body's sake love yourself tenderly—& think with gentle kindness of her who for years has been your devoted

Mary S—

Isabel says that she pictures your fairy home & its presiding Grace & wishes all good to it——

[*P. 4, side*] I have opened my letter to say that Isabel is M[rs] Douglas here—LHunt does not know my friend's name—but Mary's report will be of M[rs] D.—[*Douglas*]

ADDRESS: Mrs Hogg / Mrs Wilson / 8 Maida Place / Edgware Road—London. POSTMARKS: (1) SHOREHAM / PENNY POST; (2) A / 30 JY 30 / 1827; (3) 10. F. NOON. 10 / JY. 30 / 1827. TEXT: MS., Abinger MSS.

1. The name and address on this letter indicate that the union of Jane Williams and Thomas Jefferson Hogg took place before Mary Shelley's departure from London.

2. This letter and Mary Shelley's letters of 7 and 22 August to Jane Williams Hogg make clear that the latter was pregnant. Although biographies of Jane Williams Hogg and Thomas Jefferson Hogg make no mention of a child born of this pregnancy, a daughter was born to the Hoggs c. November 1827. The Paddington Parish Registers, The Greater London Record Office, record that the child was baptized Mary Prudentia at St. Mary's Church, Paddington, on 21 January 1829, and was buried at St. Mary's at the age of eighteen months, on 23 May 1829. Hogg's

mother and one sister were named Prudentia. (The Hoggs' second daughter, born in 1836, to whom Mary Shelley stood godmother, was named Sarah Prudentia, the first name after another of Hogg's sisters.) It is possible that the Hoggs' first daughter was named in honor of Mary Shelley.

3. "Goddaughter," that is, Dina.

4. "I am truly grateful for this pleasure—without effort I will gain this benefit—The thing was."

5. Mary Diana Dods (see 30 October {1826} to Alaric A. Watts, n. 2).

6. George Douglas, fifteenth earl of Morton (b. 1761), died on 17 July 1827 and was buried on 30 July. Since he left no legitimate progeny, he was succeeded by his cousin, George Sholto Douglas, who became the sixteenth earl of Morton (*The Scots Peerage*, ed. Sir James Balfour Paul [Edinburgh, 1909]). The will of the fifteenth earl, dated 14 August 1824, provides an annuity of £100 per year for Mary Diana Dods and an equal annuity for her sister Georgiana Dods Carter "for the love favor and affection which I leave and bear to my reputed Daughters" (Scottish Record Office, RD5 / 345, p. 416).

7. "Risking wonder."

◆

To Jane Williams Hogg

Sompting—15 August—1827

Alas, my sweet girl—how very unkind is our person to us—Your state of ill health weighs heavily on me—I can not endure to think that the Lily of the World droops—and that any thing but happiness should dwell in your blue eyes. Pray, pray take care of yourself—no wet walks to Hampstead—no yielding to the slowness of others, till coaches are lost—&c—remember all depends upon care:

Ah! how could our wrong Person have the heart to take from us the World's Splendour[1]—What a dreadful event for all & every part of habitable earth—I can conceive of no substitution that can compensate in any way for the loss we have sustained.—And foreign nations will feel it even more—for Brougham & others may continue, under the King's present liberal system, the improvements with Canning commenced—but his foreign policy cannot but feel deeply the failure of his tact & knowledge of the subject.—

In the midst of melancholy a letter from D. [*Doddy*] gives us some life—Small indeed is the thing done—[*full line scratched out*] nor do I exactly know what future course of action can be founded on it—but in some way I suppose the plan of going abroad will be put in execution—when or how must be decided when D. & Isabel meet—as yet the mere fact of the continuance of the Annuity and a possibility of something

175

more years hence, is all we know.[2] But certainty succeeding to the worst doubts, is so delightful, that we have hailed this small good with pleasure.

For myself—You say I look forward gloomily & I do. I cannot endure to return to the Kentish Town mode of things & in spite of all, I cling to my country plan—where pleasures that I love—the sights & splendours of earth & sky—will come to my door—instead of my being forced to overcome my laziness to seek them—As yet my schemes are in embryo—but will it not be a pleasant change for you in your three months widowhood[3] to come to me in my cot & enjoy country pleasures?—At any rate I shall remain in London until after the Christmas holidays—when Percy's school must be fixed upon, & I shall remove to its vicinity.

We have had clouds & rain succeeding our brilliant days & divine moonlight nights—but the rain was soft & warm—and walking yesterday night after it had ceased, though the clouds were thick & dark—we found the change delightful—& the south west wind balmy though languid.—The harvest is now getting in—so that we are losing some of our beauties;—by degrees the Bride of the Sun will throw aside her nuptial ornaments—till she assume the dark weeds of her widowhood—and the thing I fear, winter—will enwrap her.——

I have had no letters from any one except th[e] Guiccioli. She writes kindly—& speaks with great sor[row] of the loss of her Brother—which preys on her father's health. The Pope had ordered her to join her husband—which she did, but he was so intolerable in every way, that she obtained from the Santo Padre—another decree of divorce & they are separated for ever. She says she thinks of us both very often & desires tanti saluti alla gentile M.rs W. [*Williams*] ——No letter from Trelawny! What does this mean?—Have you written to Claire? I have so very many foreign letters to write that their number frightens me, & I write none.——

I wish I heard that Dina were with you—though till you gain a little strength I fear even the gentle darling would be too much for you—Give her a kiss from Marraine—& one also to my frank hearted Meddy——Remember me in the kindest way to poor dear Mammina—Ask her if there is any thing I can get for her from Brighton. Good news of the Shorediches is I fear an hopeless concern—Remember me to the Clints especially Signor Georgio.

I have no news from any one—the G's [*Godwins*] are al solito—W. [*William*] is in the country.——I have had one short note from Marianne, Harding has some hopes of Swinburne[4]——Let me hear from you soon—my lovely one—for I am all anxiety on your account—the more that peace being now around me—I wait in fear for a tempest—from which

Messer Domine guard me God bless you, my bright beauty—Isabel re-
peats God bless her—love

Ever Y^s—MS.

ADDRESS: Mrs Jefferson Hogg / 8   Mrs Wilson / Maida Place / Edgeware Road—
London. POSTMARKS: (1) [SHO]REHAM / [PE]NNY POST; (2) A / 16 AU 1[6] / 1827;
(3) 10. F.NOON. 10 / AU. 16 / 1827. TEXT: MS., Abinger MSS., Bodleian Library.
    1. George Canning died on 8 August (see [?–] 22 March [1824]).
    2. See 28 July 1827, n. 6.
    3. When Hogg would go to the circuit courts in Northumberland and Durham
(Norman, *After Shelley*, p. xii).
    4. Swinburne Hunt died on 22 September 1827.

❧

To John Howard Payne

Sompting—30 August [1827]

My dear Payne

Since it is possible that I may have the pleasure of seeing you during
my sojourn away from town, I write to tell you of a changement de de-
muere—I have been obliged to give up my lodgings to other people—&
remove next Monday to Arundel—this it is true is ten miles further from
Brighton, but a machine will easily bring you to us—Arundel is a most
beautiful town—& it & its Castle may figure well in your volumes, so
this is an additional inducement, besides the sight of your fair Friend,
to make twenty miles seem ten. It is not Mrs Williams who is with me—
but take care of your heart when you come—for though my friend is a
sweet little girl—she is married.—⟨Talking of⟩ Apropos of your ⟨dis-
trusting⟩ heart—are you not glad of Louisa's success?[1]—I must write to
congratulate—poor darling girl—how pleased she must be—& she has
so few pleasures that I am delighted that she should enjoy this one.—Any
news you send me is a god send—for our seclusion is perfect—therefore,
after all intelligence about yourself, in which I am so truly interested,
pray fill your letters with gossip.—

I wish you to do a thing for me—& if you could do it on the day
you receive this, & send me the result by return of post, you would
greatly enhance the favour.—I have heard that Colonel Lincoln (remember Lincoln) Stanhope[2] is dangerously ill—& for a particular reason (dont
try to guess it, for I defy you, I never saw him, even at the Opera, so it
is not Amore) I wish to know the truth. Will you send to Harrington
House, Stable Yard—St. James—& without mentioning names—ask—

177

Whether Colonel Lincoln Stanhope is there—or where he is—whether he is better & what is his illness—Can you do this without inconvenience—for by so doing, you will convenience me greatly.

I hope to hear, kind Friend, that you are quite well—When is it probable that I shall see you?

Most truly Yours
MS.

Remember I trust to your discretion—my name on no account must be hinted.————I do not go to Arundel till Monday—so direct your answer to me here

ADDRESS: John Howard Payne Esq. / 29 Arundel St. Strand / London. POSTMARKS: (1) SHOREHAM / PENNY POST; (2) A / 31 AU 31 / 1827. TEXT: MS., Pforzheimer Library.

1. Louisa Holcroft married John Badams (d. 1833), manufacturing chemist and a friend of Carlyle. The Payne, *Letterbook*, copy of this letter substitutes *nuptials* for *success*.

2. Lincoln Edwin Robert Stanhope (1781–1840), son of the third earl of Harrington.

❖

To Jane Williams Hogg

Somting—31ˢᵗ August 1827.

Pardon this letter—sweet Janey, it is most likely useless—but if not quite useless it is absolutely necessary—You said in your last letter that you would forward the other £5 to our new abode—this would have done very excellently if we had removed hence on Wednesday—but five days at a cabarêt will render it necessary for me to receive it here—the fear of a mistake makes me write—we quit this place on Monday, therefore will you send it by return of post—Next week I hope Whitton will be true to his word—What would I give to have no doubt of receiving my pittance to a day—however as W. [*Whitton*] has promised I ought not to doubt—Il prezzo¹ of small beer has weaned us from our village—& we long for our removal. I hope, pretty One, to hear of your entire convalescence take care of yourself—Isabel has arrived thro' care at a better state of health—She is dictating to me a thousand pettinesses of how her wrecked frame deserves not new rigging from so fair a hand as thine— but I will not write such modest proprieties—What a delight it would be if she were to attain tolerable health—Adieu—I write in a hurry as the thought came on me late that it would be prudent so to do—A thousand thanks for your speedy assistance of the half wrecked

MS.

Oime i venti son omai passato sono gia vecchia!²

ADDRESS: Mrs. Jefferson Hogg / 8 Mrs Wilson / Maida Place—Paddington / London. POSTMARKS: (1) SHOREHAM / PENNY POST; (2) A / 1 SE 1 / 1827; (3) 10. F.NOON. 10 / SP. 1 / 1827. TEXT: MS., Abinger MSS., Bodleian Library.
1. "The price."
2. "Alas the twenties have now passed I am already old." On 30 August Mary Shelley was thirty years old.

To Frances Wright[1]

Arundel.   12 Sepʳ 1827

You confer on me a very high honor by forgetting for a moment your high & noble views to interest yʳ self in me; and in addressing me rather on the score of my relations, than myself you touch the right chord to win my ⟨affection⟩ attention, & excite my interest. The memory of my Mother has been always been the pride & delight of my life; & the admiration of others for her, has been the cause of most of the happiness ⟨of my life⟩ I have enjoyed. Her greatness of soul & my father high talents have perpetually reminded me that I ought to degenerate as little as I could from those from whom I derived my being. For several years with Mʳ Shelley I was blessed with the companionship of one, who fostered this ambition & inspired that of being worthy of him. He who was single among men for Philanthrophy—devoted generosity—talent & goodness.—yet you must not fancy that I am what I wish I were, and my chief merit must always be derived, first from the glory these wonderful beings have shed [?around] me, & then for the enthusiasm I have for excellence & the ardent admiration I feel for those who sacrifice themselves for the public good.

If you feel curiosity concerning me—how much more in the refined sense of the word, must I not feel for yʳ self . . a woman, young rich & independant. quits the civilization of England for a life of hardship in the forests of America that by so doing she may contribute to the happiness of her species—Her health fails in the attempt, yet scarcely restored to that, she is eager to return again to the scene of her labours, & again to spend the flower of her life in arduous struggles & beneficent, self sacrificing devotion to others. Such a tale cannot fail to inspire the deepest interest & the most ardent admiration. You do honour to our species & what perhaps is dearer to me, to the feminine part of it.—and that thought, while it makes me doubly interested in you, makes me tremble for you—women are so per{pet}ually the victims of their generosity—& their purer, & more sensitive feelings render them so much less than men capable of battling the selfishness, hardness & ingratitude w^h is so often the return made, for the noblest efforts to benefit others.—But you seem satisfied with y^r success, so I hope the ill-fortune w^h too usually frustrates our best views, will spare to harm the family of love, w^h you represent to have assembled at Nashoba.

My absence from London prevented me probably from seeing Mr Owen.[2] it has also hindered me from receiving y^r printed papers. I have therefore only y^r letter to guide me to a knowledge of y^r settlement. Is it all you wish? Do you find the motives you mention sufficient to tame that strange human nature, w^h is perpetually the source of wonder to me? It takes a simpler form probably in a forest abode—yet can enthusiasm for public good rein in passion motive benevolence, & unite families? ⟨Nashoba⟩ it were a divine sight to behold the reality of such a picture.—

Yet do not be angry with me that I am so much of a woman, that I am far more interested in you than in (except as it is yours) your settlement. Do not excite my interest to disappoint it—Why cannot you come to England? I am near the coast—& if you crossed to Brighton, I c^d see you—At least I pray you write again—write about y^{r}self—tell me whether happiness & content repay y^r exertions. I have found that the first of these blessings can only be found in the exercise of the affections—Yet I have not found mine there—for where moral evil does not interfere— dreadful Death has come to deprive me of all I enjoyed. My life has been not like yours publicly active, but it has been one of tempestuous suffering.—now in a quiet seclusion with my boy & with the companionship of a beloved friend I repose for a few months—& such has been the uncertainty of my fate, that these seem a mighty good torn from cruel destiny & I live in perpetual fear that I shall not be permitted to enjoy it even so long.—

I fully trust that I shall hear from you again[3]—Do not, public [?spirited] as you are, turn from me, because private interests too much opress me. At least tho' mine be a narrow circle, yet I am willing at all times to sacrifice my being to it, & derive my only pleasure from contributing to the happiness & welfare of others. My sympathy is yours—let me also claim some from you that thus we may establish between us the name of friend.

With the most lively admiration I am yours

Mary Shelley

P.S. I must not forget to say, that I only received y^r letter today.—I answer it on the instant.

Text: Copy of MS. by Julia Garnett, on deposit at Houghton Library by heirs of Cecilia Payne-Gaposchkin.

1. Frances Wright Darusmont (1795–1852), philanthropist, author, and social reformer, was born in Scotland but was raised in England after the death of her parents in 1798. In 1818, accompanied by her younger sister Camilla (?1797–1831), she traveled to the United States, where she began her lifelong association with reform movements in America. In 1824 she and her sister established the Nashoba settlement in Tennessee, a community in which slaves could earn funds through their labors to buy their own liberty. Although Nashoba failed, Frances Wright continued to involve herself in other means of social and political reform. In 1831 she married Phiquepal Darusmont (1797–1855), a French educational theorist, from whom she was divorced in 1851 (for a full biography see Perkins and Wolfson, *Frances Wright*). In the summer of 1827 she had returned to Europe to recover from a serious illness and to enlist new members for the Nashoba colony. These facts and others pertaining to her anti-slavery position Frances Wright had written to Mary Shelley in her letter of 22 August 1827 from Paris (see *S&M*, IV, 1092–95).

2. Frances Wright's letter of 22 August had been hand-delivered by Robert Dale Owen (1801–77), eventually a U.S. politician and social reformer, who was the eldest son of Scottish socialist reformer Robert Owen (1771–1858). In 1826 the younger Owen had gone to New Harmony, the experimental socialist village founded by his father in Indiana. When New Harmony ceased to be a community in 1827, Owen returned to Europe with Frances Wright, whom he had met in 1826, with the plan of returning with her and others to Nashoba (see Owen, *Threading My Way*, pp. 227, 298, 302–3). The elder Owen was a supporter of Godwin's ideals and had introduced his son to Godwin in 1826 (Owen, *Threading My Way*, p. 207). It was probably Robert Dale Owen, who praised Mary Shelley in *Threading My Way* (pp. 321–24), who suggested that Frances Wright contact Mary Shelley (Perkins and Wolfson, *Frances Wright*, p. 176).

3. On 15 September 1827, Frances Wright wrote an enthusiastic response in which she set out her schedule. It would include a visit to England around 28 September, at which time she promised to meet Mary Shelley (*Garnett Letters*, pp. 99–100; *S&M*, IV, 1096–98).

To Jane Williams Hogg

Arundel   17. September [1827]

Our fates seem going on pretty equally in the crab-style, my prettiest little Girl—Since I last wrote, Isabel has been very very ill—& one day especially, endured such intense pain, accompanied by fever, that I became alarmed—she is now, I trust, convalescent—but so weak & cut up, that she requires perpetual care—surely if she had remained at Highgate, she would have died. I cannot guess at what her complaint is—but it is some real disease, of which this last is a severe attack—kept off long by quiet and care—& these two will I hope soon restore her—Our lodgings here are uncomfortable enough—& the trouble I had to prevent thunder-sound, when the dropping of a pin was agony to my poor <u>patient</u> patient was infinite—there are seven children in the house! another coming next month!—Fortunately the day before her attack I had arranged Percy as day boarder at the only decent school here, where they have no day scholars.

The weather is favourable to my invalid—& infinitely pleasant—very fine, the English call it, though my Italian prejudice will hardly permit me to call a libeccio[1] agreable—yet it is—in spite of prejudice. Our beech woods are becoming yellow, and the Autumnal tints are decorating the woodland scenery of this lovely spot—I cannot prefer autumn to the genial birth of life & beauty in spring—yet as a Menlancholy [*Melancholy*] tale as Niobe,[2] or a martyred saint, can be sublimely beautiful & interesting, so is the sear Autumn. The country is filling with people but there are no sportsmen here—for the Duke[3] preserves the game carefully—it is killed by the keeper & sent to Lord Scarey—so we have seen no short coated-Joe Manton[4] bearing divinities, from whom to obtain thro' love, what we excessively <u>wish</u> for, yet cannot get for money—pheasants & partridges.

And what are you doing, my poor darling? How are your babes? Have you moved?—how do you pass your time?—al <u>solito</u>?[5]—Now there are no courts, does the duteous Jeff. plod to temple[6] each day—and back again to his fairy-girl at five?—have you no news for me?—I have written to Trelawny & to Tom[7]—how I wish I could learn anything of the former, for I get more & more anxious about him—I hear absolutely from no one—save poor dear Papa—The Hunts never write—We do not know yet when to expect Doddy. I hope Isabel will be a little in good looks for the Sposo—she is pale & ill now & after all I am afraid that she wi[ll] hardly

182

recover, till some first rate Medical person discover her ill—there is one somewhere—but what I cannot ⟨guess⟩ divine.—

You may guess how my time is taken up—I steal an hour for writing[8] in the morning, & another for a walk at night—in truth I began to suffer in health also, but am better now—The day & night of her extreme illness shook me a good deal—poor child how very much she suffered—in her head principally—is it not strange—passing strange, Janey sweet, that when her agony almost forced screams—and her chest & head were both suffering the excess of anguish—my hand on either soothed her immediately—what would Tom say to this?—I do not believe in Magnetism[9] beyond this power, which we have exercised too often & in too flagrant cases, not to force us to ⟨believe⟩ credit it—and I think that such as it is, the power ought to be known—for no fancy gave quiet to Isabel in the midst of agony—it was a real alleviation that she felt.

I wish very much to hear how you are now, you & your darlings. Take care of yourself   God bless you   Ever Yours

MS.

ADDRESS: Mrs. Jefferson Hogg / 8 Mrs Wilson / Maida Place—Paddington / London. POSTMARKS: (1) ARUNDEL / 0620; (2) 10. F.NOON. 10 / SP. 18 / 1827; (3) F / 18 SE 18 / 1827. TEXT: MS., Abinger MSS., Bodleian Library.

1. "Southwest wind."
2. After Niobe's excessive pride in her children provoked Apollo and Artemis to kill them, she was transformed by Zeus into stone, forever remembering her sorrow. The sculpture of Niobe and her children at the Uffizi Gallery, Florence, was one of Shelley's favorite works of art (PBS Letters, #560).
3. Bernard Edward, twelfth duke of Norfolk.
4. Joseph Manton (?1766–1835; DNB), celebrated London gunsmith.
5. "As usual."
6. A reference to Hogg's law career.
7. Thomas Medwin.
8. Her novel Perkin Warbeck. On 26 September 1827, obviously in response to a request, Godwin sent her an account of the children of Edward IV for the novel (S&M, IV, 1106c–d).
9. Franz Anton Mesmer (1734–1815), Austrian mystic and physician, based on his belief in the healing and magnetic power in his own hands, developed a treatment that he named "animal magnetism" but that came to be called mesmerism. This forerunner of modern hypnosis was extremely popular for a while, although medical authorities labeled Mesmer a charlatan. Thomas Medwin introduced mesmerism to the Shelley circle at Pisa in 1820. First he, and then Jane Williams and Mary Shelley, mesmerized Shelley in order to alleviate his physical suffering from what Medwin believed to be nephritis (Medwin, Shelley, pp. 269–70).

To John Howard Payne

Arundel—23 September. [1827]

Your little note, my dear friend, is a melancholy & a painful one—you do not complain but I see all is not well with you—how hard this is! You who are so good & kind—I trust however that you are not ill[1]—with health one can struggle with much—I am afraid you work too hard & try yourself too much—let me hear that you are better, and I shall be delighted—Surely I need not make professions to you—I believe that you know me, & know that a spirit of politeness merely, would not make me write what I do not feel—and if I did not feel deep regard for you—I could not even ask you to do me services. Do not reproach me therefore for my apologies, they do not arise from any doubt concerning you—as if I felt that I could not apply to you—but kindnesses make a lively impression on me, I feel grateful, & you would not I am sure, deny me the pleasure of expressing my feelings.—

To shew you that I believe that you like to serve me, I am about to send you another commission. My friends here mean in a few days to cross the channel—they will go by Brighton & Dieppe & want a passport[2]—could you, if I sent up their names, procure it?—by so doing you would oblige me greatly. I have heard that they wont give passports in London except to the persons themselves—& that in procuring them at the Port from which they sail, it is necessary to pay—what in this case is the expence,— & will one passport, & consequently one expence, serve various members of a party travelling together?—if you could answer these questions by return of post, you would be of great service to me.

The rain is drear—Arundel is still beautiful, yet I repine at the loss of my adored summer. Adieu my dear Payne—Would I could force heaven to cause all your projects to succeed

Yours ever most truly.

MShelley

Arundel does not contain a Court Guide[3]—so will you look in one & send me Sir William Knighton's[4] address in town when you next write

ADDRESS: J. Howard Payne Esq / 29 Arundel St. / Strand / London. POSTMARKS: (1) ARUNDEL / 0620; (2) F / 24 SE 24 / 1827. TEXT: MS., Brown University Library.

1. Payne had been seriously ill in the spring (Mary Jane Godwin to Payne, 17 March 182[7], MS., Houghton Library; Overmyer, *America's First Hamlet*, p. 268).

2. Obtaining passports through John Howard Payne rather than in person pro-

tected the "Douglases" from discovery (see 25 September [1827] to John Howard Payne, 1 October [1827], and 13 October [1827]).

3. *Boyle's Court Guide.*

4. Perhaps Isabel Douglas's poor health was the reason that Mary Shelley wanted to consult this prominent physician, whom she knew through the Hunts (see MWS *Letters*, vol. I, 10 October [1824], n. 7).

❖

To Alaric A. Watts

Arundel.   25 September [1827]

My Dear Sir

I am sorry that delays of all kinds have prevented any writing of mine from appearing in your Souvenir.[1] I wish the "Lover's Leap"[2] would have been inserted, for it is a most beautiful story, & not known in English. Some time ago you asked me for two little mythological dramas of mine[3]—Do you still wish for them?   as if they suited you, they are at your service.   I have besides two or three short poems which you might have for your present volume if they pleased you.

I forward with this note a packet from M[rs] Douglas. This Lady has transmitted to me your print of the Spanish story from Stothard,[4] asking me to write for it—I fear I should now be too late—if you desire it I will write a slight sketch for it, & send it to you in the course of the week.

Permit me to thank you for the elegant Volume you have sent me—I anticipate with great pleasure the Souvenir of the present year which you speak of surpassing those which have already appeared

I am, my Dear Sir,
Your Ob[t] Servant
MaryShelley

TEXT: MS., Allison-Shelley Collection, The University Libraries, The Pennsylvania State University.

1. Watts noted in the introduction of the *Literary Souvenir* for 1827 that among items reaching him too late for that issue were those by David Lyndsay and the authors of *Frankenstein* and "A Traveller's Tale." Both "A Traveller's Tale" and "Lover's Leap," referred to in this letter, were the works of the Scottish author Leitch Ritchie (1800–1865). Perhaps Ritchie's work was introduced to Mary Shelley by his compatriot Mary Diana Dods. I have found no other reference to a connection between Mary Shelley and Ritchie, though Godwin knew him.

2. Published in *Friendship's Offering, 1830*, edited by Ritchie.

3. Mary Shelley had offered *Prosperpine* and *Midas* in 1826 (see 30 October [1826] to Alaric A. Watts).

4. Thomas Stothard (1755–1834; *DNB*), painter and book illustrator.

To John Howard Payne

⟨Arundel⟩ Brighton—25 September [1827]

My dear Payne

You will be surprised to hear that I make one of the party in question—
My friends remain at Dieppe a month before they proceed to Paris, and
they have persuaded me to pass that month with them—Say nothing of
all this to my people[1]—& if they tell you any thing let it pass current—
Our party consists—of Mrs Shelley & child—which fair person I need
not describe to you & whose signature will accompany this letter but lest
you should beleive that so divine a being could not be personated[2] by
another   I subjoin two other signatures for your choice   Mrs Douglas is
short, i.e. an atom shorter than I—dark, pretty with large dark eyes &
hair curled in the neck—Mr Douglas is my height—slim—dark with
curly black hair[3]—the passport must be drawn out for M^r & Mrs Sholto
Douglas—Mrs Carter & her two children—boys one ten the other nine—
Mrs Percy Shelley and boy[4]—

We go early next week—Monday if possible from Brighton—to
Dieppe—if there is any trouble about the passport let me know directly
as in that case we will procure it here—send it to me to Arundel where
we shall be till the day of our departure perhaps you had better send it
pr [*by*] coach—the Royal Sussex sets off at half past eight on Monday
Wednesday & Friday from the Silver Cross   Charing Cross—it ought to
come to us on Friday—Other Arundel {coaches} (Little Hampton or Bog-
nor, passing thro' Arundel) go from other places I doubt not daily—Our
address is at Mrs Cooper's Tarrant St. Arundel—Send me a letter the evening before by post to say I must expect it—but if the letter passport
enclosed w^d only be charged double—or even treble send it by post.—

We shall meet again in November—& I shall be delighted to think
that I can bestow a little pleasure where so much is so due—You are the
most disenterested of persons the rarest & best praise—

Ever Yours
Mary Shelley

Isabel Douglas.—Sholto Douglas.[5]
I return to [Arund]el tonight

ADDRESS: J. Howard Payne Esq / 29 Arundel St.   London / Strand. POSTMARKS:
(1) BRIGHTON / SE 25 / 1827 / 55; (2) A / 26 SE 26 / [182]7. TEXT: MS., Historical
Society of Pennsylvania.

  1. Godwin's letter of 9 October 1827 mentions that Mary Shelley had written to

him on 1 October (letter unlocated) "announcing a trip to the Continent, without the least hint when you should return" (see Marshall, *Mary Shelley*, II, 182–83). He explains that these plans have induced him to give her the details of his straitened circumstances and his unsuccessful attempts to borrow money.

2. The group planned to travel with one passport (see 23 September [1827]), but Payne obtained separate passports (see 13 October [1827]). Perhaps through his theater connections, Payne got two or more people to impersonate the travelers at the passport office (see 1 October [1827]).

3. Compare this description with that of 30 October [1826] to Alaric A. Watts, n. 2.

4. Probably Adeline Douglas is not listed because infants in arms could travel without passports (see 17 September [1827]), n. 8). Mary Hunt was not to be included (see MWS *Letters*, vol. II, 13 October [1827] to Jane Williams Hogg; [28–29 June 1828], n. 9).

5. The signatures are appended so that the Douglas impersonators could accurately forge their names. Sholto Douglas's signature provides further proof that this was Mary Diana Dods, as the signature is clearly in her handwriting.

To John Howard Payne

Arundel—1 October—[1827]

My friends entreat you, dear Payne, to accept their thanks[1]—they feel that I am the person who ought to be most pleased by your kindness—but they hope nevertheless that you will permit them to be grateful to you for your politeness. All seems admirably managed—and the double of my pretty friend deserves infinite praise—the signature alone is a miracle & whoever she is, pray say that we are all endebted to her.

You have written to me several times about these commissions of mine—but besides this you owe me a letter concerning yourself. Your health—your plans—your successes—do not omit to inform me of all—you are so good that you have many friends—yet not one who sympathizes more truly than I in your pleasures & sorrows.

Percy has been indisposed, so we have deferred our voyage until next Saturday. God grant us a quiet passage—Once you called me an heroine in friendship—now I am one indeed—to cross the odious sea for the sake of my pretty Isabel—sacrifices have been made—as for instance by Damon & Pythias[2]—but this in my tablets will stand above all the rest—a matchless example of fortitude, generosity—friendship and undaunted courage—pray praise me for I deserve it

Adieu believe me Affectionately Yours

MaryShelley

187

ADDRESS: John Howard Payne Esq / 29 Arundel St. / Strand. POSTMARKS: (1) T.P / DRURY LANE; (2) 12. NOON. 12 / 2. OC / 1827. TEXT: MS., Historical Society of Pennsylvania.

1. For the passports he had obtained for them.

2. In c. the fourth century B.C. in Greece, Pythias, condemned to die, asked leave to arrange his affairs, and his friend Damon pledged his own life to guarantee Pythias's return. Pythias did return, and Dionysius of Syracuse (405–367 B.C.) freed them both.

❖

To John Howard Payne

Arundel   13 October [1827]

My dear Payne

I am not at Dieppe—I have not been there—and it is uncertain whether I shall go—Your kind offices have not been vain & the separate passports were a great good, as a part of our party has crossed to France—and another part will probably sail next week.—

Meanwhile I am anxious to know how you are—what doing—what hoping—what achieving—I cannot help thinking that at last you will reap the harvest your patient labours and goodness so well deserve—tell me if your book[1] proceeds—and whether you still think of going to America—I have seen this summer one who makes me wish to see that country—one you must have heard of, Miss Wright[2] of Nashoba—the most wonderful & interesting woman I ever saw

—Do you think of visiting Brighton—shall you come over to Arundel?—Let me hear from you at any rate

Affectionately yours
MS.

ADDRESS: J. Howard Payne Esq / 29 Arundel St. / Strand. POSTMARKS: (1) T.P. / [D]evon. St Mbne; (2) [10] F.NOON. 10 / 17. OC / 1827. TEXT: MS., Pforzheimer Library.

1. Perhaps the script for a play; there is no record of a book by Payne.

2. Frances Wright's 4 October 1827 letter to Mary Shelley from London indicates that they had not yet met, and on 7 and 8 October Frances Wright was in Harrow (S&M, IV, 1099–1100; Garnett Letters, pp. 101–4). We may assume, therefore, that their meeting took place between 9 and 13 October. At the same time, Frances Wright met Isabel and Walter Sholto Douglas and provided "a letter introducing a Mr. and Mrs. Douglas, friends of Mrs. Shelley" (Garnett Letters, pp. 108–9). The introduction was to the Garnett family, whom Frances Wright had met in 1818 on a trip to America. After John Garnett (?1749–1820) died, his wife Maria (b. 1763) and two of their daughters, Julia Philippa (1793–1852) and Harriet (1794–1874),

returned to Europe, living first at Le Havre and by 1827 in Paris. The Garnett social circle included General Lafayette (1757–1834); Prosper Mérimée (1803–70); Stendhal [Marie Henri Beyle] (1783–1842); Benjamin Constant (1767–1830), Franco-Swiss politician and author, and his wife Charlotte von Hardenberg; Claude Fauriel (1772–1844), French critic and historian. All these met and accepted Mr. and Mrs. Walter Sholto Douglas, whom the Garnetts in particular befriended. In September 1827 Julia Garnett married the German historian Heinrich Pertz (1795–1876) and went with him to live in Hanover. Thereafter she kept up an almost weekly correspondence with her friends and family, which she preserved and passed on to her heirs. In 1979 Cecilia Payne-Gaposchkin, great-granddaughter of Julia Garnett Pertz, published a large portion of the correspondence in the *Garnett Letters*. The original manuscripts are now on loan at the Houghton Library. These manuscripts contain detailed information about many figures, including Frances Wright, Frances Trollope, Mérimée, Stendhal, Fauriel, Lafayette, Mr. and Mrs. Sholto Douglas, "Mr. Douglas' sister" Mrs. Carter, and Mary Shelley.

❖

To Robert Dale Owen

51 George St.   Portman Sq[1]   9 Nov. [1827]

Dear Nashobite—I send you a letter for our admirable & dear Fanny.[2] As this is foreign post day, a letter may arrive for her at N. [*Northumberland*] St.—which I will either send to you at Bedford Square—or to Liverpool—so pray, Owen, do not forget to call at the Post Office Liverpool, both tomorrow & on Sunday, for I shall direct there any thing I have to send for you.[3]—

Take care of our Fanny, dear Dale—she is neither so independant or so fearless as you think—A thousand painful circumstances may surround her, in which you may be useful to her, and which you will not discover unless you rouse yourself to perpetual attention, & resolve to devote yourself to those minute cares for her, which will win her confidence. You will say perhaps that if she confide not in you, the secretiveness is hers.—not so—we must all be sure of sympathy before we confide at all—& a woman must very highly esteem & love a man before she can tell any of her heart's secrets to him. We have no very excessive opinion of men's sympathetic and self sacrificing qualities—make yourself an exception—Inspire a belief in your lively & active interest for her—You are not in love now—one day you will be again—and the time may come when in spite of self-esteem you may fear that you are not loved in return—Now then practise yourself in such lessons as may make you loveable, if I may so express myself—& therefore the more likely to make a favourable impression—Nothing is better calculated to instil sweetness of disposition, & that best

189

& most endearing of qualities—tenderness, than constant attention to a woman, with whom if you are not in love, yet for whom you have affection and kindness—Study to please Fanny in all minutia—divine her uneasinesses, & be ever ready at her side with brotherly protection—Do not imagine that she is capable always of taking care of herself:—she is certainly more than any woman, but we have all in us—& she is too sensitive & feminine not largely to partake in this inherent part of us—a desire to find a manly spirit where on {to} lean—a manly arm to protect & shelter us—The time perhaps is not far off when Fanny may find in a lover these necessities better supplied than you can supply them—but till then, no man need be nearer—dearer or more useful to her than yourself—and every smile of thanks & approbation you win from her sweet lips, will not only be in itself a dear reward—but will assure you that you are becoming more & more capable of inspiring the best being that exists—a lofty minded, sensitive and talented woman—with love & devotion for you. I trust that you will find such an one & that thus your happiness will be secured—Sœur preçheuse[4] thus finishes her sermon—God bless you—May you have favourable Winds and a pleasant passage—speak of me at Nashoba—& do not let Fanny forget me

Your sincere Friend
Mary Shelley

Have you called at Power's[5] for me?—Mention again to Mr Walker the book for Papa

TEXT: MS., Historical Society of Pennsylvania.

    1. Mary Shelley's residence in London until her departure for Paris on 11 April 1828.

    2. Frances Wright.

    3. Robert Dale Owen, his father, and their party left from Liverpool for America shortly after this letter was written. It was arranged that Mary Shelley would collect and forward Frances Wright's letters to him to ensure their receipt (see Frances Wright to Mary Shelley, S&M, IV, 1102–5).

    4. "Teacher sister."

    5. James Power (1766–1836), music publisher at 34 Strand. Power and his brother William were Thomas Moore's musical publishers (New Grove Dictionary of Music and Musicians, XV, 174).

To Jane Williams Hogg[1]

[?51 George Street]   Thursday
Morning   [?14 February 1828][2]

Since Monday, I have been ceaselessly occupied by the scene, begun &
interrupted, which filled me with a pain, that now thrills me as I revert
to it. I then strove to speak, but your tears overcame me, while the struggle must have given me an appearance of coldness—Often—how often
have I wept at instances of want of affection from you, and that you should
complain of me, seemed the reproach of a benefactress to an ingrate.

If I revert to my devotion to you it is to prove that no worldly motives
could estrange me from the partner of my miseries—the sweet girl whose
beauty grace & gentleness were to me so long the sole charms of my life—
Often leaving you at Kentish Town I have wept from the overflow of affection—Often thanked God who had given you to me—Could any but
yourself have destroyed such engrossing & passionate love?—And what
are the consequences of the change?—When I first heard that you did not
love me, ⟨I felt⟩ every hope of my life deserted me—the depression I sunk
under, and to which ⟨in consequence⟩ I am now a prey, undermines my
health—How many many hours this dreary winter, I have paced my solitary room, driven nearly to madness as I could not expel from my mind
the ⟨circumstances⟩ Memories of harrowing import that one after another
intruded themselves. It was not long ago that eagerly desiring death—
tho' death should only be oblivion, I thought that how to purchase oblivion of what was revealed to me last July, a torturous death would be a
bed of Roses. At least, most lovely One, my love for you was not unworthy of its object—I have committed many faults—the remorse of love
haunts me often & brings bitter tears to my eyes—but for four years I
committed not one fault towards you—In larger, in minute things your
pleasure and satisfaction were my objects, & I gave up every thing that is
all the very little I could give up to them—I make no boast, heaven knows
had you loved me you were worth all—more than all the idolatry with
which my heart so fondly regarded you.

Do not ask me, I beseech you, a detail of the revelations made me—
Some of those most painful, you made to several—others of less import,
but which tended more perhaps than the more important to shew that
you loved me not, were made only to two. I could not write of these, far
less speak of them. If any doubt remain on your mind as to what I know,
write to Isabel[3] and she will ⟨tell⟩ inform you of the extent of her com-

munications to me. I have been an altered being since then—long I thought that almost a death blow was given so heavily & unremittingly did the thought press on & sting me—but one lives on through ⟨such⟩ all, to be a wreck—

Though I was conscious that having spoken of me as you did, you could not love me, I could not easily detach myself from the atmosphere of light & beauty that for ever surrounds you—I tried to keep you, feeling the while that I had lost you—but you penetrated the change, and I owe it to you not to disguise its cause—What will become of us, my poor girl— you say you love me—I heard you say so—such a speech a year ago would have been Elysium—then your expressions concerning me had not love in them. ⟨I cannot see a happy termination—some things might be explained—but—⟩

Do not think that I am not fully aware of the defects on my part that might well call forth your reprehension—or that I even do not appreciate your motives in trying for my sake to be my friend, when I really believe I was a burthen to you—Nay I see your natural goodness in the very shew of love towards me that you designed to assume—but the veil is torn now[4]—I believe you still and forever to be all that man or woman could desire as a lover or a friend, if you loved them, your very merits make my unhappiness—my sole claim on you was the entireness of my affection for you.

This explains my estrangement—how hateful I must have appeared to you all this time—While with you I was solely occupied by endeavouring not to think or feel—for had I done either—I should not have been so calm as I dare say I appeared—My first wish is to get out of a world where I have fabricated only misery for myself—my next to withdraw myself from all society—Nothing but my father, after the news of your safe accouchment, could have drawn me to town again—his claims only prevent me now from burrying myself in the country—I have known no peace since July—I never expect to know it again.

Were I to say, forget me—What would you reply? I cannot forget you; your form, in all its endearing grace is now before me—but more than ever I can only be an object of distaste to you, is it not best then that ⟨I should be forgotten⟩

you forget the Unhappy MS

TEXT: MS., Bodleian Library.

1. This letter tells of the open confrontation between Mary Shelley and Jane Williams Hogg over the latter's betrayal of friendship.

2. On 12 February 1828 Mary Shelley wrote in her Journal: "Moore is in town— by his advice I disclosed my discoveries to Jane—How strangely are we made—She

is horror struck & miserable at losing my friendship & yet how unpardonably she trifled with my feeling & made me all falsely a fable to others." Since Moore called on Mary Shelley on 9 February (Moore, *Journal*), the Monday of the confrontation was 11 February.

3. Isabel Robinson Douglas.

4. An echo of a number of Shelley's poems, including *The Revolt of Islam* 5. 38 and 9. 7; *Prometheus Unbound* 1. 539–40.

❖

To William Whitton

14 March 1828   51 George St.   Portman Sq.

My dear Sir,

I walked over to Kensington today to see M[r] Slater's school.[1] From all I have heard of it & from personal inspection, I am inclined to select it for my son. The terms are 45£ per ann. There will be a few extras, books &c.—& some things I must provide for him before he goes—His present school is by no means an inexpensive one—I trust therefore I am not indiscreet is [*in*] asking you to represent this Sir Timothy, and to mention that I shall find difficulty in making the present arrangement.[2] At the same time present my acknowledgments for his kindness to Percy, & for the provision with which he is good enought to supply me

> I am, d[r] Sir
> Your Ob[t] Serv[t]
> MaryShelley

ENDORSED: 14th March 1828 / Miss Shelley. TEXT: MS., Bodleian Library.

1. Percy Florence Shelley entered Edward Slater's Gentlemen's Academy, Church Street, Kensington, on 25 March (see 8 April [1828]). The school building is now the priory to the Carmelite Church, 41 Kensington Church Street.

2. Sir Timothy Shelley did not comply with Mary Shelley's request for an increased allowance.

❖

To William Whitton

51 George St.   Portman Sq
Tuesday   8 April [1828]

My Dear Sir

Percy went to school, to M[r] Slater at Kensington on the 25th Ult—he is now home for the Easter holidays—& is satisfied with his school & is both well & happy. I trust Sir Timothy will be pleased with my attention to his wishes & my selection for him

A friend of mine has arrived from the South at Paris—& intends immediately almost to proceed to Germany[1]—As I desire very much to profit by this only opportunity I shall have of seeing her—I intend going to Paris the day after I take Percy back to school (next Thursday)—as I shall be exceedingly anxious to return to him, I shall not remain away more than three weeks.—The opportunity is the more desirable as I join other friends who are going.—

I will let you know immediately on my return—which will not be protracted beyond the time I have mentioned.

I shall be very glad to hear that Percy will have an opportunity of seeing his Grandfather again

I am Dear Sir,
Y^r Ob^t Servant,
Mary Shelley

ENDORSED: 8th April 1828 / Mrs Shelley. TEXT: MS., Bodleian Library.

1. Mary Shelley wrote in her Journal on 11 April 1828: "I depart for Paris, sick at heart yet pining to see my Friend." It has previously been believed that Mary Shelley went to visit Julia Robinson, but these letters and the *Garnett Letters* make it evident that Mary Shelley traveled with Julia and Joshua Robinson to visit Isabel Robinson Douglas. Mary Shelley's strong feelings of friendship for Isabel Robinson Douglas were not reciprocated, as Frances Wright's 20 March 1828 response to a letter from Harriet Garnett indicates: "The D[*ouglases'*] account of Mary does not surprise me. She did not strike me as a person of sensibility, and my first impression was decided disappointment. I resisted and lost this, and became interested in and for herself, though the interest excited by her parentage and history has always held a large share in the interest I feel in her. The D[*ouglases'*] account may be all true (and my own recalled impressions would rather go to confirm it), but it makes much against them. Not only have I seen them evince the fondest kindness for Mary, but Isabel's letters, which I have seen, are in a strain of the fondest and most dependent friendship. Deficient sensibility is a negative quality, but hypocrisy is a positive one of the worst character" (*Garnett Letters*, p. 117).

It is possible that the Douglases had gone to the south of France after 27 February and returned by 30 March, since the *Garnett Letters* make no mention of them during this period. On 23 January 1828 Harriet Garnett wrote to Julia Pertz about Sholto Douglas: "He has hopes of obtaining a place in the diplomatic line—and said he hopes it may be at Hanover" (MS., Houghton Library). By February the Douglases planned to spend the summer at Mannheim and to proceed from there to Baden (MS., Maria and Harriet Garnett to Julia Pertz, 21 February 1828, Houghton Library).

To Jane Williams Hogg

Paris—Sunday   [27 April 1828]

Sweetest Janey—Since I have been in Paris this is the first day I have been out of bed—no wonder that I have not written to you—I travelled in a high fever—arrived in Paris—took to my bed—& after spending two days in it symptoms of the small pox occurred—it was kept a secret from me—I thought I had the chicken pox—it was a most virulent kind—but the journey & a warm bath on my arrival brought it out so speedily & decidedly—that the critical 7ᵗʰ day passed, on which I was very ill, I became convalescent last Wednesday & have gone on getting regularly better—I am assured by my Doctors that I shall not be in the least marked—

Could any thing be more provoking—to endanger poor Julia[1] so much, to put our friends[2] wholly under interdict[3] for the Parisians are dreadfully afraid of infection—to make a sick house of it—& then the illness over to be such a fright that it will be long before I can show myself—so much for human plans & schemes—we know what we are to do as much as Pope's Lamb[4]—One's only consolation is that they tell me I should have kept it in my blood much longer & have had it much worse in London—

How are you—quite recovered & your best prettiest & sweetest of babies

I am far too weak to write much embrace your children for me—Pray see Percy & let me have news of him speedily—present my remembrances to Jeff—How does John[5] [?passa][6] I long to know—I saw Trelawny's girl[7]—but cannot say more now than that I like her very much—she is bl[   ]

Adieu dearest—write soon & tell me all good news

Ever Affˡʸ Yours

MS

ADDRESS: Mrs Jefferson Hogg / 22 Devonshire Place / London / Edgware Road. POSTMARKS: (1) 28 / AVRI / 1828; (2) P. PAYÉ PARIS; (3) FPO / MY. 1 / 1828; (4) 12. NOON. 12 / MY. 1 / 1828; (5) [4.] EVEN. 4 / 1. MY / 1828. TEXT: MS., Abinger MSS., Bodleian Library.

1. Julia Robinson.
2. The Douglases and Georgiana Dods Carter.
3. In her letter of 22 April 1828 to Julia Pertz, Maria Garnett mentioned that she had not yet met Mary Shelley because of the latter's illness. She also comments that she does "not expect to like her. Mʳˢ D. [Douglas] has described her character to me & I have seen her letters to her most intimate friends" (MS., Houghton Library).

On 28 April 1828 Harriet Garnett informed Julia Pertz that they still had not met Mary Shelley because her illness was smallpox (MS., Houghton Library). Maria and Harriet Garnett's joint letter of 12 May 1828 to Julia Pertz states that they had met Mary Shelley the previous night and had both found her pleasing (MS., Houghton Library).

4. Pope, *An Essay on Man*, bk. 1, lines 81–86.

5. John Wheeler Cleveland, Jane Hogg's brother, who visited England in June (see [28–29 June 1828]).

6. "Travel."

7. Maria Julia Trelawny (b. 1814), Trelawny's eldest daughter, who in 1826 or 1827 was in the care of Trelawny's mother, Maria Hawkins Brereton (1762–1851). Eliza Trelawny was with her foster parents, whom Mary Shelley did not know, and Zella was with Trelawny in Italy.

To Jane Williams Hogg

4 Rue Nueve de Berry
Champs Elysèes.   16 May [1828]

My dearest Jane—My month has now gone past—how you may guess— since although well in health—& gaining strength every day, I continue sufficiently marked to make me wish to hide myself altogether—and seeing the people I have necessarily seen, has been mortifying enough— although I am interested in & pleased with several I see here[1]—French principally—the Constants I like much   he is a venerable benevolent looking old man—she a sentimental German with great sweetness of manner. The weather is divine—we are in the open air almost all day, beneath the fresh green chesnuts of the Tuilleries—theatres we have not been to—indeed I have had very little of sight seeing.—

Do you know I cannot persuade myself to return to town—to meet the commiseration—and wonder & talk of all who shall see my ugly face— I mean to hide myself till it is all over. This is a great self denial—& a great disappointment—for there are several persons now in town whom I wished much to see,[2] were I myself—and I wish to return to those who love me—but no—I shall hide myself till the mask that disguises me disappears from before me. You know that I consider it a duty to give Percy a little sea bathing every year—I wished much to pass his holidays with him near the sea—but feared it would prove too expensive—but as things have gone I can arrange it. In about ten days I quit Paris & I shall remain at Dover. M[r] Robinson—who has business there will bring my boy down to me—I shall get some country place & be quite quiet—my writing interrupted in, under the circumstances, so frightful a manner, will go on there famously; I shall ask the Godwins to visit me—and you, if possible, may steal away for a week or two—the change will do you great good, and Dina especially will be much the better for sea breezes.— Except you do this & the G's [*Godwins*] come, I shall be wholly alone— in six weeks or two months I am promised to see something white instead of red when I look in the glass, and then I shall venture to shew myself.

I wrote to Claire with directions on the outside that the letter should follow her to Toeplitz³ M^rs G [*Godwin*] has also had a letter from her, speaking of her arrangements as decided—so unless some occasion offers itself for her going as governess to the south with some family in the meantime, of which I suppose she would avail herself, ⟨I suppose⟩ we may expect her in the spring. Poor girl! I shall be very glad to contribute to her happiness. even at the expence of my liberty—

I leave Paris Monday week—this is Friday—as my stay has been pro- longed, it is necessary for me to receive here the £5 you have of mine— I am afraid that I have delayed so long writing for it, that you may find some inconvenience in sending it. If you answered me by return of post I should get your letter next Friday—if this is possible do it—if not— send it the next day—or even the next but do not delay longer writing— & if you cannot enclose the money write to tell me so & let me find it at Dover on my arrival there, directed to the Post Office.

Will you not come to me at Dover?—I think you may contrive it—I shall return to town if things go well, with Percy at the end of his hol- idays.—I think the sea air after this most vile illness will do me the great- est good—& get rid of its horrid remains quickly   But I do not like its dividing us so long—so pray—pray come to me if you can. Adieu sweet & lovely One—let me hear that you are well & the darlings also—for ever & ever I think of you with heartfelt interest

Yours
MS.

We are so far from the post that it is long since I called there—so perhaps I shall find a letter today there waiting for me from you—but I could not delay this a post longer—they will not give letters to servants & people— direct to me to the above address—

ADDRESS: Mrs Jefferson Hogg / 22 Devonshire Place / Edgware Road / Londres London. POSTMARKS: (1) P. PAYÉ PARIS; (2) 16 / MAI / 1828; (3) [12.] NOON. 12 / MY. 19 / 1828; (4) 4. EVEN. 4 / 19. MY / 1828. TEXT: MS., Abinger MSS., Bodleian Library.

1. Through the Garnetts and the Douglases, Mary Shelley met Mérimée, Fauriel, Lafayette, and the Constants (see 13 October [1827], n. 2; MSS., Garnett Letters, Houghton Library).

2. Among them was probably Lord Dillon, whose letter to Mary Shelley on 13 June 1828 expressed his disappointment that she was not coming to town. In the same letter he sent regards to Miss Robinson and asked that Mary Shelley forward to him "Miss Dodd's donation" (S&M, IV, 1111–12).

3. Claire Clairmont had traveled from Moscow to the Baths of Tuplitz, near Dresden, as companion to Madame Kaisaroff and her daughters but had quit them because of a quarrel. She found a traveling companion and proceeded to London, arriving there on 16 October 1828 (CC Journals, pp. 415–16; Claire Clairmont to Mary Shelley, 22 July 1828, Abinger MSS.).

❧

To {Prosper Mérimée}[1]

[Paris]   Samdi Soir   [24 May 1828][2]

C'est parceque je ne suis pas coquette que je vous rends votre lettre. Je ne voudrois pas garder l'expression des sentiments dont vous pourriez vous repentir apres—ni la tomoignage [*témoignage*] de ce que vous paraitra (il se peut) en reflechissant une faiblesse.

Vous demandez mon amitiè—elle est à vous. Toujours je serai votre amie, si toujours vous le desirez—si toujours (pardonnez ce façon de parler à une femme, non pas coquette mais fière) vous vous en montreriez digne. Je vous ecrirai—J'espere vous revoir à Paris—à Londres—Faites moi part de vos esperances, vos succes, votre bonheur ou si çela doit etre, de vos malheurs—vous trouverez en moi une amie simpatisante—compatisante—vraie.

Je pars Lundi. Je dois donner demain à mon amie comme le denier de mon sejour à Paris. Je suis façhèe que vous ne pourriez rester toute la soiree chez Mme Garnett.   mais je vous y verrai et encore je vous assurerai de mon Amitie

[Translation]

It is because I am not a coquette that I return your letter. I should not like to keep the expression of sentiments which you will probably repent of later—nor the evidence of what you will regard (it may be) upon reflection as a weakness.

You ask for my friendship—it is yours. Always I shall be your friend, if always you desire it—if always (pardon this woman's way of speaking, not petty but proud) you should prove yourself worthy. I shall write you—I hope to see you again in Paris—in London—Let me share your aspirations, your success, your happiness or if it must be, your unhappiness—you will find in me a friend sympathetic—tender—true.

I leave on Monday. I ought to give tomorrow to my friend as the last of my stay in Paris. I am sorry you cannot spend the whole evening at Madame Garnett's. but I shall see you there and again I shall assure you of my Friendship

TEXT: MS., Museum Calvet.

1. There had long existed an unsubstantiated belief that Mary Shelley and Prosper Mérimée were romantically linked and that with this letter Mary Shelley returned to him his marriage proposal (see Dennis M. Healy, "Mary Shelley and Prosper Mérimée," *Modern Language Review* 36, no. 3 [July 1941]: 394–96). Previously unlocated letters from Mérimée to Mary Shelley, dated 5 July 1828 through 4 February 1829, document a close if temporary relationship between them (see Bennett and Little, "Seven Letters from Mérimée to Mary Shelley"). Mary Shelley's half of the correspondence has not been located, but Mérimée's provides much information about Mary Shelley and her circle, including Mérimée's suggestion that Mrs. Douglas was unworthy of Mary Shelley's friendship.

2. In her 16 May [1828] letter to Jane Hogg, Mary Shelley indicated that she would "leave Paris Monday week," that is, 26 May. Harriet Garnett's letter to Julia Pertz confirms this departure date and the date of this letter in its reference to the same Saturday gathering mentioned by Mary Shelley: "Last night we drank tea with the Douglas to take leave of Mrs. Shelley. a flirting party. Mrs. S. flirts with Mérimée, Mrs. D. [*Douglas*] with Hallam & Fauriel, and all others, and poor D. [*Douglas*] looks sick and disconsolate" (MS., 25 May 1828, Houghton Library).

❖

To Jane Williams Hogg

Snargate St.   Over the Sluice   Dover
[5 June 1828]

Dearest Jane—At last I am again on this side of the Channel—liking it less than ever—I was, with every disadvantage of my odious illness against me, delighted with Paris—Society is nothing as an end, but as a means it is much—the means of allowing one to know of the existence of human beings with whom one can sympathize—and of which one would otherwise remain in ignorance—I have made not only acquaintances but friendships for life—One in particular—a man neither young, handsome, rich nor of high birth—but a man of talent—a poet[1]—a creature whose nature is divine—One of those rare beings in whom sensibility is joined to activity of thought—and the softest sweetness to chivalrous daring—I shall return when I can—but God only knows when that will be—-As it is I remain either here or at Hastings,[2] it is not quite decided which—You ask me why I solitudinize—my luckless disfigurement answers for me—I would not for worlds shew myself in town—besides my physician told me that sea bathing will diminish by at least a month the period of my ugliness—You would not know me—

Trelawny in England!—where?—how ardently I desire to see him—Dear dear darling—once again to find the true and good one—I shall write to Miss Trelawny[3] to learn where he is—

I am sorry you cannot join me here—I am very sorry you brood so painfully over the past—I wish I could see any possibility of bringing back a state of things gone for ever—Is it possible not to love you?—your sweetness, your grace, your ten thousand excellencies command a deep sentiment—but from the first moment we met you disliked me—apart from you your imaginations paints a being suitable to yourself, and you bestow my name on the idea—together a thousand realities that formerly disgusted you would do so again, and I, fearful of annoying by silence, by speaking, by my very looks (so was it all last winter) am any thing but myself—however we are not separated; I shall return to town after Percy's holidays & we shall see—One thing I feel—I always felt extreme difficulty in making personal confidences to you—I tried—& succeeded usually—yet in doing it I never reaped the only benefit of reposing confidence—sympathy—at least I never felt as if I did—now I cannot talk of myself to you; the being so long disfigured so long depreciated in your eey [eye] cannot pour out her heart—

Do not talk of anger & revenge—the poor child![4]   her sufferings transcend all that imagination can pourtray—they may satisfy your bitterest feelings—as I consider myself as in some sort the cause, so I devote myself to extricate her we shall see whether I shall succeed—Claire's coming will be an impediment—but if it can be, it shall—

Dearest Jane accept a sentiment of admiration, of tenderness—of a love which clings to you thro' every thing—Try not I conjure you, to force, but to lead me back—Do not I earnestly pray you, allude to the past, or the change which cannot be unchanged—let us begin again;—let me love you for all you are—& where find any thing more worthy to be loved?—By the way do not imagine now that I have any thing to conceal—it is not with the small pox painting one with ugliness that one loves or is loved—if I had met any to excite that feeling which I did not—moreover I promise faithfully to let you know when I am in love—

Adieu darling—it is useless to talk of my plans—Trelawny's arrival may change them   take care of yourself

Affectionately Yours
MS.

Can Jeff. sometimes get your letters franked for me—I am ruined in postage

Remember me to the Clints—tell him that I got his blanc d'argent[5] thro' an artist so I trust it is good—I will send it to town by M[r] Robinson when he comes & returns   Would you send to Hardings Library[6] directed to Miss Robinson—the 2 Annuals you have of mine—I want them—& M[r] R. [*Robinson*] w[d] bring them me

My address is at M[r] Dawson

Snargate St.   Over the Sluice
Dover

ADDRESS: Mrs Jefferson Hogg / 22 Devonshire Place—Edgware Road / London. POSTMARKS: (1) DOVE[R] / 5 JU 5 / 1828 / 72; (2) A / 6 JU 6 / 1828; (3) 10. F. NOON. 10 / JU. 6 / 1828. TEXT: MS., Abinger MSS., Bodleian Library.

1. This appears to be a reference to Mérimée, except that Mérimée was only twenty-five at that time. In her letter of 15 June [1828] (MWS *Letters*, vol. II), Mary Shelley again mentions her poet friend but describes him as young.

2. A seaside resort in Sussex, sixty-four miles south-southeast of London.

3. Julia Trelawny.

4. Isabel Robinson Douglas, whose "sufferings" and responsibility for informing Mary Shelley of Jane Hogg's breach of friendship are more fully referred to in Mary Shelley's letter [28–29 June 1828].

5. Lead white oil paint.

6. Two booksellers by the name of Harding are listed in London for 1828: John Harding, 32 St. James' Street, and Thomas P. Harding, 16 Chapel Street, Edgware Road (*Pigot and Co.'s Metropolitan New Alphabetical Directory . . . for Middlesex . . .* [London, 1828]).

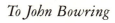

To John Bowring

Dover—11 June [1828]

My dear Sir

When I last wrote I little foresaw all the annoyances that were to overthrow ⟨all⟩ my plans. I took with me to France the small pox, which confined me immediately on my arrival, and destroyed every arrangement both of pleasure and business.

Is it now too late to write the critique I promised? if not I will set about it instantly.—I have also a request to make you—You know and I believe think well of two works "the Comedies of Clara Gazul" & the "Guzla"—Merrimèe, the author of these, is now bringing out another publication,[1] which he will send me as soon as it is printed—I expect it daily[2]—if I write an article on his works, will it prove acceptable to the W.R. [*Westminster Review*]?—I should like very much so to do.

What about LB's letters for Moore? Those you gave me are safely locked up in town—I do not intend to return to London for some time, as sea bathing is recommended to me for my perfect recovery—Would you send me the letters directed to J. Robinson Esq Park Cottage, Paddington—when they would be forwarded immediately to me—and I would return them to you as soon as copied—or will you send them immediately to Moore 19 Bury St. St. James'—the first arrangement would please me best—

Tell me how you are & what doing—I heard some very agreable intelligence concerning you in Paris—and shall be glad to be able to congratulate you upon it[3]

I am Most sincerely Yours
MaryShelley

ADDRESS: John Bowring Esq / J. Bentham Esq / 2 Queen's Square Place / London / Westminster./ POSTMARKS: (1) DOVER / 11 JU 11 / 1828 / 72; (2) A / 12 JU 12 / 1828. ENDORSED: (1) Dover 11 June 1828 / Mary Shelley; (2) Mary Shelley / 11 June 1828. TEXT: MS., Huntington Library.

1. Mérimée's witty hoaxes *The Comedies of Clara Gazul* (1828), *La Guzla* (1827), and *La Jacquerie* (1828) are all discussed in Mary Shelley's review "Illyrian Poems—Feudal Scenes," *Westminster Review* 10 (January 1829): 71–81 (see Bennett and Little, "Seven Letters from Mérimée to Mary Shelley," pp. 135–36).

2. By 27 June Mary Shelley received her copy of *La Jacquerie* and began to read it (see 27 June [1828]).

3. The Chancellor of the Exchequer had appointed Bowring a commissioner for reforming the system of keeping the public accounts, but his appointment was canceled because the Duke of Wellington objected to Bowring's Benthamite politics.

To {? Thomas Campbell}[1]

Dover 22 June 1828

My dear Sir

I enclose One or two articles—and some verses, the productions of a gentleman now abroad who wishes to contribute to the New Monthly—

He has as Mʳ David Lindsay[2] been the successful author of "The Dramas of the Ancient World"—He contributed at one time for Blackwood & for several of the Annuals—If the Articles I now send do not quite suit you, still if you were desirous of securing him & would make any suggestions as to subjects (he is in Paris) he would be very happy to attend to them; and his known talents certainly render him an acquisition of importance   Would you have the goodness to direct your reply to me to the care of Mʳ Robinson Park Cottage Paddington—& an early one would oblige me

I am, dear Sir
Your Obedient Serᵗ
MaryShelley

TEXT: MS., Pfortzheimer Library.

1. Thomas Campbell (1777–1844; *DNB*), poet, was editor of the *New Monthly Magazine* from 1820 to 1830. Campbell was also a friend of Godwin's.
2. I.e., Mary Diana Dods, also known as Sholto Douglas.

❧

To Venceslas-Victor Jacquemont[1]

Hastings   ce 27 Juin   [June 1828]

Monsieur,

Je vous donne beaucoup de la peine, j'en suis très fachée. Décachetez la lettre de Mme Douglas qui contienne un objet—faites le même de la lettre de Prosper. Si vous pouviez faire passer les simples lettres sans couper les sceau j'en serai charmée—sinon—il faut se soumettre aux stupides regles—coupez les et cachetez avant de les remettre. Je portai bien des lettre même en mes mâles, cachetées à la France, il y avait mêmes des grosses, qui contenaient des brochures et on les permettait à passer sans mot—on ne visite pas les mâles surtout d'Angleterre.

Je reçoive à l'instant une letter de Mérimée[2] qui demande réponse veuillez vous charger encore de celle ici. Son livre[3] arriva hier. Je ne fais que le commencer.

Adieu Monsieur—encore bon voyage—encore portez vous bien. Retournez sauf à vos amis. Saluez les miens à Paris.

M. S[helley]

[*Translation*]
Dear Sir,

I am causing you a great deal of trouble, I am very sorry for it. Unseal the letter of Mrs. Douglas which contains an article [*objet*]—do the same with the letter to Prosper. If you are able to pass them as plain letters without breaking the seal I shall be delighted—if not—it will be necessary to submit to the stupid regulations—break them and seal again before delivering them. I carried successfully several letters in my boxes, sealed to France, there were even some thick ones, which contained pamphlets and these were permitted to pass without examination—they do not inspect boxes, especially from England.

I have just this moment received a letter from Mérimée[2] which requires an answer—will you take charge of that one also. His book[3] has arrived yesterday. I have only begun reading it.

Adieu dear Sir—again bon voyage—again take care of yourself. Return safely to your friends. Salute mine at Paris.

M. S[helley]

TEXT: Healy, "Mary Shelley and Prosper Mérimée," p. 395.
    1. Jacquemont (1801–32), naturalist and voyager, was Mérimée's close friend. In June 1828 he visited London in preparation for his voyage to India. He returned to Paris on 2 July, left there for India on 26 August, and died at Bombay (Prosper Mérimée, *Correspondance générale*, ed. Maurice Partuerier, 17 vols. [Paris: Le Divan (vols. I–VI); Toulouse: Privat (vols. VII–XVII), 1941–64], 1, 14, 19, 30).
    2. Mérimée's response to Mary Shelley's unlocated letter sent via Jacquemont reveals many details of what she wrote about: she advised Mérimée to care more for glory as an author than for love; she had embroidered and sent him a money pouch (perhaps the "article" referred to in her letter to Jacquemont); she asked him to keep secret their correspondence; and she spoke of her own loathing for life. By 28 July Mary Shelley had written that the *Carvajal* pleased her more than *La Jacquerie* (see Bennett and Little, "Seven Letters from Mérimée to Mary Shelley," pp. 142–44).
    3. *La Jacquerie*.

❧

To Jane Williams Hogg

6 Meadow Cottages, Priory, Hastings—
Saturday   (Sunday)   [28–29 June 1828]

I am delighted, my dear Jane, to hear of your brother's arrival,[1] and the comfort that he promises to be to you. This is a good turn of fortune— God send you many such! I am very sorry that I hurt you, yet glad I confess, that I awakened your pride—I cannot tell why, but we seem to stand more equally now. It is painful to go over old grounds—I go only on what you have allowed; long you gave ear to every idle & evil tale against me—& repeated them—not glossed over—nor can I—tho' I allow myself changed, admit as just the sweeping sentence you pass over my early years—the past is dear to me—& I feel that tho' now more just to myself I was then as just to others as now   What can I say? My devotion to you was entire; the discovery caused so deep a wound, that my health sank under it—from the hour it was disclosed till my recovery from this odious illness I never knew health—You ask what good has been done—I must feel the truth a good—You speak of beings to whom I link myself—speak, I pray you, in the singular number—if Isabel has not answered your letter, she will—but the misery to which she is a victim is so dreadful and merciless, that she shrinks like a wounded person from every pang—and you must excuse her on the score of her matchless sufferings. What D. [*Doddy*] now is, I will not describe in a letter—one only trusts that the diseased body acts on the diseased mind, & that both may be at rest ere long. For the rest I look forward without hope or pleasure—it is summer weather, and so I am not often in ill spirits—I shut my eyes and enjoy—but a restless spirit stirring in my heart whispers to me that this is not life, & youth flies the while—I know the occasion and opportunity is only wanted, for me to feel some return of good—but it is vain to court these—they must come—& they will not while I am as I am now—so at least I have lost one year of my life—but I have gained so much in health—& even in good looks, when these marks disappear, that I will not too much repine,—and in a few weeks I hope not to be a fright, tho' it will take months to lose every trace.—My poor hair! it is a wonder I did not lose it all—but it has greatly suffered, and I am forced to keep it clipped still. How you would have pitied me!—

I like this place very much—the air is so pure and the sea bathing is so advantageous to Percy and myself that I earnestly desire to remain here another Month—Trelawny has written to me to return to town—I have replied by asking him to come here, and anxiously await his reply[2]—town would be odious—for I will not see people as I am. I had enough of that in Paris—we are as quiet as mice here—Papa is now down with us,[3] & returns to town on Monday—on which day we expect Mr Robinson—I do not find Percy altered—he is the same boy—without evil—& without sentiment—docile and querelous—self willed and yielding—unsocial yet frank—without one ill fold—and the open space apparently well fitted for culture but greatly requiring it.—

Poor Medwin![4]—from first to last—poor Medwin! I am glad he will not see me, or the Guiccioli would no longer be the ugliest woman he ever saw in his life[5]—I cannot say that I believe the scandal about Pierino[6]—that of the old Pope may be—but too much has been said & believed of me, for me to give ear to tales about others—I wrote to her[7] from Paris, but have had no answer—

205

The Hunts! how completely à la Marianne is the last procèdeur[8]—I suppose I should have had a visit—after her cutting me on Mary's account[9]—I can hardly pity her for she has her consolation[10]—but Hunt—What a fate—What a bitter & dread fate is his—& if we say it is partly his own fault, must one not accuse the Gods who formed him to his own ruin—it is the only comfort one has (& that a sorry one) in one's total inability to serve them, that it is impossible to render them service—I shall write to Statia—

Sontag & the Opera![11] I ought to be in London now—but that I should be as far from these delights there as here—I saw very little of these things in Paris for they were too expensive—I hope your brother will understand that happiness does not consist merely in a good dinner ⟨& g⟩ going to sleep after it—& going to bed at night,[12] but will forge amusement for his sweet sister—a brother! What a dear name if linked to affection! How I envy you—a dear Man person—on whom—the first best link not existing—one can repose as one's support in life, is a vain dream too generally. Friendships lead to love—or, quite certainly, to such scandal, as— as was my case, tarnishes the reputation and hurts the guiltless in the eyes of those with whom they would stand well—Fraternal ⟨feeli[ngs] are⟩ love is too often linked to fraternal tyranny—where it is not, it is the [   ] second blessing of life—for however devotedly one may love a woman, she can never support, defend, & protect as a Man.

Tomorrow I hope to know my fate from Trelawny—& I shall then finish this letter—God bless you, my pretty pet!—

(Sunday) No letter from our friend—I am sufficiently annoyed; the prospect of returning to town before the end of July is odious, but any thing is better than this suspense.

Dear Girl, I cannot tell you how sincerely and excessively I rejoice in the gain you have made this year. Has fortune done its worst and will it now be kind to you? To know that you are happy to see you surrounded by those who love—who worship you—to feel that your affectionate heart has a resource in this well you call it queer world is so true so real a pleasure to me that I thank our person for it as good to myself—the greatest I have had this Many a day.

You perceive I cannot say when we meet—probably next week—certainly in a month.

Affectionately Yours
MS.

ADDRESS: Mrs Jefferson Hogg / 22 Devonshire Place / London / Edgware Road.
POSTMARKS: (1) HASTINGS / JU 29 / 1828; (2) E / 30 JU 30 / 1828; (3) F. NOON. [10] / JU. 30 / 1828. TEXT: MS., British Library.

1. See [27 April 1828], n. 5.

2. Mary Shelley received Trelawny's letter on 27 June 1828 (Paul, *Godwin*, II, 300). On 8 July Trelawny wrote from Southampton that he might soon visit at Hastings, but he fixed no date (Trelawny, *Letters*, pp. 111–12).

3. Godwin visited Mary and Percy Shelley from 25 June through 1 July 1828 (Godwin, *Journal*).

4. By mid-1828 Medwin was near financial ruin (Lovell, *Medwin*, p. 225).

5. Medwin's description of Teresa Guiccioli in a letter to Mary Shelley (Lovell, *Medwin*, p. 224).

6. Count Pietro Gamba.

7. Teresa Guiccioli.

8. "Procedure, proceeding."

9. Perhaps a reference to Mary Hunt, who had accompanied Mary Shelley in the summer of 1827. At one time that summer Mary Shelley intended to keep Mary Hunt with her when she returned to London. However, Mary Shelley's 25 September 1827 plans to accompany the Douglases to Dieppe did not include Mary Hunt, and in all likelihood these plans caused Mary Shelley to send Mary Hunt home (see 28 July 1827). In 1830 Hunt referred to a secret about Mary Hunt but did not reveal what it was (Brewer, *The Holograph Letters*, p. 192).

10. Marianne Hunt had become an alcoholic (Blunden, *Leigh Hunt*, p. 328; Hunt, *Autobiography*, I, 231).

11. A "Dramatic Concert" at the King's Theatre by Henriette Sontag, Countess Rossi (1806–54), had been announced for 25 June 1828 (*Morning Chronicle*, 25 June 1828).

12. An allusion to Hogg.

❖

To Sutton Sharpe[1]

Park Cottage   Paddington
Thursday Eve^g [?October 1828][2]

You despair easily—Captain Parry[3] was not so easily deterred from seeking the Norths Pole   Will you not make another attempt—Call if you can on Saturday Morning—or fix some other day when I may have the pleasure of seeing you

I am &c &c
MaryShelley

TEXT: MS., University College, London.

1. Sutton Sharpe (1797–1843), English attorney, was a close friend of Prosper Mérimée, Stendhal, and their circles (see Doris Gunnell, *Sutton Sharpe et ses amis français* [Paris: Librairie Ancienne Honoré Champion, 1925]).

2. Mérimée asked Sharpe, who was about to return to London from Paris after a month's visit, to carry two letters to Mary Shelley and to deliver them personally. One of the letters contained some ballads by Mérimée that Mary Shelley is believed

207

to have translated, but the translations have not been located (Mérimée, *Correspondance générale*, I, 29–30). In his letter of Sunday, 5 October 1828, Mérimée informed Mary Shelley that he would send her some ballads forthwith. Mérimée's letter of 29 October 1828, in which he asks for news of "mon ami, & le votre, j'espere Mr. S. Sharpe," indicates that by that time Sharpe had visited Mary Shelley (Bennett and Little, "Seven Letters from Mérimée to Mary Shelley," pp. 147, 149).

    3. Sir William Edward Parry (1790–1855; *DNB*), English admiral and arctic explorer, published a number of works describing his explorations, including *A Narrative of an Attempt to Reach the North Pole . . . in the year 1827* (London: The Admiralty, 1828).

To { ?Charles Ollier}

Park Cottage   Monday   [?20 October 1828]

My dear Sir

    I am very much obliged to you for the books—I still keep the O'Hara Tales,[1] not having quite finished them—I certainly exonerate the Anglo Irish from the charge of impropriety—but I do not think it as clever as the Nowlans—

    If you have the set of New Monthlys & could spare me the last twelve numbers you would greatly oblige me—

    Do you think that there exists in any of the libraries here a copy of the French translation of Karamsin's History of Russia[2]—Hookham has it not—has Ebers?[3]—

    With many thanks—I am

Your Obed' Servant
MaryShelley

    Are there any new books come out quite lately, you would recommend—

TEXT: MS., Pforzheimer Library.

    1. John Banim and Michael Banim [Barnes O'Hara and Abel O'Hara], *Tales by the O'Hara Family*, 2d ser., 3 vols. (London: Henry Colburn, 1826), which included "The Nowlans."

    2. Nikolai Mikhailovich Karamsin, *Istoriya gosudarstva rossiyskogo* [History of the Russian state], 12 vols. (Saint Petersburg: Voennaia tipograffiia, 1816–29); or in French *Histoire de l'empire de Russie, par m. Karamsin*, trans. St. Thomas and Jauffert, 11 vols. (Paris: A. Belin, 1819–26).

    3. John Ebers, opera manager and bookseller, whose shop was located at 27 Old Bond Street.

To Thomas Crofton Croker

Park Cottage—30ᵗʰ October [1828]

Sir

I cannot sufficiently thank you for the politeness with which you have replied to my requests—I am very sorry that I was out yessterday evening, as then I could in person have apologized for my unceremonious application—Will you afford me another opportunity for so doing?—If you will call on Saturday Morning you will add to my other obligation by allowing me to destroy any strange impression I may have made—

By some mistake there is an error in your idea of what I want—it is the easiest way to tell you my object and then you will understand my need—I am writing a romance founded on the story of Perkin Warbeck—I have just brought him for the first time to Ireland—The Antiquary is therefore of more use to me than the historian—After all I must rest satisfied with a very imperfect sketch, as never having been in Ireland, & being very ignorant of its history, I shall fall into a thousand mistakes—to diminish this number as much as possible I have applied to you—

You seem to have imagined me employed in sober useful history instead of my usual trifling—Were I indeed the least learned I might give interest to my pages by a picture of manners & incidents little known—If I get beyond mere generalities—helped or disfigured by ⟨the⟩ my imagination I must owe it to you—

If Saturday is not convenient let it be some other day

I am, Sir

Your obedient Servᵗ

MaryShelley

TEXT: MS., National Library of Ireland.

To Charles Ollier

Park Cottage   Monday
[?17 November 1828]

My dear Sir

With many thanks I return your books—The Man of two Lives¹ is founded on a good idea—treated to great degree happily—yet it strikes

209

me to be a translation—the phrases, the thoughts—the incidents are so truly German.

I wrote to Mr Colburn the other day asking for a copy of the Last Man—he has not replied—will you obtain one for me & get it sent directed to E. J. Trelawny Esq Fladong's Hotel Oxford St.—[2]

I am Dr Sir

Y^r Obt Ser^t

MaryW. Shelley

ADDRESS: Charles Ollier Esq / 5 Maida Hill. TEXT: MS., Pforzheimer Library.
    1. James Boaden, *The Man of Two Lives*, 2 vols. (London: H. Colburn, 1828).
    2. In November–December 1828 Trelawny stayed at Fladong's Hotel, 144 Oxford Street. His 14 November 1828 letter to Mary Shelley from the hotel indicated that he wanted to read *Valperga* and *The Last Man* (*S&M*, IV, 1118).

To John Bowring

4 Oxford Terrace   3 Feb^{ry} [1829]

I have received the cheque for £5-5[1] I was unaware that the article was of such instant necessity—or that the W.R. [*Westminster Review*] would appear so soon—The subject is not France but Italy—Do you intend that I should not complete it?—At present I am too much occupied by my novel to be able to give you much time—but if you wish for my assistance & can think of some work which would only require a short easy notice I will accomplish it—& do better still for the number After—

I am very glad to hear of your child's convalescence—you are better off than poor Moore—whose only little girl will I fear hardly recover[2] & whose long protracted suffering is a sad misfortune—

I am very truly Y^s

MaryShelley

ADDRESS: John Bowring Esq / 7 North Place / Gray's Inn Lane. POSTMARKS: (1) T.P / Crawford St.; (2) 7. NIGHT. 7 / 4. FE / 1829. ENDORSED: (1) Feb 13 1829 / Mary Shelley; (2) Mary Shelley / 3 Feby 1829. TEXT: MS., Huntington Library.
    1. For Mary Shelley's January review article on Mérimée's works see 11 June [1828], n. 1.
    2. Anastasia Mary Moore (b. March 1813), Thomas Moore's second daughter, died on 8 March 1829 (Howard Mumford Jones, *The Harp That Once* [New York: Henry Holt and Co., 1937], pp. 153, 268–69).

To Edward John Trelawny

My dear Trelawny

Your letter reminded me of my ⟨mis⟩deeds of omission and of not writing to you as I ought—and it assured me of your kind thoughts in that happy land, where, as Angels in heaven, you can afford pity to us Arctic islanders—It is too bad, is it not? that when such a Paradise does exist as fair Italy—one should be chained here?—Without the infliction of much absolutely cold weather—I have never suffered a more ungenial winter—winter it is still—a cold east wind has prevailed for the last six weeks, making exercise in the open air a positive punishment—This is truly English! half a page about the weather—but here this subject has ⟨all the⟩ every importance—it is fine—you guess I am happy and enjoying myself—is it—as it always is—you know that one is fighting against a domestic enemy—which saps the very foundation of pleasure.

I am glad that you are occupying yourself—and I hope that your two friends will not cease urging you till you really put to paper the strange wild adventures you recount so well.[1] With regard to the other subject— you may guess, my dear Friend, that I have often thought—often done more than think on the subject   There is nothing I shrink from more fearfully than publicity—I have too much of it—& what is worse I am forced by my hard situation to meet it in a thousand ways—Could you write my husband's life, without naming me it were something—but even then I should be terrified at the rouzing the slumbering voice of the public—each critique, each mention of your work, might drag me forward—Nor indeed is it possible to write Shelley's life in that way. Many men have his opinions—none fearlessly and conscientiously act on them, as he did—it is his act that marks him—and that—You know me—or you do not, in which case I will tell you what I am—a silly goose—who far from wishing to stand forward to assert myself in any way, now that I am alone in the world, have but the desire to wrap night and the obscurity of insignificance around me. This is weakness—but I cannot help it—to be in print—the subject of men's observations—of the bitter hard world's commentaries, to be attacked or defended!—this ill becomes one who knows how little she possesses worthy to attract attention—and whose chief merit—if it be one—is a love of that privacy which no woman can emerge from without regret—Shelley's life must be written—I hope one day to do it myself, but it must not be published now—

There are too many concerned to speak against him—it is still too sore a subject—Your tribute of praise, in a way that cannot do harm, can be introduced into your own life—But remember, I pray for omission—for it is not that you will not be too kind too eager to do me more than justice—But I only seek to be forgotten—

Claire has written to you—She is about to return to Germany[2]—She will I suppose explain to you the circumstances that make her return to the lady she was before with, desirable—She will go to Carlsbad and the baths will be of great service to her. Her health is improved—though very far from restored. For myself I am as usual, well in health—occupied—and longing for summer when I may enjoy the peace that alone is left for me—I am another person under the genial influence of the sun—I can live unrepining with no other enjoyment but the country made bright and cheerful by its beams—till then I languish. Percy is quite well—he grows very fast and looks very healthy—

It gives me great pleasure to hear from you, dear Friend—do write often—I have now answered your letter though I can hardly call this one—so you may very soon expect another—Take care of yourself—How are your dogs? & where is Roberts—have you given up all idea of shooting. I hear Medwin is a great man at Florence—so Pisa and economy are at an end[3]—Adieu

Yours
MS.

[*P. 1, above address*]   (direct to me at my Father's 44 Gower Place—Gower St. and to Claire at 5 Carmarthen St—Tottenham C' Road {)}

ADDRESS: Edward Trelawny Esq / Ferma in Posta / La Toscane / Firenze / L'italie. POSTMARKS: (1) [?22] / G[   ] / 1829; (2) 12 / JUIN / 1829; (3) Pont / B[EAU]VOISIN; (4) GENOVA [   ]. TEXT: MS., Keats-Shelley Memorial House, Rome.

1. On 11 March 1829, Trelawny wrote from Florence to inform Mary Shelley that he was writing an autobiography, for which he wished her to provide documents and anecdotes about Shelley. He also mentioned that Charles Armitage Brown and Walter Savage Landor (whom Trelawny met in 1828) were assisting him and were "to review it sheet by sheet, as it is written" (Trelawny, *Letters*, pp. 116–18). According to Brown's son, Brown's assistance extended to rewriting Trelawny's *Adventures*, which Trelawny acknowledged by sharing with him the proceeds of the 1831 and 1835 editions (Brown, *Letters*, p. 292, n. 5). Although Mary Shelley declined to provide Trelawny with biographical data about Shelley, she did arrange for the publication of the *Adventures* by Richard Bentley in 1831 and saw it through the press because Trelawny was in Italy. Trelawny first intended to call his story *Treloen*, but in order to remain anonymous, he changed the title to *A Man's Life*. A misunderstanding, however, led to the publication under the title selected by Mary Shelley and the publishers, the *Adventures of a Younger Son*. Trelawny's intention to write a life of Shelley

was fulfilled with his 1858 *Recollections*, in which he favorably commented on Mary Shelley, and with his revised and republished 1878 *Records*, in which he viciously maligned Mary Shelley (pp. 229–32).

2. Claire Clairmont left for Dresden to rejoin the Kaisaroffs on 18 September 1829 (Godwin, Journal).

3. By September 1829 Medwin, penniless, had permanently left his wife and children. In 1830 bankers won a judgment against him for thirty thousand lire. During this period Trelawny and Brown assisted Mrs. Medwin in the tangle of financial difficulties that followed Medwin. Trelawny also provided her with funds (Lovell, *Medwin*, pp. 223–40).

◆

To Cyrus Redding[1]

33 Somerset St.   Portman Sq
Sunday [?16 May 1829][2]

Dear Sir

I am sorry to have it only in my power to reply that the portrait of M[r] Shelley to which you allude, is by no means a good one:—it is the size of life, in oils—but unfortunately very unfinished—There are however several very striking points of resemblance, and I indulge a hope that when I can afford it, a first rate Engraver might succeed in making a good print from it—I do not know any thing so disagreable or unjust as the too frequent custom of prefixing prints unworthy of the person represented—and in this case, there would be great danger, that even M[r] Heath[3] could not succeed. I should be averse therefore to having it done unless by him, & unless it were in my power to cancel it altogether if I did not approve of it—

If it had been otherwise, if the picture had been one which would only have needed fidelity and care, I should have been very happy to have furnished you with the opportunity of making an engraving   Be assured that it is not necessary to apologize to me for an application on this subject—still less from a friend of M[r] Smith—I believe also that M[r] L. Hunt is a common acquaintance

I am Y[s] Ob[ly]
MaryShelley

TEXT: MS., Betty T. Bennett.

1. Cyrus Redding noted that he was "absent from London once for nine to ten days in ten years" for a visit to Amiens and Paris. Based on an unpublished letter from Horace Smith that refers to Redding's Paris journey, we may date this visit abroad in the spring of 1829 (27 June 1829, MS., Pforzheimer Library). In Paris he

called on the Galignanis, whose *Messenger* he had edited from 1815 to 1818. Since 1804 the Galignanis had been "literary pirates." That is, with no international copyright laws to hinder them, they reprinted English books in France (see Giles Barber, "Galignani's and the Publication of English Books in France from 1800 to 1852," *The Library*, 5th ser., 16 [December 1961]: 267–86; and *A Famous Bookstore* [Paris: The Galignani Library, n.d.], a pamphlet kindly provided by J. M. Sene, former director of Galignani Librairie). During his 1829 visit, Redding agreed to write a number of introductory biographical sketches, including one of Shelley, for Galignani's compact edition of English works, and he asked his friend Horace Smith if he might include material from Shelley's letters to Smith. Smith declined because he believed that Shelley's letters were "too confidential" for publication and full of "such heterodox notions as might horrify many good folks" (Redding, *Fifty Years' Recollections*, II, 206–7). Smith's letter is dated 10, Hanover Crescent, 6th April. Smith's 6 April 1829 letter suggested that Redding might apply to Godwin, Mrs. Shelley, or Peacock for a facsimile. Whether he applied to the others is uncertain, but Redding acknowledged his indebtedness to Mary Shelley for almost all his material on Shelley (Redding, *Fifty Years' Recollections*, II, 363–66; idem, *Yesterday and To-Day*, 3 vols. [London: T. Cautley Newby, 1863], III, 108). *The Poetical Works of Coleridge, Shelley, and Keats*, with Redding's biographical essays, was published around mid-December 1829 (see Brown, *Letters*, pp. 291–92) without the frontispiece containing the poets' portraits, which, according to a notice inserted in a December copy of the book, would be ready before 15 January next (1830).

2. The earliest possible date, based on Mary Shelley's settling in Somerset Street on 13 May 1829.

3. Charles Heath (1785–1848; *DNB*), engraver and promoter of many illustrated annuals, including *Keepsake, Literary Souvenir, Book of Beauty, Picturesque Annual*, and *Amulet*.

To Sir Walter Scott

London—33 Somerset St.
Portman Sq—25 May—1829

Sir

I have been encouraged by the kind politeness you have afforded to others, and by the indulgence with which I have been informed you have regarded some of my poor productions,[1] to ask you if you could assist me in my present task.

I am far advanced in a romance whose subject is Perkin Warbeck—Of course you know that he visited the court of James IV and married the daughter of the Earl of Huntly. In consulting our historians as to his story, I have found the earlier ones replete with interesting anecdotes and documents entirely passed over by Hume &c and in the forgotten or neglected pages of English and Irish writers of a distant date I discover a glimmering of the truth about him, even more distinct than that afforded in the dissertations of the modern writers in favor of his pretentions. Your are completely versed in the Antiquities of your country, and you would confer a high favor on me if you could point out any writer of its history— any document, anecdote or even ballad connected with him generally unknown, which may have come to your knowledge. I have consulted as yet only Buchanan & Lyndsay—(the latter does not even allude to him in his history of the James's)—and among later writers Pinkerton[2]

I hope you will forgive my troubling you—it is almost impertinent to say how ⟨incongruous⟩ foolish it appears to me that I should intrude on your ground, or to compliment one all the world so highly appretiates— but as every traveller when they visit the Alps, endeavours however imperfectly, to express their admiration in the Inn's Album,[3] so it is impossible to address the Author of Waverly without thanking him for the delight and instruction derived from the inexhaustible source of his genius, and trying to express a part of the enthusiastic admiration his works inspire

I am, Sir
Your Ob' Servant
MaryShelley

ADDRESS: For: Sir Walter Scott, Bart. / Edinburgh. POSTMARKS: (1) MY / A 25 / 1829; (2) May [   ] 2[   ] / 1829. TEXT: MS., National Library of Scotland.

1. See 14 June 1818.

2. George Buchanan, *History of Scotland* (Edinburgh: Alexander Arbuthnet, 1582), written in Latin and translated several times before 1800; Robert Lindsay, *The History of Scotland (1436–1565)* (Edinburgh: Baskett Co., 1728); John Pinkerton, *The History of Scotland from the Accession of the House of Stuart to that of Mary*, 2 vols. (London: C. Dilly, 1797).

3. This recalls Shelley's self-description in Greek as "democrat, great lover of mankind, and atheist" signed in a Swiss inn album in 1816; the deed became quickly known and brought him under attack (White, *Shelley*, I, 455–56, 714).

❖

To Cyrus Redding

Somerset St.   Thursday   [?3 September 1829][1]

My dear Sir

I send you the Errata of the Prometheus—Some changes Mʳ Shelley wished made in the Adonais—and a suppressed stanza of Hellas.[2] I am tempted to offer to write a brief outline of Mʳ Shelleys life if Galignani chose—but then my secret must be kept religiously—& no alterrations made—it would {be} very short & its chief merit the absence of incorrectness—I have some hopes of the portrait—the Lady who painted it is in town & will meet Mr Davis & offer her suggestions tomorrow—but I would give the world to have it engraved here—where any defect in the drawing might be corrected & we superintend the whole—At any rate it will be better than a likeness after the imagination of a Frenchman—that is the drollest & stupidest idea—ever Man intent on selling an edition hit upon.

I am, dear Sir
Yours truly
MaryShelley

The drawing[3] is getting better & better—Pray keep them to their promise of letting me have it—I shall feel highly gratified

As it is now finished and at my house perhaps you will call   Come as soon after 12 as you can[4]

TEXT: MS., Huntington Library.

1. Godwin's Journal indicates that the only time Amelia Curran, "the Lady who painted" Shelley's portrait, was in London in 1829 and visited him and Mary Shelley was from around 19 August through 22 September. On Saturday, 19 August, and Friday, 4 September, Mary Shelley and Amelia Curran were at Godwin's. On Saturday, 12 September, Godwin dined at Mary Shelley's, and Amelia Curran called there afterwards.

2. The corrections that Mary Shelley sent Redding, except for the errata for *Prometheus Unbound*, were incorporated into Galignani's edition. Possibly *Prometheus Unbound* had already been set before the corrections were received (Taylor, *Early Collected Editions*, pp. 21–22).

3. The drawing preliminary to an engraved portrait.

4. Redding noted, "I called & was gratified at the result of my efforts to obtain the only worthy resemblance of Shelley that is extant" (Redding, *Fifty Years' Recollections*, II, 366).

***

To {Cyrus Redding}

Somerset St.   Teusday
[?September–November 1829]

My dear Sir

I have only made one correction in the MS—The whole tone of the Memoir[1] is to my mind inaccurate—but if this is the guise it is thought right that it should assume of course I have nothing to say—since it is favorable in its way & I ought to be content—I should have written it in a different style—but probably not so much to the Publisher's satisfaction—It is a mere outline & is as communicative as a skeleton can be—about as like the ⟨original⟩ truth as the skeleton resembles the "tower of flesh"² of which it is the beams & rafters—But I see no positive assertion in it that is very untrue

I am very much obliged to you for the communication & grateful to you for your reminding Galignani of his promise³

I am truly Yˢ
MS.

TEXT: MS., Pforzheimer Library.

1. Redding's "Memoir of Percy Bysshe Shelley" in Galignani, *Poetical Works of Coleridge, Shelley, and Keats*, pp. v–xi. The published memoir includes the facts of Shelley's marriage to Harriet Westbrook, his elopement with "Miss Godwin" while he was still married, his wife's suicide, and his subsequent marriage, "at the solicitation of her father," to "Mary Wolstonecraft Godwin, daughter of the celebrated authoress of the *Rights of Woman*" (p. vi). The memoir reprints, with some minor changes, Mary Shelley's introduction to Shelley, *Posthumous Poems*.

2. Perhaps an echo of "hill of flesh" in Shakespeare, *Henry IV, Part I* 2. 4. 243.

3. To give the drawing to Mary Shelley after it had been engraved (see the previous letter).

❧

To John Murray

12 November—1829   33 Somerset St.
Portman Sq

My Dear Sir

I am sorry to hear from Mʳ Moore¹ that you decline my Romance—because I would rather that you published it, than any other person.

I can assure you I feel all the kindness of your message to me through Mʳ Moore. Do you remember speaking to me about a life of the Empress Josephine Mdᵐ de Stael² &c ?—When I have got free from my present occupation, I will communicate with you on the subject, and I hope that by some plan, either of my writing for your Family Library, or in some other way, to liquidate my debt³—or I must do it even in a more usual manner—I am aware of your kindness concerning it but I could not conset that an act of civility on my part to Mʳ Moore should be brought forward as cancelling my debt to you—besides it would make me break a vow I made never to make money of my acquaintance with Lord By-

ron—his ghost would certainly come and taunt me if I did—This does
not decrease but rather enhance the value I have for your kind intention

I am dear Sir

Yours Obliged

MaryShelley

ENDORSED: 1829—Nov. 12— / Shelley, Mrs. TEXT: MS., John Murray.

1. Moore may have informed Mary Shelley of Murray's decision on *Perkin Warbeck*
on 9 November 1829 (see Moore, *Letters*, II, 660).

2. Mary Shelley apparently wrote to Mérimée of her plan to write about either
Josephine or Madame de Staël. On 4 February 1829 he suggested that both women
would be difficult subjects because of the problems of describing their active love
lives "plainly aux Anglais" (Bennett and Little, "Seven Letters from Mérimée to Mary
Shelley," pp. 151–52).

3. In response to this letter, John Murray replied that Mary Shelley had done for
him the service that he had asked Thomas Moore to request of her; that in future she
could provide further information without payment according to her "honourable
feelings"; and that he regretted rejecting her novel but looked forward to conferring
with her about other projects. He also included a receipt for £100 "value received"
(MS., 12 November 1829, John Murray; see also MWS *Letters*, vol. II, 19 February
1828).

◆

To {Henry Colburn}

13 Nov. 1829   33 Somerset St.

Portman Square.

My Dear Sir

It is now more than a year ago that I communicated to you, through
Mr Leigh Hunt, my wish to treat with you concerning a Romance on
which I was occupied on the subject of Perkin Warbeck—You asked to
see the first Volume—which I was not able to send—

I may now say that it is ready for the press; although I should not be
able to submit to inspection more than a volume and a half, you might
see the MS of the rest—requiring only to be copied by me—a thing I
am now occupied in doing—and achieve with great speed—

It will give me great pleasure if you continue to be my publisher[1]—I
may say that my present work promises, I think, to be far more popular
than the last—that I have taken great pains with it—and that the story
on which it is founded appears to me both beautiful and interesting—If
it is your desire to judge for yourself, of course I will send the part I
mention of the MS.—Only it is to be remarked that it improves in in-

terest as it goes on—And also (which I do not think) if the first vol. appear scanty to you—the materials I have for the rest, are even too much, and my principal endeavour is to compress—this indeed is one of the reasons that I write just now, as I shall have your opinion as to how far I ought to abridge the original—or not—

I may add that ⟨to no person⟩ every one to whom I have mentioned my subject judges it highly interesting—I may mention My father, Sir Walter Scott & Mr Thomas Moore—who have all highly encouraged me

I shall be glad from the reasons above mentioned to have an early reply

                                              I am dear Sir
                                              Y^r Obl^d & Ob^t
                                              MaryShelley

TEXT: MS., Pforzheimer Library.

   1. Colburn, who had published *The Last Man* in 1826, now in partnership with Richard Bentley published *Perkin Warbeck* in 1830 (see 5 January 1830).

❖

To Edward John Trelawny

                          33 Somerset St.   15 Decr 1829

My very dear Trelawny

   Your letter[1] would have occasioned me a great deal of pain had it not relieved me from my painful suspense about yourself—Is it true that I have been remiss? I thought I had been better than you by two letters—but I write a good deal and get so weary of the sight of a pen that I know I do neglect writing when I ought—besides—however a page of excuses would be ridiculous—I have ever loved—I do love you—write or not this is one of the warmest sentiments of my heart—and is it not better to feel this than to write twenty letters—Ah have pity on my miserable clouded faculties—free and enjoying beneath an Italian sky you cannot participate {   } our northern island miseries—not to talk of a climate which has outdone itself this year in rain & fogs—the peculiar situation of my relations is heavy on me—my spirits are depressed by care and I have no resource save in what sunshine my friends afford me—afford me you a little, Dearest friend—seal up words sweeter than vernal breezes[2]—flatteries if you will—warm totens [*tokens*] of kindliness—I need them   I have been so long accustomed to turn to you as the spot whence distant but certain good must emanate that a chill from you is indeed painful—I will be a good girl in return and write often—

Your last letter was not at all kind—you are angry with me   you speak of evasions—What do you ask, what do I refuse? let me write to you as to my own heart and do not shew this letter to any one—You talk of writing Shelley's life and ask me for materials—Shelley's life as far as the public had to do with it consisted of very few events and these are publickly know—The private events were sad and tragical—How would you relate them? as Hunt has,[3] slurring over the real truth—wherefore write fiction? and the truth—any part of it—is hardly for the rude cold world to handle—His merits are acknowledged—his virtues—to bring forward actions which right or wrong, and that would be a matter of dispute, were in their results tremendous, would be to awaken calumnies and give his enemies a voice—For myself—am I to be left out in this life?—if so half my objections, more than half, would disappear—for with me would depart that portion which is most painful—I do not see what you could make of his life without me—but if that is your intention tell me—and we will see what can be done—I have made it my earnest request to all who have meddled with our Shelley to leave me out—they have assented and I consider myself fortunate—I fear publicity—as to my giving Moore materials for LB's life I thought I think I did right—I think I have achieved a great good by it—I wish it not to be kept secret—decidedly I am averse to its being published   for it would destroy me to be brought forward in print   I commit myself on this point to your generosity—I confided this fact to you—as I would any thing I did—being my dearest friend and had no idea that I was to find in you a harsh censor and public denouncer—There was something false in our mutual position when you were in England—God knows I do not accuse you of being a wordling—but—alas! of course I know any, every fault must be mine—but are we not   shall we not ever be friends?

Did I uphold and laud Medwin?—I thought that I had always disliked him—I am sure I thought him a great annoyance and he was always borrowing crowns which he never meant to pay and we could ill spare—He was Jane's friend more than any ones—to be sure We did not desire a duel—nor an horsewhipping—and Lord Byron and M[rs] Beauclerk worked hard to promote peace—Can any thing be so frightful as the account you give?[4] Poor M[rs] Medwin—I shall be very glad to hear that you have done any thing for her—you if any body can—Claire is at Dresden as of course you know—she says they have had fine weather ever since her arrival—we have nothing but bad since her departure—she complains that she has not heard from you—Charles Clairmont her brother, after an unsuccessful struggle here has returned to Vienna—The Hunts are at Brumpton [Brompton] she has just had another child[5]—Jane went to see

220

them the other day—& he called at ⟨Pa⟩ my father's[6]—he is out of spirits—Your love Caroline Beauclerk married the other day[7]—well I believe—The pretty Cottagers are charmed by your remembrance—The little Invisibility preserves the little red arrangements among her bijouterie[8]—Jane is well—Nothing can be more stupid than London— Miss Fanny Kemble's success[9] is our only event—twelve guineas have been offered vainly for a private box on her nights—But while fog and ennui possesses London, despair and convulsion reign over the country[10]—some change some terrible event is expected—rents falling— money not to be got—every one poor and fearful—Will any thing come of it—Was not the panic and poverty of past years as great—Yet if parlia[ment] meet, as they say it will in January[11]—something is feared—something about to be done—besides fishing in Virginia Water[12] and driving about in a pony phaeton—

I should be very glad to hear more of your child[13]—I had thoughts— I desired to make an offer—but I dread a denial—and besides Italy is better than England for a child of the south—is she not lovely, delightful full of sensibility.

Adieu—my dear friend—have we quarrelled are we reconciled?— What is it?—I know little more than that I have never ceased being ⟨enti⟩ warmly attached to you and that I am always

Affectionately Yours
MWShelley

ADDRESS: L'Italie / Edward Trelawny Esq / Ferma in Posta / Florence Firenze. POSTMARKS: (1) [   ] AL TUR[   ]; (2) [CORRI]SPZA ESTERA DA GE[NOVA]; (3) 3 / FEBBRAIO. TEXT: MS., Bodleian Library.

1. Of 20 October 1829 (Abinger MSS., Bodleian Library; partially published in Lovell, *Medwin*, pp. 236–37).

2. Unidentified.

3. A reference to Hunt, *Lord Byron and Some of His Contemporaries*.

4. Trelawny's letter accused Medwin of folly and villainy, gave details of Medwin's desertion of his wife and daughters, and revealed Trelawny's active role in assisting Mrs. Medwin (see April 1[829], n. 3).

5. Arrabella Hunt, born 13 November 1829, died 2 December 1830 (*SC*, V, 262).

6. On 7 December 1829 (Godwin, Journal).

7. Caroline Beauclerk (1804–69) had married Robert Aldridge of Horsham on 20 October 1829 (*Burke's Peerage*).

8. "Jewelry."

9. Frances Anne Kemble (1809–93), actress and author, made her stage debut as Juliet at Covent Garden on 5 October 1829; her father, Charles Kemble, played Mercutio, and her mother, Maria Therese Kemble (1774–1838), played Lady Capulet. She won immediate acclaim and was celebrated throughout her long career. In 1833

she accompanied her father to America, and during that trip she became friends with Trelawny. In 1834 she married Pierce Butler, a Southern planter, whom she divorced in 1848 (*The Times* [London]. See also Margaret Armstrong, *Fanny Kemble* [New York: The Macmillan Co., 1938], pp. 77–101, 171–80).

10. Agitation for political reform and great economic distress, continuous since the end of the Napoleonic Wars, finally culminated in a series of reforms, including the Catholic Emancipation Bill (March–April 1829) and the Reform Bill (March 1832), which redistributed parliamentary representation in favor of the industrial and commercial classes.

11. Parliament opened on 4 February 1830 rather than as usual in January (*Annual Register*, 1830).

12. An allusion to George IV.

13. Trelawny's letters to Mary Shelley of 24–26 June 1829 stated that Zella was already with him (Abinger MSS., Bodleian Library). In fact, she arrived in Italy around 27 July (Trelawny, *Letters*, p. 129).

***

To {Charles Ollier}

33 Somerset St.   5 Jan. 1830

My dear Sir

You brought me two propositions from Mr Colburn concerning my book—One concerned the dividing of profits—I confess that this does not please me, for I am no woman of business—

The other proposal was to purchase my manuscript for £150—I accept this proposal[1]—and wish to know how soon Mr Colburn will go to the press—

You had better call on me to make the agreement—I should be glad that as little delay as possible should occur—

With many excuses for the trouble I give you—

I am Yours Obliged
MaryShelley

My father has seen Mr Colburn on the subject—and he received a letter from him about it yesterday—But the modifications occasioned by this interview none of them please me so well as the one made through you which I accept—

Nevertheless this one is sufficiently unfavorable—but I believe I know Mr Colburn enough to be satisfied that if the book succeed far beyond his expectation he will take his mistake into consideration

This will make however no part of the agreement which will simply be for the sale of Poor Perkin Warbeck for £150—

TEXT: MS., Pforzheimer Library.

1. On 21 January 1830 Mary Shelley signed an agreement that Colburn and Bentley would publish *Perkin Warbeck* in three volumes of at least three hundred and twenty pages each, to be ready for publication by 1 March 1830. The copyright would belong to the publishers, and Mary Shelley would be paid £150: £50 by a bill three months from the agreement date, £50 on the publication date, and £50 nine months from the publication date (MS., Agreement, British Library).

❧

To William Godwin

[?33 Somerset Street]   Sunday
[?17 January 1830][1]

My dear Father—Can you tell me whether Marshall[2] is in town—I shall be driven to borrow[3] I fear for I cannot bring Ollier to do any thing—I shall make another effort with him tomorrow

Y^s Aff^y
MS.

ADDRESS: W. Godwin Esq / 44 Gower Place / Fitzroy Sq. TEXT: MS., Pforzheimer Library.

1. The reference to Ollier suggests that this letter was written after Mary Shelley's letter of 14 January 1830 and before she signed the contract for *Perkin Warbeck*, on 21 January.

2. Godwin's Journal records that James Marshall called on him on 31 December 1829 and 11 February 1830.

3. Claire Clairmont wrote to Mary Shelley on 28 March 1830 that she had delayed her letter in "hope of being able to send you the money for Marshall," which suggests that Mary Shelley did borrow from Marshall at this time. Further, Claire Clairmont said that as soon as she received her salary she would send "what I owe you" (*S&M*, IV, 1124–30). Both Claire Clairmont and Charles Clairmont had borrowed money from Mary Shelley to pay for their return to the Continent (Locke, *Godwin*, p. 316).

❧

To John Murray

33 Somerset St.   Portman Sq   19 Jan^y [1830]

My dear Sir

Except the occupation of one or two annoyances, I have done nothing but read since I got Lord Byron's life[1]—

I have no pretensions to being a critic—yet I know infinitely well what pleases me—Not to mention the judicious arrangement and happy tact displayed by Mr Moore, which distinguish this book—I must say a word concerning the style, which is elegant and forcible. I was particularly struck by the observations on Lord Byron's character before his departure to Greece—and on his return—there is strength and richness as well as sweetness—

The great charm of the work to me, and it will have the same for you, is that the Lord Byron I find there is our Lord Byron—the fascinating—faulty—childish—philosophical being—daring the world—docile to a private circle—impetuous and indolent—gloomy and yet more gay than any other—I live with him again in these pages—getting reconciled (as I used in his lifetime) to those waywardnesses which annoyed me when he was away, through the delightful & buoyant tone of his conversation and manners—

His own letters and journals mirror himself as he was, and are invaluable—There is something cruelly kind in this single volume   When will the next come?² —impatient before how tenfold now am I so.

Among its many other virtues this book is accurate to a miracle   [*p. 1, cross-written*]   I have not stumbled on one mistake with regard either to time place or feeling

I am dear Sir

Your Ob^t & Obliged Servant

MaryShelley

ENDORSED: 1830 Jany 19 / Shelley Mrs. TEXT: MS., John Murray.

    1. Published 18 January 1830.

    2. The second volume was published in late December 1830 (Oscar José Santucho and Clement Tyson Goode, Jr., *George Gordon, Lord Byron: A Comprehensive Bibliography of Secondary Materials in English, 1807–1974* [Metuchen, N.J.: Scarecrow Press, 1977], p. 277).

❧

To Henry Colburn and Richard Bentley

[Somerset Street   ?4–11 March 1830]¹

Dear Sir

I send you nearly all the MS. of Perkin Warbeck—one Chapter is with a friend to correct some Irish localities² —pray let me have it back without delay—

I have just finished Cloudesley—the interest is inexpressively absorb-

224

ing—there is a truth and majesty in the delineation of the passions, and a simplicity and grace in the style different from the present day—and striking one as one reads as how infinitely superior[3]—

I am Your Ob[ly]
MShelley

ADDRESS: Mess. Colburn & Bentley / 8 New Burlington St. TEXT: MS., Pforzheimer Library.

 1. Godwin's novel *Cloudesley*, written from 29 November 1828 through 16 January 1830, was published in three volumes by Colburn and Bentley on 4 March 1830. Godwin received £450 for *Cloudesley* (Godwin, Journal; Bentley Archives, British Library, vol. 68, p. 4). This date is based on the conjecture that Mary Shelley received a copy on publication date (as did Godwin) and read quickly through it. Claire Clairmont has been credited with contributing much material to, if not actually writing some parts of, *Cloudesley* (See *CC Journals*, pp. 416–17). The fact that the manuscript of *Cloudesley* is entirely in Godwin's handwriting does not disprove this claim (MS., Pforzheimer Library). Mary Shelley's review of *Cloudesley* appeared in *Blackwood's Edinburgh Magazine* 27 (May 1830).
 2. Perhaps Thomas Crofton Croker.
 3. Mary Shelley incorporated this viewpoint in her review of *Cloudesley*.

❖

To Richard Bentley

33 Somerset St   Monday [19 April 1830]

My dear Sir

 A most tiresome accident has occurred—Copy of mine the first 44 pages of my 3[d] Vol.[1] was given to the Printer's boy some time back—And it seems the whole parcel is mislaid—of course were I not quite certain that the mistake lay with them, I should not so positively assert—that there is no doubt but that they had it—I have no other copy—And cannot imagine what is to be done—except that I do not doubt but that they will find it, if it is properly looked for—

I am Sir
Y[s] Ob[ly]
MaryShelley

ADDRESS: Richard Bentley Esq / 8 New Burlington St. POSTMARKS: (1) T.P / [N]o Oxford S[t]; (2) 7. NIGHT. 7 / 19. AP / 1830. TEXT: MS., Pforzheimer Library.
 1. Of *Perkin Warbeck*.

To Maria Jane Jewsbury[1]

33 Somerset St.   Portman Square
16 June—1830

I have been very much flattered, My dear Madam, by Mr Rothwell,[2] who assures me that you are good enough to desire my acquaintance. As your stay in town is so short, I have been induced to beleive that you would waive ceremony, and do me the pleasure of drinking tea with me either this Evening or tomorrow. May I expect you?—I enclose the autograph of Mr Shelley's handwriting which Mr Rothwell tells me your sister[3] wishes to have. I hope your sister will do me the favor of accompanying you ⟨tomorrow⟩

I am dear Madam
Your Ob^t Servant
Mary W. Shelley

ADDRESS: Miss Jewesbury / &c &c &c. TEXT: MS., Historical Society of Pennsylvania.

1. Maria Jane Jewsbury (1800–1833; *DNB*), author, who married Rev. William Kew Fletcher in 1832 and went to India, where she died of cholera on 4 October 1833. Maria Jane Jewsbury noted on Mary Shelley's letter: "This interview was brought on by R— [*Richard Rothwell*] having overestimated the force of an expression—but it is only just to say the [?*annexed*] note to Mrs Jameson [Anna Jameson (1794–1860), author] conveyed my real impression of M^{rs} S—The evening was divided between them—the most interesting of my town series." Maria Jane Jewsbury's impression of Mary Shelley was written to Anna Jameson on 18 June 1830:

As you expressed a desire to know my opinion of Mrs. Shelley, I will take the present opportunity of saying, that I rarely, if ever, met with a woman to whom I felt so disposed to apply the epithet "bewitching." I can of course merely speak of appearances, but she struck me in the light of a matured child; a union of buoyancy and depth; a something that brought to my remembrance Shelley's description of Beatrice in his preface to the Cenci. To those she loves her manners would be caressing; to a stranger they are kind and playful, less from a desire to please, than from a habit of amicable feeling. Her hilarity, contrasted with the almost sadly profound nature of some of her remarks, somewhat puzzled me. It is not the hilarity assumed by worn minds in society,—it is simple—natural—and like Spring full of sweetness, but I doubt her being a happy woman, and I also doubt her being one that could be distinctly termed melancholy. Looking over the best part of the writings of her father, mother, and husband, she is the kind of woman for them to love to describe. She reminded me of no person I ever saw, but she has made me wish the arrival of the time when I am to see her again. She is not one to sit with and think ill of, even on authority. (*Anna Jameson: Letters and Friendships*, ed. Mrs. Steuart Erskine [London: T. Fletcher Unwin, 1915], pp. 89–90.)

In her article "Shelley's 'Wandering Jew,' " *Athenaeum*, no. 194 (16 July 1831): 456–57, Maria Jane Jewsbury highly praised Shelley's "true, pure, beautiful poetry—poetry instinct with intellectual life—radiant, harmonious, and strong."

2. Richard Rothwell (1800–1868; *DNB*), Irish artist, who in 1841 painted Mary Shelley's portrait.

3. Geraldine Endsor Jewsbury (1812–80; *DNB*), author, who subsequently became an intimate of Lady Morgan (and assisted her with her *Memoirs*) and Thomas and Jane Carlyle. In 1830 Geraldine Jewsbury, in the care of her sister, was sent from their home in Manchester to London to perfect herself in languages and drawing (Susanne How, *Geraldine Jewsbury* [London: George Allen & Unwin, 1935], pp. 14–15).

To Frederic Mansel Reynolds

> Grosvenor Place—Southend
> Essex   Monday—[5 July 1830][1]

My dear Fred—I do not know whether I do not know whether I do right in send you these sheets by post—I dont know how to get them franked—Shall I enclose them to M[r] Bernal[2] if—so send me his address—number—& Christia[n] name I forget it—You shall the rest soon—& the other story also with as little delay as possible

The rain makes this place very stupid—there is no hope in this vile country unless you can shut up in one box yourself & all you wish to be with you—for out door delaissements[3]—are quite impossible

> Adieu   Yours   MS.

[*Top of page*]   I have left a space which fill up—I cannot procure LByron's poems—the quotation I want put in there is I think in the 4th Canto of Childe Harold—about the rainbows in the waterfall of Lerici—and feminine attention in misfortune[4]—put it in if it will <u>fit</u>—if not—it must be omitted

ADDRESS: For / F. Mansel Reynolds Esq / 48 Warren St.—Fitzroy Sq. / London. POSTMARKS: (1) Rochford / Py Post; (2) B / 6 JY [6] / 1830. TEXT: MS., Pforzheimer Library.

1. This lettter was written at the end of p. 9 of Mary Shelley's short story "The Swiss Peasant," published by Reynolds in the 1831 *Keepsake*, pp. 121–46, along with her story "The Transformation," pp. 18–39, and her poem "Absence," p. 39. The conclusion of "The Swiss Peasant," pp. 10–21, was sent in two packets on 10 July 1830.

2. Ralph Bernal (d. 1854; *DNB*), a politician who served in the House of Commons from 1818 to 1852 and thereby would have had franking privileges. Bernal, a regular *Keepsake* contributor, had a story and a poem in the 1831 edition.

3. *Delaissement* in English means "desertion." Given the context, this is almost certainly a mistake for *délassement*, meaning "recreation."

4. "The Swiss Peasant" was published without a quotation from Byron. I have been unable to certainly locate the quotation in Byron's works to which Mary Shelley alludes here.

To John Murray

Park Cottage—Paddington   9 August—1830

My Dear Sir

A long time ago I requested Mr Moore to communicate with you on the subject of the work it was in contemplation that I should write for the Family Library. He told me that you said that you would write to me—It is not strange that your numerous avocations should have caused you to defer this—And having been out of town, I have also delayed renewing my communication. I am now anxious to that we should agree as soon as possible on the subject—both as a means of my defraying my present debt towards you,[1] and of my earning a further sum, which from circumstances with which you are acquainted, I am very eager to do.

The subject you mentioned was the Life of Mme de Staël. On communicating with some friends of mine in Paris, I was assured by M. B. [*Benjamin*] Constant, that he would most readily give me every information in his power and introduce me to such other persons as would give me a great deal more. But nothing of this sort could be done by letter, but must necessitate a journey to Paris. I remember when I mentioned this to you—you said that you did not think it worthwhile—that you wanted an amusing not a profound book. It appears to me however necessary to make the book amusing. For a bare detail of what I could collect here, would contain nothing new or interesting—it is from anecdotes— from understanding through her friends the real and minute particulars of events, and learning through them her peculiar disposition and character, that I must form the interest of this or any other biography. By letter nothing could be done; for M. Constant had so little—and now must have so much less time[2] at his disposal that it {   } only in conversation that I could communicate with him. With these helps it appears to me that a most interesting, and were my ability sufficient, a most delightful work might be written.

As this may not enter into your plans, I have been meditating on other subjects to form a volume of your Library. Two or three have struck me. A Friend suggested the life of Mahomet—as not having been written for some years and therefore permitting novelty. I thought of the Conquests of Mexico & Peru as forming in some sort a continuation to a Life of Columbus. But the subject that struck me most, as affording scope for novelty and amusement, from the quantity and variety of materials we possess, was a history of the manners and ⟨history⟩ Literature of England from Queen Anne to the French Revolution—from Pope to Horace Walpole—To this even might follow another of Continental manners and literature during the same period—One other subject I heard in society the other day   The lives of the English Philosophers—but this would hardly be so amusing[3]

May I request as early an answer as you can conveniently give to these subjects—as my time now is tolerably unoccupied, I could easily call in Albermarle St. I confess it would give me great pleasure for a thousand reasons to contribute a volume to Your publication—The more so, as I believe though this may be vanity—that my book while it would be conscientiously accurate, would not at all fail on the score of amusement, which is one of the necessary adjuncts.

> I am, my dear Sir
> Yours Obliged
> MWShelley

Are any copies of Mr Moores 2nd Vol. made up—You may guess that I am not a little anxious to see it.

ADDRESS: John Murray Esq / 50 Albermarle St. POSTMARKS: (1) [PA]DDINGTON / EV / 10 AU; (2) 7. NIGHT. 7 / 10. AU / 1830. ENDORSED: 1830–August 9. / Shelley Mrs. TEXT: MS., John Murray.

1. This suggests that Mary Shelley had further borrowed from Murray or that she did not consider her debt of £100 cleared, although Murray did (see 12 November 1829, n. 3).

2. Almost certainly a reference to the political events in France. Dissatisfaction with ever more rigid governmental control by Charles X (1757–1836) had culminated in the 28–29 July Revolution. Lafayette had headed the radical movement, which supported him for the presidency of a French republic. Instead, Louis Philippe (1773–1850), duke of Orleans, supported by the liberal faction, was declared lieutenant general of France (30 July) and then King of the French (7 August).

3. Noted in an unidentified hand on Mary Shelley's letter: "The last suggestion capital, if M^{rs} S—be capable of undertaking it.—"

To { John Murray III}[1]

Park Cottage—Paddington   8 Sep^{br} 1830

My Dear Sir

I presume, since I have not heard from you, that you have received no communication from Mr Murray in reply to my letter. My idea has been that he intended to delay any until his return. I find however that he is not expected back for a month. Meanwhile if Mr Murray's silence proceeds from his deciding on declining my offers, I should be very glad not any longer to be kept in a suspense, which is very inconvenient to me.

May I request you at your earliest convenience, to make my desire known to Mr Murray. If he desires to postpone any arrangement until his return—yet ⟨means⟩ if he considers it most probable that then one will be made, of course I shall be most happy to wait. For I own I shall have great pleasure in contributing to the Family Library—I suggested several subjects in my last letter—I almost forget now whether some I am going ⟨now⟩ to mention were included. One subject I have thought of, is an History of the Earth—in its earlier state—that is an account both of the anti diluvian remains—of the changes on the surface of the Earth, and of the relics of States and Kingdoms before the period of regular history. Mr Murray will judge how far there is any danger of intrenching upon orthodoxy on this subject—He is aware that I have a great distaste to obtruding any opinions, even if I have any, differing from general belief, of which I am not aware—and also how far such a history would be amusing. To me these speculations have always been the source of great interest, but this may not be the public taste.

I have thought also of the Lives of Celebrated women—or a history of Woman—her position in society & her influence upon it—historically considered. and a History of Chivalry.

My friend. Mr Marshall, mentioned some time ago the idea of writing for the Quarterly[2]—and liberal as that publication has become, and clever and distinguished as it has always been, I should be very much pleased to contribute—I wrote once a Review for the Westminster—it appeared in one of the earlier numbers I forget which—it was upon "The English in Italy" and as I received a good many Compliments about it—I suppose in some degree it may be received as a specimin—if the Editor wished to have one on the subject.

I am so aware of Mr Murray's gentlemanly feeling & I must say kindness towards me, that I am sure if you will inform him how desirous I am of some kind of answer upon all these points, that he will no longer delay to furnish me with one.

I am Dear Sir
Y^s Ob^{ly} &cc
MaryW Shelley

ENDORSED: 1830 Septr 8 / Shelley Mrs. TEXT: MS., John Murray.

1. John Murray II (1778–1843) and his wife were on an extended tour of Scotland from c. 6 August to c. 27 October 1830. In his absence, John Murray III (1808–92) managed the firm (Ben Harris McClary, *Washington Irving and the House of Murray* [Knoxville: University of Tennessee Press, 1969], pp. 137–38; Moore, *Letters*, II, 695, 701).

2. The *Quarterly Review*.

❖

To General Lafayette[1]

London   33 Somerset St   Portman Sq.
11 Nov. 1830

My dear General

It is with great diffidence that so humble an individual as myself addresses herself to the Hero of three Revolutions. Yet I cannot refuse myself the pleasure of congratulating that Hero on his final triumph.[2] How has France redeemed herself in the eyes of the world—washing off the stains of her last attempt in the sublime achievements of this July. How does every heart in Europe respond to the mighty voice, which spoke in your Metropolis, bidding the world be free. For that word is said—one by one the nations take up the echo and mine will not be the last. May England imitate your France in its moderation and heroism. There is great hope that any change operated among us, will originate with the Government. Our king[3] is desirous of popularity; careless of opinions, leaning through family connexions to the liberal party—He will willingly accede to any measures for the good of the people. But our position is critical and dreadful—for what course of measures can annihilate the debt? and so reduce the taxation, which corrodes the very vitals of the suffering population of this country.

Pardon a woman, my dear and most respected General, for intruding these observations. I was the wife of a man who—held dear the opinions you espouse, to which you were the martyr and are the ornament; and to sympathize with successes which would have been matter of such delight to him, appears to me a sacred duty—and while I deeply feel my inca-

231

pacity to understand or treat such high subjects, I rejoice that the Cause to which Shelley's life was devoted, is crowned with triumph.

Your amiable family and yourself must have almost forgotten a stranger who came among you under disastrous circumstances,[4] for so short a time, and so long ago—I trust that one day it will be my fate to visit you again; meanwhile I feel satisfaction in remembering—that sick & unlike myself as I was when in Paris—yet then I became acquainted with its most illustrious citizen and that I can boast of having conversed with La Fayette

Most respectfully Y[rs]   MaryShelley

ADDRESS: For the / General La Fayette / &c &c &c. TEXT: MS., Cornell University Library.
    1. See 13 October [1827], n. 1; 16 May [1828].
    2. See 9 August 1830, n. 2.
    3. George IV died 26 June 1830 and was succeeded by his brother William IV (1765–1837).
    4. A reference to the smallpox that attacked her during her 1828 visit to Paris.

❦

To Edward John Trelawny

33 Somerset St   27 Dec[r] 1830

My dear Trelawny

At present I can only satisfy your impatience, with the information that I have received your M.S.[1] & read the greater part of it—Soon I hope to say more—George Baring did not come to England, but after considerable delay forwarded it to me from Boulogne[2]—

I am delighted with your work, it is full of passion, energy & novelty—it concerns the sea & that is a subject of the greatest interest to me—I should imagine that it must command success—

But, my dear Friend, allow me to persuade you to permit certain omissions—In one of your letters to me you say that "there is nothing in it that a woman could not read"—You are correct for the most part & yet without the omissions of a few words here & there—the scene before you go to the school with the mate of your ship—& above all the scene of the burning of the house following your scene with your Scotch enemy—I am sure that yours will be a book interdicted to women.—Certain words & phrases, pardoned in the days of Fielding are now justly interdicted—& any gross piece of ill taste will make your bookseller draw back—I have named all the objectionable passages, & I beseech you to let me deal with them as I would with L[d] Byrons Don Juan—when I omitted all that hurt my taste—Without this yielding on your part I shall experience great difficulty in disposing of your work—

Besides that I, your partial friend, strongly object to coarseness, now wholly out of date & beg you for my sake to make the omissions necessary for your obtaining feminine readers—Amidst so much that is beautiful, imaginative & exalting, why leave spots which believe me are blemishes? I hope soon to write to you again on the subject—

The burnings—the alarms—the absorbing politics of the day render booksellers almost averse to publishing at all—God knows how it will all end, but it looks as if the Autocrats would have the good sense to make the necessary sacrifices to a starving people—

I heard from Claire today[3]—She is well & still at Nice—I suppose there is no hope of seeing you here—As for me I of course still continue a prisoner—Percy is quite well & is growing more & more like Shelley—Since it is necessary to live, it is a great good to have this tie to life—but it is a wearisome affair—I hope you are happy—

Yrs my dearest friend ever
Mary Shelley

TEXT: MS. (copy), Abinger MSS., Bodleian Library.

   1. Trelawny, *Adventures* (see April 1[829]).

   2. On 28 October 1830 Trelawny had written to inform Mary Shelley that his friend George Baring, brother of the banker, had left Florence on 25 October and would go directly to London, carrying with him Trelawny's manuscript. George Baring was the youngest son of Sir Francis Baring (1740–1810; *DNB*), founder of the banking firm of Baring Bros. and Co.

   3. Claire Clairmont's letter is dated 11 December 1830 (*S&M*, IV, 1133–37).

To Charles Ollier

33 Somerset St.   Teusday   [?28 December 1830]

My dear Sir—I hope your tiresome silence is not occasioned by your being dead. Having the responsibility of M[r] Trelawny's MS. on my hands—& wishing to have a talk with you about my own affairs—I should so like to see you   Can you call on me tomorrow or when?—do let me see you tho' I am so troublesome

Y[s] Obl[d] MWShelley

Compts of the Season

ADDRESS: Chas. Ollier Esq / Frith St. Soho / 8 New Burlington St. TEXT: MS., British Library.

To Robert Dale Owen

33 Somerset St.   Portman Sq   30 Dec 1830

My dear Dale—I am tardy in thanking you for your letter[1]—yet I have thanked you a thousand times only you do not know it—for Procrastination has stolen my expression of them. Your letter gave me the greatest pleasure—first it proved to me that I was not forgotten by Fanny nor yourself—and then it gave me tidings of the former, of her success and happiness, which delighted me.

My enclosed letter to her[2] speaks of the subject that must interest us all so highly.—the triumph of the Cause in Europe—I wonder if Nations have bumps[3] as well as individuals—Progressiveness is certainly finely developed just now in Europe—together with a degree of tyrant quelling-tiveness which is highly laudable—it is a pity that in our country this should be mingled with sick destructiveness; yet the last gives action to the former—and without, would our Landholders be brought to reason? Yet it is very sad—the punishment of the poor men being not the least disaster attendant on it.

If you are good you will write to me again. When shall you again visit England? Will Fanny never come over?[4] Talk to her of me some-times   Remember me yourself—

I am Yours ever
MWShelley

ENDORSED: Mary Shelley / Decr 1830. TEXT: MS., Historical Society of Penn-sylvania.

 1. Robert Dale Owen's letter of 5 January 1830 did not arrive in England until 15 March 1830. In this letter he explains that Mary Shelley's letter of 19 August reached Fanny Wright on the eve of her departure for New Orleans and that he has undertaken to respond in her place (Abinger MSS., Bodleian Library). At the end of May 1828 Fanny Wright left Nashoba permanently to become a public speaker in the cause of political and religious reform and part owner, with Robert Dale Owen, and editor-in-chief of the *New Harmony* (Ind.) *Gazette*. She gave lectures in Ohio, Maryland, Pennsylvania, and New York and by January 1829 decided to settle in New York. Robert Dale Owen joined her there, and they continued their newspaper under the title *Free Enquirer* (Perkins and Wolfson, *Frances Wright*, pp. 207, 229, 231).

 2. See the next letter.

 3. Founded by Frans Joseph Gall (1758–1828), phrenology was a system based on the belief that thorough examination of the skull would reveal the abilities and personality of an individual. Godwin had Mary Shelley assessed by his friend William Nicholson, an amateur phrenologist, when she was nineteen days old. In 1820 God-

win was assessed by a phrenologist. However, Godwin's 1831 *Thoughts on Man* essay "On Phrenology" refuted phrenology (Locke, *Godwin*, pp. 219, 320–23). Robert Dale Owen had been introduced to phrenology in the autumn of 1827 and had been assessed by Johann Gaspar Spurzheim (1776–1832), a disciple of Gall and a famous phrenologist, and a Mr. DeVille (Owen, *Threading My Way*, pp. 331–36; Andrew Carmichael, *A Memoir of the Life and Philosophy of Spurzheim* [Boston: Marsh, Capen and Lyon, 1833], pp. 3–27).

4. In fact, Fanny and Camilla Wright had returned to Europe on 1 July 1830, first briefly to England and then to France. Shortly afterwards, they were joined in Paris by Phiquepal Darusmont. On 8 February 1830 Camilla Wright died. In July 1831 Fanny Wright and Darusmont were married. Their first daughter, born c. June 1831, died in 1832. Their second daughter was born on 14 April 1832. On 3 November 1835 the Darusmonts returned to America, where Fanny Wright resumed her public role. From 1840 to her death in 1852 the Darusmonts lived apart from each other (Perkins and Wolfson, *Frances Wright*, pp. 300, 306–7, 312–18, 326, 338–55); 12 September 1827, n. 1.

◆

To Frances Wright

33 Somerset St.   Portman Sq   30 Dec. 1830

My Dearest Fanny—Why have I not written to you so long? Not that I have forgotten you; O, no—that would be impossible.—but I have felt timid at the idea of intruding myself upon one, whose noble mind is filled with such vast interests—and whose time is occupied by such important plans. Yet dearest Fanny, amidst all your enthusiasm for the Cause,[1] there is mingled a feminine sweetness and a prompt sympathy, which, if you were nearer, would make {me} eager to claim the friendship you promised me. The Atlantic divides us[2]—Our letters can say little more than what, I trust, we feel to be true without them—that we have not forgotten each other—and that we remember with pleasure our transient intercourse. Alas! I can hardly flatter myself so far—but you I must love as a bright specimen of our sex.

Nor can I omit to congratulate you on the glorious triump{h}s achieved in Europe since you left it. France has redeemed her name. The conduct held towards the guilty ministers sets her in a bright light, and washes out the stains that Robespierre dimmed her with. Much remains to be done—in that Country—but it is impossible not to anticipate that they will finish well what they have so gloriously begun—And our dear General—the hero of true revolutions—this is the crown of his life—& may he long survive to enjoy his victory.[3] Poor Constant is gone,[4] but he was happy in beholding his party triumph. The fire is spreading from one end of Europe to the other—Russia & Prussia would assault enfranchized Belgium, but Poland rises in their path—Austria would lend his aid to his brother Anarchs[5] but Italy "Schiavi ognor frementi,"[6] keep him in check—Will not our Children live to see a new birth for the world!

Our own hapless country—but your eager correspondants must tell you every thing about that. The case seems to stand thus—The people will be redressed—will the Aristocrats sacrifice enough to tranquillize them—if they will not—we must be revolutionized—but they intend now so to do—it remains to be seen whether the people's claims will augment with the concessions—Our sick feel themselves tottering—they are fully aware of their weakness—long curtailed as to their rents, they humble—How will it all end? None dare even presume to guess.

So much for politics—Of myself I have little to say—I have added three years to my life since I saw you—And to one as keenly alive as I am, such a fact says also that I have enjoyed & suffered many things—My enjoyments shew themselves outwardly on the surfaces of things. My son is well—developing talents and excellent qualities enough to satisfy almost my maternal desires. My Father is well—enjoying a most green old age—These are circumstances to gild my life with permanent sunshine—Yet—Ah, my Fanny,—life is a toil & a cheat[7]—I love it not. If I could live in a more genial clime, it were something—but here in in my island-prison,—I sigh for the sun, & a thousand delights associated with it, from which I am cut off for ever. My youth is wasted—my hopes die—I feel fail within me all the incentives to existence—I cling to my child as my sole tie.—

Yours is a brighter lot, a nobler career. Heaven bless you in it, dear Girl, and reward you. You have chosen the wiser path and I congratulate you. Yet I feel with Spurzheim,[8] that I am made of frailer clay—and should have sunk before difficulties,—which serve to edge your heroic spirit, I should be so glad to hear of you. To learn if your exertions are their own reward—or if you have a reward beyond—Remember that in Europe you have none who loves you better than[9]—

ADDRESS: Miss Frances Wright. TEXT: MS., Indiana State Library.
    1. Robert Dale Owen's letter of 5 January 1830 gave details of Fanny Wright's activism.
    2. See 30 December 1830 to Robert Dale Owen, n. 4.
    3. Lafayette, who died 20 May 1834 (see 11 November 1830).
    4. Benjamin Constant died on 8 December 1830.
    5. Mary Shelley's use of *anarch* here recalls Byron's "Imperial Anarchs doubling human woes," *Childe Harold* 2. 14, and Shelley's "Chained hoary anarchs," *The Triumph of Life*, line 237, as well as his references to anarchs in *Lines written among*

the Euganean Hills, line 152; *Hellas*, line 318; *Laon and Cythna* 10. 5. and 9; "Ode to Liberty," st. 12, line 10.

6. "Constant clamor of slaves."

7. Perhaps an echo of Dryden: "When I consider life, 'tis all a cheat," *Aureng-Zebe* 4. 1; or Shelley, "Of parents' smiles for life's great cheat," "Ginevra," 1. 36.

8. This suggests that Mary Shelley had been assessed by the phrenologist (see 30 December 1830 to Robert Dale Owen, n. 3).

9. Mary Shelley's signature has been cut away.

To Charles Ollier

33 Somerset St.   Friday   [18 February 1831]

My dear Sir—

I have now arranged with my Father & you shall have the Memoir[1] in question—but I cannot be quite so speedy as I wished & intended—You shall have it next week—on as early a day as you can.

If M‘ Colburn desires it, my father will see him & give him every information necessary concerning M‘ Fisher,[2] so as to put a complete end to the sale of his pirated edition—My father would prefer seeing M‘ Colburn himself upon the subject, to explain the proceedings formerly used against M‘ Fisher

M W Shelley

Have they any idea of publishing Frankenstein in their edition?

ADDRESS: Charles Ollier Esq / 8 New Burlington St. POSTMARKS: (1) T.P / Tottenm Ct [   ]; (2) 10. F.N[OON. 10] / 19. FE / 1831. TEXT: MS., Pforzheimer Library.

1. Mary Shelley wrote the introductory memoir of Godwin's life for Colburn and Bentley's one-volume reissue of *Caleb Williams*, published 1 April 1831 (Lyles, *MWS Bibliography*, p. 41; Godwin, *Journal*). Godwin had sold the copyright of *Caleb Williams* to Colburn and Bentley for £50 on 19 June 1830 (Bentley Archives, British Library, Add. 46627, vol. 68, p. 69).

2. In 1824 S. Fisher, book publisher, 4 Warwick Lane, Paternoster Row, had violated the copyright laws by republishing *Caleb Williams* in five penny numbers before Godwin took legal action to restrain him (Burton R. Pollin, *Godwin Criticism* [Toronto: University of Toronto Press, 1967], pp. 110–11). In 1826 Fisher had published another unauthorized edition in three volumes.

To {Charles Ollier}

[33 Somerset Street]   Wednesday
[?February—10 March 1831]

My dear Sir—if there is another real ⟨introd⟩ edition of Frankenstein[1]—
that is if it goes to the press again—will you remember that I have a short
passage to add to the Introduction. Do not fail me with regard to this—
it will only be a few lines—& those not disagreable to C. & B. [*Colburn
and Bentley*]—but the contrary—

Yours truly
MS.

Do tell me what you have done about the MS.[2] sent you to read

TEXT: MS., Pforzheimer Library.

    1. Colburn and Bentley published Mary Shelley's revised *Frankenstein*, with its
new introduction (dated 15 October 1831), which describes the circumstances of its
composition and attributes the 1818 preface to Shelley.

    2. Probably Trelawny's manuscript, although Mary Shelley had sent Ollier arti-
cles for the *New Monthly Magazine* or the *Court Journal*.

To William Blackwood

33 Somerset St.   Portman Sq   21 March 1831

My dear Sir

    It is long ago that you told me that you should be willing to receive
articles of mine for your Magazine. Not being in the habit of writing for
periodicals—I have delayed taking advantage of your desire, though I
have often resolved so to do. I send now an article[1]—which I hope will
appear fit for insertion—if so I shall be happy to continue to communicate with you. With regard to remuneration you know the payment given
for such productions better than I—and I leave it to you—I shall be very
glad if my communications form a part of your valuable & amusing work

I am Sir
Yours Ob[ly]
M W Shelley

TEXT: MS., National Library of Scotland.

    1. Unidentified. Nor is there a record of Mary Shelley as a contributor to *Black-
wood's* in this period.

To Edward John Trelawny

1831   June 14—Somerset St—

My dear Trelawny

Your work is in progress at last[1] & is being printed with great rapidity—Horace Smith undertook the revision & sent a very favorable report of it to the publishers—to me he says—"Having written to you a few days ago, I have only to annex a copy of my letter to Colburn & Bentley—whence you will gather my opinion of the M.S.—it is a most powerful, but rather perilous work, which will be much praised & much abused by the liberal & bigoted—I have read it with great pleasure, & think it admirable—in every thing but the conclusion"—by this he means as he says to Colburn & Bentley "The conclusion is abrupt & disappointing especially as previous allusions have been made to his later life which is not given—Probably it is meant to be continued—& if so it would be better to state it—for I have no doubt that his first part will create a sufficient sensation to ensure the sale of a second."—In his former letter to me H. S. [*Horace Smith*] says "Any one who has proved himself the friend of yourself & of him whom we all deplore, I consider to have strong claims on my regard & I therefore willingly undertake the revision of the M.S." "Pray assure the author that I feel flattered by this little mark of his Confidence in my judgement & that it will always give me pleasure to render him these or any other services"—And now my dear Trelawny, I hope you will not be angry at the title given to your book—the responsibility of doing any thing for any one so far away as you, is painful, & I have had many qualms, but what could I do? The publishers strongly objected to the "History of a Man" as being no title at all—or rather one to lead astray. The one adopted is taken from the first words of your M.S.—where you declare yourself a younger son—words pregnant of meaning in this country—where to be the younger son of a man of property is to be virtually discarded—& they will speak volumes to the English reader—it is called therefore "The adventures of a younger son"—If you are angry with me for this I shall be sorry—but I knew not what to do—Your M.S. will be preserved for you & remember also that it is pretty well known who it is by—I suppose the persons who read the M.S. in Italy[2] have talked—& as I told you, your mother speaks openly about it—Still it will not appear in print—in no newspaper accounts over which I have any controul as emanating from the publisher—Let me know immediately how I am to dispose of the dozen copies I shall receive on your account—one must go to H. Smith—another to me—& to who else? the rest, I will send to you in Italy—There is another thing that annoys me especially—You will be paid in bills dated from the day of publication—now not far distant—3 of various dates—To what man of business of yours can I consign these—the first I should think I could get discounted at once & send you the cash—but tell me what I am to do—I know that all these hitches & drawbacks will make you vituperate womankind—& had I ever set myself up for a woman of business—or known how to manage my own affairs, I might be hurt—but you know my irremediable deficiencies on those subjects & I represented them strongly to you before I undertook my task—& all I can say in addition is, that as far as I have seen—both have been obliged to make some concessions, so be as forgiving & indulgent as you can.

We are full here of reform or revolution whichever it is to be—I should think something approaching the latter, though the first may be included in the last—Will you come over & sit for the new parliament?³—What are you doing?—Have you seen Claire?⁴ How is she? She never writes except on special occasions when she wants any thing—tell her that Percy is quite well—

You tell me not to marry⁵—but I will—any one who will take me out of my present desolate & uncomfortable position—Any one—& with all this do you think that I shall marry?—Never—neither you nor any body else—Mary Shelley shall be written on my tomb—and why? I cannot tell—except that it is so pretty a name that tho' I were to preach to myself for years, I never should have the heart to get rid of it—

Adieu, my dear friend, I shall be very anxious to hear from you, to hear that you are not angry about all the contretemps attendant on your publication—& to receive your further directions—

Yʳˢ very truly
MW Shelley

TEXT: MS. (copy), Bodleian Library.

1. The agreement between Mary Shelley, on Trelawny's behalf, and Colburn and Bentley to publish Trelawny, *Adventures*, took place on 9 June 1831. The bills were drawn on 17 December 1831 for £100 to be paid in four, seven, and nine months, respectively (British Library, Add. 46560, vol. 1, 14; Add. 46681, vol. 122, 59–60).

2. These included Landor, Charles A. Brown, Seymour Stocker Kirkup, George Baring and Mrs. Baring, and Lady Burghersh (Trelawny, *Letters*, p. 140). Kirkup (1788–1880; *DNB*), artist, attended the funerals of Keats and Shelley. Priscilla Anne Fane, Lady Burghersh (1793–1879; *DNB*), artist and linguist, was married to John

Fane, Lord Burghersh (1784–1859; *DNB*), in 1841, earl of Westmorland, and British minister plenipotentiary at Florence at this time.

3. In response to this letter, Trelawny wrote on 29 June 1831: "If I thought there was a probability that I could get a seat in the reformed House of Commons, I would go to England, or if there was a probability of revolution" (Trelawny, *Letters*, pp. 163–68).

4. Trelawny responded that Claire Clairmont, looking pale, thin, and haggard, had remained in Florence about ten days. He had seen her three or four times but was unable to assist her in finding a better position than she had with the Kaisaroffs, with whom she had returned to Russia (Trelawny, *Letters*, p. 166).

5. After Mary Shelley's letter of 22–25 March 1831 (MWS *Letters*, vol. II) playfully listed the marriages of a number of woman admired by Trelawny and noted that should she and Claire Clairmont either die or marry, he would be left without a Dulcinea, Trelawny enjoined her not to "abandon me by following the evil examples of my other ladies. I should not wonder if fate, without our choice, united us" (Trelawny, *Letters*, p. 162). Trelawny answered Mary Shelley's remarks in this letter: "I was more delighted with your resolve not to change your name than with any other portion of your letter" (Trelawny, *Letters*, p. 166).

To *[Charles Ollier]*[1]

Somerset St.   30 June [1831]

My dear Sir

You made me an offer from Mess. Colburn & Bentley concerning the publication of Frankenstein to which I acceded. Is it their intention to conclude that affair? If it is, you would much oblige me by ⟨tell⟩ communicating with me about it as ⟨you⟩ soon as you can—You promised me so to do early this week—⟨If⟩ It is of consequence to both parties that there should be no further delay

Yours truly
MWShelley

TEXT: MS. (photocopy), Kline-Roethke Collection (Misc. 120), Department of Special Collections and Archives, Stanford University Libraries.

1. Colburn and Bentley published the second edition of *Frankenstein* c. 2 November 1831.

To John Gregson

33 Somerset St.   Portman Sq—27 Jany 1832

Dear Sir

Mr Whitton has informed me that you will have the goodness to further any application of mine to Sir Tim^thy Shelley, and being at this moment in an embarassment that obliges me to trouble him, I shall be much obliged to you if you will communicate and second my request.

You may remember that when I signed the deed last year in Bedford Row—I applied for an encrease of income that I might send my son to a school of higher qualifications than Mr Slater's—Mr Whitton gave me hopes that this request would be complied with—I mentioned then that I had been embarassed for money ever since Percy went to school, when my income had not been encreased as I had expected. Afterwards Sir Tim^thy declined making any ⟨advance⟩ addition to my allowance, saying that he hoped that I should be able to give my son a good education on the sum I present receive.

Percy is now turned twelve years old; you may imagine that his school & taylors bills encrease every year—that his incidental expences are very great—& that to ⟨meet⟩ defray them consumes a great part of my income. To meet these calls I have but one resource which is to diminish my own personal expences as much as possible—for which purpose I have long contemplated going to a quiet spot in the country, where I could spend far less than I do now. I have been prevented, because it always demands some small command of money to make any change. I had hoped that at Xmas I might have been enabled, but found it impossible—I am forced to continue in my present abode (where I have lived nearly 3 years) my debts encreasing—and perfectly unable to change and retrench from want of such a sum as permitting me to get rid of my embarassments—would enable me to execute my economical plan. Under these circumstances I can only apply to Sir Timothy—and ask for the sum of £50, upon which I shall immediately remove—and establishing myself on the cheapest plan, continue to defray the encreasing expenses of Percy's education. If I am refused this, I am at a loss to imagine what I can do—as without an entire alteration of abode & leaving London, it is impossible for me extricate myself from my present position

Percy desires his duty & Love to Sir Tim^thy & Lady Shelley—he is a very fine boy and did his grandfather see him I am sure he would not have the heart to deny me a request which has for its ultimate object his well bringing up. I would have called on you with him, but the weather prevents my going out, & I am unwilling to delay a solicitation on which my present ⟨existence⟩ hopes of doing my duty by him depend. May I ask you therefore to forward my wishes at your earliest convenience—and I trust with success—I am dʳ Sir,

Your Obt. Servant
M W Shelley

I ought to mention perhaps that as Percy will continue with Mʳ Slater, my new abode will not be at <u>too great</u> a distance from town—sufficiently far only to ensure economy.

Percy was very much obliged to his Grandfather for some pocket money he was kind enough to send him last Easter thro' Mʳˢ Paul.[1] I hope the family are well after their affliction.[2]

ADDRESS: John Gregson Esq / 18 Bedford Row. POSTMARKS: (1) T.P / Duke St M.S; (2) 4. EVEN. 4 / 27. JA / 18[32]. ENDORSED: 27 Jany 1832 / Mrs Shelley. TEXT: MS., Bodleian Library.
   1. Georgiana Beauclerk Paul (1805–47), Mary Shelley's close friend, married to John Dean Paul (see MWS *Letters*, II, 16 February 1832).
   2. Elizabeth Shelley (b. 1794), Shelley's sister, died on 17 December 1831.

❖

To [Alaric A. Watts]

33 Somerset St.   Portman Sq   14 May—1832

Sir

I do not know whether the enclosed drama[1] will suit your Annual[2] or whether it may be considered as more befitting the beautiful Juvenile One, edited by Mʳˢ Watts[3]—If it should please you, I shall be glad that it appeared in either publication—& I refer to your usual terms, to arrange the question of remuneration

I am, Sir, Yˢ Obˡʸ M W Shelley

I may mention that this drama has been seen & liked by two or three good judges whose opinion emboldens me to send it you

TEXT: MS., The John Rylands Library.
   1. *Midas*.
   2. *Literary Souvenir* (see 30 October [1826] to Alaric A. Watts, n. 1).
   3. Priscilla Maden (Zillah) Watts (1799–1873) edited the *New Year's Gift and Juvenile Souvenir* from 1829 to 1835 (for details of the lives of Alaric and Priscilla Watts see Alaric Alfred Watts, *Alaric Watts*, 2 vols. [London: Richard Bentley and Son, 1884]).

To John Murray

Dear Sir

The more I look over Lord Byron, the less do I see what I can say in illustration—historical, since the Life so copiously treats of them—for instance in Don Juan, the only things I can discover is in Canto IV CXI—
I knew one woman of that purple school
Which the Lady C. [*Charlemont*][1] alluded to in the life—Vol II 268—But as Lady Charlemont would recognize herself in such an assertion, it would not be right to put it in—and in Canto XIV c. where the dangerous passion arising from a game of billiards alludes to Lady F. W. W. [*Frances Wedderburn Webster*] the Heroine of the Bride—and the Ginevra of the Sonnets—Of the Poems to tell you that Florence is Mrs Spencer Smith—is to tell you what you know already
"When all around was dark & drear"[2]
Was to Mrs Leigh
Thou art not false but thou art fickle
to Lady Oxford—
"Though the day of my destinys over[3]
to Mrs Leigh
Well Thou art happy & I feel
to Mary Chaworth
All this you know already—The feelings which gave rise to each poem, are so dwelt on in the Letters in Mr Moore's Life—that there seems nothing left to say on that subject.—and by printing the poems in a Chronological order, you force on the readers apprehension his state of mind when he wrote them ⟨The elegance mingled with pass⟩ the difficulty of clothing well his ideas resulting from youth—though they forced expression—which made the Hours of idleness a failure. The depth of passion, nursed in solitude—and wild romantic scenery which breathes in his poems to Thirza[4]—Who she was I do not know—I believe a cousin—at any rate she was a real person decidedly—and his feelings of misery on her death most real—I have heard him express the sensations of acute despair that produced those poems—and those "on a Cornelian heart that was broken"—Alone in Greece—his imagination imparted its fire to his feelings—and encreased their impression on his own heart, as well as bestowing greater power of language and poetry—Returned to England &

mingling with the world, a certain elegance mingled itself with his with his inspiration, and was diffused over his productions—remarkable especially in the "Bride"—Attached one after the other to women of fashion his heroines displayed the delicacy & refinement of civilization.

When he quitted England, feeling himself wronged—an outcast & a mourner—his mind took a higher flight—It fed upon his regrets—& on his injuries—& Manfred & the 3^d Canto of C.H [*Childe Harold*} bear marks of solitary ruminations in wild scenery—detached from the spirit of fashion & the world—The gaieties and incorrectness of his Venetian Life breathed their Influence in Beppo & D. [*Don*] Juan—while solitary Lido—the moon lit palaces—and the deserted ruined grandeurs of that city awakened the vein that displayed itself in the 4th Canto of C.H. in Mazeppa—in the Ode on Venice—

As his mind became more subdued—he became more critical—but his school of criticism being of the narrow order, it confined his faculties in his tragedies & Lord Byron became sententious & dull—except where character still shone forth—or where his critical ideas did not intrude to Mar—Sarcasm, before confined to his speech—now acquiring a sting from his susceptibility to the attacks made on him induced him to write the Vision—& the Solitude in which he lived at Ravenna gave birth to Deep thoughts—to Cain—and Heaven & Earth—

At Pisa he again belonged more to the English world—It did him little good—Werner he wrote chiefly because he had for many years thought it a good subject—He was very anxious to go on with D. Juan—and verging on the time when people revert to past feelings, instead of dwelling on the present—he amused himself by descanting on English fashionable life—The last Cantos of D. J. were written with great speed—I copied them[5] there were scarcely any erasures and his chief delight was in sending them to me, to date the beginning & end with the name of the same month—to prove how quickly they were composed—the opposition he met concerning the Liberal made him defy the world in D. Juan—Then it made him despise the Liberal itself, so that when he wrote expressly for it, he wrote tamely—as is the case with the Island—But, in the end, this war gave him a disgust to Authorship—and he hurried to Greece to get a new name as a man of action—having arrived at the highest praise as a poet.

I have thus run through his works, to shew you what I think and know of the periods of their composition and the moods of mind in which they were written. If you think that a few lines of their history appended to each (which you could alter & frame as you like) would be of use, you can judge by this sketch, what my view would be, & I should be happy to furnish them—but still I think, the life supplies the place of any such observations.

I write in haste. Next week I leave town for 3 Months—Would it not be better that I saw Mr Finden before I went? I have been reading Contarini Fleming—Who is the Author?^{6} I like parts of it excessively—Especially the 1st Volume—Thanks for the 6th of the Life—Permit me to remind you that the copy you gave Mrs Williams needs also a 6th Vol.— I am, d^r Sir—Y^s truly MWShelley

ADDRESS: John Murray Esq / 50 Albermarle St. POSTMARKS: (1) T.P / Duke St M.S; (2) [   ]NOON [   ] / [?10] JU / 1832. TEXT: MS., British Library.
   1. Details of Byron's association with all the women listed in this letter, with the exception of Lady Charlemont, are included in Marchand, *Byron*.
   2. "When all around grew drear and dark," the first line of "Stanzas to Augusta."
   3. "Stanzas to Augusta."
   4. "Thyrza" was John Edleston (see Marchand, *Byron*).
   5. See 3 October 1818, n. 3, and 15 October 1822 through [30 March 1823].
   6. Benjamin Disraeli, *Contarini Fleming*, 4 vols. (London: John Murray), published in May 1832 (William Flavelle Monypenny and George Earle Buckle, *The Life of Benjamin Disraeli*, 2 vols. [New York: Macmillan Co., 1929], I, 185, 194).

◆

To Maria Gisborne

Sandgate—24 August [1832]

Our letters, dearest Friend, it would seem crossed on the road—the stupidity of the people of Somerset St—so arranged, it that I did {not} get yours till last Friday.—Not being in town and unable to hunt out & see people—the best thing I could do, as it appeared to me, was to enclose your interesting & well written letter to Dr Bowring, with whom I am acquainted. I have this moment got his answer—he is at Exeter—and he tells me that in a few days he will be at Plymouth,^{1} & he adds—"I will then call on Mrs Gisborne, whom I have heard Bentham mention with tenderness—& whose visit to him was a great delight—" "I think Bentham mentioned the letter more than once" If you have not already seen Bowring, you will now expect him—and I write & send this letter immediately, that you may have previous intimation—How could you imagine that I should not be delighted to do any commission for you^2— and this one was most easily executed.

Here I am still.—Trelawny & his daughter are still with me—thank God he remains—for I do not know how I should be able to support her frivolity, but for the aid of his more amusing company.—She is amiable lively & polite, but so unidea'd—so silly in her gaiety—so childish yet overgrown in her merriment, that it is hard to bear—never was there such an opposite to her father.—He talks of visiting Plymouth, & I shall make him call on you.—You must please him—for he loves good sense, liberality & enthusiasm, beyond all things—he is too violent in his politics for me—he is radical à l'outrance³—& altogether unprejudiced—to use the common phrase—& yet as full of prejudices as he can hold—which contradiction you will have no difficulty in understanding—If you have any very pretty girl among your acquaintance, enchant him by shewing her to him—he is sadly off here—I never found so great a dearth of female beauty as at Sandgate.

My Percy is gone back to school—I love the dear fellow more & more every day—he is my sole delight & comfort—On going away he insisted on having his supper alone in his room—telling me, to persuade me, that Sancho liked an onion behind a door,⁴ & why might he not enjoy the pleasures of solitary fare?—I cannot tell you how much cleverer & more companionable he was than my present companion—We have had a good deal of rain & eternal wind; this one day has risen cloudless & breezeless on us—There is a want of wood here—but the sea is open—and the hills the most singular in the world—They are so precipitous, that they look mountains—yet three steps leads you to their summits—& when you get up one rather higher than the rest—you see them sprinkled about, in conical shapes, each distinct, with ravines between—but so low that you could almost step from one to the other—They are verdant, & covered with sheep & cattle. I am reading a little Greek—& amusing myself as well as I can—but I am very stupid—and not at all in an energetic mood—though not quite so languid as when I was in town—I am here, wishing for nothing but an exemption from pecuniary annoyances, both for myself & my father—unwilling to return to town, yet I must next Month tho' but for a short time only—I shall settle myself not far from Richmond.⁵ Jane, Jeff & her children are al Solito⁶—Will any change ever come there? None, I imagine, but what grim Necessity may bring—& I hope that that will keep afar.

You do not mention the Cholera⁷—as with us in London, I suppose you hear less of it on the spot, than we do at a distance from you—Is it not strange that it should have got to New York? And reign there so violently—fear is its great auxillary—& as that ⟨I suppose⟩ seems very great among the Yankees, that will explain it. By the bye Trelawny is America-mad⁸—a feeling with which I have no sympathy—if you have, cela vous fera fortune⁹—Have you read his book? pray do— After all his going to Plymouth is very uncertain. Let me hear from you as often as you can. You write very good letters. As is often the case with those who possessing great talents, yet find difficulty in writing—for then they do not pay us with words merely—but with ideas, concisely & energetically clothed.— If you had not been in the midst of a great town like Plymouth—when I wanted the open country so much, I should have visited Devonshire, instead of coming here—Remember me with all kind{n}ess to Signor Giovanni [*John Gisborne*], who I hope is quite recovered—take care of your precious self—Maria Carissima & love ever

Your true friend M W Shelley

ADDRESS: Mrs Gisborne / 17 Union St. / Plymouth / Devon. POSTMARKS: (1) FOLK[E]STONE / PENNY POST; (2) E / 25 AU 25 / 1832. ENDORSED: Sandgate 24th Aug. 1832 / re[   ] Do / Ans. / M. Shelley. TEXT: MS., Bodleian Library.

1. Plymouth, Devon, where the Gisbornes resided, two hundred fifteen and a half miles west-southwest of London.

2. Mary Shelley was assisting Maria Gisborne's unsuccessful efforts to publish some writing.

3. "To the extreme."

4. Though there are references to Sancho eating in *Don Quixote*, there appears to be no specific reference to his eating in private.

5. Ten miles west-southwest of London.

6. "As usual."

7. William Godwin, Jr., died of cholera on 8 September 1832 (Locke, *Godwin*, p. 333; *S&M*, IV, 1167–68). In her 20 August 1832 letter Maria Gisborne reported that cholera at Plymouth was on the wane but had taken upwards of five hundred lives (Abinger MSS., Bodleian Library).

8. Trelawny visited America from March 1833 through July 1835 (Paula R. Feldman, "Letters Unravel the Mystery of Trelawny's American Years," *Manuscripts* 32, no. 3 [Summer 1980]: 170, 183. Although Mary Shelley states that she does not share Trelawny's enthusiasm for America, she set part of *Lodore* in Illinois, which she describes in idyllic terms.

9. "That will make your fortune."

❖

To {Frederic Mansel Reynolds}

33 Somerset St.   Thursday   [?December 1832]

My dear Fred.

You have received my letter for Mrs Paul has received her Keepsake[1]—& Mr Heath is returned—I suppose he thinks that he ought not to pay because the story is not printed, but as it will be next year, I do not see why he should be so cross—I had no idea of an objection & have counted on it—or I should not be so troublesome—and he need not be so stingy—it is very unamiable—I wrote, in all hurry & expedition because you asked me—& so he rewards my complaisance—yet still I hope you will bring him to reason & I very much desire it—

One of the Keepsakes you sent me has pages omitted—& is turned topsy turvy in the binding—I sent it to a friend in the country who finds it a riddle-my-ree[2]

Adieu

Truly Yours

Obliged

M W Shelley

TEXT: MS., Jean de Palacio.

1. *Keepsakes* were published annually in November or early December. The *Keepsake for 1833* (1832) contained two stories by Mary Shelley: "The Brother and Sister, An Italian Story" (pp. 105–41) and "The Invisible Girl" (pp. 210–27). The following year, "The Mortal Immortal" appeared in the *Keepsake* (pp. 71–87) (Lyles, *MWS Bibliography*, p. 29).

2. A variant of the phrases "riddle me a riddle" and "riddle my riddle."

❖

To Charles Ollier

Harrow.   10 Feb.   [error for 10 November 1833][1]

My dear Sir

I have heard nothing from you since I left town—and you must have thought me very rude not to have written to remind you of your kind promise of visiting me—but scarcely was I established here, than I got the Influenza again—so as to be confined to my bed a week or two & to the house for a much longer time—I did not recover till the Holydays when I went to Putney & got quite well—I am here again now—& if you feel enclined this cold weather to venture to our Hill—I shall be very glad to see you—only let me know a day or two before as I visit town now & then & it would be very annoying to miss you.

Do you know when my Novel[2] is to go to the press—I am ready whenever you are. Is Godolphin by Henry Bulwer?[3] Pray tell me—Do you remember promising to lend me the newly published letters of Horace Walpole[4] when they came out?—⟨Now⟩ If you were very good & wished ⟨much⟩ to please me you would send them & ⟨Trevyllian⟩ Trevellian[5]—

which I should like to read as being by the person who wrote Marriage in High Life[6]—for me to my Father (13 Palace Y^d) ⟨who⟩. He is going to send me a parcel this week—& could include yours.

Do come here if you can find time & courage—I am in the town—any one can direct you to the house when you are here but we are too primæval for numbers

Yours truly

MWShelley

ADDRESS: Chas Ollier Esq / 8 New Burlington St. POSTMARKS: (1) T.P / Harrow; (2) 12. NOON. 12 / 11. NO / 1833. TEXT: MS., Keats-Shelley Memorial House, Rome.

    1. The postmarks indicate that 10 February is an error for 10 November.

    2. *Lodore.*

    3. Edward Bulwer's *Godolphin* was published in 3 volumes by Richard Bentley in 1833. Henry Bulwer (1801–72), English diplomat and author, was Edward Bulwer's brother.

    4. *Letters of Horace Walpole, Earl of Orford, to Sir Horace Mann,* ed. Lord Dover, 3 vols. (London: Richard Bentley, 1833).

    5. Lady Charlotte Maria Bury, *Trevelyan,* 3 vols. (London: Richard Bentley, 1833).

    6. "Lady Caroline Lucy Scott," *A Marriage in High Life,* ed. the authoress of "Flirtation" (i.e., Lady Charlotte Maria Bury), 2 vols. (London: Henry Colburn, 1828).

◈

To Edward Moxon

Harrow—22 Jany 1834

Dear Sir

Your letter in some degree puzzles me—You say "if permission could be obtained"—I have always understood that the copyright of Mr Shelley's works belonged to me. Family reasons prevent my undertaking the republication of them at present. When these no longer exist (& it is probable that they will not endure any very long time)—it is my intention to endeavour to arrange to republish them—with the addition of some letters & prose pieces in my possession. If it were then thought best to add a life—though I should decline writing it myself—I should wish to select the person I should wish to undertake the task—and whom I think I could induce to perforne [*perform*] it.

I am sorry for the delay, but it is not in my power to prevent it.—nor can I fix the term of its duration. But when I am free to follow my own wishes I shall be most happy to enter into any arrangement with you for their execution[1]   I am flattered by the offer you make & return my sincerest thanks

I am Sir
Your Ob^t Servant
M W Shelley

ADDRESS: Edward Moxon Esq / 44 Dover St / Picadilly. POSTMARKS: (1) T.P / HARROW; (2) 12. NOON. 12 / 23. JA / 1834. TEXT: MS., Pforzheimer Library.

1. Moxon again contacted Mary Shelley in 1835 about an edition of Shelley's works with a life and notes, for which he offered £600. These proposals eventually led to Mary Shelley's 1839 editions of Shelley's works (see 7 December 1838). Moxon clearly felt a proprietary interest in this project, possibly based on this letter. On 6 March 1834 Godwin wrote to Moxon after consulting with Mary Shelley to say that she would be glad if Moxon could exert pressure to stop the publication of Shelley's works in numbers (MS., Pforzheimer Library). This probably refers to John Ascham's unauthorized 1834 edition of Shelley's works (Taylor, *Early Collected Editions*, pp. 26–27).

❧

To {Charles Ollier}

Harrow   30th April—1834

Dear Sir

I am totally at a loss what to do—I cannot be mistaken as to the packages I sent—I remember the whole circumstance of looking over the MS. for the last time, making up the packets & sending them—I cannot doubt as to the correctness of this statement—I have no copy at all—& should be obliged to rewrite it—at this moment I am engaged writing for Dr Lardner[1] & am very busy indeed.—I do not see therefore how I am to enable the Printers to proceed. I know that I sent the copy—It must have arrived at Burlington St & be mislaid—the mode in which I sent it—packets regularly paged, & going on without interruption, proves that there can be no omission on my part—I stated all this above a month ago, & received no answer, & consequently had no doubt that the packets were found:—as I said there were two, directed to you—sent at the same time—Has enquiry been made at the Post Office? I really am quite at a loss what to do—and I cannot see how it can devolve upon me to take all the trouble—I feel quite sure that if proper search were made they would be found in Burlington St.

Had I nothing else to do it were still rather hard to come upon me to rewrite a portion of Manuscript which, after I had done so with the ut-

251

most difficulty & annoyance, would be found in some odd corner of Burlington St—but as it is, I have engaged myself, as to time, & the whole thing is as impossible as it is vexatious—Pray let proper enquiries & search be made   I know—I could, as the vulgar people say swear that the copy was sent & therefore there can be no doubt that it will be found if looked properly for. I am truly pained at all this annoyance as I am sure that it must be vexatious to you, but pray let the packets be properly looked for—for I do assure you that they were sent—& there can be no doubt that they are mislaid unless the fault is in the Post Office—Truly Yours

MWS

The servants remember the fact perfectly. The maid gave them early in the morning to the boy here, who always puts my letters in—& he remembers taking them & one of the packets being too large to go into the hole, & taking it into the office—Be assured therefore that you have but to look to find.

TEXT: MS., Pforzheimer Library.

1. MWS, *Lives* (1835–37), for the Rev. Dionysius Lardner (1793–1859; *DNB*), literary and scientific writer. Lardner's Cabinet Cyclopædia series, 1829–49, was contributed to by many eminent figures of the day, including Sir Walter Scott and Thomas Moore, and ran to 133 volumes. *Lives*, vol. 1, published c. February 1835, with essays by James Montgomery (1771–1854; *DNB*), poet and journalist, included essays on Dante, Petrarch, Boccaccio, Lorenzo de' Medici, Marsiglio Ficino, Giovanni Pico della Mirandello, Angelo Ferrara, Burchiello, Bojardo, Berni, Ariosto, and Machiavelli. Mary Shelley wrote the lives of Petrarch, Boccaccio, and Machiavelli; Montgomery, that of Dante. The other essays have not been attributed. *Lives*, vol. II, published c. September or October 1835, with essays by Montgomery and Sir David Brewster (1781–1868; *DNB*), scientist and author, included essays on Galileo, Guicciardini, Vittoria Colonna, Guarini, Tasso, Chiabrera, Tassoni, Marini, Filicaja, Metastasio, Goldoni, Alfieri, Monti, and Ugo Foscolo. Mary Shelley wrote the lives of Metastasio, Goldoni, Alfieri, Monti, and Foscolo; Brewster, that of Galileo; and Montgomery, that of Tasso. The others have not been attributed (Lyles, *MWS Bibliography*, p. 37).

To John Murray

Harrow—Friday   [20 February 1835]

My dear Sir

Many Thanks for the Illustrations—which are so beautiful & interesting—I am delighted at the success of your publication   I have read Boswell I am sure ten times—& hope to read it many more it is the most amusing book in the world, besides that I do love the kind hearted wise & Gentle Bear—& think him as loveable a ⟨Man⟩ friend as a profound philosopher—I do not see in your list of Authors whence Anecdotes are extracted the name of M^rs d'Arblay—Her account of Dr Johnson Mrs Thrale &c in her Memoirs of Dr Burney[1] are highly interesting & valuable—

I am so unhappy that Sir C. Manners Sutton has lost his election as Speaker[2]—It is not that I am not a Whig—I suppose I am one—but I think the Whigs have treated him most shabbily—electing him themselves as they did last ⟨Par^t [Parliament]⟩ year—They will never have such a Speaker again. I feel particularly kindly towards the Conservatives also just now as they have behaved with the greatest consideration towards my father—preserving him in his place,[3] which was about to be abolished by the Whigs & that with a manner as gracious as the deed. The Duke of Wellington & above all the [cross-written] Prince of our Orators Sir Robert Peel deserves my gratitude & has it—By the way what will the Whigs do for an orator in the Commons—I never heard Canning—& never heard any Speaker who I thought could claim the praise of a good Orator except Sir Robert Peel—his speeches have all a beginning middle & end—he rises with his subject & carries the hearer along with him—L. [Lord] Brougham I only heard in the House of Lords & his want of dignity & his insolent sarcasm towards the Peers annoyed me—

My boy is now in the 5th form & is very promising & clever & good—I am dear Sir

Very truly Y^s
MW Shelley

Text: MS., John Murray.

1. Frances Burney, Madame D'Arblay (1752–1840; *DNB*), author, edited her father's *Memoirs* in 1832. Hester Lynch Thrale (1741–1821; *DNB*) was a close friend of Samuel Johnson's.

2. Sir Charles Manners-Sutton's reelection, opposed by the Whigs, was lost on 19 February 1835. Mary Shelley was a friend of Manners-Sutton and his wife, Ellen Purves, Lady Manners-Sutton, sister of Lady Blessington (see MWS *Letters*, II, 15 August 1832).

3. In May 1833, Godwin had been awarded the sinecure of Office Keeper and Yeoman Usher of the Receipt of the Exchequer with a salary of £200 a year and housing at New Palace Yard.

To Gabriele Rossetti[1]

Harrow, 3zo Aprile 1835

Signor Pregiat[mo]

Vuol Scusare colla solita sua bontà un incomodo che la reco intorno al mio vergheggiare?[2] Sto in questo momento scrivendo la vita dell'illustre suo compatriota Alfieri;[3]—e vorrei sapere se inoltre la vita scritta da se stesso, ve ne sono altre vite o altri saggii, che mi daranno notizie pregiabili intorno al medesimo; vuol favorirmi, gentillissimo Signore Rosetti con delle informazioni.

E poi—dopo Alfieri, devo scrivere la vita del Monti[4]—della quale si sa pochissimo qui—chi fra voi altri hanno composto la vita sua?—e dove troverò quelle notizie che mi faranno consapevole degli avenimenti a lui accaduti—lettere scritte da lui, ve ne sono publicate?

Abito sempre questo paesaccio col mio figlio—così non vedo nè Lei, nè nessun de'miei amici che così raramente, che mi fa proprio disperare. Spera intanto che lei goda una buona salute—e quella prosperità che merita i talenti ed egregii pregii suoi.

Scusa questo Italiano barbarico—non sento il linguagio—non le parlo mai mai ne leggo pur sempre—ma pero che vuole! C'è una certa inusitatezza nella mia mente che mi fa sempre dire cento spropositi, quando tento di esprimermi in una lingua forestiera—tanto ne possiedo, non di meno, che basta per assicurarla che mi repeto sempre

Ammiratrice e serva sua
M. W. Shelley

[*Translation*]

Most honored Sir

Will you excuse with your usual goodness my troubling you about my [?writing]?[2] I am at this moment writing the life of your illustrious compatriot Alfieri;[3]—and I would like to know whether besides the life written by himself, there are any other lives or other essays, which will give me valuable notices concerning the same; will you favor me, my dearest Signor Rosetti with some information.

And then—after Alfieri, I have to write the life of Monti[4]—of whom very little is known here—who among you people have written his life?—and where shall I find such notices as will acquaint me with the incidents which befell him—of the letters written by him, have any been published?

254

I am still living in this wretched town with my son—so I see neither you nor any of my friends except so rarely, that I am really in despair. I hope meanwhile that you are enjoying good health—and that prosperity which your talents and distinguished qualities merit.

Excuse this barbarous Italian—I do not hear the language—I never never speak it {but} I read it constantly—but after all what do you expect! There is a certain disuse in my mind which always makes me utter a hundred blunders, when I try to express myself in a foreign language—I know enough of it, however, as suffices to assure you that I am always

Your admirer and servant

M. W. Shelley

POSTMARK: 18 PAID 35 / AP. 3 / NIGHT. TEXT: E. R. Vincent, "Two Letters from Mary Shelley to Gabriele Rossetti," *Modern Language Review* 28 (October 1932); 459–61. TRANSLATION: John P. Colella.

1. Gabriele Rossetti (1783–1854), Italian patriot, poet, and professor at King's College, London, and his wife Frances Mary Lavinia Rossetti (née Polidori) were the parents of Christina Georgina Rossetti (1830–94), Dante Gabriel Rossetti (1828–82), and William Michael Rossetti (1829–1919). Mary Shelley may have met Gabriele Rossetti through the Novellos; through Godwin, who notes calling on him on 1 September 1829 (Journal); or through the John Dean Pauls, at whose home Rossetti performed as an "improvisare one night" (MWS Journal, 24 September [1830]). It is believed that Mary Shelley gave her copy of Leigh Hunt's *Foliage* (1818), inscribed by Hunt "To Mary Wollstonecraft Shelley / from her affectionate friend the author," to Gabriele Rossetti, who in turn gave it to Dante Gabriel Rossetti (*Quaritch Auction Catalogue*, bulletin 1 [1982]: 10).

2. "To flog." This is an error by either E. R. Vincent or Mary Shelley. The word meant was probably *vergare* ("to write").

3. Vittorio Alfieri (1749–1803), Italian dramatist (see MWS, *Lives* [1835–37], II, for the life of Alfieri).

4. Vincenzo Monti (1754–1828), Italian poet (see MWS, *Lives* [1835–37], II, for the life of Monti).

❧

To Maria Gisborne

Harrow—11 June [1835]

My dearest Friend—It is so inexpressibly warm, that were not a frank lying before me ready for you, I do not think I should have courage to write. Do not be surprized therefore at stupidity & want of connection. I cannot collect my ideas—& this is a good-will offering rather than a letter.

Still I am anxious to thank S.G. [*Signor Giovanni, John Gisborne*] for the pleasure I have received from his tale of Italy a tale all Italy—breathing of the land I love—the descriptions are beautiful—& he has shed a great charm round the concentrated & undemonstrative person of his gentle heroine. I suppose she is the reality of the story.—Did you know her?— It is difficult however to judge how to procure for it the publication it deserves. I have no personal acquaintance with the Editors of any of the Annuals—I had with that of the Keepsake[1]—but that is now in Mrs Norton's hands—& she has not asked me to write—so I know nothing about it—But there arises an stronger objection from the length of the story— As the merit lies in the beauty of the details, I do not see how it could it [be] but cut down to one quarter of its present length, which is as long as any tale printed in an Annual   When I write for them, I am worried to death to make my things shorter & shorter—till I fancy people think ideas can be conveyed by intuition—and that it is a superstition to consider words necessary for their expression.

I was so very delighted to get your last letter—to be sure the Wisest of Men said no news was good news[2]—but I am not apt to think so, & was uneasy   I hope this weather does not oppress you—What an odd climate! A week ago I had a fire—& now it is warmer than Italy—Warmer at least in a box pervious to the sun, than in the stone palaces where one can breathe freely. My Father is well—He had a cough in the winter— but after we had persuaded him to see a Doctor it was easily got rid of— He writes to me himself—"I am now well—now nervous—now old— now young—"   One sign of age is that his horror is so great of change of place that I cannot persuade him even to visit me here.—One would think that the sight of the fields would refresh him—but he likes his own nest better than all—though he greatly feels the annoyance of so seldom seeing me. Indeed, my kind Maria—you made me smile when you asked me to be civil to the brother of your kind Doctor.[3] I thought I had explained my situation to you—You must consider me as one buried alive— I hardly ever go to town—less often I see any one here—My kind & dear Young friends the Misses Robinson are at Brussels—I am cut off from my kind   What I suffer—What I have suffered—I to whom sympathy— companionship—the interchange of thought is more necessary than the air I breathe I will not say. Tears are in my eyes when I think of days, weeks, Months; even years spent alone—eternally alone—It does me great harm—but no more of so odious a subject—let me speak rather of my Percy—to see him bright & good is an unspeakable blessing—but no child can be a companion especially one whose fault is a want of quick sensibility—he is very fond of me—& would be wretched if he saw me unhappy—but he is with his boys all day long, & I am alone—so I can weep unseen—He gets on very well—& is a fine boy—very stout—this hot weather though he exposes himself to the sun—instead of making him languid, heightens the color in his cheeks & brightens his eyes. He is always gay & in good humour—which is a great blessing.

You talk about my poetry[4]—& about the encouragement I am to find from Jane & my Father. When they read all the fine things you said they thought it right to attack me about it but I answered them simply: "She exagerates—you read the best thing I ever wrote in the Keepsake[5] & thought nothing of it—" I do not know whether you remember the verses I mean   I will copy it in another part—it was written for music. Poor dear Lord Dillon spoke of it as you do of the rest—but "One swallow does not make a summer"—I can never write verses except under the influence of a strong sentiment & seldom even then. As to a tragedy—Shelley used to urge me—which produced his own.[6] When I returned first to England, & saw Kean, I was in a fit of enthusiasm—and wished much to write for the stage—but my father very earnestly dissuaded me—I think that he was in the wrong—I think myself that I could have written a good tragedy—but not now—My good friend—every feeling I have is blighted—I have no ambition—no care for fame—Loneliness has made a wreck of me.—I was always a dependant thing—wanting fosterage & support—I am left to myself—crushed by fortune—And I am nothing.—

You speak of women's intellect—We can scarcely do more than judge by ourselves—I know that however clever I may be there is in me a vacillation, a weakness, a want of "eagle winged{"} resolution[7] that appertains to my intellect as well as my moral character—& renders me what I am—one of broken purposes—failing thoughts & a heart all wounds.—My Mother had more energy of character—still she had not sufficient fire of imagination—In short my belief is—whether there be sex in souls or not—that the sex of our material mechanism makes us quite different creatures—better though weaker but wanting in the higher grades of intellect.—

I am almost sorry to send you this letter it is so querulous & sad—yet if I write with any effusion—the truth will creep out—& my life since you went has been so stained by sorrows & disappointments—I have been so barbarously handled both by fortune & my fellow creatures—that I am no longer the same as when you knew me—I have no hope—In a few years when I get over my present feelings & live wholly in Percy I shall be happier. I have devoted myself to him as no Mother ever did—and idolize him—& the reward will come when I can forget a thousand memories & griefs that are as yet alive & burning—and I have nothing to do here but brood.—

Another word of Mr Budd—I should have been delighted to have been of use to him—[   ] can make no offers—prisoner as I am.   Jeff [   ] flourish—She suffers from his reserves of cha[   ] but his real good qualities make up for it—Dina [   ] growing a fine girl— Edward as yet does not develope much—he is not physically strong.— How I should like to see you & talk to you—I sometimes fancy a journey to Plymouth—What would you say to seeing me pop in some day.—The Countess Gu{i}ccioli is in England—I have such a dread of her coming to see me here—imagine the talk.—Adieu—Do write—if you ever want a conveyance—enclose your letter to me (while the Session lasts) under cover to D. [*Daniel*] Gaskell Esq M.P.[8] 5 Parliament St. but dont let it me [*be*] above franking weight—O the Heat!—how overpowering it is— Percy is gone 2 miles off to bathe—He can swim—& I am obliged to leave the rest to fate—It is no use coddling witness the fable[9]—yet it costs me many pangs—however he is singularly trustworthy & careful—Do you remember 16 years ago at Livorno—he was not born then—Do write & believe me   Ever your truly attached

friend MWS.

I sent to Mr Stephen Curtis for you the 1ˢᵗ vol. of my Lives of Italian Poets—The lives of Dante & Ariosto are not mine return it when you have done with it; it belongs to Jane.—Do you not guess why these nor those I sent you wᵈ please those you mention. Papa loves not the memory of S—because—he feels he injured him;—and Jane—Do you not un- derstand enough of her to unwind the thoughts that [*cross-written*] make it distasteful to her that I should feel—& above all be thought by others to feel & to have a right to feel—O the human heart—it is a strange juggle.—

[*P. 5, upside-down*]

A Dirge

I

This morn thy gallant bark, Love,
    Sailed on a sunny sea;
'Tis noon, & tempests dark, Love,
    Have wrecked it on the lee—

Ah Woe—ah woe, ah woe
    By spirits of the deep
He's cradled on the billow,
    To his unwaking sleep!

2

Thou liest upon the shore, Love,
　　Beside the knelling surge;
But sea-nymphs ever more, Love,
　　Shall sadly chaunt thy dirge.

O come, O come—O come!
　　Ye spirits of the deep!
While near his sea-weed pillow
　　My lonely watch I keep.

[*P. 6, upside-down*]

3

From far across the sea, Love,
　　I hear a wild lament,
By Echo's voice for thee, Love,
　　From Ocean's caverns sent

O list! O list! O list!
The Spirits of the deep—
Loud sounds their wail of sorrow—
While I for ever weep!

ADDRESS: Mrs Gisborne / Plymouth / D Gaskell. POSTMARKS: (1) FREE / 11 JU 11 / 1835; (2) Harrow / [　　　　] py P. Paid; (3) F / JU 11 / 1835; (4) [　　　]8. PAID [　　] / JU 11 / 7. NIGHT. 7. ENDORSED: Harrow 11th June / 1835 / rec. 12 Do / An 22 / Oct. 1835. TEXT: MS., Bodleian Library.

　　1. Frederic Mansel Reynolds.

　　2. The translation of the Italian "Nulla nuova, buona nuova" is traced to James Howell (?1594–1666), British diplomat, in his *Epistolae Ho-elianae: Familiar Letters* (London: H. Moseley, 1645), letter II. xviii.

　　3. In her letter of 11 April 1835 (Abinger MSS., Bodleian Library) Maria Gisborne had asked if Mary Shelley might do anything for Dr. Budd's brother, who was about to settle in London. John W. Budd was one of nine brothers, seven of whom went into the medical profession. The Budd who went up to London at this point may have been George Budd (1808–82), who became professor of medicine at King's College.

　　4. In her letter of 11 April 1835 Maria Gisborne asked why Mary Shelley had allowed her poetic talent to lie dormant and suggested that Mary Shelley write a tragedy.

　　5. "A Dirge," written out at the end of this letter, was published in the *Keepsake for 1831*, p. 85 and, somewhat revised, in Shelley, *Poetical Works* (1839), IV, 225.

　　6. *The Cenci.*

　　7. Perhaps a variant of "eagle-winged pride," *Richard II* 1. 3. 129.

8. Claire Clairmont's letter of 15 March 1832 introduced Gaskell (d. 1875) and his wife, Mary Heywood Gaskell (d. 1848), to Mary Shelley and Godwin (see *SC*, I, 153–54; Locke, *Godwin*, p. 318).

9. Aesop's fable "The Ape and Her Young Ones," which Godwin, under the pseudonym Edward Baldwin, published as "The Ape and Her Cubs" in *Fables, Ancient and Modern, Adapted for the Use of Young Children*, 2 vols. (London: Hodgkins, 1805), II, 105–14.

◆

To John Bowring

Harrow—3 Oct. [1835]

Dear Doctor Bowring

You are very kind to answer my letter in the midst of all your important avocations. One great difficulty seems to be getting books—There is no Spanish Library[1]—& one wants to turn over so many that the Longmans would be tired of buying. I own that I depended much on yours—& am disappointed at what you say—is there no getting at them?—are the cases large & are all the Spanish books in one case?—Could indeed any but yourself touch them?—I do not mind trouble—but wish to do my task as well as I can—& how can I without books?—The difficulty seems to be that from slight biographical notices one can yet the book will be more of literature than lives—& I know not how Lardner will like that. The best is that the very thing which occasions the difficulty makes it interesting—namely—the treading in unknown paths & dragging out unknown things—I wish I could go to Spain.

Many thanks for the hints you give   I am, dear Dr Bowring

Yours truly

M W Shelley

ADDRESS: Dr. Bowring M.P. / 1 Queen's Sq / Westminster. POSTMARKS: (1) T[.P] / Harrow; (2) 7. NIGHT. 7 / OC. 3 / 1835. ENDORSED: (1) Mrs Shelley / 3 Octr 1835; (2) Lo[n]don Oct 1835 / Mrs Shelley. TEXT: MS., Huntington Library.

1. Mary Shelley was preparing volume III of the *Lives* (1835–37), in which she wrote about Boscan, Garcilaso de la Vega, Diego Hurtado de Mendoza, Luis de Leon, Herrera, Francisco de Sá de Miranda, Jorge de Montemayor, Castillejo, Cervantes, Lope de Vega, Vicente Espinel-Esteban de Villegas, Gongora, Quevedo, Calderon, Ribeyra, Gil Vicente, Ferreira, and Camoens (Lyles, *MWS Bibliography*, p. 38). On 3–4 December 1835 Thomas Moore noted in his Journal: "Wrote to Lady Holland, at Mrs. Shelley's request, to ask for access to the Spanish Biography, for Lardner, and books on the subject being very rare in London. A long letter from Lady H. [*Holland*] explaining why Lord H. [*Holland*] could not infringe the rule he had laid down on

this subject. This I had prepared Mrs. S. for." On 8 December 1835 Moore wrote in his Journal: "Letter from Mrs. Shelley on the subject of the refusal from the Hollands—quotes some foreigner who says that, in England, 'chaque individu est une Ile' [each person is an island] and adds that 'some even surround the island with martello-towers.' "

❖

To John Gregson

14 North Bank   Regent's Park[1]   8 April 1836

Dear Sir

Will you have the goodness to communicate to Sir T[thy] & Lady Shelley the melancholy event of my dear Father's death—it occurred yesterday evening at seven after an illness of ten days—of a Catarrhal fever

Percy is quite well. He was to have gone to Warwick to his Tutor next Monday   His going must now be deferred till after the funeral[2]

I am, dear Sir,
Your Ob[ly]
Mary W. Shelley

ENDORSED: 8th April 1836 / Mrs Shelley. TEXT: MS., Bodleian Library.

1. Mary Shelley moved to this address c. 23 March 1836.

2. Godwin's funeral, on 14 April, was attended only by Percy Florence Shelley, James Kenney, Thomas Campbell, Dr. David Uwins, Rev. John Hobart Caunter, and Trelawny (Locke, *Godwin*, p. 345). In accordance with his wishes, Godwin was buried in the churchyard of St. Pancras as close as possible to the remains of Mary Wollstonecraft Godwin. In February 1851 their remains were removed to St. Peter's Churchyard, Bournemouth, and were interred with the remains of Mary Shelley, who died on 1 February 1851 (Paul, *Godwin*, II, 332–33); Jane, Lady Shelley to Alexander Berry, 7 March 1851, MS., Mitchell Library, State Library of New South Wales, Sydney).

❖

To Mary Hays[1]

14 North Bank   Regents Park   20th April 1836

Dear Madam

Having for some months been somewhat of an invalid—the extreme fatigue and anxiety I went through while attending on the last moments of my dearest Father have made me too ill to attend to any thing like business. By my Father's will his papers will pass thro' my hands,[2] & your most reasonable request will be complied with. There is nothing more detestable or cruel than the publication of letters meant for one eye only. I have no idea whether any of yours will be found among my Father's papers—any that I find shall be returned to you.—But my health is such that I cannot promise when I can undergo the fatigue of looking over his papers.

You will be glad to hear that one whom you once knew so well, died without much suffering—his illness was a catarrhal fever, which his great age did not permit him to combat—he was ill about 10, & confined to his bed 5 days—I sat up several nights with him—& Mrs Godwin was with him when I was not—as he had a great horror of being left to servants. His thoughts wandered a good deal but not painfully—he knew himself to be dangerously ill—but did not consider his recovery impossible. His last moment was very sudden—Mrs Godwin & I were both present. He was dosing tranquilly, when a slight rattle called us to his side, his heart ceased to beat, & all was over. This happened at a little after 7 on the Ev^{g} of the 7 ins. .

My dear Father left it in his will to be placed as near my Mother as possible. Her tomb in St. Pancras Church Y^{d} was accordingly opened—at the depth of twelve feet her coffin was found uninjured—the cloth still over it—& the plate tarnished but legible. The funeral was plain & followed only by a few friends—there might have been many more, but being private, we restricted the number. My Son, now sixteen, was among the Mourners.—

I have written these few particulars as they cannot fail to interest you.—I am obliged to you for your kind expressions of interest—your name is of course familiar to me as one of those women whose talents do honor to our sex—and as the friend of my parents—I have the honor to be, dear Madam

Very truly Yours
MaryShelley

ADDRESS: Miss Hays / 11 Grosvenor Place / Camberwell. POSTMARKS: (1) T.P / Newstead; (2) 7. Nt. 7 / AP. 20 / 1836. TEXT: MS., Pforzheimer Library.

1. Mary Hays (1759–1843), author, was the close friend of both Godwin and Mary Wollstonecraft (Locke, *Godwin*, pp. 112–14).

2. Godwin had willed: "It is further my earnest desire that my daughter would have the goodness to look over the manuscripts that shall be found in my own handwriting, & decide which of them are fit to be printed, consigning the rest to the flames." He wished her also to judge if any of the letters received by him would "be found proper to accompany my worthier papers" (Ingpen, *Shelley in England*, II, 611–12, a copy of Godwin's will).

To Henry Crabb Robinson

14 North Bank—Regent's Park
27 May—1836

Dear Sir

I am, for the benefit of Mrs Godwin, who is left unprovided by the unfortunate death of my dear Father[1]—engaged in collecting his papers for publication[2]—There is a portion of autobiography & some interesting Correspondance—Could you assist me in augmenting the latter. It strikes me that there may be many interesting letters to Mess. Coleridge, Wordsworth & yourself—which no one would object to seeing published—I have no acquaintance with Mr Wordsworth nor the Executors of Mr Coleridge—Would you kindly interest yourself on the subject—& if there exist letters that would interest the public & annoy no one to see in print, would you endeavour to procure them for me

I take a great liberty in asking you—but am induced by the long intimacy that subsisted between you & my father & Mrs Godwin & my belief that you would willingly to [*do*] the latter a service

I am, dear Sir
Your Ob^t Servant
MaryShelley

ADDRESS: Henry C. Robinson Esq / 2 Plowden Buildings / Temple. POSTMARKS: (1) Park Terrace / 2D. PAID; (2) 7 N[n] 7 / MY 28 / 1836. ENDORSED: 27 May 1836 / Mrs. Shelley, / Autograph / No publication took place—All the letters I was in possession of were applications for money—I wrote in reply that I had none but on business. TEXT: MS., Dr. Williams Library (H. C. Robinson's letters, volume for 1836–37, f. 131).

1. In order to provide for Mary Jane Godwin, Mary Shelley, with Caroline Norton's assistance, applied to Lord Melbourne for a continuation of Godwin's annuity. Melbourne declined the annuity but instead granted a present of £300 from the Royal Bounty Fund. The extant letters from Caroline Norton to Mary Shelley written during this period suggest that the two had become friends (24 August 1836; Abinger MSS., Bodleian Library; Perkins, *Mrs. Norton*, pp. 89–91). An application for funds from the Royal Literary Fund on Mary Jane Godwin's behalf was endorsed by the Rev. John Hobart Caunter. On 10 May 1836 this fund granted her £50, which she received on 16 May 1836 (MSS., Royal Literary Fund).

2. On 19 July 1836 Henry Colburn contracted to pay Mary Jane Godwin 350 guineas for Godwin's memoirs and correspondence, to be edited by Mary Shelley. Mary Shelley began this project, which she never completed, by organizing the three chapters of memoirs written by Godwin and collecting, organizing, and commenting on copies of his letters. Her notes are extensively quoted in Paul, *Godwin* (Abinger MSS., Bodleian Library). For these memoirs Mary Jane Godwin borrowed from

Sir Charles Aldiss (?1775–1863; *DNB*), surgeon and antiquary, a copy of Godwin's *Sketches of History in Six Sermons* (1783). Aldiss noted that Mary Shelley "declared she did not know he had ever written any" (MS., Pforzheimer Library). Among others whom, like Henry Crabb Robinson, Mary Shelley unsuccessfully solicited for Godwin's correspondence was Bulwer. On 8 August 1836 he informed her that he possessed only a few scanty notes from Godwin and that he could not find them because of his change of residence (MS., University of Kansas).

❦

To Thomas Abthorpe Cooper[1]

24 August—1836.
4 Lower Belgrave St.

Dear Sir

You will have heard by the public papers of the death of my dear Father, Mᵣ Godwin, which took place on the 7 April last. His strength had been failing for some months—but I thought him destined to live several years longer. His illness was a catarrhal fever—it lasted only about a week—he did not suffer much & his last moment was unaccompanied by any struggle or pain. You who knew him in his best days, will be interested in these details.

He enjoyed as I suppose you know, a small office in the pay of Government—this expired with him. Mᵣˢ Godwin is left without any resources, & my situation is such that I can do little for her. I applied for a continuance of my father's annuity for her—but his place being abolished Lord Melbourne contented himself by a present of £300. from the Royal Bounty Fund.

My father left his Autobiography up to his twentieth year—& a considerable Mass of letters & papers—I am employed in arranging these for publication for the benefit of Mᵣˢ Godwin   In my father's early journals I find mention of letters to you, particularly on theatrical subjects at the time of your first appearance as an actor in 1792—It is probable that among the accidents of a various life you have not preserved any of these but if any do exist, may I request that you will kindly furnish them for the publication I mention, to which they will add value.

You will scarcely remember me—It is many many years since I have seen you[2]—but you will remember my father and I dare trust to your kind recollections inducing you to comply with my request, if it is in your power.

Believe me, dear Mᵣ Cooper,
Ever truly Yours
Mary W. Shelley

Direct to me at Hookham's Library 15 Old Bond St. London.

ADDRESS: To be forwarded immediately / Thos A. Cooper Esq. / ⟨To the care of / Stephan Esq / Park Theatre / New York. U.S.⟩ [*In another hand*]. BRISTOL / Penna [   ]. POSTMARK: NEW YORK / OCT / 14. TEXT: MS., Pforzheimer Library.

1. Thomas Abthorpe Cooper (1776–1849), the son of William Godwin's mother's first cousin, was Godwin's ward and pupil from 1788 to 1792. In 1796 Cooper went to America, where he became a highly successful actor (Locke, *Godwin*, 33–34, 38–39; *SC*, V, 355–57; Elizabeth Tyler Coleman, *Priscilla Cooper Tyler and the American Scene, 1816–1889* [University, Ala.: University of Alabama Press, 1955]).

2. Cooper was in London from c. 9 December 1827 through c. 23 January 1828. On 17 December he played in *Macbeth* at Drury Lane. However, he was not well received by London audiences, and by March 1828 he was back on the American stage. During this London visit, he and Mary Shelley met at least once, on 23 January 1828, in the company of Godwin and John Howard Payne (Godwin, Journal; Fairlie Arant Maginnes, "A Biography of the Actor Thomas Abthorpe Cooper, 1775–1849" [Ph.D. diss., University of Minnesota, 1971]).

To {Josiah} Wedgwood[1]

4 Lower Belgrave St.   Belgrave Sq
9 Sep. 1836

Sir

On the lamented event of my dear Father's death, which occurred last spring, it has fallen to me to prepare his Memoirs & letters for the press— it is my chief wish of course to do his Memory honor—besides this, he has left his Widow without any resources, & as my situation is such that it is not in my power to do much for her it becomes my duty to bring out this work for her benefit.

My father, Mr William Godwin was intimate with your Brother Mr Thomas Wedgewood[2]—if you have any letters—especially early letters, from my father to Mr Wedgewood you would greatly serve & oblige me by giving me such as you deem fit for publication[3]—I am sure there can be none that would not do your Brother honour as I suppose a more excellent & generous Man never existed

Excuse me for this request & I have the honor to remain

Your Obedi^t Servant
MaryShelley

ENDORSED: Mrs. Shelley / 9 Sept 1836. TEXT: MS., Pforzheimer Library.

1. Josiah Wedgwood, Jr. (1769–1843), second son of Josiah Wedgwood (1730– 95; *DNB*), founder of the Wedgwood pottery works at Etruria, one hundred fifty

miles north-northwest of London. Josiah Wedgwood, Jr., continued the pottery works after his father's death.

2. Thomas Wedgwood (1771–1805; *DNB*), pioneer in photography, spent part of the fortune he inherited from his father in aiding men of genius, including Coleridge and Godwin (Locke, *Godwin*, pp. 64–65, 191, 220).

3. Josiah Wedgwood, Jr., complied. The correspondence between William Godwin and Thomas and Josiah Wedgwood, Jr., preserved in Abinger MSS., Bodleian Library, includes seven letters from Godwin, four from Thomas Wedgwood, and five from Josiah Wedgwood, all annotated for publication by Mary Shelley.

❧

To Charles Ollier

Rock Gardens—Brighton   7 Jan^{ry} 1837

Dear Sir

You will have seen my New Novel[1] advertized by Saunders & Otley. I offered it thro' you to Mr Bentley, but you would not treat till it was finished. My necessities forced me to conclude with a publisher who did not object to advances—which were the more necessary—as ill health delayed my finishing till now.

You said a New Novel might cause the remainder of Lodore to be sold—I hope still you will reap that benefit from it—Are you sure 700 are not sold & that £50 is not due to me? It would be very welcome & considering the very insignificant sum which you gave & the fair success it had—I own I think it is a little hard that the sale should stick just a few copies this side of 700—or 600 or whatever the number was—But I trust to your kindness—& sympathy with a poor Author to get me the £50 when it is possible—

I hope you are well & flourishing—I have been seriously indisposed—& came here for air & am much better

Believe me Dear Sir
Very truly yours
M W Shelley

ADDRESS: Chas Ollier Esq / 8 New Burlington St / London. POSTMARKS: (1) [BRI]GHTO[N] / [JA] 8 / [1837]; (2) [   ] / PAID / 9 JA / 1837. TEXT: MS., Pforzheimer Library.

   1. *Falkner*.

To Edward John Trelawny

Dear Trelawny—I am very glad to hear that you are amused & happy—
fate seems to have turned her sunny side to you—& I hope you will long
enjoy yourself—I know but of one pleasure in the world—sympathy with
another—or others—leaving out of the question the affections—the society of agreable—gifted—congenial-minded beings is the only pleasure
worth having in the world—My fate has debarred me from this enjoyment—but you seem in the midst of it.

With regard to my Father's life—I certainly could not answer it to my
conscience to give it up—I shall therefore do it—but I must wait. This
year I have to fight my poor Percy's battle—to try to get him sent to
College without further dilapidation on his ruined prospects—& he has
to enter life at College—that this should be undertaken at a moment
when a cry was raised against his Mother—& that not on the question of
politics but religion, would mar all—I must see him fairly launched, before I commit myself to the fury of the waves.

A sense of duty towards my father, whose passion was posthumous
fame makes me ready—as far as I only am concerned, to meet the misery
that must be mine if I become an object of scurrility & attacks—for the
rest—for my own private satisfaction all I ask is obscurity—What can I
care for the parties that divide the world—or the opinions that possess
it?—What has my life been   what is it Since I lost Shelley—I have been
alone—& worse—I had my father's fate for many a year a burthen pressing me to the earth—& I had Percy's education & welfare to guard over—
& in all this I had no one friendly hand stretched out to support me. Shut
out from even the possibility of making such an impression as my personal merits might occasion—without a human being to aid, or encourage or even to advise me—I toiled on my weary solitary way. The only
persons who deigned to share those melancholy hours, & to afford me the
balm of affection were those dear girls whom you chose so long to
abuse[1]—Do you think that I have not felt, that I do not feel all this?—
If I have been able to stand up against the breakers which have dashed
against my stranded wrecked bark—it has been by a sort of passive
dogged resistance, which has broken my heart, while it a little supported
my spirit. My happiness, my health, my fortunes all are wrecked—Percy
alone remains to me & to do him good—is the sole aim of my life. One
thing I will add—if I have ever found kindness it has not been from lib-

erals—to disengage myself from them was the first act of my freedom—the consequence was that I gained peace & civil usage—which they denied me—More I do not ask—Of fate I only ask a grave—I know what my future life is to be—what my present life is—& shudder—but it must be borne—& for Percy's sake I must battle on.

If you wish for a copy of my Novel you shall have one—but I did not order it to be sent to you because being a rover all luggage burthens—I have told them to send it to your Mother—at which you will scoff—but [   ] was the only way I had to shew my sense of her kindness. You may pick & choose those from whom you deign to receive kindness—You are a Man at a feast—Champagne & comfits your diet—& you naturally scoff at me & my dry crust in a corner—often have you scoffed & sneered at all the aliment of kindness or society that fate has afforded me—I have been silent—the hungry cannot be dainty—but it is useless to tell a pampered Man this.—Remember in all this, except in one or two instances—my complaint is not against <u>persons</u> but <u>fate</u>—fate has been my enemy throughout—I have no wish to encrease her animosity or her power, by exposing more than I possibly can to her rancourous attacks.

You have sent me no address—so I direct this to your Mother's—Give her & Charlotte[2] my love—& tell them I think I shall be in town at the beginning of next Month—My time in this house is up on the 3ᵈ and I ought to be in town with Percy to take him to Sir Tim's Solicitors—so to begin my attack

I should advise you, by the bye—not to read my novel—You will not like it—I cannot <u>teach</u>—I can only <u>paint</u>, such as my paintings are—& you will not approve of much of what I deem natural feeling because it is not founded on the New light.—

I had a long letter from Mʳˢ N— [*Norton*][3] I admire her excessively & I <u>think</u> could love her infinitely—but I shall not be asked nor tried, & shall [*cross-written*] take very good care not to press myself—I know what her relations think

[*P. 1, cross-written*] I shall soon be in town I suppose—where I do not yet know. I dread my return—-for I shall have a thousand worries. Despite unfavourable weather—quiet & care have much restored my health—but mental annoyance will soon make me ill as ever—Only writing this letter makes me feel half dead—Still to be thus at peace is an expensive luxury, and I must forego it for duties, which I have been allowed to forget for a time—but my holyday is past. Happy is Fanny Butler if she can shed tears & not be destroyed by them—this luxury is denied me—I am obliged to guard against low spirits as my worst disease—& I do guard—& usually I am not in low spirits—Why then do you awaken me to thought & suffering by forcing me to explain the motives of my conduct   Could you not trust that I thought anxiously—decided carefully—& from disinterested motives—not to save myself but my child from evil—Pray let the stream flow quietly & as glittering on the surface as it may [*p. 2, cross-written*] do not awaken the deep waters, which are full of briny bitterness—I never wish any one to dive into the secret depths be content if I can render the surface safe sailing that I not annoy you with clouds & tempests but turn the silvery side outward, as I ought, for God knows I would not render any living creature as miserable as I could easily be—and I would also guard myself from the sense of woe which I tie lead about & sink low low—out of sight or fathom line

Adieu Excuse all this; it is your own fault—speak only of yourself—Never speak of me & you will never again be annoyed with so much stupidity.

Yours truly
MS

[*P. 4, cross-written*] If you are still so rich & can lend me £20 till my quarter I shall be glad—I do not know that I absolutely want it <u>here</u> but may run short at last—so if not inconvenient—will you send it next week—

ADDRESS: Edward Trelawny Esq / 16 Michael's Place / Brompton / London. POSTMARKS: (1) BRIGHTON / JA 26 / 1837; (2)T.P / Rate 2d; (3) A / 27 JA 27 / 1837; (4) 10 Fn 10 / JA 27 / 1837. TEXT: MS., Bodleian Library.

1. In Trelawny's 8 April 1831 letter to Mary Shelley (in a passage omitted in Trelawny, *Letters*), he had written: "You must indeed be hard pressed for companions when, with such a mind as yours, you can lower yourself to the level of such animals as these. In truth you have fallen from the high estate (I mean in respect of companionship) in which I first knew you—the Robinsons and the chaffy set with which they are allied, and then such straw stuffed idols as these Hares that you appear to idolise. God forgive you, for you have much to answer for" (Grylls, *Mary Shelley*, p. 220).

2. Charlotte Trevanion, Trelawny's sister.

3. Caroline Norton's letter of 5 January 1837 concerns itself largely with her views in support of the rights of divorced women to their children; her completion of her pamphlet *Observations on the Natural Claim of a Mother to the Custody of Her Children*; and her intention to influence Parliament to change the law as it then stood. She also comments on a letter (unlocated) from Mary Shelley about the pamphlet: "It was a great triumph to me to see how <u>alike</u> what I had written & part of your letter were (what very awkward prose!) I improved the passage materially by your observation on <u>what was permitted to women, or rather excused in women when they receive any rudeness</u>: but as you are to have the trouble of reading it in print, I will not say more about it now. Perhaps you will not think I have gone far enough" (Abinger MSS., Bodleian Library; Perkins, *Mrs. Norton*, p. 133).

To Benjamin Disraeli[1]

24 South Audley St.   Friday
[?15 November–7 December 1837][2]

Dear Mʳ D'Israeli

I send you a letter to frank—I hope it will not inconvenience you—
but let it go as soon as you can.

Winter has come hard upon the heels of summer: I detest winter & all
its belongings—And the cold dispirits one sadly—Are you meditating
your Maiden speech? I wonder if you will be what you can be.—Were
your heart in your career it would be a brilliant one

Beleive me yours truly
MaryShelley

The enclosed is for

Miss Robinson[3]
Ardglass Castle
Down

TEXT: MS., Bodleian Library.

1. Benjamin Disraeli and Mary Shelley may have been introduced by Mary Anne
Evans Lewis (1792–1872), who, along with her husband Wyndham Lewis (1778–
1838), politician, befriended Disraeli in 1832. After Wyndham Lewis's death, Mary
Anne Lewis and Disraeli were married, on 28 August 1839 (for an account of her
life see Mollie Hardwick, *Mrs. Dizzy: The Life of Mary Anne Disraeli Viscountess Bea-
consfield* [New York: St. Martin's Press, 1972]). Mary Shelley probably met Mary
Anne Lewis through George Beauclerk, with whom Mary Anne Lewis had a three-
year love affair (Hardwick, *Mrs. Dizzy*, p. 65). Godwin's Journal records that Mrs.
Wyndham Lewis visited Mary Shelley at 7 Upper Eaton Street on 25 August (with
George Beauclerk) and 2 September 1834. Godwin's Journal also records visits to
him by Disraeli, who admired Godwin; thus it is also possible that it was Godwin
who introduced Mary Shelley to Disraeli.

2. This letter was written sometime between 15 November 1837, when Disraeli
took his seat in Parliament, and 7 December 1837, when he gave his maiden speech.

3. Although it has been thought that the Miss Robinson referred to was Rosa
Robinson, who later married Aubrey Beauclerk, it is more likely that this letter was
directed to Julia Robinson. On 2 February 1837 Mary Shelley noted in her Journal:
"But I will not complain—I write this but as a landmark—on Xmas Eve J— [*Julia*]
left me for A [*Aubrey or Ardglass*]." On 31 December 1837 Mary Shelley wrote in her
Journal: "Time passes—my correspondance with Julia prevents my wish to overflow
in this book."

To Leigh Hunt

41d. Park St.   Saturday
[?December 1837–March 1838]

My dear Hunt

Your promise for May is very kind & pleasant—though so far off—I shall remind you of it be assured & Jane & I shall be delighted once again to see our unforgotten & dear friend. I am sorry that Marianne cannot join us. I hope all coughs & illness will be well then—You are good & right to be careful—for Jane especially—as she has a little baby.

I hear that some friends Talfourd & Bulwer are trying to get a pension for you[1]—God grant they succeed—no one deserves it more. I am trying to get a small one for M[rs] Godwin[2]—poor as I continue to be through circumstances never changing, I have it much at heart to succeed.

I will tell D[r] Lardner to cause the Lives of the Spanish Poets to be sent directed to you at Hookhams—some day next week send for it—I am sure that of Cervantes will come home to you. Cam'oens was more unfortunate than he—but does not come home to you in the same manner   I am now writing French Lives[3]—The Spanish ones interested me—these do not so much—yet it is pleasant writing enough—sparing one's imagination yet occupying one & supplying in some small degree the needful which is so very needful.

With love to Marianne believe me Y[s] Ever Truly

MW Shelley

TEXT: MS., British Library.

1. Leigh Hunt did not receive a pension until 22 June 1847, when he was awarded £200 yearly from funds of the Civil List (Blunden, *Leigh Hunt*, p. 297).

2. Caroline Norton's letters to Mary Shelley during this period indicate that she was again assisting Mary Shelley's efforts to obtain a pension for Mary Jane Godwin (Abinger MSS., Bodleian Library; Perkins, *Mrs. Norton*, pp. 141–43).

3. *Lives* (1838–39) was published in two volumes. Volume I, published c. July 1838, includes essays on Montaigne, Rabelais, Corneille, Rouchefoucauld, Molière, La Fontaine, Pascal, Madame de Sévigné, Boileau, Racine, and Fénélon. Volume II, published in 1839, includes essays on Voltaire, Rousseau, Condorcet, Mirabeau, Madame Roland, and Madame de Staël (Lyles, *MWS Bibliography*, pp. 38–39).

To Lady Sydney Morgan

41 d. Park St.   Wednesday
[December 1837–March 1839][1]

Dear Lady Morgan

As you return none of my calls I suppose {you} cut me—which I think cross.—I send you the <u>relic</u>[2] & you may say that I have never parted with one hair to any one else. You will prize it—Poor dear fellow—he was very nice the evening I cut it off—which was in August 1822—with love to Miss Clarke[3]

Yours Ever   MShelley

ENDORSED: (1) 1840 note from Mrs Shelley The Author of Frankensten on [?sending] me a lock of Lord <u>Byrons hair</u>—; (2) Mrs Shelley / Author of / Frankenstein. TEXT: MS., Pforzheimer Library.

1. The date 1840 in the endorsement is in error, since Mary Shelley moved from 41d Park Street at the end of March 1839.

2. A lock of Byron's hair (see endorsement). In July 1832 Lady Morgan requested and received a lock of Byron's hair from Teresa Guiccioli, but on 30 January 1836 Lady Morgan wrote in her journal that she had lost the lock (*Lady Morgan's Memoirs*, 2 vols. [London: Wm. H. Allen & Co., 1863], II, 345, 412).

3. Josephine Clarke (later married to Edward Geale), Lady Morgan's niece, who accompanied Sir Charles and Lady Morgan when they removed permanently from Ireland to England on 20 October 1837 (*Lady Morgan's Memoirs*, II, 427).

To Edward Bulwer

41[d] Park St.   Sunday   [?19 February–March 1838]

Dear M[r] Bulwer

Do excuse my writing a few lines to say how very much the Lady of Lyons[1] pleased me. The interest is well sustained—the dialogue natural—one person answers the other—not as I found in Werner & Sardanapalus, each person made a little speech a part; or one only ⟨spoke⟩ speaking that the other might say something—the incidents flow from the dialogue, & that without soliloquies, & the incidents themselves flow naturally one from another—There is the charm of nature & high feeling thrown over all.

I think that in this play you have done as Shelley used to exhort L[d] Byron to do—left the beaten road of old romance—so worn by modern

dramatists & idealized the present—& my belief is that now that you have
found the secret of dramatic interest, & to please the public—you will,
while you adhere to the rules that enable you to accomplish this necessary
part of a drama, raise the audience to what height you please. I am delighted with the promise you hold out of being a great dramatic writer.—
but (if I may venture to express an opinion to one so much better able to
form them—an opinion springing from something you said the other
night) do not be apt to fancy that you are less great when you are more
facile—it is not always the most studied & (consequently) the favourite
works of an author that are his best titles {to} fame—the soil ought to
be carefully tended, but the flower that springs into bloom most swiftly
is the loveliest. I have not read your play—I would not till I saw it—for
a play is a thing for acting not the closet

I hope you will remember your promise of calling on me some Evening
& believe me

Y* truly
M W Shelley

TEXT: MS., Hon. David Lytton Cobbold, on deposit at the Hertfordshire County
Record Office.

1. Bulwer's play *The Lady of Lyons* was first produced by William Charles Macready (1793–1873; *DNB*), actor and manager, on 15 February 1838 at Covent Garden and was highly successful. The published edition, dedicated to Thomas Noon
Talfourd, was in its second edition before 11 March 1838 (Second Earl of Lytton,
The Life of Edward Bulwer, 2 vols. [London: Macmillan and Co., 1913], I, 534–36).

To Elizabeth Rumble

41.D. Park St.   Grosvenor Sq   5 April 1838

Dear Elizabeth

You must think me the most negligent person in the world—I am
afraid to think how long it is since I wrote to you—& indeed forget. All
last winter I was at Brighton for my health—& when I came back I found
the journals[1] for which I am much obliged to you—You wrote to me some
weeks ago—mentioning a mode by which I could return them. But I was
very ill of the influenza at that time & could not attend to it & have mislaid your letter; so you must let me know again. I should be obliged to
you if you would take care hereafter that these journals do not fall into
the hands of strangers. You are likely to outlive me—but if you should
not will you take care that they come back to me.

What news have you of the Reveley's? How are you yourself?—tolerably well, I hope & your house succeeding.

Mrs Hogg & her family are well as well as I & my son—though we all suffered a great deal from Influenza during this hard winter. Let me hear from you—& never make apologies for writing. Be assured, for your own sake, as well as those of our lost friends, I shall always be glad to hear from you—Believe me

Ever truly Y^s
MW Shelley

TEXT: MS., Pforzheimer Library.

   1. Taped to this letter is a a note that reads: "Mr Gisborne's Journal, and all other papers belonging to him, was left to me by his Will. Mr Reveley was very angry with Mary Shelley for asking me to let her have them on my death. Mr Reveley was not pleased with me for lending them to her (as I did) for more than two years. Mary Shelley knew that by my Will I left every thing that I possessed to Henry Reveley, son of Mrs Gisborne / E Rumble."

❖

To William Hazlitt, Jr.

41d Park St.   5 Nov [1838]

Sir

Many thanks for the Paper[1] It is astonishing to me how much can be got for 2^d—I must have every Wednesday enlivened by your sheet—& should be obliged to you to give orders that it should be sent me. I am flattered by your reprinting my Tale. Bentley & Colburn bought the Copy right of Frankenstein when it was printed in the Standard Novels.[2] Frankenstein was first published in 181⟨9⟩8[3] I think so perhaps the book is common property—but I do not know what the laws are.

Wishing you every success
I am, Sir,
Y^s Ob^ly
MW Shelley

TEXT: MS., Lockwood Memorial Library, State University of New York at Buffalo.

   1. William Hazlitt, Jr., edited *The Romancist, and Novelist's Library. The Best Works of the Best Authors*, published weekly on Wednesdays. At twopence a copy, its objective was to present literature to a wide audience. The first number included Mary Shelley's "A Tale of the Passions" (see 6 November 1822), pp. 14–16; the tenth number reprinted Shelley's *Zastrozzi* (London: G. Wilkie and J. Robinson, 1810), pp. 145–56. The weeklies were collected into a volume in 1839 and published by J. Clements. The second collected volume, published in 1840, included Shelley's *St.*

Irvyne; or the Rosicrucian (London: J. J. Stockdale, 1810), pp. 113–26, as well as works by Leigh Hunt, Washington Irving, William Hazlitt, and Charles Lamb.

2. See [?February–10 March 1831], n. 1.

3. This date is corrected several times and remains unclear. Its alterations include 1817, 1818, and 1819. *Frankenstein* was published in January 1818, but a few copies were distributed in December 1817 (*SC*, V, 366, 393 ff.).

To Edward Moxon

41D Park St.   7 Dec. 1838

Dear Sir

It gives me great pleasure to publish Shelley's poems with you,[1] ⟨& I am⟩ as I believe the publication will have justice at your hands. I am content with your offer of £200 for the edition of 2,000—but I should be glad to dispose of my entire interest & for that I think I ought to have £500[2]   I feel sure among other things that the copy right of the Posthumous Poems must be entirely mine. The M.S. from which it was printed consisted of fragments of paper which in the hands of an indifferent person would never have been decyphered—the labour of putting it together was immense—the papers were in my possession & in no other person's (for the most part) the volume might be all my writing (except that I could not write it) in short it certainly stands to reason, & I should think that it is law that a Posthumous publication must belong entirely to the editor, if the editor had a legal right to ⟨poss⟩ make use of the MS.—

I think that £500 is not too much to ask for the entire copy rights which I will take pains to render as valuable as I can. I hope you will agree to this additional sum in which case we might at once conclude.   the agreement being ⟨subject⟩ founded as you said on the present laws—⟨& to be⟩

I am dear Sir
Yˢ truly
M W Shelley

TEXT: MS., Pforzheimer Library.

1. The first volume of Shelley, *Poetical Works* (1839), dedicated on 20 January 1839 to "Percy Florence Shelley, / The Poetical Works / Of His Illustrious Father / Are Dedicated, / By His Affectionate Mother, Mary Wollstonecraft Shelley," was published late in January 1839. The remaining three volumes appeared at approximately monthly intervals, the fourth in May (Taylor, *Early Collected Editions*, p. 34).

2. Moxon agreed to £500 (see 12 January 1839; 4 March 1839; 4 April 1839).

To Thomas Jefferson Hogg[1]

41 d Park St.   11 Dec 1838

Dear Jeff—

Jane has told you I suppose that I am about to publish an Edition of Shelley's Poems—She says you have not a Queen Mab—yet have you not? Did not Shelley give you one—one of the first printed.[2] If you will lend it me I shall be so very much obliged & will return it safely when the book is printed. I want your opinion on one point. The Bookseller (Moxon) has suggested leaving out the 6th & 7th parts as too shocking & atheistical   What do you say? I dont like mutilations—& would not leave out a word in favour of liberty. But I have no partiality to irreligion & much doubt the benefit of disputing the existence of the Creator— give me your opinion.[3] Will you lend me your Alastor also—it will not go to the printer—I shall only correct the press from it. Sir Tim forbids biography—but I mean to write a few notes appertaining to the history of the poems—if you have any Shelley's letters you would communicate mentioning his ⟨author⟩ poetry I should be glad & thank you.[4] I am Yˢ Ever M W Shelley

TEXT: MS., Pforzheimer Library.

1. An altered and abridged text of this letter was published by Hogg in his *Life of Percy Bysshe Shelley*, 2 vols. (London: Edward Moxon, 1858). Omitted are the lines "I want your opinion" through "Give me your opinion." Added in Hogg's text after "Sir Timothy forbids biography" is "under a threat of stopping the supplies. What could I do then? How could I live? And my poor boy!"

2. On 12 December 1838 Hogg responded that he had loaned it to someone who had failed to return it (draft of Hogg's letter, written in Taylor's system of shorthand on verso of last leaf of Mary Shelley's 11 December 1838 letter to him, MS., Pforzheimer Library). After a number of unsuccessful attempts, Mary Shelley was able to borrow *Queen Mab* from Harriet de Boinville, who sent it from Paris on 26 January 1839 (*S&M*, IV, 1221).

In July 1814 Shelley had given Mary Shelley a copy of *Queen Mab*, in which he had written on the inside cover, "Mary Wollstonecraft Godwin, P.B.S.," and inside the other cover, "You see Mary, I have not forgotten you." On the dedication page he wrote, "Count Slobendorf was about to marry a woman, who attracted solely by his fortune, proved her selfishness by deserting him in prison." This is believed to be a reference to Count Gustav von Schlabrendorf, a Silesian, who was a friend of Mary Wollstonecraft. He was imprisoned during the Terror in Paris in 1793, but evidence shows that it was he, not his fiancée, who broke their engagement (Eleanor Flexner, *Mary Wollstonecraft* [New York: Coward, McCann & Geoghegan, 1972], pp. 180, 297). Mary Shelley wrote on the end papers of this copy of *Queen Mab*:

276

July 1814   This book is sacred to me and as no other creature shall ever look into it I may write in it what I please—yet what shall I write that I love the author beyond all powers of expression and that I am parted from him

Dearest & only love by that love we have promised to each other although I may not be yours I can never be another's—

But I am thine exclusively thine—by the kiss of love by

The glance none saw beside
The smile none else might understand
The whispered thought of hearts allied
The pressure of the thrilling hand

I have pledged myself to thee & sacred is the gift—

I remember your words you are now Mary going to mix with many & for a moment I shall depart but in the solitude of your chamber I shall be with you—yes you are ever with me sacred vision

But ah I feel in this was given
A blessing never meant for me
Thou art too like a dream from heaven
For earthly love to merit thee

The first quatrain, slightly misquoted, is from Byron's "To Thyrza"; the second quatrain is from Byron's "If Sometime in the Haunts of Men."

This signed copy of *Queen Mab*, as well as others with Shelley's notes in them, were left at Marlow when the Shelleys went to Italy in 1818 and were retained by the Shelleys' landlord, Robert Madocks, who claimed the Shelleys owed him money. Mary Shelley, through Peacock, unsuccessfully attempted to have these items returned, which explains why she had neither her personal copy nor any of the other copies of *Queen Mab* owned by Shelley. Her copy, sold at Sotheby on 13 August 1879, is now at the Huntington Library (see MWS *Letters*, vol. I, 29 September 1822 to Thomas Love Peacock, n. 4; *SC*, II, 898–99, IV, 488–91; H. Buxton Forman, *The Shelley Library* [London: Reeves and Turner, 1886], pp. 44–46; and Huntington Library *Queen Mab* [HM 114869]).

3. Edward Moxon asked for these omissions in order to protect his copyright, which he could lose if *Queen Mab* were judged, under the law, as blasphemous. Hogg said he had "no recollection of the parts" referred to by Mary Shelley, but he said that he "would omit whatever I honestly believed he would omit himself if he were—how I wish that he were—now living: whatever is shocking and irreligious, of course" (Hogg's letter draft [see n. 2 above]). Mary Shelley finally agreed to Moxon's request that the atheistical passages be removed and omitted part of canto 6 and all of canto 7. She also omitted the dedication to Harriet Shelley because she believed that was Shelley's preference (see 11 February [1839], n. 1). In mid-November 1839 (but bearing 1840 as publication date) a one-volume edition of *Poetical Works* was published by Moxon, with the omitted passages of *Queen Mab* restored (Taylor, *Early Collected Editions*, pp. 48–49; Ingpen, *Shelley in England*, II, 620–22; Dunbar, *PBS Bibliography*, p. 37). Also added in this edition were *Peter Bell the Third*, previously unpublished, and *Swellfoot the Tyrant*, published in 1820 but immediately suppressed.

4. Hogg wrote that he had no letters that would suit Moxon and also commented:

"As to biography and the history of his studies, the less said the better. It would not be expedient to tell the truth at present, and it can never be expedient to tell anything else" (Hogg's letter draft [see n. 2 above]). In her preface to *Poetical Works* (1839), Mary Shelley echoed this opinion. She wrote: "This is not the time to relate the truth; and I should reject any colouring of the truth" (I, vii).

To Edward Moxon

41d Park St.   12 Dec. [1838]

Dear Sir

I have failed in procuring a copy of Queen Mab. I think Mr Southey[1] may have one—will you ask for the loan.—but it must be quick. I have asked Mr Hookham[2] to let you know, if he can, who printed it—& you might get it from the printer.[3] I should much like to get hold of the original edition—but if I cannot for this edition I must do my best & get it for the ⟨second⟩ next. I had no idea we should have so much difficulty

Talking of our Edition with Mr Milnes[4]—he said the whole poem of Q.M. [*Queen Mab*] ought to be printed but not notes. I dislike Atheism but I shrink from Mutilation—I have not yet decided.

Will you send over the enclosed to Mr Hookham

Let me have a copy of Alastor of the first edition if you can

I am Y^s Ob^{ly}

MW Shelley

Is Mr Milnes in town do you know?
I have a notion that the Chancery Lane Main Archives may have a copy of the original edition—Could you find out & procure it.—

Are you sure Mr Rogers[5] has not a copy—Shelley sent a copy to all the great Poets of the day—will you enquire—I am sure he sent one to Southey—for he was acquainted with him.

[*On inside flap of envelope*] Would you let me have copies of your Edition of Wordsworth Southey & Coleridge[6]

ADDRESS: Edward Moxon Esq / Dover St. POSTMARK: 1838 / DE 13 / 8 [   ] 8. TEXT: MS., Fales Library, New York University.

1. Shelley at one time admired Southey and sent him copies of *St. Irvyne* and *Alastor* (Ingpen, *Shelley in England*, I, 124; II, 358–59, 464). Later Shelley was attacked by Southey for his religious and political views, and Shelley, in turn, attacked Southey (Cameron, *The Golden Years*, pp. 31, 436–38). Southey was not among the known recipients of *Queen Mab* (White, *Shelley*, I, 653, n. 11).

2. Thomas Hookham, Jr.

3. Unidentified.

4. Richard Monckton Milnes (1809–85; *DNB*), in 1863 created first baron Houghton, politician and author. Milnes was a member of the Cambridge Apostles, an association of gifted young men that included Tennyson, Arthur Hallam (1811–33), and Thackeray. Milnes knew many of the same people that Mary Shelley knew, and they may have met through any number of mutual acquaintances, including Edward Moxon, who published ten of Milnes's books, beginning with *Memorials* in 1834 (Merriam, *Moxon*, pp. 54–56). In 1838 Milnes wrote to J. W. Blakesley, another Apostle, to inquire on behalf of Mary Shelley about a private tutor for Percy Florence Shelley (MS., Trinity College, Cambridge).

5. Samuel Rogers (1763–1855; *DNB*), a renowned poet of the era and a major figure in literary circles, who counted among his friends Thomas Moore and Byron. Rogers and Shelley met first in 1817 (*SC*, V, 241 ff.) and then at Pisa in 1822 (*Table-Talk of Samuel Rogers*, ed. Morchard Bishop [London: Richards Press, 1952], pp. 194–95). Mary Shelley may have known Rogers earlier, perhaps through Godwin, whom Rogers knew and admired (*Table-Talk of Samuel Rogers*, pp. 205–6), but the first mention of him in her letters or Journal is the 30 June 1838 Journal entry in which she records that she and Rosa Robinson enjoyed one of Rogers's famous breakfasts. Sutton Sharpe, who brought some of Mérimée's correspondence to Mary Shelley, was Rogers's nephew (see [?October 1828], n. 1).

6. *The Poetical Works of William Wordsworth, A New Edition*, 6 vols. (1836–37, reissued in 1839); Southey, *The Doctor*, 3 vols., reprinted (1839); *Letters, Conversations, and Recollections of S. T. Coleridge*, 2 vols. (1836).

To Leigh Hunt

41d Park St.   Friday   [14 December 1838]

Dear Hunt

Many thanks for your kind note—I have not yet made up my mind. Except that I do not like the idea of a mutilated edition, I have no scruple of conscience in leaving out the expressions which Shelley would never have printed in after ⟨life Life⟩   I have a great love for Queen Mab—he was proud of it when I first knew him—& it is associated with the bright young days of both of us.

Thanks for your very kind offer of assisting me in my note. But it must rest on myself alone.   ⟨I do not⟩ The edition will be mine—& though I feel my incompetency—yet trying to make it as good as I can, I must hope the best. In a future edition if you will add any of your own peculiarly delightful notes it will make the book more valuable to every reader—but ⟨your⟩ our notes must be independant of each other—for as no two minds exactly agree, so (though in works of imagination two minds may add zest & vivacity) in matters of opinion—we should perhaps only spoil both—

Will you look in on me on Tuesday—with love to Marianne

Ever Yours

MWShelley

I will give your message to Jane but to poor pedest{r}ian ladies Chelsea is <u>very</u> far—especially in winter—or we should have called before.

TEXT: MS., Huntington Library.

❖

To Abraham Hayward[1]

41d Park St.   Friday   14th Dec [1838]

Dear Mr Hayward

Will you do me the pleasure to drink tea with me on Tuesday next— Will you ask Mr Sumner[2]—if you think he would like to come

Yours truly

MWShelley

ADDRESS: A. Hayward Esq / Athenaeum Club / Pall Mall. POSTMARKS: (1) T.P / Lr Brook S[t]; (2) 4 Eg 4 / DE 15 / 1838. TEXT: MS., Houghton Library.

1. Abraham Hayward (1801–84; *DNB*), lawyer and author and a friend of many literary figures, including Caroline Norton and Samuel Rogers (see 12 December [1838], n. 5).

2. Charles Sumner (1811–74), U.S. statesman. In the course of a tour of Europe (December 1837–March 1839), Sumner visited London from 31 May 1838 to 21 March 1839. His absence from London for trips to Oxford and Cambridge from 7 December through 28 December 1838 precluded his acceptance of this invitation (Edward L. Pierce, *Memoir and Letters of Charles Sumner*, 2 vols. [Boston: Roberts Brothers, 1893], I, 213, 298–300; II, 23–34). Charles Sumner and Mary Shelley met on 3 December 1838 at a party given by Lady Morgan. Sumner wrote of Mary Shelley on 4 December 1838: "I talked a good deal with Mrs. Shelley. She was dressed in pure white, and seemed a nice and agreeable person, with great cleverness. She said the greatest happiness of a woman was to be the wife or mother of a distinguished man. I was not a little amused at an expression that broke from her unawares, she forgetting that I was an American. We were speaking of travellers who violated social ties, and published personal sketches, and she broke out, 'Thank God! I have kept clear of those Americans.' I did not seem to observe what she had said, and she soon atoned for it" (Pierce, *Memoir and Letters of Charles Sumner*, II, 21). Lady Morgan's party was also attended by Samuel Rogers.

To Thomas Jefferson Hogg

41d Park St.   12 Jan^y / 39

My dear Jefferson

I hope you will not consider me indiscreet in asking your opinion & aid in a point very material to me. Moxon has offered me £500 for the copyright of Shelley's poems. ⟨Till the will is proved I cannot prevent⟩ Till the will is proved my claim to them is not established--so Moxon wanted Peacock to sign the agreement also as Shelley's Executor. Peacock said he could not without incurring indefinite risks. So I agreed that in the agreement I should pledge myself to indemnify Mr Moxon if any one else claimed the copyright as inheriting it from Shelley. Percy could be the only person. In the agreement however it is mentioned that I am to indemnify him for any expences incurred in resisting piracies—which is out of the question—for Moxon is aware, having years ago taken an opinion, that till the will is proved I cannot get an injunction from Chancery.

I enclose you my letter to him dissenting from this clause. Would you very kindly look over the agreement & see if any other objection arises. Mr Proctor[1] is Mr Moxon's legal adviser—perhaps it would be best to see him—but I must not give you too much trouble. Let me know what you think as soon as you can. Gregson would not I think refuse to see Moxon's Adviser & tell him that I am the personal representative of Shelley when the will is proved—& that Percy is such until then.

I am dear Jeff
Y^s truly
M W Shelley

TEXT: MS., Pforzheimer Library.
    1. I.e., Bryan Waller Procter ("Barry Cornwall").

To Thomas Jefferson Hogg

{41d Park Street}   Sunday E^g   [?13 January 1839]

Dear Jefferson

Thanks for the trouble you have taken—I beg your pardon for giving you so much you need not fear more.

You seem to forget that on my legal title, imperfect as it is, to what I am hereafter to inherit under Shelley's will, I have existed all this time— Sir Tim has given me nothing except as dependant on that, & I should have title as I have to the copyrights is far more obvious. Since in a very few years they will expire & so much property be entirely lost without advantage to anyone.

I shall not sign any paper the prudence of which is problematic. I cannot tell how this affair may end—but if end as I wish, I shall be able to have a house of my own a few miles from town & I think that that will be a more suitable & modest style of life than the lodgings to which I have hitherto been doomed

With many thanks for your good wishes—which accept on my part for you & yours I am

Y^s truly
MW Shelley

TEXT: MS., Pforzheimer Library.

To Thomas Jefferson Hogg

[41d Park Street]   11th Feb—[1839]

Dear Jefferson

My motive for the omission[1] was simply that when Clarke's edition appeared, Shelley rejoiced that it was omitted—& expressed great satisfaction thereon. It could be nothing to me but matter of pleasure to publish it. My motive was the purest & simplest that ever actuated any one. If convinced that I am in the wrong, it shall be restored in the next edition[2]

I thank you for your kindly expressed insinuations. I began to be fed on poison at Kentish Town[3]—it almost killed me at first—now I am used to it—& should have been heartily surprised not be have been supplied with a large dose on the present occasion you have mixed the biggest you possibly could & I am proportionately obliged to you

Yours truly MS.

ADDRESS: T.J. Hogg Esq. TEXT: MS., Pforzheimer Library.

1. See 11 December 1838. The reviews of volume I in *The Spectator* (12, no. 552 [26 January 1839]: 88–89) and the *Examiner* (no. 1618 [3 February 1839]: 68–70) both criticized Mary Shelley for her omissions. The *Spectator*, which generally attacked Shelley, also complained that Mary Shelley's preface "is rather a panegyric than

a judgment." In contrast, the *Examiner* complained of a "cold and laboured effort" in her preface and notes. Mary Shelley expressed her response to Hogg's and others' criticism for the omissions in her Journal, 12 February 1839:

> I much disliked the leaving out any of Queen Mab—I dislike it still more than I can express—and I even wish I had resisted to the last— but when I was told that certain portions would injure the copyright of all the volumes to the publisher, I yielded. I had consulted, Hunt Hogg & Peacock. they all said I had a right to do as I liked & offered no one objection. Trelawny sent back the volume to Moxon in a rage at seeing parts left out. How very much he must enjoy the opportunity thus afforded him of doing a rude & insolent act. It was almost worthwhile to make the omissions if only to give him this pleasure.
>
> Hogg has written me an insulting letter because I left out the dedication to Harriet. Poor Harriet to whose sad fate I attribute so many of my own heavy sorrows as the atonement claimed by fate for her death.
> Little does Jeff—how little does any one know me! When Clarke's edition of Q. M. came to us at the Baths of Pisa Shelley expressed great pleasure that these verses were omitted—this recollection caused me to do the same—It was to do him honour—What could it be to me?—There are other verses I should well like to obliterate for ever—but they will be printed— & any to her could in no way tend to my discomfort; or gratify one ungenerous feeling. They shall be restored; though I do not feel easy as to the good I do S—

William Clark's pirated 1821 edition did reprint the dedication to Harriet, but it was missing from some copies, including the one that reached Shelley (Ingpen, *Shelley in England*, II, 621).

  2. See 11 December 1838, n.3.

  3. A reference to Jane Williams Hogg's disloyalty (see [?14 February 1828]).

To {Charles Ollier}

41 d Park St.   13 Feb 1839

Dear Sir

You may remember when Hellas was published[1] certain verses & a portion of a note were omitted.[2] A few copies containing these were struck off—four you sent to Italy—I have given or lent them & do not possess a perfect copy—Do you? If you do & would lend it me immediately I should feel very greatly obliged

Yours truly   M W Shelley

ENDORSED: [*on separate slip of paper*] 1839 / Mrs Shelley / Park St 13th Feby. TEXT: MS., Pforzheimer Library.

  1. See 30 November 1821, n. 5.

  2. Omitted in the 1822 edition were lines 1091–93, "more bright and good / Than all who fell, than One who rose, / Than many unsubdued," and the part of

note 8 that elucidated those lines: *"The One, who rose*, or Jesus Christ, at whose appearance the idols of the Pagan world were amerced of their worship" and "The sublime human character of Jesus Christ was deformed by an imputed identification with a power, who tempted, betrayed, and punished the innocent beings who were called into existence by his sole will; and for the period of a thousand years, the spirit of this most just, wise, and benevolent of men, has been propitiated with myriads of hecatombs of those who approached the nearest to his innocence and wisdom, sacrificed under every aggravation of atrocity and variety of torture." The lines and note were restored in *Poetical Works* (1839) (see *PBS Letters*, #697, #698; and Taylor, *Early Collected Editions*, pp. 58–61). Also omitted from the first edition was the penultimate paragraph of Shelley's preface, which begins: "Should the English people ever become free they will reflect upon the part which those who presume to represent their will, have played in the great drama of the revival of liberty." The paragraph was restored by H. Buxton Forman in the 1892 Aldine Edition of Shelley's *Poetical Works* (Shelley, *Poetry and Prose*, p. 410).

❖

To Edward Moxon

41d Park St.   4 March 1839

Dear Sir

Thanks for the Second £125—which I have received—

I have heard much praise of the mode the book is got up—but regrets from all parties on account of the omissions in Q. M. [*Queen Mab*][1] I trust you will not think it injurious to the copyright to insert them in the next edition   I think it would improve the sale—

Thanks for the books—have you sent 2ᵈ Vols to those who read the 1ˢᵗ   I am, dear Sir

Yˢ truly,
M W Shelley

TEXT: MS., Bodleian Library.

1. See 11 December 1838, n. 3; 11 February [1839].

❖

To {Edward Moxon}

Layton House   Putney   4 April / 39

Dear Sir

Thanks for your parcel & the £125—which I received. The 3ᵈ vol is thin—& I have an idea that the 4ᵗʰ will be a good deal thicker; but I could not get the Printers to calculate exactly—& did not like to trust to my own idea—We shall see—I sent a week ago the order of the ⟨proof⟩ remaining poems to the printer & am in daily expectation of proofs. I told them to send them to me two at a time by the 2ᵈ post.—

Thanks for Miss Martineau's book[1] with which I am highly delighted   Her pictures are so graphic & true to nature that they interest highly. Hester is I think very finely drawn indeed. Without Miss Austen's humour she has all her vividness & correctness. To compensate for the absence of humour she has higher philosophical views   It is a very interesting & very beautiful picture of life.—I say this having read only two volumes.

I hardly like asking you for books—but if I am indiscreet you must let me know. I should like Campbells works[2]—& Philip Von Artevelte[3]— If you can easily spare them, ⟨if you can⟩ send them to me to the care of Miss Bennet 2 Wilton St. Grosvenor Sq—& they will be brought to me on Saturday.

I am dear Sir Yˢ ⟨truly⟩ Obᵗ
MWShelley

Text: MS., Duke University Library.
1. *Deerbrook,* 3 vols. (London: Edward Moxon, 1839).
2. Thomas Campbell, *Poetical Works* (London: Edward Moxon, 1839).
3. Henry Taylor, *Philip Van Artevelde: A Dramatic Romance* (London: Edward Moxon, 1834). Pages xxi–xxvi contain evaluative criticism of Shelley.

***

To Edward Moxon

Putney—2 May [1839]

Dear Sir

There was some delay at the beginning of April through my being too ill to write at all—The Printers were very impatient then—Latterly they have been slower when I was ready. In a few days now all will be finished   I very much hope the book will have great success. Remember when you think of another edition to let me know—as for several reasons I shall wish it to pass through my hands.

In a short time I should like to see you with regard to {a} volume of Letters & other prose essays[1]—which I beleive that the public will warmly welcome. I will call in Dover St. Some day when in town

With regard to the books you will deduct the price out of the sum I next receive. Certainly I did not know that Southey's[2] would be so voluminous & cost so much—& would return them but have cut open two volumes which I fear will prevent your being able to return them—& you must not lose—if their being cut open makes no difference I will return them—but keep the Wordsworth & Coleridge

I send a fresh list for distribution. I should have accepted your kind offer & delayed finishing till I was quite well—But my illness being chiefly produced by having to think of & write about the passed [*past*]—it would have revived when I return to it—and I felt that at no time could I do better than I have done now. It has cost me a great deal.

With fervent wishes for success I am, dear Sir

Y^s truly

M W Shelley

I have done as you asked with regard to mentioning the suppressions[3]—You will find one or two new poems added.

ADDRESS: Edward Moxon Esq / Dover Street / Piccadilly. POSTMARK: T.P / Putney. TEXT: MS., Henry W. and Albert A. Berg Collection, New York Public Library.

1. Mary Shelley's edition of Shelley, *Essays, Letters*, was published in mid-November 1839.

2. See 12 December [1838].

3. See 11 December 1838, n. 3. In a postscript to her preface to the one-volume edition, Mary Shelley wrote: "At my request the publisher has restored the omitted passages of Queen Mab.—"

To Leigh Hunt

Putney—Friday   [?26 July 1839]

Dear Hunt—

I am about to publish a vol. of Prose of Shelleys—This will please you I am sure—& it will not be painful to me as the other was. But I want your advice on several portions of it—especially with regard to the translation of the Symposium. I want also to know whether you would assent to the letters you published in your recollections[1] being joined to such as I shall publish—I expect you on Wednesday & will dine at 5—but if you could a little earlier to discuss these things I shall be glad. Do not disappoint me on Wednesday or you will disappoint Mr Robinson who almost worships you—besides two pretty daughters who have inherited his feeling—You need not be at the trouble of answering this letter—I only write that you may come, if you can, a little earlier, for the reason I have mentioned.

I have read your play   It is admirably written. It is full of beautiful & elevated & true morality clothed in poetry—Yet I can under understand Macready's[2] not liking to identify himself with Agolanti—his conduct—true to nature & common, being redeemed by no high self forgetting passion would not I think interest in representation as much as in reading. I long to hear of your new play[3]—

Ever truly Y^s
M W Shelley

Text: MS., Huntington Library.

1. In *Lord Byron and Some of His Contemporaries*.

2. On 1 August 1839 Hunt wrote of Macready: "I am expecting to send you news daily from Macready, who said he would write to me, and of whom I have still hopes, and greater ones, though no certainty. He would not hear me read more than one act. He says that every word requires weighing, step by step, and that he shall perhaps read the play three times over! I am told, however, by his friends, that this looks well. He was very kind and hospitable; and I floundered in a luxurious down bed, grateful and sleepless" (Hunt, *Correspondence*, I, 315). The role of the jealous Agolanti was finally declined by Macready and was performed by a Mr. Moore.

3. During this period Hunt wrote at least four plays (Hunt, *Autobiography*, II, 226). Of these, only *A Legend of Florence* and *Lover's Amazements*, a seriocomic play given at the Lyceum Theatre in January 1858, were produced (Blunden, *Leigh Hunt*, pp. 283, 330).

◆◆◆

To Elizabeth Berry[1]

Putney—3 August 1839

My dear Cousin

Mr Charles Robinson carries with him a recommendation to you from our Aunt Everina.—I will add that I have known him from boyhood that he is most honourable kind hearted excellent young man—he goes out for the purposes of advancement & any advice & kindness you & Mr Berry shew him will oblige me deeply—& be well bestowed.

I saw our Aunt yesterday—she is infirm—but is tolerable health—she is with very good people & well taken care of. I wish I could do more for her—I do what I can, but while my father-in-law lives I have little to command.   Charles Robinson will describe us to you—he knows Percy well, so if you have any curiosity about us, you have but to see & question him. I am sure you will like him—every body does—for he deserves it.

He has a good mercantile connection in this country & if put in the right way will I hope get on. Ever, Dear Cousin

Truly Y^s

MaryShelley

[*P. 1, top*]   If you write to me direct to me at Hookham's Library—15 Old Bond St. London

ADDRESS: Mrs Berry. TEXT: MS., Alexander Hay Collection, Mitchell Library, State Library of New South Wales, Sydney.

1. Elizabeth Berry (d. 1845), Mary Shelley's cousin, was the daughter of Edward Wollstonecraft (b. ?1758), Mary Wollstonecraft Godwin's oldest brother.

On 9 April 1841 Elizabeth Berry had responded to Mary Shelley's letter of 25 April 1840 (unlocated) and enclosed a letter to their Aunt Everina, whose new address she did not have. From the correspondence of Everina Wollstonecraft, Elizabeth Berry, and Alexander Berry, it becomes clear that contact between Mary Shelley and the Berrys began as a result of their mutual concern for their aunt. In Elizabeth Berry's letter of 9 May 1836 to her aunt she thanked her for sending copies of Mary Wollstonecraft's *Letters Written During a Short Residence in Sweden, Norway and Denmark* and *Mary* and commented, "I am glad that you often see Mrs Shelley, she being the only relation you have in England—I remember seeing her a very pretty little girl at Mrs Snagg's, and am sorry that although near relations we are strangers to one another—." In 1838 Alexander Berry asked Everina Wollstonecraft to send his wife's regards to Mary Shelley and to thank her for sending "her last Beautiful Novel—Falkner, which afforded her much amusement" (MS., Alexander Hay Collection, Mitchell Library, State Library of New South Wales, Sydney).

Meg Sword's pamphlet *Alexander Berry and Elizabeth Wollstonecraft* (Sydney: North Shore Historical Society, 1978) offers a factual account of the lives of the Berrys, based largely on manuscripts at the Mitchell Library. This material indicates that Edward Wollstonecraft and Alexander Berry formed a partnership as marine merchants and went to Sydney in 1819; that Elizabeth Berry (b. 1782) joined her brother in Sydney in 1824; and that she and Berry were married in 1827. The two men held land as equal partners; in the early 1820s they owned some 14,000 acres, 524 acres on the north shore of Sydney and the remainder in the Shoalhaven district (on the south shore of New South Wales, where the town of Berry is now located). When Edward Wollstonecraft died in 1832, his sister inherited his share of the partnership. At Berry's death in 1873 he owned 65,000 acres.

❖

To Elizabeth Rumble

Layton House   Putney   19th August [1839]

Dear Elizabeth

Mrs Williams[1] called on me   She seems a most amiable & agreable lady. I should wish to have been of use to her; but I live in such retirement

& so far from town, that I could do nothing. I gave her Mʳˢ Hogg's address.

I should be glad to have the copies of letters² you mention, & thankfully accept your offer of sending them to me. I want you also to do me another favour: among the papers of our lamented friends you will find a manuscript in Italian of an account of the death of the Cenci family³ If you would send me this immediately by coach I should be much obliged to you. I will take every care of it & return it very soon.

Have Mʳ & Mʳˢ Reveley arrived?⁴ I am anxious to hear how they are. I was glad to hear from Mʳˢ Williams that you were getting on very well   Take care of yourself & dont be snapt up by an unworthy man. I am always glad to hear from you. We are all well—I am Ever

Sincerely Yʳ friend
MShelley

TEXT: MS., Houghton Library.
  1. Unidentified.
  2. See 5 April 1838, n. 1.
  3. Mary Shelley wrote in her "Note on the Cenci": "When in Rome, in 1819, a friend put into our hands the old manuscript account of the story of the Cenci" (Shelley, *Poetical Works* [1839], II, 274).
  4. From Australia.

To Edward Moxon

Putney—8 Sep. [1839]

Dear Sir

I have received some proof of the new edition of poems from the printer & find some of the notes to Queen Mab are still omitted. In my observation on the omissions & restorations I have said that "I was glad to restore them as to omit them seemed to me disrespectful towards the author"—I cannot say this if there are still to be omissions.

We do not print these portions of Queen Mab and the notes because they contain truths—or because Shelley continued to maintain these opinions—but because the poem & notes are already printed & published—they cannot be cancelled, & the omissions only render our editions imperfect & mutilated. I have other reasons I own in not wishing a word he ever wrote to be lost—& above all that I should not cast a slur on them—but the first reason suffices you cannot suppress what you disapprove—why not put your edition on a par with all others by making it entire—pray give orders accordingly to the Printer

I am Yours truly

MWShelley

ADDRESS: Edward Moxon Esq / Dover St. POSTMARKS: (1) 12 Nn 12 / SP 8 / 1839; (2) PUTNEY / MG / SE [ ] / 1839. TEXT: MS., Pforzheimer Library.

◆

To Leigh Hunt

Putney   Saturday   [?5 October 1839]

Dear Hunt

Will you read the enclosed & tell me whether you object to its being printed. I do not like it I own for I do not think it in good taste—but Percy says if you do not dislike it, it ought to be printed. It is the dedication to Peter Bell.[1] If you could return me the Symposium with annotations before next Saturday I should be glad—but that day will do if you cannot be quicker—I mean to publish the letters appended to the 6 weeks tour—the question is whether the 6 weeks tour itself shall be printed—it was printed & corrected by Shelley though written by me[2]—& being once published—as a part of his life might as well appear again—What do you say?

I hope when I see you next to be in better spirits—The state I fell into last Winter too often returns on me—& I have not spirits unluckily to appear other than I am when melancholy—this is a great fault & has injured me much through life but I cannot help it but I am better now I trust—

Ever Your

MS.

Send me back these papers Michi{n}g Mallico[3] safe—I have no other copy—& send them as quickly as you can

TEXT: MS., Pforzheimer Library.

1. Shelley's satire is dedicated "To Thomas Brown, Esq., The Younger, H.F.," i.e., Thomas Moore, who had written the satires *The Twopenny Post-Bag* (1813) and *The Fudge Family in Paris* (1818) under the name Thomas Brown, the Younger, H. F. (Historian of Fudges) (see 22 January 1819, n. 8; 30 November 1821 n. 11). Following the dedication, Shelley's preface explicitly satirizes William Gifford, editor of the *Quarterly Review*, and John Murray, publisher of the *Quarterly Review*, for that publication's attacks on Leigh Hunt. In the course of this satire, Shelley humorously depicts the *Quarterly*'s view of Hunt as a "murderous and smiling villain" and a

"monkey suckled with tyger's milk, this odious thief, liar, scoundral, coxcomb and monster." These lines were omitted, one may conclude, at Hunt's request and not, as has been suggested, because Mary Shelley was fearful of attacking John Murray (see Shelley, *Poetry and Prose*, p. 322). The entire preface was first published in Shelley, *Poetry and Prose*, pp. 323–24.

2. *Six Weeks' Tour* was included in Shelley, *Essays, Letters*.

3. *Hamlet* 3. 2. 149. Shelley had signed *Peter Bell the Third* as written "By Miching Mallecho, Esq."

To Thomas Carlyle[1]

Layton House   Putney—5ᵗʰ Oct. [1839]

Dear Mʳ Carlisle[1]

Mʳ Milnes told me that you were gone to the North of England; & there I thought you were. Mʳ Hunt tells me on the contrary that you are a neighbour of his.[2] I am glad to hear that you are so near, & hope you will join him here at dinner next Wednesday[3] at the country hour of 5.———

I am Yˢ Ever
MWShelley

TEXT: MS. (photocopy), Dartmouth College Library.

1. Mary Shelley was clearly uncertain about the spelling of Carlyle's name; she first wrote *Carlise*, then changed the *e* to *l* and added an *e*. This strongly suggests that this letter was the first she wrote to him.

2. The Hunts lived at 4 Upper Cheyne Row from 1833 to 1840. The Carlyles lived next-door, at 5 Upper Cheyne Row.

3. In her [6 October 1839] letter to Hunt, Mary Shelley reminded him of her Wednesday dinner party. Whether Carlyle accepted is uncertain, but by 23 October 1839 Mary Shelley had met Carlyle's wife, Jane Carlyle.

To Leigh Hunt

Putney   Sunday   [6 October 1839]

Dear Hunt

I send you the rest of the Devil[1] that you may judge better—You see I have scratched out a few lines which might be too shocking—and yet I hate to mutilate. Consider the fate of the book only—if this Essay is to preclude a number of readers who else would snatch at it—for so many of the religious particularly like Shelley—had I better defer the publication, till all he has left is published—Let me hear what you think as soon as you can

Remember Wednesday   Yˢ   MS.

Remember I do not enter into the question at all. It is my duty to publish every thing of Shelley—but I want these two volumes to be popular—& would it be as well to defer this Essay? Send back the slips.

ADDRESS: Leigh Hunt Esq / 4 Upper Cheyne Row / Chelsea. POSTMARKS: (1) Putney S[   ] / 3py P.Paid; (2) 4 Eg / PD / OC 7 / 1839 / 4 Eg. ENDORSED: Mary Shelley. TEXT: MS., Huntington Library.

    1. Shelley's essay "On the Devil and Devils," written in ?1819–21, was not included in Shelley, *Essays, Letters* (see the next letter). For discussions of the date the essay was written see Cameron, *The Golden Years*, p. 602; and Stuart Curran and Joseph Anthony Wittreich, Jr., "The Dating of Shelley's 'On the Devil, and Devils,'" *Keats-Shelley Journal* 21 (1972), 22 (1973): 93.

❖

To Edward Moxon

Layton House—Putney
Tuesday   8 Oct. [1839]

My dear Sir

    After printing an Essay I mentioned to you on the Devil & Devils, I have changed my mind & will not include it in this publication. I think it would excite a violent party spirit against the volumes which otherwise I beleive will prove generally attractive   The printer therefore must cancel the pages.

    When this Edition is sold I think of ⟨bringing⟩ printing all Shelley's prose, which I think will make two volumes similar to the poetical works—in that this Essay will of course appear. If you read it I am sure you will approve of my leaving it out of the present publication the volumes will be large enough without—10 sheets each I trust.[1]

    I wish some fine day you would bring Mʳˢ Moxon[2] & the children to luncheon here—just let me have a line to say when—if she would do me the pleasure to come

Yours truly
M W Shelley

TEXT: MS., Pforzheimer Library.

    1. Volume 1 of Shelley, *Essays, Letters*, contains 243 pages; volume 2, 248 pages.

    2. Emma Isola (?1809—91), an orphan who was informally adopted by Charles and Mary Lamb in 1821, married Moxon on 30 July 1833 (Lamb, *Letters*, II, 290–91; Merriam, *Moxon*, p. 195).

To Leigh Hunt

[Putney]   Thursday   [?10 October 1839]

Dear Hunt

You have puzzled me much. What you <u>said</u> convinced me. You said:
"Do as Mills,[1] who has just phrased it so that the common reader will
think common love is meant—the learned alone will know what is
meant." Accordingly I read the Phædrus & found less of a veil even than
I expected—thus I was emboldened to leave it so that our sort of civilized
love should be understood—Now you change all this back into friendship—which makes the difficulty as great as ever. I wished in every way
⟨to leave⟩ to preserve as many of Shelley's <u>own</u> words as possible—& I was
glad to do so under the new idea which <u>you</u> imparted—but your alterations puzzle me mightily—I do not like <u>not</u> to abide by them—yet they
destroy your own argument that different sexes would be understood, &
thus all is in confusion

Accordingly I have left some & not others—where you seemed very
vehement—& your p. 192 I have altered & omitted as you mention—
but I could not bring myself to leave the word <u>love</u> out entirely from a
treatise on Love. With regard to your verbal corrections—this was no
hasty translation—Shelley read it over aloud several times[2]—so some
things that look uncouth, I suppose he thought, as you phrase it—<u>more</u>
<u>Greek</u>—and I like to leave it as he left it as much as possible.

After all the beauty of the piece consists in Agathon's, Socrates, & Al-
cibiades speeches—the rest are of minor importance. It is puzzling—
That's a fact as the Americans say.

I shall have other sheets so—so hope you will come to look at
them   Will you dine here next Wednesday—or Thursday— if Thursday <u>write</u> directly if I dont hear from you I shall expect you on
Wednesday.

Every truly Y[s]
MWShelley

TEXT: MS., Luther A. Brewer Collection, University of Iowa.

  1. John Stuart Mill's translations, with notes, of Plato's *Protagoras, Phaedrus,
Gorgias*, and *Apology of Socrates* were published in the *Monthly Repository* in 1834–35.
Of *Phaedrus*, Mill commented: "The dialogue derives an additional interest, from its
containing, in the form of an allegory, those doctrines, or rather ideas, on the subject
of love which, by giving rise to the vulgar expression 'Platonic love,' have made the
name of Plato familiar to the ear of thousands" (*Four Dialogues of Plato*, trans. with

notes by John Stuart Mill, ed. Ruth Borchardt [London: Watts & Co., 1946], p. 67).

2. Shelley read the *Symposium* on 4–5 August 1818, Mary Shelley on 4 August 1818. On 2 May 1820 Mary Shelley indicates that "Shelley finishes Phædrus" (*MWS Journal*).

To Mary Ellen Peacock

Putney—14 ⟨Sep⟩ Nov. [1839]

My dear Mary

I write to you a mere selfish note in a hurry. You told Percy you would look for those papers of Shelleys which your father has in his possession—When I gave them him he said they would all be kept together in one place—so I think they might be found without great difficulty. They consist of the Banquet of Plato in a small book—Defence of Poetry—Remarks in the Florentine Gallery & some others—If you could find them now directly—the favour you promised would be twice its value.

I write because I have been told you are in town; when is it likely that we shall see you—Rosa[1] sends her love—I want much to see your Rosa[2]

I am Y^s Aff^{ly}

MWShelley

TEXT: Abinger MSS., Bodleian Library.
    1. Rosa Beauclerk.
    2. Rosa Peacock.

To Edward Moxon

Putney   19 Dec. 1839

Dear Mr Moxon

I find that I forgot Sir Lytton Bulwer[1] in my list—will you forward the copy I send to HertfordSt. May Fair. I return 2 copies of the poems. I cannot send one of the 4 vols—⟨not⟩ only having one.

Thanks for the papers.[2] Do you wish for them back?—The Examiner was really good—very—The Athenaeum creditable—But the Spectator!—Its Editor must be both a goose & a coxcomb—the notion that LB. had any ⟨had⟩ hand in the Peter Bell is half-witted—the incapacity of appreciating the Defence of Poetry betrays a degree of ignorance scarcely to be parrallelled in the whole circle of criticism—to so foolish ⟨crude⟩ & uneducated a person the Fragments of Metaphysics must indeed appear devoid of meaning—he does not know his a, b, c, of the language in which they are written.

Do you not think this last sentence worthy of a sunday newspaper itself. I do.

I send you another Autograph—I want to keep the Plato yet longer—May I not?—Or could I get the Menexenus[3] any where with Latin translati{o}n?

Y[s] truly

MWShelley

Pray let me bring to your notice a poem—I have not read through—I hope you will, & that you will like it & think it worthy of

O sacred trininty—£-s-d.[4]

That is a fine tune—

TEXT: MS., Brown University Library.

1. In 1838 Edward Bulwer received a baronetcy from Lord Melbourne, thereby changing his name to Sir Edward Lytton-Bulwer, until 1844, when he inherited Knebworth and became Bulwer-Lytton (T. H. S. Escott, *Edward Bulwer* [1910; reprint, New York: Kennikat Press, 1970).

2. The *Examiner*, no. 1663 (15 December 1839): 788–89, review of Shelley, *Essays, Letters*, agrees with the opening statement of Mary Shelley's preface that "these volumes have long been due to the public" and states that "if the publication before us is an instalment only, it is a rich one, and the public have reason to be thankful." The review lauds Shelley but makes no comment on Mary Shelley's editing. The *Athenaeum*, no. 633 (14 December 1839): 939–42, review of the one-volume *Poetical Works* and *Essays, Letters* notes that the poems published in the four-volume edition with omissions now appear whole and that *Peter Bell the Third* and *Swellfoot the Tyrant* are also included. The review is critical of Mary Shelley for not publishing everything Shelley wrote and suggests that the letters should have been woven in with the poetry rather than published separately. A second review of *Essays, Letters* in the *Athenaeum*, no. 635 (28 December 1839): 982–85, declares that it now realizes that much was omitted by Mary Shelley and "since we can still only have a portion of Shelley, we do not think that the intrinsic merits of the present selection demanded their separate publication." *The Spectator* 12, no. 598 (14 December 1839): 1186–87, review of *Essays, Letters* sharply attacks Mary Shelley: "The time has been when a literary executor examined the papers of the dead with some degree of critical care, to prevent the publication of any thing inconsistent with the reputation of the deceased, or that respect which is due to the public taste, at least from third parties. But circumstances have changed all that; and now the chief consideration with any one possessing manuscripts seems to be whether the author's name is enough to sell them. This remark applies to a good part of the volumes before us, except in so far as it may be modified by Mrs. Shelley's relation to the writer, and the circumstance of her taste harmonizing with the weakest and most defective parts of his mind." It dismisses the essays

and translations as incomplete or too visionary, and the *Defence of Poetry* as "scarcely needed now." Perceiving merit in the letters, it suggests that they might have been published as a supplement to the poems.

3. One of Plato's dialogues, the *Menexenus* is a satire on the patriotic distortion of history.

4. That is, pounds, shillings, pence.

◆◆◆

To Everina Wollstonecraft

Lake of Como[1] 20 July [1840]

My dear Aunt—Yours is the only letter that I have yet received from England—it was therefore doubly welcome. I hope all will continue well with you—You do not mention Charles Robinson—By this time I hope you or his family have heard from him.[2]

We had a very long journey here. Our party consisted of Percy, I, Julian (a brother of Charles) Robinson & another young Cantab.[3] To please Julian we took a circuitous route—& thus made an interesting though long journey. On the 25. June we left Paris for Metz (look for our route in a map) by the diligence.[4] The country for the most part was eccessively fertile rich in vines & corn lands, & the year promises abundance. The Moselle runs under the walls of Metz & the town is pleasant & clean enough, but not picturesque. Another diligence took us in 14 hours to Trêves—a distance of 55 miles—this was German travelling. The driver was up & down from his seat every 10 minutes—& we delayed two hours at the Custom House on the Prussian frontier to have our luggage examined—Not that much was done—but it served as an excuse for loitering. Here too we began to experience the inconvenience of not understanding German.—It was our wish to go down the Moselle from Treves to Coblentz in a boat—there was no steamer—the passage boat plies only twice a week & had left that morning—so we & two other young men Cantabs, engaged a boat to ourselves. We ⟨did⟩ made the voyage in 3 days—it ought not to have occupied more than 2—but we were very lazy about it. One of our new companions knew a little German, which was a great convenience. The scenery on the banks of the river was monotonous but pleasing—hills of picturesque shapes—the bases clothed with vines—the summits with trees form the banks of the river—ruined towers & castles crowned the heights—& numberless villages studded the ravines. Here the Moselle wine is grown. The villages however & their inhabitants are dirty & poor—though the vineyards belong to the peas-

296

ants, the wine merchants reap the profits. After winding down the many meanderings of this river on 1ˢᵗ July we reached Coblentz—& the next day embarked on the Rhine in the steam boat for Mayence. You know how Lᵈ Byron celebrates this river[5]—& it is described in a portion of the two volumes of Shelley's works[6]—No description can equal the reality. The promontories & mountain peaks,—the castles that crown them the villages beneath—the fertility of the vallies, the various aspect of the many folded hills present an exhaustless series of landscapes—which as the sun declines grow in beauty. We went from Mayence to Frankfort by the railroad—which is comfortable & well conducted. Here we engaged a Voiturier[7] to take us to Shauffhausen in 7 days. I cannot in this letter describe the scenery in any detail—We passed though Darmstadt, Heidelburg, Carlsruhe, Baden & Freiburg. The towns are spacious airy & clean. The people courteous. The country pretty uniform; a fertile plain to the right—to the left a range of low but pleasing hills varied as usual by many a shattered tower & ruined Castle: at Heidelburg & Baden we turned in among the hills—& these places are surrounded by verdurous & woody uplands. After leaving Freiburg, the scenery became altered as we entered the Mountainous district of the Black forest. At the commencement we traversed a pass called the Valley of Hell—from the close meeting of the dark precipices between which the road winds—The country continues mountainous & varies by patches of the dark old forest, interspersed by tracts of cultivated land. At Shauffhausen we saw the falls of the Rhine—which is wondrously beautiful, & one view from a jutting platform when you look up to sky & rock through the spray & mist of the cataract is quite sublime. Our route now lay thro' Switzerland, by Zurich—the lake of Wallenstadt, Loire, Splungen across the Splungen to Chiavenna—We wound among enormous mountains—the lower Alps—through the valley of the Rhine which is now a mountain stream. The Mountains are precipitous, dark & rugged. One pass on the way from Loire to Splungen is sublime—A Mountain many hundred feet high is cleft to its base—in the depth the Rhine flows—on each side rises a bare precipice—It was considered impassable till very talely [*lately*]. Your Cyclopedia will I am sure give an account of the Via Mala—A shelf has been made by force of blasting the rock with gun powder to form the road—in parts it is protected by a parapet—in others it runs within the rock—it crosses from one side of the ravine to the other by bridges of a single arch—As you look down you see far below the torrent of the Rhine—far above the almost meeting precipices leave only a strip of sky open to the view. The passage of the Mountain of the Splungen is also very grand & the descent on the Italian side scarcely less magnificent & more beautiful

297

than the Swiss passes. The weather had been cool during the whole of our journey. On the top of the Splungen it snowed—but the sun came out as we reached Chiavenna

On the 13th we reached the shores of Como—& embarked in the steam boat. The shores of the lake are [*p. 1, cross-written*] formed of huge mountains—dark—rugged—the summits jagged—divided by deep chasms formed by fierce torrents—Half way down the lake divides in two & here the scenery of that portion called Como—(the other branch is called the lake of Lecco) becomes more mild & lovely—the bases of the vast mountains subside into hills planted with olives & vines—studded with villages & villas. Here we have settled ourselves for a few weeks. One portion of the plan of our journey was that Percy and his Friend Deffell should study for the degree they are to take at Xmas. Accordingly our lives are secluded & quiet. The mornings are devoted to study   The afternoons to boating &c—I often suffer from the terror I have of any accident happening to Percy on the water otherwise I am comfortable & happy. In the middle of September we recross the Alps—and we shall not go further than Milan southwards—all our space time & money being expended [*p. 6, cross-written*] during our long journey.

There is something strange & dreamlike in returning to Italy after so many many years—the language the mode of life the people—the houses the vegetation are as familiar to me as if I had left them only yesterday—yet since I saw them Youth has fled—my baby boy become a man—& still I have struggled on poor & alone. The weather is now hot—but there is almost always a breeze from the lake—The Evenings are delicious—The scene as I see it now from my window—the wide lake & dark high Mountains beyond all that can be imagined of grand—Nor is it less delightful to wander inland up the mountain paths among the vineyards—or under the overarching boughs of the chesnuts—catching glimpses of the lake hearing the dash of the waterfalls—while the monotonous [*p. 3, cross-written*] but pleasing song of the boat man is wafted across the lake.

I am delighted you see something of Mrs Hogg—She is very clever, agreable & kind—Her daughter is very pretty. Will you shew Mrs Hogg this letter.   Percy is quite well—He was much delighted with the more rugged & sublime part of our journey—The Via Mala & the Splungen especially—& the scenery of the lake is to his taste. He sighs a little for the society of some young persons of the other sex—but we are very solitary here—& his shyness prevents his making acquaintances as easily as other young men might.

Adieu my dear Aunt—I hope to find you on my return well—& prosperous. The account you give of the life of Hamilton Rowan is charming   I long to see the book[8]   [*P. 4, cross-written*] Among my fathers papers I found one or two letters from him to my Mother.[9]

Remember me to your kind friends & believe me

Aff^y Y^s

M W Shelley

ADDRESS: Mrs Wollstonecraft / 12 Copenhagen St. / Pentonville / London / Londres / Inghilterra. POSTMARKS: (1) MENAGGIO / 20 LUG.; (2) 27 / JUIL / 40 / 2 / NOIR [   ]HUININ; (3)[   ] / JY 29 / 1840; (4) 10 Fn 10 / JY 29 / 1840. TEXT: MS., Pforzheimer Library.

1. Mary Shelley and Percy Florence left England in mid-June 1840 for a tour of the Continent. On 22 June they arrived at Paris, where they were met by Percy's friends who were to travel with them: Julian Robinson and George Hibbert Deffell. On 15 July they arrived at Cadenabbia, on Lake Como, where they remained at the Albergo Grande until 8 September (see MWS, *Rambles in Germany and Italy*, I, 62–104, for a detailed account of their stay at Cadenabbia). On 9 September they departed for Milan, arriving there on 11 September. Their stay at Milan was unexpectedly prolonged because a letter containing funds for the Shelleys' homeward journey was delayed by the postal system and was not located until 27 September. On 18 September, however, Percy, Robinson, and Deffell, who had to return for the new term at Cambridge, left for England. Mary Shelley left Milan on 29 September and arrived at Geneva on 4 October. The next day she left for Lyons, arriving there on 6 October and proceeding to Chalons and finally to Paris on 10 October (see MWS, *Rambles in Germany and Italy*, I, 105–52).

2. Everina Wollstonecraft had written a letter of introduction for Charles Robinson to Elizabeth and Alexander Berry, in Australia (see 3 August 1839). On 4 May 1840 Robinson wrote to Everina Wollstonecraft from Sydney to thank her for arranging for him to meet the Berrys, who had shown him great kindness, and to inform her that he expected shortly to go to New Zealand as a police magistrate (Abinger MSS., Bodleian Library). Robinson remained in New Zealand, with the exception of several visits to England, until 1858, when he permanently and happily returned to live in Europe. In addition to serving as police magistrate, his career included panning for gold (1851) and farming (1853). He married in 1853, but in his correspondence he only mentioned his wife once; by 1855 he was apparently single again. In 1856 he intended to become the agent of the Ardglass estate in Ireland, at the invitation of his sister Rosa Beauclerk, but he was forced to return to New Zealand to sell land and pay debts to Alexander Berry. Robinson's letters from 18 July 1840 through 16 December 1873 recount his affairs (which apparently were never financially successful) and the development of parts of New Zealand and also make reference to the Shelleys and the Robinsons (MSS., Alexander Hay Collection, Mitchell Library, State Library of New South Wales, Sydney).

3. Colloquial abbreviation for *Cantabrigian*, for one attending Cambridge University. This reference is to Deffell.

4. A four-wheeled, closed coach that carried four passengers.

5. *Childe Harold's Pilgrimage*, Canto 3.

6. Shelley, *Essays, Letters*, II, 33–34.

7. "Public carrier."

8. Archibald Hamilton Rowan (1751–1834; *DNB*), Irish patriot, who had become a close friend of Mary Wollstonecraft's in Paris in 1794. His *Autobiography* (Dublin: Thomas Tegg and Co.) was published in 1840.

9. Almost certainly a reference to Rowan's letter dated 15 September 1797, now in the Abinger MSS., Bodleian Library. There is also in the Abinger MSS. a letter from Rowan to Everina Wollstonecraft dated 8 March 1805, which refers to the recipient's disappointment about not "having withdrawn" Fanny Imlay from Godwin's protection.

❧

To Abraham Hayward[1]

Rue de la Paix—N° 15—Paris.
26 Oct [1840]

Dear M[r] Hayward

After a very pleasant tour I am returned here where I hope to stay till Xmas. I left Italy with Infinite regret. Many a long year had elapsed since I had last saw it—but its aspect—its language—its ways of going on—its dear, courteous, lying, kind inhabitants & its divine climate were as familiar to me as if I had but left them yesterday—& more welcome & delightful than I can at all express—it was returning to my own land—a land & a period of enjoyment and I was very happy during my two months residence at Cadenabbia—on the shores of the lake of Como—opposite to Bellagio—& close neighbour to Tremezzo names rendered classical by our dear Rogers.[2]

Charles Beauclerk is gone to England and has lent me his rooms intanto[3]—which is very agreable—I had rather be in Italy than Paris—but Paris—any place better than England—& if the English are to be massacred in a Revolution[4]—bear witness for me that I think even such a death preferable to all that has ever been & ever will be my portion across the Channel—ones Enemies are not half so hurtful as ones friends—even if they murder one—This you will allow is the sublime of mysanthropy—but I cant help it.

Dear Rogers must be in grief for his friend's death. The loss of L[d] Holland[5] will be deeply felt for no man was ever better loved. I had some hopes of finding both Rogers & you here in October—as you were last year—but I suppose the threat of war has frightened you. I am not in

300

very good spirits now—& the French are out of humour with us—still if you have any agreable French friends who you think may like to form my acquaintance send them to me—if not too much trouble—and I shall be much obliged. The only English person here I should like to know is Lady Alborough.[6]

Percy is at Cambridge—he takes his degree this Jan[y7] after which it seems decided that he will study the law—which will bring me to London & keep me there. I certainly have friends I like & esteem there—& yet the very idea of being doomed to renew my London life makes me wretched. Poor as I am, it is all privation & annoyance. The think [*thing*] I like best in the world I find is travelling—were I a man I would set out directly to travel all over the world—so I would as I am, had I enough money.

Do write & tell me a little news—for I like to hear of you all though I feel as if I had no business among you. Teresa is enriched a good deal I believe by her husbands death[8]—I let H. [*Henry*] Bulwer[9] know I was here & he in return left his card which is a curiosity, it was so dirty I could scarcely read his name.

I thought of you on the Splu{n}gen and the storm of 34[10]—of which the vestiges are still so apparent. It is a sublime Pass—but the Simplon appears to me the most magnificent of any. It is in a wretched state—the King of Sardinia wants to force people to cross Arns into his own territories & will not repair it—However I passed in fine weather & was enchanted

Adieu—in spite of grumbling I shall be delighted to see you again & am Y[s] truly   MWShelley.

[*P. 4, cross-written*]   Can you give me any news of poor Col. Ratcliffe.[11] I have heard nothing of him since I left England. His indeed was a misfortune to make other sufferers ashamed to complain

ADDRESS: A Hayward Esq / 11 King's Bench Walk / Temple / London / Londres. POSTMARK: 2 / Paris / 2 / 60 / 27 / OCT / 40. ENDORSED: 26 Oct. 1840 / M Shelley. TEXT: MS., Pforzheimer Library.

1. Sections of this letter and Mary Shelley's letter to Hayward of 18 November [?1840], unlocated, were integrated and published as an "Extract" in Hayward, *Correspondence*, I, 82–84.

2. Samuel Rogers, *Italy, A Poem* (pt. 1, London: Longman, Hurst, Rees, Orme, and Brown, 1822; pts. 1 and 2, London: John Murray, 1823–28). Mary Shelley quoted from *Italy* in *Rambles in Germany and Italy*, II, 9, 83, and she dedicated the volumes to Rogers.

3. "In the meantime."

4. Mohammad Ali (1769–1849), Ottoman viceroy of Egypt from 1805 to 1848,

conquered Syria in April 1839. The British demanded that he relinquish Syria, but the French, under the ministry of Adolph Thiers (1797–1877), rejected the plan to force Ali out of Syria. On 15 July 1840, Britain, Austria, Prussia, and Russia signed the Treaty of London, under which Ali would cede Crete, northern Syria, Mecca, and Medina and would return the Turkish fleet, in exchange for Egypt as a hereditary possession and southern Syria for life. Ali rejected the terms, depending on France to support him. But when British troops captured Beirut on 9 September, panic broke out in France at the threat of war. On 20 October Thiers resigned, thus signaling France's decision against war, and on 27 November Ali agreed to the Convention of Alexandria, whereby he returned the Turkish fleet and gave up Syria for hereditary rule of Egypt.

5. Henry Richard Vassall Fox, third baron Holland (1773–1840; *DNB*), Whig statesman, died on 22 October.

6. Lady Elizabeth Aldborough, who married the third earl of Aldborough in 1777 and died in Paris on 29 January 1845.

7. Percy Florence was awarded a Bachelors of Arts on 23 January 1841 and left Cambridge on 25 January (Cambridge Exit Book).

8. Teresa Guiccioli.

9. Henry Bulwer was then secretary of the embassy at Paris and chargé d'affaires.

10. Hayward had recorded his journey from 26 August through 14 October 1834 in *Some Account of a Journey Across the Alps in a Letter to a Friend* (London: privately printed, 1834) (Hayward, *Correspondence*, I, 22–50). Mary Shelley cited Hayward's account in *Rambles in Germany and Italy*, I, 56–61.

11. Col. Jeremiah Ratcliffe, Mary Shelley's friend. In the early morning of 3 March 1840 on Wimbledon Common, Ratcliffe served as a second to Count Leon Bonaparte, reputed son of Napoleon I, in a challenge to Prince Louis Napoleon, his cousin, who eventually became Napoleon III. The duel was stopped by police, who brought all parties concerned to the Bow Street Court. Fines were levied against the participants, and news of the event appeared in English and French newspapers, some suggesting that Count Leon had provoked the duel for political reasons. Ratcliffe, who had only just met Count Leon, was reported to have gone mad at his apparent complicity in the alleged plot. The facts indicate, however, that Ratcliffe's madness began prior to the rumors accusing Count Leon of political intrigue (Dennis Walton Dodds, *Napoleon's Love Child: A Biography of Count Leon* [London: William Kimber, 1974], pp. 86–101). Mary Shelley was trying to aid Ratcliffe in the midst of the scandal and at the outset of his illness.

❖

To Abraham Hayward[1]

[Rue de la Paix—N° 15—Paris]
18 November [?1840][2]

I have two or three old friends in Paris,[3] but I have not been here long enough to make a society. A thousand thanks for your kindness. M.

Buchon,[4] from your account, I should really like to see. I like a man who talks me to death, provided he is amusing: it saves so much trouble. Sainte-Beuve[5] I like in his way. French people of a certain kind all know how to talk, and I can always get on with them. He, like all his countrymen, sighs to wash out Waterloo; they will not remember that they brought Waterloo on themselves; besides, they think War will prevent Revolution, but I believe Louis Philippe thinks that his dear subjects will beg to have both. How can they have too much of so good a thing as *gloire* of all sorts, foreign and domestic?—*les jours glorieux de la France dehors et les jours immortels dedans.*[6] The Chambers, however, seem in a body pacific. Louis Philippe was much better received than he expected,[7] which touched him to the heart, so that when he alluded to the attempts made against his own life[8] his voice was broken by tears, and the Chambers had the civility to cheer him. It was strange to see a king upon his throne cry. Fifty years ago Europe had rung with the expressions of sympathy. The French take it quietly. I know not why, but the tears came warm and quick into my eyes, and I thought as I looked at weeping royalty of the verse of Manzoni—but you will not recollect the context, perhaps;[9] it means, others besides oneself are and have been unhappy, and that is a kind of left-handed comfort now and then to the suffering. I went to see Soult's Gallery the other day. Have you ever seen it? There is an 'Assumption of the Virgin,' by Murillo,[10] worth ten thousand pictures such as one usually sees. She does not look so beautiful as Raphael's. She looks more like a martyr received into heaven; her almost tearful eyes, soft, upturned, imploring, her parted lips full of sensibility, all appear expressive of painful impressions of horror and death, and gratitude at the reward she is rising to receive; the figure is floating upwards, surrounded by all those foreshortened baby-angels Murillo delights in. She is dressed in white, not usual in a picture, but the colouring is glowing, and, like all Murillo's, is as satisfactory to the eye as harmonious music to the ear. There is a 'Birth of St. John the Baptist,' exquisite from the colouring and truth, but without ideality in the people; a little dog is sniffing at and going to play with a young angel's wing, who turns round to see who is taking the liberty. I should like to see the Quarterly[11] and am impatient to see Mrs. Norton's poem.[12] Give my love to her; I like her letters and herself, dearly, as the children say. Adieu! My love to dear Rogers.

[*Quotation, out of sequence*] Do not think me ungrateful, nor by any means unregardful of the merits of England. I never had a friend that was not English. Still she has been a stepmother to me, and I like her best at a distance.[13]

303

TEXT: Hayward, *Correspondence*.

1. See 26 October [1840], n. 1. This may be a compilation of more than one letter, or extracts from one.

2. Date and month taken from Smith, *A Sentimental Library*, p. 194. The year 1840 is established by the context of the letter.

3. The Boinville-Turner family and Lady Canterbury. At this time, Claire Clairmont was in London, working and caring for her invalid mother. On 30 October 1840 (Abinger MSS., Bodleian Library) she responded to a letter of Mary Shelley's (unlocated) and, along with other news, informed her that Rosa Robinson was to marry Aubrey Beauclerk.

4. Jean-Alexandre Buchon (1791–1846), French journalist.

5. Charles Augustin Sainte-Beuve (1804–69), French writer.

6. "The glorious days of France abroad and the immortal days at home."

7. The king had personally convened the Chambers on 5 November (*Annual Register*).

8. On 15 October a man named Darmes had fired at the royal carriage as Louis Philippe was leaving the Tuilleries. The assailant was captured and sentenced to life imprisonment (*Annual Register*).

9. Mary Shelley almost certainly would have included Manzoni's verse, though it is omitted in Hayward, *Correspondence*.

10. Bartolomé Esteban Murillo (1617–82), Spanish religious artist.

11. Hayward's essay "Prince George of Hanover on Music," a review of *Ideen und Betrachtungen über die Eigenschaften der Musik* (Ideas and reflections on the properties of music), had been published in the September *Quarterly Review*, pp. 503–15.

12. *"The Dream," and other Poems* (London: Henry Colburn, 1840). The quotation on the title page—"We have one human heart, / All mortal thoughts confess a common home."—is from Shelley's *Laon and Cythna*, canto 7, stanza 19.

13. Quotation from Smith, *A Sentimental Library*, p. 194.

❖

To Edward Moxon

15. Rue de la Paix.   Paris   30 Nov [1840]

Dear Mr Moxon

I was in Italy when I heard of this odious & unprincipled prosecution[1] I was deeply distressed—and I either wrote to you or sent you a message through Miss Robinson (I forget which) requesting you to write to me on the subject—but I did not hear from you. When My Son returned to England in October I begged him to call on you on the subject—but I am afraid he neglected to do so—Hearing nothing I hoped that the affair had blown over.—I have just received a message from you through Miss R—[*Robinson*] saying that you wish me to write to Lord Normanby[2] to express an opinion in your favour, as it will serve you. I will most willingly Do so—but fi{r}st I wish to understand clearly what

304

I had better say. I should not hesitate to tell Lord Normanby that you were averse to publishing the objectionable passages in Queen Mab—& that you did so at my request—I being prompted so to do from being assured on all sides that in these days there was no fear of ⟨mutilation⟩ proscution—that it seemed to me a mark of disrespect to my husband's Mememory [*Memory*], under these circumstances, to keep them back & that in short being written at the age of 18 they would be regarded by those who admired him with reverence due to his genius—by all with curiosity—without awakening the malice of ⟨those⟩ any. If this is the sort of representation you wish made, I will write—if not, explain. At the same time I must mention that I shall be in London about the middle of next Month (December) & if no injury will accrue from the delay, I think it would be otherwise advantageous to wait till I am in town.

I cannot express how distressed I am. Pray let me know the names of the heads of the society who ⟨want⟩ have set on foot this proscution as I shall certainly take care that they learn the contempt they inspire—I am Yours truly

MWShelley

ADDRESS: Edward Moxon Esq / Dover St. / London / Londres. POSTMARKS: (1) 2 / PARIS / 2 / 30 / 30 / [   ] / 30; (2) 1 / 2 DE 2 / [184]0. TEXT: MS., Pforzheimer Library.

1. See 11 December 1838. On 23 June 1841 Moxon was brought to trial for blasphemous libel before a special jury in the Court of the Queen's Bench presided over by Thomas Denman, first lord Denman (1779–1854; *DNB*), Lord Chief Justice. The trial was instigated by Henry Hetherington (1792–1849; *DNB*), a radical printer and bookseller, and his radical friends. Their objective was to protect radicals from discriminatory treatment under the law of libel by bringing charges against the highly respected Moxon. The specific charge was that Moxon "did falsely and maliciously publish a scandalous, impious, profane and malicious libel of and concerning the Holy Scriptures, and of and concerning Almighty God." The passages cited from *Queen Mab* were: canto 4, lines 208–21; canto 7, lines 84–97, 100–115, and a part of Shelley's second note. Moxon was defended by Thomas Noon Talfourd, who spoke and wrote eloquently in praise and defense of Shelley's genius. Though Moxon was found guilty, he was not sentenced, because the prosecution, having made its point, declined to pray judgment (see Newman Ivy White, "Literature and the Law of Libel: Shelley and the Radicals of 1840–1842," *Studies in Philology* 22, no. 1 [January 1925]: 34–47; and Thomas Noon Talfourd, *Speech for the Defendant in the Prosecution of the Queen versus Moxon, for the Publication of Shelley's Works. Delivered at the Court of Queen's Bench, June 23, 1841, and Revised* [London, 1841]).

2. Constantine Henry Phipps, first marquis of Normanby (1797–1863; *DNB*), politician and author, who was then Home Secretary.

To Richard Monckton Milnes

Rue de la Paix Nº 15
Tuesday Morn^g
[?22 December 1840][1]

Dear Mr Milnes

You bribe high for my going to the Invalides when you offer to accompany me. I heard that the shew was over on Saturday—but there is still the Catafalque I suppose—I am afraid I could not walk there & back—but if you will go with me en Citadine[2] between 2 & 3—or say at 3 I will walk back as far as Lady Canterburys where I have appointed to call at ½ past 4—Will this do?—

Two of your love Poems are supremely beautiful—

    O let not words, the callous shell of thought
    & I will not say my life was sad[3]

and I like infinitely

    They owned their passion without shame or fear[4]

I hope some day you will come & read to me again

Ever Yours truly
MaryShelley

ADDRESS: Monsieur / M. Milnes / Hotel Meurice. ENDORSED: Mrs Shelley. TEXT: MS., Trinity College, Cambridge.

    1. The context of this letter indicates that the earliest it could have been written was the Saturday after 15 December, the day on which Napoleon's remains were placed in St. Jerome's Chapel, beneath the Dome des Invalides. Milnes had witnessed Napoleon's second funeral with William Makepeace Thackeray, who published an account of the event in *The Second Funeral of Napoleon* under the pseudonym M. A. Titmarsh (London: Hugh Cunningham, 1841). Mary Shelley also attended the funeral (see 14 January 1842).

    2. "Hackney coach."

    3. In Milnes, *"Poetry for the People" and Other Poems* (London: Edward Moxon, 1840), pp. 163 and 166.

    4. In Milnes, *Poetry for the People*, p. 170.

To Edward Moxon

Penmaen   Dolgelly—N.W. [North Wales]
28 June [1841]

Dear Mr Moxon

I meant to have called in Dover St before leaving town last Tuesday—
but poor Mrs Godwin's death[1] prevented me. I did not get a new{s}paper
till yesterday when I was deeply distressed to find that the trial had come
on—& its result.[2] I have only seen the report in the Examiner & should
be very glad if you would let me have a good report—if you have one. I
cannot judge of Talfourds eloquence by this curtailed account—but it
seems to me that he took the right view—and Denman's summing up
appears excellent. Pray let me know something about it. I will write to
Lord Normanby as soon as I hear from you—& I hear whether there is
any thing you wish me to say.

The spirited & generous temper in which you have taken this perse-
cution brought on you first—by the Liberals, who urged you to publish,
& secondly by that disgrace to his party Mr Roebuck,[3] does you the greatest honour—& you must not be a sufferer if it can in any way be
prevented.

If you get any book for me keep them till I return to town at the end
of August—Any letters send here

I am Ever Y^s truly
MWShelley

TEXT: MS., Huntington Library.

1. Mary Jane Godwin died on 17 June and was buried in St. Pancras Churchyard.
The same tombstone marks the graves of Godwin, Wollstonecraft, and Mary Jane
Godwin, and although the remains of Godwin and Wollstonecraft were later removed
to Bournemouth it still marks the solitary grave of Mary Jane Godwin.

2. See 30 November [1840], n. 1. Moxon's behavior elicited a letter of apology
and support from Trelawny (Trelawny, *Letters*, pp. 209–10; see also 11 February
[1839], n. 1).

3. John Arthur Roebuck (1801–79; *DNB*), politician and radical.

To Edward Moxon

Dolgelley.   N.W. {North Wales}
14 July [1841]

Dear Mr Moxon

I know not what to say to your refusal of compensati{o}n[1] for all the expence which the Liberals have put you to. Since the evil sprung from them solely—I think you ought to let them repair it—not by a formal subscription—but by allowing them to take the fine &c on themselves. Thanks for Talfourd's speech[2]—it is very eloquent—& so conclusive that I wonder that the Jury was not persuaded by it; they ought to have been— But I suppose there was some bigotted fool among them who made them go wrong. I like some things he says about Shelley very much—& he makes out an admirable case for you—You must receive some comfort from the kind & just representation he makes of your character & position.

I shall certainly add a postscript with regard to the trial. I will send you in a day or two. I must mention that by an unaccountable oversight a poem of Shelley, printed in the Posthumous Poems is omitted in my editions it the one beginning

Rough wind that moanest loud

I think the title is a dirge—It can now be added. As to filling up the vacant space of Queen Mab—it is difficult. I object to Leigh Hunt's account—because it looks like patchwork taking a thing already printed & published. I should like what was inserted to be original. What I should like would be if Mr Hogg would write an Essay on Shelley's life & writings—original—though it might embody the substance of his Articles in the New Monthly.[3] This would cost something. Perhaps you would see him & learn what it would cost & then I would write to him & arrange it on my own account. Let me know what you think of this—

Let me have 25 copies of Talfourd's speech—send one to [*p. 1, crosswritten*] Miss Clairmont—3 Golden Sq—one to Mrs Hogg 12 Maida Vale Edgware Road—one directed to Mrs Boinville to the care of J. Flather Esq Lincoln's Inn 24 Old Square—written outside from Mrs Shelley, to be forwarded.

I am dear Sir
Y^s truly
M W Shelley

ADDRESS: Edward Moxon Esq / Dover St. / London. POSTMARKS: (1) DOLGELLY; (2) A / 15 JY 15 / 1841. TEXT: MS., British Library.

1. Samuel Rogers responded to a letter (unlocated) from Mary Shelley in c. July–August saying that Moxon was right in not accepting assistance from Mary Shelley for the penalty imposed on him (MS., Abinger MSS.).

2. See 30 November [1840], n. 1.

3. "Percy Bysshe Shelley at Oxford," *New Monthly Magazine*, January, February, April, July, October, and December 1832 and May 1833, collected and published in Hogg's *The Life of Percy Bysshe Shelley*, 2 vols. (London: Edward Moxon, 1858) (see Hogg, *Shelley*).

◈

To Elizabeth Berry

London.   14 Jany 1842

My dear Mrs Berry

Many thanks for your kind letter[1]—Correspondance goes on slowly with the Antipodes—and it is long since my letter to you. Soon after I made a trip to the North of Italy—Percy & I spent two months on the beautiful shores of the lake of Como—where he read for his degree, which he took last January. I spent a portion of last winter in Paris—& was present at Napoleon's funeral[2]—The immense assemblage of people & military would have rendered the sight exceedingly worth witnessing, had it not been for the intense cold. Being indisposed from the severe wintry weather—I preferred going inside the church where one saw little; but there was one very impressive moment—The priests had gone down the aisle to receive the coffin & returned to the music of a hymn—when there ensued a breathless silence—& then with quick step the Prince de Joinville & his staff ⟨walk⟩ passed up the aisle followed by the bier borne by the sailors of the Belle Poule[3]—⟨such⟩ a burst of martial music followed the depositing the coffin on the catafalque—such a thing seems nothing spoken of—but the actual effect—the pause in the music—the quick passage (the excessive weight of the bier forced the bearers to speed—they could not have supported it long) of the coffin really enclosing the mortal remains of the Man who once filled the world with his name & influence—& the burst of inspiriting music that followed was very fine.

Soon after Percy had ⟨passed⟩ taken his degree at Cambridge, being now 21—he wrote to his grandfather, who at last was impelled to the tardy justice of making him an allowance[4]—& for the first time since I lost my husband, now nearly 20 years ago, I began to feel a little above water in my affairs—though still my income is trifling enough—& I have a good deal of difficulty to struggle with. Last summer my father's widow died after a lingering illness—Poor Mʳˢ Godwin! It seemed strange that so restless a spirit could be hushed, & all that remained pent up in a grave. I had done all I could to help her during life—& government had given her several sums of money, so that she was above want.

Our Aunt is very comfortably placed (her address is, 7 Commercial Road—Old Kent Road London). She is with very kind people. She is very infirm—& as ever in summer she will not go out into the air, of course she is feeble & very susceptible to cold. I can never enough thank you for your kindness to her—I do not quite understand how things are managed. Mʳ Donaldson for some time refused to pay the £40 p ann. As you say that is all settled now, except that he never entirely paid up the arrears—(I understand from her that £15 is still unpaid)   However I was able to help her when she wanted it—and we determined not to worry you, but that as I understand it, a new difficulty has arrisen. She told me—& indeed I beleive I saw your letters to that effect, that from this Xmas forward you generously encreased her annuity to £50 half yearly— Mʳ Donaldson however says that he received no instructions to that effect and has only given her £40. You will best know whether this was your intention. She has never yet made the £40—suffice—however I am far from wishing to press that on you—for you have proved yourself all kindness—but it is right that you should know how matters stand. I should be glad that whatever step you take that you did not mention what I say to Everina, as she would be very jealous of my interference. But in this you will judge for yourself.

Thanks for all your kindness to Charles Robinson. I sincerely hope he will get on.   H[e] has written letters home concerning th[e] colony to his cousin Mʳ Henry Perry,[5] who is private Secretry to Lᵈ Lyndhurst[6]— These have been shewn to Lᵈ Stanley,[7] who was pleased with them & asked for copies. So it is to be hoped that something will be done to advance him. I have been reading a very interesting book lately, Captain Grey's expedition to N.W. Australia[8] which appears a very find country—far superior in irrigation & fertility to the rest of New Holland[9]—besides being perfectly healthy although within the tropics.

Poor Everina desires so earnestly to see you—& who knows whether you may not be tempted. Could you get a good vessel to carry you to Panamà, there are now regular steamers to the Isthmu[s] twice a month— This must facilitate intercourse with Sidney—I hope you will write to me again—No kindness can be so great as your writing to Everina—She quite pines for your letters, & fancies a thousand evils when she does not hear.

Adieu, my dear Cousin, I hope you & Mʳ Berry will continue to live & prosper long

Ever Yˢ MWShelley

[*P. 1, top*] Direct to me at Hookham's Library 15 Old Bond St. London

ADDRESS: Mrs. Berry / Sidney / New South Wales. POSTMARKS: (1) B / PAID / 14 JA 14 / 1842; (2) PAID SHIP LETTER LONDON / 14 [   ] 14 / 1842; (3) SHIP LETTER SYDNEY / MY* 7 / 1842. TEXT: MS., Alexander Hay Collection, Mitchell Library, State Library of New South Wales, Sydney.

1. See 3 August 1839, n. 1.

2. François de Bourbon-Orléans, prince de Joinville (1818–1900), admiral, was the third son of Louis Philippe (see 9 August 1830).

3. At his father's command, the prince de Joinville had brought Napoleon's remains to Paris from St. Helena aboard the frigate *La Belle Poule*.

4. Sir Timothy Shelley gave Percy Florence an allowance of £400 a year as a gift sometime after he took his degree on 23 January 1841 and before 14 February 1841 (Ingpen, *Shelley in England*, II, 624; MWS Journal).

5. Henry James Perry (1800–1869), barrister, was principal secretary to Lord Chancellor Lyndhurst (see below, n. 6) from 1841 to 1846 and commissioner of bankrupts, Liverpool from 1846 until his death (*Alumni Cantabrigienses*).

6. John Singleton Copley, first baron Lyndhurst (1772–1863; *DNB*), Tory politician, was Lord Chancellor under George Canning from 1827 to 1830 and under Sir Robert Peel from 1834 to 1835 and again from 1841 to 1846.

7. Edward George Geoffrey Smith Stanley, fourteenth earl of Derby (1799–1869; *DNB*), joined Peel's administration as Colonial Secretary in 1841.

8. Sir George Grey, *Journals of Two Expeditions of Discovery in Northwest and Western Australia, during the years 1837–38, and 39 . . .* , 2 vols. (London: T. and W. Boone, 1841).

9. The Dutch, who discovered and explored the west coast of Australia and parts of the north and south coasts from 1613 to 1627, called Australia New Holland. Captain James Cook, who discovered and explored the east coast during his first voyage in 1768–71, called that area New South Wales.

To Leigh Hunt

Dresden   17 August [1842]

Dear Hunt—I was delighted to get your letter—it relieved me from great anxiety. I can only say if Lord Leigh will join us it will go hard with Percy & me but that we will contribute our share to so dear & honorable a work—You may count on £10 for the Xmas quarter. I wish that I heard of other success & prosperity for you. I saw advertized, that your Poem¹ was reprinted in Galignani's weekly journal to which he transfers what he considers most worthy of our literature—When I get to Florence I shall try to see this & read your poem.

We have made a long journey since I wrote—We found here Pearson, who has set several of Shelley's poems most beautifully to Music[2] (Novello published them) & has a great Musical genius. He is very German in his Music—but there is much & beautiful Melody in some of these songs— in the Arethusa for instance & in the Spirit of Night—but they are very difficult to play. He is now writing an Opera which he hopes to have brought {out} at Vienna. Meanwhile he talks of accompanying us to Florence—towards which we shall make progress (it is a long way off) in about 10 days. The Elbe has no water for Steamers—or we had hoped for a beautiful Voyage to Prague. The drought in this part of the world is become disastrous—Every{thing} is dried up—the heat is oppressive beyond description—It is impossible to go to galleries or sights—Doing so in some small degree the other day I was knocked up & quite ill. No rain—no clouds—each day the sun makes its progress through the sky scorching & stewing—a thunderstorm never intervenes to check or change the heat—Water is sold about the town—& the people are forbidden to wash their houses, not to use the water—a superfluity of caution, I should imagine, for the Germans are not given to much washing— & there is still water in the Elbe, though it may be walked across. We regret not being among mountains—but after spending last year in a Welch Valley, rained on the whole time, it did not occur to us that we should be in danger of being broiled alive in Dresden in the Month of August.—We visited (helped by the railroad) Berlin on our way hither. The Gallery there is a very good one & admirably arranged. All things in Prussia you know are so arranged as to half convert a republican—all is done by the king[3] in the best way. There is free ingress to the Gallery to every one   Among all the pictures none delighted me so much as the adoration of the Kings by Raphael—A large picture in his first style— the colors all faded—yet what is left, the expression of the faces.—the grace & simplicity of the figures, are quite matchless—One kneeling Angel in particular—There is adoration humility & perfect self forgetfulness & such inexpressible sweetness that none but Raphael could have put on canvas. The "Mother & Child" (di San Sisto) here are very fine—but quite different—There is much more Majesty & grandeur but less simplicity & sweetness. The Magdalene you mention is very lovely—so tearful yet composed—hoping yet regretting. There are other fine Correggio[s] in the Gallery.

As I said we go towards Florence. One of our party is ordered a warm climate—I fear Florence will be scarcely temperate enough for him. Percy's friend Knox—(whom you met at our house) has a complaint of the heart—a painful disorder attended by great nervousness & distress—requiring great quiet & composure—and he has many things to worry him. He is writing & will bring out a volume of poems this Autumn[4]—a copy shall be sent you—get it well noticed if you can—and do it all the good you can. He has a true po[e]ti[cal   ][5] great sensibility—infinite facil[ity   ] deep classical knowledge & other qualit[ies   ]ppy inspiration to verse—with a great dislike to common place—I hope you will like his volume.

Percy desires to be most kindly remembered   I shall hope to hear from you—& to hear that Marianne is well & that some prosperity shines on you—Believe me dear Hunt

My letter is very stupid but you must forgive [   ] as I am only convalesc[ing] from the illness the [   ]—still very weak

ADDRESS: Leigh Hunt Esq / Edward Square / Kensington / London / Londres. POSTMARKS: (1) DRESDEN / 21 Aug 42; (2) HAMBURG / 23 / 8; (3) J / 26 AU 26 / 1842; (4) 10 Fn 10 / AU 26 / 1842. ENDORSED: Mary Shelley. TEXT: MS., Humanities Research Center, University of Texas at Austin.

1. Leigh Hunt, *The Palfrey; a Love-Story of Old Times* (London: How and Parsons, 1842).

2. Pearson had set six of Shelley's poems to music, published first separately and then as *Characteristic Songs of Shelley* (London: Novello, 1839–40). Five of these poems have been identified: "Arethusa," "Song of Proserpine," "On a Faded Violet," "To Night," and "False friend, wilt thou smile or weep . . ." (*Song of Beatrice Cenci*, act 5). He also set "Autumn: a Dirge" (1841) and "The Indian Serenade" (1841) (see Burton R. Pollin, *Music for Shelley's Poetry: An Annotated Bibliography of Musical Settings of Shelley's Poetry* [New York: Da Capo Press, 1974], pp. 91–92). In 1844 he set Mary Shelley's "O listen while I sing to thee" (see Bryan N. S. Gooch and David S. Thatcher, *Musical Settings of British Romantic Literature: A Catalogue*, 2 vols. [New York: Garland Publishing, 1982], I, 1044; and Nitchie, *Mary Shelley*, pp. 234–35).

3. Frederick William IV (1795–1861), king of Prussia from 1840 to 1861.

4. Alexander Andrew Knox, *Giotto and Francesca, and Other Poems* (London: Edward Bull, 1842).

5. There are gaps in the text because the signature has been cut out.

To Claire Clairmont

Venise   1 Oct. (2nd Oct.) [1842]
(We leave this on the 19th)

Dearest Claire—Percy got your letter at Inspruck & I have been hoping
to receive another from you here as you said you would write—a letter is
always a comfort—when from a friend—& I get so few—Jane never
writes—though I left all my little affairs in her hands when I left England—Percy hears from his Aunt[1]—& that is all. Ianthe had a boy—at
which the Esdailes rejoiced—but poor thing, she lost it immediately
after[2]—& is by no means in strong health.—We had a desperately long
journey from Dresden here—3 weeks & we never (with the exception of
Prague) slept two nights in one bed—We traversed a vast variety of scenery—& saw certainly some of the beautiful spots in the world—in the
first rank I should place Salzburgh—yet the grandeur of the Danube that
sweeps by beneath the mountains in majestic stream, renders Lintz won-
derfully beautiful. I did not take to the people—ugly, dirty & sullen
there is nothing in them attractive—the Tyrolese are better—but still
they seem to want life & spirit & above all the courtesy of the Italians.
Venice has ⟨above all⟩ excessively charmed my companions—& we remain
here in all a Month. Thanks to some introductions Laura sent me, we had
useful acquaintance, & got comfortably lodged—a little expensive for
us—but still very comfortable—with so large a party it is difficult to find
comfort, without spending a good deal for that greatly depends on the
independance of each member of the party—both Knox & Pearson are
invalids—both suffer a good deal from depression & are irritable—They
both are ill in somewhat the same way—Knox has an enlargement of the
heart, which threatens ultimately ossification, & added to this an irritation of all the nerves in the region of the heart, the most violent—He
ought to be kept quiet—but as he will write— & indeed in a certain sense
he must— quiet he cannot have, & his spirits fluctuate with his success
in composition—He, as you may, know is proud & sensitive to a fault
still we get on very well—Pearson is quite different—the illness that
threatens him is aneurism—he is much better—& I think his malady will
be subdued; it affects him most by encreasing his natural indolence,
which is excessive—he is much more openly irritable than Knox—but it
is all on the surface—he has no pride—& the fit of annoyance over he is
as gentle as a lamb—beging one to excuse him & trying to make it up
in a thousand ways—He has no more reason in him than a child—but

314

like a child is tres-raisonneux[3]—as he is utterly incapable of taking care of his own money—I have to take care of it for him—& he wants to buy a thousand things—& I wont let him, & one argues & goes over the same ground a thousand times—& when you think he is persuaded, like a child he comes back to the same point & it is all to do over again. He is a little taller than Knox—an air of indolence is diffused over all his person—his complexion is that muddy one you hate—he has a great deal of hair—about Shelley's color—only yellower where the light catches it—his eyes are grey—his nose acquiline—his features prononcèr,[4] but his face is narrow—& his chin, while it supports his face, does not deviate into width of jaw—he is as simple as a child, & to be managed like one. I like myself to have to deal with those exceedingly open characters, without stain of sulleness or concealment—still 3 young men will draw various ways at times, & I have quite enough to do to keep all well. Percy is my delight—he is so good & forbearing & thoughtful for me, that he is the greatest comfort in the world. Knox is writing a tragedy.[5] When it is finished—& (as we have every trust it will be) accepted, he will go over to England to bring it out. I dont think we shall go so soon. Helen Shelley plainly shews she is glad that Percy is away—& though that may mean that they are afraid that Sir Tim may take to him—yet they would hinder that by quarrelling with him, so it is as well that he is away on good terms.

I have made a new acquaintance here that will a little surprise you. Milnes & Leader[6] came together here—so knowing one we know both   I cannot make out whether Leader is enclined to be civil.   his manners are rather cold & repulsive, but I in a measure wish to cultivate him, because Percy wants to ally himself to the liberal party in England—& Leader, if not the wisest, is one of the most respectable among them. They asked Percy & Knox to dinner one day—& yesterday they dined with us—Milnes is gone; he set off by a Steamer for Constantinople last night—& Leader remains. He tells me that Trelawny goes on just the same, never going out—& building & cutting down trees at Putney. Augusta[7] lives in a cottage near—so the stories told of her going back to her family are not true—perhaps she went to see her father before his death.

This is all my news. Pearson is writing an Opera for a German libretto—but he wishes to write for an Italian, & I hope he will get one at Florence. He is very clever—His music is a great resource to Percy—who has added a trumpet to his stock of in{s}truments—& is taking lessons & a pretty noise is made at times—to be heard at Lido.—To Lido, by the bye, they go every day to write & bathe—I have been obliged to fight a great deal to prevent them having a gondola apiece—We have two in our pay as it is—If I saw them all happy I should be content—but I fear poor dear Knox can scarcely be so in the present position of his affairs & health—if his play succeeds it will be a great thing—& I feel sure it will.—he writes the dialogue very well—with strength feeling & poetry—A volume of his poems—including the poem you read (which I persuaded him to take back, it was too silly to allow it to be published as written by another) are now being printed & published in England— By the bye I trust that your debt to George R— [*Robinson*] is now paid I sent the money for the purpose. You have heard I suppose of Mr Robinson's death,[8] poor man—he seems to have gradually become extinct without suffering. The last I heard was that Mrs Alfred R— [*Robinson*] had gone to Boulogne & that Julia[9] was with her—poor Julia—she seems to have gained nothing by the changes in her family—Percy has rather a prejudice against her, which has prevented my wishing to see her—& besides her having told you that they had sacrificed a brilliant society for my sake utterly prevents my ever associating with her again on terms of friendship—poor thing—what benefit can she see in covering the truth with false tinsel—one cannot guess—but it is nature with some people. There was a paragraph in Galignani to say that Mrs Norton's youngest child was killed by a fall from a poney[10] I hope it is not true. Charles Dickens has come home in a state of violent dislike of the Americans— & means to devour them in his next work[11]—he says they are so frightfully dishonest. I am sorry for this—he has never travelled, & will write with all that irritation inexperienced travellers are apt feel—such as I felt in Germany—& I do dislike the Germans—& never wish to visit Germany again—but I would not put this in print—for the surface is all I know— & that does not deserve commemoration & vituperation. He is very angry because they refuse to make a law of international copyright—a law that would make his fortune—& his vehement seeking for it when in America Washington Irving says will retard its being passed for ten more years. [*Cross-written*] Pray write dear Claire if by return of post direct here—if not to Florence—& tell me what you are doing about Dina—& what you are doing yourself

Ever Affl^y

Y^s

MWS.

[*P. 1, cross-written*]

(2nd Oct.)

This letter was just going off, when I received yours.
Poor Dina—I pity her for her bringing up—her total want of self command—& above all for her attribute of fibbing—which this story about you displays so glaringly—and much I pity her for her Mother's speaking

so ill of her—I confess Jane's conduct has shocked me much. She brought it all on her child—We are all liable to do wrong & I would have forgiven that if she had borne her share of the misfortune she brought on Dina. There is no help now—Dina is married by this time—she must give lessons & get on as she can—her character may strengthen & purify under adversity; at any rate this is time to shew her kindness, & would I could serve her—but money matters go against me—It is my fate always to have poor friends—I had hoped when he came with us, that poor dear Knox would have been better off than he is—as it is my purse is exhausted—& my darling Percy's too—who is so good—however one must not complain. I shall be glad if you can lett your house & come to Florence for two months—do if you can.

I have seen nothing of Rawlinson—We frequent the piazza & some of us would be sure to see him if he made his appearance

Writing to you about Knox of course I write in the strictest confidence. He is writing a tragedy which I think will be very fine & its success make all right & well with him ⟨& then his grand intention is to pay us off⟩ I must tell you by the bye that Percy & I pay half Hunts rent—& I believe Ld Leigh will pay the other half—He is dreadfully off—writes poetry by which he gets nothing—hopes about a play, which is never acted & lives on Henry's £100 a year—I wonder if Edward will help his sister—It was a great pity that so much money was spent in sending Dina out of the way—to no purpose.

You are right in saying Venice might make me Melancholy—it did excessively at first—but I have so much to think of to keep my companions comfortable that the impression is worn off—& my great endeavour is to be in good spirits—I was a good deal worried & careworn & ill from the heat at Dresden—but I feel well here

Adieu, dear Claire, I hope Percy will write to you soon—he sends his love—I hope he will get into no love scrape here to hurt his health—that is the thing to be dreaded in this country—Adieu   Ever Y^s   MS.

ADDRESS: Miss Clairmont / Rue Neuve Clichy No 3 / Rue Clichy / Paris / Parigi. POSTMARKS: (1) VENEZIA / FRANCO; (2) VENEZIA / 3 OTTe.; (3) [   ]GUE / 10 Oct / 42. TEXT: MS., Huntington Library.
   1. Probably Hellen Shelley (see 24 April [1844]).
   2. Ianthe Shelley Esdaile.
   3. *Tres raisonneur*, "very argumentative."
   4. "Pronounced."
   5. *The Heir of Cyprus* (see MWS *Letters*, vol. III, 25 December [1842]). Knox also wrote *A Trip to Kissingen, A farce in One Act* (entered in the Lord Chamberlain's Office on 8 November 1844, British Library [Adds. 42,979, ff. 453–524]). Knox's plays appear not to have been produced.

6. John Temple Leader (1810–1903; *DNB*), political radical.
7. Augusta Goring.
8. On 15 July 1842.
9. Julia Robinson.
10. William Norton (b. 26 August 1833) died in early September from blood poisoning that developed from an injury incurred when he was thrown from his pony (Perkins, *Mrs. Norton*, pp. 56, 166–67).
11. Dickens did so in *American Notes for General Circulation*, 2 vols. (London: Chapman and Hall, 1842).

◆

To Everina Wollstonecraft

Florence.   24 Nov. [1842]

My dear Aunt—I send Mʳˢ Hogg some money by this post, so you will receive what you asked. I am sorry I cannot do more—I should much like to have sent Margaret a little present, that I might shew my sense of her Mother's[1] kindness to you—but I cannot—I hope you will be very comfortable when you get the £100 a year regularly—The tombstone it is quite out of my power to pay, as I explained in my last—it is a pity you did not keep your promise, on which I relied

We are living here very quietly & know one or two agreable people. The weather is as bad as it can be in England—so we have not gained in that. We live quite near the gallery,[2] & often visit it to see the beautiful pictures & splendid statues it contains—We are near also to the Pitti palace, which has a very fine gallery. The other day we made an excursion to Vallombrosa, a convent seated high among the mountains. The season was too far advanced, & we were caught in a storm, as we were toiling up the ravine, on our ponies—A monk received us at the convent & took us to the stranger's room & lighted a large fire, which was very welcome. The sun came out afterwards, & we descended the mountain in comfort— but had a very rainy drive back to Florence. Lady Mountcashell's two daughters by Mʳ Tighe are here. The Eldest is a very beautiful woman, with the sweetest face in the world, so kind & gentle—she made an unfortunate marriage, & has a good deal to go through—but she bears all with great fortitude & good sense. The youngest is married to an Italian—a very sensible, good man—she has two young children—& is very lively & agreable but unfortunately she has very bad health   They are the most pleasant people we know here—& we often spend our evenings with them—The eldest sings beautifully

Percy has bought a trumpet so now he has three musical instruments

318

to play upon. My health is a good deal improved—my long journey, though fatigueing at the time, has strengthened me. I hope my stay in Florence wont hurt me—for I am never so well in any town as in the Country—a great deal of fresh air & exercise are quite necessary to me. I hope you creep out in your chair[3] on fine days, & find it a comfort to you—I should be very glad to hear that you & your room looked the picture of tidiness & comfort—& that gentle exercise in your [   ] was giving you strength.

Ever aff^{ly} Y^s   MWS

TEXT: MS., Eton College.

   1. Mrs. Larkins (see 25 March–3 April 1843).

   2. The Uffizi. In *Rambles in Germany and Italy*, Mary Shelley wrote that on entering she "felt a crowd of associations rise up around me, gifted with painful vitality. I was long lost in tears" (II, 152).

   3. A large chair on three wheels for an invalid, given by Mary Shelley to her aunt (see 25 March–3 April 1843).

❧

To Elizabeth Berry

Rome   25 March (April 3^d) 1843

My dear Mrs Berry

It falls to me to acquaint you with the sad event of our poor Aunt Everina's death—if that can be called sad when released her from lingering infirmity & sickness. Still, till quite lately, she enjoyed life to a degree—& ⟨had she taken⟩ could she have been persuaded to change some of her modes of going on, I doubt not but that she might have lived some years longer. I will send you such an account as I can & I should have written this account some weeks sooner, but that I am still in expectation of a letter from England, with the latest details.

Our poor Aunt, as you know, removed from Totington to Peckham about two years ago—She took up her abode there with most excellent people—of whom, of course, she has made frequent mention in her letters to you. Mrs Larkins, especially is a woman of sound understanding, excellent comm[on] sense & a warm & feeling heart. It required no less to enable her to act the kind attentive part she did towards poor Everina. Our poor Aunt complained of little except of encreasing infirmity in her legs. While in England I did what I could for her comfort. Last June I came abroad, chiefly that as my Son does not follow any profession, I look upon travelling as the best occupation he can have while so young. Before

going away I gave Everina a Bath Chair,[1] for which she had often wished—
She could seldom be induced to leave the house, even for a turn in the
garden—and I was desirous to prevail on her to take the air, so necessary
to health & good spirits. In a letter I had from her last Autumn, she told
me that she frequently went out in it, & that if it did not prolong her
life, it would at least make her last days pleasanter. I left it in charge to
a friend of mine, Mrs Hogg, of whom Everina was very fond, to visit her
as often as she could, & to take care that she did not want for money. I
got a letter from Mrs Hogg, dated February 7th 1843—most of which I
will copy. "Ten days ago I received a note from Mrs Lissom to say that
poor Aunty was ill. I went immediately to see her. I found that she had
been seized with paralysis. Her attack is a slight one since it has not deprived her of the u[   ]ly limb; it has however weakened her very
much, & the Doctor [   ] that in all probability she will have another
attack, which will carry her off suddenly, or she may live some Months
in the same state. It is of course uncertain, but it is evidently a break up
of the system. This is sad news—but you may feel assured that she is well
taken care of, & that I will do my best to supply in some measure your
place towards her. I fear the expences of whatever kind will devolve upon
you till her next quarter comes round, as Mrs Larkins tells me that she
had not £3 left from the money she receive[d] in December—only a
month ago—but she throws her money away without consideration &
will be under no controul what ever. The Doctor lives next door & seems
to be all that is needed in the way of advice, as it is clearly a natural decay,
beyond the reach of art. She has entire confidence in, & is perfectly satisfied with him, so I shall not seek other advice, unless you wish it. She
was seized when getting up to dress herself, early in the morning. M^rs
Lissom was alarmed by a heavy fall on the floor above, & on going up,
they found her stretched on the carpet & trying in vain to get up. She
was quite sensible but incapable of motion. They sent instantly for the
Doctor. Mrs Larkins sat up with her for some nights, but as she has the
work of the house to do, she engaged a woman to sit up at nights. But
this does not seem to answer, for Aunty would have M^rs L— [Larkins] to
wait on her & would bear no one else near her. I went to see her again
yesterday, & took her some Kale & a fowl. I was anxious to see her once
more before I wrote to you. She appeared to me sinking not rapidly but
surely. You will of course write to her & to me by return of post, as I
wish to be prepared to do the right thing in an emergence [emergency].
You may feel sure that I will protect your interests, while I do all that
befits her condition & your relation to her, in your name. Poor Mrs Larkins
wages perpetual war with her on the subject of her dirt which encreases,

& begins to involve the credit of the house & her nurse—but on this point she is inexorable—nothing can induce her to be washed. If she were nearer I would see her daily, as I feel for her lonely condition—as it is I will go as often as I can. It is useless to say any thing about her habits or her expenditure neither can be altered."

The next letter I got from M.rs Hogg is dated 27 Feb. She writes:

"The sad event [   ]ce on Saturday last (23 Feb.)² at ½ past 2 in the morning.   [   ] can I call it sad. It [   ] a merciful release to the poor soul & all concerned, for she has long been beyond all con-troul. I saw her for the last time on Thursday afternoon—death was then visible written in her face. She did not know me. I took her some jelly, oranges, sponge cakes & her favourite Kale, but she rejected all food & would submit to nothing. I spare you all sad details   On the receipt of M.rs Larkins letter on Saturday, I went & sealed up her papers. M.rs Larkins will choose a spot in the cemetary near them—I gave other directions with respect to the last ceremony when I was there, & the funeral will take place next Saturday. With regard to that I shall take the sense of her friends as they seem to have correct view on all points. I will write to you at length in a few days."

For this promised letter I have waited & shall still wait some days longer that I may send you a complete account of every thing.

(April 3.d)   I have waited in vain for another letter from my friend—so I shall send off this—I shall send it to M.rs Hogg & shall ask her to add the particulars of the funeral &c &c—so that you may have a full account.³

Your last letter was forwarded to me here. Thank you for your kindness to Charles Robinson   I got a letter from him in which he mentions your most welcome present   Will you, if you write to him tell him that I will answer his letter when I return to England in the Autumn. Poor fellow—I wish I could be of service to him. When I can at all afford it I will send him out some things that may be useful to him—but though better off, the peculiar circumstances of my position make me still feel my means very narrow, especially as a nervoul illness, the effects of which still hangs about me prevents my writing & earning money. We shall remain in Italy till the Autumn. We spent the winter at Florence   The climate was very humid & warm & did not agree with me at all—making me more nervous than I had ever felt—I had always heard that the climate of Florence was bad for the nerves—but did not expect any thing so disagreable—Rome on the contrary I find very pleasant—and the city itself is so interesting & delightful, However the climate is bad in the summer—[   ] summer months we [   ] passing the sea side near [   ]

What did you say to my Aunt about her idea of your having Sarah

Wakefield out.[4] I believe her to be an excellent & intelligent young woman—& worthy of a better fate than she is born to—I respect her for her kindness & zealous attentions to poor Everina; for you must in some degree know how arduous a task it was to attend on her. Mrs Larkins deserves great thanks—& I hope to shew her one day in a more tangible way my sense of her kindness—but that time which one has been bid expect so long seems as far off as ever. My husband's family are strange people. Sir Tim himself is enclined to be kind but is held back by his wife who is fearful that her second son should not get all that it is possible for him to have. Percy is so reasonable so fond of me—so amiable, cheerful & affectionate that he is delight & consolation of my life—giving comfort at last after a long series of struggle & lonely suffering.

Adieu—pray write to me—to Hookhams—I hope your health is better believe me

Ever truly Y^s MaryShelley

ADDRESS: Mrs Berry / Sidney / New South Wales. [*By Jane Hogg; see below, n. 3*] Mrs Berry / Sidney / New South Wales. POSTMARKS: (1) X / PAID / 22 AP 22 / 1843; (2) Maida Hill; (3) PAID SHIP LETTER LONDON   22 AP 22 / 1843; (4) SHIP LETTER / AU[   ] / [   ]. TEXT: MS., Alexander Hay Collection, Mitchell Library, State Library of New South Wales, Sydney.

1. See 24 November [1842].
2. Saturday was 25 February.
3. Following is Jane Hogg's letter to Elizabeth Berry:

April 22nd—43.

My dear Madam

According to the wishes of my friend Mrs Shelley, I write to comfort you with the assurance that your poor Aunt although unblessed with the presence of dear relatives to receive her last wishes met with every attention and care from Mrs Larkin, and the lady with whom she lived—The former attended upon her night, and day, with indefatigable zeal; and she would receive neither food nor medicine from any other hand: she, and the nurse only were with her in her last moments, during which, she appeared to suffer acutely from inward convulsions. She was buried in compliance with her wishes, at St. Pancras close to her sister. The good people with whom she resided having but slender means applied to your Agent Mr Donaldson for the amount of her annuity due up to the period of her decease, which would (with the sum sent by Mrs Shelley) have covered all expences, but Mr Donaldson declined making any advance without authority. I cannot speak too warmly in praise of the constant care and attention your worthy relative received at the hands of Mrs Larkin. I regret that the great distance between us, did not permit me to be with her as often as I wished and should have felt this still more had I had less confidence in the kind people she was with—With a hope that yourself and Mr Berry are quite well,

I remain yours truly

J. Hogg

4. On 4 January 1842 Elizabeth Berry wrote to Everina Wollstonecraft indicating the difficulty of then bringing a servant out from England. She explained that government funds for such emigration were by that time exhausted and all emigrants had to pay their own passage, which Sarah Wakefield apparently could not afford (MS., Alexander Hay Collection, Mitchell Library, State Library of New South Wales, Sydney). Records show that Elizabeth Berry did employ Catherine Henessy, age eighteen and newly arrived in Sydney in 1844, as a housekeeper, her initial term of three months to be compensated by £11 plus board and lodging. The cost of her passage was defrayed by "Bounty" (*Governor's Despatches to Secretary of State for the Colonies* 46 [September–December 1844]: 823, Mitchell Library, State Library of New South Wales, Sydney).

<hr/>

To Edward Moxon

Rome—7 May [1843]

Dear Mr Moxon

A thousand thanks for your letter, which was very welcome—The introductions from the Severns' were exceedingly useful—Will you put up the other half of this sheet in an e{n}velope & send it by post to her.

I see by the papers that poor Southey is no more.[1] Dying as he did—his mind first—the loss will be the less felt & lamented. I congratulate Mr Wordsworth on the Laureateship.[2] a royal favour well bestowed at which every one must rejoice. May I ask you to interest yourself—as soon as decorum permits, in obtaining those letters of my husband that I once mentioned to you. Shelley addressed them to Southey from Italy in 1821[3]—I would not have them published for the world; & Mrs Southey will oblige me very greatly by letting me have them. If she has the feelings of a gentlewoman she will at once—as they relate solely to Shelley himself—& were written in confidence. I shall be very much obliged to you indeed if you can succeed in this negotiation for me.

I am very sorry that no good writers are exciting attention in England. I wish I could do as you ask, & am flattered by the wish. All the time I was at Florence I suffered greatly in my health—& was incapable of any mental exertion. I am quite well now at Rome—& should be glad to employ myself in that way this summer—but I [sca]rcely think I shall be able—we shall see. Nothing can be so delightful or inspiriting as this divine country—I should like to remain till next spring—but I am afraid we shall return in the Autumn—to go North in the Winter appears cruel.—By this time you may have seen Mr Milnes, who visited Rome on his way from Upper Egypt—& can give news of us. Give my love to

323

Mr Rogers & tell him that his friends the Rios' have been an inestimable resource to us—we have been almost near each other—This will soon I am sorry to say no longer be the case as they pass the summer at Bologna. He indeed is already gone—He got a cold which degenerated into a Tertian[4] before he thought of medical advice—a little of that sen[   ] way the fever—but he left Rome as soon as he was convalescent to gain strength. Mrs Rio & her children join him next week. I hope you & your family are all well. Tell Mrs Norton I should be excessively delighted to get a letter—if she directs to the care of Mess. Cini Florence I am sure to get it—Ever tru{l}y Y^s

MShelley

[*P. 1, top*]   direct to me aux sonis des M.M. Freres Cini Florence

ADDRESS: Edward Moxon Esq / Dover St. / Piccadilly / London / Inghilterra / Londres. POSTMARKS: (1) DIREZIONE DE ROMA / 12 MAG / 43; (2) SARD / 21 / MAI / 43 / PONT-DE-B; (3) T.S.; (4) S / 23 MY 23 / 1843. TEXT: MS., Pforzheimer Library.

1. Southey died on 21 March 1843 after protracted mental and physical illness (Kenneth Curry, *Southey* [London: Routledge and Kegan Paul, 1975], p. 62).

2. Wordsworth, who received the offer of the Laureateship within ten days of Southey's death, first declined, saying that his advanced age would not allow him to perform the duty of writing poems for state occasions. On 3 April 1843 Sir Robert Peel indicated to him that he had "nothing required," and Wordsworth accepted (Mary Moorman, *William Wordsworth: A Biography*, vol. II, *The Later Years* [Oxford: Clarendon Press, 1965], 559).

3. The location of these letters is not presently known. Shelley's letters to Southey in *PBS Letters* are taken from earlier publications.

4. A fever or ague marked by a paroxysm every third day.

To Edward Moxon

White Cottage   Putney   20 Sep. [1843]

Dear Mr Moxon

I wrote to you soon after my return—but learnt afterwards that you were out of town—I hope when you return you will come down & see us. You are pretty sure to find me—I seldom go out.

You asked me about writing—it is a serious question to me—but I hope as winter comes on to have strength—& dont despise me if I say I wish to write for I want money sadly. I dont want it for myself—that is I dont want it so much as to impel me to write—but I do for another purpose[1]—which will make me exert myself. But now—Is it a novel or a romance you want?—I should prefer quieter work, to be gathered from other works—such as my lives for the Cyclopedia—& which I think I do much better than romancing—Something, God willing, I must do, if you fancy it worth your while to set me to work.

Will you thank Mr Talfourd for the kind present of his pleasant book—Where is Mr Rogers? I will visit town to see him though for no one else.

Did I tell you, there were no letters of Mr Southey among Shelley's papers—he destroyed those he received—I should be glad of those Mr Taylor can find

I hope you & yours are all well

Ever truly Y^s

MaryShelley

ADDRESS: Edward Moxon Esq / Dover Street / Piccadilly. POSTMARKS: (1) FULHAM; (2) 4 Eg 4 / SP 21 / 1843 / B. TEXT: MS., Henry W. and Albert A. Berg Collection, New York Public Library.

1. In August 1843, while Mary Shelley was in Paris, Claire Clairmont introduced her to a group of Italian expatriates, in exile since 1831, including Ferdinando Gatteschi. Mary Shelley believed Gatteschi's writing talents were thwarted by lack of money, which she tried to supply. In 1845, he used her letters to him in an attempt at blackmail (see MWS *Letters*, I, 30 August 1843 [?16–24 September 1845], ff.).

To Edward Moxon

Putney—2⟨6⟩7 Sep. [1843]

Dear Mr Moxon

A few words you let fall made me reflect & look over some notes I made. And the spirit moves me to put together a journal of my late tour—which long and varied affords scope—Many facts of expences I can tell which will be useful—but above all—my 6 weeks tour[1] brought me many compliments & my present Twelvemonths tour will, I feel sure, procure me many more. This sounds vain, but is not. I distrust myself & often lose advantages natural to me thro' this distrust—The 6 weeks tour—& among my novels Lodore—were written off hand & have pleased most.—I mean therefore to make my present work as light—as personal to myself—& as amusing as I can. I think you will like it as a reader—as a publisher I hope it will meet your approbation. I am working fast—but then I work best—since fast ever comes with me from the inspiration of & pleasure I take in the subject—I told you I wanted money—not for myself—but for a purpose most urgent & desirable I want it—I shall work fast therefore—& I hope you will prepare to receive the offered MS. graciously & generously—as usual.—

Ever truly Y^s

MaryShelley

ADDRESS: Edward Moxon Esq / Dover Street / Piccadilly. POSTMARKS: (1) FULHAM; (2) 8 Nt 8 / SP 27 / 1843 / A. TEXT: MS., Luther A. Brewer Collection, University of Iowa; envelope, Pforzheimer Library.

1. MWS, *Six Weeks' Tour* (see [25 October 1814], n. 1, and ff.).

To Leigh Hunt

Putney   20 April 1844

My dear Hunt

The tidings from Field Place seem to say that ere long there will be a change—if nothing untoward happens to us till then,—it will be for the better.

Twenty years ago in memory of what Shelley's intentions were—I said that you should be considered one of the legatees to the amount of £2,000.[1] I need scarcely mention that when Shelley talked of leaving you this sum he contemplated reducing other legacies—& that one among these is (by a mistake of the Solicitor) just double what he intended it to be[2]—

Twenty years have of course much changed my position—Twenty years ago it was supposed that Sir Tim^{thy} would not live five years. Meanwhile a large debt has accumulated—for I must pay back all on which Percy & I have subsisted as well as what I borrowed for Percy's going to college. In fact I sca{r}cely know now how our affairs will be. Moreover Percy shares now my rights—that promise was made without his concurrence—& he must concur to render it of avail—nor do I like to ask him to do so till our affairs are so settled that we know what we shall have—whether Shelley's uncle may not go to law—in short till we see our way before us.

It is both my & Percy's great wish to feel that you are no longer so burthened by care & necessity—in that he is as desirous as I can be—but the form & the degree in which we can do this must at first be uncertain

From the time of Sir Timothy's death I shall give directions to my banker to honour your quarterly cheques for £30 a quarter—and I shall take steps to secure this to you & to Marianne if she should survive you—

Percy has read this letter & approves—⟨& we both⟩ I know your real delicacy about money matters & that you will at once be ready to enter to my views—& feel assured that if any present debt should press if we have any command of money, we will take care to free you from it.

Anxiety we shall not have for neither Percy or I will allow ourselves to be anxious where matters of ⟨delicacy⟩ necessity or [are] not concerned— but worry & business enough we shall have.

I believe we are going into Hampshire on Monday—When we return we hope to see you—& Percy will call to see how you are, and I hope find you all better

> With love to Marianne
> Affectionately Y˅
> MaryShelley

TEXT: MS., Humanities Research Center, University of Texas at Austin.

1. See 30 October 1826 to Leigh Hunt.

2. Claire Clairmont was bequeathed £6,000 outright and an annuity from an additional £6,000 during her life, which she could extend to another person whom she might name. This latter provision, included in Shelley's will of 24 September 1816, was probably in anticipation of the birth of Allegra; it is likely that given the amounts of his other bequests, Shelley, after Allegra's death, would have rescinded the annuity had he lived longer. In June 1835 Samuel Amory responded to two letters (unlocated) of Mary Shelley's inquiring about the annuity, and he confirmed that Claire Clairmont and whomever she designated were entitled to it (26 June, 30 June, Abinger MSS., Bodleian Library; a copy of Shelley's probated will, dated 18 February 1817, is in the Pforzheimer Library).

To Thomas Jefferson Hogg

Putney   24 April [1844]

Dear Jeff—

We hear that poor Sir Tim is falling from the stalk like an overblown flower—free from pain—quite comfortable, Hellen says, he has gradually lost strength appetite—sight & hearing & speech—breath only now remains.[1]

I ⟨suppose in⟩ should be sorry to {   } any thing imprudent—Of course we wish to be proper to Lady S. [Shelley] & just to John[2]—but he I am sure perhaps she will take every possible advantage—

But I conclude there is nothing to be done in the very first instance Gregson has all our papers—every one gives him a high character—& he has always shewn himself friendly.

But if you think any thing ought to be done, tell me.   A solicitor
from Horsham yesterday called with an introduction from Mr Beauclerk—who give us every information—but I did not think it proper to
ask any questions. It is likely enough that the same country solicitor wont
do for us & John—

All I mean by this letter is, that if there is any thing you think we
ought to do, that you will be so kind as to let me know.

Y^s truly

MaryShelley

TEXT: MS., Pforzheimer Library.

    1. On 24 April Percy Florence received the following note from his Aunt Hellen
Shelley announcing Sir Timothy Shelley's death: "My dear Father died this morning
at 6 o clock So quietly that his last breath was Scarcely heard   John has promised
to write to you & Says that he will invite you to his house for the Funeral but if you
prefer coming to us I need not assure you of a welcome   I will at all event write
again when any thing is settled   Mr Gregson will be here this Ev^g if he is in
Town   Pray remember us to y^r Mother & believe Me to remain My dear Percy Your
Aff^{te} Aunt Hellen Shelley" (Abinger MSS., Bodleian Microfilm, Bodleian Library).

    2. John Shelley.

❖

To Claire Clairmont

Saturday—Putney   27 April [1844]

Dearest Claire

I saw Gregson yesterday & all things seem to go smoothly enough—
Only I think it will be necessary for you to come over very soon. Gregson
can borrow any sum of money for us at 3½ per cent—& therefore we shall
raise money for the legacies &c & pay every thing off directly. You must
be here soon to settle what to do with your money—which will require
great consideration & care   You are very prudent in money matters—in
all matters of self denial—but do not fall into the Charybdis which has
swallowed so many fortunes & ruined so many lone females—trying to
get a large percentage for your money. However that is all matter for after
consideration. How do you stand now—do you want money for your journey?—If so let me know & I will send some. We have had none yet but
on Monday must get some.

Gregson thinks it a great shame that Percy is not named in Sir Tim's
will—at least that he did not leave him the securities I signed[1]—I did
not expect it & therefore we are not disappointed. The good of our po-

328

sition is that money can be got now on such easy terms of interest   Percy goes down to the funeral with Gregson on Monday—

I am very anxious to know where you can come—we have absolutely not room in this house—I cannot bear for a minute that you should be in wretched London lodgings—what can be done?

Do write & tell me that you get my letters—for since you wrote to tell me you were going directly to M^m de Maistre you have not written—from M^m Ivanoff I hear you were gone to St. Germain—But whether you are there now or whether you have received my letters I cannot tell.

Lady Shelley is left sole executrix—The girls have made up to them about £2500 each & all that Sir Tim could leave he has left to Lady Shelley during her life—strictly entailed on John & his children afterwards— John grumbles excessively at his Mother having every thing for life—but as he comes in for a good fortune & she is above 80—no great harm is done—But it shews the fruits of a heartless bringing up.

I am truly anxious to know when you can come—Would you like a lodging near us?—but that is so far from town—It is too bad not having a room to offer you—but such is the case—as you will see when you come.

Percy has bought a half decked sailing boat for the river & is deep in her rig—& happy.

God bless you dear Claire—answer this letter directly—Percy is happy to think he shall see you, without going to Paris which he detests.

Adieu   Aff^ly ys

MWShelley

ADDRESS: Madlle / Mlle de Clairmont / ⟨Rue Ne Clichy No 3 bis⟩ / ⟨Rue de Clichy⟩ / à Paris.   [*In another hand*] à st Garmains / Grand rue du p[ecq] / chez Mme Bertrand à St Germain En laye. POSTMARKS: (1) T.P / Putney N.O; (2) H / 27 AP 27 / 1844; (3) 2 ANGL[   ] 2 / 29 / [A]VRIL / 44; (4) ST. GERMAIN.EN.LAYE. 6E DIST / 29 / AVRIL / 44. TEXT: MS., Huntington Library.

1. For the repayment of the funds Sir Timothy Shelley had provided since 1823 (see 9–11 September [1823]).

❧

To Claire Clairmont

Putney   4th June [1844]

Dearest Claire—I am very sorry to hear you are so ill—especially as I had flattered myself that you were getting better—I hope being with Lady Sussex[1] suits you & does you good.

I fear, my dear Claire—we cannot serve you about your money & that you must come over. The burthens on the estate amount to £50,000—if money were scarce this w^d pretty nearly ruin us—as it is—it is necessary to pay them in such a way as will fall lightest. The thing we are advised to do is to raise the whole sum at once on mortgage which we can do at 3½ per cent—even so we have to pay nearly 2,000 a year interest—& 500 a year Lady Shelley's jointure—this joined to the necessary expences attendant on the care of an estate leaves Percy any thing but rich. A second mortgage is always to be greatly avoided & is very expensive. When we have raised the £50,000 to pay all—what could we do with four of yours?—only put it in the funds; which you can do as easily as ourselves—I am afraid dear Claire you must be satisfied with receiving at once the legacy of £12,000—& though just now money brings a low rate of interest—things may change & you may do better by & bye. Mrs Hare talks of putting some portion of her money in the Austrian funds which give 5 per cent—I am far from advising this or any thing that may not be safe. But there could be no harm in writing to your brother & asking his advise as to placing say £2,000 in the Austrian funds. I sincerely wish I had a room to ask you here—but we have not. You talk of coming to Boulogne in August—that is in your way here—& the trip may do you good.

The £50,000 is now being raised—I cannot tell you when it will be done—as these things are uncertain—A month or six weeks, I imagine is the time—By that time you ought in some way to understand what to do. Write to Mr Amory—to Mr Rawlinson to Mr Sanford. I will myself speak to the two latter, if you like, & hear what they have to say. You ought to write at once to Amory—It will cost you no trouble just to say "I expect my legacy to be paid in about a Month   can you advise me how to invest the whole or a portion in a safe manner at tolerably good interest—better that is than the funds." Coming over here might do your health good— If you could continue to be any where at all comfortable. You are within 6 hours of us at Boulogne—& if you came here, at any time you might be at Boulogne in 6 hours. From the little I have seen it looks as if our rents were more likely to be lowered that [than] raised—at least the leases of two of the best farms end at Michaelmas & the tenants ask to pay a less rent—& the farms are to be surveyed to see whether that is fair.

We are at this moment returned from Field Place where we were invited—They were all immensely civil—& Lady Shelley told Percy that she was sorry she did not know me before—Why then did she not?   Hellen however seems to have some heart, & speaks of her brother with enthusiasm. Field Place itself is desperate—it is so dully placed— & so dull a house in every way. Lady S. [Shelley] does not stay there—&

people say (London people I mean) that I ought to persuade Percy to live there—but how can I?—he would either spend all his money in going away from it—or be forced from sheer ennui to make love to the dairy maid. He shrinks from it—& no wonder—& for me, it would avail little whether I had 300 or 3,000 a year if I am to vegetate in absolute solitude—I have had too much of that. We shall see what we shall do. Lady S. has taken it till Michaelmas at all events, so we have time to reflect.

Percy is very well indeed—M[rs] Nicholls[2] is still in Ireland. Edward is rather a despair—however Peacock will get a place for him in the India House—& he it is to be hoped will work.

John Shelley has quarrelled with his Mother because Sir Tim left her so much. This of course renders her more enclined to be civil to us.

(I have heard that the Belgian funds give 4 or 5 per cent & are safe—but I cannot advise on these points—What is safe for a man, is often so unsafe for a woman—because he hears more what is going on & can be more on his guard.) I think that you had better at once make arrangements to come over here in 3 weeks—and take advise at [as] to what to do with the money—but I would have you write to Amory in the way I mention directly—You may remember When in Paris I spoke about your leaving some of your money with us—which you negatived then in the most decided manner.   Now [cross-written] that the 50,000 is raised, it is impossible—besides you must imagine that with such a burthen of debt, we must very very careful

Adieu Claire—Kind Compts to Lady Sussex.

Affcf[y] Y[s]

MS

TEXT: MS., Huntington Library.

1. Mary-Margaret, Lady Lennox (informally, Lady Sussex), wife of Lord Sussex Lennox. Gatteschi, described by Claire Clairmont as a scandalous adventurer, and Lady Sussex became lovers in 1844 (CC *Journals*, p. 220, n. 56; MWS *Letters*, III, 29 November 1842, ff.).

2. In January 1844 Mary Peacock married Lt. Edward Nicholls, who drowned in March 1844.

❧

To Richard Monckton Milnes

Putney   Wednesday   [?19 June 1844][1]

Dear M[r] Milnes

Poor Campbell is dead—£300 a year pension returns to Government—Do you think that Sir Robert Peel would be enclined to consider M[r] Leigh

331

TEXT: MS., Pforzheimer Library.

1. The references in this letter make it clear that Mary Shelley is discussing Hunt's *Imagination and Fancy; or Selections from the English Poets* (London: Smith, Elder, Co., 1844). The preface to the volume is dated 10 September 1844, and Hunt's correspondence indicates that he distributed copies of the volume c. 15 November (Hunt, *Correspondence*, II, 3).

2. In his introductory essay, "An Answer to the Question, 'What is Poetry,'" he refers to Dante and quotes from the *Inferno*, Canto 31, on pp. 12–16.

3. "My vision was greater than speech can show, which fails at such a sight, and at such excess memory fails. As is he who dreaming sees, and after the dream the passion remains imprinted and the rest returns not to the mind; such am I, for my vision almost wholly fades away, yet does the sweetness that was born of it still drop within my heart. Thus is the snow unsealed by the sun; thus in the wind, on the light leaves, the Sibyl's oracle was lost" (Dante, *Paradiso*, trans. Charles S. Singleton [Princeton: Princeton University Press, 1975], p. 375).

4. John Keats, "Ode to a Nightingale," in Hunt, *Imagination and Fancy*, pp. 341–44.

❧

To Marianne Hunt and Leigh Hunt

Putney   Friday   [?10 January 1845][1]

My dear Marianne

I wish you could be persuaded to go tomorrow to Severns to see his picture of Shelley. The nose is any thing but right—if you w^d only cut out one with your scissors[2] you would set it right—The mouth is defective—& so is the shape of the face—do look at it, if you can contrive—He goes out of town on Monday—

In haste

Yours truly
MShelley

Dear Hunt

Would you be so good as to give Knox an introduction to Charles Mathews[3]—He wishes to see him on the subject of a Comedy & w^d be greatly obliged of a line from you as introduction. Will you send it here tomorrow if you can—by post—Do you know where he is living at present

Yours truly
M Shelley

Knox says he will walk over to you with this himself

TEXT: MS., Bodleian Library.

1. The date is based on the following letter dated Monday 5 [error for 6] January

334

1845 from Severn to Leigh Hunt: "I am most anxious to have your opinion on my picture of Shelley which will be finished tomorrow—next week I go to Scotland, but before I leave I am most desirous to compleat my work, even including your valuable hints so if you can oblige me with a visit by the middle of the week I should be very glad" (MS., Bodleian Library).

2. See 17 December 1816, n. 4.

3. Charles James Mathews (1803–78), actor, whose wife, Lucia Elizabeth Mathews, Madame Vestris (1797–1856; *DNB*), managed Covent Garden Theatre.

❧

To {Alexander Andrew Knox}

[Putney   ?16–24 September 1845]

My dear Friend—

Putting the thing into the hands of you & your legal adviser[1]—I shall of course be guided by you.

Certainly it looks as if they would make no great use of my letters—but who can tell? They were written with an open heart—& contain details with regard my past history, which it w^d destroy me for ever if they saw light—possibly even if left to themselves they never may.

I suppose M Delessert[2] objects to acting unless you are well recommended—but I feel very doubtful of getting the letter from Trelawny—he is in Devonshir   I write to him by today's post & I will get the procuration—yet if my name is not to be used—wherefore?—Indeed I feel puzzled—but I put myself in yours & M. Peronne's hands—only keep my name secret I conjure you.

I do not understand what you mean by my leaving Putney—Since you have decided to act in this way—I shall certainly open no more of his letters, but forward them to you—but I if I left Putney the letters w^d be forwarded—you say dont start without consultation—consultation with whom? I have no human being to speak to—You fear perhaps his coming over he has no money for such a trip.—However as soon as I have got Trelawny's answer—& got the procuration I think I will go—In one way I dont think Claire's notion of my coming boldly to Paris a bad one—only it costs money—& might cause me to be talked of. I think therefore I shall take a trip as soon as I get your answer to this—explaining what you mean by consultation.—I will calm myself—the feeling that I shall open no more of his letters nor answer any is very calming

I think with Claire that his debts are not much—except a quantity of trifling to trades people but he wants the means of subsistence—& could not come over here I guess—However I shall go when I get an answer to this—perhaps before—but when you tell me to do a thing let me have an inkling <u>why</u>—or I hesitate   Especially when you add dont start without consultation—My idea is running with Percy to Broadstairs[3] where M[r] Rogers is—to stay a few days or more as I may like—

I think my plan as detailed w[d] succeed—but I leave it to you—You speak dreadful things of G—[*Gatteschi*] that he is a villain & only wants money of <u>course</u>—but do you know that his acts are so infamous as you say?

I am better in my head— my general health is suffering somewhat from the past suff{er}ing but not having to read any more nefarious letters or to write to him quiets me much—Dont forget to have the portrait[4] sent back—just done up & directed & sent without a word

M. Delessert & no Frenchman ought to see what he has written about expected commotion in Italy—It is a falsehood of course—but one's conscience must be clear of any betrayal of that sort—

It is all very dreadful—but being out of my hands, I will do my best not to think of it—Only as my name is not to be mentioned I do not see the use of the procuration—but you shall have it.

How kind—how more than kind you are—Heaven bless you—Dont worry yourself too much—I will take it all quietly now—I was reading the other day—The worst part of any evil is the fear of it—& fear too [*took*] so violent a possession of me—but I am better[5]

TEXT: MS., Huntington Library.
    1. Almost certainly the M. Perrone referred to later in this letter.
    2. Gabriel Delessert (1786–1858), banker and prefect of police under Louis Philippe. His wife, Valentine Delessert, and Prosper Mérimée were lovers from 1836 to c. 1848 (A. W. Raitt, *Prosper Mérimée* [New York: Charles Scribner's Sons, 1970], pp. 92, 110–11, 162, 226).
    3. A seaside town and urban district of the Isle of Thanet, approximately seventy-two miles east of London.
    4. Unidentified.
    5. The letter is incomplete.

❧

To Claire Clairmont

Thursday
[25 September 1845]   Putney

My dearest Claire—You are very kind to write so kindly—Beleive me in all the torturing pangs which I endured when this blow came, next to my Child, I felt for you & hated myself for bringing annoyance & injury on you—God grant you do not suffer—If indeed you find a talk arise, come over to us till it is worn away. You are hopeful in your letters & Knox praises much the sagacity of your views—I have told him to do nothing without consulting with you—& have put the whole affair in his hands. God grant him success—I shall open no more letters from G— [*Gatteschi*]—so indeed I shall not be a fair judge—but you will be consulted—he may fail in getting the perquisition[1]—G— instead of vituperation & threats may take to entreaty. I do not think that his views of extortion are so large as Knox fancies—I think 10,000 fr—is the outside—he would be content with half the sum—but the difficulty still is to get the letters at one blow—unexpectedly—without giving him an opportunity of abstracting any. There is another thing as I have told dear Knox—I have (after fancying him a hero & an angel & martyr—& because of the last covering him with benefits) looked on him as a sort of Matacini[2]—his hidious letters of menace made this name too honourable for him—but still he was driven by necessity—Necessities, if in part created by foolish vanity, yet rendered acute by the want of means for procuring his daily bread. But Knox uses expressions with regard to him that makes one's blood run cold—If indeed he is sunk in vice & infamy—I should regret that he ever touched another franc of mine which ought to be expended on worthier objects.—I do not know what to think with regard to Lady Sussex—her being at Boulogne looks as if she had not broken off all intercourse with him—& yet I think they have quarrelled—& as you say that speaks ill for him, as her generosity has been far more unbounded than mine. She sold her furniture—she got money on all sides—& when she came over here to London M[r] Rawlinson says that she was shabily dressed & evidently distressed for money—he has evidently drained her of every penny—but I think both their tempers being violent they have quarrelled—after all if he be the wretch described, even she w[d] sicken of him—nor could he endure the views of respectability & labour (such as going to Paris & giving lessons) which she opened to him to save him. Well, you saw his last letter to me—he is still waiting & utterly perplexed by my silence—but at last he will become furious—when he can hope no more, he will be eagre for revenge—however if my letters can be recovered, he can do me no great mischief—& if he be sunk as low as Knox describes, he can do nothing except curse—If he be still receiving money from Lady Sussex he might think of coming over here & therefore I wish a watch kept over the passports—for I would go far away on the instant—I ought to go now—but the weather is cold—& to the excessive agitation I suffered, has followed

337

a reaction of quiet & apathy which renders it very difficult to do anything. However I think if the weather does not change to bad again that tomorrow or the next day I shall go to Broadstairs for a few days—& then even further off—I cannot hope that all this wretched affair will end quickly—When it is over I shall breathe—meanwhile now is the moment—when G— is beginning to get desperate when dear Knox must watch for me more than ever & avert calamity from me & mine.

You see our plan of going abroad is overturned—for with difficulty could we have afforded it before, & now this miserable affair swallows up so much that we cannot manage it—the wretched season we have had & are still having makes this sacrifice seem greater & Mrs Hare being there————but it is all my own doing so basta.————Meanwhile I must tell you of another thing, which if it holds, reconciles me to staying—but say nothing about it to any one as yet—Percy has a plan of reading with a Conveyancer[3] & studying the law, as James Campbell is doing. He says he feels the want of an object—that all his friends are doing something & he is doing nothing—besides as he wishes to go into parliament he thinks this will be preparation. In short his income not being enough to permit him to yacht or to indulg{e} in careless expenditure he feels unoccupied—& cut off & isolated   He is spurred on also by worthier ambition. He promises me that if he begins he will go through with it for one year. This will at least give him information—develope his understanding, habituate him to habits of business & be the very best preparation for the House. You see this plan necessitates our taking a house in town (as will also his being in parliament as I hope he will be)   We must besides have some sort of piêd-a-terre in the country—some little cottage of our own—so that I need not be confined to town, but run down to my garden & chickens whenever I like—our cottage in the country must be on a very inexpensive plan & our house in town no great things. Percy prefers commencing on his plan this winter to going abroad, & so I suppose it will be—& for myself once extricated from this miserable affair, I may regard myself happy indeed in doing my best to make Percy's house happy. I have I confess a distaste to bringing myself into contact with society—which has ever been the source to me of mortification. When I go abroad I know I shall like what I get, new scenes & a fine climate—but unless I were far richer so to give dinners in my position, it is very difficult to get good society round one in London—However I have lived for these last 2 years so recluse a life that I am losing the faculty of conversation or of making one at all in company   It is as well to make a complete change & we shall see how things go.—We shall have to take & furnish a house—to choose one is difficult—to find a house

in a good quarter (& it is as well to be here as in a bad one) not too dear—
& large enough—for I must manage a spare room for you—We shall
see—for our means after all are very limited—& my first care & resolution
is to keep within them.

I have just got yours—a thousand thousand thanks. Put Knox at ease
on one point—I put the thing in his hands—& told him I should do
nothing—I have done nothing. I answered G's letter but enclosed the
answer to Knox to do what he liked with—he need not fear my com-
mitting him—I shall not again [*envelope, inside*] open a single letter coming from Rue de la B— [*Bienfaisance*]⁴ but send them to Knox—no more
have come. I cannot now answer you long letter every line of which is so
kind & welcome—I will only say that I doubt not that you will be attacked—not now at this minute, but later—but later you will wish to
come over here about your Opera box—we shall be settled in London (if
nothi[ng] dreadful happens) & do you come over to us—after a short time
they will forget us—at least so far as to hinder them from active injury—
if Lady S—[*Sussex*] does continue with them G's wants being less—so
will his mischief—O my letters once out of his hands—& I must submit
to what other ills he can create & not mind—God bless you dearest
Claire—I am better for the attack of my head is gone off—Evʳ Yˢ—

ADDRESS: Madlle / Mlle Clairmont / Rue des Marionniers No 8 / Passy / Paris.
POSTMARKS: (1) Putney S. [   ]; (2) TZ / 25 SP 25 / 1845; (3) 2 ANGL. 2 BOULOGNE /
27 / SEPT. / 45; (4) PARIS / 27 / SEPT. 45. TEXT: MS., Pforzheimer Library.

1. A search ordered by law for the discovery of a person or of incriminating
documents.
2. "A slightly mad but lively person."
3. A lawyer who prepares documents for the conveyance of property and inves-
tigates titles to property.
4. Identified as Gatteschi's residence in Claire Clairmont's letter of February
1844 (Abinger MSS., Bodleian Library).

❖

To Claire Clairmont

Brighton   Tuesday Evᵍ
[14 October 1845]

My dear Claire—Is it not all wonderful? Knox's firm & admirable conduct—his success—the authorities consenting to so desperate a step—
all—all is wonderful—& the more I hear the more I admire & am grateful—tho' too humiliated by the part I played, & by being the cause of

so much disagreable labour to exult. Poor Lady S— [*Sussex*] what can become of her! poor poor thing—what a situation—he cannot hurt her but who will help her?—for she is such an enemy to herself—how much she must now be enduring   What a monster it is—His conduct to her is so a thousand times worse than all. How did he make the acquaintance of Lady St. Germains?[1] And how idiotic has been his conduct; but lying & driving to desperation those whose services he wanted—& falling into utter ruin—It is dreadful to think that such a wretched being exists. It is strange—how strange the whole thing next to the immeasurable comfort of getting out of such nefarious hands. I rejoice for Knox's own sake that he succeeded—poor fellow worrying himself about my money &c— certainly I regret the large sums spent on so worthless an object—for I would so much prefer that were spent so as to benefit the deserving—but in escaping from such snares one cannot count pence   I do not write to Knox because I imagine he will have left Paris—if not tell him what I say—How glad I shall be to see him—what a change in me—I was nearly out of my mind when he went.

We leave this place on Thursday—I dont think now Percy's heart in danger but he wants to be occupied & following up his plans—the weather is warm & fine   The sea beautiful & so healthy—but we must go—& I am not in the humour to repine at any thing just now

Martini too ruined! What can be the end of all this? & he might have been respectable surrounded by friends—& even with this tie between him & Lady S— he might always have been above want—but he could not be satisfied—You may imagine that as yet every new account sent by Knox fills me with surprize & conjecture—I shall be glad to hear from you—I sincerely hope you will not be worried—if you are, you must come over, till the storm passes—for your sake it were better he were conducted to the frontier—& really when a man thus turns to stab with poisoned daggers those who desired & exerted themselves to benefit him, pity is a sin—besides he will not be worse off in one place than another he must fall into ruin on all sides—for he brings ruin on himself by his crimes—poor Lady S—   She indeed I do pity—I run on dear Claire saying nothi{n}g to the purpose—but can not compose my thoughts it is all so strange—but after a time his affairs will run in a new channel & he will forget the wild dreams awakened by foolish kindness—& sink far below our level—Meanwhile if you are annoyed or frightened come over would I could say to my house—but you know I have no room—still if you can come we could get a room near—& you could have the little room next my bedroom to sit in—at any rate you would be among us all— Goodnight—Percy is gone to a ball tonight   I am afraid it will be stu-

pid—he sadly wants to marry—I wish I could find a wife for him meanwhile occupation is the best thing—he feels this & wishes to occupy himself—he is so right minded—he ought to be happy—if he gets a
tolerably good wife he will be—God grant that he find such a one

Nothing can be so ridiculous as the newspapers—the bubble of the
day is to project railroads—not a quarter of the numb{e}r (not a tenth)
can be executed.   meanwhile they are the subject of gambling & will be
the ruin of thousands—for no one but a person versed in the science &
on the spot can do other than lose—the papers meanwhile publish 3 & 4
sheets of advertisements about them & this brings in a large sum to them
& to the revenue—

ADDRESS: Madlle / Mlle Clairmont / Rue Ne Clichy—No 3 bis / OC 15 / 1845; (2)
D / PA[ID] / 16 OCT 16 / 1845; (3) AN[GL   ] BOULOGNE / 18 / OCT / 45. TEXT:
MS., Huntington Library.

    1. Lady Jemima Cornwallis (d. 1856) married Edward Granville, third earl of St.
Germans (1798–1877; *DNB*) in 1824 (*Burke's Peerage*).

❧

To Alexander Berry

Putney   Oct. 24 1845

My dear Sir

    I was much grieved to hear of my poor Cousin's death[1]—Some years
ago our Aunt Everina told me that she did not consider herself in good
health—but in these days, life is so prolonged, that I hoped she would
be long spared to you. Such a companion, the friend & wife of years, is
never to be replaced—& so good a woman is a loss to the world. My regrets will reach you so long, long after the event that I will not prolong
them, to renew in you painful impressions. I had hoped that my Cousin
would have come over here, & that I should have seen her.

    I am afraid that many of my letters are lost.—I never received any an-
swer from my Cousin to any of the letters announcing poor Everina's
death, which took place in the Spring of 1843. Your & her kindness to
her was indeed great, and a comfort to me, who would otherwise have
been quite overwhelmed by the demands of one who had no consideration
for others. As it was she died a good deal in debt—as I wrote to poor M[rs]
Berry, and I was much inconvenienced & should have been far more, had
it not been for the kindness of the very excellent women in whose house
she died—who waited long for their money—tho' they could ill afford to
do so. I wrote also last year to announce the death of my father-in-law; I

341

cannot now exactly remember the date of my letter—sometime in September / 44, I think. Perhaps the letter has reached you since you wrote. You will see by that, that my Son has indeed inherited the family honours, but only a small portion of the family wealth—it would be a long story for a letter—but it is enough to say that by the exceeding injustice of his Grandfather, his estate is burthened by a heavy mortgage, & his means lessened more than one half of what they ought to be. He is of a happy cheerful disposition—& feels no discontent—tho' I do for him. I am in hopes he will get into parliament at the next election—but we are obliged to be very ⟨careful⟩—moderate & modest in our way of life. He has lett the family seat in consequence, & lives quietly in my cottage. He is upright, intelligent & amiable—so I have every reason to consider myself blessed—since with opposite qualities his fortune, were it even such as he is duly entitled to, would avail nothing either to happiness or honour.

I have to thank you for kindness to my friend Charles Robinson. Percy heard from him not long ago (he also appears by no means to receive all the letters written to him) he is much discontented with his lot[2]—& in this shares the feelings of the whole colony—but the Governor is recalled, so it is to be hoped things will go better—

Thank you for your kind promise of writing to me again. If there is any thing I can do for you in this country pray command me.   I hear your colony is reviving—We here are on the eve of changes. Sir Robert Peel is most ready to make them if his party would let him. While crops & harvests went well he could do nothing. But this disease among potatoes will famish Ireland. It can no longer send over its corn to us—& they say the ports are to be opened in England to foreign corn—but it is said that the supply from the continent (the demand not being expected nor provided for) will be very small. After a very wet, cold, dreary summer, I am in some hopes that we shall have a mild winter—that will lessen the sufferings of the poor—but if hunger is felt more than usual in Ireland, the coming months will prove critical—& must curb a party who forces the government to be illiberal—it may occasion my friends the Whigs to return to power—Every party is obliged to confess that the Whig administration in Ireland was singularly wise & successful.

I have written a long letter for me—for I suffer much from nerves, & am obliged to refrain almost entirely from writing. I shall hope to hear from you—& am ⟨dear⟩ Mr Berry

Yours truly   MaryWoll^{ft} Shelley

[*P. 1, top*]   Direct to me at Hook{h}am's library 15 Old Bond St. London

ADDRESS: Alexr Berry Esq / Sydney / New South Wales. POSTMARKS: (1) B / PAID / OC 2[   ] / 1845; (2) SHIP LETTER SYDNEY FE* 20 / 1846. TEXT: MS., Alexander Hay Collection, Mitchell Library, State Library of New South Wales, Sydney.

1. In his letter of 30 April 1845 Berry had informed Mary Shelley that Elizabeth Berry had died on 11 April 1845. Berry indicated his plans to establish a new cemetery, in which a vault would be built and both his wife's and her brother Edward's remains would be placed. This letter is the beginning of a correspondence between Berry and Mary Shelley that continued until her death; subsequently, Jane Shelley continued the correspondence until Berry's death in 1873, when his remains were interred with the remains of his wife and brother-in-law (MS., Alexander Hay Collection, Mitchell Library, State Library of New South Wales, Sydney; see also 14 January 1842, n. 1).

2. Charles Robinson had written to Alexander Berry on 27 April 1845 indicating that he would resign his post in New Zealand because "it is impossible to live upon the £140 a year I am paid, in such a manner as to preserve the respect that is necessary for the proper performance of my duties." In his next letter to Berry, dated 16 June 1845, he sent his condolences for the death of Elizabeth Berry; said he had written to Mary Shelley to inform her of the death; and indicated that he would leave New Zealand in two to three months (MSS., Alexander Hay Collection, Mitchell Library, State Library of New South Wales, Sydney).

❦

To Thomas Hookham[1]

Putney   Oct 28—[1845]

My dear Sir
From what Mr Finch[2] said I hoped to fine [*find*] a line from you telling me what you thought of the man who called on you & the letters in his possession. Can they be any among those lost with other things in Paris in 1814—I should like to know what you think about the matter. He did not call today. Does he want the letters bought of him—or what?

Yours truly
MShelley

Do you know whether Macauly[3] has written in the Edinburgh—any paper about the breaking of the peace of Amiens—or are there any good political articles in the Edinburgh (on our policy with France) relative to the years 1800 to 1805. If so would you be good enough to send them.

TEXT: MS., Henry W. and Albert A. Berg Collection, New York Public Library.

1. This is the first of eleven letters to Thomas Hookham that concern George Byron (1810–82) and the forged and original Shelley/Mary Shelley letters he marketed. George Byron, who claimed to be the legitimate son of Lord Byron (whose

letters he also forged), came into the possession of a large number of manuscript letters, including Byron's and the Shelleys', upon the death of a bookseller named John Wright on 25 February 1844. He subsequently made copies of these letters and other, already published letters and successfully sold them to Mary Shelley; Percy Florence Shelley; William White, a bookseller, who sold some to John Murray; and Edward Moxon, who bought some at auction. Moxon published some of the "Shelley letters" with an introduction by Robert Browning in 1852 but removed the volume from circulation when the letters were discovered to be forgeries. George Byron's copies were apparently well-executed, leading to considerable confusion about the authenticity of a number of Shelley and Byron letters. For a comprehensive study of George Byron see Theodore G. Ehrsam, *Major Byron: The Incredible Career of a Literary Forger* (New York: Charles S. Boesen; London: John Murray, 1951).

2. Unidentified.

3. Thomas Babington Macaulay (1800–1859; *DNB*), historian. I have found no essay by Macaulay on the peace of Amiens in the *Edinburgh Review*.

To Thomas Hookham

Putney—30 Oct. [1845]

Dear Sir—I have written to Mr Peacock about this affair—did you give his address in John St—for as our friend B [*Byron*][1] prefers the dusky hours he may not find him at the I. H. [*India House*]—

Most likely he will call on you again—& then the best possible thing w^d be for you to possess yourself of the letters at once. As to his saying he w^d give me mine that is all talk—he wants to sell them & to get money—he knows they are stolen & my property, & he is afraid they will be taken from him—& yet he cannot make up his mind how to ask or what to ask. In treating with a fellow of this sort a 3^d person is so much better   If you can get the letters at once for £20 get them & I will pay it at once—I dont think he ought to have more—& should be glad if half the sum sufficed.

We must not shew any great desire the man must feel that he can get something, but not much.

As those he shewed you are only a small portion of those lost, has he any more?

I should be very glad indeed if he saw you that you should settle it all yourself—I dont like seeing him—for he seems a disreputable person—and with such a third person manages things so much best—He wont give any letters—of that be assured.

I leave it to you to judge how to manage him if you see him—but it would be a very good thing if you got the letters out of his hands at once. I am so very truly obliged to you for the trouble you have taken

Y^s truly
MShelley

TEXT: MS., Henry W. and Albert A. Berg Collection, New York Public Library.
   1. I.e., George Byron (see 28 October [1845]).

❦

To Thomas Hookham

[?Putney]   Monday Ev^g [?3 November 1845][1]

Dear Sir

I send you the rascal's letter. This is the note that we wish you to send the man.

15 Old Bond St.

Sir

If you will call here on Monday Ev^g at 5 o'clock—I will communicate further with you on the subject of the Shelley letters & you will most probably receive the assistance you require on your giving up all the letters you had when you called upon me before—be so good therefore to bring them all with you.

I will call on you on Monday about one—but send this letter as soon as need be before 8 Monday A.M.

Y^s truly
MaryShelley

TEXT: MS., Henry W. and Albert A. Berg Collection, New York Public Library.
   1. This tentative date is based on the contents of the letter. The following Monday was 10 November. As the following receipt by G. Byron indicates, by 12 November he had received £30 for an unspecified number of letters, thereby concluding this phase of his dealings with Mary Shelley:

Sir

   I beg to acknowledge the receipt of thirty Pounds, and most solemnly declare once more that I cannot receive that sum otherwise than as a loan to be repaid in the course of twelve months. Please to give this assurance to Mrs Shelley. Circumstances prevent me from signing my name in full, but I trust you will mention to Mrs Shelley (as far as circumstances admit of it) the conversation I had with you.

G. B. ——————
London
Nov^{ber} 12, 1845.

To Thomas Hookham

Dear Sir You are very good to take all this trouble—the Rascal's notes make me sick

I went to see Peacock today—& meant to see you tomorrow, but I fear I shall not be able—so I write & being very tired will just succin{c}tly say what I can on the subject. Peacock says I did wrong to give any money—I am sure I did so in offering so much so readily. I am far poorer than any one knows or this rogue c^d be made beleive—not that he would care, so he got the money, whether I could well or ill afford it—but fancying me richer than I am makes him exorbitant.

Peacock says the fellow has brought himself within the law—he had better take care—he does not live at Greenwich certainly (for whatever he says must be false of that be sure) I wish he could be followed.

However to the point of course I would give £5 for the letters—but to offer this would be unavailing—& besides I fear he has many more—to offer so much per letter (one pound for instance) w^d be the only way—but this I would only give for Shelley's own—for the rest a pound a dozen w^d be enough.

Still we must not offer—He must be told that ⟨I cannot treat with him⟩ I demand all the letters as mine—or say what you will—I wish him to be made understand that I consider that he is playing the rogue & that he will make nothing by me—Thus he may be brought to the terms I have mentioned. I cannot afford to give more or I might be fool enough to do it—but I cannot

Have an eye to any auctions of autographs—will you be so good.

One pound per letter of Shelley's own

for all others half a crown—

but do not offer this I entreat. Let him bully & threaten a little more, & feel that I will do nothing & then he may avail himself of what I will do. The more letters he writes us—& the more blackguard & threatening they are, the better.

I dont beleive he has the impudence to take the name of Byron generally—tho' a swindlers name is only an alias of course

Ever Y^s MShelley

TEXT: MS., Henry W. and Albert A. Berg Collection, New York Public Library.

  1. The tentative date is based on "Feb. 28 / 46" written in pencil on the first page of this letter. Since Friday was the twenty-seventh, the twenty-eighth is probably the date of receipt of the letter.

&

To Thomas Hookham

Putney   Friday Ev^g
[?27 February 1846] (*b*)¹

Dear Sir

  A few more words—I mentioned £1 a piece for any letters of Shelley—
⟨I take it for granted that even if you have already written to this fellow
you have not mentioned this specifically because⟩ one or two things suggest themselves to me on this. I see you mention 8 letters of Shelley dated
1816—Are these to me? because otherwise I would not treat in the same
manner or on these terms—they must be <u>bona fide</u> letters <u>to me.</u>

  As to a fragment of an unpublished poem it is of course only a bit of
copy—& not worth regard

  (Except that I desire to possess every scrap in Shelley's hand—& if you
treat, you w^d bargain for <u>all</u>)—

  2 letters of M^{rs} S—do you mean Harriet—I doubt that they are hers—

  In fact the rest are mere private papers—of which the rascal could
make no possible use—but he must <u>give all up</u> or he will receive <u>no</u>
<u>money.</u>

  I fear he has <u>many more</u>

  The way we must manage is to demand all at so much a letter—Nothing unless he <u>give all</u>—but as I doubt Shelley's are bonâ fide letters to
me—in which case <u>I</u> w^d only give £5 for all—but it is better to treat at
so much per letter—

  Above all let me beg of you to shew every <u>backwardness</u> to treat at all.
I am not afraid of the rogue—he has more cause to fear me—& I would
buy these simply for the pleasure of having them—but cannot afford to
pay high for any pleasure & must therefore go without if he prove
impracticable.

  At so much <u>per</u> letter remember—as he has more & will come again—
& not more than I mentioned before.

TEXT: Medwin, *Shelley*, xviii–xix.

1. This tentative dating is based on Medwin's response of 17 May. In 1845 Medwin began his biography of Shelley, which was published in late August or early September 1847 (Lovell, *Medwin*, pp. 311–13).

2. In the preface to Shelley, *Poetical Works* (1839).

3. Although Medwin wrote to Mary Shelley several more times in regard to his biography, it appears that she purposely did not reply, believing that he was trying to extort money from her. However, his 17 May letter (Abinger MSS., Bodleian Library) only indicates that he intended to continue with the project:

Horsham   17th May 46

Dear Mrs Shelley

You tell me that my letter has surprised & pained you.—Why it should pain you I am at a loss to guess, & had thought that it was pretty generally known that I had long been engaged in this work.—

When you say that you have vindicated the memory of Shelley & spoken of him as he was—you seem to imply that I shall take a different course.—I have latterly met with Gilfillin's Gallery of Literary Portraits—& De Quincey's review of the same.—I am disgusted with your English writers with their accursed Cant—their cold false conventionalities—their abominable Claptrap—They should take a lesson from the Germans—I should like to show you a book just published, entitled Bürger Ein Deutscher Dichterleben—Poets are not to be squared by the rule and measure of ordinary mortals.—But how bright does Shelley's character come out—What a glorious creature he was, how infinitely above all those methodical hypocrites—that bow-bow at him.—

I remember seeing when we were at Pisa a work of considerable length that Shelley wrote, a book of History of Xst why do you not publish it.—How did he differ in his opinions from Paulus & Strauss and the Rationalists, who felt the theological chains in Germany—& drag from them the Divinity of Xst.—What does Ronge the new Luther teach—? Why you are 100 years behind the Germans—I speak not out {?of} my own Profession of Faith—Every one has his own & should have—but of the narrow-minded intolerance that reigns here.—Every Visit I make to England disgusts me more & more with it, & were it not that I come to see my dear old Mother I would never set foot in it again.—Germany is my foster Mother & there I have passed the happiest part of my existence.—there I mean to lay my bones.—It is cheap also to be buried there!!

But to return to your letter—You cannot suppose that I shall undo the arrangement I have made for the publication which will take place in about a month or 6 weeks at latest.—& you shall have a Copy among the first—It will be translated in Germany by a friend of mine a most accomplished person a Lady who has done more justice in her translations to our Lady Poets than any other I know of Mad. de Ploennies—& who has admirably rendered some of Shelley's Minor Poems.

My hands are so cold that I can scarcely write & this is the middle of May.

Yours truly
TMedwin.

PS. I am much grieved to hear that you are still suffering from ill health, & think you do right to try the air of Italy, which I hope & trust will restore you— I think when I was here last Autumn you had such an Intention—

I saw Howitt when I was in town last week—& have promised to dine with him—I think you know Mary Howitt.—They were neighbours of ours in Baden—for a winter. He tells me of a work entitled Homes & Haunts of Poets.—Of Course Shelley will find a place there.—The Visit I paid last year to Field place was a melancholy one. The place dismantled—the family scattered.—& who about to inhabit it—a London Alderman!

To Leigh Hunt

24 Chester Sq   Wednesday   [?3 June 1846]

My dear Hunt

I am much obliged to you for your kind expressions. I am totally indifferent on the subject you mention—& it has never given me an uneasy moment—An attempt to extort money finds me quite hardened—I have suffered too much from things of this kind not to have entirely made up my mind. I told Mrs Hogg, because as she had known Captain Medwin it was possible that he might make some sort of communication to her—but I never dreamt of answering his letter or taking any notice of his threat. The fact is he could not find any bookseller to publish his trash, so he thought, by working on my fears, to dispose of it to me. Unfortunately for his plan & for my own comfort I have had too much experience of this sort of villainy & his attempt is quite abortive. He may certainly find a bookseller to publish a discreditable work—but really I cannot bring myself to care the least about it.

As far as I recollect the note unanswered was an invitation to dinner—but the current of my life & thoughts has been so interrupted of late, that I do not remember any thing about a letter—I have suffered a great deal of painful illness—& am still a complete invalid. My chief illness, neuralgia, keeps my nerves in so painful a state, that repose & quiet are the only goods I am capable of enjoying, or which I covet. In the hope of getting better, Percy & I spent 6 weeks at Cowes—but I returned no better—However as it is chiefly Neuralgia the physicians make small account of my illness—Percy has been exceedingly anxious & was unspeakably attentive to & careful of me—I shall get away from town as soon as I can—for as I cannot see any society, there is nothing to keep me here

351

I am delighted to hear of your new employment and I hope it is a good in every way—If you ever come into town pray call on us—we shall be very glad to see you   Percy desires his kindest remembrances   I am Y^s Aff^{ly}

MShelley

TEXT: MS., Pforzheimer Library.

❖

To Thomas Hookham

[Baden-Baden]   Saturday
12 Sep. [1846] (*a*)

Dear Sir

I of course expected this sort of thing to happen—And you know how totally hardened I am against this ⟨sort⟩ species of rascality. Mr Byron[1] has of course got other & will get other copies—& to keep these is of no avail—I am not sure that the best mode of action is not to let him have them again (except that one w^d not voluntarily put them in his hands)—& defy him to make any use of them—for what use is it to make a fuss about keeping one set of copies, when having another, he can make as many as he likes? O course I wish you in my name to relieve Mr Holcroft from all onus on the subject. It is very disagreable to be brought into contact with M^r H— [*Holcroft*] whose letter is disgusting to me, tho the feeling that dictated it had something of good in it—he is not of course such a person as Mr Memoir—but he is ⟨a person I do⟩ one with whom I do not wish to come in contact—Say every thing civil from me to him—& tell him that I hold the efforts of such swindlers as Mr Memoir in such contempt that my impulse is to defy them, without more comment or care.

I have written to a young friend of Percy's & mine Mr Knox with whom I wish you to talk over the matter before you act—He is a lawyer very clear-sighted—& I should depend on his advice on the subject   I fancy—he will counsel defiance merely—as w^d Peacock & Jefferso{n}— and indeed under the circumstances it seems, in the last resort, ones only resource—so it may be better to begin with it.

I am very much obliged to you for your kindness in all this. Your friendship for Shelley ⟨& that you [   ] are⟩ naturally leads you to

wish to serve his Name—and I am obliged to you for all the zeal & kindness you have shewn me.

The great thing will be avoid police reports & police Magistrates—

I am dear Sir

Yours Very truly

MShelley

My health is, I trust slowly mending—but I am still far from well—I
will preserve carefully Mr T. Holcroft's letter   Do not let him come in
contact with Mr Knox.

Don't put via Belgium or via any thing out side your letter

My address is

153 Promenade

Baden-Baden

ADDRESS: Thos Hookham Esq / 15 Old Bond St. TEXT: MS., Henry W. and Albert
A. Berg Collection, New York Public Library.

1. See 28 October [1845]. At this point several new figures appear in the course
of George Byron's new offer to sell letters to Mary Shelley. Thomas Holcroft appears
to have served as an intermediary, but one friendly to Mary Shelley (see correspondence below). The swindler Memoir was, in fact, George Byron himself (Ehrsam,
Major Byron, p. 27).

The Berg Collection holds two letters from Holcroft to Hookham:

3 North St.

Tuesday

15/8./46

My dear Sir

Acting on the maxim, "Fas est ab Hoste doceri" I copy for your guidance
the legal interdict wch I recd from Mr Byrons Solicitor in re Shelley Papers—

15 Old Bond Street

Sept: 15, 1846

"Sir

I hereby give you notice not to deliver the letters, copies of letters, or any
other papers you obtained (received) from Mr Byron to that person or any other
person or persons without the written authority of Mrs Shelley, her heirs representatives or other persons authorised to act on her behalf, the said copies of
letters &c—being her sole property—

I am Sir

Your obed^t Ser^t

(Signed) Thos Hookham."

I have slightly modified the terms to suit the circumstances—I need not say
how sincerely I appreciate your prompt and efficient service yesterday—I write
this in Case when I Call you should be out or engaged—

Yours faithfully

Thos Holcroft

353

The date "15/8./46" at the top of this first letter from Holcroft is almost certainly an error for "15/9./46." And the maxim may be translated as "It is right to be taught even by an enemy."

The second letter follows:

3 North Street—Friday   [?September 1846]

Dear Sir

A Summons has issued from Bow Street out of this Byron-Shelley business—It is returnable on Monday at Two—Can you by any means conveniently attend? as it is possible the question may turn upon your former agency in the Matter—I am at Hampton Court fishing which will account for the tardiness of this notice—

Your mo. ob. Srv^t
Thos Holcroft

To Thomas Hookham

153 Promenade   Baden-Baden
12 September 1846 (b)

Dear Sir

I authorize you to possess yourself of & to keep possession of the copies of letters (my property) which you mention to me—as they are mine by law & cannot in any way be published by any one else. I will of course take care to guarantee you against the consequences of your acting in this manner for me.

I am dear Sir
Yours truly
MaryShelley

TEXT: MS., Henry W. and Albert A. Berg Collection, New York Public Library.

To Alexander Berry

24 Chester Sq—London   29^t March 1847

Dear Mr Berry

Charles Robinson dined with us today—& I enquired whether he had heard from you—he had not—so it is a long time since a letter has reached us. Charles remembers your kindness with much gratitude & I am ⟨so⟩ thankful to you for being so good to a friend of mine that we both wish you not to forget us—& Charles looks forward to the time when he may have the pleasure of seeing you again—His plans are still uncertain—for he has not yet got a place & feels very impatient—tho' his friends bid him be patient & that he will be sure to get one—Had he arrived while the Tories were in office he would not have had to wait so long—but the Whigs are noted for only giving places to Greys & Howards—people of their own kin—Still Charles is so well recommended both by his own personal character & by the influential friends he has that I sincerely trust that there is no doubt but that he will be recompenced as he deserves.

Just now indeed politics are in a strange position & the famine in Ireland[2] engrosses the attention of Government. The universal scarcity felt on the continent of Europe as much as with us—has so raised the price of corn that the fears of the Protectionists are for the present allayed—but it is fearful to think of Ireland & the million a Month sent her from England—& the unfortunate propensities of the people who, in the hopes of money from this country, can scarcely be induced to sow seed for next harvest. All parties here shrink from the load of responsibility—in Government & no one I fancy envies Ld John Russell—not even Sir Robert Peel—

I sincerely hope that Percy will get into parliament next election—but the dissolution will not take place till next Autumn.—Your late Governor Sir George Gipps[3] is dead you see—but before this he had lost the power of injuring the Colony—The recall of Sir Eardly Wilmot[4] is now a principal colonial subject. Lord Stanley[5] having moved that Mr Gladstone's[6] dispatch recalling Sir Eardly should be printed. Lord Stanley's own speech is looked upon as doing Sir Eardly no good—& Mr Gladstones dispatch recalling him is, I am assured, a curious specimen—he tells Sir Earlly that ⟨there is⟩ he has been accused—& that he has been defended—& that he does not know which is the true statement—but "there is something between certainty & uncertainty" & on that he founded his recall. There are rumours of changes in the modes of governing the colonies—& Lord Grey is very active & intends to be very reforming[7]—You will know best whether he will do any good. Charles Robinson tells me he got a Sidney Newspaper the other day—if it came from you he thanks you. How does the plantation round Mrs Berry's & her brother's tomb thrive? I am interested on that subject & shall be very glad to hear from you—I am Y^s ever truly   MShelley

[*P. 1, top*]   Percy desires to make your acquaintance at least by a friendly message. We hope all is going on well with you

[*Envelope, inside*]   The mourning seal is for Lady Shelley—Percy's grandmother—Her death makes him some what richer

ADDRESS: Alexander Berry Esq / Sidney / New South Wales / Australia. POSTMARKS:
(1) T.P. / Ebury; (2) PAID / CO / 30 MR 30 / 1847; (3) SHIP LETTER SYDNEY / JY*
26 / 1847 / SYDNEY. TEXT: MS., Alexander Hay Collection, Mitchell Library, State
Library of New South Wales, Sydney.

1. "29" is superimposed over "22."

2. The 1846–47 famine in Ireland resulted from the failure of the potato crop,
which was destroyed by blight. An outbreak of typhus followed the famine, causing
vast numbers of deaths. Emigration was the chief means of escaping starvation and
epidemic, and the population of Ireland fell from 8.5 million in 1845 to 6.55 million
in 1851.

3. Sir George Gipps (1791–1847; *DNB*) became governor of New South Wales
in 1838 and resigned in early 1846. He was much criticized for asserting the absolute
right of the crown. In the 1840s Gipps clashed with sheep owners because he wanted
to keep unoccupied land for future generations, while the sheep owners wanted the
land then. There was general economic depression, which began to improve in 1847.
Gipps died in England on 28 February 1847. In his 1 August 1847 response to this
letter, Berry said that though Gipps was dead, the evil he had done was not (MS.,
Alexander Hay Collection, Mitchell Library, State Library of New South Wales,
Sydney).

4. Sir John Eardly Wilmot (1783–1847; *DNB*), lieutenant governor of Van Die-
men's Land (Tasmania), was held responsible for the terrible conditions of the large
convict population. He was superseded on 13 October 1846 and died on 3 February
1847.

5. Edward George Geoffrey Smith Stanley, fourteenth earl of Derby (1799–1869;
DNB), statesman, was Colonial Secretary under Peel.

6. William Ewart Gladstone (1809–94; *DNB*), statesman and author.

7. Berry responded that he believed Lord Grey "influenced by the insane theories"
of Gipps; that Wilmot was comparatively innocuous; and that no great country had
been "so misgoverned" as had the British Empire since the reform bill, as evidenced
by the people starving in Ireland and in New South Wales (1 August 1847).

To Leigh Hunt

11 July [1847]   13 Bedford Sq   Brighton

My dear Hunt

I see Medwins "Life" advertized as about to be published by Newby[1]—
Of course it will be a most blackguard Publication—tho' I do not think
he will make it as scandalous as he threatened.

Allow me now to ask you as a mark of friendship & kindness to me,
to use all your influence to prevent <u>any notice whatever</u> being taken of it
in the Newspapers

I have had another letter from him in which he says he expects it "to
make a great hubbub." & "cares nothing at all for critics"—Notoriety is

the aim of such a fellow—or rather Money which he hopes to gain thro'
Notoriety.   That the press should cavil, set right, or expose or censure
his work is the thing he aims at. I must earnestly desire that it may fall
dead born. Will you use your influence with Mʳ Fontblanque—I think
he will not be averse to complying with my wishes—but alas!—A newspaper Editor is so fond of publicity but do if it be possible contrive that
no respectable paper—& above all the Examiner should take the slightest
notice of it—

As you know he offered last year not to publish if I would pay him
£250 for his silence²—his letter was a threatening one—to which I returned no answer—The other day I got another, not in the same tone &
offering to send me the book—but when a Man has once acted towards
me as a rascal I have no further communication with him & did not answer him—I dare say it will prove a most empty and stupid production   Whatever it may be, I shall not read it.

Do not disturb your head by answering me—only act for me in enforcing
silence whenever you can & you will benefit me. I am getting stronger
but these things are not good for nervous disorders—I hope you have
changed the air [cross-written] the best thing for invalids

Ever Affʸ Yˢ

MShelley

Pray tell Mʳ Fontblanque that last year Medwin wrote to me to say his
book would contain things disagreable to me but that if I would pay him
(he did not specify the sum, but made it appear something more than
£250—) he wᵈ suppress the book & enter into an agreement never to
publish on the subject in question—

Of course I returned no answer to so ruffianly a letter

You will know best whether it be not better to speak to Mʳ Foster [For-
ster] than to Mʳ Fontblanque³—I am not acquainted with Mʳ Foster—but
I am sure he would listen to you & above all not serve the aims of such a
fellow as Medwin by taking any notice of them his aim being to make
money by publishing scandal.

TEXT: MS., Pforzheimer Library.
   1. Advertisement appeared in the *Examiner* of 10 July 1847, p. 448:

Mr. [T. C.] Newby's New Works by Popular Authors
   1. *Life of Shelley* by Captain Medwin, Author of "Conversations with Lord
      Byron," Ec. Just ready, in 2 vols.

   2. See [?13–16 May 1846], n. 3.
   3. Albany Fonblanque (1793–1872; *DNB*) and John Forster (1812–76; *DNB*),
writers, were editors of the *Examiner*.

To Leigh Hunt

13 Bedford Sq   Brighton   Thursday
[?22 July 1847]

Dear Hunt

You are very kind indeed—I believe, as you say, the Life was never so injuriously written, but for the sake of extorting money, he tried to frighten me—& a Man who could commit that sort of low crime is capable of any thing. Tho' not so injurious—I am sure the book will be a disgrace to dear Shelley's name & an annoyance to all connected with him—& that it should be passed over in silence is the most honorable way in which the press can act.

For the rest, dear Hunt, I leave it to you—I agree with you that pushing the Matter is only to awaken attention. For myself the Man's letter & the advertisement[1] disturbed me greatly & nervous as I am made me ill—but having got over that I shall dismiss the whole affair from my mind & shall only be too grateful if it is not dragged before my eyes by articles in the Newspapers. I will not read a line—I will not look at the book if I can help it—I hope Mr Newby will not send it to me—for I dislike doing a rudeness but I should send it back directly—The attempt to extort money outlaws the Author in my eyes—but I do hope the book will not be sent me. I should counsel you not to read it—I am quite sure that it is a vulgar disgusting production. He says that it is slashing—& will make a hubbub—O the delight & joy of Silence   If only I could command that with regard to it—It is all I ask.   I leave it all to you—but would not give the book the importance of Your taking too much trouble or notice.

I hope Marianne is fast recovering, & that I shall soon hear of your changing the air which is the best remedy for all illness—especially to Convalescents

Ever truly Y^s
MShelley

TEXT: MS., British Library.
   1. See 11 July [1847].

358

To Charles {Robinson}

[?24 Chester Square]   Monday
[?18 March 1848]

Dear Charles

Percy called yesterday, but did not find you. Will you dine here one day this week (not tomorrow) & you will see Mʳˢ St— John¹ who is a prize indeed in the lottery ⟨not as rich⟩ being the best & sweetest thing in the world—She is not however nearly as rich as Rosa² was told

I have had long letters from Mʳ Berry, which I shall answer at the end of the Month

Yˢ truly
MShelley

TEXT: MS., Pforzheimer Library.

1. Jane St. John (1820–99) and Sir Percy Florence Shelley, who met in 1847, were married on 22 June 1848 (see Mary Shelley's letters to them of that date). Heretofore, very little has been known about Jane Shelley's background. She was born Jane Gibson, one of nine children of Ann Shevill (?1790–c. at least 1866) and Thomas Gibson (1759–1832), banker of Newcastle-on-Tyne (and not, as commonly indicated, a member of the clergy). Jane Gibson's parents apparently never married, and the baptismal records of the first three of Ann Shevill's children—Harriet, Isabella, and Ann (d. 1865)—state that they are the illegitimate daughters of Ann Shevill and Thomas Gibson, banker. Jane's other siblings' baptismal records, as well as her own, indicate only the name of their mother, as spinster.

Thomas Gibson's will provided for the mother and surviving children of "my friend Ann Shevill." To each child he left £5,400, the boys to receive their legacy at age twenty-one, the girls upon marriage. Upon the death of Thomas Gibson, Jane and Edward, a favorite younger brother, were sent to live with their father's sister and her family, the John Speddings, at Bassenthwaite, a few miles south of Keswick, in the Lake District, where she reports having seen Southey and Wordsworth.

In 1841 Jane Gibson married Charles Robert St. John (1807–44), son of George Richard St. John, third viscount Bolingbroke and fourth viscount St. John (1761–1824), and his second wife, Isabella Antoinette (d. 1848). George Richard St. John had at least fifteen children, the first and last three of whom were legitimate, by two marriages and one alliance. Charles Robert St. John was among the last three, although a number of his older siblings were illegitimate because his father was already married when he entered a "private" marriage in 1795 with his second wife. (His parents were officially married in 1804, after the death of George Richard St. John's first wife.) Between these marriages, George Richard St. John had four children with Mary Beauclerk, his half sister. (His mother, the former Lady Diana Spencer [1784–1808; *DNB*], out of an alliance with Topham Beauclerk [1739–80; *DNB*], gave birth to Mary Beauclerk in 1766, thereby causing George Richard St. John's father to divorce his mother. Lady Diana, who married Topham Beauclerk in 1768, was

359

therefore a grandmother of two families important in Mary Shelley's history: the Beauclerks and the St. Johns.

Jane St. John was widowed in 1844 when Charles Robert St. John died of a protracted illness. No children were born of this marriage. Charles Robert St. John, however, had fathered an illegitimate son, named Charles Robert St. John, to whom Jane St. John became guardian.

Unpublished as well as published accounts suggest that the marriage of Percy Florence and Jane Shelley was a happy one. For Mary Shelley, the match was ideal both for her son's sake and for her own, since she and Jane Shelley formed an unusually strong bond of mutual love and admiration. With her son's marriage, Mary Shelley's circle was increased to include the Gibson and St. John families, with whom Jane Shelley was on close terms (I am indebted to Canon Brian Carne and William L. Jacob for kindly providing me with their careful research on the St. John and Gibson families, which has largely appeared in the *Reports of the Friends of Lydiard Tregoze*. Other sources include: unpublished letters of Jane Shelley, Alexander Berry, and Sir Charles Nicholson [Alexander Hay Collection, Mitchell Library, State Library of New South Wales, Sydney]; Maud Rolleston, *Talks with Lady Shelley* [London: George G. Harrap and Co., 1925]; and Public Record Office, Carlisle).

2. Rosa Beauclerk, Charles Robinson's sister.

❖

To Augusta Trelawny

24 Chester Sq   10 June [1848]

My dear Augusta

Trelawny told me when I saw him in the winter that you would be glad to see me if I visited your neighbourhood (as I did last Autumn—but was then too ill to seek anybody) & therefore I think you may not be displeased to hear from me.—This is a most interesting moment to me, for Percy is about to be married. He is most fortunate in his choice—She is a young Widow. She married 7 years ago one of the St. Johns—She says one devoid of the defects of the family—perhaps Trelawny knew him at Florence—Charles a younger brother of Ferdinand—however he was in ill health all their married life & lived in the country in England—he died 5 years since

She is in herself the sweetest creature I ever knew—so affectionate so soft—so gentle with a thousand other good qualities ⟨too long⟩—she looks what she is all goodness & truth. She has no taste for society & will thus participate in Percy's taste for a domestic quiet life & now as a married man he will settle at Field Place. She has a little money.

When I saw Trelawny I fancied another match might have come about

360

which would have suited him as little as this suits him well—for he is not fitted to guide & tutor a young girl—while his present choice is but little younger than himself.

I have often heard of you from James Campbell—Your present house is beautiful I hear—& I well know in what a lovely county it is placed—Your children thrive & are beautiful—& all goes well with you.

You will even after so a long time have lamented dear Georgina.[1] She was a great loss to me & her death was a cruel one—arising from accidental causes—& taking her from us, just as we were rejoicing to think that her health was restored. Her son was away at the time—he is now travelling in the East.—I could write you a long gossiping letter about old acquaintance if you cared to receive it—I shall be glad if ever I am able to make a trip to Chepstow again—I liked it so much when I was there

You know of course that James Campbell's projected marriage is quite off. I beleive now that he could even see the young lady without danger—so completely is the spell broken—but he will not be exposed that danger.

Remember me kindly to Trelawny & beleive me to be

Affectionately Y^s

MaryShelley

ADDRESS: Mrs Trelawny / Keven Ila / Usk / Monmouthshire. POSTMARKS: (1) [   ] / JU—12 / 1848; (2) USK / 13 [   ]. TEXT: MS., Bodleian Library.
    1. Georgiana Beauclerk Paul died on 25 December 1847.

◆◆◆

To Sir Percy Florence Shelley

[24 Chester Square]   22 June [1848][1]

Darling Percy
    You are very happy—so with a thousand blessings I am

Y^s happy &

Affte   Mother

TEXT: MS., Pforzheimer Library.
    1. The wedding day of Percy Florence Shelley and Jane St. John. The wedding took place at St. George's, Hanover Square. The marriage certificate was witnessed by Mary Shelley, Anne Hare, and Edward Gibson, the bride's brother, and lists Jane St. John's residence at that time as Marnhull, Dorset. The ceremony was performed

by George Frederick St. John (1795–1867), eldest though illegitimate son of George Richard and Isabella Antoinette St. John (see [?18 March 1848], n. 1). George Frederick St. John had both a Bachelor of Arts (1816) and a Master of Arts (1823) from Balliol. In 1820 his father had purchased the patronage of Manston Church, Dorset, for his son, who presided there until his death (Canon Brian Carne, report no. 9 [1976], *Reports of the Friends of Lydiard Tregoze*).

❖

To Jane, Lady Shelley

[24 Chester Square]   22 June [1848]

My own dear Child

You forgot your Watch—I keep it for you—but send the key of Your dressing case

A thousand blessings on you my darling Jane   I know you will make Percy happy—Please God, you will be happy together

Affectionately Y^s
MaryShelley

ADDRESS: The Honble / LadyShelley. TEXT: MS., Pforzheimer Library.

❖

To Alexander Berry

24 Chester Sq   30 June [1848]

Dear Mr Berry

You are very good to write me such long & really interesting letters. You live, you say, a hermit's life—but your writing has all the vivacity of youth—& shews the deep interest you take in your Country & its welfare. A Colony—where one can at once perceive the operation of the social laws—presents a wide field for enquiry & the acquisition of knowledge. At the same time there is melancholy attached to it—the melancholy spectacle of misgovernment. This is particularly mortifying in the cases of such men as Sir G. [*George*] Gipps & Lord Grey—for they mean well, while they do so much mischief. We boast of our improved lights[1]—& our books overflow with philosophical principles, yet our public men perpetually make the grossest mistakes, & all they do, had better be left undone. Lord Grey has always been called a crochetty man—a Man of schemes, who will neither hear nor see reason (speak it ever so loud, look it ever so big) against his own preconceived ideas. At the present moment he has given a grievous specimen of this defect with regard to the West Indies.[2] You will see the details in the papers, so I need not fill my paper with them. The matter will, it is beleived ruin him as a public Man. The Whig Ministry are likely to resign, when left in a minority on the sugar question—probably no other Ministry will be formed, & after 24 hours they will return to office—but Ld Grey, it is to be supposed will be left on the way side. And who will be his successor? & what new plans will he try to work out. He will not be a Saint, it is to be hoped for Saints are most of all to be dreaded from their fatal habit of always confiding in Men who talk their talk, however incapable or dishonest they may be— Our colonies are just now of the mightiest import, while strange & ⟨mighty⟩ fearful events are in progress in Europe. Barbarism—Countless uncivilized men, long concealed under the varnish of our social system, are breaking out with the force of a volcano & threatening order—law & peace. In Germany the bands of society are entirely broken—no rents are paid—the peasant invades the Chateau—& would take it—were it worth his while—as it is, he demands a dinner & it is given him. In France how unscrupulous was the flattery that turned the heads of the working classes & produced the horrible revolt just put down. With us the Chartists have lowered themselves greatly for the present—but tho' their demonstrations are at an end, their numbers are on the encrease & before many years there will be surely great great changes in England. (I have just seen the Times—the Ministry have a majority about the sugar, So there will be no change yet)—But now let me turn to private matters. You say in your letter "Were you a young Man of Percy's age & fortune you w^d devote yourself to scientific pursuits & the improvement of your estates, instead of embroiling yourself in politics." These words have reached us at an opportune moment—When I wrote last in March, Percy was canvassing the boro of Horsham—he was then a single Man, Now he is married— he has given up politics & is about to settle in the country—on his estate. He has made a most happy marriage. The lady was a Widow. She was a Miss Gibson—married to the youngest son of the late Lord Bolingbroke   Her husband was an invalid & died after 2 years a period she spent nursing him with the tenderness of a Mother—She had no family. She is very pretty—but that is her least merit. I never knew any one so good, true & affectionate. She never thinks of herself—all her thoughts are spent on those she loves—her tastes are quiet & domestic. Percy deserves so good a wife—& please God they will be long happy together & I hope to share their happiness living at Field Place with them occupied by improving the estate & being of use to the tenants   She has a fortune

To Isabella Baxter Booth

Cadinabbia on the Lake of Como
26 May 1850

It is long, my dear Isabel, since I have written to you & before this I expected to have given you tidings of my return to England. Thank God, We have every reason to think that the object of our journey is accomplished and that Percy's dear Wife has got over her alarming malady— This is a great blessing—& unexpected during the winter—when she was constantly ill, & we suffered the greatest anxiety. The remedies & medecine given only served to weaken her; At last she consulted a German Homeopathic docter—of course you know about them & their infinitesimal doses—Although Jane is as by magic recovered, I do not quite give credit to his invisible medecine—but rather to his having recourse (without my knowledge) to the hazardous experiment of cold water applications. As Jane's illness has become almost entirely one of weakness—this method gave her strength & health. She yet suffers from nervous attacks—but the dangerous symptoms are all gone—& as she gains strength—We trust that every thing will get right. As LadyShelley took little Nothings to cure here—I, having long come to the conclusion that all Medecine did me harm,—followed her example—but not with like success—I was far from well all the winter—they say my illness is rhumatism of the nerves—& Nice with its dry, irritating air was not fitted to sooth them. With short intervals I suffered very much both through spring & winter—& have indeed just this last day or two, got over a severe attack—It renders me very weak & helpless—but I still live in hopes of getting the better of it some day—If no untoward accident occurs,—& if I can live almost entirely in the open air   Unless more is the matter than the docters suppose—inability to walk & nervous spasms are my chief ills—bad enough sometimes

When I was feeling tolerably well, I found Nice very pleasant—from its scenery & the pretty rides—I could mount a donkey though I could not walk—& with an intelligent, indefatigable country girl as a guide I often took longer rides than I ought over hill & through ravine—& wood:—When I was well enough to do this, it was very delightful—for every view was varied—& sea & Mountain formed a thousand changing landscapes.

Our winter was fine—but with March came the cold winds—& there never was such a spring—I hope it has not been as proportionately bad

366

with you. At Nice it never rains scarcely—& this year it did not at all—
Vegetation was retarded & the winds blinded is [us] with dust when exposed to it.—Here in the North of Italy they have had continual rains
for two Months.—It was this circumstance that rendered the plan of returning home by the Alps a bad one at this time of year—but Percy &
Jane set their hearts on it—& here we are—We have been here a week—
waiting to hear that the pass of the St. Gothard is open—Of this last
week—4 or 5 days have been of pouring rain; during this new one in
which we are entering we hope to have sunshine & towards the end of it,
to be able to cross. Percy & I were ten years ago—ten years which have
made me old—& the changes found here have forced Percy to feel that
boyhood is indeed passed—Yet we have found the old alive & very little
altered—but the stalwarth & youthful—many of them dead & the children sprung up to men & women.

And your—dear Isabel—how is it with you? Is your health better?—
You have such clever docters in Scotland—cannot they put you on a plan
for getting rid of your illness?—Your daughter & her little brood,[1] how
are they? And Mr Stuart—do his Mills prosper—& his people thrive under his energetic & most laudable endeavours for their improvement? I
shall be so glad to hear from you. I wrote to my friend (entrusted with
furnishing you with the Times) & he said that they had been sent [*p. 1,
cross-written*] regularly & that the fault must be in the Post Office—& that
he would write to you & Try to set it right—I hope he succeeded—Remember me to M^r & Mrs Stuart—I long to be at home—tho' just now
feeling pretty well—with the sun shining the blue lake at my feet & the
Mountains in all their Majesty & beauty around & my beloved children
happy & well, I must mark this as a peaceful & happy hour

Affectionately Y^s
MaryShelley

TEXT: MS., Pforzheimer Library.

   1. Catherine and Joseph Stuart had nine children in all, including James (1843–
1913), the oldest, educator and Member of Parliament, and Isabella (b. 1847), poet
(James Stuart, *Reminiscences* {London: Cassell and Co., 1912], p. 62).

To Octavian Blewitt

24 Chester Sq   15 Nov. 1850

My dear Sir

I have received a letter from my Friend, Mrs Booth, which causes me to trouble you with a request—I hope you will excuse me.

It is several years since, thro' your kind interference, Mrs Booth received a donation of £30 from the R^{L} [*Royal*] Literary Fund. Once she got £50 from the Queen's Bounty—& these are the only contributions that she has received since her husband's death—Her daughter helps her—but her daughter has a large family & is by no means rich, so that Mrs Booth is of course in penurious circumstances. In addition she had a very severe & dangerous illness two ⟨years ago⟩ months ago, & the expences necessitated have made her poverty more bitter & pressing.

You know in how many ways David Booth benefited the literature of this country by his talents and industry. His widow has lost her health by a faithful attendance of years upon him, aff{l}icted as he was by Epilepsy, which at last caused his death. His Malady demanded a care & courage in nursing, which for a women to undertake & go through with alone, demanded heroic exertion—She persevered to the last, at the sacrifise of her own health.

No one can be more deserving of the aid of your excellent Institution, both on account of her late Husband, her own sufferings in his behalf, & the careful economy of her life. If you would be good enough to represent these things, Would not a further donation be awarded?[1]   It would be a good deed, & you would help a meritorious & grateful person.

Sir PercyShelley as well as myself have been absent from town, since I had the pleasure of seeing you, Indeed we were abroad for a year

You will oblige me greatly by taking Mrs Booth's circumstances into consideration—& furthering her wishes. My Son desires his best Compliments and I am, My dear Sir,

Yours truly
MaryShelley

TEXT: MS., Royal Literary Fund.

1. On 18 November Octavian Blewitt responded that Mr. Booth had received £120, and Mrs. Booth £50, and that the regulations of the Royal Literary Society would not allow any further relief to Mrs. Booth (Archives, Royal Literary Fund).

CHRONOLOGY

1797

29 March. William Godwin and Mary Wollstonecraft marry at Old St. Pancras
Church, London

6 April. Godwins take apartment at 29 The Polygon; Godwin takes rooms at
17 Evesham Building, Chalton Street

30 August. Birth of Mary Wollstonecraft Godwin

10 September. Death of Mary Wollstonecraft

15 September. Burial of Mary Wollstonecraft at churchyard of Old St. Pancras
Church

1801

5 May. Godwin meets Mary Jane Clairmont

21 December. Godwin marries Mary Jane Clairmont, who brings with her a
son, Charles, and a daughter, Clara Mary Jane (later Claire)

1803

28 March. William Godwin, Jr., born

1807

13 November. Godwins move to 41 Skinner Street

1808

January. Mary Godwin's *Mounseer Nongtongpaw* published

1812

7 June. Mary Godwin is sent by Godwin to live in Dundee with the family of
a Scottish friend, William Baxter

10 November. Mary Godwin returns to Godwin's Skinner Street home for a visit
with Christy Baxter

11 November. Mary Godwin meets Percy Bysshe Shelley and his wife Harriet
Westbrook Shelley at Skinner Street

1813
3 June. Mary Godwin and Christy Baxter return to Dundee

1814
30 March. Mary Godwin returns to Skinner Street from Scotland
13 May. Mary Godwin and Shelley meet again
28 July. Mary Godwin and Shelley, accompanied by her stepsister Claire Clairmont, elope to the Continent
July–August. Travel through France, Switzerland, Germany, and Holland; source of *History of a Six Weeks' Tour*
13 September. Mary Godwin, Shelley, and Claire Clairmont return to London
October–November. Shelley in danger of arrest for debt
30 November. Birth of Charles Shelley, Shelley and Harriet Shelley's second child

1815
5 January. Death of Sir Bysshe Shelley, Shelley's grandfather
22 February. Birth of Mary Godwin and Shelley's premature daughter
6 March. Death of premature daughter
April. Chancery suit to establish Sir Timothy Shelley's rights over disposal of Sir Bysshe's estate
13 May. Provisional settlement with Shelley's father, Shelley to receive £1,000 per year; Shelley arranges for estranged wife to receive £200 per year
June. Mary Godwin and Shelley tour southern coast of England and Devon
August–. Mary Godwin and Shelley reside at Bishopsgate
Winter. Shelley writes *Alastor*

1816
24 January. Birth of William Shelley
February. Alastor published
23–24 March. Godwin refuses to see Shelley when he calls at Skinner Street
April. Second Chancery suit regarding Shelley's grandfather's estate; Claire Clairmont and Byron become lovers
3 May. Mary Godwin, Shelley, William Shelley, and Claire Clairmont depart for Switzerland to meet Lord Byron
?16–23 June. Mary Godwin begins *Frankenstein*; Shelley and Byron travel around Lake Geneva
21 July. Mary Godwin, Shelley, and Claire Clairmont to Chamonix
29 August. Mary Godwin, Shelley, William Shelley, and Claire Clairmont leave for England

8 September. Mary Godwin, Shelley, William Shelley, and Claire Clairmont return to England and lodge in Bath

9 October. Fanny Godwin commits suicide

10 December. The body of Harriet Shelley, who committed suicide by drowning on 9 November, is discovered

15 December. News of Harriet Shelley's suicide reaches Shelley

30 December. Mary Godwin and Shelley marry at St. Mildred's, Bread Street, London

1817

12 January. Birth of Claire Clairmont and Byron's daughter, Allegra

January. Mary Godwin and Shelley move to London

January–July 1818. Chancery suit over guardianship of Shelley and Harriet Shelley's children, Ianthe and Charles

March. Shelleys reside at Albion House, Marlow

27 March. Shelley denied custody of Ianthe and Charles in Chancery Court proceedings

April–December. Mary Shelley finishes *Frankenstein* and begins *History of a Six Weeks' Tour*

May. Shelley writes *Laon and Cythna*

2 September. Birth of daughter Clara Everina Shelley

December–January. *History of a Six Weeks' Tour* and *The Revolt of Islam* published

1818

1 January. Frankenstein published

January–February. Albion House sold; Shelleys and Claire Clairmont move to London

11 March. Shelleys, Claire Clairmont, and Allegra depart for Italy

4 April. Arrive in Milan

May. Shelleys and Claire Clairmont to Pisa and Leghorn; meet Gisbornes

11 June. Move to Casa Bertini, Bagni di Lucca

17 August. Shelley and Claire Clairmont go to Venice and Este

5 September. Mary Shelley and children join them at Este; Shelley begins *Prometheus Unbound*

24 September. Death of Clara Shelley at Venice

29 October. Allegra sent to Byron in Venice

5 November. Shelleys and party travel to Rome and remain until late November; leave for Naples

1819

March. Reside in Rome

May. Shelley begins *The Cenci*

7 June. Death of William Shelley in Rome

June. Move to Leghorn, then Villa Valsovano, near Montenero

August. Mary Shelley begins *Mathilda*

October. Reside at 4395 Via Valfonda, Florence; meet Mr. and Mrs. Mason

12 November. Birth of Percy Florence Shelley

1820

January. Move to Casa Frasi, Pisa

March–April. Mary Shelley begins *Valperga; or, The Life and Adventure of Castruccio, Prince of Lucca*; *The Cenci* is published

April–. Mary Shelley writes mythological drama *Proserpine*

c. May. Mary Shelley writes mythological drama *Midas*

June 15. Move to Leghorn

August. Move to Casa Prinni, Bagni San Giuliano; *Prometheus Unbound* published

October. Reside at Palazzo Galetti, Pisa

November. Meet Emilia Viviani

1821

January. Shelleys meet Edward and Jane Williams

February–March. Shelleys move to Casa Aulla, Pisa; Shelley writes *Epipsychidion*

May. Return to Bagni San Giuliano; *Epipsychidion* published

October. Return to Pisa

November. Byron arrives in Pisa

1822

January. Edward John Trelawny arrives in Pisa

31 January. Godwin accepts Mary Shelley's offer to publish *Castruccio* for his benefit

20 April. Death of Allegra

30 April. Move, with Williamses, to Casa Magni, San Terenzo

16 June. Mary Shelley has miscarriage

1 July. Shelley and Edward Williams sail to Leghorn to welcome Leigh Hunt and family to Italy

8 July. Shelley and Williams drown in Gulf of Spezia returning from Leghorn

20 July. Mary Shelley and Jane Williams remove to Pisa

16 August. Shelley's body cremated at Viareggio

11 September. Mary Shelley to Genoa; rents Casa Negroto

17 September. Jane Williams leaves for London

20 September. Claire Clairmont leaves for Vienna

3 October. Byron arrives in Genoa; settles in Casa Saluzzo

4 October. Hunt and family join Mary Shelley at Casa Negroto

1823

21 January. Shelley's ashes interred in the Protestant Cemetery, Rome

6 February. Sir Timothy Shelley writes to Byron to offer to assume the guardianship of Percy Florence Shelley if Mary Shelley relinquishes custody; refuses Mary Shelley support

19 February. *Valperga* published

25 February. Mary Shelley refuses Sir Timothy Shelley's offer regarding Percy Florence Shelley's custody

? July. Mary Shelley writes her poem "The Choice"

24 July. Byron and Trelawny sail for Greece

25 July. Mary Shelley and Percy Florence Shelley leave Genoa for England

28 July. Presumption; or, The Fate of Frankenstein, drama by Richard Brinsley Peake based on Mary Shelley's *Frankenstein*, opens at the English Opera House

11 August. Second edition of *Frankenstein*, arranged by Godwin

12–20 August. Mary Shelley in Paris

25 August. Mary Shelley returns to London

29 August. Mary Shelley attends performance of *Presumption*

3 September. Whitton advances Mary Shelley £100

8 September. Moves to 14 Speldhurst Street, Brunswick Square

27 November. Mary Shelley receives repayable allowance of £100 per year from Sir Timothy Shelley

Winter. Begins *The Last Man*

1824

19 April. Death of Byron in Greece

June. Mary Shelley's edition of *Posthumous Poems of Percy Bysshe Shelley* published; Sir Timothy objects strongly; by August 22, after the sale of more than three hundred copies, Mary Shelley agrees to suppress the remaining copies in order to retain allowance for Percy Florence

21 June. Resides at 5 Bartholomew Place, Kentish Town, near Jane Williams

9 July. Views Byron's body before burial

August. Allowance of £200 per year from Sir Timothy Shelley begins

1826

23 January. The Last Man published

August. Spends month in Brighton with Jane Williams

14 September. Death of Charles Bysshe Shelley; Percy Florence becomes heir to baronetcy

1827

May. Allowance increased to £250 per year

2 June. Mary Shelley and Thomas Moore renew acquaintance

July. Discovery of Jane Williams's betrayal

July–October. Mary Shelley at Sompting, Arundel, with Isabel Robinson and Mary Diana Dods ("Mr. and Mrs. Walter Sholto Douglas")

September. Percy Florence Shelley attends day school in Arundel

End of October. Moves to 51 George Street, Portman Square

1828

11 February. Mary Shelley reveals to Jane Williams that she knows of her betrayal

25 March. Percy Florence Shelley attends Mr. Slater's school, Kensington

11 April. Mary Shelley to Paris to visit "Douglases"; ill with smallpox; meets with Prosper Mérimée, General Lafayette, and others in Garnett circle

26 May. Leaves Paris

June–August. Recuperation at Dover and Hastings

7 August. Resides at Park Cottage, Paddington, with Robinsons

16 October. Claire Clairmont returns to London

15 November. Reunion with Trelawny

24 December. Moves to 4 Oxford Terrace, London

1829

May–January 1830. Secretly assists Cyrus Redding in publication of the Galignanis' edition of Shelley's poems in Paris

May. Moves to 33 Somerset Street, Portman Square

1 June. Allowance from Sir Timothy Shelley increased to £300 per year for Percy Florence Shelley

18 September. Claire Clairmont leaves for Dresden

1830

5 February. William Godwin, Jr., and Mary Louisa (Emily) Eldred marry

13 May. The Fortunes of Perkin Warbeck published

July. Resides at Southend

August–October. At Park Cottage

1831

November. Revised edition of *Frankenstein* published

1832
Proserpine published (*Midas*, her other drama, first published in 1922)
mid-June–mid-September. Resides at Sandgate
8 September. Death of William Godwin, Jr.
29 September. Percy Florence Shelley enters Harrow

1833
May. Mary Shelley moves to Harrow; Percy Florence Shelley becomes a day
     student
4 May. Godwin awarded sinecure as Office Keeper and Yeoman Usher of the
     Receipt of the Exchequer and moves to 15 New Palace Yard

1835
February. First volume of *Lives of the most Eminent Literary and Scientific Men of
     Italy, Spain, and Portugal* published
7 April. Lodore published
October. Second volume of *Lives of the most Eminent Literary and Scientific Men of
     Italy, Spain, and Portugal* published

1836
7 April. Death of William Godwin
April. Mary Shelley moves to 14 North Bank, Regents Park, London

1837
February. Falkner published
March. Mary Shelley moves to 24 South Audley Street
October. Percy Florence Shelley enters Trinity College, Cambridge
November. Mary Shelley moves to 41d Park Street, Grosvenor Square

1838
c. August. Sir Timothy lifts the ban he imposed on Mary Shelley's publication
     of Shelley's works
August. First volume of *Lives of the most Eminent Literary and Scientific Men of
     France* published

1839
January. Beginning of periods of illness for Mary Shelley that last until her
     death in 1851
January–May. Publication of *Poetical Works of Percy Bysshe Shelley*, 4 volumes
March. Resides at Layton House, Putney

August. Second volume of *Lives of the Most Eminent Literary and Scientific Men of France* published

November. Publication of Mary Shelley's edition of *Poetical Works of Percy Bysshe Shelley*, 1 volume

December. Publication of Shelley's *Essays, Letters from Abroad, Translations and Fragments*

1840

June–early January 1841. Tour of the Continent with Percy Florence Shelley and his friends: Cadenabbia, Milan, and Paris

1841

January. Resides at 84 Park Street, London; Percy Florence Shelley graduates from Trinity College

February. Gift from Sir Timothy Shelley to Percy Florence of £400 per year

17 June. Death of Mary Jane Clairmont

1842

June–30 August 1843. Tour of the Continent with Percy Florence Shelley, Alexander Knox, and Henry Hugh Pearson: Kissingen, Berlin, Dresden, Venice, Florence, Rome, Paris

1843

September. Moves to White Cottage, Putney

1844

24 April. Death of Sir Timothy Shelley; Percy Florence Shelley inherits title and estate

July. Rambles in Germany and Italy published

1845

September. Attempted blackmail of Mary Shelley by Ferdinand Gatteschi

October. Attempted blackmail of Mary Shelley by George "Byron"

1846

c. March. Moves to 24 Chester Square

1848

22 June. Sir Percy Florence Shelley and Jane St. John marry

August. Moves to Field Place

1849

September–May 1850. To Continent with Percy Florence Shelley and Jane
   Shelley: Paris, Nice, Cadenabbia

1851

1 February. Death of Mary Shelley, Chester Square; buried, St. Peter's,
   Bournemouth, near Percy Florence Shelley and Jane Shelley's new home at
   Boscombe. In compliance with Mary Shelley's wish that she be buried
   beside her parents, the remains of William Godwin and Mary
   Wollstonecraft are removed to St. Peter's. Percy Florence Shelley died on 5
   December 1889, Jane Shelley on 24 June 1899; both were interred in the
   same grave as Mary Shelley and her parents.

SELECTED BIBLIOGRAPHY

WORKS BY MARY SHELLEY

Mounseer Nongtongpaw; or the Discoveries of John Bull in a Trip to Paris. London: Proprietors of the Juvenile Library [M. J. Godwin & Co.], 1808. Four editions published by Godwin. Two editions published in the United States.

With Percy Bysshe Shelley. *History of a Six Weeks' Tour through a Part of France, Switzerland, Germany, and Holland: with Letters Descriptive of a Sail round the Lake of Geneva, and of the Glaciers of Chamouni.* London: T. Hookham, Jun.; and C. and J. Ollier, 1817.

Frankenstein; or, The Modern Prometheus. 3 vols. London: Lackington, Hughes, Harding, Mavor, & Jones, 1818. Revised with an introduction by Mary Shelley. 3 vols. in 1. London: Henry Colburn and Richard Bentley; Edinburgh: Bell & Bradfute; Dublin: Cumming, 1831.

Valperga; or, the Life and Adventure of Castruccio, Prince of Lucca. 3 vols. London: G. and W. B. Whittaker, 1823.

The Last Man. 3 vols. London: Henry Colburn, 1826.

The Fortunes of Perkin Warbeck, A Romance. 3 vols. London: Henry Colburn and Richard Bentley, 1830.

Proserpine, a Mythological Drama in Two Acts. In *The Winter's Wreath* for 1832. London: G. and W. B. Whittaker, [1831].

Lodore. 3 vols. London: Richard Bentley, 1835.

With James Montgomery and Sir David Brewster. *Lives of the most Eminent Literary and Scientific Men of Italy, Spain, and Portugal.* Vols. I and II. The Cabinet of Biography, edited by the Rev. Dionysius Lardner, vols. 86 and 87. London: Longman, Rees, Orme, Brown, Green & Longman; and John Taylor, 1835.

Lives of the most Eminent Literary and Scientific Men of Italy, Spain, and Portugal. Vol. III. The Cabinet of Biography, edited by the Rev. Dionysius Lardner, vol. 88. London: Longman, Orme, Brown, Green & Longmans; and John Taylor, 1837.

Falkner: A Novel. 3 vols. London: Saunders and Otley, 1837.

Lives of the most Eminent Literary and Scientific Men of France. Vols. I and II. The Cabinet of Biography, edited by the Rev. Dionysius Lardner, vols. 102 and

103. London: Longman, Orme, Brown, Green & Longmans; and John Taylor, 1838–39.

Rambles in Germany and Italy, in 1840, 1842, and 1843. 2 vols. London: Edward Moxon, 1844.

The Choice—A Poem on Shelley's Death. Edited by H. Buxton Forman. London: Privately printed, 1876.

Midas. In *Proserpine & Midas. Two Unpublished Mythological Dramas by Mary Shelley.* Edited by A[ndré] Koszul. London: Humphrey Milford, 1922.

Mathilda. Edited by Elizabeth Nitchie. Chapel Hill: University of North Carolina Press, 1959.

Mary Shelley: Collected Tales and Stories, with Original Engravings. Edited by Charles E. Robinson. Baltimore: Johns Hopkins University Press, 1976.

WORKS EDITED BY MARY SHELLEY

Posthumous Poems of Percy Bysshe Shelley. London: John and Henry L. Hunt, 1824.

The Poetical Works of Percy Bysshe Shelley. Edited by Mrs. Shelley. 4 vols. London: Edward Moxon, 1839. One-volume edition with postscript. 1840.

Essays, Letters from Abroad, Translations and Fragments, By Percy Bysshe Shelley. Edited by Mrs. Shelley. 2 vols. London: Edward Moxon, 1840 [1839]. 2d ed. 1841.

OTHER WORKS

Bennett, Betty T., and William T. Little. "Seven Letters from Prosper Mérimée to Mary Shelley." *Comparative Literature* 31 (Spring 1979): 134–53.

Cameron, Kenneth Neill. *Shelley: The Golden Years.* Cambridge, Mass.: Harvard University Press, 1974.

Cameron, Kenneth Neill, and Donald E. Reiman, eds. *Shelley and his Circle, 1773–1822.* 8 vols. Cambridge, Mass.: Harvard University Press, 1961–86.

Clairmont, Claire. *The Journals of Claire Clairmont, 1814–1827.* Edited by Marion Kingston Stocking with the assistance of David Mackenzie Stocking. Cambridge, Mass.: Harvard University Press, 1968.

Dowden, Edward. *The Life of Percy Bysshe Shelley.* 2 vols. London: Kegan Paul, Trench & Co., 1886.

Dunbar, Clement. *A Bibliography of Shelley Studies: 1823–1950.* New York: Garland, 1976.

Gilbert, Sandra, and Susan Gubar. *The Madwoman in the Attic.* New Haven: Yale University Press, 1979.

Gisborne, Maria, and Edward E. Williams. *Maria Gisborne & Edward E. Williams, Shelley's Friends, Their Journals and Letters.* Edited by Frederick L. Jones. Norman: University of Oklahoma Press, 1951.

Holmes, Richard. *Shelley: The Pursuit.* London: Weidenfeld & Nicolson, 1974.

Ingpen, Roger. *Shelley in England: New Facts and Letters from the Shelley-Whitton Papers*. 2 vols. London: Kegan Paul, Trench, Trubner & Co., 1917.

Ketterer, David. *Frankenstein's Creation: The Book, the Monster, and Human Reality*. English Literature Studies No. 16. Victoria, B.C.: Victoria University Press, 1979.

Levine, George, and U. C. Knoepflmacher, eds. *The Endurance of Frankenstein: Essays on Mary Shelley's Novel*. Berkeley and Los Angeles: University of California Press, 1979.

Lyles, W. H. *Mary Shelley: An Annotated Bibliography*. New York: Garland, 1975.

Marchand, Leslie A. *Byron: A Biography*. 3 vols. New York: Alfred A. Knopf, 1957.

Marshall, Mrs. Julian [Florence A.]. *The Life and Letters of Mary Wollstonecraft Shelley*. 2 vols. London: Richard Bentley & Son, 1889.

Mellor, Anne K. *Mary Shelley: Her Life, Her Fiction, Her Monsters*. London: Methuen, 1988.

Murray, E. B. "Shelley's Contribution to Mary's *Frankenstein*." *Keats-Shelley Memorial Bulletin* 29 (1978): 50–68.

Nitchie, Elizabeth. *Mary Shelley: "Author of Frankenstein."* New Brunswick: Rutgers University Press, 1953.

Norman, Sylva. *Flight of the Skylark: The Development of Shelley's Reputation*. London: Max Reinhardt, 1954.

Palacio, Jean de. *Mary Shelley dans son oeuvre: Contributions aux études shelleyennes*. Paris: Editions Klincksieck, 1969.

Paul, C. Kegan. *William Godwin: His Friends and Contemporaries*. 2 vols. London: Henry S. King & Co., 1876.

Polidori, John. *The Diary of Dr. John William Polidori*. Edited by William Michael Rossetti. London: Elkin Mathews, 1911.

Rolleston, Maud. *Talks with Lady Shelley*. London: George G. Harrap & Co., 1925.

St Clair, William. *The Godwins and the Shelleys: The Biography of a Family*. Boston: Faber & Faber, 1989.

Sanborn, F. B., ed. *The Romance of Mary W. Shelley, John Howard Payne and Washington Irving*. Boston: Boston Bibliophile Society, 1907.

Shelley, Lady Jane, ed. *Shelley and Mary*. 4 vols. London: Privately published, 1882.

Shelley, Mary. *The Journals of Mary Shelley, 1814–1844*. Edited by Paula R. Feldman and Diana Scott-Kilvert. 2 vols. Oxford: Clarendon Press, 1987.

———. *The Letters of Mary Wollstonecraft Shelley*. Edited by Betty T. Bennett. 3 vols. Baltimore: Johns Hopkins University Press, 1980–88.

———. *The Mary Shelley Reader*. Edited by Betty T. Bennett and Charles E. Robinson. Oxford: Oxford University Press, 1990.

Shelley, Percy Bysshe. *The Complete Works of Percy Bysshe Shelley*. Edited by Roger Ingpen and Walter E. Peck. Julian Edition. 10 vols. London: E. Benn, 1926–30.

———. *The Letters of Percy Bysshe Shelley*. Edited by Frederick L. Jones. 2 vols. Oxford: Clarendon Press, 1964.

Small, Christopher. *Ariel Like a Harpy; Shelley, Mary and Frankenstein*. London: Victor Gollancz, 1972.

Spark, Muriel. *Child of Light: A Reassessment of Mary Shelley*. Hadleigh, Essex: Tower Bridge Publications, 1951. Revised and republished as *Mary Shelley*. New York: E. P. Dutton, 1987.

Sunstein, Emily W. *Mary Shelley: Romance and Reality*. Boston: Little, Brown, 1989.

Veeder, William. *Mary Shelley and Frankenstein: The Fate of Androgyny*. Chicago: University of Chicago Press, 1986.

Walling, William A. *Mary Shelley*. New York: Twayne, 1972.

White, Newman Ivey. *Shelley*. 2 vols. London: Secker & Warburg, 1947.

Wollstonecraft, Mary, and William Godwin. *Mary Wollstonecraft, A Short Residence in Sweden, Norway and Denmark*, and *Memoirs of the Author of The Rights of Women*." Edited with an introduction and notes by Richard Holmes. London: Penguin Books, 1987.

INDEX

Mill, John Stuart, 293, 293–94n
Milnes, Richard Monckton, 278, 279n, 291, 315, 323, 332n; letters to, 306, 331; *"Poetry for the People" and Other Poems*, 306nn
Mohammad Ali, 301–2n
Montgomery, James, 137, 140n, 252n
Monti, Vincenzo, 254, 255n
Moore, Anastasia Mary, 210, 210n
Moore, Thomas, 37n, 43n, 82n, 91n, 133n, 170, 171–72, 172–73n, 190n, 192–93n, 202, 210, 210n, 217, 218n, 219, 220, 224, 228, 229, 244, 252n, 260n, 261n; *The Fudge Family in Paris*, 290n; *The Twopenny Post-Bag*, 290n
Morgan, Sir Charles, 272n
Morgan, Sydney, Lady, 272n, 280n; letter to, 272; *The Life and Times of Salvator Rosa*, 145, 146n
Morton, George Sholto Douglas, Earl of, 174, 175n
Mountcashell, Lady. *See* Mason, Margaret
Moxon, Edward, xxiii, xxix, 251n, 275n, 276, 277n, 279n, 305n, 209n, 344n; letters to, 250, 275, 278, 284(2), 285, 289, 292, 294, 304, 307, 308, 323, 324, 325
Moxon, Emma Isola, 292n
Murillo, Bartolomé Esteban, 303, 304n
Murray, John, 25, 26nn, 27n, 33n, 82n, 86n, 118n, 119, 120n, 218nn, 229n, 230–31, 231n, 290n, 291n, 344n; letters to, 217, 223, 228, 244, 252
Murray, John, III, 231n; letter to, 230

Napoleon, 306, 306n, 309, 311n
Napoleon III, 302n
Newby, Thomas Cautley, 356, 357n, 358
New Harmony Gazette, 234n
New Monthly Magazine, 202, 203n, 308, 309n
New Year's Gift and Juvenile Souvenir, 243, 243n
Nicholson, William, 234n
Nicolls, Edith, 365, 365n
Nicolls, Mary Ellen Peacock, 365nn; letter to, 365
Nitchie, Elizabeth, 122n
Norfolk, Bernard Edward, Duke of, 183n
Norman, Arthur M. Z., 109n
Norman, Sylva, 152n
Normanby, Lord, 304–5, 305n, 307
Norton, Caroline, 256, 263n, 268, 271n, 280n, 324; *"The Dream," and other Poems*, 303, 304n; *Observations on the Natural Claim of a Mother to the Custody of Her Children*, 269n
Norton, William, 318n
Nott, George Frederick, 83, 85n
Novello, Joseph Alfred, 140n
Novello, Mary Sabilla Hehl, 140n, 155
Novello, Mary Victoria, 140n

Novello, Vincent, 140n, 155
Novello & Co., 140n, 312

O'Hara, Barnes and Abel. *See* Banim, John and Michael
Ollier, Charles, 48n, 50, 52n, 54n, 60n, 71n, 81, 84, 86, 114n, 154n, 164n, 223, 223n, 238n; letters to, 142(2), 153, 162, 208, 209, 222, 233, 237, 238, 241, 249, 251, 266, 283
Ollier, James, 71n, 154n
Ollier, Marla Gattie, 142n
Opera Glass for Peeping into the Microcosm of the Fine Arts, and more especially the Drama, The, 162, 162n
Owen, Robert, 181n
Owen, Robert Dale, 180, 181n, 190n, 234n, 235n, 236n; letters to, 189, 234
Owen, William, 50
Owenson, Sydney. *See* Morgan, Lady
Oxford, Lady, 244, 246n

Paris, John Ayrton, 348n
Parke, John, 104–5n
Parry, Sir William Edward, 207, 208n
Pasta, Giuditta, 155
Paul, Georgiana Beauclerk, xx, 243, 248, 361
Pauls, John Dean, 255n
Payne, John Howard, xix, 151–52nn, 158n, 159n, 160nn, 162n, 184nn, 187n, 265n; *Brutus; or, The Fall of Tarquin*, 159, 160–61n; letters to, 151, 158, 159, 177, 184, 186, 187, 188
Payne-Gaposchkin, Cecilia, 189n
Peacock, Edward, 331, 365
Peacock, Mary Ellen, letter to, 294
Peacock, Rosa, 294, 294n
Peacock, Thomas Love, xxix, 2n, 5, 14n, 20n, 23, 24n, 29, 32, 33, 33nn, 45, 46n, 48, 48n, 50, 51, 52n, 64, 71, 81, 86, 95, 103, 106, 113nn, 121, 122n, 138, 168, 281, 283n, 344, 346; letter to, 111
Pearson, 312, 313n, 314
Peel, Sir Robert, 253, 324n, 331, 342, 355
Pepe, Guglielmo, 67n
Perrone, M., 335, 336n
Perry, Henry James, 166n, 310, 311n
Pertz, Heinrich, 189n
Pertz, Julia Garnett, 188–89n, 194n, 195n, 196n, 199n
Pindar, Peter, 26n
Pinkerton, John, *The History of Scotland from the Accession of the House of Stuart to that of Mary*, 215, 215n
Plato: *Menexenus*, 295, 296n; *Phaedrus*, 293, 293n, 294n
Platt, Mr., 19n
Polidori, John William, 17n
Pope, Alexander, 195, 196n

Power, James, 190, 190n
Power, William, 190, 190n
Presumption, or the Fate of Frankenstein (Peake), 136, 140n
Procter, Bryan Waller, 153n, 281, 281n; letter to, 152

Quarterly Review, 230, 290n, 303, 304n

Raphael, 312
Ratcliff, Jeremiah, 301, 302n
Rawlinson, Mr., 330, 337
Redding, Cyrus, xxiii, xxviii, 213–14n, 216nn; letters to, 213, 215, 216; "Memoir of Percy Bysshe Shelley," 216, 217n; *The Poetical Works of Coleridge, Shelley, and Keats* (ed.), xxiii, 214n, 217n
Reiman, Donald H., 23n
Rennie, Eliza, 164n, 165n
Reveley, Henry, 36, 36n, 38, 54, 56, 84, 93, 274, 274n, 289
Reynolds, Frederic Mansel, 227n; letters to, 227, 248
Ricci, Apollonia, 61, 62n
Ricci, Carlotta, 61, 62n
Rios, The, 324
Ritchie, Leitch, 185nn
Robberds, J. W., 325n
Roberts, Daniel, 87, 88n, 93, 98, 100, 103, 116, 117, 145
Robinson, Alfred, 166n
Robinson, Charles, 287, 299n, 310, 321, 342, 343n, 354, 355, 364; letter to, 359
Robinson, Eliza Agnes, 166n
Robinson, George, 166n, 316
Robinson, Henry Crabb, 4, 264n; letter to, 263
Robinson, Isabella. *See* Douglas, Isabella Robinson
Robinson, Joshua, xix, 166n, 194n, 196, 205, 286
Robinson, Julia, xix, 166n, 194n, 195, 270n, 316
Robinson, Julian, 166n, 296
Robinson, Louisa, 166n
Robinson, Mrs. Alfred, 316
Robinson, Rosa. *See* Beauclerk, Rosa Robinson
Rochefoucauld, François, Duc de La, 161, 161n
Roebuck, John Arthur, 307, 307n
Rogers, Samuel, 278, 279n, 280n, 309n, 324, 325, 336; *Italy, A Poem*, 300, 301n
Romieux, Aimée, 26, 27n, 32, 33n
Romieux, Louis, 33n
Roskilly, Dr., 43
Rossetti, Christina Georgina, 255n
Rossetti, Dante Gabriel, 255n
Rossetti, Frances Mary Lavinia, 255n
Rossetti, Gabriele, letter to, 254

Rossetti, William Michael, 255n
Rossini, 69, 71n
Rossini, Giacchino, 84
Rothwell, Richard, 226, 226n
Rousseau, Jean-Jacques, 16
Rowan, Archibald Hamilton, 300nn; *Autobiography*, 300n
Rumble, Elizabeth, 274n; letters to, 273, 288
Russell, Lord John, 355

St. Croix, Marianne, 50, 52n
Sainte-Beuve, Charles Augustin, 303, 304n
St. John, Charles Robert, xxvi, 359n, 360n
St. John, George Frederick, 362n
St. John, George Richard, xxvi, 359n, 362n
St. John, Isabella Antoinette, xxvi, 362n
St. John, Jane Gibson. *See* Shelley, Jane Gibson St. John, Lady
Sanford, Mr., 330
Schlabrendorf, Count Gustav von, 276n
Schwalb, Madame, 117
Scott, Sir Walter, xvi, xxi, 137, 219, 252n; letters to, 34, 214; *St. Ronan's Well*, 145, 147n
Severn, Arthur, 332n
Severn, Joseph, 123, 124n, 332n, 335n; letter to, 332
Sgricci, 69, 71n
Shakespeare, William: *Hamlet*, 291n; *Macbeth*, 265n; *Richard II*, 259n
Sharpe, Sutton, 207nn, 279nn; letter to, 207
Shelley, Charles Bysshe, 21n, 24n, 91n, 111; death of, 168, 168n, 169
Shelley, Elizabeth, Lady, 243n, 261, 327, 329, 330, 331
Shelley, Harriet Westbrook, xxiii, 2n, 7n, 9, 21nn, 22n, 217, 277n, 283n, 347
Shelley, Hellen, 314, 315, 317n, 327, 328n, 330
Shelley, Ianthe, 2n, 21n, 22n, 24n, 91n, 314
Shelley, Jane Gibson St. John, Lady, xxvi, 343n, 359, 359–60n, 361n, 363–64, 365, 366; letter to, 362
Shelley, John, xxv, 327, 329, 331
Shelley, Mary Wollstonecraft: death of, xxvii; devotion to father, xiv; elopement with Shelley, xi, xiv, 1–2nn; female friendships of, xviii–xix; health of, 261–62, 348, 348n, 349, 351, 351n, 353, 360, 366; marriage to Shelley, 21n, 217n; motherhood and, xvi–xvii. Works: "Absence," 227n; "The Brother and Sister, an Italian Story," 249n; "A Dirge," 258–59; *Falkner*, xiii, xxi, 266, 266n, 288n; *Frankenstein*, xii, xvi, 17n, 18, 27n, 34, 34n, 124n, 145, 185n, 237, 238, 238n, 241, 241n, 274, 275n; "Illyrian Poems—Feudal Scenes," 202, 202n; "The Invisible Girl," 249n; *The Last Man*, xiii, 154n, 157n, 162, 162n, 210n, 219n; *Lives*

Taylor, William, 325, 325n
Thackeray, William Makepeace, 306n
Thiers, Adolph, 302n
Thistlewood, Arthur, 56, 60n
Thomas, Mrs., 123, 124n, 125n
Thrale, Hester Lynch, 253, 253n
Trelawny, Augusta, letter to, 360
Trelawny, Edward John, xv, xx–xxi, xxviii,
    86–87, 88n, 93, 94n, 97–98, 101–2, 103,
    103n, 104, 106–7, 108nn, 113, 114, 116,
    117, 128–29, 131, 132, 133, 133n, 134,
    155, 156n, 161n, 176, 182, 200, 201,
    205, 206, 207n, 210, 210n, 222n, 233,
    233n, 238n, 241nn, 246–47, 248n, 261n,
    269n, 307n, 315, 335, 360–61; letters to,
    123, 143, 211, 219, 232, 239, 267.
    Works: *Adventures*, 212n, 240n; *Recollections*,
    213n; *Records of Shelley, Byron, and the
    Author*, xxi, 88n, 213n
Trelawny, Eliza, 196n
Trelawny, Maria Julia, 196n, 200
Trelawny, Zella, 196n, 222n
Trevanion, Charlotte, 268, 269n
Turbati, Mrs., 144

Uwins, Dr. David, 261n

Vincent, E. R., 255n
Virgil, *Georgics*, 41
Viviani, Emilia, xxx, 69–70, 120n

Wakefield, Sarah, 323n
Walker, William Sidney, 88n
Wallack, James William, 136, 140n
Walpole, Horace, 249, 250n
Watts, Alaric A., 163n, 165n, 166n, 185n;
    letters to, 163, 185, 243
Watts, Priscilla Maden, 243, 243n
Webb, Mr., 38, 44, 79
Webb & Co., 39n
Weber, Karl Maria von, 155
Wedgwood, Josiah, 265n
Wedgwood, Josiah, Jr., 265–66nn; letter to,
    265
Wedgwood, Thomas, 265, 266n
West, John, 17, 18, 19n

West, Joseph, 19n
Westbrook, Eliza, 22n
Westbrook, Harriet. *See* Shelley, Harriet
    Westbrook
Westbrook, John, 21n
Westminster Review, 157, 157n, 202, 202n,
    210, 230
White, William, 344n
Whitehead, Ellen, 144, 146n
Whitton, William, xxiv, 9n, 111, 113n,
    114n, 137, 140n, 154, 168, 169, 174,
    178, 242; letters to, 193(2)
William IV, 232n
Williams, April, 87n
Williams, Edward, xviii, 82n, 83, 85n, 86,
    87–88nn, 93–94, 94n, 95n, 97, 98, 100,
    103, 103n, 106, 110, 112, 113, 114, 115,
    129, 133n, 143, 160n
Williams, Jane. *See* Hogg, Jane Williams
Williams, Mary Ann, 138, 141n
Williams, Mrs., 288–89
Williams, Rosalind (Dina), xviii, 85n, 316–17
Wilmot, Sir John Eardly, 355, 356n
Wilson, Sir Robert, 15n
Wolcott, John, 25, 26n
Wolff, Henry Drummond, 165n
Wollstonecraft, Edward, 288n
Wollstonecraft, Everina, 288n, 310–11, 319–
    20, 321–22, 323n, 341; letters to, 296,
    318
Wollstonecraft, Mary, xiii, xiv–xv, 2n, 262,
    299, 300n; *Letters Written During a Short Res-
    idence in Sweden, Norway and Denmark*, 288n;
    Mary, 288n
Wordsworth, William, 263, 323, 324n; *Poeti-
    cal Works* (1836–37), 278, 279n, 286, 286n
Wright, Camilla, 181n, 235n
Wright, Frances, xiv, xv, 181nn, 188n, 189–
    90, 194n, 234n, 235n, 236n; letters to,
    179, 235
Wright, Gabrielle, 115, 117, 123
Wright, John, 244n

Xenophon, 133n

Ypselanti, Alexandros, 72–73, 73n